CENTER STAGE

Sea Urchin Press • P. O. Box 10503 • Oakland, Ca. 94610

CENTER STAGE

An
Anthology
of
21 Contemporary
Black–American
Plays

Edited by Eileen Joyce Ostrow

Center Stage: An Anthology of 21 Contemporary Black-American Plays copyright © 1981
by Eileen Joyce Ostrow.
Library of Congress Copyright Registration Number: TX 828-293.
Introduction copyright © 1981 by Sandra L. Richards.

Cover photograph copyright © 1977 by Frank Stewart: photograph of Kim Weston-
Moran and Arick James during a performance of *Transitions for a Mime Poem* by Owa.
Directed by Stephen D. Agins at the New York Theatre Ensemble, July 1977.

Cover & book design, typesetting, & paste-up by Eileen Joyce Ostrow.
Typeset and printed at the West Coast Print Center, Berkeley, Ca. 94703.

The publication of this first edition of *Center Stage* was funded in part
by a grant from the National Endowment for the Arts.

Library of Congress Catalog Card No.: 80-53143
ISBN: 0-9605208-0-5

First printing, March 1981, 1,200 copies.
Second printing, April 1983, 2,000 copies.

Address inquiries to the publisher:

> Sea Urchin Press
> P. O. Box 10503
> Oakland, California 94610

This collection is dedicated to the reader

EDITOR'S PREFACE

IN THE EARLY FALL of 1979 this book consisted of one script in hand and the vague notion of creating a whole anthology. I began my search for scripts by contacting three individuals actively working in Black Theatre in the San Francisco Bay Area: Jan-Taylor Blythe, Artistic Director at Black Repertory Group in Berkeley and Program Director of New Arts Experience—the Group's workshop for new playwrights; Sati Jamal, filmmaker, director, and, at that time, Artistic Director of United Projects, Inc., housed at the Western Addition Cultural Center in San Francisco; and Sandra L. Richards, then Artistic Director at the Oakland Ensemble Theatre.

Through Jan's, Sati's, and Sandi's open and friendly sharing, a new world of theatre opened up for me. I obtained accessibility to playwrights, directors, university professors, and became aware of relevant publications and community theatre groups throughout the country. From this strong start, I was able to explore different avenues (including doing legwork at the Oakland Public Library, which provided up-to-date information).

Dr. Lloyd Richards, Dean of the Drama Department at Yale University, took the time to refer me to individual playwrights I otherwise would not have known.

For knowledge of the legal matters involved in Small Press Publishing, I contacted Bay Area Lawyers for the Arts (a nonprofit organization in San Francisco). The further assistance of Attorney Howard Moore, Jr. was invaluable. Ishmael Reed (writer, publisher) and Gundars Strads, both of whom are with the Before Columbus Foundation, freely shared their expertise in the official aspects of book publishing.

On the actual bookmaking/design/production end, I received instruction from David Bullen and benefited from the continuous support and know-how of my fellow staff members at the West Coast Print Center: the director Don Cushman, Wendy Bogin, Josh Cullander, Don Donahue, Mary Ann Hayden, Scott Kane, and Wendy Welsh.

To all the above-mentioned individuals who willingly shared their resources and expertise, to the National Endowment for the Arts for helping fund the first edition of this publication, and, of course, to the playwrights themselves, I express thanks.

Eileen Joyce Ostrow
Oakland, California
1981

Eileen Joyce Ostrow, printer, publisher, and professional educator, has taught in California and holds several teaching credentials on levels ranging from preschool to Junior College and Adult School. She received her B.S. degree from the University of Michigan, and has earned M.A. degrees from San Francisco State University (Special Education for the Neurologically Handicapped) and from Mills College (English). Her graduate work in English was concentrated in the area of American literature, with a background of study in Black-American literature.

Other interests include aquatics, dance, and computers. Ms. Ostrow's current involvement in the book making process encompasses letterpress and offset printing and typography in relation to book design—the development of "the book and the printed page as art forms."

With the exception of decisions made in the area of book design and a few authorized changes made for consistency or clarity within each script, there have been no editorial or textual changes—the scripts are presented as the playwrights have submitted them. Each playwright's style of presentation, breaks in delivery of speech, spelling choices, and so on transmits a feeling for how the work is to be interpreted and, thus, is of considerable value to readers, actors, and directors.

NOTE ON THE SECOND PRINTING

THE RESPONSE TO CENTER STAGE has been fantastic. Along with making current scripts by contemporary writers available, *Center Stage* is helping expand the lines of communication among creative artists. Since the publication of this volume in 1981, previously unpublished plays which otherwise might not have reached producers, directors, and audiences are being performed coast to coast. The included scripts, so vital and exciting, are but a sampling of the playwrights' work. New creations continue to be written and performed.

Word has spread about the existence and value of this collection. Despite the limitations that inhibit small presses in the areas of promotion and distribution (due to lack of capital, inaccessibility of standard channels of exposure, etc.), *Center Stage* is being purchased by individuals, universities, libraries, theatre groups, and college classrooms throughout the country and abroad.

The public's interest in this anthology warrants its continued publication. Thus, it is with this spirit of enthusiasm that the second printing of *Center Stage* is borne.

Eileen Joyce Ostrow
1983

CONTENTS

INTRODUCTION

IN 1964 *Dutchman* burst upon the American theatrical scene and helped to launch a movement. Its author, Amiri Baraka (LeRoi Jones), graphically demonstrated in his own literary and non-literary activities the ways in which art could be utilized as a weapon for social and political change. He challenged others to do likewise, and the results were in part the Black Arts and the Black Theatre movements. Given the intense interest generated by these movements, which were a corollary of the Black Power movement, publishers recognized a market for Black literature, and several anthologies of Black plays appeared. Those anthologies published in the late '60s through mid-'70s tended to fall into one of three categories: works which unabashedly reflected their authors' commitment to a nationalist perspective; historical collections which brought back into print plays from earlier decades; and the middle-of-the-roaders which combined earlier plays with those contemporary ones which anthologizers may have considered less "strident" and more within the American mainstream.

Center Stage indicates some of the roads Black Theatre has travelled since the mid-'70s. Simply stated, the virtue of this anthology is its diversity. These playwrights come from all parts of the United States as well as the Caribbean. Some have been practicing their craft for over thirty years, while others have not yet reached age thirty.

Their collective theatre background attests to the breadth of the Black Theatre movement and its commitment to developing playwrights. The general public may be unaware that very often would-be playwrights lack opportunities to have their works performed or even read aloud, and being without a company which will allow them the space to explore, fail, or succeed, they give up before achieving an accurate sense of their abilities. Happily for us, many of the playwrights represented here have been nurtured by writers' groups like the Frank Silvera, New Lafayette, and Negro Ensemble Company playwrighting workshops in New York; the Congo Square and Free Southern Theatre writers' workshops in New Orleans; and the Black Writers and New Arts Experience workshops in the San Francisco Bay Area. Not to be forgotten either is the part Black colleges have played, for several of the authors have been associated with theatre departments at Howard, Atlanta, Spelman, West Virginia State, and Tougaloo. A lucky few have been encouraged in their work by receiving such prestigious national awards as the Lorraine Hansberry, Kennedy Center National Black Playwrights, Eugene O'Neill Memorial Theatre Playwrighting Competition, and the Squaw Valley Community of Writers Conference.

The reader will find here full length plays, one acts, character sketches suitable for actor scene study, and scripts which fall somewhere in between. Some of the plays are clearly the work of accomplished playwrights; others represent the efforts of authors in the early stages of their development who have nevertheless mastered the hard, fundamental requirements of dramatic form and earned the right to call themselves playwrights. The range of issues tackled is quite impressive: Often these playwrights take chances in subject matter and style which we would have thought heretical or irrelevant during that earlier period when the ideological battlefields were clearly drawn.

Seemingly, the horizons of today's playwrights are more personally defined, if we look at plays like Edwards' *Three Fallen Angels,* Foreman's *Daddy's Seashore Blues,* or Hobbes' *You Can't Always Sometimes Never Tell* where the central issue is love, whether it be among a husband-wife-male friend trio, a middle-aged couple, or a brother and sister. Similarly, in plays as different as Mason's *The Verandah* and Owa's *Transitions for a Mime Poem* the focus is on the personal rather than the public. The former play dramatizes the ravaging destruction a family brings upon itself by virtue of its belief in racial and caste distinction in 1930s' Jamaica, while Owa's argues that a meditatively derived sense of centeredness or self-knowledge is the essential base from which political or social action flows.

Even in those plays where elements from the outside world invade the home with disastrous consequences—a familiar '60s' theme if we think of plays like *Clara's Ole Man* or *The River Niger*—the perspective has changed. Sharon Stockard Martin and Jacques Wakefield use in *The Moving Violation* and *Perceptual Movement* the filter of the Absurd and demand that we acknowledge the ways in which totally irrational forces and the individual's private nightmares combine with recognizable social injustices to threaten his integrity.

Martin's and Wakefield's pieces along with Owa's mime poem and Welch's choreopoem, *Hands in the Mirror,* manifest a stylistic mode which only a select group of Black playwrights has chosen to employ. Their plays demand that theatre artists work against the persistent human desire to impose rational explanations on experience, and they challenge artists to create instead a style which, while it may already have its counterpart in Black music, has yet to become a tradition within Black Theatre. Given the intelligence and craftsmanship evident in these scripts, theatre companies must not be afraid to continue to support these playwrights even while in some instances encouraging them to mold their abstract styles into forms that are truly unique yet indigenous to Black cultural values.

Then there is a group of plays whose most impressive quality is economy. Hunkins' *Revival*, Jackson's *In the Master's House There Are Many Mansions*, Cooper's *Loners*, Shine's *The Woman Who was Tampered with in Youth*, along with Williams' *A Christmas Story* and Rhodes' *The Trip* all manifest an economy of setting, language, and character. These playwrights are masters—mistresses, actually in that only one of these six plays is by a man—of form, so that the plays are almost like piano finger exercises, sufficient evidence of skill to leave us crying "more" and hungering for full length pieces by these authors.

Their scripts are particularly suited for use in acting and directing workshops where two-person scenes and tightly crafted one acts are seemingly always at a premium. They require simple, uncomplicated sets and a minimum of props; characters have discernible objectives and yet are drawn with a complexity which makes them rewarding for actors and directors. But at times their simplicity is deceptive: How, for example, does one in a workshop setting satisfactorily cast the roles of the two elderly grandmothers and ten-year-old grandchild in the Williams play? To what extent does gender shape perception in the Cooper and Shine plays; how does the student handle the question of authorial intent vis-à-vis directorial interpretation?

Within this anthology there are also links with the past that are refreshing and amplify our sense of the literary history of Black Theatre. Louis Rivers' *More Bread and the Circus* may remind one of the 1930s' *Big White Fog* in its evocation of an atmosphere of social erosion and family tension centering around the son's belief in Communism, but whereas the latter play is built upon a cause-effect premise, Rivers' easy-going, deceptively meandering plot structure is current with the randomness we have come to expect in life. Wesson and Stiles extract underlying truths from some of the old stereotypes, while Alexander strikes out for new ground entirely. The result is hilarious in *Miss Cegenation* and sobering in *No One Man Show* as we root for the heroine to recognize the ways in which her strength robs family members of opportunities to develop self-sufficiency. By contrast, the net effect is chilling in *The Hourglass*, for the mother, usually portrayed in Black playwriting as a figure to be venerated or castigated for her loving excesses, has been drawn here as a malevolent force seeking revenge.

In Richard Wesley and the Molettes, whose plays have appeared in some of the earlier anthologies, and in newcomer Dianne Houston, the '60s' assumption of the individual's responsibility to contribute to the health of the community continues to shape the perspectives from which they view the world; yet these authors are by no means stuck in the past. Wesley effectively dramatizes in *The Sirens* the destructively different ways in which young Black men and women are taught to view their futures, and though he uses the familiar dramatic subject of the whore on the block, he treats these women with a loving sensitivity sorely absent from plays of the '60s. Barbara and Carlton Molette proceed in *Noah's Ark* from the social macrocosm to the individual microcosm; they foresee a future "flood" of increased suppression of civil liberties and by implication raise the question of the nature of a Black American response to an overt appropriation of African resources. Houston, on the other hand, reverses the process in *The Fisherman*, for she dramatizes how rage and love can be channelled outward into meaningful social action.

But more important than any differences or similarities is the fact that this anthology is proud testament to the valuable developmental work Black companies have been doing nationwide. I have been fortunate enough to read two of these plays in earlier drafts and can attest to the fact that the published versions are stronger and more interesting. The two authors have benefited, as I am sure have their counterparts whose work is contained here, from the opportunity to gain feedback from other writers and from actors, directors, and audience members; they all have had the chance to hear their words, to see them living and moving about the stage, to learn what it is actors, directors, and technicians do. And, in those workshops where public critiques or question and answer periods have been part of the playreading format, audiences have also benefited by being able to exchange ideas and articulate those visions of themselves which they hope to see reflected in the artists' work.

In these hard economic times when Black Theatre itself is becoming a severely endangered species, it is crucial that both artists and audiences find ways to strengthen the commitment to developmental programs. We are fortunate in that *Center Stage* allows theatre artists to share materials outside their limited geographical areas. What is needed, of course, is to institute a more formal method of exchange of materials between the various playwriting workshops and to publish those scripts which have won some of the national awards mentioned above. In this way playwrights will obtain for a given script second, third, or fourth productions, and they will be encouraged in their resolve to write for the theatre. In this way the public will have its conception of itself stimulated, made more complex and enduring.

The publication of this anthology is an important step in the process of communication and cultural definition. For this we can all be grateful.

Sandra L. Richards
Stanford, California
1981

Boston native Dr. Sandra L. Richards has a background of experience in academic, professional, and community theatre. At Stanford University, where she currently holds a joint appointment, Richards serves as acting assistant professor in the Drama Department and director of the Committee on Black Performing Arts. Before joining Stanford, she taught drama at the University of California at Santa Barbara, at San Francisco State University, and at the University of Santa Clara; she also directed the Black Actors Workshop of the American Conservatory Theatre (ACT) in San Francisco; and she served as artistic director of the Oakland Ensemble Theatre, one of the leading Black community theatre groups of professional caliber in the San Francisco Bay Area.

ROBERT ALEXANDER

ROBERT ALEXANDER IS A PRODUCT of both an urban and suburban upbringing. And that strange but not so unusual atmosphere created a street wise, bourgeois Black man who in turn spawned a cast of complex characters, neither villains nor heroes, which allow people to read about Blacks in a relatively unexplored light.

Photo by Doug Jenkins

Alexander's parents set the stage for an artist to enter by exposing Robert to a wide variety of art forms, and his mother wrote poetry and recited it to him. Robert began writing seriously in high school under the direction of his English teacher Constance Sullivan.

While attending Oberlin Robert became the protégé of Calvin Hernton, noted essayist, poet, novelist, and playwright, who encouraged the young writer and at the same time scathed the babyfat painfully from his early pieces. During his Oberlin career Robert spent a year at Columbia where he further developed his playwriting and novel writing skills under the tutelage of Damon Kenyatta and John O. Killens .

After graduation he moved home briefly, spending enough time in the Washington D.C. area to pick up a literary critic bride and decided to seek his fortune in the writer's new frontier—the West Coast. While living in San Francisco he made literary connection with Ahmad Shabaka, who directed four of Robert Alexander's plays in the Bay Area. Alexander has also been sponsored by First World Productions headed by Sati Jamal.

In addition to *The Hourglass,* other plays by Robert Alexander include, *The Sandman and the Dreamer, Trespass, Threshold, Home Free, The Darkroom,* and *Sympathy Flowers.* Alexander's East Coast, Midwest, West Coast background can be viewed in his characters, who have such intense interactions in stories that need to be told. I am sure he will burn a place in American and International Theatre.

Carolyn Alexander
1980

THE HOURGLASS

Robert Alexander

CHARACTERS

MAMA: *Lena Fletcher, in her 70s, confined to a wheelchair.*

MARY FLETCHER: *A registered nurse, 30 years old.*

WENDELL JORDAN: MARY's *fiancé.*

REVEREND PIKE: *Good looking preacher in his 30s.*

DORA FLETCHER HARRIS: MARY's *older sister. The oldest of the three kids.*

CLIFFORD FLETCHER: MARY's *older brother.*

Set Direction: The set should include a living room to the left and a kitchen area to the right. Other imaginary rooms are offstage, right of the kitchen. Living room should include a fireplace with a mantelpiece. The hourglass is centered on the mantelpiece, and pictures of CLIFFORD FLETCHER, SR. *and* JR. *(one of each), are be placed on both sides of the hourglass. The furniture should include an old lamp and lamp table, a sofa and chair, and a coffee table. Leave ample space for* MAMA's *wheelchair to maneuver. Kitchen area should have at least a cupboard (essential), a stove, and a kitchen table and chairs. A big sign hangs over the kitchen entrance saying "WELCOME HOME CLIFF."*

ACT ONE

MARY's *busy dusting off the mantelpiece, getting the house in order for a party. She has on a bright party dress with an apron over it.* MAMA, *on the other hand, is wearing her every day attire, a grungy sweater. A shawl covers her lap and legs.* MARY *hums her favorite church hymn, "Rock of Ages," as she dusts: "Mmmm . . ."*

MAMA: Girl, you've been dusting the same spot for the past fifteen minutes.

MARY: *(Stops humming)* Maybe you should help me instead of complaining.

MAMA: You just be careful with my hourglass. It's the world to me.

MARY: Suppose I break it, Mama?

MAMA: I'd think twice if I were you.

MARY: Suppose I shatter your little world, Mama? What would you do then?

MAMA: You talking out your head, girl.

MARY: Naw, you talking out of your head, fussing over this silly thing. Ever since Daddy died you been fussing over this thing. I'm going to town Monday, Mama, to get us a clock. I can't tell time by this silly thing.

MAMA: Well I can. It's quarter to eight and Wendell should have been back with your brother by now. I don't know why you sent that fool to meet Clifford instead of going yourself.

MARY: And leave this house work to you?

MAMA: You got a lot of sass today, huh girl? You feeling your oats cause your brother coming home? This ain't like you.

MARY: I'm tired that's all.

MAMA: Gal, you too young to be tired.

MARY: Cleaning and fetching for you is enough to age anybody.

MAMA: You ain't doing me no favors.

MARY: All right then. Let's suppose I just move someplace else.

MAMA: Where?

MARY: Don't worry about where? How would you handle this house by yourself.

MAMA: *(Softer)* Come on Mary. Don't talk like that. You know you all I got left.

MARY: Then why don't you treat me with some respect?

MAMA: Okay. Starting this week, Mary. I'll start doing you better.

MARY: And how many times have I heard that?

MAMA: I mean it this time. I'm turning over a new leaf.

MARY: You don't mean it, that new leaf will be old and dry in five minutes.

MAMA: Hey watch what you doing. Be careful with my pictures.

MARY: Don't you think you should change your clothes now? You look like a scarecrow in that get up.

MAMA: Please, Mary, let me wear what I got on.

MARY: But it looks so drab. Can't you put on something pretty, something soft and lady-like.

MAMA: You forget I'm paralyzed, don't you?

MARY: No, Mama. How can I forget? You can't do nothing for yourself. You working me to the bone. I be so whupped when I come home from the hospital every night it's pitiful, only to come and play nurse to you too. It just ain't fair, Mama. When to hell am I supposed to rest?

MAMA: You act as if I got this way on purpose.

MARY: I ain't blaming you, Mama. *(Looks up)* I'm blaming the Lord.

MAMA: Maybe if you stop singing to him so much, things would be better. Maybe he don't care for your singing and this his way of saying so.

MARY: Somebody got it in for me. That's for sure.

MAMA: *(Soft)* I love you, Mary. Of all my chillen I love you the most. Don't think I'm gonna forget the way you stayed by my side. Other chillen might've put they poor mama away. But not you, Mary. You been such a good daughter. I'm gonna leave you a fortune when I die.

MARY: Shit!

MAMA: I'm serious. I'm gonna leave you my entire estate. *(Gestures with her hand)*

MARY: Keep it, Mama. This is one thing I hope you take with you.

MAMA: Say what?

MARY: When we bury you, we gonna bury the house too!

MAMA: Don't bury me, honey, cremate me like we done your father.

MARY: Yeah. Then we gonna cremate this house too.

MAMA: What you talking about. This a good house.

MARY: What do you know?

MAMA: I know it paid for. That what I know. That make it a good house.

(MAMA and MARY laugh)

MARY: You awright, Mama. Sometime you make it worth the trouble. But other times, Lord.

MAMA: I can't help it, Mary. You know how it is when you getting on in age and you get them funny ways. Ways that seems strange to other people.

MARY: Like that hourglass.

MAMA: That hourglass is my life now. I keep turning it over and over, measuring my life with each grain of sand. Ever since your daddy died, it's the only thing that's meant anything to me. It keeps our old love going. And when I'm gone, I hope you keep it going for me too.

MARY: When you gone, Mama, I'm getting a clock.

MAMA: Girl, if you get a clock, I won't let you rest for a minute. I'm gonna spook the hell out of you. You'll still feel me like I still feel your daddy. He with us now. Right in this room. Can't you feel him. Creeping up, crawling around, talking with that whiny voice.

MARY: Sometimes I think you're crazy, Mama.

MAMA: *(Sinister laugh)* Maybe I is. *(Pause)* Say, Mary, do me a small favor and fetch me my favorite cup.

MARY: Please, Mama, don't start drinking now. That's the last thing I need.

MAMA: Well just stand there then. I don't need no cup. *(She pulls her bottle from under her shawl and takes a swig)* You care for a chug? (MARY *frowns at her)* Do you some good.

MARY: You want to be drunk when Clifford comes.

MAMA: I don't care if Clifford sees me drunk. Who is he to judge me? Been away all this time.

MARY: Now don't start fussing at him when he gets here. Cliff had his career to think about.

MAMA: You call acting a career? I ain't ever seen the nigger on TV.

MARY: I just hope you'll be nice. *(Pause)* I ran into Auntie today. I told her Cliff was coming home.

MAMA: Mary, I hope you didn't invite her.

MARY: No, Mama, I didn't. But I think you should have. She's your sister, after all. *(Pause)* But I did invite Reverend Pike.

MAMA: That old fuddy duddy. Well you uninvite him.

MARY: It's too late, Mama. Besides, he's one of Cliff's friends. They were high school chums.

MAMA: Now that's an odd pair. *(Pause)* Reverend Pike kinda sweet on you, ain't he?

MARY: *(Fixing a floral arrangement)* I guess so. How does this look?

MAMA: It looks fine. What does Wendell make of you and Pike?

MARY: He don't make nothing of it, ain't nothing happening.

MAMA: Not yet.

(MARY rolls her eyes, followed by a long pause)

MARY: Mama, would you stop getting in the way. *(Pause)* I'm so excited I can hardly wait to see Clifford's face.

MAMA: Where is Dora and Frank? They should be here by now. Don't they know we trying to surprise Clifford?

MARY: Mama, would you stop worrying. Besides, you know how Clifford is. He might not want us fussing over him.

*(The doorbell rings—*MAMA *hides her bottle)*

MAMA: That better be Dora.

*(*MARY *opens the door.* REVEREND PIKE *enters wearing a three-piece suit)*

REV PIKE: Hello, Mary, am I late?

MARY: Oh, no, you're the first one here. Can I take your jacket or get you anything?

REV PIKE: Don't bother. I'll just have a seat. How are you, Mrs. Fletcher?

MAMA: *(Hamming it up)* Well, if it ain't the good Reverend Pike. What a surprise. Come to do a little courting, Reverend?

REV PIKE: Well, actually I . . .

MAMA: *(Cutting in)* I think it might' nice of you to drop in on Mary like this. She's been saving herself for someone nice like you. *(Pause)* You've been saving yourself too, haven't you, Reverend?

MARY: Mama, please.

MAMA: These folks around here are mighty lucky to have such a fine preacher, and still not married. My, my, my, what you and Mary waiting for? The resurrection of Jesus Christ?

REV PIKE: Well, actually . . .

MARY: *(Cuts in)* Ignore her, Reverend, she's on the sauce again.

MAMA: Mary is thirty years old, pushing fifty, and still ain't got no husband. Least I was married by a respectable age. I didn't have them whispering old maid behind my back.

MARY: But you had them whispering some other things, didn't you?

MAMA: It must be mighty lonesome living in that big house all by yourself, now that your mama done passed away.

REV PIKE: True, it can be lonely sometimes.

MAMA: *(Cuts in)* You don't have to be lonely. Although Mary may not look like much, she's one hell of a housekeeper. And you know what they say, you ain't never been loved until you been loved by an ugly gal. She'll bend over backwards to give you what you need when you need it.

MARY: Are you through making a fool of yourself?

MAMA: Shut up gal, I'm trying to get you a husband. *(Pause)* Care for something to drink, Reverend? *(Pulls out her bottle)* It'll loosen your joints.

REV PIKE: Maybe later, Mrs. Fletcher, after we eat. When do you suppose Clifford will get home?

MARY: Any minute now. I sent Wendell to get him. He carried a snapshot of Cliff so he'd recognize him.

REV PIKE: Oh, I forgot Wendell never met your brother.

MAMA: I told her to meet Cliff herself instead of sending a perfect stranger.

REV PIKE: I would have met Cliff if you had asked.

MARY: I wish I had known that, I just assumed you'd be too busy. I'm sorry, Reverend.

REV PIKE: That's another thing, Mary. Call me by my first name, Tommy. We don't need all of these formalities sticking between us.

MAMA: Uh, I can go in the other room if you want some privacy.

MARY: You stay put, Mother.

MAMA: Y'all need some time alone. Ain't that right, Reverend?

REV PIKE: There's no need for pretense, Mrs. Fletcher. I've been infatuated with your daughter ever since I laid eyes on her singing in the choir.

MAMA: Sings like a bird, don't she? God sure gave her a set of pipes.

REV PIKE: Yes, he did. He was pretty generous all the way around.

MAMA: I think I smell your rolls burning, Mary. I better go check on 'em.

MARY: No, Mother, I'll . . .

*(*MAMA *rolls into the kitchen and eavesdrops)*

REV PIKE: *(Grabbing* MARY's *arm he sits her down on the couch)* You've been dodging and ducking for a long time, but sooner or later you're gonna have to face it. I might be a man of the cloth, but I'm still a man. And I'm determined to get my way in matters of the heart.

MARY: But I'm seeing someone, Reverend.

REV PIKE: I know about Wendell, and he's an admirable man. But you could still do better.

MARY: Better, Reverend, in what way?

REV. PIKE: I am the best catch in town.

MARY: The best catch. I didn't know you were so vain, Reverend.

REV. PIKE: My name is Tommy. And vanity is the last thing I'm guilty of. Now, Mary, I think the time has finally come for us to both admit that we got a lot in common besides the church.

*(*REV PIKE *stares into* MARY's *eyes—he tries to force a kiss, but she turns her head, making him angry. He tries again, planting a medium length kiss on her lips.* MARY *responds)*

MARY: *(Looking down)* I'm embarrassed, Reverend. Embarrassed and surprised.

REV PIKE: Surprised at me or at yourself?

MARY: I never been unfaithful to Wendell. In fact we're engaged, only . . . we could never set a date. There's always been a lot of tension between Mama and Wendell. Every time we try to make a move, she gets in the way.

REV PIKE: Like a convenient obstruction. Face it, Mary, if you really loved Wendell, your mama couldn't keep you from being with him.

MARY: *(Looking at* REV PIKE *knowingly)* Maybe you're right, Reverend. There's something about being in the house with Mama. The way she bottles you up. But it's not just this house. Sometimes I feel it throughout the town. It's as if someone put an invisible dome over this town. A dome that can only be broken by a chosen few. Why do you suppose Clifford is coming back?

REV PIKE: Homesick, I guess.

MARY: Homesick is too easy. Besides, that don't fit Clifford. It's as if some force was pulling him back. You know, Reverend, this may sound strange, but I've known all along we would be sitting together like this one day. I dreamed it once. I tried to wash it from my mind, but that image of us wouldn't go away.

REV PIKE: So why fight it? *(Long pause)* How about going out with me tomorrow night?

MARY: Before we rush into anything, let me talk to Wendell.

(MAMA reenters. MARY turns around startled)

MAMA: *(To MARY)* Don't you think you ought to put the food on the table. Folks should be here any minute.

MARY: You're right, Mama. Excuse me, Tommy.
(MARY goes into the kitchen)

MAMA: I see you and Mary finally hit it off. I want you to know how much it pleases me.

REV PIKE: I'm glad to meet your approval Mrs. Fletcher. I hope it's not premature. Your daughter doesn't know what she wants.

MAMA: But her mama do. Say, Reverend, would you do me a small favor?

REV PIKE: Sure.

MAMA: *(Points to the mantelpiece)* Would you be kind enough to turn that hourglass over for me? It's not right to let time stand still.

REV PIKE: No problem. *(He does as instructed)*

MAMA: I'd turn it over myself if I could just stand up. You don't know how much it hurts me being in this chair.

REV PIKE: I know how you feel, Mrs. Fletcher. But the Lord is watching over you. Remember blessed are the meek for they shall inherit the earth. *(Pause)* You know, I like this hourglass. It's a quaint novelty piece. How long have you had it?

MAMA: A little over five years. Bought it right after my husband died. It's my tribute to him. I think of him every time someone turns it over.

REV PIKE: That's beautiful, Mrs. Fletcher. That's really wonderful the way you're still devoted to him. He was a lucky man.

MAMA: You flatter me too much, Reverend.

REV PIKE: *(Picking up the picture of her husband)* This is a good picture of your husband. I see why you loved him. He was a very handsome man, especially in his Army uniform.

MAMA: He had his faults, and we been over some . . . *(Pause)* rough roads together. Always moving the kids from place to place, until we ended up here. I don't want to bore you with the past, Reverend. Dora says that's my main problem. I'm obsessed with the past. She think I'm crazy keeping this hourglass. Crazy for talking about my husband all the time.

REV PIKE: *(Picking up and looking at the other picture)* Clifford looks just like your husband.

MAMA: The spitting image. He just like his daddy for the world. I swear both of them used to work me to the bone. Neither willing to lift a finger to help me. But I got 'em now. I got 'em, don't I?

REV PIKE: What do you mean, "you got 'em?"

MAMA: Pay me no mind, Reverend. I'm just babbling to myself. *(The door bell rings. MARY reenters, setting a platter of food on the table)* I sure hope that's them now. I'm tired of waiting.

MARY: I'll get it, Mama. *(MARY opens the door, and DORA enters dressed in high style and carrying an expensive piece of luggage)* Hey, Dora. Girl, how you doing?
(They embrace)

DORA: I'm making it. How about you?

MARY: Same as always.

MAMA: Well, we just glad to see you make it. Sure took you long enough.

DORA: Is that all you got to say to me? *(Pause)*

MAMA: *(Sweet)* I was only jugging with you. You looking good. Like you living in the rich house.
(They embrace)

DORA: Thank you, Mama. How you doing?

MAMA: I'm feeling all right. Mary been real good to me.

MARY: Where's Frank? Parking the car?

DORA: *(Sitting)* He couldn't come.

MAMA: You mean you drove here by yourself. Something wrong between y'all?

DORA: Everything's fine, Mama. He's just backed up in work. Running a cleaners is a headache. There're a lot of dirty clothes in Chicago.

MAMA: And a lot of dirty people if you know what I know. I know what kind of cleaning up he's doing if he a man.

DORA: What you trying to say, Mama?

MAMA: Nothing girl, I ain't saying nothing. What you say, Reverend?

DORA: Forgive me, Tommy. Sorry for not speaking. You here to see your running buddy, Cliff?

REV PIKE: Yeah, you know me and Cliff. We go back to high school. We were a terrible pair.

DORA: Y'all stayed in trouble. But I'm glad you found God. You know I figured you should have a church in Chicago by now. You too good for this town.

REV PIKE: Wellington suits me fine, really. I'm happy here.

DORA: I don't see how y'all can take it.

MAMA: Everybody ain't looking for bright lights, Dora.

DORA: Do bright lights scare you, Mary? Is that why you stay in this hick town?

MARY: Where do you get off coming in here putting us down? Living in Chicago don't make you better than us.

DORA: It's not that I'm better. I got better opportunities. You could have 'em too. If you'd move to the city. A woman with your background in nursing would have an easy time finding work.

MAMA: Sho' has gotten stuffy in here.

MARY: Yeah, I hear you, Mama. They say Chicago is the windy city. But it just blowing hot air.

DORA: Stay small minded. Hell if I care.

MAMA: You got anything that needs tending to in the kitchen, Mary?

MARY: You can see how my cake is doing.

MAMA: Gladly. *(She goes into the kitchen, eavesdrops, and drinks)*

DORA: Now wait a minute. Who does Mama think she's fooling with that cutesy wootsy act? You know she ain't helped you since Daddy died.

MARY: Can't she have a change of heart?

DORA: Not short of a transplant. If I was you, Mary, I'd pack my bags tonight and ride back to Chi-town.

MARY: And what in the hell am I supposed to do with Mama?

DORA: You know what to do about Mama.

MARY: But I can't do that.

DORA: It's either that or throw your own life away.

MARY: Reverend, she expects me to put Mama in the old folks home. What kind of daughter would think like that?

REV PIKE: *(To DORA)* Why do you want to put her away?

DORA: Because she's out of her skull.

REV PIKE: She seems perfectly normal to me.

MARY: Thank you, Reverend.

DORA: She's sure got y'all psyched. Aren't you tired of waiting on Mama?

MARY: Someone has to do it.

DORA: I don't understand you, Mary. You remind me of Jesus, dragging your cross to your own crucifiction. Mama is crazy. Face it. She hasn't budged from this house since Father died. *(Stands)* How can you stay here, without a radio, without a TV, no telephone, without a clock. Hey, Tommy, Mama tells time by looking at that hourglass. Now is she crazy or is she crazy?

MARY: So I should dump her crippled? She can't walk. Is it her fault she can't walk?

DORA: Maybe. It sure happened mighty suddenly, and we don't know how or why. She say she fell down, but I can't buy that. All I know is that Daddy died, and she said to hell with it all. To hell with walking. To hell with working. And to hell with living. She won't leave the house for nothing. She cut herself off from the world. Frank says Mama's problem is all up here. *(Points to her head)*

MARY: What does he know?

DORA: Mary, Mama is using this cripple thing to keep you here. She old, and I can understand her being afraid of being left alone, but she going about it the wrong way. You leave Mama today, and she'll be up walking tomorrow. *(Significant pause)*

REV PIKE: Mary, Dora may have a point there.

MARY: Well, I think it stinks.

DORA: Look, when Cliff gets here, I think you should talk to him. He's got something to tell you.

MARY: What?

DORA: You'll find out soon enough.
(Doorbell rings)

MARY: This has got to be him now. *(She looks out the window)* It's him. Y'all want to hide and say "surprise!"

DORA: To hell with that, just open the door.
(MARY waves her finger at DORA threateningly before opening the door. CLIFF enters the door carrying modest luggage)

MARY: *(Embracing CLIFF)* We were wondering if you was coming or what.

CLIFFORD: Hey, Mary, give me some sugar. Damn it's good to see you. Dora, come here.

DORA: Oh Cliff, God you look so much like Daddy, it almost scare me.

CLIFFORD: Goddamn, you look like you living on easy street with those clothes. Fingers painted. Where's that old man of yours?

DORA: At home making me some more money.

CLIFFORD: I'm sorry he couldn't be here. I want to see the brother.

REV PIKE: Hey, but look who is here.

CLIFFORD: *(Doing a double take)* Tommy? Tommy Pike, is that really you, man?

REV PIKE: You know I'd be here to see you.

CLIFFORD: So what's happening. You still got the girls tied 'round your little pinkie?

REV PIKE: Now that was you that had all the girls. I couldn't even scrape up any leftovers.

MARY: He's a preacher now, Cliff.

CLIFFORD: Aw, man, don't tell me that lie . . . are you serious? *(Pause)* So, how's the rest of the gang?

REV PIKE: I'm the only one left. Fred, Ron, those guys all moved to Chicago. And Robert's out on the West Coast making all the money.

CLIFFORD: Well, I'll be goddamned. Everybody got the hell out of Dodge.

MARY: Where is Wendell? Is he parking the car.

CLIFFORD: Wendell? Who's Wendell?

MARY: He was supposed to meet you at the bus depot.

CLIFFORD: Well, I didn't see him. I took a cab.

MARY: That sure is strange, I wonder what happened?

CLIFFORD: It's anybody's guess.

REV PIKE: So how was Europe, Clifford? Tell the truth now.

CLIFFORD: Europe is Europe, you know. It was a good scene for a while, but you know, it's time to be home.

REV PIKE: Do they treat the brothers good over there?

CLIFFORD: Depending on where you're at. Just like here.

DORA: It musta been good—we didn't think you'd ever come back.

CLIFFORD: Hey, well, touch me, feel me, cause I'm back. This is really me. *(Pause)* Say, where the hell is Mama? Y'all hiding her?

MARY: Oh, wow. She's in the kitchen, I'll get her. *(Goes to the kitchen)*

CLIFFORD: I see y'all put a sign up there for me and got a nice spread on the table. So where y'all hiding the booze? *(Breaks into a British accent)* We drink only the very best gin in old London town.

DORA: There's something I never told you about Mama. I didn't . . . I never . . . I thought it would have cleared up by now. But it hasn't.

CLIFFORD: Is something wrong?

DORA: I'm afraid so.

MAMA: *(Enters pushed by MARY)* Well, it's about time you come home boy. Look at you, looking skinny as sin. Ain't they fed you over there in Euu-rope. *(CLIFFORD is astounded—significant pause—mouth agape)* Well, what you got to say for yourself?

CLIFFORD: When did this happen? *(He drops down to be at MAMA's level)*

DORA: Right after Father died. She's been in that chair for over five years.

MAMA: If you had come home like you was supposed to you would have known this.

CLIFFORD: *(Puts his head on MAMA's lap)* Mama, I'm sorry, really I am.

MAMA: Don't say sorry now, it's past the time for feeling sorry.

CLIFFORD: What have the doctors said?

MARY: She hasn't seen one.

CLIFFORD: In five years?

DORA: Cause she could walk if she really wanted to. She playing possum, Cliff. She know it, and I know it. I sent a specialist down here to examine her, and she knew he was coming too. So what does she do? She locked him out the house.

MARY: Mama's old fashioned. Doctors frighten her, that's all it is.

DORA: Still ain't no reason for her being a recluse.

MARY: She's proud, Dora. She got too much pride to let this town see her confined to that chair.

DORA: Proud my ass.

CLIFFORD: Now wait. Let Mama tell it.

MAMA: Naw, let 'em go on. I'm seeing something. I'm starting to see who to leave in my will and who to leave out.

DORA: *(Powerfully)* What could you leave us, Mama? That wheel chair, that hourglass, this lame excuse for a house?

(MARY slaps DORA in the face. DORA stares bitterly at MARY, holding the side of her face while MARY trembles violently. Long significant pause)

DORA: She got you so sucked in there's no saving you.

(MARY turns her back to DORA. She stands next to REV PIKE, grabbing hold of his hand)

MAMA: Well Cliff, your coming home got things all stirred up. What you got to say for yourself?

CLIFFORD: What can I say, Mama? That it's good to be home?

MAMA: Well, for starters you can explain why you didn't come home for your daddy's funeral.

CLIFFORD: Why? That was five years ago.

MAMA: I need to know, boy. Mary told me she reached you over the phone.

CLIFFORD: Mama, I was playing Othello at the Royal Academy in London. It was the first time in the spotlight, Mama, and I didn't want to give it up. Not then, not for something I couldn't change.

MAMA: So Othello was more important than your family. Move away from me, Cliff, I don't want you slobbering on me. *(CLIFFORD moves away from her. Long pause)* Somebody turn that hourglass over for me. It ain't right to let time stand still.

REV PIKE: I'll turn it, Mrs. Fletcher. *(He turns it over)*

DORA: See, Cliff. This is the hourglass I wrote you about. Mama claims she can tell time down to the minute from looking at it.

MAMA: Ain't nobody made me a liar yet. *(Pause)* Thank you, Tommy.

CLIFFORD: *(Shouting for attention)* Hey, is this a party or what?

DORA: This ain't no party, Cliff. This is Daddy's wake. Since you couldn't make it earlier, Mama suspended time just for you. Ain't that how it is, Mama? This is Daddy's wake. Am I right?

CLIFFORD: Nonsense. This is a party. A celebration of life.

DORA: It ain't no party, Cliff. Do you see any happy faces? Do you hear any music playing? It ain't no party. I tell you it's a wake. Daddy's wake. *(Long pause)*

CLIFFORD: What have I come home to?

(Everyone looks away. WENDELL *limps on stage. He has a brace on one leg. A flask of whiskey in a brown bag sticks up out of his back pocket. He knocks on the door.* REV PIKE *answers it.* WENDELL *is drunk)*

REV PIKE: Hey, Wendell, come on in. Everybody was worried about you.

WENDELL: *(Enters)* Mary, I didn't see your brother. You sure he's coming today? *(He stumbles as he approaches her)*

MARY: Am I the only sober person living in this town. Damn. *(She goes into the kitchen)*

WENDELL: What's she mad at me for? What did I do?

MAMA: Nothing, that's just it.

CLIFFORD: I'll go talk to her.

*(*CLIFFORD *goes into the kitchen.* WENDELL *looks at the snapshot* MARY *gave him)*

WENDELL: Hey, that's the man right there. Ain't that him? *(He shows* REV PIKE *the picture)*

DORA: Poor Mary. What does she see in this child?

MAMA: Y'all might as well eat this food. Ain't no point in letting it waste.

WENDELL: *(Grabbing a plate)* Good idea, Mrs. Fletcher.

(Lights dim over the living room and get brighter over the kitchen)

MARY: You don't have to come in here.

CLIFFORD: Mary, what's going on in this place?

MARY: Why you want to know?

CLIFFORD: Because it's frightening—everything I'm hearing and what Dora's been writing. I'm worried about you, Mary. And who is that Wendell guy? Where did he come from?

MARY: He's my fiancé.

CLIFFORD: Him?

MARY: Is something wrong with him?

CLIFFORD: Hey, if he turns you on, who am I to butt in?

MARY: I don't know what turns me on. I don't know what turn on is. Why did you come back here, Cliff? Why now?

CLIFFORD: I felt something was pulling me back.

MARY: Well you should have stayed away. Life here has been miserable.

CLIFFORD: So I see.

MARY: Dora said you came back because you had something to tell me.

CLIFFORD: Dora said that? I don't know what she's talking about.

MARY: Well we can ask her. Or you can tell me yourself. Now which do you prefer?

CLIFFORD: *(Trying to make up something)* Oh, I remember now. She wants us to help plan a surprise party for Mama in Chicago. You know, at her house. Frank is gonna cook some ribs and . . .

MARY: *(Cutting in)* Stop lying, Clifford. You already know Mama ain't leaving this house for nothing. Now quit playing with me.

CLIFFORD: I can't tell you, Mary. Not now. Not after seeing Mama sitting in that chair.

MARY: So it's about Mama, huh? *(*CLIFF *nods "yes")* I'm gonna get Dora in here and find out what all this secrecy is about. *(Goes to the kitchen door)* Dora come in here. We want to talk to you.

*(*DORA *jumps up and enters the kitchen)*

MAMA: What's going on in there? Y'all having a private party?

MARY: Tommy do me a favor and read to Mama. Something from the bible.

MAMA: You ain't putting me to sleep.

*(*REV PIKE *keeps Mama preoccupied so she won't try to eavesdrop)*

MARY: Dora, you said Clifford had something to tell me. But he won't. I know it's something about Mama. Now are you gonna tell?

DORA: Cliff, you promised.

CLIFFORD: Well, I changed my mind.

MARY: I'll get it out of Mama.

CLIFFORD: Okay. I'll tell you. I guess it's best that you know. You better sit down.

MARY: *(Sits down)* I'm sitting.

CLIFFORD: *(Looks around)* I better sit down too . . . *(He stalls)*

MARY: I'm waiting . . .

DORA: Mary, what Cliff wants to tell you is that Mama isn't really your mama. Now don't you feel a fool for getting stuck?

CLIFFORD: *(Stands up)* Thank you, Dora. Now let's go back in there and get something to eat.

MARY: Sit down, Cliff. Dora, are you serious? *(*DORA *and* CLIFF *nod their heads in affirmation simultaneously)* Of all the weird, stupid shit I done heard in my life. You guys have outdone yourselves. *(Starts to cry)* I don't believe you.

CLIFFORD: But, it's true.

MARY: Then prove it. Get Mama in here.

DORA: I don't think that's such a good idea. You'll never get her to admit she's not your mother, just like you'll never get her to admit she can walk.

CLIFFORD: You really believe she can walk?

MARY: Let's deal with one thing at a time. How do you know she ain't my mama?

DORA: Look, I'm old enough to remember whether Mama carried you or not. Clifford is too.

CLIFFORD: That's right. I was there when we

found you on the doorstep with a note saying John Fletcher is the father of this child, signed the mother.

MARY: That's funny, y'all. Y'all really had me going for a minute.

DORA: I'm not cracking a smile, Mary. I'm as straight-faced as I can be. The woman you running around fetching for ain't your mama. If you leave tomorrow there's no reason for you to feel guilty.

MARY: She's the only mother I know. So if what you saying is true, it don't change a thing. I'm gonna keep on taking care of her.

DORA: Why?

MARY: Because neither one of you will. Besides, if she's not my mama, why in the hell did she raise me?

CLIFFORD: The note said Daddy was your father. So we kept you.

MARY: Why would Mama keep me knowing I'm some other woman's baby? Huh? Knowing I'm the offspring of one of her husband's flings. Mama ain't the type to sweep things under the rug so easy. The whole story sounds shabby to me.

DORA: Well, it's true. She ain't your mama. She ain't even Clifford's mama.

CLIFFORD: *(Astounded)* Say what?

DORA: She ain't your mama either. Didn't you know that?

CLIFFORD: Bull shit.

DORA: You mean Daddy never told you?

CLIFFORD: Told me what?

DORA: We found you the same way we found Mary. Daddy was your father, but somebody else was your mama. I thought you knew.

CLIFFORD: I knew about Mary. I was here the day she came. But I always thought she was my mama.

DORA: Daddy said he was gonna tell you. I thought that was why you went away, 'cause you couldn't face the truth.

CLIFFORD: I went away, because I couldn't stand this place. And I advise you to do the same, Mary.

MARY: And leave Mama by herself?

DORA: *(Loud)* She ain't your mama, damn it.

MARY: *(Loud)* That's what you say.

MAMA: *(Yelling from the other room)* What y'all doing in there? Don't be messing with my liquor.

CLIFFORD: You mean to say she ain't my mother either?

DORA: I can't prove she's my mother either. Being born is a blur to me.

CLIFFORD: What would make her want to raise us, knowing we come from someone else? Knowing Papa was screwing around.

MARY: *(Getting up)* I'm gonna ask her myself.

CLIFFORD: *(Moving to block the door)* No, Mary, not just yet.

MARY: But I got to know. This is a shock to me.

CLIFFORD: I know it is. But use tact. That's the only way to get anything out of Mama.

DORA: He's right.

MARY: You mean, all this time I been lovin' and caring for this woman who ain't no kin to me?

DORA: Right. If you decide to leave tonight, there's no reason why you should feel guilty.

MARY: But somebody has got to stay with her. You're her daughter, Dora. And you're not gonna care for her.

DORA: Me and Frank don't have the time or the space for Mama.

CLIFFORD: I'll take care of her.

MARY: *(Sarcastic)* Oh, that's real big of you. You'll be with her for a week, then you'll be off again.

CLIFFORD: Come on, Mary.

DORA: Caring for Mama requires patience, Cliff.

MARY: You won't last a week around here. Wellington is too dry for someone like you.

DORA: Yeah, you're an actor. This is not the place for you.

CLIFFORD: I'm not an actor anymore. I've given it up. I want to do some other things, like trying my hand at writing. I got a novel inside me that I want to get out. Wellington is the perfect place. It's quiet. I can think and write without being disturbed.

DORA: Not with Mama around.

CLIFFORD: I know how to deal with Mama. Besides she one hell of a story herself. Give me some time with Mama and I'll put this puzzle together. Anyway, this is supposed to be a party. Mary, put a smile on your face.

MARY: How can I, Cliff?

CLIFFORD: For me, please. Act like you're happy I'm home, even if all I brought you was bad news. Yeah. That's better. Dora, you too. Now come on, let's go in there and act like one big happy family, okay?

(They get up and go into the other room. They are greeted with hostility by MAMA*)*

MAMA: What y'all in there talking about all this time? Y'all plotting on how to spend my money after I die?

DORA: You got to die first.

MAMA: Oh, so you was plotting on how to kill me.

CLIFFORD: Don't be silly, Mama.

*(*MARY *stares at* MAMA*)*

MAMA: What's wrong with you, Mary? Why you staring at me like that?

MARY: *(Snaps out of it)* Sorry, Mama. Just thinking, that's all. *(She gets her sweater and starts to exit)*

WENDELL: Hey, Mary, you still coming over to-night? *(MARY does not respond. She exits)* What's with her?

DORA: Come on. Clifford is here, let's celebrate.

(MAMA shrugs her shoulders as they continue to eat)

REV PIKE: *(Making room for CLIFF)* Come on, Cliff, I'll fix you a plate.

Lights out, Curtain

ACT TWO

Scene 1

Same set direction. The following day. CLIFFORD *and* DORA *are sitting in the living room, talking.*

CLIFFORD: Do you think Mary will like it in Chicago? She sure changed her mind quite suddenly.

DORA: Finding out Mama ain't her mama got something to do with it.

CLIFFORD: And you ain't got no idea who my real mother could be?

DORA: Daddy should be here to explain this shit. All I know is that he once told me about this real serious affair he had when he was living in Newport News. The girl couldn't have been more than sixteen. I mean they really had the hots for each other. Anyway, this girl suddenly disappears. I mean, the old man looked everywhere for this child, but he couldn't find her, so finally he just gave up. Then one day he goes out to get the milk off the front porch, as usual, only to find you out on the porch, wrapped in a basket with a note attached saying the same goddamn thing Mary's note was to say a few years later in another town.

CLIFFORD: It's unbelievable. I mean, that it could happen twice. Two times in two different cities.

DORA: Look, honey, it would come as no surprise to me, if I found out it happened three times.

CLIFFORD: Is that why you're so cold to Mama?

DORA: Ain't a thing here to prove that she is my real mother. Me and that woman don't look nothing alike. How do I know I wasn't left on the doorstep? Bad things always happen in threes, you know. But that's not why I'm cold to her. I'm cold because I think she can walk. It upset me seeing her mess over Mary. I want to be kind to Mama, she raised us, but now something about her bothers me. Maybe it's just our egos. We grate one another.

(MAMA enters, followed closely by MARY, carrying luggage)

MAMA: What y'all in here yapping about?

CLIFFORD: Nothing, Mama.

MAMA: Can't nobody sleep in this house for y'all two yapping. Boy, don't you know your voice carry?

CLIFFORD: Sorry, Mama.

DORA: You got everything, Mary?

MAMA: I still don't like the idea of you running off like this.

MARY: I know, Mama. It was a hard decision for me to make.

MAMA: I don't understand y'all kids today. None of y'all appreciate the value of being at home. One come and the other go. Lawd, what done got into y'all?

CLIFFORD: Well, Mama, at least I'm here now.

MAMA: Boy, hush. I'm talking to your sister. Mary, you ain't gonna like it up there in the city.

MARY: I got to go see for myself, okay?

DORA: *(Picking up her bag)* I better take these things out to the car.

MAMA: Dora, I don't appreciate you coming in here, influencing Mary like this.

MARY: Mama, Dora had nothing to do with my decision. I had been thinking about it for a long time.

MAMA: You mean, you was just waiting for your brother to get back here so you could run off and have yourself a hot time.

MARY: Mama, there's no point in explaining anything to you. You're gonna think what you want to think. No matter what I say or do.

DORA: Come on, Mary. Let's just get in the car. Mama, you take care. *(MAMA shuns her)* Cliff, you take care of Mama and yourself. Maybe we'll get together sometime so you can tell me all about Europe. *(They hug—DORA exits)*

MARY: Mama, looks like this is it. *(She kneels down to kiss MAMA, but MAMA turns her head and wheels away)* Okay, have it your way then. Cliff, call me if something goes wrong.

CLIFFORD: Okay, Mary. *(They hug)*

MARY: Now, I got to break the news to Wendell. I'll see y'all. *(She exits)*

CLIFFORD: So long, Mary. *(Long pause)* Well, Mama, looks like it's just you and me now.

MAMA: *(Sarcastic)* Who would have ever guessed?

CLIFFORD: Well, Mama, what is it gonna be for breakfast?

MAMA: Whatever you fix will be fine.

CLIFFORD: No, Mama. I meant what were you gonna fix for breakfast? I can't cook.

MAMA: Don't hand me that. You a grown man now. I know you had to cook for yourself over there.

CLIFFORD: No, Mama. Not me. I don't know what to do in a kitchen.

MAMA: No wonder you came back so damn skinny.

CLIFFORD: My women did my cooking for me.

MAMA: Your women? What you doing over there, messing with them women for? I hope you ain't brought back nothing.

CLIFFORD: Nothing but a suitcase full of memories, Mama.

MAMA: Wish you had settled down now, don't you?

CLIFFORD: Sometimes, Mama, sometimes.

MAMA: You and that Mary. First you run off and stay away for eight years. You don't hardly write, you act like you don't know us, and now Mary want to go and do the same.

CLIFFORD: Don't be hard on us, Mama. We only doing what we felt we had to do.

MAMA: You speak for yourself. That damn Mary just do what she's told. She ain't got it in her to think for herself.

CLIFFORD: Look, Mama. I really am starved. Can't you fix me something?

MAMA: Boy, I can't see the stove top. I'll burn your food to death.

CLIFFORD: So what if it's a little well done?

MAMA: You ever eat burnt eggs before? Boy, you better get in there and fend for yourself.

CLIFFORD: What about you?

MAMA: Don't worry about me.

CLIFFORD: *(Looking around)* Sure is quiet around here. Guess this is the perfect place to write.

MAMA: What you talking about? Write what?

CLIFFORD: Didn't I tell you, Mama? I'm gonna write a novel. A novel about a Black-American expatriate living by his wits in Europe.

MAMA: What was it like over there, anyway? You must've felt kind of funny being around all them people, talking that different talk. How did you understand 'em?

CLIFFORD: Well, I was in England for the longest time so I didn't encounter any language difficulties there. But I really didn't have that much of a problem in Paris or Copenhagen either. I always managed to run into people who spoke English. And I was able to pick up a phrase or two, here and there. I spoke survival French. You would have liked it, Mama. They really treated me like I was something special.

MAMA: You are special, Clifford. You my only boy. That makes you special.

CLIFFORD: Yeah, but over there I was really special. Over there I had everything a black man could ask for. Fine clothes, beautiful women, respect from my fellow artists.

MAMA: Seems like you threw away a lot by coming back.

CLIFFORD: In one sense, yeah.

MAMA: If it was so good then, why did you decide to come back?

CLIFFORD: I guess for the same reason I left, Mama. You know, the alluring call of the unknown. I went away seeking adventure, excitement, and to be alone in a strange place so I could get to know myself. So I go over there for a few years. I meet people, I hang out, I do a few plays, Then it all becomes a routine after awhile. The excitement wears off. All of a sudden America, Wellington, you, Mary, and Dora excite me to the point of wanting to come home. It's a vicious circle, Mama. When you're here you want to be there, and when you're over there, you want to be here.

MAMA: Well, I hope you don't run off again.

CLIFFORD: Me too. I'm tired of running from place to place.

MAMA: Just like your daddy. He had us moving from town to town before we finally settled here.

CLIFFORD: Come on. It was the Army that kept us moving around. They kept on transferring him.

MAMA: But your father volunteered. Every time something new came up he was the first to volunteer.

CLIFFORD: Why would he do that? It was frustrating for me to keep getting readjusted to a new place, new school, new people all the time. It was hell.

MAMA: *(Turns away)* That's something between your father and me.

CLIFFORD: Well, he's dead now, so we can talk about it.

MAMA: Let's just say he had his reasons for wanting to move. *(Turns)*

CLIFFORD: What kind of reasons. We always knew in advance that where we was going was really no better. Sometimes he acted like his life depended on getting relocated. I remember how cranky he used to get until he knew for sure we were moving. Now, why was that, Mama? I know that's why I got the hell out of Copenhagen, women were driving me crazy.

MAMA: Talk with some respect about your father, boy. You know he ain't never had no other women.

CLIFFORD: Let's not pretend, Mama.

MAMA: Is that why you come back here? So you can say unkind things about your father to your mother before she dies?

CLIFFORD: You're dying, Mother?

MAMA: Any minute now.

CLIFFORD: *(Goes to couch)* Well, I'm glad I got a good seat, 'cause I sure don't want to miss this.

MAMA: Don't play with me, boy.

CLIFFORD: *(Looks around)* What time is it, Mama? I'm supposed to meet Tommy for lunch this afternoon. You must have a clock in here somewhere.

MAMA: There ain't a clock in this house. Hasn't been one since your father died.

CLIFFORD: That's right, you tell time by looking at that hourglass.

MAMA: *(Points to the mantelpiece)* According to it, it's eleven o'clock. Why don't you turn it over for me.

CLIFFORD: *(Picks it up)* Whoops. Almost dropped it, Mama.

MAMA: You be careful with that thing.

CLIFFORD: I better get breakfast in town and keep on to Tommy's. I'll be back sometime this evening.

MAMA: 'Fore you go, honey, would you go into the kitchen and fetch me my favorite cup?

CLIFFORD: Okay, Mama.

(He goes into the kitchen. MAMA yells to him)

MAMA: Honey, while you in there, would you put a couple of pieces of bread in the toaster for me? I'd do it myself if I could just get around the way I used to.

CLIFFORD: *(Yells back)* Okay, Mama.

MAMA: Oh yeah, and put a little butter and some of that strawberry preserves on it for me, okay?

CLIFFORD: Okay, Mama.

MAMA: Ms. Taylor made that strawberry preserves. She come over here last month with a big jar of peach preserves and strawberry preserves. Me and your sister tore through that peach preserves like it wasn't nothing.

CLIFFORD: *(Reenters with the toast and the cup)* Here's your toast, Mama, and your cup.

MAMA: *(Pointing to the lamp table)* Just set that down over there. *(MAMA takes out her whiskey bottle and pours the liquor into the cup)*

CLIFFORD: Oh, so that's what you do for entertainment.

MAMA: A little catnip never hurt none.

CLIFFORD: Well, I better get going.

MAMA: You try to be back here by six o'clock. That's when I want you to fix dinner.

CLIFFORD: I can't cook. Will you get that into your head.

MAMA: You'll learn. You'll get plenty of practice around here. Oh yeah, one other thing. Mary may or may not have told you this. But after dinner each night, you have to give me my bath. I can't bathe myself on account of my paralysis.

CLIFFORD: Naked?

MAMA: Unless you want to save time by washing me and my clothes together.

CLIFFORD: *(Distressful)* I'm not looking forward to any of this.

MAMA: Mary ain't been gone a hot second, and I miss her already.

CLIFFORD: So do I, Mama, so do I.

Lights out, Curtain

Scene 2

Same setting. Months later. MAMA *is in the kitchen setting the table. A new clock is on the kitchen wall.* CLIFFORD *is in the living room reading a letter.*

MAMA: Clifford, your breakfast is on the table. It's getting cold. *(Pause.* CLIFFORD *goes into the kitchen absorbed in his letter. He says nothing to* MAMA; *he just reads the letter)* Clifford, your eggs are getting cold.

CLIFFORD: *(Still looking at the letter, puts a forkful in his mouth and immediately spits it out)* Uck. They're cold.

MAMA: I told you they would be.

CLIFFORD: Why did you let my eggs get cold? Fix me some more. *(He shoves his plate across the table toward his mother)*

MAMA: Clifford, you know how hard it is for me to cook. I can barely see the top of the stove.

CLIFFORD: *(Still looking at the letter)* So, get out of the chair.

MAMA: Look, Cliff, God don't like no ugly.

CLIFFORD: If that's the case, you'll never get to heaven.

MAMA: Look, Clifford, just get me my cup. I could stand a drink. *(*CLIFFORD *surprisingly gets up and gets her cup, but instead of giving it to her, he teases her by putting it within her grasp, then quickly moving it away when she tries to grab it. A yo-yo effect. This goes on for a few seconds)* Goddamn you, Cliff. Keep the cup. I don't need it. *(She takes out her bottle and drinks from it directly.* CLIFFORD *just laughs)* Who you laughing at?

CLIFFORD: Nobody, Mama, nobody.

MAMA: You're evil. Just like your father, for the world. God is gonna punish you.

CLIFFORD: I'm being punished, living with you.

MAMA: Who is that letter from? Let me see it.

CLIFFORD: *(Tossing the letter at* MAMA's *feet)* It's from Mary.

MAMA: You bastard.

CLIFFORD: I know. I know all about my roots.

*(*MAMA *picks up the letter and reads it, ignoring his last comment)*

MAMA: So, Mary's in Hawaii now, and she's found a job as a nurse. Chicago must have been too rough on the girl. But she sounds happy now. Hawaii . . . that fits her.

CLIFFORD: As soon as it wears off, she'll be back. You can count on it.

MAMA: What makes you so certain?

CLIFFORD: I came back, didn't I? *(Cynical laugh. CLIFFORD gets up)*

MAMA: Where you going now?

CLIFFORD: *(Starts singing)*
When I die, bury me.
Hang my balls on a cherry tree.
If they grow, let me know.
I'll be listening on the radio.
(More giggling. CLIFFORD reaches behind the sofa and pulls out a bottle of whiskey) Say, look what I found.

MAMA: Nigger, what you doing going in my hiding place, messing with my liquor?

CLIFFORD: A little catnip never hurt none. Here's to you. *(He clinks his bottle against his mother's bottle and takes a swig. Then he picks up the hourglass and starts tossing it, then inspects it closely)* You know, it's funny how some things change with time. I mean, it's crazy the way things have a way of reversing themselves. *(Pause)* Look at us. It used to be you and Mary. Now it's just me and you. *(Turns to MAMA)*

MAMA: *(Wheels away)* Don't remind me. I loved it when Mary was here. Those were better days. I wish she'd come back so it could be just like the good ol' days.

CLIFFORD: Don't rack your brain. Forget about the past.

MAMA: How can I? The past is all I have. My life is all behind me now. It done slipped through my fingers like those ashes in the hourglass. *(Pause)* You hate me, don't you Cliff?

CLIFFORD: No, Mama. I don't hate you.

MAMA: Then how come you treat me the way you do? *(Pause)* Now I know what it must've been like for Mary.

CLIFFORD: Explain yourself.

MAMA: Never mind. If only Mary would just come back. I'd treat her differently.

CLIFFORD: No, you wouldn't. You'd treat her the same way. You wouldn't be able to help it. That's the way you relate to Mary. And this is the way I relate to you. And if Daddy came back, he'd be no different either.

MAMA: You didn't like your father, did you Cliff?

CLIFFORD: I don't know, Mama. I got mixed emotions. I know one thing. I didn't like the way he treated you.

MAMA: You don't treat me no different

CLIFFORD: *(Ashamed)* I know, Mama. I can't help it. It's in me to treat you like this.

MAMA: You was the worst child God ever put breath in.

CLIFFORD: I know . . . remember the time I locked you out of the house?

MAMA: I damn near froze to death. Didn't you hear me calling you?

CLIFFORD: Yeah, I heard. Only I pretended not to.

MAMA: Just like your father. He claimed he never heard a word I said either.

CLIFFORD: I know, it used to make me sick, too.

MAMA: But you'd go and do the same thing. Didn't you ever feel bad about doing me the way you did?

CLIFFORD: Sometimes I did. But I tried not to trip on it. You know, when I first got to Europe, I got involved with this Swede. Blonde hair, nice tits, no ass, a little money, no brains. Bitch used to chase me all around town. Popping up when I least expected. Anyway, she reminded me of you.

MAMA: In what way?

CLIFFORD: There was something desperate about her. I mean, she wanted so desperately to be loved. Just like you. You wanted Daddy to love you, but he didn't. Anyway, the girl went crazy. She tried to kill herself, and she ended up in a mental hospital. I got depressed for a while. I started blaming myself. And it was then that I realized that you were the first woman I ever mistreated. My own mother. Ain't that nothing? I wanted so badly to be different from Daddy. But I couldn't help myself. You know, he made me lose all my respect for you. He told me, "Your mother is just another broad. She's just a slut with a cut in her butt." "Don't get tied to no woman. You'll regret it forever. Love 'em and leave 'em. Find 'em and fuck 'em. Forget 'em when they're gone," he used to say. "The only person you can love is yourself. Man is the most perfect of all God's creations, and woman is the lowest, foulest of them all. Why else did God give them periods? To punish them." You want to know how old I was when he first told me all of this? Seven. Seven years old. And he was telling me all this in front of his drinking buddy, Jasper.

MAMA: Oh God, don't remind me. I couldn't stand that man. Where was we living then?

CLIFFORD: At Fort Belvoir. Yep, that damn Jasper was always hanging around. Saying yes to everything Daddy ever said. Looking at me like I turned him on. I remember the time Daddy made me take my pants down in front of Jasper. You were out back, hanging up the laundry. Jasper and Pops were in the front room, drinking wine and beer, waiting for the baseball game to come on. Daddy said, *(Stage lights should get dim. In his father's voice)* "Come here, boy. Pull down your pants. Let me get a look at your family jewels." *(Pause)* I pulled down my pants. I didn't know what for. All of a sudden, Daddy and Japser start laughing. He says, "Ain't that the tiniest thing you ever laid your eyes on? You ain't gonna get nothing with that little cherry picker. What you call that thing, boy?" I said, "A pee-pee." They really started laughing then. "Come here, boy. Come closer. I want to show you something." *(Difficult for* CLIFFORD *to tell)* All of a sudden the old man was taking down his pants, and I was confronted with this thing. This big, black, ugly thing. He said, "This here ain't no pee-pee, boy. This here is a dick. Look at it, boy. Be proud of it. This is your creator." I could hear Jasper splitting his side, saying how crazy Daddy was for doing this to the kid. "I'm just educating the boy, that's all. Touch it, boy. It won't bite. Go ahead and touch it. Don't be afraid." *(Voice over—Little boy)* "No, Daddy, no." *(In the old man's voice)* "Get down and worship this thing. This is your God, your creator. Get down on your knees and kiss it." *(Returning to the present)* I ran from him as fast as I could. Nobody could make me do that, nobody, nobody, not even the old man. The bastard. I hated him for that.

(Significant pause. The lights come up)

MAMA: I'm sorry, Clifford. I didn't know he did that.

CLIFFORD: Don't be sorry, Mama. Be glad I survived that shit.

MAMA: I don't understand why your father would do something like that.

CLIFFORD: I do. I understand now, he really wasn't proud of his thing. He was mocking it. He saw it was something that ruined his life. Got him into trouble all the time. He wasn't proud of it's size. He was ashamed. *(Pause)* You see, Mama, I know you ain't my real mother. I been playing a game with you. A game without rules and a game without a winner. Sorry, but we both lose.

MAMA: *(In shock; hesitating)* When . . . how long . . . who . . . you mean, you knew all along?

CLIFFORD: Dora told me the night I got back. Mary knows about herself too.

MAMA: So that's why she tore out of here. I told y'all to never tell her. And I told Dora not to tell you.

CLIFFORD: But why, Mama? What did you have to gain?

MAMA: I wanted to keep you, that's all. I wanted to raise you like you were my own.

CLIFFORD: But why Mama? You should have hated us. Daddy ran around on you and we were living proof.

MAMA: Please, Cliff. Let's not talk about it. You were right. We should forget the past. What's done is done.

CLIFFORD: *(Shaking* MAMA*)* But Mama, I got to know. That's why I stayed here as long as I have, waiting for the moment of truth. Waiting for this moment. Now tell me. Why did you have to keep us?

MAMA: I kept you because you was the part of my husband that did not belong to me. To keep him, I had to keep you. Both of them girls loved your father. There was something about him that drove women wild. Drove my sister wild too. Drove my best friend wild. They all got a little piece of his sweet candy. But me, he belonged to me, and I was determined to keep him. *(Pause)* I remember your mother. I remember how she came to me one afternoon her stomach full with you. She said she was looking for John Fletcher. He was the father of this child in her stomach. I asked her in. Sat her down, we had some tea. I asked her how old she was to find out she was just fifteen. Did you hear me? Fifteen. She had her suitcase outside. She had come to live with us since her parents kicked her out. I didn't mind at first. The thought didn't upset me. I mean, I felt sorry for her. I wasn't even mad at her. But then she started getting pushy. She said she wanted your father to herself, wanted me to pack my bags and get out. I told her she was crazy if she thought that she could get me to leave. "I'm John Fletcher's wife. I got the papers to prove it. You can't fuck with me as long as I got the papers on his ass. I don't care who he screw or what he do, he's still my husband. And you can't run me off." I convinced her she was wasting her time. I'd never give him up. I knew she'd never be happy. I wouldn't let her be happy with my husband for a moment. As long as I had the papers on him, I'd be there, making life miserable for them. I convinced her to give you up. I had money then. Money that my father left to me. Money that your father was waiting to get his hands on. I used some of that money, and I supported that girl myself while she was pregnant. Kept her away from your father in a motel in another town. I made her promise to give you up when you was born. She promised to leave you on my doorstep with a certificate of birth saying I was the mother.

CLIFFORD: But why? Why did you feel you had to keep me?

MAMA: Because if she had kept you, your father would have felt some kind of obligation toward her. Believe me, his attention was already divided enough. I didn't need him running to be with you and your mama ever' five seconds. Oh, the baby's sick. Oh, he needs new shoes. Shit. You crazy if you think I could put up with some shit like that. Hell, I'm glad I bought your ass. Especially after you turned out to be a boy. That kept your father home for a while. He was fascinated with you. You brought us such joy, for a while.

CLIFFORD: Then he was out on the streets again. And then came Mary. The same way, no doubt. Huh, is that how it went?

MAMA: Exactly.

CLIFFORD: What about Dora? Who's child was she? They say things happen in cycles of three. *(No response from* MAMA*)* What about Dora, Mama? Who's child is she? Are you her mother. Answer me, woman. Who's Dora's mother? *(Long pause)* You said Daddy drove your sister wild. Your best friend too. Is one of them Dora's mama, or are you? Where is Auntie anyway?

MAMA: She's still living in town.

CLIFFORD: How come you don't talk to her. I never could understand that . . .

MAMA: Would you turn that hourglass over for me? Would you, honey? It's not right to let time stand still.

CLIFFORD: *(Irate)* Fuck this damn hourglass. Answer me!

MAMA: You know, after your father retired from the army, he never did an honest day's work, the damn buzzard. Never lifted his finger to do shit. Why in the hell do you think we moved to Wellington? This house was left to him by some uncle he didn't even know. Your father was an officer and all them years he was in the army, he had us living on base somewhere so he wouldn't have to pay a cent for rent. Do you know why your father married me? For my money, honey. Dat nigger spent ever' waking hour thinking and plotting at how he was gonna get next to my money. He spent half his years waiting for me to die.

CLIFFORD: I never knew you had any money. I thought we was living off of Daddy's pension after he retired.

MAMA: We was. That's why he was so damn bitter. That's why he treated me like a piece of shit. He found out I spent my money. Spent it on you and Mary.

CLIFFORD: Your father left you money, but what about Auntie? What did he leave her?

MAMA: Son. Do like I ask, and turn that hourglass over for me. Would you, please?

CLIFFORD: *(Being careless with the hourglass . . . pointing it at* MAMA*)* Okay, Mama, only if you be straight with me and tell me the whole damn thing. *(His eyes flash)* Daddy loved Auntie, didn't

he? Is she Dora's Mama? Didn't Auntie follow us no matter where we lived? Was she Dora's mama?

MAMA: *(Snatches the hourglass from his hand)* Your father sure was one lazy bastard. He never lifted a finger for me, the buzzard. But I got his ass now, and he's working all the time. *(She displays the hourglass victoriously)*

CLIFFORD: What? What do you mean he's working all the time?

MAMA: Ain't you wondered why nobody ever showed you his grave?

CLIFFORD: I guess I never thought to ask. I'm sorry.

MAMA: There is no grave, Cliff. I had your father cremated, and I mixed his ashes with some sand, and I put his ass in this hourglass. Now he's working all the time. *(She turns it over displaying it)* Work for me, honey. Work! It make Mama so happy to see you working so hard.

CLIFFORD: *(In shock)* Why, that's insane.

MAMA: Maybe it is, maybe it ain't.

CLIFFORD: You're crazy, Mama.

MAMA: *(Victoriously)* But I got his ass now, don't I? Nigger think he can screw all over creation.

CLIFFORD: But he's dead, Mama. He's dead. What good is he doing you dead? *(*CLIFFORD *takes the hourglass)* Can this hourglass keep you warm at night? Let go of the past. Be glad he's dead. Let him rest, wherever he may be.

MAMA: I'll never let him rest.

CLIFFORD: *(Looking like he will break the hourglass)* Let him rest, set him free, Mama, or else I will.

MAMA: *(Stands up, coming toward* CLIFFORD*)* No, Clifford. Don't break it. It's mine. *(She shakes it out of his hands)*

CLIFFORD: *(Astonished)* Mama, you can walk. You can walk, Mama. You can walk.

MAMA: *(Hugging the hourglass)* There, there baby. It's alright. Mama won't let Clifford hurt you. He's a bad boy, a real bad boy.

CLIFFORD: *(Snatches the hourglass from* MAMA*)* Give me that damn thing.

MAMA: No. Give it back. It's mine. *(*MAMA *lunges for it, but* CLIFFORD *smacks her. Smacking her, he drops the hourglass, and it breaks.* MAMA *says, in shock)* You hit me, Cliff. You hit me. You hit your mother.

CLIFFORD: You ain't my mother, you ain't nobody's mother. You probably can't have no kids. You're sterile, lifeless, just like that . . . *(He looks down at the hourglass)* that hourglass.

MAMA: *(Looking at the hourglass)* You broke it, Cliff. You broke my hourglass. *(Hysterical)* You bastard. You monster. I'll put a curse on you for this.

CLIFFORD: *(Sitting down, nonchalant)* It was for your own good. You'll thank me one day for breaking that thing and getting you out of that chair. I was hoping you weren't pretending. I was hoping Dora was wrong. I'm disappointed in you. You nearly ruined Mary playing this cruel game. *(Long pause)* I better sweep this up.

MAMA: Just get out, Cliff. I don't care where you go, just as long as you get out!

CLIFFORD: Don't be mad at me, Mama, please. There's still time. We can forgive each other and go on living like a real mother and son. Besides, you're the only mother I know.

MAMA: I'm not your mother, Cliff, you remember that.

Lights out

Scene 3

Same set. One afternoon, weeks later. MAMA *and* MARY *are sitting in the parlor.* MAMA *is back in the wheelchair.* MARY *is clad in her nurse's uniform. The clock is gone. The hourglass has been replaced.*

MAMA: I sure am scared when you go to work, Mary. What they put you on that night shift for anyway? You belong on the day shift.

MARY: Look, I was lucky I got my job back, period.

MAMA: Well, it ain't fair to me. I got to be alone in this house all night while you at work.

MARY: Mama, I went back to them begging for my job back. Shoot, I had to take what they gave me.

MAMA: I don't see why you left in the first place. Did Clifford say anything to you that caused you to leave?

MARY: No, Mama.

MAMA: Look at me, girl. You sure he ain't said nothing to you about me?

MARY: Mama, we been over this a thousand times. What did you think he would say?

MAMA: Nothing, nothing. I just wanted to know why you took off the way you did, that's all.

MARY: Like I been telling you, Mama. I left because I had to do some thinking.

MAMA: But did you have to go so far to think?

MARY: Mama, sometimes it's good to get away. I wish you'd understand.

MAMA: Oh, I understand, you just don't care about me none. If it wasn't for Tommy, you wouldn't have ever come back.

MARY: Mama, I care about you, honestly. *(Pause)* Guess what, Mama, I picked out a new dress for you for the wedding. Tommy gave me the money, and I'm picking it up today on the way to work.

MAMA: I don't know what for, I'm not coming to y'all's wedding.

MARY: So, we're bringing it to you. We decided to have it here.

MAMA: Not in my house you ain't. Ain't nobody getting married here. You get that notion out of your head now, girl.

MARY: Well, we'll talk about it later. I'm running late for work.

MAMA: 'Fore you go, would you do me a small favor?

MARY: What is it, Mama?

MAMA: Would you turn that hourglass over for me?

MARY: Okay, Mama. *(Turns it over)* Anything else?

MAMA: That's all. *(Pause)* You know, it's funny, but I think of Clifford every time you turn that thing over.

MARY: Do you?

MAMA: Yep. *(Pause)* I wonder why he left home again? I thought he was going to stay. Didn't he say he was gonna stay?

MARY: Maybe he was bored here. Clifford's the restless type, you know.

MAMA: He don't ever write us to see how we're doing or nothing. Is he coming to your wedding?

MARY: Who knows, Mama? Who knows?

MAMA: *(To the audience, smiling)* Lord knows, I sure don't know.

Lights out

Curtain

JOAN "CALIFORNIA" COOPER

A NATIVE CALIFORNIAN, Joan "California" Cooper performed her plays for her family and friends before she was five years old—a secret writer putting them in a drawer for years. Joan was discovered by Nora Vaughn of the Berkeley Black Repertory Theatre several years ago and has been building an enthusiastic following since. Mrs. Vaughn feels Joan has a natural talent. Her plays have been produced several times in Berkeley, Oakland, and San Francisco, as well as on television. Thus far, Joan has written thirteen plays, three acts as well as one acts. Some titles include: *How Now; The Unintended; Everytime It Rains; Ahhh, Strangers; System, Suckers, and Success;* and *The Mother.* Joan is also writing a book of short stories and is interested in writing for film.

Joan "California" Cooper feels this way about her writing: "I am grateful to those who write about our lack of freedom and associated problems of being Black. *But,* I feel that even if a person is free, there are still great problems to be borne. I like to write about the things that effect each and every person and race. Common problems. Birth, death, love, lonliness, pain, ugliness, a disability, hunger, hate, and hope. Consequently, ninety percent of my plays can be played by any nationality with just a slight change in accent or a few words. I have two plays that are definitely Black; I think in Black, so they sound Black. But, mostly, *they are just human.*"

About Cooper's plays:

. . . Her subject matter is timely, relevant, and meaningful; her themes so universal that everyone can relate to them. And she creates warm, true to life characters easily identified with, characters that one finds oneself immediately becoming involved with, bigger than life characters who transcend social, racial, and cultural classifications.

Charlie L. Russell

. . . I have seen the work of Ms. Joan "California" Cooper both written and performed on the stage, and . . . I consider it superb. Ms. Cooper is a talented, highly imaginative, creative play-wright and artist.

Alice Walker

I feel Ms. Cooper's writing in inciteful, well developed, and exhibits the talents of a fine playwright whose works certainly deserve more exposure.

Nora B. Vaughn, Executive Director
Black Repertory Group

I can't hold it any longer! I have to rant and rave, sing and shout, holler it from the roof tops about the latest one act play now appearing at the Black Repertory Group Theatre. Entitled *The Loners,* this beautifully written piece of work by Joan "California" Cooper is nothing short of perfection!!

Crystal V. Rhodes
Review in *The California Voice*

LONERS

Joan "California" Cooper

CHARACTERS

COOL: *A man of 37 years or so. Nice looking. Dressed a little country or very sharp, depending on locale. Puffed up with self, egotistical. Some dissipation showing.*

EMMA: *A plain woman, 30 years or so. Shy but with inner strength. Simple and direct. Clean and neat.*

MR. WILSON: *45 years or so. Quiet, neat, unafraid but sympathic. In love with* EMMA.

JOE: *A tired man about 43 to 47 years of age. Laughs with customers but lonely and silent within self.*

TAN TAN: *About 45 years old. Combination waitress and lady of the night. Not necessarily a prostitute. Broke, takes money from men. Lonely. Likes* COOL *but gloats at his misfortune.*

OLD LADY 1—RETHA: *About 65 years of age. Neat. Was a swinger, and the ravages of time and dissipation show, though she thinks she may still look good. Unmarried.*

OLD LADY 2—MATILDA: *About 67 years of age. Looks good, neat, prude, wise, and is nosy.*

CAB DRIVER

Setting: Second class bar, second class neighborhood. Arrangement to taste of director, but not an elaborate bar, not the worst. Lights shall do most of the work on the characters. Bar faces stage with four or five stools. The usual beer and liquor signs, some lit. Two tables near upstage, two chairs each. It is semi-dark, with lights on the characters speaking after EMMA *comes in. This is anywhere in the world.*

A PLAY IN ONE ACT

Scene 1

The scene opens early afternoon, three or four o'clock, but the bar is dim. COOL *is having a beer and talking to the bartender* JOE *in a cozy, laughing, and bragging manner.* JOE *is doing busy work and listening and talking intermittently.*

COOL: Yeah man, I lost last week in that crap game, but I caught up on things last night!

JOE: You was lucky, man!

COOL: Well . . . you gotta stick with things, man!

JOE: Sometimes . . . sometimes not! I don't like em, them games, cause somebody always get mad or somethin and somebody gets hurt!

COOL: *(Pulling out small gun)* This here keep me from gettin in too much trouble! I ain't never had to use it! But I lets everybody know I got it!

JOE: *(Nervous)* Man! Put that thing away! I don't like them things! Only a fool carry a gun! Put that thing away! Take it outta here even!

COOL: Cool it, man! *(Putting gun away)* I ain't crazy! I always know what I'm doin! And that's all you have to do! Know what you doin! If you can't tell a snake from a worm . . . you betta stay out the jungle! *(Laughs at his own joke)*

JOE: You gotta point there! *(Returns to wiping glasses, etc.)* But you got to go a long way on this here earth to get out the jungle! But you know what? I don't see how you fellows have enough money to gamble with, drink with, still eat and still sleep somewhere . . . and dressin clean . . .

COOL: Ain't nothin to it!

JOE: Well, it beats me! I have ta work!

COOL: Reason ain't nothin to it is cause half the time most of these jokers *owe* everybody! But I don't! I do a little work sometime though. Can't tell that lie and say I don't!

JOE: I know you work sometime! I know you *have* to cause don't nobody want to lend you nothin! You don't pay back!

COOL: That's a lie!

JOE: Man, this is me . . . I been here . . . I know what's happenin!

COOL: You don't know everything!

JOE: At least, you ain't tryin to pimp none!

COOL: Uh-un! That's a fools game!

JOE: Course you probly can't no-how!

COOL: Brother . . . I can do whatever I want to do!

JOE: (Grunts—poking fun at COOL) Huh!

COOL: Damn right! That just ain't my game!

JOE: (Pleasantly, holding arms stretched out) That's what I was sayin . . . it ain't your game!

COOL: Ain't 'cause women don't like me! I ain't never had no trouble with women! You know that!

JOE: Everybody always think I know so much.

COOL: Cause you say you do! You know somethin else, man? I loves women! All of em!

JOE: I see you tryin too, anyway!

COOL: Man, I saw a woman the other day, I wanted to jump outta my car and make love to her right on the sidewalk! Make her feel better than she ever felt in her life. . . . But I was cool. Got too many women now I can't get rid of!

JOE: Bad luck just follow you around!

COOL: That's cause I'm a strong man. I ain't weak! Women don't like weak men! And I got a strong, smooth, good, hard body!

JOE: It's sposed to be a good thing if you love yourself!

COOL: Well, I sure do! And women do too! They good to me too! (Proud laugh) They . . . some of them . . . give me money (Primps) and presents.

JOE: That's kinda sad man, taking a poor woman's money . . . probly welfare money!

COOL: They ain't all poor! (Leans over bar confidentially) I got one . . . you know that lady with the . . . no, I better not mention her name . . . she too well known!

JOE: Huh!

COOL: She give me all kinds of things . . . man, I got more shirts and suits . . . and that good men's cologne! I got plenty of that!

JOE: I must be doin somethin wrong!

COOL: All you got to do is tell em how pretty they are! They all want to hear that! Even the real down home, plug ugly ones. now that ain't hard for me cause I love all of em! But I know them! I knows women! I don't let them get ahead of me!

JOE: You know, them women can wear you out, man!

COOL: (Laughing) Yeah man, you right! Sometime I wish I was four men . . . then I could spread myself out more! Travel all over the state and make more women happy!

JOE: Man . . . I think you think about screwing too much!—if you need to be four men!

COOL: It's all in what you can handle! Right now, I can handle things two times a day . . . some days.

JOE: Seems like a man with your tastes can be kinda ruled by women . . . if they all he thinks of . . .

COOL: Nope . . . ain't true! Sometimes I don't fool with none at all. No . . . I know I have to rest my body sometimes . . . a day or two.

JOE: No shit?

COOL: No shit! That's why I like married women. They can't always get out, and they got someone else to take up the slack! I don't even really care if a woman I got has somebody else sometime cause I'm pretty busy myself and can't always get to em! . . . in time . . . you know what I mean?

JOE: What's happenin with that nice little woman you was fooling with . . . Emma? Wasn't that her name?

COOL: (Bored) Yeah.

JOE: Emma Tatum . . . ole Tatum's daughter.

COOL: She all right! Now! There's a example for ya! She been my woman for goin on eight years now! We got two babies!

JOE: You marry her?

COOL: Marry? Man, you crazy or somethin? What's that?

JOE: Oh . . . then she got two kids!

COOL: I recognize them boys! They my boys! I didn't try to lie! It's so straight, we ain't never even talked about it!

JOE: You take care of them?

COOL: (Whining) Man . . . I ain't got enough money for nothin like that! It's hard out here! It takes all I got to keep on going on!

JOE: Course, it's probly hard out here for her too! Well . . . I repeat, she got two kids!

COOL: She manages . . . I go over there every now and then.

JOE: And try to make another baby?

COOL: Naw, . . . I ain't gon make no more babies! I give her a little piece now and then . . . cause I want to keep her a good woman! (Smirk)

JOE: I see your reasoning.

COOL: I think I love her, sometime . . . more then all the rest!

JOE: Golly! She's lucky!

COOL: Yeah. . . . You know, I tried her sister out first . . . but she don't know that! Nobody do! The sister never did tell, bless her pretty lil soul! She got a ole man she don't want to go up side her lips if he knew! She wasn't so hot in the bed no way! Not like little Emma! Emma was a virgin, man! That's Allllllllll mine! Bet I'm the only man in this town can say that bout their woman! She my main stay!

JOE: Man . . . you got a hell of a philosophy! You

go to church?

COOL: Man, we ain't talkin bout church! Talk about church on Sunday! We talkin bout screwing now! I ain't tryin to get no religion! I'm tryin to get some "givin"! You sposed to go to church when you sad! I ain't sad! My life is just what I want it to be! I got Emma, my two sons . . . every man wants a son . . . I got *two!* And I got a woman who give me things so I stay clean, and I get all the mojo I want!! Now what I got to pray for? Lord already done give me everything a good man needs!

JOE: But what about them . . . the women . . . what do they have? What does the mother of your sons have?

COOL: *Me!* But man, I can't be goin over there too much! It's too dead and borin over there! Ain't no excitement! I'm too . . . young . . . to live like I'm old and sad . . . and through.

JOE: Through what?

COOL: Through lovin women! Havin fun! Gimmie another drink man!

JOE: Well . . . they say everybody knows what's best for themselves!

(*The telephone rings*)

COOL: Well, I sure do know what's best for me! (*Checking himself in the mirror*)

JOE: (*Answering phone*) Yes . . . he is here . . . hold on a minute . . . . (*Listens*) Well, whatever you say, lady . . . . (*Listens*) O.K . . . . Goodbye. (*To* COOL) That was a lady asking for you, but she didn't want to speak to you . . . say she comin on over.

COOL: Oh shit! Who was it man?

JOE: Forgot to ask . . . and she didn't say. But she sure got a sweet voice.

COOL: (*Smiling*) I can't even get away for a little while to myself . . . . The girls just won't let sweet daddy alone.

JOE: When you got it, you got it!

COOL: Riiiiiight.

JOE: Say, I'm getting hungry, I may leave you here while I run next door to grab a take-out. It's the slow time a day anyway.

COOL: Yeah, go head man, gotta wait for the lady anyway!

JOE: I hope she ain't no mad lady! Don't want no fightin up in here.

COOL: Man, ain't nobody wanta hurt me! They wanta keep me! Any woman I have . . . man, she mine . . . . I don't worry bout all that stuff you talkin bout!

JOE: (*Picking up stick and waving it*) That's good, cause I keep my peacemaker here for all drunks and fools! But man . . . maybe you oughta worry bout somethin! Least about the one with your

two kids, man!

COOL: What are you today . . . the preacher? Man, I think about her! She is my ace in the hole! I know she is a good woman, a good mother . . . and everything! And one of these days . . . I'm gonna . . . I'm gonna marry her! I'm just savin her for the last . . . cause I know she gon be there . . . . Ain't . . . goin . . . nowhere! . . . with her little quiet self.

JOE: Them quiet girls surprise you sometime!

COOL: All kinda girls surprise you sometime! You got to learn more about women fore you can tell me anything!

Scene 2

At this point TAN TAN *walks in, tired and dejected, shopworn. About 45 years of age, says she's 34. Wrong wig, dress black, shoes red, purse red—or as director sees her.*

JOE: Tan Tan!! What's goin on?

TAN: Ain't nothin goin on! And don't call me Tan Tan! My name is La Tanya!

COOL: (*Mimicking*) "La Tanya"!

TAN: Nobody say nothin at all . . . to me!

COOL: What's the matter, pretty? You look fine, but you don't sound fine!

TAN: Gimmie a straight shot, Joe! A double! And half is on you!

JOE: No, no half ain't on me! I can't afford your habits! (*He pours*)

TAN: Oh yes you can! You make plenty money offa me!

JOE: Well, you know I must be standin back here for somethin, don't ya? I ain't here for my health!

TAN: Well, comin here don't help mine either, but I come!

COOL: You come cause it's your business to come! If you don't have someplace to get them lonely fools you catch, you starve to death on that waitress pay!

TAN: I ain't never tried to catch you!

COOL: I may be a loner . . . but I ain't lonely . . . and I ain't a fool either, Darlin!

JOE: You both loners . . . always by yourself till you catch somethin!

COOL: Man, don't put me in her place! Sex is somethin she make her livin with . . . for me, sex is somethin make my livin worth livin! She got to make somebody go home with her . . . I got to fight em off! (*To* TAN TAN) You my girl though Tan Tan . . . La Tanya . . . I'll pay for her drink! Maybe one day you'll do me a favor!

TAN: Ain't nobody's girl! I'm a woman! And I

don't do no favors in bed!

JOE: Right on, Mama!

COOL: Fair exchange ain't no robbery! But you ain't got to think of me! I got more now than I can use! I'll be an old man fore I get to you!

TAN: Leave me alone, Cool! I don't feel good!

JOE: *(Kindly)* What's the matter with you, woman?

TAN: It's my baby! My daughter.

COOL: That pretty young lady you got? Comes down here to get you sometime? Sure is a fox!!

TAN: Well, this fox of mine ain't smart like no fox! She done got pregnant!

JOE: Damn! Another one down!

TAN: She thinks she "looooooves" him . . . and I can't tell her nothin!

JOE: Maybe they do love each other, Tan!

TAN: I can deal with the baby. That happened to me too. What I can't deal with is when we went over to his house to see what we was goin to do about everything . . . you know . . . the money and everything. *(To JOE)* Gimmie another drink.

JOE: *(He does)* That's right! It takes money . . . and everything!

TAN: Well, we sitting there talking . . . the kids get it together and everything . . . they want to get married. So I say "fine, if that's what you want"! Then this juke-head man, his father, says "How do my son know that this is his doin?" And I say, "How do you know your son is your doin?"

COOL: You layed somethin on his mind!

TAN: Well . . . that made me mad! Men always get righteous when a baby shows up . . . then they want a little integrity from a woman . . . . But if they kept a little integrity on the tip of that thing they use to make them babies with, wouldn't nobody have to get unrighteous!

COOL: Don't forget . . . it was Eve bit that apple!

TAN: You ever make love to a apple?

COOL: I don't have too!

TAN: And eatin apples don't make you pregnant!

Scene 3

At this time the two older ladies come in. MATILDA *is a righteous older lady.* RETHA *is a swinger from the past.* MATILDA *is holding on to* RETHA, *pulling her back, as they come into the bar.* RETHA *heads straight for the bartender.*

RETHA: On come on, Matilda! We ain't gon do nothin but order a cab! What's wrong with you, girl?

MATILDA: There's a phone on the corner . . . we can call our own!

RETHA: This bar probly got a direct line . . . why waste a dime? *(Flirty)* Bartender, can you call us a cab, please?

JOE: Why certainly ladies! Right away! *(He does)*

MATILDA: It's dark in here! I can't see a thing!

RETHA: What you want to see?

MATILDA: I like to know what's goin on around me! Ain't no tellin what's creepin round in this dark!

RETHA: *(Moving MATILDA to table)* You ain't never known what's goin on round you, Matilda. Now rest yourself, everything's all right!

COOL: Afternoon, ladies!

RETHA: *(Big smile and pats her hair)* Evening! *(Giggles)*

MATILDA: Humph! You better quit speakin to strangers!

RETHA: Oh, for Pete's sake, Tilda! Relax, girl!

MATILDA: How am I goin to relax when I know I am in the devil's house?! And the good Lord is sittin somewhere wondering why I'm lettin you lead me outta my own good mind!

COOL: Would you ladies like a taste on me . . . a coke or somethin? While you wait? Cool you off . . . . That's my name "Cool".

(MATILDA gasps loudly)

RETHA: *(Flirts with him)* Why, I believe I will, Mr. Cool.

MATILDA: *(Indignant)* Well, I believe I won't! *(To RETHA)* I don't do nothin like this, Retha!

RETHA: I know . . . cause it show, Tilda! But maybe you shoulda . . . make a woman out of you.

MATILDA: Drinkin alcohol and talkin to strangers make a fool out of you, not a woman! Most you find in bars is crazy people and people with no where else to go! Just loners and looneys!

RETHA: Lord! *(To JOE)* I'll have a sloe screw, please.

MATILDA: *(Gasps loudly)* Retha!!

RETHA: Give my sister one too! Please!!

MATILDA: No he ain't gonna give me no sloe screw! He ain't gon give me nothin! *(Starts away but RETHA grabs her)*

RETHA: It's hot outside! It'll taste good, and then the cab will be here and we can go.

MATILDA: Get behind me Satan! All right, but give me a tomato juice with a little gin in it. *(Indicates large taste with fingers)* Retha, you get me into more things!

RETHA: *(Smiling)* Yeah . . . ain't you glad?

TAN: Have the drink, honey . . . you may be dead tomorrow!

MATILDA: I wouldn't have a drink on my mind or in my hand if I thought I'd be dead tomorrow! *(Gets the drink and drinks it up fast)*

CAB DRIVER: *(Peeking in door)* Anyone call a cab?

JOE: Yeah! Be right out! Cab's here, ladies!

RETHA: *(Picking up* MATILDA's *glass; it's empty)* It's a good thing. You might hurt yourself, Tilda! Thank you, Mr. Cool.

MATILDA: Don't lick the bottom of that glass, Retha!

RETHA: Oh Tilda, you always messin things up when I'm enjoying myself! What's a little drink?!

MATILDA: *(Moving out)* I'm the oldest and you look older than I do!

RETHA: *(Moving out too)* Looks don't make me happy!

MATILDA: Well, if drinking makes you happy, you won't be unhappy for the next six thousand years just riding on what you done already drank!

RETHA: I wish you quit tryin to save me and let me live!

MATILDA: You been livin sixty years! Don't you know you better get ready to die? Come on here! *(Going out door)* Let's get to church!

RETHA: *(Looking back sadly)* Bye.

(After ladies leave, everyone laughs)

TAN: That old lady sounds just like my mother!

COOL: That old lady sounds like everybody's mother!

TAN: She had her points though.

JOE: She does look a lot better than Retha though. Bet she feels better too.

TAN: That was nice of you, Cool, buyin them two ole ladies a drink.

COOL: Never can tell whether one of them old biddies have some money! The fast one might be comin back!

Scene 4

EMMA *enters and looks around.*

COOL: I wish the broad on the phone would come on in! I got things to do!

JOE: Maybe this is the lady.

COOL: *(Turns around and is shocked to see* EMMA*)* Emma! Emma, what you doin here?

EMMA: I come to talk to you, Cool.

COOL: *(Annoyed)* Well, it sure coulda waited till I got out to the house to see you! I don't like you comin down here!! *(Looking at* JOE *and* TAN, *trying to steer* EMMA *to door)*

EMMA: No... it couldn't wait. *(Tired, strained voice. Never gets angry during this talk. Slightly sad until* WILSON *talks)* You haven't been out there in two weeks.

COOL: Well, let's go, I'll take you to the bus stop, and we can talk while we wait for your bus! What I owe you, Joe?

EMMA: No, we can talk here.

COOL: No? *(To* EMMA*)* Are you telling me what to do? Woman, I'm your man! Don't question me! *(Glances over his shoulder at* JOE *to see if he heard that)*

EMMA: Let's sit at this table. *(Passes by* COOL *and sits)*

COOL: *(Surprised)* What's wrong with you, girl? *(Capitulates)* Well, all right. But only for a minute, I ain't got much time. I... uh... got... uh ... a little job I got to do. *(He sits)*

EMMA: I think I'll have a drink, Cool. Something ... pretty.

COOL: I ain't got much money, Emma!

EMMA: Well... I'll pay for it!

COOL: *(Glances at* JOE. *Quickly)* I'll pay for it! Hey Joe! Bring the little woman a drink! *(To* EMMA*)* Where you get money to buy a drink?!

JOE: *(Coming over)* Well, it's little Ms. Tatum! I haven't seen you since you was going to high school. How you doin?

COOL: She doin fine! What you want, Emma? give her a...

EMMA: Hello, Joe. I'm fine. I'll have a Tom Collins, please.

(Another man walks in, MR. WILSON, *mature, quiet, looks around and has a seat at the other table)*

JOE: *(Moving over to* WILSON*)* Mr. Wilson.... How you doin, Sir? What can I bring you?

WILSON: I'll have a Tom Collins, Joe. How are you and your family?

JOE: Fine, Mr. Wilson, fine. Tom Collins comin right up!

COOL: What is it, Emma? Now I ain't got no money! *(Trying to speak so no one can hear)* I just gave you twenty dollars a week ago!

(The lights have dimmed in the back bar and the light focus is on the table with EMMA *and* COOL—*or as director sees it)*

EMMA: Ten dollars.

COOL: Was it ten dollars? Well...

EMMA: Two weeks ago.

COOL: Well, I still ain't got no more today.

EMMA: I didn't come for money, Cool.

COOL: Well, what is it then, My kids sick?

*(*JOE *serves drinks and exchanges a few words, very few, quietly with* WILSON *while* EMMA *and* COOL *talk)*

COOL: *(Agitated)* If my son's sick, what you doin out here at a bar? You oughta be home with them! Not out here!... in no bar!

EMMA: The kids aren't sick, Cool.

COOL: Well... O.K. I want you to take good care of my sons, Emma—don't want them sick!

EMMA: Everything is all right, Cool.

COOL: *(Confused)* Well... what you doin comin down here to talk to me for? You sposed to wait till I get out there to talk to you!

EMMA: I had to talk to you today. I didn't know when I'd see you so . . .

COOL: Now Emma, don't give me no speech about marriage. I told you I am goin to marry you . . . someday. But not now! I'm not ready to come out there and spend my life. I got to get ahead and do somethin big for my sons. But when I gets bothered like this, you breaks my stride! I got a big business deal . . .

EMMA: Cool, I want . . .

COOL: Emma, don't make me mad! I don't want to get married now! I have my life to live! Now you choose your way . . . and I'll choose my way!

EMMA: All right, Cool. *(Exasperated)* Cool, Cool, stop a minute . . . give me a chance to talk.

COOL: O.K. . . . But whatever it is, I ain't got much time right now!

EMMA: I, Cool, I just thought it would be fair to talk to you . . . if you busy . . . *(Attempts to get up)*

COOL: You done come this far! Stop being stupid! Hurry up! But I don't like *my woman* comin in no place like this! Don't come again!

EMMA: *(Bangs table with fist, first sign of emotion)* Then be quiet! *(COOL is surprised, hushes)* Now . . . I think I did everything I could to give our . . . love . . . a chance.

COOL: Emma, don't worry, I'm satisfied with you . . . you don't need to do nothin else . . . just stay out there in the country at your papa's.

EMMA: We've been . . . happy a little. But I've been unhappy a lot. *(COOL looks around to see who hears)* But that don't make me mean and mad at life, or you, anymore.

COOL: That's good . . . *(He pats her hand)* Emma, that's good.

EMMA: But I believe in people bein happy . . . if they can . . . in life. That's why I never really bothered you. But now I want to be happy.

COOL: Things gonna get better, Emma.

EMMA: I'm not gettin any younger . . . and you always tole me to live my life cause you was livin yours.

COOL: *(Laughing)* And someday they gon come together . . . get it? Come together?

EMMA: *(Not laughing)* I know . . . there are gentle . . . nice . . . kind men in the world. Men who give love to their woman. I wants to be loved.

COOL: I be out there in a few days, Emma . . . be cool.

EMMA: I want somebody . . . grown up, mature . . . somebody who cares about me and my sons. You know . . . I'm learnin a lot from my sons! And I hope I'm teachin them somethin about life . . . and women and love.

COOL: You a good mother, Emma, but you got to stay *home* to be a good mother!

EMMA: I want them to be tender and affectionate . . . like their father.

COOL: *(Pleased, preening)* Why sure . . .

EMMA: It's gonna be very important to them. See . . . I have learned that it's O.K. to kiss somebody's ass . . . but only if that ass belongs to you. See . . . some people can love . . . and some people can't! Those that can't are always lookin for some love to stuff into their heads and pockets out from other people's hearts. While those what can love is always givin . . . always givin. *(Shakes head slowly and sadly, then brightens)* But when you get two givers . . . together . . . Lord, you really got somethin!!

COOL: What you been readin, Emma? I tole you stop readin all that trash!

EMMA: A lot of things start with mother's love . . . and father's love.

COOL: I love my kids!

EMMA: *(Not hearing him)* That's where you have to learn to love first, sometime. *(Looking at COOL)* For a long time, I thought I loved you. People been tellin me they love me . . . while all the time I be tellin you I love you. They show me, I show you, and let the people who love me suffer.

COOL: You been messin round on me, Emma?

EMMA: Cool . . . I waited to see you *(Takes a long drink)* because *(Looks at him)* I wanted to tell you . . . I am gettin married.

COOL: Now I just got through tellin you that I . . .

EMMA: Not to you . . . Cool . . . to someone else.

COOL: *(Stands up, knocking over the chair. WILSON rises too)* Woman, are you crazy?!!

EMMA: Now don't get excited, Cool, and we can talk. Otherwise, I'll have to leave.

COOL: *(Sitting back down, WILSON sits also)* You ain't going *nowhere!!*

EMMA: No . . . that's where I been! I ain't goin there no more. Now let's finish this out.

COOL: You damn right! We gon finish this out!

EMMA: *(Still not angry)* Now let me talk. We've never had much time to talk. When you come to see me, talkin ain't much on your mind. And if we did talk . . . it was just games. You never took the time to think about if what you gave me was what I needed or what I just took.

COOL: Well, you was happy, and you loved me.

EMMA: I was not happy, and I don't love you anymore. Life with you ain't life.

COOL: *(Ugly)* Well, in them nights when we was alone you sure did seem to be enjoying yourself!!

EMMA: Oh there were times, Cool. *(Puts her hand over his)* But in the good times, I was burdened with all the things I had to try to understand. *(Removes hand)*

COOL: *(Defensive)* What did you have to try to understand?

EMMA: You way pass me, Cool. You have your own dreams.

COOL: You got that right!

EMMA: I know.

COOL: What's this about marriage? What you talkin about? Who did you meet that would marry you? . . . And take care of my kids . . . my sons?!!

EMMA: Nobody.

COOL: *(Laughing)* Well then . . .

EMMA: Cool . . . let me talk and try not to interrupt me. This is not easy for me.

COOL: Don't say nothin you'll be sorry for! I may not come to see you for two more weeks!

EMMA: You know I go to church, regular, because that's the place I choose to find my wisdom . . . find my way . . . and for years I been prayin for what I want . . . for what every woman wants, I think.

COOL: Let's talk bout this marriage you talkin bout doin.

EMMA: *(Interrupting him)* What I'm sayin is you are not enough for me. *(COOL looks around again at JOE and TAN. EMMA looks in space)* Ohhh, I was lonely. Many times I looked in the mirror and said what a fool I was. So many things I wanted to *do* . . . before the children and after the children. Many times I wanted to make love *(Looks at COOL)* in the middle of the night or . . . early in the morning . . . or even in the afternoon on the grass, in the rain, in the creek, in the tree . . . . Not just sex, Cool . . . love. But you wasn't there. You were with me when you wanted to be 'cordin to your feelings, not when I needed you to be . . . 'cordin to mine.

COOL: Well . . .

EMMA: Sometimes you were too tired . . . you come where I was so you could sleep . . . or eat . . . and when you wake up, you'd be on your way out.

COOL: What has that got to do with gettin married, today?

EMMA: It's the reason I found somebody else.

COOL: *(Stands up and knocks chair over again. WILSON stands also)* Somebody else!!! What you mean? You been givin my . . . *(Remembers JOE and where he is, grabs the chair and sits down again)* . . . you been givin my stuff away?

EMMA: Not yours, Cool. Mine! I was born with this!

COOL: To who? When?

EMMA: If you're quiet, I'll tell you . . . if you're not . . . I'll go.

COOL: Baby, you ain't gon nowhere!

EMMA: Cool, I know I ain't so good lookin, and I know fellas like the good lookin kind. But I can't worry bout that cause I'm young, and I got a lotta feelings that I left up to you to satisfy . . . but you didn't. I don't feel like sleepin around . . . so . . . well . . . while I was doin housework for the church members . . . I met . . . someone . . . else!

COOL: The preacher?!

EMMA: No . . . but a very nice gentleman, who was very kind to me, helped me in lots of little ways, big ways too. He was patient with me, treated me like I was somebody special!

COOL: They all do that to get what they want! You just a fool to go for that!

EMMA: He didn't change with the first baby . . . and he still hasn't changed! He still treats me that way, and it's been six years now!

COOL: *Six years!* You been goin with me seven years! You been foolin round with somebody else for six years?! I oughta kick your ass!

(WILSON stands up and starts over, and JOE does too)

JOE: O.K. Cool, don't want no mess in here!

COOL: *(Raising hand)* Ain't no mess, man! This bitch here . . .

WILSON: Watch your language, boy!

COOL: Sit down old man, this is my business! I ain't gon hurt her, not now, anyway!

WILSON: See that you don't!

(Everybody sits. JOE goes back behind bar)

EMMA: Cool, how many women you had in six years?

COOL: That's different! I'm a man! But why did you do this to me?

EMMA: *(Softly)* Because he showed me what it felt like to be a woman. Get valentine cards, birthday presents, soft underwear . . . rub you to sleep . . .

COOL: *(Incredulous)* You been "sleeping" with em?

EMMA: . . . make love to you like you're both there . . . . Think of you . . . for no reason at all and stop by to see if there is anything he can do for you. *(Laughs lightly)* Buy you pretty toilet paper or perfume, not because you need it, but because he knows you use it! Make you feel like you both somethin . . . not just him!

COOL: *(Grinning)* Who is he? I'm gonna tell him who I am!

EMMA: I told him about you . . . . How I wished you and I would get married a long time ago and have a life together.

COOL: *(Satisfied)* What the fool say to that?

EMMA: He never said one word about us . . . no matter what I said. I liked him for that. In fact, Cool, over the years . . . he's been there when the kids are sick, when they have to do somethin or, oh, just whatever came up . . . so that I piled up so much likin for him that it turned into love without my even realizin it.

COOL: *(Disbelief)* You love him?

EMMA: I love him.

COOL: *(A moment's silence)* What you gonna tell my kids?

EMMA: I don't have to tell my sons anything, Cool.

COOL: *(A moment's silence)* I want them to know who their father is.

EMMA: They have always known who their father was. Their father knows them and they know their father. It's my fault they been apart.

COOL: *(Suspicious)* What you mean "your fault"?

EMMA: *(Places hand over COOL's)* Cool, I never told you those were your children. You just thought so because you thought you were the only man in my life.

COOL: *(Almost crying and shouting)* Woman, don't you . . . shit on my life! Don't you take everything from my life and leave the shit!

EMMA: But we aren't your life, Cool. *(Scared, but trying to be kind)* Your life is out here. You didn't even know my sons knew who their father was because you've never been close to them. We have a whole life apart from you and you didn't think enough of us to see it!

COOL: You lyin! Why you take my money?

EMMA: Because I let you take my body.

COOL: You lyin bout my kids.

EMMA: No . . . I'm not lyin, Cool,

COOL: Them's my kids, Emma!

EMMA: No . . . *(Skaking head sadly, but you know it's the truth)* they're not your sons. They are my husband's children. They carry his name on their birth certificates. He was the one who was there.

COOL: *(As he talks he lunges and strikes EMMA, and she falls from her chair. JOE starts out, WILSON grabs him)* Don't do this to me! . . . Don't do this to me!

EMMA: *(From floor)* I didn't do nothin to you, Cool. . . . Nothin but what you ask me to. *(WILSON stoops to help her up)* I got to go now.

COOL: You ain't goin now . . . . You done come in here and strip me of everything in my life!

EMMA: *(Being helped up, brushing her clothes off)* Everything in your life? We wasn't nothin to you!

COOL: *(Almost crying, angry)* Yes, you were, yes you were! I was goin to spend my old age with you and them kids!

EMMA: They wouldn't be kids anymore, and I wouldn't be young anymore, and you probly be sick and wore out and through livin. *(Starts leaving)* Take care of yourself, Cool.

(COOL grabs EMMA, and she falls to her knees. COOL raises his fist to strike her—JOE reaches for COOL's arm—WILSON pulls his gun and puts it to COOL's head)

WILSON: Don't hit her, man!

COOL: *(Standing up, hysterical)* You bitch! You musta had everybody laughing at me! Whoring round callin it housecleaning! You don't know who the daddy of them bastards of yours is!

(WILSON tries to come between them, lifting EMMA up. EMMA is frightened and shocked)

COOL: *(Not realizing about gun)* Get the hell away from here, man, I'm talkin to my woman!

WILSON: You talkin to my wife! And I'm not gonna let her be another bitch outta your mouth!

COOL: Your wife! *(Shocked, then laughter)* You married this old man?

EMMA: Yes! The Lord blessed me with a *man!*

COOL: *(Starts to reach for her again)* If I catch you . . .

WILSON: You gonna have to catch up with your head first, cause if you make one more move to hurt her . . . you gonna be lookin up at yourself from the floor! *(Now COOL realizes gun)* I hope when you get my age . . . in a few years . . . you do as well as I have. Come on, Emma . . . *(They move to door)* let's go get our sons and go home where there is peace.

COOL: I'll marry you now, Emma, *(Reaching for her)* tomorrow morning, today . . . I'll marry you now . . . don't take my sons . . .

EMMA: *(The last thing before she goes out)* You got to understand, they are not your sons, Cool.

COOL: *(To WILSON)* Take her then, ole man . . . I had her first!

WILSON: That's right . . . and I'm glad you didn't have enough sense to hold on to her. You coulda had my sons too . . . and I'm glad you didn't have enough sense for that either! It really was all your choice for a long time. *(Leaves)*

COOL: *(Rushing to door, hysterical)* Get out of here! Get out of here! You think you got something, but you ain't got nothin!

WILSON: *(From outside)* That ain't me, Cool, that's you that ain't got nothin!

Scene 5

Everything is quiet in the bar. JOE and TAN are dead still. COOL remembers them, and wiping his nose and eyes with his arm like a child, he tries for bravado.

COOL: You see that bullshit, man? I didn't want to hurt that ole man! Shit! Who needs her? But them are my sons . . . she's lyin, man . . . she be back . . . she gon need me! But I'm a loner . . . can't stand that kinda shit! I'm a loner! *(Breaking down a little)* But she be back. But I don't need her! I ain't gon take her back! When them kids grow up, they know who they real daddy is! Gimmie a drink, man!

(As JOE *fixes a drink,* COOL's *body jumps as if with a shot—it's the completion of his breakdown. He grasps the bar, arms stretched out and leaning on the bar, he sobs, deep, wracking sobs as he slowly crumbles to his knees on the floor.*

COOL: I . . . don't . . . want . . . to . . . be . . . a . . . *loner!* I . . . don't . . . want . . . to . . . be . . . a . . . *loner!!!*

*(*TAN *gets up from her stool, picks up drink, and drinks it.* JOE *shrugs. Gloatingly,* TAN *leans down to help* COOL *up . . . he lets her)*

TAN: Come on, honey, you need some company . . . . Come on with Tan Tan. *(NOT said with the attitude of "everything will be all right")*

(As they slowly walk, COOL *stumbles a little, leaning on her, a sad, sad sight. The lights slowly dim out)*

End

GUS EDWARDS

FROM THE CARIBBEAN, Gus Edwards was born in Antigua, grew up in St. Thomas, Virgin Islands, and migrated to the U.S. in 1959. He has lived in New York City since then, studying theater, earning, and living, and, in general—trying to survive. He was an actor before he became a playwright, but he has also done other kinds of work—everything from being a boutique store manager to stevedore.

The year 1977 became a banner year for Mr. Edwards when both The Eugene O'Neill Memorial Theater and The Negro Ensemble Company chose his works to include in their production schedules for that season. The plays generally were received with enthusiastic critical acclaim. And since that time, his works have been produced all over the United States. He has won best playwrighting awards and was the recipient of a 1979-1980 Rockefeller Foundation Playwrights Award. Currently, he is the resident playwright of The Negro Ensemble Company.

A list of his works include, *The Offering, Black Body Blues, Old Phantoms,* and the current *Weep Not for Me* (scheduled for a 1980-81 production).

Mr. Edwards, who says he has no thoughts or philosophies concerning his own works, prefers a comment written by Douglas Turner Ward, the artistic director of The Negro Ensemble Company: "Gus Edwards is a unique talent and a playwright of great originality. His territory is the outer boundaries of the Black experience. He portrays people isolated from the mainstream of Afro-American life, functioning on the borderline of existence, yet depicts them with such compelling intensity and force until they command primary attention. They focus on a brutal urban world suffused with sexuality and the ever-present threat of violence. But they are depicted with the controlled passion of a true artist. Moreover, he refuses to indulge in facile moralizing. He does not try to tell us what to think, but provokes thoughts' exercises."

THREE FALLEN ANGELS

Gus Edwards

CHARACTERS

WILLIE HARRIS: *A friendly looking black man in his late 20s. He weighs about 175 pounds and shows the remains of what once was a very powerful body.*

MIRIAM HARRIS: WILLIE's *wife. An attractive, serious woman in her middle twenties.*

EDDIE LEE: *A drifter, two years younger than* WILLIE. *College bred. A slight physique.*

Setting: The play is set on an empty stage with several sitting and standing platforms. Everything is a deep gray (the floor, the sky, the walls, etc.). Occasionally a few props are brought on by the cast—they are indicated in the text.

A PLAY IN ONE ACT

Scene 1

When the lights come up, EDDIE *and* MIRIAM *are dancing.* WILLIE, *her husband, is reclining on a platform across from them, sipping a drink and letting the slow, bluesy music the band is playing go to his head.* EDDIE *has* MIRIAM *pressed very close to him; both are moving gracefully to the music.*

MIRIAM: Please . . . you're holding me too close.

EDDIE: No-oo-oo.

MIRIAM: What?

EDDIE: I ain't letting you go. You feel too good. *(He holds her closer)*

MIRIAM: I'm telling you . . . don't hold me like that.

EDDIE: Fight if you want. I ain't letting you go.

MIRIAM: What's the matter with you? You drunk.

EDDIE: No, I wish I was, but I'm not.

MIRIAM: Then let me go before I call Willie and make a scene here.

EDDIE: Call him. I don't care. Understand something, Miriam. I ain't letting you go. *(A pause)* I love you.

MIRIAM: You crazy.

EDDIE: I love you.

MIRIAM: You just met me. Tonight.

EDDIE: I love you.

MIRIAM: I am married.

EDDIE: I know.

MIRIAM: You and Willie supposed to be friends.

EDDIE: We are.

MIRIAM: And this is the way you talk to his wife?

EDDIE: Yes.

MIRIAM: Eddie, please let me go.

EDDIE: Never.

MIRIAM: Eddie . . . please . . .

EDDIE: No, Miriam, no.
(The music stops, and abruptly MIRIAM *breaks away and goes toward* WILLIE. EDDIE *follows her)*

WILLIE: Nice. That band plays some nice sounds.

EDDIE: Yeah.

MIRIAM: Willie, it's getting late. Let's go.

WILLIE: You want to?

MIRIAM: Yes.

WILLIE: *(To* EDDIE*)* You want to?

EDDIE: I don't mind.

WILLIE: What time is it?

MIRIAM: Nearly two. Let's go.

WILLIE: Okay, if that's what everybody wants.

MIRIAM: That's what everybody wants.

EDDIE: Yeah.

WILLIE *stands up, he is a little drunk and has trouble standing.* MIRIAM *supports him.* EDDIE *doesn't move to help.* MIRIAM *and* WILLIE *leave with* EDDIE *walking behind them.*

Scene 2

The stage is in darkness for a moment. A work whistle blows. It is the lunch whistle. Lights come up on another section of the stage. WILLIE *and* EDDIE *are sitting and eating on a platform in work clothes, lunch boxes are in front of them.*

EDDIE: Hank has a hard-on for me in the worst way, man.

WILLIE: You pay attention to that fool, that's why.

EDDIE: I can't ignore him. The son of a bitch is there every minute. "Eddie, faster! Eddie, slower! Eddie, move your ass." His night don't go right unless he's bugging me about something. Look at tonight. I wasn't doing nothing.

WILLIE: You was throwing packages on the belt when he told you not to.

EDDIE: Who the fuck can see that belt under there? You don't have time to look, especially with that asshole yelling out over that microphone, "Move your ass, move your ass."

WILLIE: He's ridiculous on that microphone.

EDDIE: He's got an ego problem. That's what he's got.

WILLIE: The union goin' change all that microphone shit when February comes around.

EDDIE: They got to. It ain't right, that man sitting up there on his ass calling out to people on that mechanical thing like he was some kind of electric god or something.

WILLIE: They goin' fix that. I heard them union fellows talking.

EDDIE: I wish I was union.

WILLIE: Come February, we will be.

EDDIE: I wish we was union right now. You know what I'd do if we were union? You know what I'd do? I'd walk up to that fucking Hank and I'd punch him in the goddamn face then step back and watch him hard in the eyes. *(Pause)* I can't do it because if I hit him now, I'd lose the goddamn job. *(Pause)* Jesus Christ, I wish I was union.

WILLIE: Hank ain't no child. You think you could take him if it come to that?

EDDIE: I don't know. I ain't no fighter. *(Pause)* Anyway, I ain't about to hit him. I need this job too bad.

WILLIE: I ain't ever made money like this before. So this job okay with me.

EDDIE: I ain't ever worked like this before.

WILLIE: You some kind of college boy, ain't you?

EDDIE: I had two years, then I dropped out.

WILLIE: My wife, Miriam, is college. The whole four years. Me, I went as far as sixth grade in school.

EDDIE: But you know something. You know how to box.

WILLIE: The Army teach me that.

EDDIE: Me. I don't know shit. *(Pause)* Willie, teach me how to box. Teach me how to do all

that bobbin' and weavin'. How to knock a faggot like Hank on his ass if the chance ever come up.

WILLIE: You serious?

EDDIE: Yes, I'm serious.

WILLIE: Okay, whenever you want.

EDDIE: Fine. What time you got?

WILLIE: Time to catch some zees before that lunch whistle blows.

WILLIE *lies back on the platform.* EDDIE *closes up his lunch box and sits and stares out at the audience for a while. The whistle blows, and the lights go out.*

Scene 3

Another part of the stage. WILLIE *and* EDDIE *are seated together.* EDDIE *looks very tired, very out of it.*

WILLIE: You tired?

EDDIE: Yeah.

WILLIE: Muscles aching?

EDDIE: All here, *(Indicates the back of his neck)* and here. *(His shoulders)* That last bunch of boxes just about do me in.

WILLIE: Let me try something, see if it help make you feel better.
(He takes EDDIE's *shoulders from behind and massages them with his fingers—then he does the back of his neck)*

WILLIE: Feel better?

EDDIE: Yeah . . . yeah . . . much much better.

WILLIE: Your muscles are tight. You ain't used to working hard, baby.

EDDIE: I told you, until this job I used to be an office worker. In fact, when I applied for this job, I thought it was paperwork. The form said platform clerk and naturally I assumed . . .

WILLIE: Yeah . . . you assume.

EDDIE: Anyway, I'm doing it and I ain't doing too badly except now and then when my back hurts. *(Pause)* Tell you the truth. When I took it I didn't think I could stick it out. It ain't the kind of work I want to do all my life, but right now I don't mind it.

WILLIE: I like it. I think a man could get rich just doing this if he smart and he don't spend every penny of what he make every week. With what my wife bringing in from teaching and what I bring in from here we could have everything we want plus a few a the extras.

EDDIE: Things are different when you're married. Me, I only got myself to worry about.

WILLIE: I like being married. Miriam is a good woman. A smart woman.

EDDIE: I know . . .

WILLIE: You ever had a steady girl?

EDDIE: Sure.

WILLIE: A lot?

EDDIE: No. Not a lot. But enough to know a little bit about them.

WILLIE: What you doing Sunday?

EDDIE: Nothing.

WILLIE: Want to come over the apartment? We could sit and talk and watch some T.V.

EDDIE: Okay.

WILLIE: I'll get Miriam to fix some dinner. We'll make a day of it.

EDDIE: Okay.

WILLIE: Get yourself together. I think I hear the train.

EDDIE: At last.

Lights

Scene 4

In another area—a bed. EDDIE *is seated on it wearing slacks and an undershirt.* MIRIAM *is standing close by surveying the place.*

MIRIAM: This is where you live.

EDDIE: Yeah. This is it.

MIRIAM: It ain't much.

EDDIE: I ain't no millionaire.

MIRIAM: The least you could do is keep it clean.

EDDIE: It's clean.

MIRIAM: It's a mess. It's a goddamn mess.

EDDIE: Then I'm sorry.

MIRIAM: I don't care.

EDDIE: Miriam . . .

MIRIAM: What . . . ?

EDDIE: Come here.

MIRIAM: . . . no.

EDDIE: Miriam. *(He rises)*

MIRIAM: Stay . . . stay over there.

EDDIE: No . . . I can't.

(She is facing the audience. He walks up behind her and embraces her)

MIRIAM: This ain't right. *(He caresses her)* This ain't right at all.

EDDIE: I got to kiss you. I got to know what it's like.

(He takes her face in his hands and brings it to his)

MIRIAM: You spoiling me, Eddie. You spoiling me for my husband.

They kiss, a long tender kiss. They break and kiss again. Afterwards both move away from each other. Slowly MIRIAM *begins to unbutton her blouse. She removes it and hands it to* EDDIE. *She steps out of her skirt;* EDDIE

takes that. They stand looking at each other for a moment, then MIRIAM *goes to the bed, gets under the covers and waits for* EDDIE. *Lights go down as he joins her.*

Scene 5

In an empty clearing, center stage, WILLIE *stands with boxing gloves on. After a moment,* EDDIE *joins him, also wearing boxing gloves.*

WILLIE: Okay. I'll only block and try to keep you off. You try and hit me. Okay?

EDDIE: Right.

(They begin. EDDIE *goes at him and tries in every way to hit him, but* WILLIE *is too skillful. He blocks and he dances and something pushes* EDDIE *away, but he never strikes him or tries to)*

EDDIE: Break! *(*WILLIE *stops)* I'm tired.

WILLIE: Tired?

EDDIE: Yeah. This is your game, remember? I'm just a beginner.

WILLIE: Take your wind. Next time we start I'm going to hit you to show you how open you are. I'll hit you as much as I could just to show you where you should cover up.

EDDIE: You gonna hit me hard?

WILLIE: As hard as you hit me. I'll let you set it. Ready?

EDDIE: Yes.

*(*WILLIE *steps up and begins to punch. As he boxes, he talks)*

WILLIE: *(Jabbing* EDDIE *constantly in the face)* Your face is wide open, baby. Cover is up. Not good enough, I can still see it . . . . Now for your stomach, 'cause you coverin' your eyes and can't see nothin' . . . . Now your head 'cause you let that go again. *(He goes in and hits* EDDIE *all over, confusing him as to where to cover first)* Use your hands. Hit back. Fight back. Hit back.

*(*EDDIE *tries and falls. He tries to clinch.* WILLIE *breaks, pushes him away and fires straight at his head.* EDDIE *slips the punch and* WILLIE *is off balance,* EDDIE *throws one, knocking* WILLIE *down)*

EDDIE: Willie . . . I'm sorry . . .

WILLIE: *(Getting up; he's angry)* Don't be sorry. Prepare to fight. You a pro now. Let's see how good you really are.

EDDIE: Willie . . . Willie . . .

WILLIE: *(Punching viciously at the air in front of* EDDIE*)* Don't talk. Defend yourself.

*(*WILLIE *goes into a crouch and menacingly goes toward* EDDIE. EDDIE *stands his ground grimly and fires as hard as he can at* WILLIE. WILLIE *knocks it away. He does it again and again; each time* WILLIE *knocks it away, moving up and measuring like a matador)*

WILLIE: You in trouble, ain't you, baby? You can't hit me and I sure as hell can hit you. *(EDDIE tries again and WILLIE blocks it again)* Here it come! *(WILLIE throws out a decoy; EDDIE goes for it. WILLIE poises the big one and EDDIE covers up in a little ball, waiting for it to land. WILLIE never fires. WILLIE is suddenly pleasant)* What kind of defense is that? I come after you and you close up like a flower? *(EDDIE looks up, perplexed)* Hold your hands up. Face me.

EDDIE: You—you ain't angry?

WILLIE: No. I was faking you out. See how you'd react under pressure. I was giving you a test.

EDDIE: And I failed.

WILLIE: You tried, but you let me scare you.

EDDIE: I thought you was really angry.

WILLIE: About what? A fall? I been knocked down a lot of times. They don't bother me no more. Let's take a break. Now I'm out of breath. *(WILLIE pulls the strings of his gloves with his teeth. He goes to help EDDIE take off his)* Man, you shaking.

EDDIE: Yeah.

WILLIE: Don't let anybody scare you like that, man. Least of all, me. I'm your buddy, baby. I am. I love you, man. Believe me, I do.

EDDIE: I believe you.

WILLIE: Come—I'll get us something to drink.
    (As they leave the stage, we hear WILLIE's voice)

WILLIE: *(Offstage)* When I finish teaching you, nobody on that waterfront will be able to beat you, and that's a fact.

Scene 6

A small Christmas tree with tiny colored lights that blink on and off. For a moment the stage is empty while the tree goes on and off. Then MIRIAM comes out with several packages. She puts them under the tree and waits. Way in the distant background we hear a record playing Christmas music. She waits for a while, absorbed, in the mood.

MIRIAM: Willie. Eddie. What taking you so long?

WILLIE: *(Appearing laden with gifts)* Here—here—
    (EDDIE arrives behind with two packages)

MIRIAM: You damn fool. Look at you. You look like a drunken Santa Claus.

WILLIE: *(Doing a Louis Armstrong)* Ho-ho-ho. I'm from the North Pole, motherfucker. This is for you and you, *(He gives EDDIE two boxes)* and some more for you. *(MIRIAM gets four boxes)*

MIRIAM: Oh my God. Well, here's yours, *(She gives him three)* and Eddie.
    (EDDIE takes his from her)

EDDIE: Merry Christmas, Willie. Merry Christmas, Miriam. *(He gives each one a package)*

(All stand watching each other and smiling)

MIRIAM: Well, what're we standin' round like fools for? Let's open them.
    (All fall on their packages and begin tearing them apart)

MIRIAM: *(Holding up a dress)* Oh—Willie. That's so nice. *(Holding up a purse)* Eddie—this thing ain't real leather, is it?

EDDIE: Yes.

MIRIAM: Eddie—Eddie—oh God—you shouldn't spend your money like that.

WILLIE: Baby, look at this. It's that car set I been looking at. Eddie got it for me.

EDDIE: I hope you know how to build it.

WILLIE: Build it? I could put this thing together in my sleep. Man, this is nice. Thanks. Thanks a lot.
    (EDDIE opens one of his packages. It's a radio. He goes over to WILLIE and smiles at him. For the rest of this package-opening, the gratitudes should be mimed while the volume of the Christmas music is raised to drown out their voices. At the end all drink a toast and music goes down)

MIRIAM: That sofa ain't too comfortable, but it's all we got.

EDDIE: I'll manage.

MIRIAM: Good night, Eddie.

EDDIE: Good night.

WILLIE: See you in the morning.

EDDIE: Yeah.
    (Arms around each other, WILLIE and MIRIAM leave the stage. EDDIE removes his shoes and his shirt and is about to lie down when WILLIE reenters in his pajamas)

WILLIE: You asleep, baby?

EDDIE: No.

WILLIE: Man, she just told me and I had to tell you. I goin' to be a father. We getting a baby!

EDDIE: Congratulations.

WILLIE: This has got to be the best Christmas I ever had. *(Pause)* Well—good night.

EDDIE: Good night, Willie.
    (Christmas music. EDDIE stands up and goes to a window to look out. He is there for quite a while before MIRIAM appears behind him)

MIRIAM: He told you, didn't he?

EDDIE: *(Not turning)* Yeah.

MIRIAM: Are you happy?

EDDIE: I don't know.

MIRIAM: I'm happy. He's happy. Why can't you be happy?

EDDIE: 'Cause . . . 'cause . . . I don't know why.
    (They stand for a long moment without speaking. Then EDDIE turns away. He's trying hard not to cry)

EDDIE: I think I'm going . . . going away.

MIRIAM: Eddie . . .

EDDIE: Yeah, I am. I'll go back on the road . . . see

what the rest of the country look like.

MIRIAM: Eddie—

EDDIE: Yeah. Yeah—that's the thing to do.

MIRIAM: Because of this . . .

EDDIE: Yes . . . no . . . no.

MIRIAM: Eddie, don't play games.

EDDIE: This ain't no game.

MIRIAM: You really want to go.

EDDIE: Yeah.

MIRIAM: And you ain't goin' write or try to call nobody.

EDDIE: No.

MIRIAM: What about Willie?

EDDIE: No.

MIRIAM: *(Suddenly annoyed)* You just goin' walk out of our life like the way you walk in?

EDDIE: Yes—why not?

MIRIAM: Well—it ain't right. It ain't goddamn right—!

EDDIE: Miriam. Miriam, nothing ever been right. Nothing.

MIRIAM: Do me a favor, Eddie.

EDDIE: What?

MIRIAM: Don't run away tonight. Do it after the holidays. Willie expect to see you here in the morning. Don't spoil Christmas for him. He like you too, you know. He like you as much as I do, maybe even more. So—don't spoil it for him.

EDDIE: I won't . . . I wouldn't.

MIRIAM: Thanks . . . Eddie . . . thanks.

(She goes over to him and they kiss tenderly)

MIRIAM: Merry Christmas again.

EDDIE: Merry Christmas.

MIRIAM: Good night.

EDDIE: Good night.

She leaves. EDDIE *stands looking out at the audience for a long time. Christmas music comes up. The curtain descends.*

End

FARRELL J. FOREMAN

FARRELL FOREMAN'S CREDO simply stated is, "Only fools and madmen are pleased with themselves. No wise man is good enough for his own satisfaction." Mr. Foreman found that quote while riding the subway in his native Philadelphia. Oddly enough, he did not start in theatre as a writer. The acting bug bit F. J. at an early age. In fact, to this day he is quite sure he is the first Black actor to portray Zorro in the projects.... "My friends and I would produce movies on Saturday. Well, we never really had an inch of film or camera, but it was real enough for us. Yeh, I guess we were some pretty different kids. A couple of guys would get some boxes from the neighborhood supermarket and take toilet tissue cardboard rolls and stick them in the end of the box and attach a drawing of a local networks call letters on the side, and we were off..."

People have had stranger beginnings in the theatre...but beginnings are only just that, beginnings. While at Villanova University Mr. Foreman started writing poetry. In 1970 a small collection of these works were published under the title, *Null & Void."* He called the book that because he figured that the English profs comments would closely resemble the title. One professor didn't agree and submitted a poem to the *Atlantic Monthly* Poetry Competition. Professor James J. Mitchell later said to Farrell, "Look, as far as your writing is concerned, be true to your mistress and she'll never leave you." As far as I can tell, from that moment on Mr. Foreman has been faithful. In 1978 his play, *The Ballad of Charley Sweetlegs Vine,* won The Lorraine Hansberry Award for Playwrighting. In 1977 he received honors for a one act entitled, *Teachers Lounge.* Mr. Foreman has published poetry in Antioch's *Imprint* magazine, Northern Illinois University's magazine, *Tower,* and in many other publications. He is the author of the articles, "On Being a Writer," and "Sambo Might Be Dead but...." Both were published in *Encore* magazine, the periodical of the National Association of Speech and Dramatic Arts. He also writes a column for *The Rockford Midwest Observer. Daddy's Seashore Blues* won honors in the Wichita State University Playwrighting Contest, and in 1980 won the Samuel Goldwyn Award for Creative Writing. "This play is about folks trying to make it. Folks trying to run away. Folks trying to love when it would be a lot easier to hate. Black people fall in love...they also have to survive. Most ordinary folks are just trying to get by with a little happiness. Some are doomed to fail, but they aren't any less human for trying."

DADDY'S SEASHORE BLUES

Farrell J. Foreman

dedicated to Cool Russ & Weasel, too

FOLKS

RAY: *Black man, 48 years old, still handsome although alcohol is taking its toll.*

BABE: *Black woman, 52 years old, you'd never guess her age unless you looked directly into her eyes. She drinks and snorts and smokes, but it doesn't seem to be bothering her really. Together* BABE *and* RAY *are like two old cats circling each other wondering who will get to the last meal first.*

SKEETER: *Black man, in his late 30s, dresses like he is 22.*

GAIL: SKEETER's *girlfriend, in her late 40s and spreading.*

SONNY: RAY's *son, 27 years old, low-cut afro, clean-cut on the outside.*

Place: One bedroom apartment in a high-rise building on the boardwalk in Atlantic City, New Jersey. Atlantic City at this time is preparing for the advent of gambling. Still, it is winter in a summer resort, gray, cold . . . dingy. The sea seems to be the only constant. It is 1977.

A PLAY IN THREE TIDES

TIDE ONE

At rise RAY *rushes in with a bag of groceries.*

RAY: He call yet? *(Putting the bag on the counter)*

BABE: *(A little high)* Nope! Ain't nobody called at all. You better sit down and relax. By the time he gets here you'll have had a heart attack.

RAY: We got any mixers around here?

BABE: We got plenty in the refrigerator.

RAY: I don't see nuthin here. Where the hell are they???

BABE: Calm down, baby. Calm down. I'll show you. *(She goes to the kitchen)* See . . . right on the door where you put them. *(She saunters back to the couch)*

RAY: *(Angry)* Why you got to go and get drunk before he comes? Huh?

BABE: There it is, see?

RAY: Answer me! *(Grabbing her by the wrist)*

BABE: *(Ripping away)* I drink all the time. You ain't never said nuthin before. Just cause your snot ass kid is comin don't mean that I got . . .

RAY: *(Slapping her)* Shut your filthy mouth! *My boy is comin! And you ain't slingin shit on him comin here for a visit!*

BABE: Baby, why you hit me?

RAY: *(Awkward)* Look, I just want stuff to be right. That's all. Come on and sit down. How about a drink? It'll *calm your nerves, baby!*

BABE: I'm already drunk.

RAY: Yeah, well I need one. *(Goes over to the kitchen and fixes a drink. After he mixes the drink, he walks over to the window and looks out at the sea)* Funny how far out the tide is. Way out. This summer these waves will be breaking right under the pier. Humph, summer. Lookin at this barren dead gray who'da thought there could be a summer at the seashore. *(Taking a sip of his drink)*

BABE: It won't be long, baby. Pretty soon everything will be open for gambling. The neon lites will be blinking all nite. This joint will be jumpin and then, sweetie, you and me will be in the money.

RAY: Still got grand ideas about pushin all that shit of your friend's, huh?

BABE: Why not? Who else gonna be able to make the New York connections but me? We'll be rollin in money.

RAY: Just don't have none of that shit out when my boy comes.

BABE: Listen to this mess. He ain't here, you'll do

36

anything. Now it's hi and mighty time. You full o shit.

RAY: Just like you. That's all you talk about, *money and dope!* When you gonna get some money, how much you gonna blow, what you gonna do with it. Don't you think of anything else? We ain't never once had an intelligent conversation.

BABE: Who wants to do a whole lotta talkin? I want to live. Do things. Have fun. How you gonna have fun talkin? Let's go out.

RAY: *(Ignores her. He seems to be in his own world)* I usta get paint jobs in the summer. About April or so I'd get these leaflets printed up with my prices. Wait a minute, *(Suddenly coming to life)* I think I got some in a drawer someplace. *(Goes to a kitchen drawer)* Yeah, here it is . . . fifty-nine dollars for a house front. Of course that depended on how many stories, the woodwork and so forth. Hell, back then paint wasn't but seven dollars a gallon. Finish a front in half a day. That was easy money. My boy would do the low work and I usually did the high stuff. It really got good when I started advertising in the local papers. Them houses in the Deerwood section didn't hardly have nuthin to paint, just door jams and window frames. Quick money. He was funny about goin up on the ladder though. *(Laughing)* Shit, one day there was this wasps' nest in the corner of one of the eaves that had to be painted. When the wasps saw him . . . you ain't never seen somebody come down a ladder so fast. Whew . . . hahahahahaha.

BABE: Let's go do somethin.

RAY: *(Ignoring her)* Yeah, that boy. He usta help me sell trees on the avenue at Christmas time. *(Pause)* People don't hardly buy real trees anymore. All this artificial shit.

BABE: Let's go down to the club.

RAY: Are you kiddin?! I gotta at least wait till he calls. Did I ever read you the poem he wrote about me? Huh?

BABE: I don't wanna hear no damn poem. You *done read it to me fifty times!* Let's go out. *(Pleadingly)*

RAY: I know it's here somewhere. *(Starts searching)* Did you see it?

BABE: Fuck you.

RAY: Fuck me! Bitch, you best watch yo mouth. *(Goes offstage to search for the poem)*

BABE: *(Calling to him)* C'mon baby, let's go on down to the club. He won't be here for awhile. C'mon.

RAY: I'll be out as soon as I find the paper. Here it is! *(Offstage)* Listen to this! *(Entering)*

BABE: Shit!

RAY: If you'd read more maybe your life wouldn't be so lopsided.

BABE: I got you, baby!!

RAY: *(Looks at her a second)* Listen. *(He begins to recite)* "It takes time, poppa, a long time. Understanding nestles deep down within young people, it just takes time to blossom. It takes time to see what it meant to you to sit on the back porch steps, sippin that coffee before we went out on a paint job. It takes time to see what it meant to you standin on the corner selling them trees on the avenue, I can't forget the pine smell nor the spirit there. It took time to see just who Santa Claus really was. I remember you wakin me up with a wet washcloth . . . get up, son, when you could hardly stay awake yourself, but you hadta run. It takes time but I ran into mine." . . . That's what my boy thinks of me. Ha, dat's right. Well . . . say somethin . . . *(She is silent)* Go on, say somethin. *(Walks over to her)* Don't you think it was nice . . . huh??

BABE: I wanna go out.

RAY: Yep, that's my son. *(Ignoring her)*

BABE: Let's go!

RAY: We ain't goin nowhere.

BABE: I don't see why I got to sit around here and wait for your piss ass son . . . he never wrote you, not even when I wrote that letter for you . . .

RAY: Shut Up!

BABE: Come to think of it, you ain't heard from him in six years, so why the big thing now?

RAY: You ain't never had no kids. You don't know what it means. *(Pause)* You don't even like kids . . .

BABE: Why you say that?

RAY: It's true, ain't it?

BABE: I don't like no burdens, No extra burdens.

RAY: That's what's wrong with you now. It's unnatural for a woman not to like kids.

BABE: How the hell would you know what's natural and unnatural.

RAY: I know a woman is supposed to like kids.

BABE: Bullshit.

RAY: I got some pictures of him when he was little too. I'd bet he'd git a kick outta seein them. I wonder if I can find them. *(He goes off searching for the pictures)*

BABE: I almost got married once. *(Low, quiet)*

RAY: What? You say you knew where the pictures wuz?

BABE: I said I was almost married once.

RAY: *(Appears in the door . . . then sits down beside her)* You say somethin about marriage?

BABE: *(Takes a drink)* I said I almost got married once.

RAY: Oh . . . where's my drink?

BABE: Over there . . . *(Pointing)* He was nice. Strong and tall . . . and had a smile somethin like yours. He wanted babies too. Somethin wrong with men that all they wants to do is make babies ...babies. Me and him we usta do things... live...that was a fun-lovin man. Soft and gentle ... *(RAY is looking straight ahead)*

RAY: How come you never married?

BABE: None o your gotdamn business!

RAY: Cause he wanted kids. Ain't dat right... huh?

BABE: So what?

RAY: So you couldn't deliver, *that's what! That's the whole gotdamn point!*

BABE: The point is you ain't exactly a model parent either. Look, what are we talkin about this for?

RAY: You brought it up.

BABE: I didn't bring up nuthin.

RAY: How can you sit there and say that when you started all this shit talkin about my boy?!

BABE: Your boy, your boy...now everything is your boy! Was it your boy that paid the rent for this funky apartment?? Huh?? Was it your boy that puts them rags on yo back, huh?? Who puts the coins in your pocket? Who buys the liquor around here...

RAY: Alright, that's enough.

BABE: Enough...who...what...enough?!!!!

RAY: I think you maybe need to go out! You crackin up. You just mad cause you ain't got your jollies off lately. C'mere baby... *(He reaches for her to kiss, and she shoves him away and gets up. He follows her and tries again)* C'mon, sweetmeat, I got somethin for you.

BABE: Git the hell offa me, Ray!!

RAY: *Touchy! Real touchy!*

BABE: I just want us to have some fun, that's all. I don't wanna see you hurt either.

RAY: What you mean, see me hurt?

BABE: How many times has he promised to visit you?

RAY: There you go again. The boy is busy. He got his schoolin to attend to. He ain't got time to run down here every time he'd like.

BABE: He visits his mother, don't he?

RAY: *(On the defensive)* That's different. He just came and visited his momma when she was sick ...that's all.

BABE: You foolin yourself, Ray. Why keep foolin yourself? The boy has got his own life and you got yours.

RAY: You just sayin that cause you *ain't got no kids.* You don't know how much this boy thinks of me.

BABE: I know the only time he writes is when he needs money.

RAY: Now, you know you lyin. He calls at least twice a month.

BABE: I must not be here when he calls.

RAY: You think maybe he's having some trouble findin the place?

BABE: Ain't but one boardwalk.

RAY: You ain't no help at all. I think I'll call the bus station to see if his bus got in. *(Going to the phone. BABE is sitting on the couch. She picks up the poem and looks at it. She then places it on the table. RAY returns)* They say the bus is forty-five minutes late. He'll be here soon.

BABE: That's plenty of time, baby. We can go out to my girlfriend's...you know, Gail...you always said you liked her and her man, Skeeter.

RAY: Yeah, that nigger is funny. 'Member when I bet him he wouldn't put his head in the fish tank they had cause they had piranhas in there. The fool did it. It was at that New Years party they threw.

BABE: I remember. You wanna go?

RAY: Nah. Suppose his bus comes in earlier? Nah, I better stay here. You got any cigarettes?

BABE: No.

RAY: Stay here while I walk down to the corner and pick up some. *(He exits)*

BABE: Shit!

She walks over to the phone and then goes over to the coffee table and picks up the poem again and looks at it. She finds some matches, lights the paper and watches it slowly burn in the ash tray. The lights slowly fade.

TIDE TWO

When RAY comes in, BABE is laid out on the sofa.

RAY: Did he call? *(She doesn't respond)* Did he call? Shit, she's sleep. *(Mumbling to himself)* Let me go call the station. *(He makes the call)*

BABE: *(Begins to wake up)* Ray...that you? *(He doesn't answer)*

RAY: *(Shouting)* What the hell you mean you don't know what the delay is! Ain't the bus supposed to be in?! Look lady, let me talk to your boss. I don't give a good gotdamn what the schedule says, just let me talk to your...what...the bitch! *(Slams the phone down)* Everything's goin to hell! You know that?!

BABE: Wha'?

RAY: I called the station just now and I can't even get a decent answer as to when the bus is coming in. What is happenin in this country? Even Greyhound's gittin unreliable.

BABE: Are you sure he's comin in on Greyhound?

RAY: Am I sure? Now why in the hell would I call em if he wasn't comin in that way?!

BABE: I just asked. You ain't got to git so smart!

(Gets up and goes to the bathroom)

RAY: Smart! I'm talkin about the damn operator down at the station. What are you talkin about?

BABE: *(From the bathroom)* Nuthin!...Never mind...*(Comes out)* I don't know why you get so worked up over that anyway. He'll get here when and if he gets here. I doubt if you live that long anyway. The way you actin you might have a stroke any minute now.

RAY: I just don't like bein treated like dirt, that's all. That woman was plain nasty and it wasn't no call for it. Shit, I'm law abidin. I pay my taxes.

BABE: Nigger, you ain't made no money in two years to pay taxes. What you mean, pay taxes?

RAY: You know what I mean. You always givin me two for one. You don't never support what I say.

BABE: That's cause you wrong most of the time.

RAY: Sometimes you make me want to bust you right upside your head.

BABE: *(Quickly now)* And then you come to your senses and realize how foolish that would be. Right?

RAY: Maybe I oughta just go pop you one for spite.

BABE: Don't go takin out on me what that woman said to you on the phone. I ain't in it. If you wuz smart you'd sit down, calm down and smoke some of this weed. *(She is rolling a joint)*

RAY: That's all you do. Smoke weed and snort shit up yo nose.

BABE: It beats doin nuthin. Here. *(Handing him the joint)* Take it.

RAY: *(A little hesitant in taking it)* Not bad. Maybe I shoulda did this earlier. *(Pause)* Ya know, since the boy's outta school now, he might be considerin comin and stayin for a while.

BABE: So?

RAY: I'm just sayin it cause there's gonna have to be some changin goin on around here.

BABE: Like what?

RAY: For one thing, them grand plans for being the queen of drugs might have to change.

BABE: What we gonna live on, dreams?

RAY: I can git my old waiter job back with the hotel, and with what I git from the aid, we'll make out alright.

BABE: You must be crazy. I ain't livin on that shit. Besides, you ain't never worked nowhere more than three days straight.

RAY: I'm sayin it's gonna be different.

BABE: How's it gonna be different? It's gonna be worse. Livun with no money. You must be kiddin. That's what we doin now.

RAY: Who said we ain't gonna have no money? I tole you I get a check, and I'll just go back to the hotel, that's all.

BABE: I can't live on that chump change. What's more, you can't either. What are you gonna do when your liquor money runs out? You ain't the type that begs for wine money on the corner, or are you tellin me you can swallow your pride?

RAY: You must be high already! With tips and stuff we'll do alright.

BABE: If you think I'm gonna support you and your son you crazy!

RAY: *(Low)* You been doin it!

BABE: What you say?

RAY: Eh, nuthin. Just that if the boy stays here he'll probably work. Hell, for all we know he's already got a job.

BABE: You live in a dream world. You know that? A big fat dream filled world. All you wanna do is sit around here and cry and whine about what happened in your past. You even cry in your sleep. You know that?

RAY: You lyin. I ain't never cried in my sleep.

BABE: I ain't got to lie, nigger. I done watched it enough times. First, it was your ex-wife, then it was some woman, then it was your son. You walk around here like you don't know what you gonna do from one minute to the next.

RAY: Just shut up, woman.

BABE: Just shut up woman, be quiet woman, I'm gonna slap your face woman, that's all you ever say. It don't change nuthin. *And* you ain't slappin me no more.

RAY: I done tole you about tellin me what to do. For that matter, why in the hell don't you just leave. Just git out. Split. Huh? I'll tell you why, cause you ain't got no place to go either. Don't nobody want your ass but me and sometimes even I don't want you. Dat's right, *no place.* You ain't got one damn friend, one damn relative, one damn nobody but me that you can go. That's why you here. This is the last stop. Ain't dat right? Huh? Don't want to admit it, do you? I'm all you got. And if you think it's a shitty bargain, well, that's too damn bad...what you better start doin is figurin out how to stay on my good side or I might just throw your ass out.

BABE: Shit!

RAY: You heard me. Just throw your ass right on out.

BABE: What would you do when you git the shakes? What would you do when the money runs out? What would you do if that shortness of breath comes back?

RAY: My boy will take care of me.

BABE: You a fool, Ray. He ain't even here yet. What makes you think he wants to be weighted down with an old man for?

RAY: I ain't old and besides, he's my son.

BABE: Yeah, he's your son. He's your one and only. I only hope he ain't as selfish and self-centered as his daddy.

RAY: Yeah, yeah. Why don't you cook somethin?

BABE: You just ate not too long . . .

RAY: I know, but I'm hungry again and besides, the boy is probably gonna be hungry when he gets in.

BABE: He ain't comin.

RAY: *Say it one more time and you ain't gonna recognize yourself in the mirror!*

BABE: What do you want to eat?

RAY: I don't know, just put somethin on.

BABE: Suppose I fix a sandwich?

RAY: Fine. *(She goes to the kitchen and begins to prepare the sandwich)*

BABE: You want mayonnaise on your sandwiches.

RAY: You know I always have mayonnaise on my sandwiches.

BABE: Sometimes you change. Sometimes you want just mustard, then there's times when you want both mustard and mayo, and then there's times when you want neither.

RAY: Alright, you made your point. *(Reaches for a deck of cards and starts to shuffle them)* Let's see what the cards got to say today. *(He deals himself and a fake hand of draw poker. Looks into the kitchen to see if she is watching and then proceeds to peep at the dummy hand)* Well! This looks pretty good . . . think I'll play with these.

   (BABE comes from the kitchen and places the sandwich on the table in front of RAY. She picks up the dummy hand)

BABE: I'll take three cards.

RAY: What are we playin for?

BABE: You makin my sandwich.

RAY: You're on. *(Deals her the three cards)* If I win . . . *(Hesitantly)* I want some poon-tang right now.

BABE: What you got.

RAY: You wanna bet some more?

BABE: Make it easy on yourself.

RAY: How bout hangin from the chandelier in the bedroom?

BABE: Nigger, you crazy.

RAY: Well? How bout it?

BABE: How we gonna hang from the chandelier?

RAY: Not we, you!

BABE: Bet something reasonable.

RAY: Alright . . . how bout a fifth of Old Crow?

BABE: Fine. What you got?

RAY: Three aces. *(Grinning)*

BABE: Not good enough, four threes.

RAY: Damn!

BABE: Let's go git that sandwich.

RAY: If I didn't know better, I'd think you was cheatin.

BABE: You the one always tryin to cheat. I know you looked at the hand before I even picked it up. You just knew you wuz gonna win, didn't you? Hahahahahahahahah.

RAY: What kind of sandwich do you want.

BABE: *(In an affected tone)* Well, let's see. I would like hot pastrami with swiss cheese and a number of black olives on the side.

RAY: We ain't got no pastrami. And *(looking around the refrigerator)* we ain't got no black olives either.

BABE: That ain't my problem. A bet is a bet.

RAY: You think you so damn smart.

BABE: You agreed to the bet.

RAY: But that ain't no fair. You can only make a sandwich with what's in here.

BABE: Aw, da little baby can't find the things to make mommie's sandwich with. Aw, tch, tch, tch, too bad. Make it, sucker. Hahahahahahaha.

RAY: Look, I'll make the sandwich with what's in here, okay?

BABE: Hell no! A bet is a bet. Ain't that what you always say?

RAY: That ain't fair.

BABE: Okay, okay . . . don't have no heart attack over it. Make it with what you got.

RAY: That's all you wuz gonna git anyway.

BABE: You know somethin . . . you a sore loser. As long as you win, everything is cool. But as soon as you lose, everybody else is wrong and unfair. You just a big baby . . . *(Calling him)* Ray.

RAY: Yeah.

BABE: Why don't I call up some of the people from your job. We could have a party. It could be a welcoming party for your son.

RAY: I don't want a bunch of niggers in here actin crazy when my boy gits here. *(He brings the sandwich from the kitchen. It is a piled-high mess)* Here. *(Placing it on the table)*

BABE: What am I supposed to do with this?

RAY: Eat it . . . stick it in your ear. I don't care.

BABE: I can't eat this.

RAY: Then don't.

BABE: You a rotten chump. You know that?

RAY: Yes, darling. *(Smiling)*

BABE: I don't see why you wouldn't invite some folks over to meet *your boy*.

RAY: We got things to talk about. I don't want no crowd. *(Reading a newspaper)* Looks like they gonna break ground for a new hotel soon. Boy, I wish I could get a piece of one, just one of them casinos. Do you know how much they bring in a day?

BABE: Lots. Look, as soon as the suckers come down here to blow there money they gonna also be willing to spend on other pleasures as well.

RAY: That's where you come in, right?

BABE: Right! I know once they start comin in droves we can make a fortune, a fortune!

RAY: What about all the trouble that junk brings with it—all kinds of sick motherfuckas knockin on the door all hours of the night.

BABE: Look, dummie . . . you don't service the riff-raff. You make sure that the folks is reasonably cool. 'Sides, I'm only gonna deal in coke and smoke. Heroin has too much heat attached to it.

RAY: I don't want none of that shit around me.

BABE: You been likin it so far.

RAY: So far ain't nobody been bangin on the door all hours of the night.

BABE: You worried about nuthin.

RAY: We'll see about that when my boy gets here.

BABE: *(Phone rings)* I'll get . . .

RAY: It's him. *(Running by her)* I'll get it. *(Brushing past her)*

BABE: Damn.

RAY: Hello. Yeah. Skeeter? Shit. Yeah, I'm alright, nigger. What you up too? Yeah. Well, we okay . . . come on up. Later . . . *(Going back into the living room)* That was Skeeter. He's comin up.

BABE: Good! Tell him to bring Gail.

RAY: You tell em.

BABE: I'm gonna call her. *(Going to the phone)*

RAY: *(Hollering after her)* And don't stay on that damn phone so long! Sonny might be tryin to get through!

BABE: Hello, Gail . . . Hi, how you doin, girl . . . yeah you comin up with Skeeter? Good. Yeah bring a bottle, girl. Yeah . . . c'mon. *(Going back to the living room)* Gail's coming too.

RAY: Damn. That's the babblinest broad I ever met.

BABE: Stop talkin about my girlfriend.

RAY: It's true.

BABE: I don't talk about them strange old folks you hang out with so don't talk about my friends.

RAY: My friends ain't old, besides they ain't into that dope stuff. That's the only reason you call em old. Just because you like it don't mean everybody else has to. My friends like to drink. So what?

BABE: That's right they like to drink. They ain't never once brought no liquor here. Shit. They come in and drink everything in sight. If they was liquor in the fish tank they'd drink that too. Them old men is nasty anyway. They always tryin to hit on me behind your back.

RAY: Who's tryin to hit on you? It's just in yo mind. Ain't not a one of em ever tried anything. You stay so damn drunk you wouldn't know if somebody hit on you or not.

BABE: Not drunk, high.

RAY: Drunk, high, what's the difference?

BABE: The difference is that I ain't stumblin around here knockin over stuff. Them niggers break up everything and ain't never got no money to pay for nuthin.

RAY: That ain't true and you know it.

BABE: It is so. That ole . . . eh . . . Westley broke my lamp last time he was here. Nigger been here three times since and ain't never offered to pay for nuthin.

RAY: He ain't got no money.

BABE: Then he shouldn't have broke that lamp then.

RAY: How people gonna know what they doin when they drunk . . . well?

BABE: Then they shouldn't drink, they should smoke.

RAY: Aw, forget it.

(The door buzzer rings)

BABE: It's them. I'll get it. *(She goes to the door and opens it. GAIL and SKEETER enter)* Hey, what's happenin?

SKEETER: Nuthin lady . . . nuthin. Hey, my man Ray, what's happenin?

RAY: Nuthin man . . . nuthin.

BABE: So, what you been up to girl? *(Taking their coats)*

GAIL: Not too much . . . tryin to make it, you know.

BABE: I know, honey . . . I know.

GAIL: Here's the Old Crow for the *old crows*. You got any smoke, girl?

BABE: You know I got my stash.

SKEET: Old Crow, my ass.

RAY: Yeah . . . Babe has been runnin that old shit all day, man. She forgets that young johnson I been whippin on her lately.

SKEET: I hear you talkin, man. *(Slapping five)*

BABE: If it's so young, then how come I forget it?

GAIL: Git him, girl . . . git him . . . hahahahahaha.

RAY: Dat's alright . . . it'll be a cold day in hell for you get some more.

BABE: I can wait, honey . . . I can wait.

SKEET: The job is gettin dead, man. I'm lookin for a second hustle. With all these suckers comin into town, there's gotta be somethin.

GAIL: Girl, I been checkin out some new coats downtown. They got a sale on at Clamon's Department Store.

BABE: Yeah . . . how much?

GAIL: Well, the ones with fur collars were goin for two-fifty.

BABE: *(Rolling a joint)* What?

GAIL: They were marked down from three eighty-nine.

BABE: That don't sound bad at all.

RAY: How bout some glasses so us old crows can drink some of this Old Crow? Hahahahahahaha.

SKEET: Yeah.

BABE: I'm comin. *(Bringing the glasses)*

GAIL: Girl, this is some good bo.

BABE: Yeah, it ain't bad. Bout a month ago I had some that was worse than that. Y'all want to play some cards?

GAIL: Not really.

SKEET: How bout some Monopoly?

BABE: Hell no. Everytime Ray plays he gets serious as hell and wants to fight if you buy somethin he wants to buy.

RAY: Aw hell, you get mad all the time when I win.

BABE: It wouldn't be too bad if you didn't cheat so bad.

RAY: I ain't never cheated at Monopoly!

BABE: Everytime we play somethin you got to cheat. You just can't play to enjoy the game.

SKEET: You do be cheatin, man.

RAY: Alright . . . alright, . . . I won't cheat none.

GAIL: I'll believe it when I see it.

BABE: I'll play on one condition . . . Gail is the banker.

RAY: How I know she can count?

GAIL: Oh, I can count. I'll make sure there's no embezzlin from this bank.

RAY: I'll get the game. *(To BABE)* It's in the back, ain't it?

BABE: Yeah. *(RAY goes into the back and looks for the game)* Ray's son is supposed to visit today.

GAIL: *(Amazed)* Ray's got a son?

BABE: Yep, a twenty-seven year old responsibility.

SKEET: He never mentioned that he had a boy.

BABE: You'd never know it here.

GAIL: What's he like?

BABE: Look at you. Got the hots already and you ain't never seen him.

SKEET: This woman stays hot.

GAIL: You like it.

SKEET: Dat's right, honey, just keep it on a back burner.

GAIL: C'mon Babe, what's he look like?

BABE: I ain't never seen him.

GAIL: Oh shit.

BABE: Just hold your horses, you may get to meet him yet. He's due in any minute. Hey, Ray, what's takin you so long? It's in the closet where the rest of the games are. Anybody want more ice?

SKEET: Yeah, I do.

BABE: Be right back.

SKEET: That's strange that Ray never mentioned his boy before.

GAIL: Maybe he just don't like talkin about him.

Lots of people don't talk about their pasts. There might be all kinds of shit in the closet he don't want to remember himself.

SKEET: True. Hey Ray, c'mon man. I'm ready to take all you suckers to the poor house. *(Slapping and rubbing his hands together)* First time we played this game I went bankrupt first. That ain't happenin today, baby.

BABE: *(Returning from the kitchen)* If you manage your property and money the way you did last time, you gonna be broke again.

GAIL: I got faith in him, Babe. This time I think he'll set a record for "fastest to the po house."

SKEET: No way.

RAY: *(Reentering from the bedroom, carrying the Monopoly game. To BABE)* I wish you'd put shit away so that somebody could find it. I had to dig through half the shit in the closet. Under shoes and handbags, and all kinda crap.

BABE: You found it, right?

RAY: This time I'm gonna be the old shoe. Babe, whata you want?

BABE: The thimble is fine.

SKEET: I got the brim.

RAY: What about you, Gail?

GAIL: There ain't nuthin left but the car.

RAY: Then that's it. Okay. *(To GAIL)* Give up the cash. You supposed to be the banker.

GAIL: Alright. Here's your stash . . . *(Handing the money to RAY)* and yours . . . *(To SKEETER)* and to the lady . . . *(To BABE)* and now me . . . *(To herself)*

SKEET: I think you shorted me a hundred bucks.

GAIL: Don't start no shit, nigger. Count your money again.

SKEET: Yeah . . . you right . . . these hundreds stick together.

RAY: Where's my fifty . . . I ain't got no fifty dollar bills here.

GAIL: Let me see. Okay . . . here.

(RAY winks at SKEETER)

BABE: I seen that damn wink. You cheatin already.

RAY: Ain't nobody cheatin here. You just paranoid. C'mon, roll the dice, let's see who goes first . . . wait a minute, before you do that what rules is we playin by. We better get this straight first cause last time we got to arguin over stuff that didn't matter.

BABE: You was cheatin then and it did matter.

RAY: I was not cheatin.

SKEET: What's the rules?

BABE: If we go by strict rules, you can't buy houses or hotels until you have all three or two in a series of spots. If we play the other way, as soon as you land on somethin you have the option to buy and can immediately put up property on the spot.

42

GAIL: I don't care. But I know if we play the second way we run out of houses and hotels fast.

SKEET: So what? It makes the game more interesting.

BABE: No loaning each other money.

RAY: *(Amazed)* What you mean, no loanin each other money. It ain't nuthin in the rules that says you can't loan folks money if you want.

BABE: It's cheatin.

RAY: *How the hell is it cheatin!*

BABE: *Because it is!*

RAY: You don't know what you talkin about.

SKEET: We keep this up and ain't nobody gonna play nuthin. I vote we play easy rules.

RAY: Me too. What about you, Gail?

GAIL: It's okay with me.

BABE: What's okay with you?

GAIL: Easy rules, I guess.

BABE: Okay, let's play. Roll to see who goes first. Go head, Skeeter.

SKEET: *(Rolling)* Let's go, baby . . . double sixes. *(He rolls snake eyes)* Damn.

RAY: *(Rolling)* Here we go . . . be nice to daddy . . . yeah, nice . . . not bad. Okay, hot shot, your turn.

BABE: *(Rolls the dice quickly)* Six.

GAIL: Let's see what I can do. *(Rolls the dice)* Twelve! Yeah, now that's more like it. Okay, I'm first, Ray's second, Babe's third and you, dahling, is last. Let's go! *(Rolling)* Seven . . . chance . . . go directly to the nearest railroad, and *I'm buying it!!*

(The lights black out. When the lights rise, it is four hours later. Everyone is somewhat tired. RAY has gotten edgy and testy because he is beginning to sense that his son, SONNY, is not coming. SKEETER and GAIL have noticed this and have not mentioned the son at all. BABE has not brought the subject up either. To make matters worse, RAY hasn't been doing well in the game. He is losing, and if he lands on Park Place or Boardwalk again, he will be finished. When the light rise, he is on North Carolina and about to roll the dice)

RAY: *(Rolling the dice)* Well, here we go. Shit. I'm out. I couldn't win today if I had cheated.

SKEET: One down, two more to go!

GAIL: You land on my property one more time and you had it as well.

SKEET: You ain't got that much yourself.

GAIL: I don't know, *(Counting the money)* the banker has done pretty well, so far.

BABE: Yeah.

RAY: *(Going to get a drink)* I wonder why.

BABE: What's that supposed to mean?

RAY: She ain't never played this well before.

BABE: Go on, spit it out.

RAY: Well, you wuz always volunteering your ad-vice on what she should buy . . .

BABE: That ain't got nuthin to do with it.

SKEET: *(To GAIL)* Babe has been helpin you a lot.

RAY: And some of them discussions was designed to block me and Skeeter out.

BABE: That's the name of the game, ain't it?

GAIL: *(Menacingly)* You sayin we was cheatin, Ray.

RAY: That looks like the color of the cards to me.

GAIL: *(Throwing the dice at RAY)* I knew you was gonna pull some jive shit like this. Every time we come up here you always make sure you win. No matter how you do it, you win. Well, this time you got a taste of the loser's soup. *Don't like it, do ya? You can't stand it, can ya?*

SKEET: C'mon girl, it ain't all that much.

GAIL: Oh yes it is!! Everytime we come up here this old bastard cheats us blind!! Well, this time I got tired of it!! I did a little cheatin of my own!!

BABE: *You was cheatin?* Shit, what difference does it make? I'm tired of playin this shit anyway.

RAY: See, I tole you they was cheatin.

SKEET: They, they who?

GAIL: You can't stand it when somebody gits the goods on you. Can you, Ray?

RAY: Aw, go to hell.

GAIL: You won't be able to have your son visit you there. Will ya, Ray.

(BABE, shocked, opens her mouth to say something but cannot speak)

SKEET: Why don't you shut up, Gail!

RAY: What you say?

SKEET: You're drunk.

RAY: *(Dead sober and serious)* I asked you a question.

BABE: She ain't mean nuthin by it, Ray.

GAIL: I said your damn son ain't comin to visit you in hell!

RAY: You must be crazy, bitch! *(Lunges for GAIL, but SKEETER grabs him)*

SKEET: C'mon man, she don't know what she sayin, she's drunk as hell.

RAY: I'm gonna break her gotdamn head.

BABE: Y'all better get outta here.

SKEET: Go head, Gail. I can't hold this fool forever.

GAIL: I'm leaving. *(Exits)*

SKEET: *(Releases RAY)* Look, I'm sorry things got outta hand.

RAY: Just go, man.

SKEET: *(Near the door)* I hope your boy comes.

(RAY turns to look at him)

BABE: *(To SKEETER)* Don't bring that bitch back here no more.

(SKEETER exits)

RAY: That was your bright idea invitin them up here. You tole em about Sonny too.

BABE: Just lay off. If we had went out insteada sittin up here, none of this woulda happened . . .

no, you insisted that we wait, *wait, wait, wait. I'm tired of waiting.*

RAY: Nobody asked you to wait.

BABE: *(Walking over to* RAY*)* Look at me, Ray. *(She turns him around)* He ain't comin. You hear me, *he ain't comin!!!*

> *(In that instant* RAY *slaps her.* BABE *slaps him right back with equal force.* RAY *holds her by the shoulder and then lets her go. He goes and sits on the couch.* BABE *goes back to the kitchen. She is fixing a drink. There is a piercing silence.* BABE *brings a drink from the kitchen)*

RAY: Why do you stay?

BABE: *(Pause)* You always think you the only one with memories. I got memories too. Just cause I don't talk about em every five minutes don't mean I don't have any. I had a love . . . a real love once. You know them little dinky coffee shops on Fifth Avenue?

RAY: Yeah.

BABE: That's where I met him. He wasn't a real pretty man or anything like that. He just had a proudness . . . a strength, and yet I could see right through to him. He asked me could he join me for coffee, and I don't think I said anything, but the expression on my face must have told him it was okay. He talked about his job and how he was real good at makin his deliveries on time. He was square. I mean a Class A Number One Square. He didn't even smoke when I first met him. I think he made somethin like one twenty-five a week. He had a little money saved too. The first time he took me out it was to one of them steak houses. That steak was as chewy as salt water taffy. It didn't matter. He was the first person I ever really felt comfortable with. It was like we was real good friends. I didn't talk much at first, but after a while I'd open up. I was making good money then so I had a fairly decent place. He didn't want me to know where he lived. At first I thought he was married. Later I found out he lived in a real dump. Yeah, a dump. Worse then this joint. When I confronted him with it, it was almost over right then. Hahahaha. He got real mad. By then it didn't matter at all. He coulda lived at the city dump. I didn't care. You know where we went for our honeymoon? We just stayed in the Taft Hotel. *Yeah.* That's right. We stayed about a week. I really had a nice time too. He took me over to Rockefeller Center and taught me how to ice skate. That was funny. I musta fell fifteen times. He'd just pick me up and hold me until I'd fall again. It was nice . . . we moved into this dinky flat up in Harlem. We worked on it though. Was the first home I ever really had. You know that fool wouldn't let me work. I almost went crazy up in that little place. Sometimes I'd take walks and then I usta go over to the Y for classes. I never finished high school, and he encouraged me to take classes. When my girlfriends saw me they couldn't believe it. They usta come by to just see if it was true. Some of em was jealous, and I guess it was kinda unbelievable . . . me settlin down. I was happy . . . for a while though. It was like I had a light on inside. I just felt real good. It was nice until . . . well, until we had trouble makin it.

RAY: You had trouble makin it with a man?

BABE: That's what I said, stupid! I don't know what was wrong. I was happy enough. We didn't have much, but the trouble really came when the doctor told me I couldn't have any kids. I hid it from him as long as I could. He really wanted a family, hell, I really wanted a family. I ain't have nobody . . . nobody . . . and I wanted the kids for him as well as myself. The nite I tole him his face was strange . . . cold, like everything went dead inside him. He didn't say nuthin at first. Then he wanted me to see other doctors, and I did but it was always the same. One night I tried to get him to accept the idea of adoptin kids. He said he didn't want nobody else's baby. That's when he took to stayin out and drinkin all the time . . . and then one nite he jest never came back. I waited awhile, but it was no use so I just left. Went back to clubbin and havin a ball. But even that wasn't what it used to be. Still ain't. It just seemed like one big circle . . . never-ending. Then I came here and met your ass. You were real nice in the beginning, baby.

RAY: Can't be nice . . . too nice with a woman like you. Hell, you'll run all over a man if you had the chance.

BABE: Who's runnin over you? And if you was bein run over you'da been long gone. You talkin shit, nigger. This is the best you ever had it.

RAY: You ain't the best of nuthin. Your problem is you don't know what a family is. I had a family. Folks who care about each other . . . willin to do for each other. We had some good times . . . real good times. I felt like I was doin alright by the world . . . yeah . . . alright, then, I don't know . . . it jest crumbled like so much plaster in my hand. Bills . . . bills . . . no money comin in. Shit, every time I got a decent break the shit blew up in my face. One time I got on at the post office . . . yeah . . . this committeeman set it up for me. I lied on the application, though. I tole em I didn't have a record. When they found out, I was dismissed. That never happened to Sam though.

BABE: Who's Sam?

RAY: He's a guy I was raised with. Hell, he was left

property by people he hardly knew. He's got a big house too. Doin well.

BABE: He probably saved and sacrificed. You ain't never sacrificed nothin in your life. That's why you feel you ain't got nuthin.

RAY: How the hell you know what it is to sacrifice?

BABE: I know. I would've given anything to have that baby.

RAY: I'm gonna call the station again. *(Goes into the other room and makes the call. Returns as if stunned)* She said the bus came in two hours ago.

BABE: Face it. He ain't comin.

RAY: *(Stunned)* Don't say that shit again.

BABE: I'll say it again. *I'll shout it to the treetops, he ain't comin. You hear? He ain't comin!* (RAY *starts to chase her)*

RAY: Shut your gotdamn mouth!

BABE: He ain't comin!! He ain't comin!! He ain't commmmmmminnnn!!!*(She runs into the back bedroom and slams and locks the door)*

RAY: *(Banging on the door)* He is comin, he is comin, he is gotdammit . . . he's comin! I know it!! *(On his knees, screaming outside the door)* He's comin, he's comin, I know it . . . I know . . . *(Weeping and sobbing)* I know it.

BABE *opens the door and pulls* RAY *up and in. They slowly fade into darkness.*

TIDE THREE

It is later that night, about midnight. RAY *enters from the bedroom and turns on the living room light. He sits on the couch and lights a cigarette. A few minutes later* BABE *comes and joins him.*

BABE: Why you up?

RAY: Simple . . . I can't sleep.

BABE: *(Sits beside* RAY *on the couch)* You want me to fix you somethin?

RAY: Nah.

BABE: You got somethin on your mind?

RAY: I always got somethin on my mind.

BABE: You know what I mean.

RAY: *(Restless, he gets up and goes to the terrace and looks out at the sea)* Dat sucker never misses a beat . . . a wash really. Just rollin up and down and out . . . up and down and out. Humph. Sometimes I can almost tell where it's all comin from. It's past pretty. The sea is the beautifulest thing I know. It was funny . . . the first time I went deep sea fishing. I ain't never know quiet and well, eh, peace like that. Just no sound. You had to really strain to hear the water lappin against the boat. I mean you could hear folks

casting their reels out and that tickin sound but nuthin else. When I hooked that sucker, Babe, it was somethin, man. He was fightin, really fightin for all he was worth, and so was I. When I brought him up on the boat, well, I didn't want him. I wanted to throw him back, but he was much too big for that . . . it was the whole fight, me, him, the sea, that's what I wanted, not a dead fish on the floor of some boat . . . strange thing, the sea. Real strange . . . I wanted to fish more by and by but there just never was any time.

BABE: Plenty of time.

RAY: You ever been in a new car, Babe? I mean your own new car.

BABE: No, I always had somebody to take me where I wanted to go.

RAY: Well . . . that new smell is somethin. It's the upholstery. You know it's new and it's yours . . . all yours. Glidin down the street and . . . it's like bein on top of the world. A fifty-seven Dodge. That's when they had the fins and the push-button automatic transmission. Man, that was a beautiful car. That money went fast. Then the only thing I wanted to do was make that feelin last.

BABE: What feelin?

RAY: It's like knowin you got enough money to do whatever you want. You ain't got to be duckin bill collectors or nuthin. I guess it's the security rich people have. Kinda strong . . . nobody can touch you. I'd take the kids for rides all the time.

BABE: Why you always talkin like everything is over?

RAY: *(As if shocked back to reality)* It is.

BABE: No it ain't. You can still . . .

RAY: Be happy? Now that's a good one. What is there to be happy with? Fo'?

BABE: For yourself.

RAY: Maybe.

BABE: If you would spend as much time workin on the here and now maybe you could have a little happiness.

RAY: You a dreamer.

BABE: You the dreamer. Mopin round here and talkin bout the past all the time.

RAY: Yeah, maybe.

BABE: I hate to see you hurt, Ray . . . but you got to accept the fact that the boy doesn't care. The sooner you do the better.

RAY: I don't know.

BABE: Look, I'm goin back to bed.

RAY: Go head. Who the hell asked you to get up in the first place! *(*BABE *goes back to the bedroom.* RAY *goes and sits on the couch. There is a knock on the door.* RAY *goes to answer it)* Who is it?

SKEET: Skeeter.

RAY: What the hell do you want?

SKEET: I just want to talk to you, man.

RAY: You know what time it is?

SKEET: Yeah, I know, I just gotta talk to you, that's all.

RAY: *(Still standing in the doorway)* Well????

SKEET: You got a drink?

RAY: Yeah. It's on the counter.

SKEET: *(Fixes the drink and goes past* RAY *to the living room. He takes off his coat)* Look man, I came to apologize for Gail.

RAY: What!

SKEET: She don't know what she's doin when she's drunk. I know she didn't mean what she said. It was just the liquor talkin, that's all.

RAY: If she can't hold her liquor she shouldn't drink, that's all. Besides she was kinda right. The boy didn't come.

SKEET: I'm sorry.

RAY: What are you sorry about? You ain't got nuthin to do with it.

SKEET: That ain't the only reason I come up, though.

RAY: Well, finally. Let's hear it.

SKEET: I been watchin you for a while with the cards. You look pretty good . . . damn good. Well, it's this couple. Comes down here every year at this time. Both of em is old as hell. Anyway, they love to play poker . . . high stakes poker . . . you know, five hundred dollars table stakes. Now I know the old bats carry plenty of cash. They just rich and ain't got nuthin to do with the money. When I'm waitin their table in the dining room they always askin me to scare up a game. I don't know enough to take em but you do. Look, all I want is half.

RAY: Half! You must be crazy. Forty percent.

SKEET: You got a deal.

RAY: When and where you want to set up the game?

SKEET: Here. All you got to do is clean up a bit and tell Babe to lay off the heavy language and everything'll be cool.

RAY: Don't worry about that. Just get those suckers up here. What time?

SKEET: About six. *(Walking toward the door)*

RAY: Yeah. I'll be ready.

(SKEETER exits. Lights fade out on RAY at the door. At rise he is sitting at a card table marking the cards and then resealing the decks. The place appears to have been cleaned. BABE is just getting up and has slept all day. It is about 5:20 p.m.)

BABE: What the hell happened here? Place looks nice. What's goin on, Ray?

SKEET: We, my dear, are about to make a big score.

BABE: What?

RAY: Skeeter was up here last night. He found these suckers that was ripe for the pluckin.

BABE: What's the catch?

RAY: Ain't none. All I got to do is take the money. According to Skeeter, they is *loaded.* Oh eh . . . I had to go into your stash to finance this little move.

BABE: How much, Ray?

RAY: How much what?

BABE: How much is this gonna cost?

RAY: *(Getting up to comfort her)* Look, it ain't gonna be long. It shouldn't take me more'n five, six hours at the most to take these suckers. Honey, you know . . .

BABE: *(Shouting) How much, Ray?!*

RAY: *(Throwing the cards down)* I needed it all gotdammit!! You can't run these cons without some setup money!!

BABE: You took *all my stash?!* All??

RAY: Look . . . I can get these old toads for at least ten grand. Then I can get you your money back and everything will be peaches and cream.

BABE: Peaches and cream my ass!! That was my stash money!!

RAY: You mean money for that gotdamn dope! Yeah dope, Well, this way we can make some money clean and sweet. We ain't got to worry bout no hard time or nobody knockin on the door or nuthin.

BABE: It was my money. Mine . . . . You had no right to take it. No right.

RAY: No right? What you mean, no right? You the one always sayin I ain't never doin nuthin, ain't never into *nuthin,* well . . . I'm doin somethin . . . I'm gonna git us some real money.

BABE: I don't believe what I'm hearin. You gonna take our last chance and give it away to some old dried up people who don't even need it! No, you got to do better than that.

RAY: It's the best I can do. And I'm gonna do it and that's all there is to it. You know you a funny one just like all the rest; when the chips is down you don't wanna support a man, you just want to tear him down.

BABE: Don't try that bullshit with me. *I don't wanna hear it.* All I wanna know is what do we do when you lose? What the hell we gonna live on then?

RAY: I ain't gonna lose. Relax, it's in the bag . . . in the bag.

BABE: I don't know what to say.

RAY: Don't say nuthin. Just git dressed and look presentable. We got to make these folks think we're fairly secure, as they say. We will be after we take they cash . . . that is.

BABE: What am I supposed to do?

RAY: You, my dear, are to smile and look like a nice hostess. I am supposed to be a, how do they say it, ah yes, a gentleman of means. Put on that black dress and make sure you don't go round here cussing like a sailor. Got it?

BABE: You are absolutely nuts, and I'm just as crazy to go along with it.

RAY: You really ain't got no choice.

BABE: *(Calm and low)* Oh, I got a choice.

RAY: *(Serious)* Look, I just want this one. Let me have this one. If it don't work I wouldn't blame you if you split. I wouldn't blame you at all. *(BABE just looks at RAY. SKEETER is banging on the door)* Come on in, Skeeter!

SKEET: How you doin, Babe? *(BABE says nothing, just goes past SKEETER and into the bedroom and slams the door)* Ray, look...she ain't gonna fuck this thing up, is she? I got a lot ridin on this thing.

RAY: She got as much ridin on this as you. *(Staring dead at SKEETER)*

SKEET: I was just askin, man.

RAY: And I was tellin you.

SKEET: You almost ready?

RAY: Yeah. I gotta go out and pick up some brandy, though. What kind did you say the old farts liked?

SKEET: They always orders eh, this Cour-ve-sore stuff.

RAY: Cour-ve-sore! Sound like some rotgut shit.

SKEET: I don't know. All I know is that's what they asks for and that's what they gits.

RAY: They carry that at Mike's package goods store?

SKEET: I don't know, You better go uptown and check. You all set?

RAY: Is pig pussy pork?

SKEET: *Alright!!!* *(They slap hands)* I'll check you out a little later.

RAY: Okay. *(SKEETER exits. RAY continues to mark and seal the decks of cards. BABE comes in from the bedroom. She has changed into a blue dress and she looks real good)* Hey...lookin good, sugar. *(He gets up and goes over to hug BABE)* We got time for a little nooky beforehand.

BABE: No nooky! Damn, for a man dats almost fifty you sure don't act like it.

RAY: What's a man fifty supposed to act like?

BABE: Not like no twenty year old.

RAY: Who says? Who says I can't act and feel young?

BABE: All I'm sayin is you supposed to be more reserved, more laid back. You don't wanna scare the man away.

RAY: I don't wanna put him to sleep either.

BABE: You know what I mean. Zip me up. *(RAY*

obliges, playing with her bare back) Cut it out or you won't be doin no gamblin.

RAY: Okay, okay. Look, leave the connin to me. You just be a fine gracious hostess. Don't hang around the table. Don't look over the man's cards. If you git bored, just go in the bedroom and look at TV or somethin.

BABE: If I get that bored I'll just go over Gail's.

RAY: Don't be goin over there and stayin all damn day and night. I need you here. Look Babe, after this we can have a ball. We can go out every nite for a month. Just hand on and help me pluck this chicken.

BABE: How long do you think it'll take?

RAY: Depends on how good he is. It takes a few hours, we might be here all night...depends. You don't wanna take em too fast cause then they gits suspicious. We'll see. We'll see. Babe...how bout goin to the package goods store and pickin up some eh...eh...what's this stuff, eh... Cour-ve-sore.

BABE: What is that?

RAY: Skeeter says it's some kind of brandy. It's supposed to be real good. Here, take fifty dollars. You better get a couple a bottles. No tellin, these folks might be real lushes.

BABE: Look who's talkin?

RAY: Just go head now. And git me some beer. I'm gonna need somethin to git me through this. Hurry back.

BABE: *(Exiting)* I will.

(RAY is arranging the table and cleaning up. He fixes himself a drink. There is someone at the door)

RAY: Come on in, Skeeter. It's open. *I said come on in. (The door opens and it is RAY's son, SONNY. RAY's back is to the door)* What's up, Skee...is that you, Sonny? Sonny...Sonny...Sonny...(Runs to him on the balcony...they hug)* It's good to see ya, boy. Good to see ya.

SONNY: How ya been, Pop?

RAY: Oh, I'm doin alright. How you doin? *(Suddenly angry)* Why in the hell didn't you call me? Where the hell you been? I been expectin you since yesterday. Boy, you know somethin, you ain't got no respect. I don't know what your momma's been tellin you but that ain't no way to treat your father, and another thing, a gotdamn phone call couldn't a been too much to ask! I oughta whip yo ass! You think...

SONNY: Pop...

RAY: ...you too damn grown, don't ya! I can...

SONNY: Pop...look, Pop...

RAY: ...still whip yo ass, boy! Shit! I was worried! I didn't know what the hell had happened!

SONNY: Pop...Pop...I got held up an extra day in Philly.

RAY: That ain't no damn excuse! *(Grabbing* SONNY *by the arm)* Boy, I oughta whip . . . *(He grabs and hugs* SONNY *again. When he releases him he just looks at him a moment)* You want a drink?

SONNY: What you got?

RAY: What you want?

SONNY: Vodka and orange juice.

RAY: That's what your momma used to drink. *(Bringing the drink)* Which reminds me, how's your momma?

SONNY: She's alright. She's gettin around a lot better since the operation.

RAY: That's good. How long you gonna stay, boy?

SONNY: Just a coupla days. I'm at a hotel a coupla blocks from here.

RAY: I'm in the middle of some real important business right now, but it shouldn't take but a day.

SONNY: Got a big game, huh?

RAY: Who said anything about a game? I got some business, that's all.

SONNY: Okay . . . okay.

(BABE comes in. She has a bag with her)

RAY: Babe . . . could you git it?

BABE: Yeah, I got it. That stuff is expensive.

RAY: Oh eh, Babe . . . this is Sonny, Sonny this is Babe.

BABE: *(She sees* SONNY *and remembers)* Glad to meet you. Your father has tole me a lot about you . . . you gonna be in long?

SONNY: Bout three days.

BABE: Good, then we'll get to know each other a little. S'cuse me a minute.

SONNY: Is that the lady you wrote me about?

RAY: Yeah . . . well, that's the lady that wrote you for me about her . . . well, you know what I mean.

SONNY: Yeah, I kinda figured that wasn't your handwriting.

RAY: *(Embarrassed)* Yeah well . . . how's school?

SONNY: *(Uneasily)* It's okay. You live with her, Pop?

RAY: Yeah.

SONNY: This ain't a bad place.

RAY: *(Looking out the terrace window)* It ain't bad at all. In the summer you got prime beach property. Hell, sometimes I feel like I'm a rich guy on my own private beach. You can see straight out to the horizon.

SONNY: You workin this year?

RAY: On and off. This past summer was a good season, but it's slow now. Should be pickin up soon, though. What you gonna do when you get outta school?

SONNY: I'm not sure yet. Probably just bum around for a while.

RAY: Bum around! Boy, you better latch onto a job quick.

SONNY: I'll be alright.

RAY: Alright how? You know somethin, you young folks crack me up. Got the whole world at yo feet and don't know what to do with it.

SONNY: Just cause you got a degree don't mean you got it made.

RAY: You sure as hell got a better chance than us over the hill folks.

SONNY: Who the hell is over the hill?

RAY: Don't be cussin at me boy. I'm still your father.

SONNY: Look, Pop. I'm a grown man . . . . I can talk like I want.

RAY: Is that so? You ain't so grown that I can't whip yo ass! Maybe you think that education yo got makes you better'n me, but as long as I got strength you better watch yo jibes. As I was sayin, try and start work on a job now cause pretty soon ain't nobody gonna have nuthin.

SONNY: Is that what *you* doin?

RAY: I'm doin what's best for me.

SONNY: So am I.

RAY: You don't know that.

SONNY: There it is. Y'all always run that crap.

RAY: Look, I have been there. I'm there now. You might like to argue with it but what I'm sayin, I sayin from experience.

SONNY: I've had some interviews.

RAY: And . . .

SONNY: They want experience. I tell em I been in school. They tell me . . . sorry.

RAY: Well shit, I didn't say it was gonna be easy. You gotta keep tryin. You sure didn't get my stubbornness, boy.

SONNY: It ain't that simple.

RAY: You make it hard on ya'self. It's simple to me. How old are you?

SONNY: I'll be twenty-seven next month. So?

RAY: Damn, that's almost thirty! It's time you thought of settlin on a career.

SONNY: I don't see why there's such a rush. I don't think it's the kind of decision you just up and make and that's it. First off, I ain't that sure what it is I want to do. Secondly, there's more than just me to worry about anyway.

RAY: What you mean, boy?! You got somebody pregnant! Oh shit! Just tell her it ain't yours, that's all.

SONNY: I ain't got nobody pregnant. I need some money for . . . eh . . . a business I'm startin.

RAY: What kind of business?

SONNY: Well, we ain't sure yet.

RAY: Who the hell is we?

Some buddies and me.

RAY: Boy, you ain't makin a whole lotta sense.

First, you tell me you don't want no job and now you tellin me you want to start a business?! Somethin ain't right.

SONNY: Look, you got some things to do. I don't wanna talk now. Why don't I come back later?

RAY: Why can't you tell me now?

BABE: *(Entering from the bedroom)* How do I look?

RAY: Well? *(The apartment buzzer rings)* Who is it?

SKEET: Skeeter.

SONNY: I better go.

RAY: Look, I'll meet you a little later. I want to hear more about this.

SONNY: Yeah okay.

(SONNY exits. SKEETER enters)

RAY: Well, where's the mark?

SKEET: He's comin, he's comin.

(The lights fade out. At rise there are a few whisky bottles laying about. Smoke is in the air. About twenty-five thousand dollars has changed hands. RAY has won it all. He has just shown the mark to the door. It is 7:00 a.m. in the morning)

RAY: Yessir . . . thank you . . . take care now. *(Closing the door. RAY walks back to the table very guardedly and sits down. Then he jumps up and throws the money in the air)* Haha! I did it! I did it! Hahaha. What do ya think of that, Babe. *Twenty-five thousand big ones. Did you hear me?!!! Hahahahahaha.*

BABE: I hear you, Ray. I hear you.

SKEET: You gotdamn right! I knew this man was tough. I knew it! You had him runnin the minute he sat down, Ray.

RAY: Oh no, this cat was foxy. It's just that he was dealin with the master fox, dat's all.

SKEET: I'll drink to that . . . the master fox. *(They all raise their glasses in a toast)* Now I suggest we get this money up on this table and divvy up. What you say, Cap'n?

RAY: Well . . . I says so myself . . . yessir I do. Haha.

SKEET: All I wanta know is how'd you know when he was bluffin and when he wasn't?

RAY: Well, sometimes his left eye would twitch and another time he'd kinda twiddle his thumb when he had a good hand. It took awhile, but once I caught on to his style of play, I could figure out when I'd need a boss hand to win. In the beginning, though, I had to take my time. I just couldn't beat his brains out from the beginning or it'd look funny. Had to ease up on em and then snuff em out.

SKEET: You know there's plenty more like him. We could make a fortune.

RAY: Just hold on, youngster.

SKEET: What you mean, youngster?

RAY: Just because we hit an old man and got away don't mean we startin no business. I been around too long to fall for that shit.

SKEET: Aw Ray man, we could make a fortune. All we gotta do . . .

RAY: This is it for me. One hit an I'm gone.

SKEET: Man, you passin up a good opportunity.

RAY: I know what I'm passin up . . . . *Jail!*

SKEET: Well, if you change your mind, let me know.

RAY: I won't . . . count your money. I don't want you goin down the street screamin I cheated you.

SKEET: It's all here, believe I can count. Well, it was a pleasure.

RAY: I enjoyed it. *(SKEETER exits)* Well is that all you can do is sit there and look foolish?! *(BABE jumps into RAY's arms)* Now that's better . . . much better. *(Goes back over to the table and grabs a stack of money)* Here, this is what I owe you. I always pay my debts. Hahaha.

BABE: Since when?

RAY: Since I got fifteen thousand big ones. That's when.

BABE: Let's go out and celebrate.

RAY: Baby, we gonna celebrate like we ain't never celebrated before.

BABE: This is only the beginning, baby. As soon as I make my connections we can make a fortune!

RAY: Ain't no need for you to make no connections now.

BABE: What you mean?

RAY: There ain't no need for you to be dealin nuthin.

BABE: I ain't stoppin just cause you won some money. That's chicken scratch compared to what we can be makin.

RAY: I don't wanna be around no dope dealin.

BABE: Look Ray, we can bring this in every day.

RAY: It means trouble . . . and runnin from the law.

BABE: How in the hell you think we been livin all this time? You think I been walkin outta here and pickin money off a money tree? Look, it took time but I've built up all the contacts and all the drop points. It's simple and we'll be rich as hell.

RAY: Maybe I ain't been heard or you ain't been listenin right. I'll just say it one more time . . . I don't want no more dope here.

BABE: You are stubborn, Ray. But this time you're wrong. I don't wanna live like this forever. I want better things. And we ain't twenty-seven anymore, Ray. Just think about it, that's all. Just think about it.

RAY: There ain't nuthin to think about. Look, I'm goin out, you comin?

BABE: No.

RAY: Suit yourself.

(RAY exits. Lights fade out. At rise BABE is sitting on the couch nursing a drink and a joint. The apartment buzzer rings)

BABE: Come in! It's open!

(*The door opens and* SONNY *enters*)

SONNY: Is my old man here?

BABE: No.

SONNY: Well, how you been, Babe? Been awhile hasn't it?

BABE: Doesn't look like it's been long enough.

SONNY: Aw Babe, don't sound so sour. We did all right when we was doin business. Didn't we?

BABE: Why didn't you ever mention your father?

SONNY: Why should I? This was business between you and me, remember. I should've known it was you when he was writing those letters. I recognized your handwritin but I couldn't figure where I had seen it before.

BABE: You still ain't said why you never told me Ray was your father.

SONNY: When we was in business you didn't know him so what difference did it make . . . shit . . . I lived with the man for years in the same house and hardly saw him . . . it wasn't like I never knew him, it's just that there was gaps . . . big gaps . . . chunks of what seems like years now . . . we just didn't know each other. Boy, did I want to know that man. Seems like everybody else's pappy was out there . . . playin . . . my old man was always workin or somethin . . . somethin . . . shit . . . that's what my momma used to say when I got too inquisitive as to where Pop was. "Your father's doin somethin, boy," she usta say. Even then it didn't sound right, and her eyes, they didn't look right . . . it didn't matter . . . it don't matter . . . look, all that matters is that we do business.

BABE: You still the rotten young pup you always was, ain't you?

SONNY: Look Babe, ain't no need to insult. Some big money done fell in your lap. All you gotta do is rake it in.

BABE: It's that simple, huh?

SONNY: Don't go tellin me you done went soft on us, Babe.

BABE: Soft on what?

SONNY: Nah . . . I wouldn't believe it.

BABE: Believe what? What are you talkin about?

SONNY: Nuthin.

BABE: You want a drink?

SONNY: Why not? (BABE *goes to get the drink.* SONNY *begins to look around the apartment*) Looks like the old man was on his remodeling kick. He usta do a lot of this at home . . . when he was there. Everybody liked our house. Most people couldn't figure out how a nigger could build some of the stuff he built . . . so Babe, what have you been up to for the past three years aside from bein little miss happy homemaker? (BABE *hands* SONNY *his drink.*

He taste it) Umm. Just like I usta like em, remember honey?

BABE: Cut the shit. How long you plannin on bein here?

SONNY: Well, I don't know. Depends now. I wouldn't think of leavin without us rekindling our old flame.

BABE: It's out, boy. It's been out.

SONNY: I don't know about that.

BABE: I think you oughta leave soon . . . like yesterday.

SONNY: Now Babe, that ain't no way to treat a father's only son. Hahahahaha.

BABE: I don't want you to tell your father nuthin.

SONNY: Why Babe? You think my daddy would be upset to learn that his little woman had been screwin around with his only son?

BABE: You still got your filthy mouth.

SONNY: He won't be none the wiser if you play your cards right.

BABE: And if you keep your mouth shut.

SONNY: No reason for me to blab, that is unless you are uncooperative.

BABE: What you want?

SONNY: A business relationship, pure and simple.

BABE: You must be crazy. Your father sees you hangin around and it won't take him two seconds to figure out what his precious son is doin. Besides, he don't wanna be around no dope.

SONNY: I ain't plannin to hang around. Besides, it ain't been botherin him recently so why should it now.

BABE: I ain't been dealin recently.

SONNY: Oh I see . . . this is not time to become a goody goody, Babe. Too much money is on the line. I got people in three cities lined up. All you got to do is deliver.

BABE: Git it from the connection you was usin after me.

SONNY: Can't do, honey. Besides we both know you can get the best.

BABE: Look, it's been awhile . . . even my contacts is dry. I can't get you nuthin.

SONNY: I don't think you was listenin, Babe. *You are gonna deliver.*

BABE: I don't like being threatened.

SONNY: And I don't like being threatening. He don't haveta know nuthin, and he won't suspect nuthin if you watch yourself and be cool. Who are you tryin to fool, Babe, this ain't you. True blue till the end and all that shit. I know a fellow rattlesnake when I see one.

BABE: You're too young to know anything.

SONNY: I wasn't too young once.

BABE: What do you think it's gonna do to your old man when he finds out?

SONNY: It don't matter.

BABE: It don't matter?! All your father talks about is his son . . . his great son . . . what a joke, what a joke. Hahahahahaha.

SONNY: What are you talkin about, woman?

BABE: Your father thinks you're the best that ever came down the chute. If I had a dollar for every time he's talked in praise of his precious son I'd be rich right now.

SONNY: You bullshittin.

BABE: I wish I was. That don't mean nuthin to you? He sees himself through you. Everything he's ever hoped for himself you can get or have.

SONNY: He's a fool cause I don't have nuthin yet. You believe in that fool, don't ya . . . you do, don't ya, Babe? He never tole you about the time I saw him at the movies . . . yeah, *at the movies!!!* He tell you about that? What do you think I felt like twelve years old . . . begged him . . . *begged him to come to walk with me, to do somethin* . . . well, he came, he came and he wasn't alone either. I sat there and I knew where he was and all my friends and their pops knew too. Course, nobody said nuthin, oh no, eyes say it all, baby . . . eyes that just looked at me on the way home, and looked and looked. I couldn't ever really stand him after that . . . after it wasn't him but what I wanted in a pop . . . when I got older it didn't matter one way or the other . . . we painted houses, we sold trees, we . . . well, I couldn't get that outta my mind and I know that later there were others and others, and as I got older I kind of understood that but there just never seemed to be time for me.

BABE: He don't see it that way. I guess the thing . . . the most important thing you got is your youth. You got it alright and you about to pee it right down the drain.

SONNY: And what was you doin not too long ago?

BABE: The same thing. Course I ain't never been to college.

SONNY: What's college got to do with it?

BABE: I guess nuthin. You can be a crumb from wherever or whatever.

SONNY: When we was in bed you never worried about me being a college boy.

BABE: No . . . I didn't. You were cute and I was havin fun foolin with a fool. Just a fantasy, like a dream that came to its end. I woke up. It looks like you didn't.

SONNY: We could have it again.

BABE: What! *(Looking at him incredulously)* You must be nuts.

SONNY: C'mon, Babe. Once you get down under again it won't make no difference.

BABE: You're pretty sure of yourself, aren't you?

SONNY: One of Pop's teachings. *(Comes up behind*

BABE. *She moves away. He tries to force himself on her)*

BABE: Nigger, you better back off.

SONNY: Babe, you don't know what you're missing. *(He tries again, this time* BABE *struggles fiercely, and just after,* RAY *comes in. He has been drinking)*

RAY: What's goin on? *(Silence)* Ain't nobody hear me? What's goin on . . . gotdammit?

SONNY: Nuthin, Pop.

RAY: Don't give me that nuthin pop stuff. *Babe?!*

BABE: Eh, nuthin Ray, Sonny here just had too much, that's all.

RAY: Y'all been smokin that shit, haven't ya? *Answer me, gotdammit!!!*

BABE: Eh yeah, we had a little weed, and he couldn't handle it.

RAY: I oughta kick your ass for givin my boy that shit. You know he don't mess with that shit. Ain't that right son? . . . Well . . .

SONNY: Yeah, Pop. Uh huh.

RAY: Well . . . since we all here together we can have a nice talk.

BABE: *(Trying to leave the room)* Maybe tomorrow, Ray. Sonny wants to talk to you alone.

RAY: *(Grabbing her)* Naw . . . anything me and my boy here got to discuss we can do it right with you. Ain't that right, son?

SONNY: Of course, anything you say.

RAY: You want a drink?

SONNY: Nah.

RAY: What about you, Babe?

BABE: No.

RAY: Nobody drinkin but me. Humph. Well, I'll carry on for the both of us. So . . . what was y'all takin about when I busted in . . . eh?

BABE: Nuthin Ray . . . nuthin, we was wonderin why you was takin so long.

RAY: All that hollerin and screamin over me?! Nah. Had to be somethin more juicy than that. C'mon boy, you ain't said nuthin. You can tell your daddy, now can't ya?

SONNY: Wasn't nuthin . . . just talkin.

RAY: Looked to me like it was a lot more than talkin. C'mon you can tell your old man . . . can't ya?

SONNY: It ain't like that.

RAY: It ain't like what?

SONNY: Like what you saw.

RAY: You know the last time you lied to me you was nine years old, and there was a good reason for the lapse of time until now . . . if you remember I whipped yo ass. You tellin me I got to whip yo ass again . . . boy?

SONNY: You ain't in no condition to whip nobody's ass. I came here to talk to you about somethin important.

BABE: Look Ray, it ain't no need to go and . . .

RAY: C'mon woman, the boy is trying to say somethin, you'll have your turn.

SONNY: I needed to borrow some money for a business I'm gonna be startin soon.

RAY: What kind of business?

SONNY: What difference does that make?

RAY: Since I'm lendin the money . . . a lot.

SONNY: Then forget it.

RAY: Now wait a minute boy . . . not so fast. You came all the way down here for somethin so you gonna have to tell me what it is.

SONNY: I said it.

BABE: You want somethin to eat, Ray?

RAY: No I don't want *shit* to eat. I'm waitin, boy.

SONNY: Look, I need some money, and if you ain't got it I can go somewhere else.

RAY: You on junk, boy?

SONNY: I ain't on nuthin.

BABE: Why can't you just accept what he's sayin, Ray?

SONNY: He's hardheaded and drunk, for one.

RAY: I got a suspicious nature, that's all. And as far as being drunk is concerned, I done more drunk than you ever done in your life, boy! You hear me?! *In your life!!*

SONNY: I'm leavin. I'll come back when you makin sense.

RAY: *(Blocking his way)* You ain't goin nowhere yet. I ain't finished talkin. You supposed to respect your elders. *Ain't dat right, Babe!*

BABE: Yeah. Ray, you gettin upset. You shouldn't. Why don't you just relax until you can think right and then it'll be cool.

RAY: Be cool! Yeah, be cool. Yeah I'm gonna be cool all right. Sit down, boy. *(SONNY goes back and sits)* Since I walked in here everybody's been sayin it ain't like you think. Well, what's it like?

BABE: Before . . . I . . . met you I had somethin goin with Junior.

RAY: Junior . . . Junior who?

BABE: *Sonny!* . . . He used to move stuff for me. Two years before I ever saw you, Ray.

RAY: So all that time you was tellin me you was in school you was in the street sellin junk.

SONNY: Not all the time.

RAY: *What?!*

SONNY: I was in school some of the time, then I dropped out.

RAY: So all the time . . . the time I thought you was doin right you was turnin into a bum.

SONNY: I ain't never had to wait on no tables. *(RAY quickly slaps SONNY. SONNY raises his arm)*

RAY: Go head, boy. Go head.

SONNY: Don't hit me again, ole man. I ain't ten years old no more.

RAY: If I thought it would help you I'd do it. You ain't worth it.

SONNY: How you know what I'm worth? You wasn't never there.

RAY: When I could be, I was. You wasn't never lacking for nothin.

BABE: Ray, this ain't the time for . . .

RAY: This is the best time, honey, the best time. Right about now you're feelin I wasn't shit as a father . . . *(To SONNY)* Ain't that right?!! Well, that may be . . . but before you go judging your ole man, you better take stock of yourself, boy. Take stock. All this time you was the one glimmer of anything right in my life. You was part of me and in a real way, all of me. I was livin through you, boy. Every accomplishment, however small, that you had I felt I was a part. To be honest, I felt good. My life lately ain't resembled no pretty thing . . . in fact it ain't never been all the way right. I guess it just wasn't meant so . . . but you, you got it all, you still . . . well . . . that part is up to you. Yeah, I know I wasn't there a lot when you was growin up. There are a lot of reasons . . . but I ain't apologizing for shit. I did what I had to do. Some of it was wrong as hell but I did it and I know it. Now this dope thing, Babe says it's the comin thing, could make big money. I don't like it. Never did. But like you say, you a man and you can do what you want. Well, I'm sure as hell a man and I don't want the shit around me. And another thing, as long as you ever live in this life or the next, if you even sneak up on the idea of hittin me, drawing breath will become a great problem for you. You get my meaning? Now please get out.

SONNY: I'm gone. *(Exits)*

BABE: You hungry?

RAY: Why is it every time somethin happens you figure I'm hungry?

BABE: Cause you are.

RAY: *(He looks at BABE a moment)* Yeah, I guess I usually am.

BABE: *(In the kitchen, fixing RAY a sandwich)* You did believe what I said about . . .

RAY: I don't wanna hear no more. *(As he talks, the lights lowly fade)* I just don't wanna hear no more. *(It is late at night, and RAY is smoking a cigarette, looking out the terrace window. BABE is on the couch)*

BABE: What are you thinkin?

RAY: About us.

BABE: Well . . .

RAY: I don't know.

BABE: You think there was something between me and Sonny?

RAY: *(Just turns and looks at BABE)* Is there?

BABE: What do you want me to say?

RAY: The truth.

BABE: *(Hard to say)* I love you.

RAY: *(Turns back to the window)* You ever just stand here and look at the sea?

BABE: *(Sitting on the couch)* Oh . . . damn.

RAY: . . . it's there . . . shining, foaming and looking like it could take on the world. From here it's like it goes on forever like time. Shame people don't be like that.

BABE: Didn't you hear me, nigger, I said I loved you.

RAY: I heard you. Babe . . . I . . . you might think I'm jokin but nobody's ever said that to me. Yeah, I was married and I think my wife loved me, but she never said it. I guess after awhile it was the furthest thing from her mind. Maybe it wasn't right from the beginning . . . I just didn't care after awhile. You know, when you do care, it's too late.

BABE: So you still love your wife?

RAY: No. Hahaha. Why'd you ask me that?

BABE: When you sleep, sometimes you call her. I feel real helpless then cause I feel I can't do nuthin.

RAY: And that boy . . . I don't know what happened.

BABE: You didn't know Sonny, Ray. You just thought you did.

RAY: And you did.

BABE: That was low, Ray. You know what I meant.

RAY: You *(Sarcastically)* gotta give me some time, my dear. It takes awhile to get use to the idea that my son was pushin stuff. Didn't you know he was my son when you met me?

BABE: *(She goes to the kitchen drawer and then comes back to* RAY *with a photo)* Was I supposed to know by this? He was twelve when this was taken, right? Huh?

RAY: Yeah.

BABE: I knew Sonny was your son when he walked into that door.

RAY: When he came you sure had a sick look on your face. Why didn't you tell me then?

BABE: What good would that have done? You wouldn't have felt any differently. With that temper of yours, no telling what you might have done.

RAY: I guess you're right.

BABE: Ray, is it too late for us?

RAY: Depends on where you're goin. Haha.

BABE: Would you be serious.

RAY: Be glad I can still laugh. Ain't been too much funny around here lately. I guess I was puttin too much stock in somethin other than myself.

BABE: You ain't dead, you can still try livin the way you want.

RAY: It ain't gonna be easy. You already know what livin with me is like.

BABE: Yeah, hell. Haha.

RAY: I'm serious.

BABE: Oh, now you're serious. I'm listenin.

RAY: We ain't gonna have much money, but we'll make it. You gonna have to give up them ideas of wearin furs for a while. We ain't gonna be eatin no hot pastrami with black olives either . . .

BABE: *(She comes to* RAY's *arms)* Keep talkin, I hear you, daddy.

RAY: No dope. No coke . . . marijuana cool. But none of that hard shit.

BABE: Right.

RAY: . . . We both can get work. After a while I wanta start fishin again.

BABE: Ray . . . we got to go out once and awhile.

RAY: You're right, being cooped up in here don't help us none.

BABE: You know we're both kinda crazy. We sound like two newlyweds or somethin.

RAY: You ain't no newlywed, that's for sure.

BABE: Nobody said you wuz a young buck either.

RAY: I'm younger than you.

BABE: You wouldn't know it to look at your wrinkled face.

RAY: I ain't got as many wrinkles on my face as you got on yo ass.

BABE: You know somethin, you a crazy ole fool.

RAY: Just like you, Babe. *(Hugging her)* Just like you.

Blackout

DWIGHT HOBBES

DWIGHT HOBBES IS A BROOKLYN-BASED author, singer-songwriter, and actor. In 1969 he co-wrote *Dayman*, a Chime Records single for which Thom Modeen composed the music. The same year, Dwight's poem, "Captive Monk of the Highlands," won Suffolk County's Prose and Poetry Contest. Dwight entered high school after that and wrote steadily for the literary club's magazine until 1970. Then came SUNY at Stony Brook and the role of Clay Williams in a local community production of *Dutchman*.

Photo by David La Tierre

Hopeful of someday penning another record, he picked up guitar, playing university and local coffee houses with a set of originals, interspersed with Buffalo Springfield and Love. WUSB aired several of the performances. Before dropping out, he studied a semester with playwright Lewis Petersen.

Singing appearances on WSNL-TV landed an LIU scholarship at the Merriweather Campus, Long Island where Dwight says, "I finally stretched out, sat down, and began to work on scripts. *Pain in the Midst,* my first, was a Chester Himes/Frank Chin-influenced one acter. Broadway-television actor Samuel E. Wright performed, directed by Steven D. Nash. It was a terse, sentimental statement of one man's futile attempt to defend his woman's honor. Heh-eh-eh. Against her will."

While Hobbes completed three other manuscripts, under the tutelage of Arthur Sainer (playwright-critic) then David Scanlan (director-playwright), only *You Can't Always Sometimes Never Tell* saw the light of production. New York actor Jack Poggi directed. There were nominations for the Lorraine Hansberry Playwrighting Award and, as an actor, The Irene Ryan Award. "Due to severe lack of guts I never entered the finals. However, it was just as well." He enrolled in poet Norbert Krapf's workshop. Krapf and a woman remembered only as Colette offered extensive criticism on the short story "One Going, One Staying." As a result, it was rendered salable. It ran in the January 80 issue of *Essence.*

At the Merriweather Campus, a friendship was struck up with novelist-poet Dan Levin. "He figuratively dried me behind the ears." There was another workshop, which produced a log of song lyrics, poems, and stories. Dwight Hobbes graduated LIU/C.W. Post Center in 1979.

"Then I really went to school. Selling shoes in Harlem. I have what I feel is a murderously devastating play in mind about my experiences there." Hobbes' philosophy is, "Keep the demos and manuscripts in circulation. Life is doing."

His current projects are writing the screenplay of his novel manuscript *Renegade: Journey of a Rock Messiah,* "and finding a job."

YOU CAN'T ALWAYS
SOMETIMES NEVER TELL

(L'amour des deux enfants égarés)

Dwight Hobbes

*to my family, especially Aunt Janet
and Mr. Maurice J. Beckles,
and to every Walker, every Jeanette
caught in the crux*

CHARACTERS

JEANETTE   WALKER

*Setting: The living room of a middle class
apartment dwelling. Central Islip, Long Island.*

ACT ONE

Scene 1

Spring afternoon. JEANETTE *stands d.r.c. watching* WALKER *sleep in the sofa bed. She wears tennis shoes, jeans, and a t-shirt.*

JEANETTE: Wake up a minute? Walker? Please? *(He grunts)* Nigger get up. *(She nudges him)*

WALKER: Am I on the couch?

JEANETTE: You're in it.

WALKER: Leave me alone. Unn.

JEANETTE: Don't lay there and groan with your crusty self. Open your eyes a moment.

WALKER: Why?

JEANETTE: I want you to see something.

WALKER: My head.

JEANETTE: "Poor thing." Look at this. Tell me what you think.

WALKER: What is it?

JEANETTE: The sooner you look at me the sooner you can go back to sleep.

WALKER: *(Cracks his eyes)* You got on a wig.

JEANETTE: I know. What does it look like?

WALKER: A wig.

JEANETTE: Thanks buddy. A lot.

WALKER: Y' welcome. *(Turns over)*

JEANETTE: Come *on*. Tell me your opinion.

WALKER: Don't yell, woman. I tol' y' my 'pinion.

JEANETTE: Does it look like my hair?

WALKER: No. Yours is straighter.

JEANETTE: You *know* what I *mean*.

WALKER: Looks fine, looks great. Lea' me alone. *(She hits him)* Hey! Ohh.

JEANETTE: Your honest opinion, if you didn't know it was a wig.

WALKER: Good morning.

JEANETTE: I hope so.

WALKER: Well, iss not bad. Yours is better.

JEANETTE: That ... is the wrong answer. Never mind. Go back to sleep. I knew better than to ask you in the first place. *(Examines it)*

WALKER: Then why did you? What time is it?

JEANETTE: *(Without consulting the clock)* I don't know. Hnh. May've done better to save the money.

WALKER: Will you look on the counter and tell me ... *(She looks at him)* what time it is?

JEANETTE: This cost eighty-five bucks.

WALKER: So? They cheat you?

JEANETTE: I don't like it so much either.

WALKER: Put on *Soul Train*?

JEANETTE: It's over.

57

WALKER: Hunh?

JEANETTE: "Hunh?" It's after eleven. Quarter of one.

WALKER: Missed my program.

JEANETTE: Big deal, you miss it every week.

WALKER: For once, you could've got me up to see it.

JEANETTE: Nigger, for once you could've slept in your bed. You've a clock.

WALKER: *(Threatening)* Ah.

JEANETTE: "Ah." 'Sides, you ain't missed a thing. But some crispy critters from Philadelphia . . . spinning around, wavin' their hands. . . . Paws.

WALKER: You watched it? Who from Philadelphia? Bluenotes? The Ojays?

JEANETTE: Mn. Yeah, Ojays. And Tyrone Davis.

WALKER: Tee was on and you let me sleep—

JEANETTE: You worked all day. And went guzzling all night. *(He moves to rise)* Walker!

WALKER: For the sake of all that's holy, I want the TV guide. If my body offends you, please get it for me.

JEANETTE: Where?

WALKER: I don't know . . . someplace. On the set or by the set. Or near it or . . . grown woman. Acts like she never saw a naked man.

JEANETTE: *(Gets it)* Never mind what I've seen and what I haven't. I'm your sister.

WALKER: Mm-hn, your mama's daughter.

JEANETTE: What was that?

WALKER: You're a prude. Thank you.

JEANETTE: Mm-hn.

WALKER: I wouldn't tell the world you spent— what? Eighty-some dollars . . . on that thing. *(Discovers seltzer packets and water glass, napkin over it)* Thank you.

JEANETTE: It's all right. I won't make it a habit.

WALKER: Well, anyway, thanx.

JEANETTE: You said that.

WALKER: I don't know about you. You wanted your hair in a fro. Then you didn't want to mess with it. Y' wanted to cut it. And punked out on the way to the beauty shop. Now this here.

JEANETTE: It looked good on the dummy in the window. It might look good on the one watching. What the hell, it was an idea.

WALKER: Hope I don't bet no idea cost that kind of money. Well you got it right, dummy. My dummy prude sist—

JEANETTE: *(Putting guide over his face)* Shut up. *(Crosses d.r.)*

WALKER: Put it on? Seven? *(JEANETTE does)* No sound? Please . . . and put in your lip. If you do I'll take you shoppin'? Wanna go to the mall? After I get up we'll go to Smithaven.

JEANETTE: Sure all right. *(Goes offstage)*

WALKER: *(Sits up)* Gotta go de bookstore. God . . . I don't know do you listen to a weekend alcoholic . . . but Um grateful you stopped me from orderin' another double. 'Preciate it from the bottom of my stomach.

JEANETTE: What are you mumbling in there?

WALKER: I said to God—*(JEANETTE enters)* would he send some lovely angel to rub my back.

JEANETTE: Heh-eh-eh. *(Cross u.l. to dinette)*

WALKER: How 'bout it?

JEANETTE: Mm-mn, you can't behave yourself.

WALKER: Promise. I'll be the havinest self you ever saw.

JEANETTE: *(Stand u.l.)* You wouldn't know how. *(Amused)* I'm fixin' breakfast. What you want to eat?

WALKER: I'll make a deal with you.

JEANETTE: Right, one of your deals.

WALKER: Honest. On the level.

JEANETTE: If the devil made a deal with you, "on the level," you'd have his pitchfork and tail, which I look for sometimes. And he'd end up with snowshoes and an overcoat. No thank you. *(About to enter the kitchen)*

WALKER: Oh my back. My poor aching back. That I bent over boxes with all week.

JEANETTE: What's your deal, old man?

WALKER: Applesauce.

JEANETTE: What?

WALKER: I will buy the biggest jar of it you can find in the store.

JEANETTE: The supermarkets are open.

WALKER: All day, I know.

JEANETTE: No hidden clauses. No fine print.

WALKER: No print.

JEANETTE: Swear?

WALKER: Mm-hn. Ohh.

JEANETTE: Shush. *(Crossing)* All right, slick. It's a deal.

WALKER: Ahh.

JEANETTE: Motts. Not some brand X. *(Straddling him)* The real thing.

WALKER: What you want is what you get. Look into these eyes and tell me they can't be trusted.

JEANETTE: They can't. Roll over.

WALKER: Yes ma'm.

JEANETTE: You not worth the powder it'd take to blow you away, you know that?

WALKER: Un-hunh. Ohh.

JEANETTE: Settle down.

WALKER: Uhhh.

JEANETTE: Don't enjoy it too much. This isn't one of your little friends.

WALKER: Whose fault is that?

JEANETTE: Starting already. You promised not to tease me.

WALKER: Um not. You think I'm mean? Be terrible to lead such a nice girl on. 'Specially with your sexy bo— *(She punches him)*... body. *(She pounds his back)* Mnh. Ow.

JEANETTE: Just can't learn. Will you stop?

WALKER: Yes, girl. That hurt.

JEANETTE: It was supposed to. By the way, you have one left.

WALKER: Hnh. One what?

JEANETTE: Rose called last night.

WALKER: Black Rose or white Rose?

JEANETTE: *(Dryly)* Rosemary Cummings.

WALKER: Thanx.

JEANETTE: She know you call her that?

WALKER: Well she couldn't deny it. She's white and that's her name.

JEANETTE: She said to call her.

WALKER: I will.

JEANETTE: Uh . . . say.

WALKER: Mn?

JEANETTE: Can I ask you something? *(He tries to see her)* Put your head down. *(Helps him down)* Is there a difference?

WALKER: A difference in what?

JEANETTE: Between. White and black?

WALKER: Women?

JEANETTE: No, artichokes.

WALKER: . . . Mn. Yeah, I suppose there is.

JEANETTE: What?

WALKER: Sure, why?

JEANETTE: Which is better?

WALKER: Better than the other? Heh-eh-eh. That's one question there'll never be an answer to.

JEANETTE: A safe one, you mean.

WALKER: I mean what I said. Safe or otherwise. If you talkin' about bein' in bed—and I do assume you to be speakin' about that—

JEANETTE: Okay.

WALKER: I can't tell which is better. An' I never met anybody who can that wasn' lyin'.

JEANETTE: Un-hunh.

WALKER: Don't "un-hunh" me. Um sayin' don' nobody know. Some folks like chocolate ice cream. Some like vanilla. Who's gon' say one's better.

JEANETTE: All right. Which do you . . . "prefer?"

WALKER: Mn. I'd hate to think my sister was growin' up a racist.

JEANETTE: I'm already grown. Don't beat around the issue, tell me.

WALKER: I like 'm both better.

JEANETTE: You full o—

WALKER: 'Cause they got different things. Really, y'all got the same things. *(She shoves him)* Heh-eh-eh. But . . . if you're in bed . . .

JEANETTE: *(Tentative)* Mm-hn.

WALKER: Sometimes you like a girl with lips.

JEANETTE: You serious?

WALKER: As a heart attack. And sometimes you want a skinny little mouth.

JEANETTE: Nigger, please.

WALKER: Please what? You ast. I jess told y'. Lips happen to make a difference. Dependin' what you do with 'm. Other than that, ain't it all rhythm? Anybody can learn to move.

JEANETTE: Never mind. Take it out the physical. All right?

WALKER: Mm-hn. Lower. A little more.

JEANETTE: *(Goes higher)* If you had a kit . . . from which t' make a woman any way you wanted . . .

WALKER: Mm-hn.

JEANETTE: . . . which color would you reach for? When you made her skin?

WALKER: Whichever I got my hands on first.

JEANETTE: You say that. Would you reach for brown?

WALKER: Maybe.

JEANETTE: Or . . . heh-eh-eh . . . flesh.

WALKER: I said I don't know.

JEANETTE: All right.

WALKER: You settin' me up. And it'd be funny . . . if you was kidding.

JEANETTE: I am not serious.

WALKER: No, hunh?

JEANETTE: What if I was! I'd have a right. Ever see men look at white women? Y'd think they're somethin' special. An' when nobody's watchin'? Niggers' tongues fall out their head for some pale skin . . . and string hair. Fall to their knees! Don't deny, I see it *on* 'm.

WALKER: Can't help what you see them do. Maybe me too once in a while. Iss a fact of life. Whiteys get jungle fever and we get rabbit fever. No big—

JEANETTE: Speak for yourself.

WALKER: For myself, I don't see why your dandruff is in such an uproar. Life goes on. The world keeps on spinnin'.

JEANETTE: Spins a little lopsided I think.

WALKER: Always will . . . . What're you gonna do about it, step off? Slow it down? By yourself.

JEANETTE: Shut up. *(Rises)* Call that girl. Then you can get up off my applesauce.

WALKER: *(Stretches)* Mmm.

JEANETTE: Are you going to call her?

WALKER: *(Lies back)* Right after my shower.

JEANETTE: Which will be when *Bandstand* is over. I can get her on the line.

WALKER: I'll call.

JEANETTE: Wouldn't be me.

WALKER: What?

JEANETTE: Said how you want these eggs? Scrambled? Or somethin' nice for a change?

WALKER: Over is just fine. Thanx.

JEANETTE: 'Welcome. *(Sourly)* You know, I can cook.

WALKER: I like 'em—

JEANETTE: Over easy. What I said was it wouldn't be me who was third on your list when you get around to it. After your show, after you shower. Though I don't fault you for that. Your funky body need to be under some water. It'd reach clear to her house. Burn up the wires goin' through.

WALKER: "Hah-hah." *(Sniffs himself anyway)*

JEANETTE: Wouldn't be me—

WALKER: I heard you.

JEANETTE: . . . who you didn't call for a month of Sundays! If you don't want to see her, you ought to say so.

WALKER: *(Up, cross d.r. turning off set)* Please. Don't spend that kind of money on something again. 'Least before you talk to someone. Good lord gave you a whole head of hair free. Didn't cost a nickel. *(Off)*

JEANETTE: It was foolish. Some people are Angela Davis and I guess some just aren't. Still. If I had a head of her hair. *(U.l. looks through dinette window)* When I was little I had that doll. You know the one. Momma brought it home. And we sat there with a giant box of Crayolas. *(Amused)* Trying to color it to look like me. It had the longest hair. And you couldn't tell me it wasn't the loveliest thing I ever saw. Momma was no help, either, with "See? The long strands. Like our's. Keep in mind that you aren't just anybody's little nigger. Your hair is as good, so you're as good . . . as any white girl. Just darker. Hear?" . . . I heard. Took that stuff out in the street and got the stew beat out of me. You didn't say other little colored girls wouldn't be as pleased with your attitude as I was . . . . In that run down neighborhood, she sends a child through the door with garbage in her head . . . . Know what I think really? I think that woman felt so cheated being only high yella she convinced herself, deep in her heart, that I was dipped in something. Lord knows what. She meant to bring out the clean, pure whiteness of her little brown baby. If it killed us both. *(Eggs crackle)* Shit. *(Off to tend to them. He enters with pants, without shirt, drys under his arms. Puts set on)* Afraid they're a little rubbery.

WALKER: It's alright. Y'know the hot water is gone? Right in the middle of my hair the damn water runs out. Girl, you got to take shorter showers, smaller baths or somethin'.

JEANETTE: *(On)* Have you been in the bathroom?

WALKER: Mm-mn. N' I stepped out for a wet towel to wipe under my arms.

JEANETTE: I've been talking to you.

WALKER: Oh?

JEANETTE: We were having a conversation.

WALKER: I say anything good?

JEANETTE: I'm gonna knock you into the middle of next week.

WALKER: Heh-eh-eh. What did I miss?

JEANETTE: . . . Not much. Me and that silly doll I used to have.

WALKER: You mean the time we sat in the middle of the floor and *(Digs in his ear)* put a brown crayon to Barbie?

JEANETTE: Yeah.

WALKER: What about it?

JEANETTE: If she was bound and determined I be white, why did she marry him in the first place?

WALKER: Beats the hell out of me. *(Sits)* Mm shake it baby, don't break it. Wrap it up, I'll . . . . Y' know you should drop all this about what Mom did and didn't want. And what kind of lady splibs get they nose open for.

JEANETTE: Heh-eh-eh.

WALKER: You not the first, or the last, black girl to wish she passed for Pam Grier. Or who're you so crazy about? Angela. She is she, y' know, and ye is ye. The train is never gon' meet.

JEANETTE: Lord, twain. Never the twain shall meet.

WALKER: Like I said. Now come in and watch TV.

JEANETTE: Soon as I finish burning this food. *(Off)* You want bacon? Toast?

WALKER: Just slap some egg between two piece-o' bread.

JEANETTE: Alright.

WALKER: *(Aside)* Thanx.

JEANETTE: *(Same)* Mm-hn.

WALKER: And butter and pepper and sliced tomato on it? Come and see this.

JEANETTE: I can't.

WALKER: Yes you can. Before they change the picture.

JEANETTE: *(Partly on)* What?

WALKER: Talk about kicking the hell out of a stereotype.

JEANETTE: Is it the same fool you always pick on?

WALKER: Yeah.

JEANETTE: Ask me to make something then call me out for simpleness.

WALKER: You didn't miss your call as a secretary. You could've never been a waitress. Bad disposition.

JEANETTE: Rub it on your—

WALKER: Here he comes. You gotta see'm.

JEANETTE: I do. Everytime you watch this show.

WALKER: Whoever said we all got rhythm never saw this rascal.

JEANETTE: Never seen you. Talk about sloppy on the floor.

WALKER: Not on nation-wide television I'm not.

JEANETTE: Leave him alone. Do you want tea? Coffee?

WALKER: Bring me a beer?

JEANETTE: There's none here. Like your stomach didn't already feel like shit.

WALKER: Stomach's o.k. My head has a elf on it. Swingin' a sledge hammer. Ping ping.

JEANETTE: A self-respecting elf wouldn't go "ping ping" or anything else over that pickled brain. The rising fumes'd have him drunk for a week. *(Giving him tray)*

WALKER: They're Irish. They like to get drunk.

JEANETTE: That . . . isn't funny. I'll hit your head. And it'll be more like slam bang.

WALKER: Hell, everybody I know likes to get drunk. Cept you. Thanx.

JEANETTE: Mm-hn. *(He eyes o.j. suspiciously)* It isn't hemlock.

WALKER: . . . I can make more money with a high school diploma.

JEANETTE: What inspired this stunning realization? Been watching the commercials?

WALKER: When I was with Burke this mornin'. His sister was into it about him and me goin' back to finish school. . . . I guess at night . . . she has pull at the Wilke Sports Company. We could get in line for some jobs.

JEANETTE: Liftin' boxes and puttin'm down is pretty much the same at one place as another.

WALKER: Wouldn' lift no boxes. Push a pencil across a piece of paper. Wear a tie. *(She's amused)* Laugh. When the eagle flies, take home be a hundred seventy.

JEANETTE: Over one ten? Can't beat it with a stick. This is after you go to school for a trainees course.

WALKER: Mm-mn. Regent's diploma. Then I train. On the job. We go over as bottom of the barrel. Load skids and what not. They interview potential pencil pushers in late summer. Meantime—

JEANETTE: You'll qualify with a diploma. . . . I smell a rat in the cheese cake. *(He grunts questioningly)* You're going to change jobs for just an interview. For a chance to make money. Not an opportunity.

WALKER: I din' tell you his sister just married the fella in charge of hirin' and firin'.

JEANETTE: Personnel?

WALKER: 'S what I said. All I have to do is learn a language.

JEANETTE: Thank God you may not lift things till you're old. Or till your back and shoulders go.

WALKER: I don't know. Can I see myself around a lot of office nigros?

JEANETTE: Instead you'll work on a factory floor your whole life? Be foreman . . . someday? Maybe. You better see yourself around'm. It makes sense to be one. Don't it?

WALKER: Alright, don't go to hell with yourself.

JEANETTE: You'd've got that paper when you were supposed to, if he wasn't always down your neck.

WALKER: I'm responsible if I quit. That man never ran my life.

JEANETTE: Ran you clean out of it. Anything you wanted . . . that he wanted you to do . . . to spite him . . . you wouldn't do it.

WALKER: We goin' to the store?

JEANETTE: . . . Alright.

WALKER: Don't do me a damn favor.

JEANETTE: The way you asked.

WALKER: . . . Wanna go to a clothes shop?

JEANETTE: Boutique?

WALKER: For a skirt. Or somethin'. How 'bout it?

JEANETTE: I dunno. I'm not sure I want a new skirt.

WALKER: Good. Drink your juice. *(Rise, finishing his)* Think I'll spend some cash on my girl.

JEANETTE: *(Fisheye)* If you say.

WALKER: I do. These I'll wash when we get back.

JEANETTE: Bottoms up.

WALKER: Come on.

JEANETTE: You're rushing me. I won't go anyplace before you comb that head . . . I'll bring this. *(Wig)* Maybe they'll take it back.

WALKER: You don't want it you don't have to keep it. Say. Know who wore a wig?

JEANETTE: No.

WALKER: Your girl Angela.

JEANETTE: Come on.

WALKER: I bullshit thee not.

JEANETTE: That's not all her hair?

WALKER: Ain' none of it her's. Ever see the photograph when she got arrested?

JEANETTE: Mm-mn.

WALKER: Hair is straight. And pinned back.

JEANETTE: Heh-eh. I'll be damned.

WALKER: Didn't look half as nice as yours.

JEANETTE: Thank you.

WALKER: Why you thankin' me? You don't know what it looked like. Her hair might've had crow shit in it for all you know.

JEANETTE: *(Jabs him)* Nh!

WALKER: *Nh!* That hurt.

JEANETTE: I meant it to.

WALKER: . . . Yeah?

(Chases her off stage)

61

Scene 2

She enters with articles. Clothing box, bag.

JEANETTE: Well it isn't fair. Do you think it's really fai—*(Turns. He is entering)* I do more talking to myself when I speak with you.

WALKER: I ripped my shirt. *(Drops small bag on knick knack table. Holds small wound in his shirt tail)*

JEANETTE: Mn?

WALKER: On a fucking loose nail.

JEANETTE: Who are you talkin to, with that language?

WALKER: Who do you—...Who tol'm t' put a loose nail stickin' out the door? Umma get the hammer and pull it out. Ripped my damn shirt.

JEANETTE: It will heal.

WALKER: Easy for you to say. Iss my shirt.

JEANETTE: If you buttoned it. But you must walk around with flying behind. You think you have a chest. *(She crosses off d.r., tired)*

WALKER: It's summer. *(Closes door, returns to table)*

JEANETTE: Coincidentally.

WALKER: *(Opens drawer)* My favorite fucking shirt.

JEANETTE: Never mind what you do in it. And I told you about your mouth. Should I come in with some soap?

WALKER: *(Aside, absently)* Come in here with a bar of soap...*(Needle, thread)* you'll see all the interesting places there are to put it.

JEANETTE: Hunh?

WALKER: *(Phone)* Said would you answer that. I got my hands full.

JEANETTE: *(Rings again)* Mm-hn.

WALKER: Look good, girl.

JEANETTE: Shut up. Hello?...Hi, fine and you? *(He shakes his head)* He's really up to his elbows in suds, doing the breakfast dishes. Can he call you right back when he's done? Okay. Bye-bye. *(Hangs up)*

WALKER: Cute—

JEANETTE: I couldn't say you were out. We passed Split-Cedar St. coming off the parkway. She had to see the car.

WALKER: ...A woman with some pride would wait till she was called.

JEANETTE: One with any sense would've cut your ass loose by now.

WALKER: "Watch your mouth. Watch your mouth."

JEANETTE: I would've let you go a week before I met you.

WALKER: Put on channel eleven? *(She does)*

JEANETTE: You're a bum. I love you.

BOTH: But you're a bum.

WALKER: What isn't fair?

JEANETTE: Hunh?

WALKER: "Hunh?" What were you beatin' your gums about in the hall?

JEANETTE: *(Holds* Essence*)* This.

WALKER: Mn?

JEANETTE: *Cosmopolitan*...in...black-face. Rather brown face.

WALKER: How many copies would they sell with Beneatha McCoy on the cover?...I wouldn't buy it.

JEANETTE: A model. A creamed coffee colored... doll. Someone sees this and it says, "Use the hair goods with 'soooul!' If you can't be an apple pie girl, sweet potato will do.

WALKER: Says all that?

JEANETTE: If you pay attention.

WALKER: Then don't.

JEANETTE: You can be replaced. By an empty chair.

WALKER: Bye nigger.

JEANETTE: Back here. For a woman, isn't there a better example than...Miz Off-white America?

WALKER: Do you need an example?

JEANETTE: Don't give me word for word. I mean a reinfocement I can pick up and see myself in. Not...one of these deluded aspirants to lily-whitehood.

WALKER: Buy *National Geographic*.

JEANETTE: Shit in your hat. Then pull it down over your ears. Where y' going?

WALKER: Heh-eh-eh. *(Crossing)* Out of ear shot. *(Off)*

JEANETTE: Go to the toilet, I'll loan you my base-ball cap....As bad as the rest. Anything two shades off a banana make y' horny as three toads on a rock. If you expect Mandy to clean your mess, think again. *(He returns)* That sits in the homes of people trying to maintain an identity. And pass it on to their young. Should a whole race see themselves...like this?

WALKER: No room for a whole race in my head. Barely got space for me. You want identity?

JEANETTE: ...What have you got behind you?

WALKER: *(With* National Geographic*)* Have all you want.

JEANETTE: Cute.

WALKER: I always say. Give'm what they tell you they want, they'll hand it back everytime. You don't like the imitation Breck Girl?

JEANETTE: She uses lip thinner. And a little nose vise at bedtime. Are you saying the alternative is this?

WALKER: Yeh.

JEANETTE: You telling me, in this day and age, folks are ashamed of their looks?

WALKER: They ain't especially proud.

JEANETTE: You're kidding.

WALKER: If I'm lyin' I'm flyin'. And if black was as beautiful to us as we say, we'd get a lot more like them bunnies runnin' roun' ne bushes in mother-motherland. Skip all the Sassoon, Cardin and pickin' out hair. Don't no Africans wear their hair all puffed out. Or it'd catch more lice than you or I would know what to do with.

JEANETTE: People in Africa wear fros.

WALKER: In the cities I'm sure.

JEANETTE: You talking about the ones in the jungle?

WALKER: Ain't they the ones that's black? The city ones too busy tryin' ne be like the niggers they see on TV. And in American magazines. "With they nat'ch'l together." Mm-hn. If you want true essence, honey, get within chucking distance of a spear. *(She crosses d.r.)* Where y' goin'?

JEANETTE: To put on shoes.

WALKER: What's wrong?

JEANETTE: Nothin'. How you know all about who's what?

WALKER: I watched *Roots*. Didn't you watch *Roots*?

JEANETTE: I can't stand a wise ass.

WALKER: A book in the lib'ary. I got it sittin' on my shelf. Called "The Continent That Gave Birth To A World."

JEANETTE: *(Crossing off)* The country that did what?

WALKER: Continent. Look, y' don't need the book. *(TV)* Man I could've caught it from here. You need a basket?

JEANETTE: Is it the Yankees?

WALKER: No, the Reggie Jackson show. Hope his candy bar is better than his fieldin'. Or iss a sorry tastin' piece o'—

JEANETTE: *(Enters with books)* Leave him alone, he tries. Is Chris Chambliss coming up?

WALKER: Boston's at bat. What you got?

JEANETTE: This was holding up your window. If a burglar found it there wouldn't be a stick of furniture left.

WALKER: You look nice.

JEANETTE: Well thank you. I was going to ask.... See? He caught it.

WALKER: Barn door's closed, damn horses already gone. Turn around. Let me see y'.

JEANETTE: Don't look close.... It's got a nice cut. It bells.

WALKER: Mm-*hn*.

JEANETTE: I asked you not to—

WALKER: Very sorry.

JEANETTE: It goes with just about anything.

WALKER: How about nothing?

JEANETTE: *(Hits him)* I'm glad you like it!... Seriously. It looks alright.

WALKER: Snug around the waist. Shows off your hips. On a scale of one to ten ... twelve.

JEANETTE: No one wants to hear something "shows off her hips."

WALKER: An' everybody wears something that does.

JEANETTE: Where should I hit you with this?

WALKER: What's that other one?

JEANETTE: *Oui, monsieur. (Tosses French book)*

WALKER: Basic Conversational—Mm-hn. *(Discards it)*

JEANETTE: It was in the back of my closet. From Mrs. Grillet's class.

WALKER: Mm-hn.

JEANETTE: What's the score?

WALKER: They'll put it up.... Un-hunh. He let'm go in front. Two to one.

JEANETTE: Move over. I wanna see'm catch up.

WALKER: So walk around.

JEANETTE: I like this side. *(Minces)* "Woof woof woof."

WALKER: Watch TV

JEANETTE: Heh-eh-eh. Grouchy little chi-chi baby. Pull in your lip.

WALKER: Keep it up. I'll put a mojo on Chambliss an' make him strike out.

JEANETTE: No you won't. You want him to get a hit. For the Yankees.

WALKER: Sit still.

JEANETTE: *(Bass voice)* "Woof woof." Think you finished the dishes?

WALKER: Unh?

JEANETTE: You were supposed to call somebody?

WALKER: Let me alone.

JEANETTE: She's upset ... probably. Why don't you talk to her? ... You're gonna be a daddy!

WALKER: Just full of piss aren't y'. *(Hits her with pillow)*

JEANETTE: Heh-eh-eh. Come on. Why won't you talk to the girl?

WALKER: She's serious.

JEANETTE: About you? She has rocks in her head. You've never been able to keep a girlfriend.

WALKER: She wants me over to eat with the family.

JEANETTE: "Guess who's coming to—"

WALKER: Right. Can you dig it?

JEANETTE: Go. You can stand to put on weight. *(Commercial)* ... Why in the world would anyone want to look in the mirror and see this? *(Picks up magazine)*

WALKER: *(Tired of it)* I don't *know*.

JEANETTE: I shouldn't raise such hell.... But I get pissed.

WALKER: True. If you thought it kept from lookin' white you'd wear a bone in your nose. Did it never occur to you ... why you look the way you do? Why they'd want you for a cover?

JEANETTE: *(Touching her hair)* Yeah, because—

WALKER: Cause iss natural.

JEANETTE: . . . What?!

WALKER: And if you stick a wig on . . . your real, natural hair that you was born with . . . is still under it.

JEANETTE: White blood is natural to those who had it in the beginning.

WALKER: Somebody told you that. Every nigger alive is got some.

JEANETTE: Every light one.

WALKER: Dark too. Colonel Beauregard put it to Luti Mae back in the plantation bushes and we all show it. Regardless to how we feel our heart don't care. It keeps pumpin' the stuff. Can you crawl back up the chute for a replacement order? We might as well go on and like what we have. We get nothing else.

JEANETTE: That doesn't mean I have to accept it as natural.

WALKER: *(Watches set)* Life'll be a lot easier if you did. Lite beer. Doesn't fill you up. Tastes like hell too. How about a game?

JEANETTE: . . . They could've explained these things when we were children.

I don't think it was expalined to them. Hard to fault Mom. It's not somethin' she'd think to say. But the motherfucker.

JEANETTE: Your father.

WALKER: I had no say in that. Never met a nigger in life hated so much to see hisself. A college educated big deal. Nothin' but a house boy in dashikis and J.C. Penney slacks. Passed the mirror doin' fifty. When he stood still it took a half-hour for him to like what he saw . . . . You can bullshit the old looking glass but beauty's in the eye of she who beholds. When his wife finally beheld that he was a nigger . . . like us . . . well then she just had to admit that she, herself, might be one too. She let go. And he fell flat on his ass. It flipped him out even more when she went in his biology books. Were you around for that.

JEANETTE: Standin' where you are now.

WALKER: *(Smile)* When she had to admit she couldn't get no all white baby, it was her last straw. Nutcase city . . . . How'd your boy do?

JEANETTE: He's not up yet. You say it's natural blood.

WALKER: It ain't Kool-Aid. Iss not a disease. I'm here. You're here. Ain't jacksquat to be done about a thing. Irregardless t' whose blood is what—

JEANETTE: Well, in a case like mother—

WALKER: Yes, and the mother . . .

JEANETTE: *(Dryly)* Say it again . . . . In a specific

instance, how much would be in each of us. From each of—

WALKER: Who can say? Maybe I got more of him. Less of her.

JEANETTE: And I got it the other way.

WALKER: And we both got custody of the furniture. May we sit on it, living our days in peace. . . . Damn both of 'm to hell. *(Crosses)* Wanna sip?

JEANETTE: You're gonna share your game brew with me?

WALKER: I didn't say you c'd have it. Do you want a sip? That's some.

JEANETTE: Yes, I want some. Gimme.

WALKER: Instead of waitin' for them to fall apart on themselves, we should've gone somewhere. It was enough to drive you crazy. Is that the end of my beer?

JEANETTE: Mm-hn. Thank you very much.

WALKER: *(Grabbing her elbow)* You wasn't suppose to get but some, damn it.

JEANETTE: Hey. *(Spills it)* Damn. Look what you did.

WALKER: You had the can, who told you drink it all anyway.

JEANETTE: *(Dabbing)* Shut up.

WALKER: *(Watching set)* You had to be a pain in the butt. *(She unbuttons blouse)* That's what happens. *(Notices her)* For cryin' out loud, you spilled a little. It wasn't half the—

JEANETTE: I'm going to smell of beer. *(Rise, cross)*

WALKER: He did it. A hit. With somebody on base. I'll be damn'.

JEANETTE: Who did?

WALKER: That damn Jackson. He drove in Rivers. If Chambliss does anything the Sox will have trouble. Don't stand there. You'll smell of beer and turn into something. Go sterilize yourself.

JEANETTE: Go scratch your— . . . Man is he cute. Hey that's not fair. *(Perched on mattress edge, holding blouse)*

WALKER: Be glad for what you get.

JEANETTE: They're walking him. It isn't fair.

WALKER: It's not smart either. With Munson nosin' around the bat rack.

JEANETTE: Later for him. I want to see Chambliss get a hit. Shut up.

WALKER: Well, call the station. They'll stop the game for you. And make that bad old pitcher serve a nice fat one to Chrissy.

JEANETTE: I said sh— . . . Come on. Get one too close.

WALKER: But you didn't ask nice. You didn't say—

JEANETTE: Please. For the sake of all that's holy. Please be quiet.

WALKER: With sugar and a cherry on—

JEANETTE: Nigger if you don't close your mouth.

They walked him. I asked you to shut up when I was watching Chris Chambliss, didn't I?

WALKER: I don't recall.

JEANETTE: But you couldn't.

WALKER: Oh be glad he got on. If I was gon' be mean I'd've put the whammy on, so they strike his ass out.

JEANETTE: *(Hits him with blouse)* Don't you say that about him. Um gonna bother the hell out of you now.

WALKER: Don't. They're just about to go ahead. *(She hangs blouse in front of him)* I can't see. *(He moves, she moves)* It smells.

JEANETTE: "It's just some, not half the can."

WALKER: I don't care, I can't s— It's a hit. *(He moves, she moves)* Girl, move.

JEANETTE: Don't call me a girl.

WALKER: *(Pins her arms, watching game)* Wanna make your next birthday party? I missed it. Munson comes through with two out and I miss it.

JEANETTE: Next time leave me alone when I tell you. Ow.

WALKER: Sorry. *(Lets go)* No, I'm not. *(Reaches. She moves)*

JEANETTE: Now what's right is right. You bothered me when I tried to watch. I only got even.

WALKER: *(After her)* Don't give me that. Intention pass not the same as a hit. With men on.

JEANETTE: *(They circle)* Yeah, well I'll . . . I'll . . . make it up to you.

WALKER: How?

JEANETTE: You can bother me again. Next time he's up and gets a walk, I'll let you bother me.

WALKER: Think you're funny. Think you're cute. Umma beat your behind. *(Reaches)*

JEANETTE: No! *(Scrambles over bed)* Hey, you're really mad. Be nice.

WALKER: See how nice I am to the seat of your britches. If you had'm on.

JEANETTE: Now I'm your sister. Come on.

WALKER: Where we goin'? The longer I chase you the worse you'll get it. *(Reaches. She moves)*

JEANETTE: Touch a hair on me and I'll tell Rose to come here for dinner. Heh-eh-eh. Both of'm.

WALKER: You do and Ill—

JEANETTE: *Turns on him, tickling)* What! *(Pins him)* Now what do y' say?

WALKER: Y' can't keep me here forever.

JEANETTE: Mm the nigger has a point. I can't sit here all afternoon. And he'd promise anything to get up. It's true. You can catch the devil but you can't keep him . . . . Just have to sit here until I decide what to do. *(Jabs him)* Don't struggle so. I'm tring to think. And . . . *(Straightening her skirt)* don't look at me.

WALKER: You got your momma's legs.

JEANETTE: Sh.

WALKER: Got her chest too.

JEANETTE: Watch yourself. Besides I have more.

WALKER: Heh-eh-eh. That ain't sayin' nothin'. *(She punches him)* It's sayin' a pound! *(Chuckles)* Iss sayin' you got more than two peanut halves on a bread board. *(She slugs him)* Ohh.

JEANETTE: Wanna say somethin' else?

WALKER: No. Except they look a little nice from here. Not falsies.

JEANETTE: Heh-eh-eh. (!) How would you know about her— . . . . How do you know?

WALKER: Seen her in the shower.

JEANETTE: You looked at her in the—

WALKER: When I was nine years old.

JEANETTE: Oh . . . hnh. You'd probably do it today.

WALKER: No, you're more fun. Close your mouth, I'm teasin'.

JEANETTE: Are you? Hunh? Do you see me in the shower!

WALKER: Yeah. Right through the closed door. Spilled a little on your skirt. Gonna take that off?

JEANETTE: Where?!

WALKER: Hah!

JEANETTE: Aw lemme up.

WALKER: Not on your life.

JEANETTE: Please. I just got this new. It has to be washed off.

WALKER: Be quiet. Ain' nothin' spilt on you.

JEANETTE: You lied. I'll smack your face.

WALKER: With what?

JEANETTE: Come on. Let me go . . . . Please? Sugar and a cherry.

WALKER: You ain't got a cherry.

JEANETTE: Walker C. Smith!

WALKER: Heh-eh-eh. Mm?

JEANETTE: This isn't funny.

WALKER: *(Simply)* Okay. *(Up. To kitchen)*

JEANETTE: You're not mad?

WALKER: No, I'm crazy. But it's okay.

JEANETTE: Hunh? . . . Look, I'm sorry. I'm so sensitive. You didn't say anything all that bad. God didn't strike you dead.

WALKER: God don't know what I was thinkin'.

JEANETTE: What's wrong?

WALKER: Let's go to bed. *(She recoils)* . . . Can I have a cigarette?

JEANETTE: On my dresser. *(He exits. She stands a moment. Retrieves the blouse, puts it on. Unbuttons it again. He enters, crumpling empty pack)*

WALKER: *(Simply)* If you waitin' on me to say "sorry," don't hold your breath.

JEANETTE: Don't be. Hell. What's an old cherry between us . . . . Just . . . why did you say that?

WALKER: What the hell is why? I said my mind.

Ain' no reason.

JEANETTE: It surprised me ... out of nowhere that way. Do you approach all your girls that way. I was put off by how you said it. Not by what you said. It's a nice idea.

(He slips an arm under her blouse and unhooks her bra)

ACT TWO

Scene 1

Evening. In bed.

WALKER: How do you feel?

JEANETTE: About what?

WALKER: Are you sorry?

JEANETTE: Not the least bit.

WALKER: No?

JEANETTE: You crazy? I feel fantastic.

WALKER: Good.

JEANETTE: What about you?

WALKER: I'm fine.

JEANETTE: Heh-eh, mm-hn. You have an extremely nice back. I approve.

WALKER: It's the one I've had since I was born.

JEANETTE: And it has nice muscles in it. Sue me. ... Je t'aime, beaucoup.

WALKER: How do I say, "You're great in ze sack"?

JEANETTE: Through very loose teeth.

WALKER: I see.

JEANETTE: *Vraiment? Est-ce que je suis bonne au lit?*

WALKER: Come again?

JEANETTE: *(Smirks, nudging him)* Stop. "Really." Am I?

WALKER: Heh-eh-eh. Yes.

JEANETTE: Better than her?

WALKER: Hol' it.

JEANETTE: It's crass, crude and a bad thing to say. But I want to know. Hell. I can't be jealous. You're my brother, no my lover.

WALKER: Lady, don't look, but your brother has just become your—What the hell is funny?

JEANETTE: You're right. We're lovers. I think that's pretty damn outrageous .... But answer me.

WALKER: An old saying goes, "If you need to ask—"

BOTH: "You don't want to know."

WALKER: But Um not gon' say that. Comparing yourself in love is dangerous.

JEANETTE: What?

WALKER: Since, from that point, you want to constantly relate to being better than.

JEANETTE: Who doesn't?

WALKER: Needing to be better ... makes your

head big. The joy of love is in being small and safe together. At the moment. Instead of comparing, you create a one of a kind experience.

JEANETTE: Mm-hn.

WALKER: Take applesauce.

JEANETTE: And do what?

WALKER: You've never wondered if it's as good as anything else. From the first taste, it was satisfying in and of itself. Because it was ...

JEANETTE: Applesauce.

WALKER: I rest my case.

JEANETTE: Your case needs a—

WALKER: P.S. This fussin' and frettin' you doin' lately would feel much better if you listen between your knees.

JEANETTE: Wait.

WALKER: That's where the center is. That tells you there's no need to compare and there's no need to get very hung up in images.

JEANETTE: One thing. Does it speak English?

WALKER: Makin' fun.

JEANETTE: You telling me crotches talk?

WALKER: Yours has since you were a moment old. Ever listen?

JEANETTE: I suppose I don't.

WALKER: Or there wouldn't've been all this eighty-five dollar hogwash over ... how you look. As a woman you are all the identity you will ever have.

JEANETTE: Rap on.

WALKER: Heh-eh-eh.

JEANETTE: Can you always make it last so long? *(He nods)* No wonder she calls.

WALKER: Nice. What happened to a woman wants a man with more on his mind?

JEANETTE: That's alright, how do you do it?

WALKER: Taking notes?

JEANETTE: Yes. Just answer.

WALKER: Breath and muscle control.

JEANETTE: As simple as that?

WALKER: That simple. Like hitting a ball. It's an instinct.

JEANETTE: The more we do it and the longer it lasts ... the better I'll hear this center?

WALKER: I think so. I really don't know. *(Rolls over on French book)* Son of Jesus!

JEANETTE: Why do you say that! The savior didn't have any children.

WALKER: Maybe none that they told you of in church. *(Setting French book aside)* Look it up. Every other page in the good book is begettin' where somebody ain't suppose to be gettin' it. The whole while he peddled gospel door to door. He didn't leave a holy ghost or two when the man of the house wasn't home?

JEANETTE: This is Jesus. We're talking about the

same man. Last name of Christ?

WALKER: That wasn't his name, it was his job. A title. His name was probably Rebenowitz. Or Goldstein.

JEANETTE: Walker, bless yourself. Heh-eh.

WALKER: Beg pardon?

JEANETTE: If he had a son. Why is it you're the only one ever heard of him?

WALKER: After what they did to the old man? Would you speak up and say "Hey, I'm the son of—?"

JEANETTE: *(She shoves him)* Heh-eh-eh. What you lookin' for.

WALKER: There used to be a bible around here.

JEANETTE: What you gonna find there?

WALKER: A precedent. It must go on all the time.

JEANETTE: Why?

WALKER: I don't know.

JEANETTE: Gettin' nervous for your soul?

WALKER: I haven't done nothin' I'm ashamed of. An' I'll tell God or anybody else who asks me. . . . I'll bet they've done it in the encyclopedia.

JEANETTE: Bet you they haven't. Who could get comfortable in one of those? Boy would they be surprised.

WALKER: Who?

JEANETTE: Who do you think?

WALKER: Oh to hell with them. *(Sourly)* She's in the nut house and he's back cruisin' bars for the grayest lookin' trim he can find. Either of'm walked in the door it wouldn't mean a thing.

JEANETTE: Sorry I brought it up. *(Picks up French book)* Mn.

WALKER: What?

JEANETTE: Would you like to work on some French?

WALKER: Then what?

JEANETTE: Anything you like.

WALKER: Lemme see this . . . . "Ets-vus"?

JEANETTE: *Mais non. Etes-vous.*

WALKER: Hmn.

JEANETTE: I want to hear your vowel sounds. Ah. *(He repeats) Exactement. Bien. Repetez. Eh. (Same) O. (Same) Eu. (He repeats, despite himself)* Purse your lips.

WALKER: *(Fisheye) Eu.* I sound like a faggot.

JEANETTE: So, if you get the job? . . . Just pretend something is funky. Like your upper lip.

WALKER: . . . *Eu.*

JEANETTE: See? Didn't hurt a bit? *Merci. Splendide, monsieur.*

WALKER: That's what I want. How to say sixty?

JEANETTE: *Soixante.*

WALKER: And? *(Points)*

JEANETTE: *Neuf.*

WALKER: "Nuff"?

JEANETTE: Mm-mn. *Neuf.*

WALKER: Heh-eh-eh. *Ma cherie,* hows about a little of ze *soixante*—

JEANETTE: *(Covers his mouth)* How about taking that laugh to the laundry. Leave your mind over night. Ah . . . you're fun.

WALKER: Heh-eh-eh.

JEANETTE: But—

WALKER: Hm?

JEANETTE: You have a temper. Don't get your *derriere* on your shoulders. It's a fact. You sack trouble up. Until even little things upset you. Badly. And you climb all over someone.

WALKER: So?!

JEANETTE: There . . . I wouldn't want it to ever by my child you got angry with. You haven't got . . . just a boiling point.

WALKER: Like a normal person.

JEANETTE: Don't put words in my mouth . . . . I meant you can be absolutely cruel.

WALKER: Says you.

JEANETTE: At the mall. When you looked in that man's eyes. You would've grabbed him. Because he didn't want to give me a refund. The emotion dissolved from your face. I was afraid.

WALKER: Of me?

JEANETTE: I was. I have been before.

WALKER: Come on. You didn't want the thing. You not supposed to keep it.

JEANETTE: Stores don't usually make that kind of exchange. We were asking him for a favor.

WALKER: So I should've been meek.

JEANETTE: They shall inherit the earth.

WALKER: They can have it.

JEANETTE: Never mind anyway. I was daydreaming. We couldn't have kids. The blood would be bad . . . . Otherwise I could spend a lot of time around you.

WALKER: You spend half your life around me now.

JEANETTE: That's true. But I've never seen you like this.

WALKER: Like what?

JEANETTE: Don't be stupid. You understand me.

WALKER: I haven't changed.

JEANETTE: Mm-hn, you have.

WALKER: Neither have you.

JEANETTE: Don't tell me.

WALKER: We just stopped pretending we weren't attracted to each other. Ain' a thing different about us. Except that.

JEANETTE: That's enough. It's dumb, but you're more . . . here.

WALKER: Mm-mn.

JEANETTE: You are so.

WALKER: Am not. *(Cross)*

JEANETTE: Are you getting up?

WALKER: Jeanette, let me alone . . . For a minute? *(Fixes a drink)* Hey . . . Lady . . . . Was there ever somebody inside yourself with you?

JEANETTE: No, I can't say there was. Why?

WALKER: I feel like that . . . a lot.

JEANETTE: Hunh?

WALKER: Like somebody I always recognize . . . and don't want to see . . . is in the reflection.

JEANETTE: You're being melodramatic. Come lay down.

WALKER: Ain't tired.

JEANETTE: Are you in the scotch?

WALKER: Mm-hn.

JEANETTE: We just bought it.

WALKER: So Um just gon have some.

JEANETTE: . . . Then have it here?

WALKER: If you want to live a certain way. If your values are the same as everybody around you . . . you have a little piece of them in you.

JEANETTE: What's this about?

WALKER: There's an identity problem, right? When you're not sure how much control you have over who you are. There's no crisis when you don't know who you are and like it that way. You got trouble, capital T, thank you, when you know who you are and don't like what you know.

JEANETTE: Quit. You're making word jokes. Or beginning to see the world through Dewar's colored glasses. It's too late for either. Come to bed.

WALKER: I guess you can't always sometimes never tell. But to look in this glass . . . I see somebody who could really be as white as he's not.

JEANETTE: You been thinking too hard. Anybody who looks will tell you you're black as spades.

WALKER: I am? We have a deck of cards around here?

JEANETTE: You know what I mean.

WALKER: Yes! And I'm tired of it.

JEANETTE: Give me a break.

WALKER: Not from you. From . . . everywhere. Am I how I look? Really? Am I what anybody tells me I am from what they see?

JEANETTE: Hnh?

WALKER: I know what I'm talkin' about! Anybody . . . listens to what society says. The law is two per cent colored blood makes a nigger. Them who make laws see mesceg— . . . miss—

JEANETTE: Miscegenation.

WALKER: As situation where their ego would be tainted, heir self-concept would be fucked, if they called dark white people . . . dark white. They had to call'm light black. And what they said . . . we said about ourself . . . . Don't no one tell me who I am. Mm-mn, I wouldn't never pass. Cept maybe as black. Like you do. Yeah.

When you use incorrect English to consider yourself using nigger talk. That's when you're around certain of your friends.

JEANETTE: What are you trying to prove?

WALKER: I'm telling you! There's part of a white boy in that reflection. The lips ain't very thick. The nose isn't really broad. And that pretty hair's not all wool. He drives his Celica . . . uses Chaz . . . dreams mostly about women whose hair comes in red, blonde and brunette. Buys *Players* if it's out but doesn't *miss* an issue of them rabbits. Learning French to get a job where y' can wear a sharp suit to work and relax on weekends with a tall cool glass in hand. The way it is in the advertisements. Them things say what I want from life. From the inside out. What bein' a man is. Umma say somethin' that might bother you. People think you're fine. Everybody in life is attractive in relation to how close they are to white. No matter what Johnson's products tell us. Or how much self-identity gets lip service. In the bowels of the so-called blackest ghetto, the alleged black man will go for the woman with the whitest features, dark or lightskinned he can find. The guiltier he feels for wantin' in, the darker he may go but he *goes*. Cause Benetha McCoy is got big feet with corn's on them. And greasy ham-hock breath. She walks like a neanderthal. I don't want her. Anybody who says he does is a liar . . . . Maybe you don't like to think about it but your job typin' in that office you didn't get because you look like a mau-mau. But because you talk, walk and smile accordin' to *Hoyle* . . . *Cosmopolitan* . . . and . . . *Essence* . . . that thing. Hefner giveth and he taketh away. That's life in this world, from one end of it to the other. If I read books forever. All the ones in creation. I ain't never gonna cut off my "good" hair. Don't wanna learn to throw spears for a livin'. Bein' black, truly, don't appeal to me. *(Refill)* Nope. Do not appeal to me worth a damn. Gon' stay a pretty nigger and gon' like it. But how much of this is me. And how much is a white boy? I don't know.

JEANETTE: Well I hope you haven't awakened the building. Stop arguing and come here. Now? *(He crosses)* Forget white people. And there's no white boy inside you.

WALKER: Inside us all—

JEANETTE: Well I tell y' what. Don't be racist.

WALKER: Hunh?

JEANETTE: Regardless how much of that fella you're worried about happens to be there. You wouldn't throw Burke out of the house because he's white. Why do it to him? *(Taps him)* It's not his fault how he is. He didn't have a lot to say in how he got like that. Another thing. You didn't invent cheese cake. You happen to like the taste. Doesn't mean you can't appreciate *(Kiss)* devil's food . . . . I'll testify to that. It doesn't do a bit of good to sit up and drink my half of the liquor. *(Arms behind his neck)* Or *(Wink)* to buy a wig. Or complain about what's beyond your control. Magazine covers. Does it?

WALKER: *(Smile)* No *(Cries . . . . She holds him. Lifts his face)*

JEANETTE: Well. Are the front of someone's trousers getting a little tight? . . . Loosen up. You're in friendly hands.

Scene 2

Afternoon. Bed is returned to sofa. He's reading. Head in his lap, she reads French.

JEANETTE: There won't be any law on the test.

WALKER: So?

JEANETTE: Put that down and let me hear your vowels.

WALKER: You're close enough to'm. Listen.

JEANETTE: Come on. *(He rattles them off)* Tres bien. Now—

WALKER: There's nothing in there on marriage law.

JEANETTE: . . . So?

WALKER: *(Returns book)* Mm. It has to change from state to state.

JEANETTE: What do you need with the law?

WALKER: Curious. Ah well. Feel like going out?

JEANETTE: To the library? No thank you . . . . On a daily basis, give or take goofing off now and then . . . by the time of the exam we can cover all we need.

WALKER: I promise to learn the whole book when we get back. But let's go somewhere. Like to the stadium?

JEANETTE: They don't play till tonight.

WALKER: Great. We'll go in and hang out all day. Yes. If we're early enough for batting practice, Chris might let you touch his moustache.

JEANETTE: "Hah-hah." Do you want to?

WALKER: Sure, tickets are on you.

JEANETTE: Oh?

WALKER: Yeah. You got eighty-five dollars.

JEANETTE: Fair enough.

WALKER: Can you go like this? Or must the princess consult her wardrobe?

JEANETTE: *(He crosses)* Bring me a light jacket, trife.

WALKER: You talkin' to me?

JEANETTE: You answering?

WALKER: *(Enters)* When the Lord made lip, he gave it all to black women.

JEANETTE: So you'd have something to aim at.

WALKER: Hnh. Y' know, y' know—

JEANETTE: Hn?

WALKER: The Yankees are in Boston.

JEANETTE: Jerk.

WALKER: *(Smile)* We can still go. It's only four hours to Fenway Park.

JEANETTE: *(Sarcastically)* Why don't we leave this minute?

WALKER: Just cause the game is out of town . . . . Still. We'll go to Shea.

JEANETTE: I been to the circus when I was little.

WALKER: They're not as bad as all that. *(She gives him the fisheye)* Well okay they are. Let's go anyway. If just for a flick.

JEANETTE: All the way to the city for a movie . . . . What's playing out here? *(He crosses for paper)* My clothes are always dirty when I come back from Manhattan. You know what I'd like to do? Forget going anywhere. I want to lay around the house. Enjoy each other's company.

WALKER: The company will still be here when we get back. I want to do something. If only to go out and count clouds.

JEANETTE: There's a bug in your ass.

WALKER: *(Smile)* Alright, alright. Get the set. *(She crosses for chess set)* You know who we haven't seen in a while?

JEANETTE: Keith and Leslie. I'll bet they're free today.

(Phone rings)

WALKER: I got it! Hello? . . . Hi. We're on our way out the door.

JEANETTE: Who are you lying to?

WALKER: *(Covers phone)* Never mind. *(Into phone)* Don't raise your voice to me. Better. What's wrong?

JEANETTE: Girl hasn't had a word since he can last remember. "What's wrong?"

WALKER: I haven't been busy. She's been polite enough to say I was. Or that I was in the bathroom—

JEANETTE: Hey!

WALKER: But I've been here.

JEANETTE: She has feelings—

WALKER: I haven't wanted to speak with you. I been taking time to myself. To go over some personal things. Mm-hn. Other than you . . . . You're not a thing, no. I mean to say— . . . . Whether I meant it or not. The point is I don't want to see you.

JEANETTE: Damn.

WALKER: I don't have to give you a reason. Have you ever heard me make a commitment or a obligation . . . . Never mind what you thought. You make assumptions. Don't you know these things never work out? Um gon' put the phone down in a few minutes. Maybe you'll listen to what I say between now and then. I hope—

JEANETTE: I hope you hang the hell up.

WALKER: Neither you or I make the money it takes to put an inter-racial family beyond the reach of intolerant neighbors. I never said anything about marriage neither. And Um not going through the hell and heartache of a renegade romance in this blue collar town for anything less. A minute ago I said I'd hang up. Rose, good—*(Hangs up)*

JEANETTE: You were talking to a person.

WALKER: I were. Till she hung up the phone.

JEANETTE: A person . . . is a human being . . . who feels.

WALKER: That mean me?

JEANETTE: . . . I don't know.

WALKER: I did and said the way I felt was necessary.

JEANETTE: You were as rude and disgustingly ill-mannered as a child!

WALKER: A child.

JEANETTE: And not a very old one.

WALKER: Well I did what I had to.

JEANETTE: You cut someone dead like a rotten tree branch. Would it be that way? Would you do it to me?

WALKER: It wouldn't be necessary.

JEANETTE: You don't know that. Is this the way? If so just please don't do it over the phone. I'll want to be close enough to spit in your face.

WALKER: . . . I could've considered her. And been nicer . . . dragged out what was inevitable. I was afraid she'd ask questions. Before she got around to it I wanted to be off the line.

JEANETTE: What fucking question?

WALKER: . . . Whether there was somebody else.

JEANETTE: Right now, I wonder.

WALKER: Jeanette!

JEANETTE: . . . What are we gonna do? Can we stay together?

WALKER: *(Beer)* Well we're not supposed to. We can.

JEANETTE: I don't mean just incest. I'm nervous . . . about you. There's no doubt about my needing to sleep with you. But to make myself open to the possibility of the same thing happening that you did to . . . to—

WALKER: You don't know it's going to happen that way. You don't know it's gonna happen!

JEANETTE: For us . . . it has to happen sometime.

WALKER: As long as it's not today what do you care?

JEANETTE: I care. You aren't just a guy who, if we don't get along, can just walk away and I'll chalk it up to experience. We live here. When you or

me pull away, there'll be no place to pull away to.

WALKER: Quit frettin' on it. There's no need to do anything now.

JEANETTE: Before we're in over our heads. Shouldn't we?

WALKER: I am in—

JEANETTE: Things can go back to normal. They'll straighten out. Yes.

WALKER: By acting like we don't want to be anything more special than family . . . . Okay . . . I'm goin' out for a while.

JEANETTE: *(Despite herself)* Where?

WALKER: Someplace!

JEANETTE: Alright . . . . Can I come?

WALKER: Why?

JEANETTE: No reason. Never mind. See you later.

WALKER: . . . Are you mad at me?

JEANETTE: I'm not angry with you. Maybe I need to be alone too.

WALKER: See y'.

JEANETTE: Not if I see you first. *(Wink)*

WALKER: *(Forced laugh)* Right. *(Exit)*

JEANETTE: Girl . . . get a grip on your shit. Because you been in his bed it is still him . . . . If he has the sense to get distance, do the same. Before he gets back, God. Because this is not cool.

Scene 3

Evening. He enters. She has a beer.

WALKER: Hi.

JEANETTE: Hello.

WALKER: Don't excite yourself.

JEANETTE: Would you care for a particular tone?

WALKER: Since you in my beer, nice will do fine.

JEANETTE: You may have it back. Where have you been?

WALKER: . . . What?

JEANETTE: Where were you?

WALKER: . . . At the bar.

JEANETTE: The bar?

WALKER: B-a-r.

JEANETTE: Doing what?

WALKER: What else, getting my hair cut.

JEANETTE: You bastard, don't you know the time?

WALKER: . . . Mm-hn.

JEANETTE: You didn't put ten cents in a telephone.

WALKER: So?

JEANETTE: Why not?

WALKER: What's your problem? I never call. Why the devil should I've called? I went to the Gold Coast Inn then I stopped at Schroe's for a sandwich, a beer and to bullshit. When was I supposed to call you? What was I supposed to say?

JEANETTE: That you weren't coming right back.

WALKER: I didn't say I was. I said I's going out. Is it odd for me to go in the car and take a drive?

JEANETTE: . . . No.

WALKER: *(Lying)* What, I didn't hear.

JEANETTE: No!

WALKER: So what's wrong?

JEANETTE: I feel hurt.

WALKER: . . . Why?

JEANETTE: You didn't come home in the afternoon. Or for dinner. I didn't know what happened.

WALKER: What did you expect?

JEANETTE: . . . Nothing.

WALKER: That's what happened.

JEANETTE: I thought you were . . . cruising.

WALKER: If I was, if I wasn't—

JEANETTE: It's not my business. Sue me. I was jealous.

WALKER: You was what?!

JEANETTE: I said sue me!

WALKER: Don't loud on me. I wanted things to go on like it was. But you—

JEANETTE: I know.

WALKER: So you can put this on hold.

JEANETTE: I swear you bleed ice water.

WALKER: Me?

JEANETTE: You walk out, stay out. And sashay in here like it was alright. Didn't you feel like taking time to sort your feelings?

WALKER: I don't have to sort anything.

JEANETTE: Just withdraw, say nothing. Who knows how you feel? Can I read minds?

WALKER: What do you want to hear?

JEANETTE: How you feel! I called myself being close. I don't know you.

WALKER: You need to know so damn much . . . . I don't wanna be your fuckin' brother. I want to put my hands on you. And to do it again. And again and again.

JEANETTE: . . . I couldn't keep away from you.

WALKER: Some states have common law marriage. No judge, no license. No preacher to please. Nobody but us and God would know the difference.

JEANETTE: Do you want that?

WALKER: Don't you?

JEANETTE: Answer me straight. Don't offer me a bill of goods like the one you sold her.

WALKER: . . . Listen. Till last night I was alone. Nobody knew me. That made me look at you a lot different . . . . How long I would look at you like this . . . . I can't tell you with a straight face. I can't.

JEANETTE: And it could end up like it with . . . . what's're name?

WALKER: I hope not . . . . It could.

JEANETTE: . . . No. I like being your friend. Besides anyway, if I married you I'd surely die of guilt.

WALKER: Yeah. You would . . . . So let me pack a brew for the road.

JEANETTE: Mm-mn. That wouldn't make sense. There are rooms at the Y. I'd like to get one and look around . . . eh . . . the city.

WALKER: I heard things about girls who like to stay at—

JEANETTE: I mean I want to stay in midtown, while I shop for a place . . . . You really gonna live here?

WALKER: It's a nice place. 'Sides what about the furniture?

JEANETTE: I hate the furniture. We didn't buy it. You scared to lose the security deposit?

WALKER: Naw I ain't scared.

JEANETTE: . . . Don't stay here.

WALKER: I won't . . . . but I'll think a lot about you . . . . You want to leave first thing in the morning?

JEANETTE: Let's get out now.

WALKER: I don't see why not . . . . I'll come back for anything I need. Got your keys? *(Crosses off to bedrooms)*

JEANETTE: Will you get my toothbrush and whatever is in my top drawer? Throw it in a bag for me? *(Looks room over)* Is there anything here I can't live without? *(Picks up "Continent That Gave Birth . . .")*

WALKER: Hey. Can you remember? Ye is ye and Angela is she. Iss just as well the train stay like it is.

JEANETTE: *(Picks up French book, writes in it)* Can I forget? . . . Keep somethin' in mind, hn? . . . Don't let the people around you make you cut off your nose. Cause you know the only one who gets spited.

WALKER: Who you think you talkin' to? Heh-eh-eh. Want me to drive you in?

JEANETTE: Mm-mn. Would you drop me at the station?

WALKER: Sure. You should check a schedule. We may have to wait a while.

JEANETTE: Baby, I don't care.

WALKER: *(Returns as she is writing)* What are you up to?

JEANETTE: Just something to remember me by. Read it sometime.

WALKER: *(Takes book)* "Je t'aime."

JEANETTE: It means—

WALKER: I know what it means. Come on.

They exit

71

DIANNE HOUSTON

Photo by Brenda Gilmore

DIANNE HOUSTON, born July 22, 1954 in Washington D.C., began her professional career as an actress. Having received early training at D.C.'s Workshops for Careers in the Arts, Ms. Houston went on working with several theatre companies, including the City Street Theatre of New York, and the Ebony Impromptu Theatre Company, based in Washington D.C. Ms. Houston launched her career as a director while a student at Howard University, where among other local and regional awards, she was honored as best director for two consecutive years for her productions of *Ladies in Waiting,* by Peter DeAnda; *Black Images/Black Reflections,* by K. Collie; and a showcase production of *The Sistuhs,* by Saundra Sharpe. These productions marked the beginning of a professional association between Ms. Houston and composer Latteta Brown, with whom Ms. Houston has written several now popular children's songs and a three act children's musical based on the tale of Peter Rabbit.

Ms. Houston has taught at Duke Ellington School of the Arts, served for two years on the Theatre Panel for the D.C. Commission on the Arts, and has taught theatre and photography at community centers throughout Washington, D.C. Ms. Houston is actively involved in children's theatre, and is co-director of The Children's Theatre Funshop, a company which has performed in New York, at Wolftrap, and locally in Montgomery County public schools. Equally at home and adept as an actress, director, and playwright, Dianne Houston is currently directing for stage, performing, and writing for educational television.

The Fishermen is Ms. Houston's first full length straight dramatic play and was one of three finalists in the Kennedy Center/Karamu House division of the National Black Playwrights Competition, in which thousands of plays were entered. It successfully premièred in Washington, D.C. in April of 1980 at The New Black Alley Theatre.

The Fishermen was inspired in part by the death of one associate and the imprisonment of a friend during the so-called "Hanafi Takeover" in Washington D.C. In the words of the play-wright, "When the Hanafi Takeover happened, this play was in its infancy. Only the end of it had been written. I didn't know where it was going, what the whole story would be. Then the Takeover began, and I was besieged with feelings of hurt, of rage, of grieving. One friend was dead, and another dear friend had been accused of murdering him. I was enaged at the violence that had precipitated the whole thing happening in the first place. Many innocents dead, and one man, from whom I had only known a peaceful softness, was, by virtue of his commitment, being held high as an example of the ugliness of terrorism, of violence, of fear. It was a tapestry of victims. Both the living and the dead. *The Fishermen* was born of a need to say 'hey look . . . these are *human* people here!' It does not tell the story of the Takeover, nor does it parallel the lives of the people and events involved. It attempts to break up stereotypes . . . to put an end to 'bad' and 'good.' To show that passion and/or grief unanswered can, and does turn to violence, to exploded rage and grief. It is dedicated to my two friends—who's names will go unmentioned here—because we are all capable of being either one or both of them. We are *The Fishermen*.

Latteta Brown, composer of the score and theme for *The Fishermen,* is a concert flutist, composer, songwriter, vocalist, arranger, and performer. She is the author of a series of Flute Method books, and, with Ms. Houston, is the co-author of *New Age Songs for New Age Children,* a child/family song book. Ms. Brown also co-heads The Children's Theatre Funshop, and with Ms. Houston has written *The Tale of Peter Rabbit: A Musical Re-telling,* a three act musical.

THE FISHERMEN

Dianne Houston

PRODUCTION NOTES

There is music (including a theme), composed for The Fishermen *by composer Latteta Brown, that must be used whenever* The Fishermen *is produced. The music is played at four different times throughout the play—Part One is a haunting, sung melody that sets the mood for* Act One *(and, therefore, for the entire play); Part Two is a beautiful flute and piano lullaby used once at the top of* Act Three *and again to set the* Epilogue; *Part Three is another arrangement of the sung theme, which closes and gels the* Epilogue. *The music and other information can be obtained through contacting Dianne Houston (see previously listed address).*

Intermission should be after Act One *only. It is the only natural break in the play.*

In the Epilogue, *if flowers are used at all, the only roses should be those carried by* MAMA E.

CHARACTERS

RUTH TYLER: *A small yet strong and energetic Black woman. She has a soft face and eyes that do not belie her capacity for the humor, intensity, and fury that are also hers. She is a woman of passion, given to impulse. A housewife in her mid-40s, she lives with her husband, son, and mother. Not given to moodiness,* RUTH *knows that she is either intensely right or wrong.*

MAMA E: RUTH's *mother. 90, going on 300. Spry and sharp. She knows humor, knows how to laugh, and knows that wisdom is lived rather than learned through books. She is her own repository of knowledge, and her own decider of what is fact.* MAMA E *moves mostly through the aid of her wheelchair, a high-backed wooden model circa WW II. At other times she stands or walks with the aid of a cane.*

JEREMY TYLER: RUTH's *son. At 21,* JEREMY *is in transition: The dreams of the boy; the man-child; becoming the lifeblood, reality, and substance of the man.*

NEWS COMMENTATOR (VOICE)

NEWS REPORTER (VOICE)

LEE WATKINS, JR.: JEREMY's *closest friend.* LEE *is angry, threatened, and threatening. He is afraid and needs (though is afraid of) love and loving. Instead of seeking understanding,* LEE *seeks out solutions to having been misunderstood. His right leg is in a cast: A broken ankle due to a too hasty, too eager introduction to martial arts.*

MILTON TYLER: *A minister and Black community leader for over 20 years.* REVEREND TYLER *is* RUTH's *husband, or rather,* RUTH *is* REVEREND TYLER's *wife. A handsome man,* MILTON TYLER *has a face befitting an actor or a politician: It is wise, is pained, knows tenderness, but scarcely ever does it tell what it has seen or all it knows. A bit reserved, heady, or lofty,* MILTON's *ministerial demeanor hides a man hiding a fuse, already lit.*

POLICE SERGEANT (VOICE)

SIX HOSTAGES

THREE ARMED POLICEMEN

POLICE VOICE

VOICE OF MAYOR SHILLET

Time: Mid-1970s

Place: An American City or Township

ACT ONE

Scene 1

Setting: The Tyler living room. It is large, as opposed to being small, yet not unusually large or roomy. There is comfortable sitting, standing, and walking space, with an air of such benefits being thought out and planned. The furniture is a mix of styles: An almost antique high-backed wheelchair; a modern yet not new sofa; a lamp table complete with Bible and family photographs; a hand-crafted, homemade coffee table proud with varnish; and an inconspicuous yet ever present television set. There is also a man-sized easy chair and ottoman, a wall of bookshelves, and the other walls are adorned with awards, citations, plaques. Upstage, just right of center is a swinging door that leads offstage into the kitchen. Upstage left is an exit to other rooms in the house. At left center there is a stairway, going up; and at down left, opening downstage is the main, front entrance to the house. The television is on, and MAMA E sits in her chair before it, dozing. The sounds of a rainstorm can be heard, and RUTH enters, carrying cut garden roses (wet), a vase, and doily. Her dress is sprinkled with raindrops, and her face and arms are also wet. She has a towel over her shoulder.

NEWS COMMENTATOR: Temperatures will continue in the mid–eighties today and tomorrow. Experts predict a ninety per cent chance of rain . . .

RUTH: You hear that, Mama? Ninety per cent chance of rain. *(She laughs)* Well, they're more on the ball than usual. Only ten per cent off! Shoot, it's rainin' so hard out there I was lookin' round for Noah! Almost crushed my roses. I wasn't gonna pick 'em either, they looked so pretty on the bush, but I had to do somethin'. Poor things looked like they were drownin'. *(She has placed the roses on the lamp table, steps back to admire them, and starts drying herself)* I swear, I wonder where those weather people sit that they can't see outside. Seems to me they'd have a window. Any fool can see it's rainin', and they still talkin' about a ninety per cent chance! Makes 'em look awfully stupid, Mama, don't you think? Don't you think so, Mama? Mama? *(She turns and sees MAMA E fast asleep)*

NEWS COM: The Nation's unemployment level has soared again to seven point six per cent. A recent survey showed that sixty per cent of the seven point six per cent unemployed are Black, twenty per cent of the remaining forty per cent are White, and the remaining twenty per cent of the seven point six per cent of the national total are of . . .

RUTH: Mama! *(Crossing to her, turns off TV)* Remind me not to ask you what's happenin' in the news.

MAMA E: *(Wakes up. Groggily)* Uh . . . what? *(Fully conscious)* Ruth! Child, what are you doin' standin' all over me? You know it ain't right to stand over top somebody while they's thinkin'!

RUTH: *Thinkin'!* Mama, you were asleep!

MAMA E: And why's the TV off? Ain't it time for the news?

RUTH: The news was on, Mama, but I . . .

MAMA E: You don't listen to the news you'll never get a head. Got to know what's goin' on in the world. You got to learn things.

RUTH: *(Dryly)* Yes, Mam. Well, I've certainly learned one thing.

MAMA E: What's that? *(Gestures to RUTH to turn TV back on. RUTH does)*

RUTH: Not to wake you while you're "thinkin'"! *(She heads back to roses. TV sputters, statics, and then clears)*

NEWS COM: In the local news, Rev. Milton Tyler, prominent leader in the Black community, was interviewed today concerning rumors of his forthcoming appointment to the city council seat left vacant by the late Harry S. Dowell. If appointed, Rev. Tyler would be the first Black to serve on the city council. Here is Aaron McRan . . .

RUTH: *(Overlap)* Milton, Mama! They talkin' about Milton!

MAMA E: Shhh!

(RUTH runs over to TV)

NEWS REP: Rev. Tyler, how do you feel about the rumors of your being appointed to city council?

MILTON: Well, I . . .

RUTH: *(Overlap)* Don't he look good!!!

MAMA E: Shhh!

MILTON: I've never taken any stock in rumors. As my public record shows, I am a man of fact. Fact and action. Not rumor.

RUTH: Sock it to 'em, Mil!

MAMA E: Shhh!!!

NEWS REP: . . .but you must have some inkling as to whether or not you're actually being considered . . .

MILTON: *(Overlap)* I know only that Mayor Shillet is a wise and dedicated man and that he only wants the best for his cabinet, for this city.

NEWS REP: Based on that, do you see yourself as a contender? As one of the best? The best?

MILTON: I try.

RUTH: Whooo wheee! Give it to 'em, Milton. Tell

'em everything. Tell 'em nothin'!

MAMA E: Will you be quiet!

RUTH: Oh, it's gone off now, Mama. *(Clicks off set)* Wasn't he fine? Ain't Rev. Milton Tyler just the finest, most groomed, most polished, most sophisticated, most splendid, pretty nigga you ever seen in all your life? Ain't he?

MAMA E: There's more to the world than just your husband, Ruth. Turn that set back on.

RUTH: More? Who needs more? Who wants, who cares about more? Milton's gonna get that seat, Mama. Just you wait and see. A Black man at the head of city council. And my Black man at that! Mama, don't you know what that means?

MAMA E: It don't mean no immediate changes around here, that's for certain. No chauffeur, no doorman, and it looks like I'm always gon' have to turn this TV on myself. *(She does, it statics, she grimaces, turns it off)* No, no . . . this ain't gonna be the Blue Room. It's still gonna be your house.

RUTH: Mama, I don't mean changes like that. I mean political, social changes. With Milton in office, ain't no tellin' what good can happen for our people.

MAMA E: Shoot, you mean *your* people.

RUTH: Oh Lord, here we go . . . Mama, when are you gonna stop with that "your people versus my people" kind of foolishness?

MAMA E: When your people stop acting like dang fools!

RUTH: What do you mean "fools"?

MAMA E: I mean fools, just like I said. Half of 'em swear they African, and got no reason to know or to remember anybody who ain't; and the other half is either already hippie white or is so far into being equal that they done forgot what it is inside that makes 'em Black in the first place. It ain't just a tan, you know.

RUTH: I know, Mama, but that's two extremes. What about the middle?

MAMA E: Ain't no middle. No room for one. Ain't in fashion.

RUTH: Mama, what about Milton? He's . . .

MAMA E: Milton's an exception.

RUTH: Jeremy then.

MAMA E: Jeremy's an exception. Still ain't no middle.

RUTH: Mama, the exceptions to what you call fools do not all live in this house.

MAMA E: Obviously.

RUTH: What?

MAMA E: You live here, don't you?

RUTH: Yes.

MAMA E: Well, did you hear me call your name? *(Starts laughing)*

RUTH: Mama, you're crazy.

MAMA E: Maybe so, but I ain't no fool! *(Laughs again)*

RUTH: *(Balling fist)* If you wasn't my mama! . . .

MAMA E: *(Also balls fist)* Mine's straighter, stronger, and carries less guilt! *(Both laugh. JEREMY enters through the kitchen door, soaked, muddy, and carrying a large cardboard box)*

JEREMY: Ma, where can I put these so they can dry out?

RUTH: Put what, Jeremy? *(She turns and sees him)* Lord, boy, where you been to look like that?

JEREMY: Over at the church, Ma. I got clothes in this box that need drying out.

MAMA E: Looks to me like *you* need dryin' out.

RUTH: I hope you didn't track mud all the way in here.

JEREMY: No, I took my shoes off in the kitchen.

RUTH: Well, so much for the kitchen floor. Stay there, stay right there till I get some newspaper. Otherwise you and your box'll be drippin' all over the floor in here.

JEREMY: It's a wood floor, Ma.

RUTH: And I don't want it to sprout. Stay there and do not move one inch till I get back. *(Exits through kitchen door)*

JEREMY: *(Urgently)* Ma!!

(RUTH's scream is heard. JEREMY winces. MAMA E gets up. RUTH comes back through door)

RUTH: Jeremy, how many times have I asked you to please let me know when someone else is in the house?

JEREMY: I tried, Ma. It's only Lee.

LEE: *(Looks through doorway over RUTH's head)* Sorry, Mrs. Tyler.

(MAMA E sits back down)

RUTH: It's all right, Lee. Child, you just as much a mess as him.

LEE: Yes, Mam.

RUTH: Well, you stay put too, then! 'Scuse me. *(She ducks under his arm. Door closes, leaving only MAMA E and JEREMY in the room)*

MAMA E: Where'd you say you'd been, Jeremy?

JEREMY: Over at the church, Mama E.

MAMA E: What's happenin' over at the church to get you and that other boy so muddy?

JEREMY: We were doing a little construction, Mama E. Part of the fence had fallen down.

MAMA E: Part of the fence?

JEREMY: Yes Mam.

MAMA E: Had fallen down?

JEREMY: Yes Mam.

MAMA E: So you and Lee, Jr. fixed it?

JEREMY: *(Laughs)* Yes, Mam.

MAMA E: Umm hmm. *(Pause)* Jeremy . . .

JEREMY: Yes Mam?

MAMA E: I don't recall no kind of fence around

your father's church.

JEREMY: *(Laughing)* It wasn't Papa's church, Mama E. What are you, a detective?

MAMA E: Maybe. *(More laughter)* Jeremy?

JEREMY: Yes Mam?

MAMA E: Who's church was it?

JEREMY: Church of the People, Mama E. Reverend Akbara's church.

MAMA E: Rev. Akbara? Haven't I heard his name before?

JEREMY: Probably. He was my history professor at school. Both Lee and I took his course. That was my second year. Almost four years ago.

MAMA E: And now he's got a church.

JEREMY: Yep.

MAMA E: What's it called?

JEREMY: Church of the People. It's over on Second and Abeline. He's reconverted an old building over there.

MAMA E: Church of the People.

JEREMY: Yes Mam. That's right.

MAMA E: 'S got a steeple on it?

JEREMY: No, not yet.

MAMA E: Uh huh. It's got a cross, though, huh?

JEREMY: No.

MAMA E: One of them stars with six points?

JEREMY: No Mam, Akbara's not Jewish.

MAMA E: Well, what kinda church is it, then?

JEREMY: It's not quite a church, yet, Mama E. *(RUTH enters with newspaper for the floor and a towel for JEREMY)* Thanks. *(He dries his head)* He wants it to grow into being a church so he can involve more of the community in the things he wants to do.

RUTH: Things who wants to do?

JEREMY: Rev. Akbara. He runs the free food program up in Crown Heights, and he's just started a clothing drive. That's what all these clothes are for. Been helpin' Lee get 'em together. Lee's already a member of the church.

(LEE opens the door)

LEE: Okay to come in now?

RUTH: Yes, if you're dry. *(LEE enters, using crutches)* How's that foot doin', Lee Jr.?

LEE: Doin' fine, Mrs. Tyler. Still hurts a lot though, sometimes.

RUTH: For the life of me, Lee Jr., I just don't know what made you think you could break a board with your foot!

LEE: Two boards.

RUTH: That's even worse! *(Shakes head)* I swear, sometimes it's like I got *two* sons.

LEE: *(Smiling)* We're all brothers and sisters anyway. *(To MAMA E)* Good evening, Mrs. Jones.

MAMA E: Good evening, Brother Lee. *(They all laugh. To JEREMY)* Finish tellin' me 'bout this Ack-bo...

JEREMY: Akbara.

MAMA E: *Who-ever* and his church.

JEREMY: Well, about four years ago, Akbara was fired...

LEE: Quit!

JEREMY: *(Looks at LEE)* ...quit his job at the university and started out on his own. First, he...

RUTH: Jeremy!

JEREMY: Huh?

MAMA E: *(Disturbed)* Shoot!

RUTH: Sorry, didn't mean to cut you off, but all this time you were talkin', I forgot you didn't know!

JEREMY: Know what?

RUTH: Your father, Jeremy. Milton was on TV!

JEREMY: Yeah? Papa?

RUTH: *(Overlap)* They interviewed him, Jeremy. Asked him how he felt 'bout all them *rumors* that he was gonna get that council seat.

JEREMY: Rumors!

RUTH: Awww, but he handled 'em so well, Jeremy. Told 'em he took no stock in rumors, and, oh Jeremy, he was so grand! He looked so dignified, so handsome!

MAMA E: Ruth, that boy don't give two hoots how handsome his daddy looked! That's your foolishness, girl.

JEREMY: *(To LEE)* My mother's in love with my father.

LEE: That's fortunate.

RUTH: That's more than fortunate, that's rare! Ain't too many women can lay claim to lovin' their husbands as much or as well as I do mine!

MAMA E: Ruth!

RUTH: It's true! Ain't gonna hurt these boys at all to hear it. They both grown. They ought to know what to look for in a good woman.

MAMA E: Certain things are just not...

RUTH: I ain't talkin' about bed, Mama. *(Looks at JEREMY and LEE)* Ain't nothin' I can tell them about that they haven't already found out themselves.

MAMA E: Lord, Jesus...

RUTH: I just want these two clowns to understand that a good woman is not just good to you...

MAMA E: Sweet Jesus...

RUTH: ...she's good for you as well. She'll bear up with you through the hard times and brighten up the best. *(Pauses)* Stop prayin, Mama! Ain't nothin' lewd about the truth.

MAMA E: The truth the way you see it would send us all to Hell. Ain't no need to be talkin' to children...

RUTH: Ain't no *children* in here. Besides, somebody got to tell 'em.

LEE: Don't worry, Mrs. Tyler. I'm sure Jeremy's

gonna bring home a lady just like you. *(Smiles at* JEREMY*)* Ain't you, buddy?

JEREMY: *(Looks at* LEE*, surprised at his statement. He studies* LEE*'s smile, then aware that an answer is expected of him, replies)* Uh, yeah . . . *(Perking)* If I don't, Mama probably won't let her in the house!

RUTH: I ain't that choosey!

JEREMY: Oh yes, you are too! Between you and Mama E . . .

MAMA E: Me! What did I do?

JEREMY: *(To* LEE*)* You remember Amale, the South African girl in our history class? *(*LEE *nods)* Well, I brought Amale home for dinner once, and after introductions were made, Mama E. looks Amale dead in the eye and says, "Girl, your mama give you that name?" *(They laugh)*

MAMA E: That's 'cause every other used-to-be-Joe what came in here was tryin' to pass themselves off as some kinda would-be African.

JEREMY: It was just a name, Mama E.

MAMA E: Names is important! Tell a lot about the soul. Besides, I already told you . . .

JEREMY: I know, I know, you don't care who I bring in here long as she's clean, healthy, got a good mind, and goes to church.

MAMA E: That's right.

JEREMY: I could bring home a tidy, well-mannered, Catholic hippopotamus, and Mama E. wouldn't mind one bit.

MAMA E: Not if you fool enough to bring one home!

RUTH: Yeah, well she better be yard or toilet trained. Got enough mess in here just lookin' after you. The last thing I need is hippopotamus shit all on my floor!

MAMA E: Ruth!

RUTH: Lord, pardon my sailor's mouth. I'm a sinner through and through! *(Laughing)* I just don't like no hippopotamus shit, Lord, that's all!

MAMA E: And to think you're a preacher's wife!

RUTH: Awww Mama, even heaven needs a break.

*(*MAMA E *pointedly ignores her)*

MAMA E: Jeremy, tell me more about that church you and Lee Jr. come from today.

JEREMY: I don't know that much more to tell you, Mama E. Lee's the one.

RUTH: Mud's dried up and made more mess . . . *(Exits to kitchen)*

MAMA E: Oh, shush up! What you know 'bout it, Lee Jr.?

LEE: Well, he's been preaching for a while now. Got a pretty good sized following and lots of volunteers.

MAMA E: This . . . following . . . that what you a part of, Lee?

LEE: Yes Mam, for over a month now.

MAMA E: You meet every Sunday?

LEE: Not just Sunday, Mam, any day of the week. Rev. Akbara believes that the time for prayer is when it moves you, and that can be any time, so he holds his sermons the same way. Sometimes Sunday, sometimes Monday, they can be anytime. Sometimes there's no sermon at all.

MAMA E: Seems like a pretty funny way to run a church. How's he keep his congregation together? Keep 'em strong?

LEE: Well, we're not exactly a congregation. We're called workers. Workers of the Church.

RUTH: *(Reenters with dustpan and broom)* Now, that's exactly what I need around here. Some *workers*. Who's this you're talking about?

JEREMY: Rev. Akbara, Mama. You should meet him. I think you'd like him.

LEE: I don't think so.

RUTH: Why not?

LEE: Well, I'd rather not say, Mam, but I just don't think you would.

RUTH: You know, you've always been strange, Lee Jr. . . . Akbara, Akbara . . . it's a wierd name, but I swear I've heard it before.

LEE: Probably so, Mam. He's in politics, just like Rev. Tyler.

RUTH: That don't mean a thing, Lee Jr. There's half a zillion wierd named would-be politicians. Besides, Rev. Tyler ain't exactly into politics yet. Mayor's still got to make an official announcement, and then Milton's got to be sworn in. You do think they got to swear him in, don't you?

JEREMY: Don't know, I guess so.

RUTH: *(Pleased)* Good!

MAMA E: Blue Room it is.

RUTH: Shush, Mama. Ain't nothin' of the kind. It's just that I know Milton'll get that seat. He's a good man, got an excellent record, and everybody likes, or at least respects him. Besides, the mayor's got to pick a man the people would accept, and since the majority of the people are Black, he's the most logical choice. Ain't no other Black man better suited or even equally suited for the job than Milton Tyler!

JEREMY: Here, here! Three cheers for Rev. Milton Tyler's chief campaign manager. Hip, hip!!!

RUTH *and* MAMA E: Hooray!

JEREMY: Hip, Hip . . .

RUTH *and* MAMA E: Horray!

JEREMY: Hooray—Hooray!

*(*RUTH *and* MAMA E *start to answer but get confused. All except* LEE *break into laughter)*

MAMA E: Boy's crazy as his mother!

RUTH: What's the matter with you, Lee Jr.? You too grown up to laugh?

LEE: *(Quietly)* There's Akbara.

(Laughter stops)

MAMA E: What you say, boy?

LEE: There's Rev. Akbara. He's every bit as suited for that job as Rev. Tyler, and he just might get it, too.

JEREMY: Hey, cool out, Lee . . .

RUTH: Boy, do you know what you're sayin' in my house?

MAMA E: Easy daughter.

RUTH: Easy Hell! You bite your lip, Lee Jr. and you bite it good. Don't nobody come in here bad-lacing Milton or anybody else in this house!

LEE: I'm not "bad-lacing" the Rev., Mrs. Tyler. I'm simply stating a fact.

MAMA E: Take my advice you'd swallow your facts and bite your lip while you still got one to bite.

JEREMY: Come on, Lee. *(Moves as if to go)*

RUTH: No. Stay right here, Lee Jr. Tell me 'bout these facts you say you got!

JEREMY: Ma, do you really think . . .

RUTH: I want to hear them. Go on, Lee.

LEE: Mam, I don't really think it's the right time to . . .

RUTH: You damn right it's not the right time! Ain't no time ever the right time to bad-lace anybody in my house. 'Specially not Milton. Not when he's so close . . . when his chances are so good. Nobody in this town deserves that position more than Milton, and ain't no two-bit fake African nigga preacher gonna even cross his path.

LEE: Akbara's got good chances. He's been in operation almost five years!

RUTH: That's nothin'! Milton's had his church going on twenty years now, and his congregation is more than half the Black folks in town.

LEE: Numbers don't mean nothin' if they're all a bunch of toms!

MAMA E: That's enough!

RUTH: Get out of here, Lee Jr.

JEREMY: What's the matter with you, man?

RUTH: *(Screaming)* Get out!

LEE: Yes Mam. You comin', Jeremy?

JEREMY: *(Uncomfortable)* Yeah. We told him we'd finish putting up that fence.

RUTH: Told who?

JEREMY: Akbara.

RUTH: Oh, so you workin' for him too?

JEREMY: Mama . . .

RUTH: Well, then you get the hell out too! I don't want to hear nothin' more about that nigga in my house, so if you goin', get the hell out now, and don't race no horses comin' back.

MAMA E: Ruth . . .

JEREMY: It's okay, Mama E. Come on man.

(They exit. There is silence for a while)

MAMA E: Ruth . . .

RUTH: I don't want to hear it, Mama.

MAMA E: Jeremy is your son!

RUTH: I know that. And I know perfectly well how to deal with my son, if that's what you're wondering.

MAMA E: You sure about that, girl?

RUTH: I am not a girl, and I don't care who's mouth it comes out of, I'll not have anybody bad-lacin' Milton's chances at that seat.

MAMA E: Jeremy didn't bad-lace nothin'!

RUTH: No, but he's going down to that preacher's church now, ain't he? Ain't that bad enough?

MAMA E: Ruth, you don't know nothin' about that man then what Lee Jr. told you, and that ain't fact—just his opinion is all.

RUTH: He shouldn't have said nothin'—fact or no!

MAMA E: He's young, Ruth.

RUTH: And since when did he start callin' you Mrs. Jones? Ain't it always been Mama E?

MAMA E: The boys' grown now.

RUTH: Well, which one is it, Mama? Young, or grown? Jeremy still calls you Mama E!

MAMA E: Jeremy's my grandson! What else he gon' call me?

RUTH: I'm sorry, Mama, I don't know, I guess I'm just not thinkin' right.

MAMA E: You got your head up in the Blue Room.

RUTH: *(Snapping)* That ain't so!

MAMA E: No?

RUTH: No, Mama. I want Milton to have that seat more than anything I've ever wanted in my life, except that Jeremy be born all right. And Milton wants it, Mama. He needs it. It's power, Mama. A man needs power, Milton does. And I want it for him. And ain't no damn nigga preacher gon' take it away from him or me! I mean it!

MAMA E: Now Ruth . . .

RUTH: When I was pregnant that first time, and we got married, Milton broke his back tending for me. He didn't have to. Didn't have to marry me at all. But he did, Mama, he did. Milton built this house practically by himself, Mama, so we could have a decent place to live—not that your old place wasn't decent, Mama, it just wasn't *your* place, or his.

MAMA E: I know that, child. And I'm grateful.

RUTH: Mama, he did everything for me. Sometimes too much. Treated me like an invalid sometimes, and I'd have to push him away. That hurt him, Mama, I know it did, but he'd always come back smilin', ready to help more. Poor Milton, always smilin', always gettin' pushed back away. He didn't understand that havin' a baby ain't painful—not for the whole nine months anyway. *(Pause)* When the baby died, was born dead, seemed like Milton died some too. Wasn't no-body's fault, the baby dyin', but Milton seemed to take it all on himself. It was like he had nothin' left to live for, like all his life was gone. He was still a good provider, but it seemed like our life together was more work for him than joy. He didn't laugh no more. He didn't smile. I knew he loved me, but his feelings seemed to be lost somewhere, tumblin' around inside. He was like a shadow, Mama. A man without the sun. It got so I prayed I'd do anything just to see him smile again. He touched me three times in five years. It was the third time that Jeremy was conceived—I prayed for that baby, Mama. Prayed he'd be born alive and healthy. Prayed for the baby's sake, and for mine—for Milton's—that things would change. That he would smile again. And he did, Mama. When the baby came, he was a happy man. Started comin' back to life. Started living again. That's when he started the church up, started his whole civil rights campaign—that's when everything started, Mama. Everything he is today. And Milton deserves this position, Mama. He's worked for it long and hard. It ain't like it's an award or somethin', Mama. He needs it. It's a new beginning, just like Jeremy was for him. A chance for him to smile again.

MAMA E: *(Looking at* RUTH*)* His smile been fading lately?

RUTH: *(Looks away)* Sort of. *(Wipes her eyes)* It's the pressure, Mama. All the things he has to do.

MAMA E: You talk with him about it? *(Ruth shakes her head)* Husbands and wives do talk, you know.

RUTH: Now, what is that supposed to mean?

MAMA E: It just seems to me that if you took a little more time to talk sensibly to the man instead of always telling him how great he is . . .

RUTH: He is a great man, Mama!

MAMA E: Sometimes I think you think he's too great. Sometimes on Sundays while he's standin' up there preachin', I wonder is it really God you praisin', or is it him?

RUTH: All right now, Mama . . .

MAMA E: Ruth, baby, any marriage . . .

RUTH: I have had twenty-seven years of marriage, Mama. Not any marriage, but this one! I should think by *this* time I should be able to define for myself what marriage is and what it is not. By myself, Mama. Without any help from you.

MAMA E: Very good, Ruth.

RUTH: Twenty-seven years, Mama. You know, that's over twice what you and Daddy had before he died. *(Realizes that she has wounded* MAMA E*)* I'm sorry, Mama. I didn't meant to . . .

MAMA E: *(Recovers)* Don't worry about it, daughter. Fussin' with you keeps me young.

RUTH: Keeps you young?

MAMA E: Umm hmmm. Next to your stubbornness and catty ways ain't nobody ever gon' call me old fashioned!

RUTH: Mama?

MAMA E: Yes? That's me.

RUTH: Why don't you turn the TV back on and go "think" some more to yourself? I like you much better that way.

MAMA E: That's not half a bad idea, Ruth. *(Yawns)* I got things I need to think about. *(She turns on the set, leans back in her chair, and closes her eyes.* RUTH *watches her then goes back to tending her roses)*

RUTH: *(Looks out window)* Rain done slacked up. Getting late though. Milton should be comin' soon, 'less another meetin' holds him up. *(Finishes arranging roses)* Mama, you like these? *(No answer)* Mama, I know you heard me. You ain't thinkin' that hard yet.

MAMA E: I heard you, Ruth. *(*RUTH *goes to her)*

RUTH: Well, do you like them?

MAMA E: *(Opens her eyes, sits up, and leans back away)* Where'd you get those roses, Ruth?

RUTH: From the garden, Mama. From the rose bush in the yard.

MAMA E: You cut that bush?

RUTH: Mama, they were drowning. The rain was beatin' 'em to death!

MAMA E: Better to have let them be. Don't you know it's bad luck bringin' cut flowers in the house?

RUTH: So you say. Don't nobody think like that but you. Besides, these flowers came from my own garden. Now what bad luck can that bring?

MAMA E: Cut is cut. And once they's cut they starts to dyin'. If I was you, I'd . . .

RUTH: Well, you ain't me, and they're stayin' right here. They look right pretty next to the pictures of Milton and Jeremy. Brings out their colors. Know what I mean?

MAMA E: Ruth, I been thinkin' . . .

RUTH: *(Fondling pictures)* Jeremy looks so cute next to his papa.

MAMA E: I *said* I been thinkin', Ruth!

RUTH: Of course you have—the TV's on.

MAMA E: Don't be smart! *(*RUTH *looks at her. Is quiet. After a moment* MAMA E *continues)* I said I been thinkin' . . . thinkin' 'bout what you said this morning about there being a middle. A middle ground.

RUTH: Yes?

MAMA E: Well, I'm thinkin' there just might be one though not quite way you see. *(*RUTH *crosses to her.* MAMA E *looks towards her, then away)* The middle ground is the old folks. A bridge of old souls between two sets of fools. Folks what grew up on slavery's tailcoat. What knew what hard work was, and what it meant. Folks that knew the ways of nature and listened to her signs, *(Looks at roses)* her warnings. You and Milton, Ruth—you're children of the middle ground. You got hopes and dreams and aspirations that put you off in a set off by yourself. You and other people like you. What's left then is the old folks. The middle ground. Here to cheer you on or pick up the pieces when you fall. Folks like you and Milton, and even Jeremy are dreamers, to the right or left of either side of fools. The middle ground is dead, or dying. The middle ground is me.

RUTH *watches as* MAMA E *leans back, closes her eyes, and goes to sleep. Slow fade.*

Scene 2

Setting: The Tyler living room, same day, later that night. MILTON *enters, very tired, rumpled, through the front door. He takes off his raincoat, hangs it on a hook and removes his shoes. He carries a small black metallic box, which he handles very carefully, and after some thought, places it on a shelf between two stacks of books. He loosens his tie, then turning, his eye is caught by an over-large note pinned (or taped) to the large armchair. In large letters it is addressed "Rev. T." He picks up the note, opens it, and reads it aloud.*

MILTON: "Dear Mil, Dinner's in the fridge and so is some fresh iced tea. The only thing that's warmed up for you is waiting for you upstairs and will cuss you out if you don't wake her up when you get home! I love you. Where the hell you been? Sincerely, Guess Who?" *(He laughs)* Guess who! My reason tells me that it wasn't Mama E! *(Laughs again)* Guess who. *(Tenderly)* Crazy lady. *(He leans back and stretches in the chair. Noticing the roses, he picks them up, inspects them, replaces them, and picks up and studies the photo of himself holding his son. He studies it for a long time; meanwhile, sounds of the back door opening are heard. It closes, and* JEREMY *enters through the kitchen door)*

JEREMY: *(Seeing* MILTON*)* Hello, Pop.

MILTON: Um? What?—Oh!—Jeremy! Hello, hello! *(Shakes head)* Whew! I was gone there for a minute!

JEREMY: *(Seeing photo)* Boning up on some heavy nostalgia?

MILTON: No, to tell the truth, one minute I was looking at this, and before I knew it, I was right in the middle of tomorrow's press conference.

JEREMY: *(Looking at photo)* An insult to be sure to the handsome fellow on the right.

MILTON: Apologies to be certain to the handsome, short, rather fat fellow on the right.

JEREMY: That's not fat, that's muscle.

MILTON: On a two year old?

JEREMY: Baby muscle.

MILTON: Never in your wildest baby dreams! That is pure babified poundage! *(They laugh)* Oh man, what time is it?

JEREMY: Ten to twelve. You just gettin' in?

MILTON: Yep. Dang reporters had me all day, doin' nothin'. Deacons' meeting at five. Hospital till seven, and then wound up back at the church trying to work on Sunday's sermon.

JEREMY: Got a press conference tomorrow, too, huh? I heard about the one you had today.

MILTON: Well, tomorrow's pretty much the same thing, except the Mayor will be there. Not a press conference really, just a bunch of people asking questions they already know the answers to.

JEREMY: Mama said you were pretty impressive.

MILTON: Your mama would be impressed if I sold toe shoes to an elephant!

JEREMY: So would I. Seriously, though, Pop, Mom said you were looking and doing very well.

MILTON: I have to. You think I can afford *not* to look well on TV in this town? This country even? I've got to look well, speak better than the reporters, and act as if the questions they ask are of any consequence at all. One slip up. One mistake, Jeremy, is all they need.

JEREMY: All who needs? The reporters?

MILTON: The reporters and every White person in this town. Plus every Black.

JEREMY: Black folks too? Come on, Pop, the folks in this town all love you. You're everybody's favorite son.

MILTON: Believe that myth if you want to, but just today, right after that TV thing, one of our distinguished racial members made it his business to jump to his feet and shout at the top of his lungs that Milton Tyler was a coward. A dark skinned White man with no heart for the people. Said that the people wanted *Akbara* and would see him get the seat.

JEREMY: Akbara!

MILTON: Yeah. You've heard the name?

JEREMY: Yeah, I . . . I've heard it. He . . . uh . . . used to teach at the university.

MILTON: Well, "Reverend" Akbara and I go back a nice long way. He was full of crap when I first met him, and he's full of more crap now. Only now he's got a little clan of big mouthed idiots doing his lying for him.

JEREMY: You know him well?

MILTON: Oh, from four or five years back. Too

long for me. Knew him since he first blew into town with his idea for a free food program. Ah, the same program that's just getting started now.

JEREMY: He started it five years ago?

MILTON: Oh yeah. Five whole years—give or take a month or two. . . . Akbara came to me and the Deacon's board trying to get us to help him get his project off the ground. Well, naturally, we said we'd help him. Crown Heights is way out of my district, so I was glad to see somebody trying to help those people out. The church raised two thousand dollars, all members' donations. Akbara took it and was back in three weeks saying it was not enough. We understood his problem, and from our own pockets got up another four hundred dollars for his project and offered him the services of one of our Deacons to help get his project in full swing. Deacon Parsons went with him, and for a while we heard nothing more about Akbara, or his project. Then one Sunday, after service, Deacon Parsons pulled us all into the meeting room and told us there was no way under heaven he would go back and work with Akbara again. It seemed like Akbara cussed too much for the Deacon. Too much cussin' and not enough prayin' is what the Deacon said. Now, we'd have been content to just send in another Deacon to take Brother Parson's place, but then he told us that what bothered him the most was that he couldn't see how the money Akbara had was being spent on food. Said he thought Akbara was buying guns instead.

JEREMY: Buyin' guns! Pop, you know how Parsons exaggerates . . .

MILTON: Exactly. Which is why I took it upon myself to visit Akbara's set-up myself. I didn't see any guns, but since I didn't see any food program either, I asked him, as a representative of the church, just how the money was spent. Well, damned if that nigga didn't go up on me like I had cussed his mama out! Man called me every name in the book and then some so low a toad wouldn't use 'em! Took off his coat and was ready to fight me.

JEREMY: You fought him?

MILTON: No. I turned and walked away, or tried to.

JEREMY: *Tried* to?

MILTON: Akbara ran at me—hit me so hard he knocked me down.

JEREMY: So you *did* fight him!

MILTON: No! *(Looks at his son)* . . . I didn't. *(Defensive logic)* There's no point, Jeremy, in fightin' a fool. It won't change him. Why waste your time? I didn't fight him. I walked away.

JEREMY: Oh . . . I see . . . uhh . . . you had any deal-

ings with him since then?

MILTON: Not directly, but yes.

JEREMY: How?

MILTON: *(Looks at JEREMY then gets up)* About three months later, Jeremy, a woman came crying, literally crying to me in my office at the church. Said her boy had been arrested and was being held without bail. *(Starts to pace, stretch)*

JEREMY: What'd he do?

MILTON: Robbed a store. Henson's, the big Jewish grocery on thirty-third.

JEREMY: A grocery store?

MILTON: Yep. The store was closed, and the boy had obviously been there for some time before somebody reported it. An off-duty cop tried to interfere and ended up with his brains all over the loading dock. Shot three times in the head. When the police arrived, the boy started running like he was trying to catch up with somebody. They caught him, and the boy gave up without a fight. Police say he just stood there while they disarmed him, never said a word as they took him away. Not a word. Now Jeremy, you know as well as I do that everybody knows there ain't no money kept in a store after it closes. If there is, it's kept in a safe. That boy never went near the safe, and had no tools on him anyway. He hadn't come there for money.

JEREMY: Well what!!!

MILTON: Food! The boy had sixteen boxes of canned goods lined up on the loading dock when the police arrived. Sixteen! And that's not all. The boy's gun had not been fired. Not recently. Not at all. Somebody else shot that cop. The same somebody that was going to transport sixteen boxes of food!

JEREMY: Akbara?

MILTON: It had to be. The police never proved anything because the boy wouldn't talk. I don't mean wouldn't confess—I mean wouldn't talk, would not utter one sound. Even when they told him he'd do time for armed robbery *and* murder, he never said a word. That's when his mama came to me. She wanted me to try to get the boy to talk so he could clear himself, do shorter time. The police had told her that if he'd name names, they'd drop the murder charge against him.

JEREMY: Did you go?

MILTON: Yes. *(He begins to pace again, stopping at the bookcase and fingering the metallic box during his speech)* I went that afternoon. The boy was sitting on the edge of his bunk, looking very sad, very afraid. When he saw me coming he scooted back on the bunk so far it seemed like he was trying to go through the opposite wall. I talked and talked to him, and finally he started to loosen up. He started crying, no sounds, but just tears, Lord, what tears! I came closer to him, telling him everything would work out, and it seemed like he believed me, or wanted to. Like he wanted to talk but was afraid to. I tried to help him along, talking to him, soothing him. I asked him who's idea the whole thing had been, and for a minute he looked like he was going to tell me. Then his face changed. The tears vanished as if they'd never been, and the face that had looked so sad, so fearful was glaring at me with all the hate a scared Black boy can know. He opened his mouth and started calling me the same filthy names I'd heard three months before.

JEREMY: Akbara!

MILTON: That's what I said. And no sooner than the name had passed my lips, that boy was up on me, and it took three policemen to get him off. The boy never said anything more after that. He was convicted for both theft and murder, but he didn't serve much time.

JEREMY: He was paroled?

MILTON: No. He was found in his cell at the State pen—dead. He hung himself.

JEREMY: And Akbara never said or did anything?

MILTON: No. Why should he? Nobody had anything on him. And as long as that free food and whatever else he's dishing out keeps coming, he's a saint in the people's eye. Incapable of wrong. A true Black soldier.

JEREMY: Holy shit.

MILTON: My sentiments exactly. However, being a man of the cloth and all that, I shall refrain from voicing that particular phrase. *(Yawns and almost drops box)* Oops, must be more tired than I thought.

JEREMY: What's in that box, Pop? I've never seen it before.

MILTON: I just dug it out of the church storeroom yesterday from the same place I chucked it almost twenty years ago. It's nothing really—just an old war souvenir. Something to remind me that I survived. *(He places the box back on the shelf, hesitates as if he would like to say more about it, then decides not to)* I'm very tired. Think I'll turn in now, *(Yawns)* though I know I'd sleep better if I had some idea what Sunday's sermon is going to be about. Tried to work on it some this evening, but nothing would come. Everything sounded like reruns of something I've said before.

JEREMY: Need some help?

MILTON: No, Buddah, that's okay.

JEREMY: Buddah! You haven't called me that since you could pick me up!

MILTON: Since I could pick me up! I'll have you know... *(Moves as though to pick up* JEREMY, *but*

realizing his son's height and weight, thinks better of the idea) ... oh, well.

JEREMY: *(Laughing)* Buddah!

MILTON: Well, it fit you then. You were such a verbal, philosophical little kid. I always thought you'd be a preacher. Ever give it any thought?

JEREMY: To tell you the truth, Papa, I haven't given much thought to anything since I got out of school. My carpentry and my wood shop are enough to keep me going right through here. When I want to do something else, I will.

MILTON: You'd make an awfully good one. Preacher, I mean.

JEREMY: I thought at one time I'd try it. Not in the conventional sense, though. Not so much emphasis on God. People tend to run "God" into the ground, you know? A lot of false imagery. Even calling God a He, or even a She is limiting, and therefore not the whole truth. Seems to me that people should just see God as a Power. Something greater than they are but who's in their corner, on their side. Something to really trust, really believe in. With all the easy weaponry and super bombs around that people know about, people ought to know that there's something more ... greater than man's power. If not, why not just worship bombs instead?

MILTON: Some people do. Well, you've given me an idea for Sunday's sermon.

JEREMY: Yeah?

MILTON: Yep. For the zillionth time. Someday I'll stop saying no when you ask if you can help me.

JEREMY: *(Laughing)* Remember the first time?

MILTON: How could I forget? It was the first sermon I gave as full Minister, some fourteen years ago. Easter Sunday, too.

JEREMY: You bribed me into helping you, remember?

MILTON: Oh yeah. It was the only way I could make sure you'd stay awake. Lord, Lord, I was so nervous, memorizing that thing. Felt sure I'd blow it, put the whole congregation to sleep. You were my trial audience. Must have gone over that thing fifty times with you. And you sittin' up each time sayin', "That's good, Daddy, try it again!"

JEREMY: Shoot, I was finishing off Mama's pound cake. The longer you talked, the more I got to eat. Finished the whole thing, then Mama came down.

MILTON: And Lord, how she threw a fit. Not just because her prize cake was gone, but because I'd kept you up with me half the night.

JEREMY: I went to bed mumbling that sermon. Knew it by heart.

MILTON: *(Nods)* Sure did.

JEREMY: And Sunday, I was right there next to Mama. Mouthing every word.

MILTON: You remembered?

JEREMY: Heck, yeah! I was waitin' for you to slip up so that I could get my chance.

MILTON: Lord, no! And I almost messed up, too!

JEREMY: Ummm hmmm, sure did. And I was ready, but you covered yourself with "Hallelujahs" till you got back on the right track.

MILTON: You remember all that?

JEREMY: Sure. In fact, the following week when I was back at school, during recess, there was a dead bird on the baseball field. Well, I remembered my Daddy's sermon on death and dying—the Resurrection—and I'll have you know I gathered the entire second grade and preached a sermon around that thing—yes I did! Same lines you used. Had half the class scared to death themselves! *(They both laugh)*

MILTON: What did your teacher say?

JEREMY: Nothin'! She'd been at Sunday's service so this was just reliving it for her. When I called for Hallelujahs, . . .

MILTON: You didn't.

JEREMY: Oh yes I did! When I called for hallelujahs, she was right there, one arm raised, hand waving, swinging from side to side—giving me "Praise the Lord" right back.

MILTON: Oh no!

JEREMY: Everybody was moving. The kids were scared their teacher'd gone beserk! But just like church, everybody was too scared to leave. Could have gone on forever, 'cept for one thing.

MILTON: What's that?

JEREMY: Well, Miss Patterson, the teacher, didn't like it none when I started passing my lunch box for collections!

MILTON: *(Laughing)* Oh Lord!

JEREMY: Yep. Had almost a dollar ninety-six cents. Big time! Before I passed it to her. Something told me I shouldn't have, 'cause when she grabbed that box . . .

MILTON: She grabbed it?

JEREMY: Heck, yeah, and was almost halfway into her pocket before she opened her eyes and realized where she was!

MILTON: *(Doubled in laughter)* Oh no, no, no!

JEREMY: Lord, she paddled me so hard and then threatened the whole class that if we ever told anyone about her she'd have us all put out of school!

MILTON: That why you never told me about it?

JEREMY: No, I knew I could have told you. Paddling or no paddling, I was proud of what I did.

MILTON: Then why?

JEREMY: Truth of the matter is, I was too proud to.

MILTON: Too proud!

JEREMY: Yep. I was awfully sleepy when I helped you memorize your text, and though I knew it all by heart that Sunday, when I got back to school I'd forgotten many of the words—had to make up some of my own.

MILTON: That would have been okay.

JEREMY: Okay for me, sure—but not to share with you. For you it had to be perfect, and it wasn't. So I just kept my little adventure to myself.

MILTON: You're somethin' else, boy. All that over a bird.

JEREMY: Umm hmmm. A robin.

MILTON: Wish I'd been there to hear it.
(JEREMY looks at MILTON, stands, and walks across the room, facing upstage. He stops, finds his ground, and turning around, begins to reenact the sermon)

JEREMY: Brother Robin Redbreast. . . . How . . . tell me *how* did you fall so low?

MILTON: *(Laughing)* Oh no! Help me! Save me!

JEREMY: Ye that have soared, and known the flight of life, despair ye not in death, for death itself is but yet another journey. Over farther seas. And higher mountains than you've ever flown before! Can I get a Witness?

MILTON: All right! Can *I* get a Witness?

JEREMY: You got it, Pop.

MILTON: All right! *(Joining sermon)* And ye that are bereaved—weep not for those departed. For your tears, they do not help them . . .

JEREMY: Do not guide them on their way. But instead, tears tend to hinder, to hold them close, to slow down their journey from this earth.

MILTON: Make not your bind twixt life and death with sorrow . . .

JEREMY: But with support! For the soul is recently moved from its familiar temple and may be afraid to venture forth.

MILTON: Speak then not of your own bereavement—but of the bereavement of the dead. For they have lost so that they may gain, and your support is needed to help them on their new way.

MILTON *and* JEREMY: Speak then—not of your own losses to those closed, unmoving eyes. Whisper not your grief beside that closed and lonely coffin. Say not, say not, "Come back my love." But say instead, though it may pull the very life-strings of your heart . . . say instead, in tenderness, "Fly on, my love. Be free." Can I get a Witness?

JEREMY: Yes! Can I get a Witness?

MILTON: Oh Yes! *(They pause, look at each other)* Hallelujah!

JEREMY: Praise the Lord!

MILTON: *Hallelujah!!*

JEREMY: So Brother Robin—spread your wings and fly again.

MILTON: Yes!

JEREMY: On the winds and wings of God!

MILTON: Yes!

JEREMY: Soar into the atmosphere!

MILTON: Yes!

JEREMY: The stratosphere!

MILTON: Yes!

JEREMY: The hemisphere!

MILTON: *(He stops)* The hemisphere?

JEREMY: Well, I was only in the second grade! Hell if I knew what any of those spheres meant! I was just preachin'!

MILTON: You sure were doin' that!

JEREMY: Can I get an Amen?

MILTON: *(Laughing)* Amen, Jeremy, Amen!

RUTH: *(Enters in robe from upstairs)* What's all this noise down here? That you, Milton?

MILTON: *(To JEREMY)* Now she's gonna act like she ain't seen me in so long she's forgot what I look like! *(To RUTH)* No dear, it isn't Milton. It's a great big talking Grizzly Bear right here in your living room.

RUTH: Well that's one grizzly bear better slide a bear hug over this way before he winds up a trophy! *(MILTON laughs, goes to RUTH, picks her up, hugs her. JEREMY exits into kitchen. RUTH, shrieking)* Ahh! Help! Put me down, you beast! *(He does, she punches him)* Not here, you fool, *upstairs!*

MILTON: Please my dear—we have a guest!

RUTH: *(Looking over his shoulder)* What guest?

MILTON: A travelling minister. Reverend Jeremy ... *(He turns, sees no one)* He's gone! Where'd he go? He was just right here! Jeremy! Jeremy!

JEREMY: *(Appears in the kitchen doorway, solemn, sad)* Yeah?

MILTON: What happened? What the hell is wrong with you?

JEREMY: It's nothing, Papa—really.

RUTH: It's me, Milton.

MILTON: You?

RUTH: Ummm hmmm. We had a kind of run in earlier today. Jeremy's friend, Lee Jr. was sayin' some things I didn't like—and well, you know me—I got hot and threw both of 'em out.

MILTON: Oh?

RUTH: Yes. And I'm sorry, Jeremy. I really am. What Lee Jr. said didn't have a thing to do with you.

JEREMY: It's okay. Forget it, Mom. Really, just forget ...

MILTON: What kind of things was Lee Jr. saying?

JEREMY: It was really nothin', Papa—you don't ...

RUTH: It was awful, Milton! Boy called you and us and the congregation a bunch of toms. Said some

other reverend would probably beat you out of that council seat!

MILTON: What!

RUTH: Uhh huh! Some crazy sounding name. What was it, Jeremy? Jeremy?

JEREMY: *(Quietly)* Akbara.

MILTON: Akbara!

RUTH: Ummm hmmm. And see, Jeremy hadn't said nothin'. Even tried to keep Lee Jr. quiet. But when ...

JEREMY: It's okay, Mom. Forget it—please—okay?

MILTON: When what?

RUTH: Well, when Jeremy was gonna go with him to finish building on that fence ...

MILTON: What *fence?*

JEREMY: Akbara's fence.

MILTON: You mean to tell me you've been working for that man?

JEREMY: Not working for him. Just helping him get settled in his ...

MILTON: Why didn't you tell me this before?

JEREMY: It's not important, Pop.

MILTON: It damn sure is important. You are my son.

JEREMY: I'm also a grown man.

MILTON: Regardless. What's it gonna look like with my own flesh and blood aiding my opposition?

RUTH: Your what?

MILTON: Opposition, Ruth. *Opposition*, Jeremy. Akbara's the only Black man in this town with half a chance at getting that position over me. The man's probably out there now, *campaigning* for himself! I told you that, Jeremy.

JEREMY: But I didn't think you meant he was seriously campaigning ...

MILTON: You think I thought he was *playing* with me?

JEREMY: But you didn't seem all that phased by him. You said he was a fool, a liar!

MILTON: Fools and liars have a lot of pull in this country—or hadn't you noticed that?

JEREMY: Dad, I ...

MILTON: I can't have it, Jeremy. It's just too risky. Akbara knows what he's doing in getting you to help him out.

JEREMY: He didn't *get* me. I came with Lee.

MILTON: I don't care if you came with Jesus!

RUTH: Milton!

JEREMY: I only helped the man to build a fence.

MILTON: It doesn't matter what you do. You're my son. That's what matters to him. He'll use you to get that position over me.

JEREMY: Dad, there are some things he's doing that are okay.

MILTON: Like what? The free food program?

JEREMY: Well, yeah.

MILTON: Even after what I told you?

JEREMY: Just based on what I've seen, Pop.

MILTON: I swear, Jeremy—sometimes I think you spend too much time shut off in that damn woodshop of yours. What you see don't count for nothin'! It's what you *know!*

JEREMY: He is *feeding* people!

MILTON: That man feeds people on anger. Feeds people on lies, on his own guilt, his own hate! That the kind of diet you like, Jeremy?

JEREMY: No, but . . .

MILTON: But what?

JEREMY: Look, I told the man I'd do some construction work for him, and I'm not going to *not* do it just because you say. I'll weigh everything all over again and find my own reasons to go . . . or to stay.

MILTON: Or *stay?*

JEREMY: Or stay!

MILTON: *(Furious)* Listen boy . . .

MAMA E: *(From upstairs)* Milton . . . Jeremy . . . somethin' wrong? What's happenin' down there?

RUTH: I'll go tend to Mama. *(Exits)*

MILTON: *(Softer, tired)* Jeremy—I can't afford to have you connected with that man, with Akbara. I've got more interviews tomorrow. Akbara will no doubt be there, and I can't have that man use public TV to throw your name up in my face, Jeremy! I . . . I need to know tonight, no, *right now*, Jeremy—exactly what it is you plan to do.

JEREMY: *(Slowly)* I don't know.

Lights fade slowly, MILTON *in silhouette, special on* JEREMY.

Scene 3

Setting: Morning. Basement of Akbara's church. Planks, wood crates, etc. are piled up, or propped up, or strewn about. Some are marked as to what they will be used for. Others appear to be waiting. The aura of the shop is one of waiting. It is LEE'S *workshop. Planks bar the sunlight trying to come through a dusty window.* LEE *moves a plank to allow more light in then joins* JEREMY *in disassembling crates and pulling nails out of old boards.*

LEE: I don't know, man. It just doesn't seem like Akbara. I mean, if the brother was one of Akbara's workers, Akbara would have fought tooth and nail to keep him from gettin' sent up at all.

JEREMY: Yeah, maybe.

LEE: Maybe? You gotta be kiddin', brother. The main thing Akbara teaches is that we have to be loyal to each other. Stick together for the cause. You know that, right?

JEREMY: Yeah . . .

LEE: Right. So knowing that, do you really think he'd let that brother be sent up without a word— with no support?

JEREMY: Well, man . . .

LEE: He couldn't have been one of Akbara's people or Akbara would have . . .

JEREMY: No man, he wouldn't have!

LEE: What?

JEREMY: Not if Akbara himself was in danger. Not at the risk of getting sent up to jail himself!

LEE: You're crazy, man.

JEREMY: No—uh uh—listen. How many times has Akbara said himself that no ship can run without it's captain?

LEE: Aww man, he just says that to teach the kids in the program about the values of leadership.

JEREMY: *Who's* leadership, Lee?

LEE: Anybody's leadership.

JEREMY: Anybody's, Lee?

LEE: Okay, okay, Jeremy! So he's talking about himself. So what? The man's entitled . . .

JEREMY: To send some kid out on a "holy mission" for him, leave him, see him get busted and still not lift a finger to help him . . .

LEE: For the sake of the church!

JEREMY: Beginning to see it now?

LEE: Look, man, lots of kids get caught trying to rob stores.

JEREMY: Of *food*, man?

LEE: Yeah.

JEREMY: *Sixteen crates* full? No transportation? Alone? With just a gun?

LEE: *(Lowering his voice)* Okay, man, okay—be cool. Look, let's just drop it, okay? Neither one of us has any proof that Akbara was or was not involved. And even if he was, that was five years ago. What difference does it make now?

JEREMY: The boy killed himself, Lee!

LEE: So what? Lots of people do.

JEREMY: So what happens when Akbara sends *you* on one of his "missions." Suppose you get caught, man. What happens to your support?

LEE: I'm sure I'd get it. Besides, even if I didn't, one thing my dear old daddy taught me just before his final contradiction, is that suicide can be very detrimental to your health. He even went so far as to illustrate the point.

JEREMY: Your father killed himself, Lee?

LEE: I don't know. Some say he did. Could have been murder. But if he did, well those are some footsteps, buddy boy, that I definitely do not intend to follow in. Got my drift?

JEREMY: Yeah.

LEE: So don't worry about me, old buddy. I'll be fine. . . . *(Teasing)* But what about you man? Suppose he wants to be sending you?

JEREMY: Sheeee-it! . . . He'd better think again! *(They both laugh)* Besides, I'm pullin' out, man, for a while.

LEE: *(Serious)* What?

JEREMY: Till this city council stuff is over. My dad's up for it, Akbara's up for it—so me—I'm staying clear of all this stuff till it's over and done with.

LEE: But you can't just up and leave, just like that!

JEREMY: Why not? I've done all I can do for now anyway—'cept those boards over there, and I can finish them up today. That's it. Plus rounding up those clothes drying over at the house—

LEE: I don't believe you, man.

JEREMY: What? Why not?

LEE: You mean your commitment stops with some old boards and some dingy shirts? I don't believe you, Jeremy. It ain't real for you.

JEREMY: Look Lee, you know I've never been into Akbara's movement like you have. I mean—look, you've joined his church—you're a member. I just . . .

LEE: Came along for a free ride.

JEREMY: I wouldn't exactly call all the work I've been doing here a free ride!

LEE: Man, that work is payment for all you've been taking out of here.

JEREMY: Wait a minute—hold it. Something's been twisted all around. As I see it, brother Lee, these are my hands, my tools, my sweat, and my time. All I've taken away from here is my own fatigue, and splinters.

LEE: What about the teachings, man? The things Akbara has said, man, in his lectures.

JEREMY: What lectures? The only things Akbara has ever said to me are, "Nice work, little brother," or "I like your craftmanship, little brother," or "Little brother, why don't you go fix the—

LEE: Okay, man.

JEREMY: It's true. He may come and drop pearls of wisdom at your feet, but all I've heard from him is how fortunate he is to have found good help!

LEE: Jeremy . . .

JEREMY: And what's all this "little brother" stuff anyway? He addresses me the same way he does the kids in the food program!

LEE: It's because you're not initiated.

JEREMY: *What?*

LEE: You're not initiated, little broth— I mean, Jeremy. Only the initiated are called by their proper names.

JEREMY: I notice he calls you Lee . . .

LEE: That's because I've passed the first level of initiation. I've been accepted as a member of the church.

JEREMY: Accepted? I thought all you had to do was *join* the church.

LEE: No. I was accepted. I passed the first in a series of initiation tests. Every member of the church has passed initiation.

JEREMY: Yeah? Well what about all those people who come to his lectures at night? They initiated too?

LEE: No. They're not really members. They're the general public, and they're welcome any time. But to actually function within the structure of the church, you have to become a member.

JEREMY: And you're a member? *(LEE nods)* Sounds weird, man. Like a cult or something.

LEE: It's more like an army. The first level, the "boot camp" of the church is the mental level. That's where the history and basic philosophy and theology of the church are taught. I took History of Revolt and Social Structure from Akbara back in school—so all I had to do to pass that was just review. The second level I passed too. *(Looks at his foot)* It was harder though. Lots of physical training stuff.

JEREMY: Yeah? *(Takes another board)* Like what?

LEE: Army guerilla type stuff, man. Survival techniques. Shooting, hand to hand combat, fasting for long periods of time. Lots of emphasis on endurance of physical pain.

JEREMY: He taught you all that?

LEE: No, a brother from the service. Akbara supervised the fasting part, but the rest was taught by an ex-full-fledged US Marine. *(Laughs and salutes)*

JEREMY: If you wanted pain, man, why didn't you just join the Army full out?

LEE: This way I can get the training without having to kill some yellow or brown skinned brother to get it. I can put it to good use right here at home where it counts. Fending off the pigs that surround and harrass us . . .

JEREMY: *(Laughs)* Man, you sound like a poster out of 1968.

LEE: *(Grabbing him)* What you trying to say, man?

JEREMY: *(Freeing himself)* Nothin', man. Except that for a minute you sounded like the old rev—

LEE: The revolution isn't dead, little brother. Oh, it may be sleeping for pretty boys like you with preacher daddies and nice houses to go home to. But it's never slept for me, man. It's never slept for me. In fact, if anything, man, it's more awake than ever, and's about to take another turn.

JEREMY: What turn is that, Lee?

LEE: *(Quiet, yet intense)* Tomorrow, Jeremy. Tomorrow I take part one of my third level initiation. *(Pauses)* I won't be Lee no more, man. Lee Watkins, Jr. will be dead. Dead just like Lee Watkins the first. 'Cept in Lee Jr.'s place there won't be a cold gray slab like the one that marks his father. In Lee Watkins, Jr.'s place will be a new man with a new name. Lee Watkins, Jr. will be over. And a new man's revolution will have just begun. *(There is silence.* JEREMY *places board back against the wall)* You understand me, man?

JEREMY: Yeah man, I do.

LEE: For half my life I've carried a dead man's name around, Jeremy. A dead man. A man who died in my mind a long time before he made it to the grave. And once he made it, the name lived on. In me. *On* me! I couldn't move without it, couldn't even talk to myself without hearing it. I hated it, man. Hated it! Know what I mean?

JEREMY: Yes.

LEE: That's why you shouldn't leave, man. Not for nothin'. For any length of time.

JEREMY: What? Why?

LEE: Because you understand. . . . Look, Akbara likes you, Jeremy. He wants you in the church. And since you took his course already, all you'd have to do is study—just review a little bit, man, and you'd be first level just like that! With your carpentry skills, man, you'd be an asset. We need craftsmen as well as fighters. Akbara *wants* you, man!

(There is silence for a moment, then Jeremy speaks)

JEREMY: What's the second part, Lee?

LEE: Second part?

JEREMY: The rite, man. The initiation. You said you take the first part of level three tomorrow—the naming, like you said. That's pretty serious business, man. What's the second part?

LEE: I don't know.

JEREMY: You don't know?

LEE: *(Angry)* No man, I don't!

JEREMY: Are you crazy, man? You mean you're gonna go this far, change your whole life, and *not know* what's coming up ahead?

LEE: *(Quietly, cautiously)* It's a secret ceremony, Jeremy. That's all I know, and I'm not supposed to repeat that. It's between me and Rev. Akbara, or whoever he appoints to bring me in. It's the highest ceremony, Jeremy, and even after it's over, you're not supposed to tell anybody what it is. There's only one thing left after that, and that's to bring another member into the church as a confirmation of your faith, your allegiance to the church and to Akbara.

JEREMY: Where does it all happen, Lee?

LEE: In Akbara's private chambers.

JEREMY: When?

LEE: Whenever Akbara or whoever's going to

bring you in decides you're ready. Listen, I haven't even gone through phase one of third level yet.

JEREMY: Yeah, well just make sure phase two ain't some excuse for your Rev. Akbara to peg you in the butt!

LEE: *(Swings a board at him—*JEREMY *ducks, jumps clear)* I ought to kill you, man! *(Swings again)*

JEREMY: Hey be cool, Lee! Put the board down, man!

LEE: Don't call me Lee no more mothaafucka! Don't call me nothin' anymore!

JEREMY: Hold it—simmer down, man! *(*LEE *swings again, looses the board, grabs a crutch)* Calm down, man, before you hurt yourself!

LEE: Ain't nobody gonna hurt but *you,* mothaafucka! Nobody but you!

(He swings again, JEREMY *ducks under the crutch and comes up—grabs it and* LEE, *and pins him to the ground under the crutch.* LEE, *trying to break free)* I'll kill you, man! I'll kill you!

JEREMY: *(Softer)* Easy, brother, easy. Just calm down, man, calm down.

LEE: *(Sobbing)* I really ought to kill you, man!

JEREMY: No man, you ain't gonna kill me. You're gonna breathe easy and calm down, man. Then I'm gonna let you up. You hear me? You hear me, Lee?

LEE: *(Struggling to get up)* Don't call me Lee no more, man! *(Sits up facing* JEREMY*)* Lee Watkins, Jr. is dead!

JEREMY: *(Restraining him)* No man, he isn't. *(*LEE *struggles,* JEREMY *holds firm)* Lee Watkins, Jr. is still alive—

LEE: No!

JEREMY: Yes! And he's my friend, man. My friend. *(Loosens his hold on* LEE *and becomes tender in touching him)* He's my friend, man. And I love him. *(Takes* LEE's *face in his hands)* I love him. Hear what I said? And no matter what he calls himself, I'm still gonna love him. No matter what he has me call him, he's still gonna be my friend. You got that? You got that?

LEE: Yes.

JEREMY: All right. *(He embraces* LEE, *rocking him, stroking his back, his neck, holding him . . .)*

LEE: I'm scared, man . . . Jeremy. I'm scared.

JEREMY: I know. Easy now, Take it easy. I know.

LEE: Jeremy . . . man, think about it. If you joined up, we could work *together—*

JEREMY: I can't do that, man. I told you—

LEE: Because of your *father,* man?

JEREMY: It's not his decision, Lee. It's mine.

LEE: You can't leave, man. You just can't. Akbara wants you, man. And I need you.

JEREMY: I'm not leaving *you.* But I am leaving this

cult or church or whatever it is. *(Pauses)* I'm leaving now. You can come with me if you want to. Take a little time to relax—think things over. Or if you don't want to . . . to think—if you're all decided, then come on and share some fresh air, some good feelings with your friend over here.

LEE: I'd like to, but I've got some things I uh—need to study, Jeremy. For tomorrow . . . you know?

JEREMY: I gotcha, brother. *(Pauses)* Hey look, I know you're frightened, that there's a whole lot going on through your head. I can't stay, but you know where you can reach me. *(Looks at him)* I love you man. I'll always want to help you out in any way I can. Any time. *(Pauses)* Lee? *(LEE doesn't answer)* Lee?

LEE: Yeah?

JEREMY: You understand me?

(LEE hesitates, then looks up at JEREMY. Eye contact)

LEE: *(Softly)* Yes.

Slow fade

ACT TWO

Scene 1

Setting: The Tyler living room, late afternoon. MAMA E sleeps in her chair by the TV set. RUTH and JEREMY are upstairs. Noises of furniture being moved are heard. The TV drones on with some endless talk or game show—barely audible above the noise of JEREMY and RUTH. JEREMY enters coming down the steps, carrying a huge mirror. RUTH is right behind him. Both of their voices are heard.

JEREMY: I got it, Ma, I got it.

RUTH: Now be careful Jeremy, that mirror's as old as my mother.

JEREMY: You hear that, Mama E? Oops!

RUTH: Jeremy!

JEREMY: I got it, I got it—just a little slip, that's all.

RUTH: A little slip!

JEREMY: *(Down the stairs)* Shhhh, be quiet. You'll wake up Mama E.

RUTH: She ain't sleepin'. *(Also down)* She's thinkin'! Ain't you, Mama? *(MAMA E doesn't answer)* Well Lord, I finally caught her when she's sleep. *(To JEREMY)* It's a good thing too. She'd have a fit if she knew I was movin' her bedroom downstairs. Don't care what she says though, Mama's too old to be going up and down those steps. Besides, the den's got more sunlight, and it's got its own door to the porch. Now go on and move

that mirror in there. It's the last piece, and it's gonna make that room look just like her room looked upstairs. Careful now.

(JEREMY exits—side doorway, carrying mirror)

MAMA E: *(Eyes still closed)* Think you're pretty dang smart, don't you?

RUTH: *(Startled)* What?

MAMA E: *(Calmly)* If he breaks that mirror, I'll break your face.

RUTH: Mama!

MAMA E: *(Laughs)* Well now that I've been evicted, might as well go check out my new cell!

RUTH: Mama—you're awful!

MAMA E: Thought you knew that by now. *(RUTH crosses to MAMA E and wheels her into the room)* Jeremy—come on out now. I'm comin' in and I intend to be indecent. You've been warned.

JEREMY: *(Coming out as they go in)* Got you loud and clear, Mama E. You ladies call me if you need something else moved. *(He moves into living room, stoops to cut off the TV when the doorbell rings. He answers it. LEE enters)* Lee! Hey—*(Hugs him)* How you doin', man?

LEE: *(Starts to say something, says something else instead)* Uh, fine, man. Listen, I came to get those boxes of clothes we left over here . . .

JEREMY: Oh yeah, man. Come on in. I'll get 'em. I almost forgot. Hang-tight for a minute. *(Runs upstairs)*

LEE: Yeah. *(He stands rather rigidly, formally, in the living room. RUTH and MAMA E's voices are heard in the other room)*

MAMA E: I don't care what you say, I ain't sleepin' with my feet pointing to the north! My head's been north for ninety years and I ain't changin' now! I don't intend to die and meet Jesus with my feet!

RUTH: All right, Mama. Here—I'll turn the bed around!

MAMA E: Got to do more than that. Got to make it up all over again, the other way!

RUTH: Okay, Mama. I'll do it now.

MAMA E: *(Leaving room)* Good. Call me when you finish. *(She heads into living room. JEREMY heads back downstairs carrying a box of clothes. MAMA E stops short upon seeing LEE)*

LEE: Good afternoon, Mrs. Jones. How are you?

MAMA E: *(Continuing to her TV set)* I believe I'm doin' right fine, Lee Jr.

LEE: Abdullah. *(JEREMY looks at him)*

MAMA E: *(Looking at LEE)* What's that?

LEE: Abdullah, Mam.

MAMA E: *(Looking around)* Somebody sneeze? *(JEREMY hides a laugh)*

LEE: No Mam. I said Abdullah. Instead of Lee Jr. I've changed my name.

MAMA E: *(Studying him)* Changed your name?

LEE: Yes Mam.

MAMA E: To what?

LEE: Abdullah. Abdullah ben Kahim.

MAMA E: Come again?

LEE: Abdullah ben Kahim.

MAMA E: Abdullah ben Kay...

LEE: Kahim, Mam. Adbullah ben Kahim.

MAMA E: Um, um, ummm, *(To* JEREMY*)* What does that make you? Tonto? *(*JEREMY *breaks up laughing.* LEE *looks embarrassed—stern)*

JEREMY: *(To* LEE*)* I'm sorry, man, but "Tonto"— *(Laughs again.* LEE *looks uncomfortable, but as* JEREMY *tries to sober himself,* MAMA E*, having placed her handkerchief over her glasses, begins humming the theme from the* Lone Ranger, *cracking* JEREMY *up and further infuriating* LEE*)*

LEE: I take part two tonight, Jeremy! *(Ineffective, he repeats himself...louder)* I take part two tonight! *(*JEREMY *sobers)*

JEREMY: Come on, man, we can talk upstairs.

LEE: Okay. *(Both head upstairs)*

MAMA E: Abdullah... *(Both freeze)*

LEE: Mam?

MAMA E: There's somethin' in a name, you know. More than just sounds and letters. You know that?

LEE: Yes Mam, I do.

MAMA E: A name has a place on somebody. Has it's meanin'. Name's 'sposed to fit you. Fit just like your skin. You know that?

LEE: Yes Mam.

MAMA E: You know what my name is?

LEE: No Mam. Not past Mrs. Jones or Mama E.

MAMA E: Jones don't count. It's my married name. Married name ain't worth much. It's the name you're born with makes a difference in your life. Jeremy, you don't know my name, do you?

JEREMY: Not past Mama E. You told me once but—

MAMA E: You don't remember. I told you when you was still a little baby. Whispered it in your ear. Whisper still there to remind you if you listen hard enough.

JEREMY: Mama E, I don't recall anybody ever callin' you by your first name.

MAMA E: First names are sacred. When I was born, my Daddy whispered my name into my ear. My mama had whispered it to him, and God had whispered it to her. A name was somethin' special. To be held on to, like a little piece of music all your own. My family name—last name you call it—was—*is* Rose, just like the flower. It were my father's name his father give him while still in slavery. A secret name. Known just between

them. Name to pass on to his family when he had one—if he lived that long. Those days, the name you known by was the name the massa had. My granddaddy and daddy was both on the Jessup Morton plantation—so when my daddy was born, his *known* last name was Morton. His *real* last name was Rose. Like a long line of slave Black men who answered to Jackson, or Washington, or Morton—but knew they real names was somethin' else. Was somethin' wild and beautiful and free. My daddy's name was Rose.

JEREMY: And your name, Mama E?

MAMA E: *(Looking at him)* Throughout my life, I've answered to many names. Earline, Lena, Earla May.... But the name my daddy whispered into my ear was Early. Early, like when the sun comes up, like the frost before the snow. Early May Rose. That's what he called me. That's what Mama whispered to him. It's what my mama called me till the day she died. She called me Early. Early May.

JEREMY: Early May Rose.

MAMA E: Now don't you go 'round sayin' it. It isn't yours to say. Name stays sacred, holds its meanin' when it's only used at the proper time. Jacob Jones, your grandpa—man I married, didn't know his other—his real name, and wouldn't accept mine. You ask me, that's why he died so young—wasn't but fifty-five—and me older than him! Man need to know his name. You remember that, Lee Jr., I mean—Abdullah.

LEE: Yes Mam, I sure will. Thank you, Mrs. Jones.

MAMA E: Umm hmm—Abdullah—

LEE: Yes Mam?

MAMA E: It's Mama E.

LEE: Yes Mam! Thank you, Mama E!

MAMA E: Don't mention it. Now git on up where you goin' fore you talk me half to death. *(To* JEREMY*)* You too, Kimosabe. Go on now—git! *(They laugh, exit upstairs,* MAMA E *goes back to her TV set)* Lord, Lord...Abdullah! Why not somethin' more simple, like Thistle, or Briarwood, or Rose? I guess I...

RUTH: *(Enters from back room)* Mama, I—*(front door opens.* MILTON *enters)* Milton! *(She runs to him, hugs him, and backs off)* What happened to your face?

MILTON: Nothing, Ruth. What time is it now?

RUTH: Nothing! *(She touches his face—he winces)* Milton, it looks like somebody punched you right in the—

MILTON: I said *nothing*, Ruth. Now turn on the TV please, it's time for the six o'clock news. *(He removes his coat, turning so that his face is downstage. He has a large bruise below his left eye.* RUTH *turns towards TV,* MAMA E *waves her away)*

MAMA E: I got it.

(MAMA E *clicks on set.* RUTH *turns back to* MILTON. *He has a handkerchief out, dabbing his bruise.* RUTH *comes to him)*

RUTH: Oh Milton! *(He turns away from her, gestures for her to listen to the news,* MAMA E *turns it up)*

NEWS COMMENTATOR: Mayor Abraham Shillet announced his choice today as to who will fill the city council seat vacated by the late Harry S. Dowell. These and other stories coming up on the six o'clock news.

MAMA E: Jeremy! Come on down here! Your father's gonna be on TV!

JEREMY: Comin'!

RUTH: You don't know that, Mama. The commentator only said—

MAMA E: I do know what I do know. *(Looks at* RUTH) Since when you start being skeptical?

RUTH: I'm not skeptical, Mama, I *(Sees* LEE *entering with* JEREMY. *To* LEE) I didn't know *you* were here.

LEE: I'll be leaving now, Mam.

MILTON: It's all right boy, sit down.

RUTH: Milton, I told Lee Jr. not to step foot in this house again and—

MAMA E: That ain't Lee Jr. That's Abdullah. Now hush and listen to the news. (RUTH *looks perplexed, then obeys)*

NEWS COMMENTATOR: Mayor Abraham Shillet announced that for the first time in almost a century, a Black man will fill a city council seat. Rev. Milton Tyler will fill the seat vacated by the late Harry S. Dowell. Mayor Shillet had these comments:

VOICE OF MAYOR SHILLET: Milton Tyler—Rev. Tyler is the best possible man to fill this job. His significant contributions and dedication to the Black and poor communities in this city have singled him out as the best possible choice. He is, a good man.

JEREMY: That's great, Pop! *(Turns and sees him)* What happened to your face? *(LEE looks also.* MILTON *says nothing, points to TV)*

NEWS COMMENTATOR: There were others, however, not so pleased with the Mayor's choice. Rev. Akbara of the Church of the People, a relatively small Black sector in town, and several of his followers rose loud objections to the mayor's decision. Akbara demanded to use the mayor's microphone to air his views, and when denied permission, stood on a conference table and shouted, and I quote "He's a White man. Tyler's a White man. A coward. A White man in Black skin. That's why he got the seat. The Mayor's scared of a real Black man. Scared of a man like

me." End quote. Mayor Shillet had no answer, but Rev. Tyler took the microphone. Before he could speak, however, Tyler was struck in the face with an ashtray thrown by Akbara. A mêlée erupted with Akbara's followers battling police and newsmen. Rev. Tyler did not require hospitalization as was feared, and when asked if he would press charges, said he was undecided at that time. Akbara and seven followers are being held meanwhile at at the city jail pending formal charges of assault and disturbing the peace. In the world news today . . . (MAMA E *turns TV off)*

RUTH: Undecided! That crazy nigga half knocks you out, and you're undecided?

LEE: *(To* JEREMY) I didn't know about any of this. I swear I didn't—

MAMA E: I believe you, boy.

RUTH: How can you not be decided? That man hurt you! And he shamed you on TV!

MILTON: The man shamed no one but himself!

RUTH: You got the ashtray!

MILTON: What would you have me do? Throw it back?

RUTH: You could have done somethin'!

MILTON: What!

RUTH: Said somethin'! When they asked you, you could have said somethin'! You always have before!

MILTON: There was nothing decent to say!

RUTH: Decent! You think what he said was *decent?*

MILTON: Ruth—

RUTH: He called you a *coward!*

MILTON: What's the matter, you believe him?

RUTH: I didn't say that, Milton.

MILTON: No, but you *feel* it! You feel it! You're not sorry that stupid nigga hit me in the face. You're embarrassed! Embarrassed for me. For poor Milton layin' there bleeding in front of all those big White folks.

RUTH: That isn't so, Milt—

MILTON: Isn't it? Or is it that you're embarrassed for *yourself.* What will the sisters in the pews say about your husband now? No more pretty nigga, no more he-god. Just a coward. Poor you. Poor first lady of the Union Baptist Church.

RUTH: Milton . . .

MILTON: *You* wanted all this. I did all of this for you. *(Silence)*

MAMA E: Excuse me. *(Leaves the room)*

RUTH: *(She is intense, yet silent. She busies herself with her hands, looks up at* MILTON, *then back at her own hands)* Now Milton, *(Voice steady)* I know you're tired; I also know that you're upset. I also know that though you won't let anybody touch you, *(Voice builds)* that you are in a lot of pain. *(Voice back steady)* But if you, Milton, if you think for one moment I'm going to stand here and let you dump all that kind of crap on me—then you are out of your tired, upset, too-stubborn-to-be-touched, crazy mind. You hear me? I've supported you, Milton. Been behind you all the way. Note that I did say *behind* you. I'd much rather have been beside you—but no, Milton Tyler was the limelight. And he didn't share his glow with *anybody*. He wouldn't. I've done what I could, from behind you. Ain't much one *can* do from the behind, but to push. And be support for somebody to fall back on. Just like a *(Crosses to* MILTON's *chair)* a easy chair—you know? Wide, open arms—nice soft bottom—know what I mean? You sit on it and you hardly even notice that it's there. 'Cept that it feels nice. And you know it loves you *(Cynically)* 'cause it feels so good. And the chair don't mind, 'cause it's a chair, and it's just doin' what a chair is supposed to do. But you know what, Milton? It's only a chair because you said it was. Said it was a chair to you. Somebody else may call it an elephant. Or a bongo drum, or a canoe, and treat it like one. That's called perception, preacher. Got to have a mind for that. But to you—it's just a chair. Somewhere nice to rest your butt! And for that misconception, for that lie, Milton, I am sorry. I have been your chair too long. See, Milton, I really am an eagle. An eagle with a hard bald head, and giant wings, and *talons*—that could pick you up and drop you over the edge of the earth any old time I choose. I am an eagle. Playin' like a chair—because you needed one. But you were too dumb, too blind to see the feathers under the cushion. Too bad, Milton. Too damn bad, and too unlucky for you, Milton. You ain't got no chair no more. *(She heads upstairs)*

MILTON: *(Sorry)* Ruth I—

RUTH: And 'bout this position, Milton. Congratulations. I am glad, I only wanted for you what you wanted for yourself. You could've been a fisherman, you know? I like fish. Or stayed a carpenter. Or been a garbageman. Or a junk-man—

MILTON: Stop it, Ruth!

RUTH: And if I was you, buddy—I'd press charges. . . . If not, you're sayin' he had a right to hit you. It ain't a question of if *I* believe what he said about Milton. It's do *you* believe it! It's on you. *(She looks at all)* Goodnight. *(Exits upstairs.* MILTON *stands, walks uncomfortably. Fumbles with his handkerchief)*

JEREMY: I'll get you some ice for that, Pop.

MILTON: *(Nods, voice husky)* Thanks. (JEREMY *exits)*

LEE: I'm sorry they hurt you, Mr. Tyler.

MILTON: *(Looking at him)* What's your connection with him, Lee?

LEE: Abdullah . . .

MILTON: *(Pauses)* Oh, I see. *(They look at each other.* MILTON *turns away.* JEREMY *reenters with the ice)*

JEREMY: Here, Pop.

MILTON: Thank you, son. Jeremy . . . you think I'm a coward?

JEREMY: No, I don't think—

MILTON: Even though I didn't say something back to him? Though I didn't try to ram his ugly words back down his ugly throat?

JEREMY: That doesn't make you a coward, Pop. You're just not a violent man.

MILTON: Then why didn't I say something. When I was back on my feet why—

JEREMY: You said yourself that you couldn't think of anything decent—

MILTON: And a preacher is supposed to be a decent man! *(Silence)* Right?

LEE: *(After more silence)* I got to be leaving, sir. *(Moves to go)*

MILTON: Abdullah!

LEE: Yes sir?

MILTON: Is a preacher a decent man?

LEE: Yes sir.

MILTON: *(To* JEREMY*)* And is a decent man violent?

JEREMY: When—if he needs to be.

MILTON: You think I needed to be?

JEREMY: Look Dad, that's your problem to work out. I can't tell you. I don't know. You decide what you are. I sure don't see you as a coward.

MILTON: No?

JEREMY: No.

MILTON: You're right. I'm not.

JEREMY: What?

MILTON: I am not a coward. *(Pauses)* But I am afraid.

JEREMY: Of what?

MILTON: Of letting loose the violence in this decent preacher man. *(Looks at* JEREMY *and* LEE*)* You don't understand me. You, Jeremy—all you see before you is your father. And you, Abdullah, a preacher man is all you see. There's more. Much more. *(He pauses, and during his next speech makes use of the entire living room)* I didn't *want* to be a preacher. Didn't start out that way. You might say preachin' was the furthest thing from my mind. And I wasn't always, as you just called me, Jeremy, a nonviolent man. Don't know if there are any. How can there be any in this world when even breath is violent? When I was your age, younger, I was a fighter. Not in a ring or in a gang—just a unique kind of solo fighter. Alone, and always ready to throw a fist. Bar fight, street brawl. Even jumped into muggings and robberies. Not because I cared about the poor dope being robbed, but because it smelled like violence, and that was enough for me. I took nobody's side but violence. That same cat I defended on Monday, I might beat to a pulp on Tuesday night. It didn't matter. I was dynamite in the real sense of the word. With a short fuse—growing shorter . . . self-explosive—self-lit. I had one friend. His name *(Pauses)* was Michael. *(To* JEREMY*)* Your middle name. He was a whole lot like me, and I loved him very much. Michael was the only man I ever touched, that I didn't have to hit. *(Laughs)* Oh we were awful. Notorious from one end of town to the other. Milton and Michael, those crazy boys, *(Fakes punches)* watch out! *(Laughs)* When the war broke out, the town was only too glad to be rid of us. We were the first in line to enlist! I remember the day we were leaving, 'bout to step onto the train, and this old White lady came over to us, grabbed Michael by the shoulder, and kissed us both on the cheek. "God bless you," she said, and looked at Michael. "Our people are grateful for strong, healthy boys like you." Then she kissed us both again. Me and Michael looked at each other, then back at that little crooked nosed White lady and fell out laughing. Her people? Her people! We didn't give a damn about no *Jews!* We were on that train because the army was a good job, and a good excuse to fight. We laughed—oh how we laughed. Laughed on the train, laughed at that little bit of training they gave us at the camp. It was wonderful. We were getting paid to have these White chumps teach us things we both already knew. How to duck and keep your head down. We already knew that kind of stuff. What made us both stop laughing is when they handed us each a gun. We were street fighters, where the action is hand to hot hand, flesh to sweatin', breathin' flesh. This gun, this rifle, was a new thing. So slick, so heavy and cold. To hold it was like courting Death. And to fire like every ejaculation through every willing pair of legs I'd ever known. It was God, was hell, was heaven. I held Violence in my hands. Michael and I fought together, always side by side. We were too crazy to split up. Both of us laughin' all the time. Then Michael, he, he stopped laughin'. Something about the smell, he said. The smell of warfare, of the bloody bodies of our own men being carried back in. He stopped laughin' all right. And he started acting real scared. His eyes would be wide open and he'd start cryin'—cryin' out his and Jesus's name. "Michael, Jesus, Michael." I'll never forget it. He went on and on like that. I would come to him and hold him. Hold him, rock him, rub his back, his chest. He'd stop cryin' and be okay for a while, then the cryin' and the shakin', and the prayin' would start up again. "Michael, Jesus, Michael," like he was makin' sure that heaven knew his name. When we took turns sleepin', he'd sleep holding on to my leg. If I'd ever had to run, we'd both have been done for! Used to rib him about it in the morning, and he'd swear it wasn't so, but it was. He even kissed me once. . . . *(Pause)* He was so scared he . . . *(*MILTON *turns to look at the boys, turns away, touches his face)* Michael died in St. Lo. The last battle for us both. We were under command to rush this hill, and were waiting for the signal to charge—when Michael started actin' all strange, like he was falling all apart. "The smell man, the smell!" he kept saying—and was twisting and turning all about. I was trying to crawl over to him to keep him quiet when the signal came and Michael took off, runnin', yellin', and screamin' into an open field. The field was mined. I tried to stop him and was shot in my shoulder and below my knee. I went down just as a big explosion went off over, above my head. The last I saw of Michael was a billion bloody bits blown up—hair, flesh, bone, blood and all, into the sky. I remember screaming, "Michael!" and his blood spraying across my face—inside my mouth. I swallowed him. Michael, Jesus, Michael. Screaming out your name—did heaven hear you? Did you tell them who you are, who you were? *(*MILTON *looks at the boys and gets out the black metallic box)* I want to show you boys something. *(They come closer, then fall back as* MILTON *opens box and pulls out a grenade)* This boys, is my life. Or used to be. It was the only thing I had of value, of any strength, or force. It's all I brought home with me. When I got out of the Army, when I came home, back here, I was a crazy man. Not violent and crazy, just crazy and lost. I met your mother, Jeremy, and things were better for a time. I had a good job in a sawmill and did carpentry on the side. It paid well and was noisy enough to keep my mind off of any real thoughts. Your mama got pregnant, and I was a happy man. I built this house, Jeremy, almost completely by myself. I know it ain't perfect, but it was mine. I was a happy man, son. Married your mama, brought in Mama E. Treated your mama like she was a princess—no, a queen. My queen. . . . When the baby died, was born dead, I was no longer a happy man. Barely a man at all, I was back to crazy. Didn't speak, smile, say boo to nobody, not even your ma. I used to take this box, and open it at night, when nobody was around. I would take this out and rub it, like a ritual, every night, and look at it, caress it, feel it like it was another part of me. My excrement. My snot. My semen, maybe. I would stroke it till my hands got warm, chaffed and rugged from the friction in my palms. I would rub it faster, harder, faster, hoping that maybe the friction from my hands would bring me to a final climax. One, great, final act of violence—sending me sky high, blown into a billion bloody bits—irretrievable. I waited, time and time again, but nothing happened. I was frustrated, and in a rage sometimes I took your mother, exploding instead inside of her.

JEREMY: Papa—

MILTON: It's true! And from one of those times, those explosions, you were made, and you were born.

JEREMY: That's enough, Pop, I'm sorry, I—

MILTON: (*Facing, touching* JEREMY) When I saw you, I knew I had to be somebody. Be somebody, for you. More than a crazy man. I put that black death back in it's box and started looking for something greater. A greater power that I could give—hand down to my son. I read books—politics, philosophy, religion. Then I came upon that story in the Bible. About how Jesus passed the brothers casting their nets upon the sea. The stormy sea that held no reason, no answer to man's life. Just perpetual and subtle violence in the movement of its waves. And them, challenging it. Casting out their nets to catch fish. Perpetual and hopeless, just like me. Then Jesus came and told them He'd make them fishers of men instead. Fishers of men. Of hope, and dreams. Fishers of a greater power. Greater than the sea. Greater than all else. And they followed him. And so did I, Jeremy. That's why I am what I am now. A preacher. Man of God. Fisher of men. Because it's the only power that I know. Because I can't make an atom bomb or a nuclear warhead. Maybe I'm a preacher because it's the next best thing.

(*There is silence for a while*)

LEE: I'll be going now, Rev. Tyler. Jeremy, I'll catch you later on.

MILTON: If you're going up by Crown Heights, Abdullah, I'd be glad to give you a ride.

LEE: No thank you sir, I can make it.

MILTON: You can't hop all the way, Lee—I mean Abdullah . . . (*Pauses*) Oh, well, I'm headed down to the police station. See you boys later on. (MILTON *exits. There is silence for a while*)

LEE: (*Softly*) I take part two tonight, Jeremy. (JEREMY, *still engrossed in his father's words, does not, cannot answer.* LEE *exits*) See you later, man.

JEREMY: Yeah, later. (*Realizing* LEE *has gone, through door*) Hey, take care of yourself, okay? (*He closes the door and slowly reenters the living room. He stares at the grenade box and opens it. He tries but*

cannot bring himself to touch the grenade. Closing the box, he reaches instead for the photo of his father and himself. He studies it. Softly) A fisherman.

Fade out. See production notes for music.

ACT THREE

Scene 1

Setting: Nighttime. The Tyler living room. Same night. JEREMY *is asleep in the easy chair, still clutching the photograph.* RUTH *enters from upstairs and sees* JEREMY *sleeping. She watches him for a moment as she descends the stairs, comes to him, starts to wake him, but watches him instead. She is seeing his breathing, his face, his body. She feels mother-proud and serene. Her face changes to sadness as she gently takes the photo, replacing it. He stirs, slowly awakens.*

JEREMY: Mama?

RUTH: (*Kisses him*) Yes, it's me.

JEREMY: Pop home yet?

RUTH: No, he isn't. I don't know when I should expect him. Hope he's all right.

JEREMY: He's all right. He'll be back home in a while. (*Looks at her*) He loves you, Mama.

RUTH: I know he does, Jeremy. This afternoon, I, well, I guess I couldn't take no more of what he was tellin' me. All that crazy talk about it bein' all for me. I couldn't take it, Jeremy. (*Softly*) You understand?

JEREMY: Yes, Mama, I do. And don't worry. What you said to him was right.

RUTH: You really think so?

JEREMY: Would I lie? Besides, you know it was.

RUTH: I don't know, Jeremy. I want to help him so much. (*Pause*) You know?

JEREMY: What you told him tonight was probably more help than anything you've ever said to him before.

RUTH: What makes you say that? I didn't give him anything but my anger—and I was plenty mad. Wasn't nothin' else but anger there.

JEREMY: Don't you love him?

RUTH: Of course I do.

JEREMY: Then it was there, too. Your anger was a gift.

RUTH: Some kind of gift!

JEREMY: The best kind. You said yourself you took the chair away—

RUTH: Oh please!

JEREMY: And made him stand. Made him deal with the fact that he's standing on his own two feet. The gift of his own strength, Mama. Can't give much more gift than that.

RUTH: Never thought of it that way. I've always thought of anger as destructive, you know—breakin' up friendships, marriages, love affairs.

JEREMY: If it's the truth, doesn't much matter how it comes out. Long as it does.

RUTH: Preacher's son.

JEREMY: And son of Eagle! *(They both laugh)*

RUTH: Jeremy, what is it you want to be doing? You know, with your life?

JEREMY: Live it, hopefully.

RUTH: I'm serious.

JEREMY: So am I. It's tricky business, life. I ain't gonna be a philosopher, that's for sure. Just sittin' and talkin'. That's not for me.

RUTH: What is?

JEREMY: If I had one wish, Mama, *(Smiles)* I'd be a lighthouse—a black one. Strong and solid and black as night. Looking out at the world over the sea. With one bright white/yellow beam that I could shoot out if I wanted to—guiding ships all safely home. I think I'd like that. Seeing, knowing everything.

RUTH: And nobody seeing you?

JEREMY: They'd see me when my light shines.

RUTH: Well, I guess that's about normal for most people. When they want to be seen most is when they're shinin'.

JEREMY: Or sending out messages for help.

RUTH: Lighthouse might not be such a bad idea.

JEREMY: Of course not.

RUTH: 'Course, it could stand a few revisions in design.

JEREMY: Like what?

RUTH: Oh, like an eagle's nest, for instance.

JEREMY: Oh yeah?

RUTH: Ummm hmmm. And we'd have to call you dark house for sure. Be a terrible blow to your ancestors. Having evolved all this way just for you to choose to become one tall, lonely darkie! Your grandma'd have a fit! *(Laughs)*

JEREMY: Ma, how old is Mama E?

RUTH: Almost ninety-one. Why? You worried about her?

JEREMY: Sort of. She's awfully frail.

RUTH: You ever worry about me?

JEREMY: About you?

RUTH: Ummm hmmm.

JEREMY: Naw . . . but I think about you a lot.

RUTH: Oh, go on!

JEREMY: It's true. This time of year, springtime, always puts me in mind of you, Mama.

RUTH: You sure it ain't just women in general?

JEREMY: That too, maybe. But there's a certain smell, after it rains—the blend of flower smells in the air, that bring back feelin's of when I was a

little boy clinging to the hem of your dress and twistin' it all around. Like when I used to help you in the garden. Whenever there's a spring rain, I always think of you.

RUTH: That true, Jeremy?

JEREMY: Uh huh. But I *worry* about Mama E.

RUTH: Don't you worry *none* about her, Jeremy. That old lady's got more spunk, more streak of lean and *mean* in her to outlive us all.

MAMA E: *(Enters)* That's right! Now move over. It's eleven o'clock, and I want to hear my news. *(Turns on TV)*

RUTH: *(Laughing)* See what I mean? *(Phone rings)* I'll get it.

JEREMY: Where's your bathrobe, Mama E?

MAMA E: I'll get it later. Shush now, here comes the news.

JEREMY: I'll get it for you.

MAMA E: No, sit down! Shush now, here it comes. *(JEREMY reaches for his jacket on the arm of the couch, starts putting it on MAMA E)*

NEWS COMMENTATOR: In tonight's news, a shoot-out at the central precinct cell block has left one person dead and three others injured. This story and others following—

JEREMY: *(Overlap)* Papa!

MAMA E: What!

RUTH: Jeremy, your father's on the phone. He's all right, but there's been a gunfight at police head-quarters.

JEREMY: I know, I know!

RUTH: Three policemen were injured, Jeremy, and Jeremy . . .

JEREMY: What?

RUTH: Rev. Akbara's dead.

JEREMY: What!

RUTH: Milton says it just happened a few . . .

JEREMY: *(Rising)* Give me the phone. *(Takes it)*

RUTH: Ain't nobody on the line. Milton had to put me on hold. Switchboard's probably got their hands full tryin' to . . .

MAMA E: Shhh!

(JEREMY hands the phone back to RUTH and goes back to TV)

NEWS REPORTER: *(Mid-sentence)* . . . are in critical condition. How did it happen. Sergeant?

POLICE SERGEANT: Well, we were moving the prisoner to another cell when he attacked the three policemen escorting him and fired on them with a gun taken from one of the policemen's holsters. Three of my men were wounded, one critically, before the suspect was overpowered.

NEWS REPORTER: By "overpowered," you mean shot?

SERGEANT: No, the suspect was tackled to the ground. Before he was tackled, he shot himself.

NEWS REPORTER: Shot himself?

SERGEANT: That's right.

NEWS REPORTER: The dead man was Rev. Akbara of the Church of the People, who was being held in connection with an assault on policemen and reporters earlier today at a Mayoral press conference. We asked the sergeant in charge why such a man, already being charged with assault, would have been without handcuffs.

SERGEANT: Oh, he had handcuffs. Police regulation. He had them on all right.

NEWS REPORTER: We asked the sergeant, who preferred to remain unnamed, how it was possible for a man in handcuffs to shoot three policemen and then turn and shoot himself. The sergeant said he had no comment on the matter and said he was only telling it as he saw it happen. This is W. Mackleby...

JEREMY: Liars! They killed him, they know they did! Probably shot their own men as well! How's he gonna attack all three officers at the same time? And shoot himself while handcuffed? Come on. They're *lyin'*; (*Rises*)

MAMA E: What you aim to do?

RUTH: Jeremy, your father said if Lee Jr. comes by here, tell him to stay put. Police are out lookin' for members of Akbara's group. Said they got the word there might be some kind of retaliation. It ain't safe out there for Lee.

JEREMY: Where is Papa?

RUTH: He's gone now. Said he'd be home later on.

JEREMY: Did he say anything else?

RUTH: Yes. (*Tired*) He said he saw the body...

JEREMY: And?

RUTH: Said there was blood and bruises all over it. Like they beat him somethin' awful.

JEREMY: Beat him to death! (*Reaches for jacket*)

MAMA E: Where you goin'?

JEREMY: I've got to find Lee.

RUTH: What makes you think it's any safer out there for you?

JEREMY: It ain't never safe, for anybody! I'll be all right. (*Exits—front door*)

RUTH: (*Calling after him*) Jeremy! (*Folding*) Lord, Lord Jesus!

MAMA E: A little less moanin' and some out and out prayin' might be more help.

RUTH: Mama, I don't believe you. How can you stay so calm, so unmoving...like you already know everything.

MAMA E: (*Looking at* RUTH) I'm the middle ground, remember? It's my job, my place, to know.

Fade out

Scene 2

Setting: Tyler living room, almost morning. MAMA E *is wide awake in her wheelchair, deliberately inconspicuous.* JEREMY *and* MILTON *enter through front door.*

JEREMY: I looked everywhere for him. Couldn't find him anywhere.

MILTON: I didn't get much further with that sergeant. Still swearing up and down that Akbara killed himself.

JEREMY: But you saw the bruises!

MILTON: And the blood.

JEREMY: They won't get away with a lie like that. I went up to school tonight, lookin' for Lee, and the whole dorm and student center were filled with folks talking about what happened. They're talking about holding a demonstration down at the police headquarters, staying there till somebody gets up off of the truth.

MILTON: They'll be waiting forever, Jeremy.

JEREMY: What?

MILTON: Those people are paid, professional liars. And they've got privacy, power, and Justice on their side. Remember they're the ones who saw what happened.

JEREMY: But you saw...

MILTON: I'm just one nigga preacher. My word against all theirs... (*Shakes head*)

JEREMY: Well, what are you gonna do?

MILTON: Jeremy, I get sworn in at twelve noon today. The second after I take that oath, I'm calling for a complete investigation.

JEREMY: Twelve Noon! By that time they could have done anything. Even make Akbara's body look like he beat up himself!

MILTON: There's nothing else to do.

JEREMY: Oh yes there is. (*Crosses to phone*)

MILTON: What are you doing?

JEREMY: Calling school. When I was there they asked if I would lead the demonstration. I'm calling to tell them yes and that we'd better make it very early.

MILTON: Put that phone down!

JEREMY: What?

MILTON: (*Taking phone*) With my son leading a demonstration against the police, just how great are my chances at still being sworn in?

JEREMY: (*Looks at him, takes phone back*) That's your problem.

MILTON: (*Stops him from dialing*) Your demonstration won't help anything, Jeremy. But I can!

JEREMY: Noon is just too far away!

MILTON: But I'd be in the position to help!

JEREMY: And by that time, several other people could be dead! There's so much police action

around Akbara's church that you can't get anywhere near it. The members are like sitting ducks
in there!

MILTON: They wouldn't fire. The police surrounded a demonstration I led here once. They
bluffed, but wouldn't fire. No one was hurt.

JEREMY: Of course not. They *like* you. You're a
good nigga! (MILTON *slaps him.* JEREMY *looks at
him, pauses, then tries to dial again*) Shit! Busy!

MAMA E: Jeremy... (*Both men turn, surprised*)

JEREMY: (*Tense*) Yes, Mama E?

MAMA E: I got a message for you. From Abdullah.

JEREMY: Abdullah!

MAMA E: Yes. He came by here not long after you
left. Limpin' somethin' awful. I told him to stay.
he wouldn't stay, though.

JEREMY: What'd he say? What was the message,
Mama E?

MAMA E: Said to tell you, "City Hall—seven
o'clock." Said you'd know what he meant.

JEREMY: Well, he's wrong, I don't know. Did he
say anything else?

MAMA E: Ummm hmmm. Told me he loved me.
Thanked me for callin' him by his name.

JEREMY: That's all?

MAMA E: Umm hmmm. That's it. (*Nods her head,
begins to cry*)

JEREMY: Mama E? You cryin'? What's the matter?

MAMA E: I didn't want to tell you. Didn't want to
tell you that.

JEREMY: You mean what Lee—Abdullah told you?

MAMA E: Didn't want to tell you none of it. Been
sittin' here all night, just thinkin'—noddin' back
and forth. Hopin' you wouldn't even come home
so I wouldn't have to tell you anything. Didn't
want to. Swear I didn't.

JEREMY: Why not, Mama E? Why not?

MAMA E: It's them damn cut flowers, Jeremy.
Lord, wish I was dead!

JEREMY: Mama E—what is it? What's the matter
with you? What's wrong?

RUTH: (*Enters from upstairs*) Mama? Mama, what's
the matter? What you cryin' for? Help me,
Jeremy. (*They try to lift her*)

MAMA E: Leave me alone. Will you? Long as
you're alive, He's gonna use you. Ain't nothin'
you can do.

RUTH: Who's usin' who? Mama, you're not makin' sense!

MAMA E: Leave me alone. If you want to help me,
just help me to my room.

RUTH: Okay, Mama, okay. (*She helps* MAMA E;
both exit to her room)

MILTON: What's troubling your grandmother?

JEREMY: Something about cut flowers or something. I don't know. (*Starts to dial again*)

MILTON: Jeremy—

JEREMY: Huh?

MILTON: I'm sorry I hit you.

JEREMY: (*Pauses*) That's okay. (*Continues dialing*)

MILTON: No, it's not okay. I'm sorry.

JEREMY: (*Hangs up, dials again*) Okay. Apology
accepted. (*Hangs up*) Damn!

MILTON: Line's still busy?

JEREMY: Yeah. All of them. Well, one thing's for
sure. There's going to be a demonstration tomorrow, and I won't be leading it. At this rate, I'll be
lucky to find out when it starts! Damn!

MILTON: (*Touching him*) I'm really sorry, Jeremy....

JEREMY: (*Jumping back*) Damn it, Papa! Didn't
your father ever hit you before?

MILTON: Once.

JEREMY: Well, did you hate him for it?

MILTON: No.

JEREMY: All right then. I don't hate you for it
either. So get your paranoia off my back, okay?

MILTON: I did hate him though.

JEREMY: What'd he do? Tie you up in pink silk
ribbons and put you in a box? (*Their eyes meet.
Silence*)

MILTON: You love Lee Jr., don't you?

JEREMY: Yes.

MILTON: As a brother?

JEREMY: (*Angry*) Did you love Michael "as a
brother"?

MILTON: What are you trying to say?

JEREMY: Oh, I don't know. You tell me! You're
the one who said Michael was the only man you
could touch instead of hit! You said that you held
him, rocked him, that he kissed you! At least he
screamed out, "Michael Jesus Michael!" What
was it, Papa, that you were too *afraid* to say?

MILTON: (*Raises his arm to hit* JEREMY *again.* JEREMY
catches his fist. Eye contact, then MILTON *drops his
eyes*) In my whole life, my father only hit me
once. Only one time. Never again after that.
(*Pauses*) He had made this bird house, built it
himself from one piece of hollowed wood,
carved sixteen tiny portholes in it, and stuck it on
a pole on the front lawn. My papa loved that bird
house. Would sit and watch it for hours every
day. He would touch it, pat it like it was made of
flesh, not wood. He tried to get me to like it,
(*Shakes head*) but I hated it. Hated it. One morning, Papa wasn't around, and I was on my way
with my pail of slop to feed our one big hog, and I
stopped and watched the thing. A family of robins had landed on the feeder tray around the
house. Two adult birds and three babies, hardly
able to fly. I watched them. Then took my pail,
swung it round and round and round and let it

fly, full force at the robins and the house. It knocked over the birdhouse, splintered it, and four of the five robins got away. The fifth one, one of the babies, lay fluttering in the slop. I went over to it, picked it up. Its neck was broken. Its beak was still, and its eyes stared straight ahead as it's wings beat, then lay flat open—shaking, trembling as its life poured out of it into my hands. . . . I didn't hear my father coming. I looked up from the robin, into my father's face. Tears were still flowing as he hit me and I went down. Went out. I stayed there in the pig slop all day, almost all night. When I came to, I was dizzy—couldn't move. Papa had carried me into the house and put me on his bed. The doctor was there and Papa was cryin' and saying over and over and over how sorry he was. How much he loved me. How much he hoped I wouldn't hate him for what he did. I didn't hate him. Not for slugging me. He never built another birdhouse. I hated him for that.

(Silence)

JEREMY: Papa, do you love me?

MILTON: Of course I love you, Jeremy. What kind of a question is that?

JEREMY: An honest one. I want to know.

MILTON: Jeremy, you're my son—

JEREMY: Never mind that! Taking the son part out of it—do you love *me?*

MILTON: Yes.

JEREMY: Why?

MILTON: Dammit, Jeremy—I built this house for you and your mother. I've gone hungry so you could eat. If it was cold, you weren't! When there was one bed, it was yours. This whole house, with my bare hands. . . .

JEREMY: It's a birdhouse, Papa.

MILTON: What do you mean?

JEREMY: Look, I'm not going to pretend that I'm not grateful for all you've given me, because I am. I'm grateful. But it's a birdhouse, Papa. And the holes have gotten so small that I can't fit in or out.

MILTON: What are you saying?

JEREMY: That I love you. That what I'm feeling's not your fault. All that talk about casting your nets out over the ocean, having them come back heavy, empty, and wet. Well, you found a smaller ocean, where you could control all of the fish—but you failed to realize one thing. Among the catchings in your net, there is a son. A son, who's not just another fish, but a fisherman, just like you. I love you, Papa, because I see you. Your nets are empty, and you're afraid.

MILTON: Afraid of what?

JEREMY: Afraid that son Jeremy's going to love Lee the same way you were afraid to love Michael, and how you wanted your father to love you. With strength, tenderness, and courage. With all it takes to be a man. To love a man. To love yourself. You're afraid that I'm going to love, Papa, and that somehow that's going to leave you all by yourself.

MILTON: That's not true!

JEREMY: Isn't it? Or don't you need anybody?

MILTON: I don't need anybody! Nobody! Not even you!

JEREMY: No? Then why don't you just go hold your grenade? I'll get it for you. *(He crosses to shelf,* RUTH *enters)*

RUTH: Jeremy . . .

JEREMY: It's gone!

MILTON: What?

JEREMY: The grenade—the whole box is gone!

MILTON: Let me see there! . . .

RUTH: Jeremy!

JEREMY: Huh?

RUTH: Your grandma said she had one other thing to tell you.

JEREMY: Yeah? What is it?

RUTH: She said Lee Jr.'s changed his name.

JEREMY: I know that already. It's Abdullah ben Kahim.

RUTH: No, she says he's changed it again.

JEREMY: To what?

RUTH: She says to tell you it's Abdullah ben Akbara now.

JEREMY: Akbara!

*(*MAMA E *enters)*

MILTON: Somebody's taken it! It's gone!

JEREMY: Jesus—City Hall! *(Grabs jacket)*

MAMA E: *(Crying)* Jeremy!

JEREMY: I got to, Mama E! *(Exits—front door.* MAMA E *sobs and collapses.* RUTH *and* MILTON *catch her)*

MILTON: Where's Jeremy going? What's happening, Mama E?

RUTH: What is it, Mama? What is wrong?

MAMA E: *(Sobbing)* Lord, Lord—why me? I told you. It's them flowers. Never should'a brought no rose in here!

MILTON: *(Looks at* RUTH*)* I don't understand.

Blackout

Scene 3

Setting: A disheveled office in City Hall. There is an elevator upstage center. The only light comes from semi-closed window blinds. LEE *is alone, armed with a sawed-off shotgun, a revolver, knife, and several rounds of ammunition. Around his waist is strapped the grenade. Upstage right, slightly ajar, is the door to a storeroom, through which a glimpse of bound hostages can be seen. Police sirens are heard, and the red glare from the flashing lights atop police cars bounces and skids below his face. He holds a phone receiver by his ear. He is nervous, tense. A* POLICEMAN *talks through a megaphone outside, below.*

POLICE VOICE: Give yourself up, Watkins. You haven't a chance in hell in there. Throw your guns out.

LEE: *(Through phone)* I ain't throwin' nothin' out nowhere—'cept to blow you all to bits. You understand? Now I told you, I'll trade you body for body. Six live hostage bodies, for one live nigga-killin' cop body. Understand? As a matter of fact—you can deliver that killer cop body *dead* or alive to the church of the People, and you get six live hostage bodies back. If not, they gon' die! Get it?

VOICE: You're crazy, Watkins!

LEE: Abdullah! The name's Abdullah! *(Puts phone down)* What the hell, names are sacred anyway. *(He starts shaking the tension out of his body, his neck, arms, and hands. The sound of the elevator in motion whirls him around into a mass of armed tension again.)* Shit! *(Into phone)* I'm warning you—whoever you're sending up here in that elevator, I'm killin' 'em!

VOICE: You're crazy, Watkins! We haven't sent anybody up—*(Aside)* What? Well, how the hell did that happen? *(Back to megaphone)* Listen, Watkins—*somebody* is on their way up. We didn't send 'em. We don't know who it is. Don't shoot, Watkins! You hear me, Watkins!

LEE: *(Puts phone down)* Yeah, I hear you. You think I'm really crazy, don't you? *(He positions himself on the floor—ready to fire at the elevator. The elevator comes up to the floor, stops.* LEE *cocks and aims shotgun. The door opens. Nothing happens.* LEE *waits, shifts position. Still nothing. He belly crawls, keeping his aim at the elevator, over to its far side. Raising himself full height alongside the elevator door, he crouches, swings his body around—rifle into elevator, ready to fire. An arm grabs the rifle and pushes it up)*

JEREMY: Hold it, man! *(Shotgun blasts ceiling. Both duck)* Glad you looked first. Somethin' told me not to stick out my head and say hello!

LEE: Nigga, do you realize I could'a killed you?

VOICE: *(Overlap)* What's happening in there, Watkins?

JEREMY: I realize that you didn't!

VOICE: Watkins!

LEE: Man, how the hell'd you get up here?

JEREMY: I came in downstairs with the press, took the backstairs to the sub-basement, and the service elevator up.

LEE: And just how do you plan to leave?

JEREMY: With you. *(*LEE *stiffens;* JEREMY *takes a step forward)* Lee . . .

LEE: Abdullah!

JEREMY: Abdullah, man, then—shit! I didn't come up here to argue with you over a name!

LEE: Then what you here for?

(Window breaks as tear gas cannister is shot in. LEE *covers it with his jacket, throws it back outside)*

VOICE: You still in there, Watkins?

LEE: *(Into phone)* Try that again mothafucks and I'll drop you a secretary! *(To* JEREMY*)* This ain't no fuckin' game, man. Why you here?

JEREMY: You left a message where you were.

LEE: Didn't mean you had to come!

JEREMY: Look man—you don't stand a chance in here! *(*LEE *looks at him, looks away)* They ain't gon' turn that cop over. They're not even saying who he is. . . . Probably was more than one cop anyway.

LEE: So what you sayin'?

JEREMY: I'm sayin' you don't stand a chance in here, man. They ain't givin' *nothin'* up! What's the sense you dyin' in here?

LEE: What makes you so sure I'm gonna die?

JEREMY: Be real, man. These honkies ain't gon' let you live! Not if you use that thing and kill somebody. Give it up, brother!

LEE: *(Laughs)* You know—Jeremy, you're a good man. A good nigga. You too damn much like your father!

JEREMY: And you're too damn much like yours!

LEE: What? How?

JEREMY: Suicidal. You've got one foot in the grave. The mere fact that you're a nigga up here with a gun makes you a target, man . . . for anybody. Honkies, bored Black folks. Don't make no difference if you use that gun or not. The fact that you have it makes folks with and without guns want to kill you. You're not the hunter, man, not the hero. You're the game. You're more a victim now than Akbara ever was. 'Cause the whole world is watchin', man. Waitin' for you to slip.

LEE: Stop it, Jeremy! Stop it, man! *(He is trembling, looses his grip on the gun and lets it slip, falling, himself, into* JEREMY*'s chest.* JEREMY *holds him)* They killed him, man. They killed him!

JEREMY: I know, brother, I know.

LEE: I didn't want you to be involved, man. It's too dangerous. I was scared, man. That's why I left the message with Mama E. I had to know somebody knew where I was, man. I'm sorry, Jeremy. I'm sorry, man . . . I—*(Begins to weep)*

JEREMY: *(Rocking him)* It's okay, man. It's gonna be all right. *(Weeping too)* I'm here now, man. We'll get out of this some way.

LEE: Ain't no way, Jeremy. We're both dead men. I'm sorry man—Oh God, I'm sorry, Jeremy.

JEREMY: Shhh—We'll be all right, man. Listen. First step is putting those hostages on the elevator —all together, and tell the folks outside we're sending them down.

LEE: We?

JEREMY: Much as I may wish, I'm not invisible, man. I'm a part of this now too.

LEE: I won't let 'em book you, man. I'll tell 'em it was me!

JEREMY: Later for that, brother. Let's get out of here breathin' first! Start roundin' up those people. *(LEE opens door to storeroom/closet and starts bring out hostages. He blocks open the elevator door and starts putting them inside. JEREMY speaks into telephone)* Hello. This is Jeremy Tyler. I am Rev. Milton Tyler's son. I am here with Abdullah. We are sending all hostages down to you by elevator —alive.

VOICE: Good work, Jeremy. *(JEREMY winces)*

JEREMY: In return, I want only that my—my friend Abdullah and I leave this room, this building, unharmed. We will surrender. You can take both of us in. We will offer no resistance. *(Pauses)* It's over now.

VOICE: Place your weapons on the floor of the elevator with the hostages when you send them down. Then come on down yourselves. Hands over your head. You read me?

JEREMY: Yes. *(Puts down phone. Turns to LEE)* They're all gonna fit in there?

LEE: They better. *(He squeezes them in. JEREMY goes for rifle)* Hey, what you doin' man? *(JEREMY places rifle in the elevator)*

JEREMY: He says we got to do it. It's our ticket out of here.

LEE: It's crazy man! Jeremy!

JEREMY: It's what he said.

(LEE looks at him for a moment, then places his revolver, knife, and bullets in. He removes the grenade from his belt and sneaks it into his pocket)

LEE: All set.

JEREMY: *(Picks up phone)* They're coming down. *(Hangs up phone)* God help us. *(JEREMY removes the elevator doorstop and pushes button, sending elevator down. Door closes. JEREMY comes over to LEE)* Well—that's that. *(They stand in silence for a moment. LEE moves back towards the window. Fingers grenade)* Ain't nothin' to do now but wait. *(Sees grenade)* Hey, what you doin', man?

LEE: I ain't gon' be caught here with *nothin'*, man. I don't trust 'em. At least this way we'll have a chance. *(JEREMY starts towards LEE)*

JEREMY: They ain't gon' try nothin' now . . . *(Elevator door opens—POLICE with guns drawn)*

LEE: Jeremy! *(JEREMY turns)*

POLICE: Freeze!

LEE: No! *(Pulls pin on grenade, rears back to throw it)*

JEREMY: Abdullah! *(All freeze, slow fade)*

NEWS COMMENTATOR: Two Black terrorists and three policemen were killed early this morning in an explosion that . . .

VOICE OF MAMA E: *(Wailing)* Jeremy!

See production notes for music.

ACT FOUR—EPILOGUE

Setting: A funeral home. Traditionally furnished. It is in two sections: the reception room, and the chamber room which houses the coffin. A turntable, or revolving set should be used here as it is essential that the scene be viewed from two opposite perspectives: from the reception room looking into the chamber, and from the chamber looking into the reception room. Our first view is of MAMA E. *She is sitting in the center of a sofa in the reception room, facing the audience. She holds her cane, and something wrapped in a handkerchief is in her lap. Her wheelchair stands by the u.r. exit from the reception room, in temporary disuse, but ready to be used if needed. Directly behind her we see the wide opening to the chamber room. We see the casket and people passing by it.* RUTH *is seated, facing upstage.* MILTON *stands beside her, accepting condolences and nodding "thank you's" to mourners. The last mourner leaves, passing out through the upstage portion of the reception room. We can tell by Milton's back that he is weeping.* RUTH *is slowly rocking back and forth. She stands, and they both exit the chamber room, entering the reception room.* RUTH *comes to* MAMA E. *Her voice is husky. Her face is grief.*

RUTH: Mama, we fixin' to leave now.

MAMA E: What for? *(Looks at RUTH. RUTH drops her head, wipes her eyes)* All the people gone?

MILTON: Except us three.

MAMA E: And Jeremy.

MILTON: And Jeremy, Mama E.

MAMA E: You think I'm senile, don't you? Well, I ain't. I know Jeremy's dead.

RUTH: Mama, please . . .

MAMA E: It's just that I been remembering that sermon you gave us all. All 'bout death bein' a beginnin'. Just another part of life. A journey. You remember, Milton?

MILTON: Yes. That was many years ago.

MAMA E: Well, it's still true, ain't it?

MILTON: Yes, of course.

MAMA E: Good. 'Cause I got somethin' to tell Jeremy to help him on his way.

RUTH: What?

MILTON: Now, Mama E—

MAMA E: Don't Mama E me, preacher. I know that boy, and I know you. He wasn't expecting to die—all blown—

RUTH: Mama!

MAMA E: It's different when you die in bed—from illness or old age. You kinda know you're goin'. Got time to get prepared. Jeremy didn't know nothin'. He's gonna need some help. *(She stands, heads towards casket room)* You all can stand gawkin' if you like. Or if you listen, you might learn somethin'. It's private, but I don't think Jeremy will mind. *(She walks slowly towards chamber, the stage turning with her as she walks. By the time she reaches the doorway, the stage has fully turned, and we see her entering the chamber, with RUTH and MILTON lingering behind her in the doorway. She approaches the casket, looks into it, then pulls a chair up beside it)* Jeremy, this is your Mama E. Your Ma and Papa think I'm crazy, but I know you don't. Jeremy, there ain't much any of us can take with us when we die, 'cept the knowledge that we's dyin'. But you didn't even have that, so I come to give you some advice. You can take it or leave it—but I've done a lot of travellin' in my day—so I know what I'm telling you is right. Ain't no good to over-pack, Jeremy. Take only what you need. I ain't died yet, so I don't know, or don't remember if the journey's long or short. But I know one thing for certain—you got to take the best you got. I don't mean no college education, ain't gonna do you no good, won't ease your soul. And don't go packin' all the things that made you angry in your life. Anger's a thing of this life here. No need bringin' it to the next. But, Jeremy, there is one thing I feel you should take with you. And that is, Jeremy, that you remember that you knew how to laugh. How to laugh and enjoy laughter. Not many folks know how, but you did. Remember that you knew laughter, and that you knew how to smile. That'll ease you. When you're journeyin' on, that'll ease you on your way. It don't make no difference if the laughter turn to tears if you start to missin' folks. That be all right. That be fine. Just remember that in your lifetime, you knew how to—knew how to smile and how to laugh, gut-deep, with feeling. Whenever I can, Jeremy, your Mama E'll be laughing too, right with you. I'll help you anyway I can. You know that. I'm your Mama E. One more thing, Jeremy. *(Whispers)* Now, if anybody ask you—your name is Jeremy Michael Tyler-Rose...you understand? You tell 'em now. And Jeremy, if you see my mama or my papa where you goin'—tell 'em—Early May say hello. *(MAMA E unwraps one of RUTH's garden roses she has wrapped in her handkerchief and places it on the coffin)* Have a good trip now. Goodbye, Jeremy. Goodbye, Son. *(She gets up and leaves out, looking at MILTON and RUTH as she passes by. In passing)* Next.

MILTON: *(Looks at RUTH, then ventures in. He sits, stands, paces, and sits again)* Jeremy, I—*(Voice breaks, face breaks—very tender)* I love you. This is probably the last sermon I will ever give, and it's not really a sermon, Son—it's just the only way I know. *(Pauses)* A father always knows his son, Jeremy. Whether he wants to deal with it or not, a father always knows his son. I love you, and I know you. From the time you beat so wildly, a rage in my loins, and went streaming into your mother, I knew you. You were the sum total of everything I'd ever dreamed of, and more. You were my life, yet not my life, and you fascinated me. From the point of your conception, you *became,* and brought your own life force along. I knew you, as you grew, a swelling—a lump in your mama's belly. Now *(Pause)* you're the lump in my throat—Jeremy—I loved you. Your mama used to smile, real warm, and pat her tummy, like she had some kind of special secret just between her and you. I didn't mind. I let her keep her secret. 'Cause I knew you too, and I knew it was just a matter of time before I held you in a new way—in my arms, close to my heart. I know, I know, I know I've said it many times—but—I love you, Jeremy—You will always be my son. Unless of course someday we find our roles reversed, and I come springing, streaming, flying out of you. I'd like that. You'd make one hell of a good father. But it's not time for that yet. No, you've got somewhere else to go. Something wonderful to do. It's time to stream again, Jeremy. You're entering a place as dark and warm as the womb from which you entered into this world. My world. And you must stream. For at the end of that stream, there'll be light, Lord, there'll be light, Jeremy. As full and brilliant as your own. There *will* be *Light!* A father knows his child, my son. And I know that you are strong. Go with God and use that strength as only you and God know how. I love you, Jeremy. Know that son. For my love will stream with you as you yet soar to higher places! A son always knows his father. A father, always knows his son. *(Kisses him)* Goodnight, Jeremy. *(He stands, looks at his son. Runs his hands over his own face, sighs, starts to leave, then turns, remembering)* Say not, say not, "Come back my love," but say instead, though it may pull the very life-strings of your heart . . . say instead, in *tenderness,* "Fly on, my love. Be free." *(Pauses)* Can I get a Witness?

(MILTON exits into sitting room. RUTH enters, shakily, unsure of herself. She hesitates, then sits, looking away from casket)

RUTH: Jeremy, I—I *(Looks into casket)* Oh Lord! Lord! *(She breaks down. MILTON, in doorway starts to go to her but is stopped by MAMA E)* Jeremy, this is the hardest part, you know? I ain't never been one for lettin' anything go—dresses, ticket stubs—but Lord Jesus, my own son? It's hard, Jeremy, it's hard. You know, the first steps you took when you were just this high—I was scared to let go of you even then. So scared. And when you did it—took those first five steps across the room to your Daddy's arms—I'd been so scared, I was ashamed. Then, your Daddy turned you around and pointed you towards me. Lord, I thought I'd . . . anyway . . . you were all happy, your little mouth all smilin' and wet with joy. I was happy too, but as you took those first steps towards me—something *happened.* My heart was frozen with some crazy kind of fear you wouldn't make it. That you'd fall, and you nearly did. Your feet got all turned over and tangled, and you just stood there for a moment, wobbling all about. I reached out to grab you, but you caught yourself and just sat down. And looked at me. Just *looked* at me. I went back to where I'd been kneeling and just waited. There were a few more bumps and tumbles, but you made it. You came to me all smiles, gigglin' and gurglin' and fell into my arms. And me, Jeremy? I started cryin'. I was so ashamed, Jeremy, so ashamed. Oh, not because you'd fallen, but because I, in my fearfulness, had almost not allowed you to fall. I had wanted you to walk for me. But you walked for you, Jeremy, for yourself. That's the way it should be, you know? . . . Mama says all things have a reason, ain't no need worryin' 'bout things once they's said and done. But I swear, Jeremy, every time I think about that boy with that grenade and those policemen . . . liars, I want to . . . ! Ain't no wrath like a mama's wrath when somebody's hurt her child! That anger is my birthright—don't care what nobody says. . . . I used to watch you in your bed as you slept. Watch you in the still, soft, moonlit darkness that surrounded your crib, in silence, as though beholdin' a miracle. Those tiny eyes, so full of life would be tightly closed and dreamin'. Your hands would open and close on your blanket, as though you were clutchin' on to some dream, some piece of lullaby that was tryin' to slip away. I'd stand there and all my tiredness, my achin' feet and all would just give way, and I would feel renewed. It was as if the Spirit of the Lord, God Himself had whispered, "Woman, be relieved, for this is a beautiful baby." *(She laughs)* 'Bout right through here you'd say, "Awww, Mama." I ain't tryin' to make out like you still a baby, like you never grew up and became a man. But you'll always be my baby, my child, my son to me and ain't no way to get around that. And here I am, sittin' watchin' you again—'cept there ain't no moonlight, and you ain't just sleepin'! Oh Lord, Jeremy, I don't want to hold you. I know the Lord's got things planned for you I ain't even heard of—but it's hard. It's just so hard. It's part of my growth too, I guess. There's a lot more to life than what is seen—I'm learnin' that. God bless you, Jeremy. You're in His hands. He's watchin' and listenin' now. You learned to walk once, and you can do it again . . . and can't nobody stop you. If they try, you just *look* at 'em, Jeremy. You just. . . . *(She stops, looks softly at Jeremy, and breaks down)* Oh God, it's hard—it's so hard for a mama to let go! *(She slides to the floor sobbing into a handkerchief. Presently, she feels herself being helped, lifted up. She responds, rising)* Thank you, Milton. *(She turns, seeing no one near her and MILTON still out in the hall. She nods her head as if understanding something)* Oh . . . thank you, Jeremy.

"The Fishermen" theme (see Production Notes) begins as RUTH exits slowly through the door, meeting MILTON and MAMA E there, and the three of them exit offstage. Lights lower in the reception room. A soft blue special light fades on the coffin as the theme fades, and the sounds of thunder and a fresh spring rain begin.

Fadeout

End

LEE HUNKINS WAS BORN in New York City. She's been writing since 1960. Lee's always daydreaming about how it would feel to be a full-time writer, typing until the wee hours of the morning with a pot of coffee on the stove and a box of Cracker Jacks by the typewriter. But, she's got to earn a living, so the wee hours are presently limited to sleeping. She's worked for the Social Security Administration since 1948, and in five years she'll finally be able to stop dreaming and become a full-time writer. She's had no formal training as a writer, and although she wrote poetry from the time she was fourteen, she never thought much about writing as a career. Actor/director, Maxwell Glanville had (and still has) a community theatre in Harlem. Lee joined his group and learned her craft from the ground up. Working with props, painting sets, working sound and lights, she began to realize all the technical details that go into a production. Words like plot, structure, dialogue became more than just words to her.

Lee's first production at the American Community Theatre was a three act play called, *The Square Peg*. This was followed by two more full length plays, six one act plays and monologues. She moved out of Harlem in 1963 and didn't see her old neighborhood again until almost ten years later. It had changed over the years, and this filled her with a longing for "The good old days." She wondered if she had to go back to the changed Harlem, could she still relate to it. This question prompted a new play, *Hollow Image*. Lee realized that a lot of Black women had their roots in Harlem but had moved on to become successful, and in the climb up the ladder had not looked back. Knowing that her theme was both universal and very important, she felt it should be seen by as many people as possible, and television was the answer. She'd never tried her hand at television writing but assumed it was not that different from writing for the stage. Using a book on television technique, she accepted the challenge. There were a lot of rejection slips between 1973 and 1977, and she'd almost given up when she heard about the Eugene O'Neill Writers Conference in Waterford, Connecticut. She submitted *Hollow Image,* and lo and behold, it was selected for the 1978 National Playwrights Conference. She saw her play rehearsed, taped, and come to life by the enthusiasm and dedication of a group of talented actors and a director with insight, Merrily Mossman. The dream wasn't over. About a month after the conference ended, Lee was notified that she had won the ABC Theatre Award, which consisted of $10,000 cash award and the right of ABC to option the script. On June 24, 1979 the ABC Theatre presented *Hollow Image*, a Titus Production, directed by Marvin Chomsky. When her name appeared on the television screen, Lee cried and wished that her parents had lived to see the beautiful happening. Her brother, Bernard Hunkins, whom Lee refers to as "my rock of Gibraltor," cheered her up by saying, "Mom and Dad are somewhere watching. Mom's fluttering around like a nervous peacock, and Dad's trying to calm her down."

Lee's still working full-time and writing evenings and weekends, presently working on a television drama and a stage play. For relaxation she practices yoga, plays chess, and goes disco dancing. She also attends lectures on Religious Science, being a firm believer in positive thinking. She has to laugh when people refer to her as "an overnight success." If twenty years is overnight, then time does really fly.

Lee says, "What's really kept me from being discouraged is my family and a group of friends who mean more to me than all the money or success that this life has to offer. I'd like to be considered a writer. Not a woman writer or a Black woman writer—just Lee Hunkins, playwright with no color or sex attached. But I've learned a lot in the past two years. There aren't that many opportunities for Black actors. This means that we, the writers, have to get off our rear ends and write for them. My idea is to write comedy, drama, whatever it takes to keep Black people in front of an audience or on a television or motion picture screen. My goal is to write material that Black people can relate to and watch with pride and dignity—material that people of other nationalities can watch and from which they can learn what makes us tick. I don't have any worldly possessions to leave behind, but if I can accomplish my goal, then I think I'm leaving a valuable gift . . . man's understanding of his fellow man."

REVIVAL

Lee Hunkins

CAST

TYLER: *Black man, about 55 years old. Carries himself proudly. He is quiet spoken, but firm.*

JED: *White man, about 35 years old. Cynical, selfish type. Not easy to get along with.*

CHUCK: *White man, 25 years old. Kind, considerate, easy going type.*

LENNY: *Black man, about 20 years old. Thin, sickly type. Admires* TYLER. *Leans on* CHUCK *for his strength. Loves to play the harmonica.*

A PLAY IN ONE ACT

Scene opens in a clearing near the railroad tracks. The sound of a train whistle is heard in the distance. TYLER *is gathering small pieces of wood for a fire.*

JED: Tyler! Hey Tyler, where are you?

TYLER: Over here in the clearin'.

(JED *enters carrying a fresh chicken in a plastic bag. He holds it up for inspection*)

JED: How about that?

TYLER: Looks good. What took you so long?

JED: Tried to talk the farmer out of it. Finally had to chop some wood for him.

TYLER: Where's Chuck and Lenny?

JED: We split up. Thought we'd get more food that way. (*Laughs*) 'Member the last time we went beggin' and . . .

TYLER: We don't beg!

JED: But Tyler . . .

TYLER: We ask . . . we don't beg.

JED: Ask . . . beg . . . 'long as we get somethin' to eat, what's the difference?

TYLER: Pride . . . we still got that.

JED: That don't put food in my gut, so who needs it?

(TYLER *sits down and opens his sack. He pokes around until he finds a Bible.* JED *sits down next to him and rolls a cigarette*)

TYLER: No sense cookin' the chicken till the others get here.

JED: They might be awhile yet. (*A beat*) You know we could . . .

TYLER: We'll wait for Chuck and Lenny and split it four ways.

JED: Goddamn it, Tyler! Sometimes you scare me. You guess what I'm thinkin' 'fore I say it.

TYLER: Nothin' scary 'bout it. Just know you that's all.

(TYLER *starts reading the Bible*)

JED: You been readin' that Bible for the past five years. Ain't you finished it yet?

TYLER: I keep readin' it over.

JED: Expectin' the end to change? (*Laughs at his own joke*)

TYLER: I'm hopin' the change will be in me.

JED: How's that?

TYLER: Forget it.

CHUCK: (*Offstage*) Tyler!

JED: Near the tracks! Just keep walkin'. Hope they got some bread or rolls to go with the chicken.

TYLER: Gettin' choosy?

JED: Ain't no harm in wishin'.

(CHUCK *and* LENNY *enter. They are empty handed except for a sack that* CHUCK *is carrying over his shoulder.* LENNY *flops down; he is tired and out of breath*)

JED: What'd you get?

CHUCK: Nothin'.

JED: Not even some stale bread, or a pie?

CHUCK: Damn it, Jed, I said nothin'!

JED: Okay . . . okay, don't get all riled up about it.

LENNY: It was my fault. I started feelin' sick again.

JED: Why didn't you go on? Lenny could have

107

found us by himself.

CHUCK: He had the shakes. I didn't want to leave him alone.

TYLER: You got to see a doctor, Len.

LENNY: I'll be all right. Just need an old jacket or coat to keep me warm. The Hawk's havin' a good time blowin' thru the holes in this sweater.

CHUCK: Maybe when we hit the next town, they'll have a mission house. Should be able to get some clothes there.

TYLER: He still needs a doctor.

JED: Doctors ain't free.

CHUCK: So, we'll do some odd jobs and get the money.

JED: What's with you anyway? You share your food with him, and just last week you gave him those wool pants.

CHUCK: They fit him better.

JED: You're lyin'. They was your size!

CHUCK: He's sick. We got to look out for him, that's all. Nothin' wrong with that, is there Ty?

TYLER: It's a kind thing you're doin'. Jed ain't reached his good point yet.

(LENNY *takes a paper out of his pocket*)

LENNY: A lady give me this paper. I was shamed to tell her I couldn't read.

JED: (*Takes the paper from* LENNY. LENNY *plays the harmonica softly*) "Come to our Annual Revival Meetin'. All men of God, come and talk to the people. Everybody welcome. Friday, January 15th. Six o'clock. The big tent on the North side of town."

CHUCK: It's only 'bout a mile from here. We passed it on the way. Ty, do you think we could go?

TYLER: Guess it'd be all right.

JED: (*Flinging the paper back to* LENNY) We can't go in that place. Who do you think we are? Good, upstandin' pillars of the community? We're bums lookin' for a handout and the next train headin' west!

LENNY: We ain't askin' to join the church. We just want to listen.

CHUCK: And that paper says all are welcomed.

JED: *All* don't include us, and don't you know any other songs? Always playin' the same damn tune.

LENNY: I like this one. (*Continues playing the harmonica*)

CHUCK: We could sit in the back row and . . .

JED: I ain't goin'.

TYLER: You afraid of religion, Jed?

JED: Don't need it. (*A beat*) Let me see that paper again.

(LENNY *gives him the paper*)

JED: (*Continuing*) They want men of God to preach.

CHUCK: So?

JED: Why don't Tyler preach to them?

CHUCK *and* LENNY: Yeah, Tyler . . . that's a good idea!

TYLER: I'm not a man of God.

JED: You believe in him, don't you?

TYLER: Yes.

CHUCK: You know the Bible like the back of your hand.

LENNY: You're always tellin' us 'bout Moses and all those other people, and you talk real good too.

CHUCK: Come on, Tyler . . . do it!

TYLER: No. We ought to be movin' out tonight. Try a new town . . . maybe find a doctor for Lenny.

JED: You afraid of religion, Tyler?

(*The two men look at each other for a second.* TYLER *turns away from the group. They watch him, waiting for him to speak*)

TYLER: My mama use to take me to church every Sunday mornin'. Reverend Otis would work himself into a sweat, and the people would start jumpin' and shoutin'. I'd sit there with my eyes closed, listenin' to every word. Use to say I was gonna be a minister too and tell people how to find God.

LENNY: Was he lost?

TYLER: I thought he was. Time I was fifteen, things started goin' bad for me. I got into one fix after another. It hit me too late that God wasn't lost . . . I was. Jed's right. Ain't nobody gonna listen to what a bum has to say.

CHUCK: But they don't know who you are.

LENNY: You can go in first so they won't see us together.

TYLER: These rags will tell it all.

LENNY: You said Jesus didn't wear fancy clothes.

TYLER: They're liable to run us outta town.

LENNY: They stoned him. Tyler you ain't like us. It's like you got somethin' inside that's fightin' to get out. When you read from the good book and talk to us 'bout havin' faith . . . it gives me a good feelin' inside. It's like . . . I know I ain't much, but God's lookin' out for me too.

CHUCK: I feel the same way. So does Jed, 'cept he's too stubborn to admit it.

JED: Never mind all this bullshit, are you gonna do it?

TYLER: My jacket's torn under the arms.

CHUCK: Just don't get carried away with your preachin' and fling your arms up.

LENNY: I'll shine your shoes with some old fashioned spit and polish.

JED: Well good buddy, sounds like you're all set . . . nothin' to stop you now.

(TYLER *looks at the three men. He is undecided. He touches the Bible*)

TYLER: Wonder what time it is?

CHUCK: Sun's goin' down . . . must be 'bout five-thirty or six.

TYLER: Guess we better be goin' then. Don't want to be late for my first sermon.

CHUCK and LENNY: *(In unison)* He's gonna do it! Hot damn!

TYLER: On one condition . . . we go in together.

LENNY: But Ty . . .

TYLER: Together . . . or not at all.

(LENNY and CHUCK nod their heads in agreement)

JED: Guess you'll be breakin' up with us now. Maybe get the notion to take up preachin'.

TYLER: 'Cause of one revival meetin'? I just want to know if I can.

LENNY: But there'll be other towns, won't there Ty?

TYLER: Other towns, and other tent meetins'.

(LENNY is happy. He starts playing his harmonica. CHUCK picks up his sack and slings it over his shoulder. He and LENNY start walking in the direction of the meeting)

CHUCK: Comin', Reverend Tyler?

TYLER: Don't start playin' the fool now. *(CHUCK laughs. He and LENNY walk offstage. LENNY is still* playing the same tune on his harmonica. TYLER *puts his Bible in the sack and ties it up)* Comin' Jed? *(JED doesn't answer.* TYLER *picks up his sack and starts to walk off. He stops and turns toward* JED*)* Man's got to have somethin', Jed. Even if it's just a dream . . . he's got to have somethin'. So long.

(TYLER walks offstage. JED *appears to be fighting a battle within himself. Suddenly he grabs the chicken and stuffs it in the sack)*

JED: *(Shouting loudly)* Hey Tyler!

TYLER: *(Offstage)* Yeah?

JED: Wait up. *(TYLER comes back and stands at a distance, waiting for* JED. JED *ties up his sack)* I'll . . . I'll walk a ways with you. Ain't goin' to no revival, but it can't do no harm to just walk a bit. *(JED walks over to* TYLER. *The two men look at each other.* TYLER *smiles, and* JED *is embarrassed. Walking away)* If we goin' . . . come on.

JED *exits quickly.* TYLER *looks around . . . he thinks for a second . . . then nods his head as if to say that what he's about to do is right. He exits. The sound of* LENNY *playing the harmonica can still be heard. A train whistle can be heard growing louder, drowning out the music, as the curtains close, and the stage goes to black.*

End

CHERRY JACKSON

A philosophical sketch:

We have been sent, and so we come, toilet-trained, holding up our clean hands to our masters.
Our faces uplifted, with smiles, expecting to be validated—lest we die.

THE PERIOD BETWEEN the womb and the tomb is a brief one, and so it is essential to squeeze the life out of every moment lest we be taken to our graves kicking and screaming—ill-prepared for the other side of life. The records show that many who have gone before us were not ready. And if those records were spread out before us and we were to study them, then we would see that some who objected were justified in their complaints, for it takes a whole natural lifetime to see into this thing here.

Even when the veil is snatched from our eyes through some wonderful daily miracle or a sudden moment of tragedy, the snag of our nails grabs it and pulls it back into place again. And so the brave ones of us peer through tattered holes—seeing clear flashes from time to time. And those of us who are not so brave long for the comfort of our mothers' wombs.

The not so brave are justified too. For there is scarce little time in one life span to heal the breach which splits us at birth. Can you see the pink blanket waiting to receive the infant

She—and the blue blanket wanting to welcome the He. Can you see the rich being put over here in this corner—and the poor over there. Can you see the sign which reads, "All men, women, and children over here—and niggers over there." We do have a poor beginning, and we do suffer from it.

The infant is taken from the mother's womb and is carried, kicking and crying, to the nursery—given a formula when what it wants naturally is to be put to the mother's breast. When we are small children, our parents want us to be safe and behave ourselves. But what we really want is to learn by doing and taking risks, and this is sometimes confused with misbehaving. When we are a little older, the Board of Education wants us to come to school and sit down and listen in order to be trained. But what we really want then is to run wild and test our muscles, scream, and listen only to the sound of our own voices. If we should survive this period, then our teachers and professors want us to study so we will pass our examinations and become professionals. But we want to continue playing. If we should emerge upright through all of this, then the entire system hits us broadside. The preacher wants us to pray to save our souls. The policeman wants us to follow the law, but we are hard-put to do it for we are a lawless nation. The boss wants us to pay attention to production so that profits will increase. The politicians want our vote for the same reason. The devil wants our soul, but we are not yet ready for hell.

But what is it that we want. Society would have us believe that we want comfort. That almost all of us want to be comfortable. The term is almost as prevalent as bad air. The politicians will say, "I am not comfortable saying this thing or that thing to my constituency. They believe that I am building cathedrals—It is uncomfortable for me to tell them that I am really digging ditches."

Society wants us to think that we want comfort—But I don't think we do. Dare I say that there is nothing comfortable in the midst of an orgasm. But who would give up the joy for comfortability. To let go of our fears and hostilities is not comfortable, but in order to live fully we must do it. To explore the unknown is not comfortable, but who would give up exploration and knowing for comfort. When I am comfortable, I usually am put to sleep or lapse into a light stupor.

It is sometimes difficult to go against the tide. The community wants us to pick cotton, but we want to grow strawberries. Cotton is not red, or plump, or sweet. What ought we to do then. There is so much pressure to pick cotton. As for me, I will grow strawberries and take what heaps of cotton may be put upon my head for doing it.

Cherry Jackson
August 14, 1980

IN THE MASTER'S HOUSE
THERE ARE MANY MANSIONS

Cherry Jackson

CHARACTERS

TYRONE WILLIAMS: *The Deceased, age 29 at the time of his death.*
LARRY JAMES FLETCHER: *A childhood friend of* TYRONE'*s. He is 26 years old.*
MR. FULLER: *Funeral home director and mortician. He is well on the other side of
middle age and very protective of his business which he inherited from his father,
who started it and built it up during the 1940s and 50s.*

All three men are Black.

*Music: Snare drums (for brushing effect) & percussions; organ; bass. The different instruments are
used for transitions and are an integral part of the play.*

Prologue: The color motif, so far as it is carried out in the outer clothing of TYRONE *and*
FLETCHER, *is taken from the traditional Chinese theatre. The Chinese actors, however, wear
different color masks rather than clothing to symbolize the characters they are portraying. White
usually represents power and destruction, yellow represents cunning, and black symbolizes trust-
worthiness, servant-like behavior, and loyalty.*

*Setting: All the action takes place in the mortuary. The setting is the front office and the embalming
room of a small mortuary for black people in the flat-lands of the Fillmore district around Fillmore
and O'Farrell streets in San Francisco. The time is around 11:00 in the morning, early June,
1976.*
   Right center stage is an ordinary embalming table on which rests the remains of TYRONE
WILLIAMS. *The body is dressed in a white silk suit with yellow silk lining, a yellow silk shirt, a
white tie, and white leather platform boots. The body is covered neatly from shoulder to foot with a
white sheet.*
   *Up stage left is a small area suggesting a front office with a counter and telephone and a
glass-panelled door leading out onto the streets.*
   The embalming room (where TYRONE *is) is small, but all the necessary equipment and supplies
are present. On the portable chrome table at the right back wall we can see on the top shelf a tangle of
tubing that has been washed but not yet put away. On the second shelf are embalming fluids. On the
bottom shelf we can see different kinds of tools used for embalming such as clamps, scissors, needles,
etc. The gravity pitcher is still resting in its rack which is suspended from the ceiling; the tubing
suspended from the pitcher has been tied off. At left back stage is a small enclave which suggests a
supply room, but the audience cannot see the interior.*
   *At left back against the wall near the door is a small table with a chair. Resting on the table are a
pen and a large, open guest book for the visitors to sign. This ensemble is usually found in the main
viewing room, but* MR. FULLER *has not had time to set up the viewing room yet. Near the enclave is
a waist-high stool with a pile of folded terry cloth towels on top. There is a small white door at back
center stage, and it leads from the main office and opens into the embalming room.*
   *Neither the embalming room nor the front office area is somber. Both are well lighted and suggest
an air of everyday business rather than of a mournful mortuary.*

A PLAY IN ONE ACT

Scene 1

As the curtain goes up, the first action is in the embalming room with MR. FULLER *in a business suit rushing around picking up dirty towels and putting them into the supply room. While he is in the supply room, there is an impatient five sharp raps with a coin on the glass panel of the front door.* MR. FULLER *rushes out of the supply room, straightening his coat and brushing his hands as he hurries out the white door, through the front office, towards the front door. As he rushes towards the door, the embalming room lights go down but not out, and the lights in the small front office come up. Before* MR. FULLER *reaches the front door, there are another five sharp raps with the coin on the glass panel.*

MR. FULLER: *(Agitated, hurrying to door)* Yes, yes, I'm coming. Don't knock the door in! *(Mutters under his voice)* Damn fool!

(Goes to the front door and slides back the big main lock, then twists the smaller bolt lock to admit FLETCHER. FLETCHER *is dressed in a black cotton suit, black shirt, black tie, has a black silk handkerchief in the breast pocket of his coat, and wears a small black cap. A black silk armband on his left upper arm signifies the death of someone close. He is of medium height, well-built, and clean shaven.)*

FLETCHER: *(Entering, obviously nervous and tries to couch his nervousness in joke as he enters. Speaks in a loud and giddy voice)* What y'all got everything so locked up here for? If yo' clients ain't satisfied, ain't no danger in them jumping up and running out of here is it? *(Laughs nervously at his own joke as he looks around the office)*

FULLER: *(Obviously not amused, locks the door behind* FLET.*)* Are you the young man who called me from the Greyhound bus station an hour or so ago:

FLET: *(Becoming more serious now)* Yes, I...I... *(Lowers his voice a little)* came up here to pay my last repsects to my friend, Tyrone Williams.

FULLER: *(rushed, business-like)* Yes, yes, I just finished Mr. Williams. In fact, I haven't had time to move the remains to the main viewing room yet. We'll have to rush you through this. It's getting on towards mid-day, and after twelve on Friday and Saturday it's just impossible. My helper has been out for two days sick, and I've had to do everything myself.

FLET: Was my friend pretty well shot up?

FULLER: *(Going behind the counter and taking out a big account ledger)* Just about everyone who comes in here is pretty well shot up. Why don't you come over to the counter for a minute. I need some information before you go in. Now what did you say your name was?

FLET: Larry James Fletcher.

FULLER: Now let's see...Mr. Larry James Fletcher. *(He writes* FLET*'s name in the big book)* Now where do you live, Mr. Fletcher?

FLET: Greensville, Texas.

FULLER: *(Writes in book again)* And where were you born?

FLET: Same place.

FULLER: *(Writes and continues in business-like manner)* And what is your social security number?

FLET: *With pride in having committed his number to memory, he rattles it off in military fashion)* six-four-two-dash-four-six-dash-six-six-one-four.

FULLER: *(Records number)* Place of employment?

FLET: *(Hesitatingly answers, begins wondering)* Uh, Mr. Wallace's Orange Grove.

FULLER: Marital Status—

FLET: *(Becoming suspicious and a little angry with all the questions)* What?!

FULLER: Are you married?

FLET: *(Angry now and showing it)* No I ain't, and it's none of your business if I is. *(His anger mounts along with his voice)* I just came in here to see my friend—I didn't come in here to sign up for no welfare!

FULLER: *(In a very matter-of-fact, business-like voice)* Well you may not want to get on welfare, but the fact is that your friend *was* on medi-aid and they are paying for his burial, and this is the form that I have to fill out for everybody viewing the body. If I don't give them the information, they don't give me my money for working on him. *(Getting weary now and wants* FLET *to answer the questions or be on his way)* Now, I suggest if you don't want to cooperate...

FLET: *(Still angry but broken and tired, snaps back in an angry voice)* Okay, okay... *(Pauses, heaves a big sigh)* I ain't got no wife, no kids, and I ain't got no mansions, no jet airplanes and no yachts neither!

FULLER: *(Pretending to be friendly)* Date of birth—

FLET: 4-27-49.

FULLER: *(Relieved)* Okay, now that ought to do it. Now just place your right thumb... *(Takes* FLET*'s thumb and presses it on the thumb print pad)* on this pad right here, Mr. Fletcher, and we can press down gently. *(FLET obliges without comment)* That's it now. *(MR. FULLER leads* FLET*'s thumb to the line on the bottom of the form and presses his thumb* *to print)* Now we just place it on this bottom line here and press. See—no ugly ink stains or anything—nothing to wipe off. Now just give me your signature at the X here, and we'll be all set.

(FLET signs the form and lets the pen slide from his lifeless hand into the book. He looks up slowly and realizes it is time to go in and see his friend. His fear of the dead returns. The organ music comes up slowly and softly in the background. FLET. recognizes the old tune as "Nearer My God to Thee." He has heard this tune on several occasions all through his childhood and mostly on sad occasions. The tune sets the fear in him as MR. FULLER puts the book and forms away)

FULLER: *(While motioning FLET towards the direction of the door leading to the room where TY is)* Please follow me, Mr. Fletcher, this way.

(Now MR. FULLER has fallen silent, as though speech had never been a part of his experience, as he leads FLET. up to the door. FLET pauses before the closed door; he is rigid with fear)

FLET: Is . . . is it cold in there?

FULLER: *(Now with grave dignity)* No, son. Go on in and make your peace.

FLET *stiffens with readiness as MR. FULLER opens the door for him to enter. The lights go out in MR. FULLER's office and go up bright in the embalming room.*

Scene 2

MR. FULLER, *with a motion of the head, urges FLET in. As FLET enters, he spots the chair and table just inside the door against the wall. He quickly takes off his cap in such a way as to hide the right side of his face so that he will not have to look at his friend just yet. He stares at the open book on top of the table to avoid reality.*

FULLER: *(Seeing FLET's hesitation suggests)* If you want to, Mr. Fletcher, you can sit down here and sign our guest book.

(The sound of signing anything more sends a shiver through FLET.. MR. FULLER sees this, slowly closes the door behind him, leaving FLET. alone with his friend. The organ music, which has been quietly playing, now goes down and out. As FLET is not able to collect himself, he sits down very rigidly with his back to his friend. While clutching his black cap in one hand, he scribbles something in the guest book with the other. The snare drums with percussions come up softly in the background. TYRONE sits up naturally, swinging his legs over the side of the table. FLET suspects something but doesn't look. TY's actions are not at all frightening or unnatural. TY knows that FLET is there, and he knows perfectly well how

frightened FLET is. In fact, ever since the bullet that killed him entered his body, he has had perfect knowledge of everything around him. FLET clutches both sides of the table and turns his head a little and stretches his eyes to look over his right shoulder. TY hops down from the table with a thump. FLET is terrified and holds on to the table for dear life. TY straightens up, pulls his clothes into place. He is about the same size as FLET and is a perfect picture of life. There is nothing death-like about him. TY knows that it will be a delicate challenge to abate FLET's fear. He walks slowly but deliberately over to FLET's right, giving FLET a wide berth. FLET looks at TY now for the first time, not believing what he sees. Fear has frozen his buttocks to the chair and his fingers to the table. There is no danger of him running. Drums and percussions go down to marginal but not out)

TYRONE: *(Appealing to FLET)* Hey, Fletch, man— it's me. *(Laying his fingers on his own lapels)*

FLET: *(At the sound of TY's voice, his mouth drops open and his disbelieving eyes are fixed on TY. With great effort, manages to raise his right finger pointing towards TY, and shaking his head in disbelief, stammers)* You . . . you . . . ain't . . . you . . . you ain't Tyrone.

TY: *(Jumps back a little ways and cocks his chin in a gentle scold)* Come on man, it's me! Your old buddy Tyrone. *(Makes a step towards FLET, but sees FLET's fear mount, so he retreats)* Hey man, what you want me to do to prove it?

FLET: *(For the first time mustering a little courage, he comes forth with a flood of words, moving more to the edge of his chair and pointing at TY)* You ain't Tyrone —you can't fool me. Dis here is some kind of trick or something. *(Gains more confidence now as he goes on)* You and dat *(Pointing out towards MR. FULLER's office)* old bastard out dere done cooked dis up to get some free money from de gubment. *(TY starts to appeal, but FLET's confidence keeps coming, even to the point where FLET stands up, being careful to put the chair between TY and himself. The music goes out; FLET rushes on)* Naw—naw, you ain't my friend. My friend was killed by the po-lice four days ago. And you ain't never seen no nigger gettin' up waltzing around after he done been hit by no three-fifty-seven mag.

TY: *(Walking around in a small circle, one hand in his pocket, scratching his head for another idea of approach —Idea! He turns to face FLET and appeals)* Okay, okay, Fletch. You remember when we used to shine shoes on Broad street in front of the five- and-dime? *(FLET nods his head but still not trusting)* You remember Cracker Willis and what he used to do to us when we shined his shoes?

FLET: *(With a little nostalgic smile he looks at TY)* Yeah, that old son-of-a-bitch never gave us nothing more den a nickel.

TY: (*Knows he's winning* FLET *over now*) And what was the song we made up about him?

FLET: (*Trying to remember and smiles as the memory of the song comes back to him. He starts to establish the rhythm of the tune as he remembers it. He places his right foot on the rung of the chair and begins to beat out the rhythm with his hand on his thigh. Percussions and brush come in marginally*)
Willis is so ugly
Willis is so po'
We ain't gonna
Shine his shoes no mo' . . .
(FLET *forgets the next lines, tries but can't remember.* TY *comes in and helps with two or three words to get* FLET *going again*)

TY: He gives us . . .

FLET: (*Takes it up again*)
He gives us a nickel
When we charges him a dime
We gonna take dat nickel
And stop us his behind.

TY: You remember the dance we made up?

FLET: Yeah . . . (*Reluctantly*) You mean de dance about Ol' Man Willis?

(TY *begins a soft-shoe dance reminiscent of the childhood dance they made up and repeats the rhyme as he dances. After the first few lines,* FLET *reluctantly picks up the rhyme and joins in the dance, mirroring* TY)

TY:
Willis is so ugly
Willis is so po'
(FLET *joins in*)
We ain't gonna
shine his shoes no mo'.
He gives us a nickel
When we charges him a dime
We gonna take dat nickel
and stop up his behind.
(*Music goes down and out. Both men laugh.* FLET *forgets himself for that instant. But his suspicion returns.* TY *sees this and acts quickly so as not to lose the ground he has already gained*)

TY: And . . . and where did we used to go every other Thursday night?

FLET: (*Suspect*) Never mine me tellin' you—you tell me where we use to go every other Thursday night?

TY: (*Very precise*) We used to go down to the city auditorium and slip in to watch the wrestling matches.

FLET: (*Amused with his next question*) And who wus tag team champions when you got dat hickie put on yo' head fu sittin' in the White folks' section?

TY: (*In an amused fashion feel the spot on the left back side of his head as he remembers*) Let's see . . . it was . . . (*Pauses, then in TV quiz show fashion, quickly points at* FLET *as he says*) Green Hornet and the Reptile vs . . . let's see . . . (TY *unbuttons his jacket, puts one fist on his hip, and cups his chin with his other hand as he walks around. But just as* FLET *starts to show some glee in trapping* TY, TY *remembers with a whirl and shoots the name at* FLET) Sugar Sweet George and Kenny!

FLET: (*Also in TV quiz show fashion*) Dat's right! (*Regroups himself quickly and, in trial lawyer fashion, demands more of* TY) Never mine who wus vers'n who—who won de championship?

TY: (*Buttoning his jacket, perfectly confident and relaxed*) Sugar Sweet George and Kenny. (*Waits to see* FLET*'s reaction*)

FLET: (*Looking more closely at* TY Not so self-assured any more. Slowly, doubtfully*) Yeah, yeah, dat's right—but . . . but (*More confused now than doubtful*) how you . . . (*Stands behind the chair, holding the back of the chair with both hands. In pleading fashion*) Is dat you, Tyrone?

TY: Yeah, man—yeah, it's me. What you think I've been trying to tell ya.

FLET: But . . . but dey told us you wus dead. (*A slow, knowing smile breaks across* FLET*'s face*) Hey, Tyrone—Tyrone—you smart ass nigger . . . you up to yo' smart ass tricks again . . . goddamn it, man. (*For the first time starts in the direction of* TY *for the palm-slap greeting.* TY *puts out his two hands, palms up*) Dey told us you wus . . . (FLET *comes down with his palms on* TY*'s, and* TY *grasps* FLET*'s two hands for an instant*) . . . dea . . . d. (FLET*'s body goes rigid as he makes contact with* TY*'s cold hands.* FLET *snatches his hands back immediately and folds his arms so that his fists are under his arm pits. He squeezes down on his fists with his arms to lend stability to himself. Peers into* TY*'s eyes*) You cold, Tyrone. (*Puzzled, sad*)

TY: (*Matter-of-fact but still friendly*) So I'm cold, man. So what? It's still me.

FLET: (*Draws back a little now, but not so frightened as he is puzzled*) Den . . . (*Pointing at* TY) den you is dead.

TY: (*Losing a little patience now*) Yeah, yeah . . . I'm dead. (*Stretches out hands and lets them drop to his side*) You found me out. (*Little sarcastic laugh*) I'm stone dead.

FLET: (*Still not entirely letting go of the idea that this whole thing is a ruse*) Well if you so cold and dead, how come you ain't ashy? When niggers gits cold, dey gits ashy. I know dis as a fack.

TY: (*Scratching his head*) Well, let me put it like this . . . . (*A little smile falls over his face*) Let's just say I got a lot of lanolin on me . . .

FLET: What!

TY: And a lot of lanolin in me! *(Smiles)* Old man Fuller knows his job, don't he? Don't I look as good now *(Smoothing down his hair)* as I did when you and me used to be over at the Do Drop Inn after work throwin' down them shots of I. W. Harper's?

FLET: *(Relaxing a little more)* Shit, if you ask me, you look a damn lot better, *(A little jealous)* and I ain't never seen you in no white silk suit while you wus live. Look like you doin' mo' better when you's dead den you wus when you wus liv'n. *(Admiringly inspects* TY's *suit from close up.* TY *is not impressed but lets* FLET *have his moment)* Man, dis here is de real McCoy, huh? *(Touches* TY's *arm and circles him in an admiring fashion)*

TY: *(Straddling the chair and sitting down)* Yeah, Mama went way in debt for all this. I didn't need no white suit, but Mama didn't know no better.

FLET: Yo' mama got plenty sense, Tyrone, but she wus always like dat about you, gettin' you everything all de time and taking care y'all. I remember dat las' time you got in trouble with ol' man Westley. Yo' mama had you and yo' brothers out of dat town over night. Next thing we heard of you, y'all wus in San Francisco. Yeah, yo' mama always took care of y'all, all right. I wish my mama would help me some. *(Gets a little angry at his own mother)* She ain't never tellin' me nothin' but, *(Puts his hands on his hips and mocks his mother's voice and motions)* "Git outter dis house and make some money. Git outter dis house and fine yo' self a job." *(Back to his own voice)* Goddamn! You think I was the laziest nigger in Greensville. *(Now earnestly tries to convince* TY*)* Well, I ain't. I'm one of de few niggers left in dat town wants to work. Ol' man Wallace tol' me dat outter his own mouf. He may be a cracker, but he give you credick. Dem young dudes who come back from Viet Nam ain't go do no work. Dey ain't go do nothin' sep sit aroun' and blow dat weed all day. Why, I'm de only nigger in dat town who can pick a ring roun' dem wet-backs comin' over dere in pickin' season. In fack, I wus de only one who got a raise durin' de whole pickin' season. Ol' man Wallace even put me in charge of some of dem suckers who wus sluffen off. And I ain't sayin' dat I ken speak none o' dat Es-pan-ñole, but I got de work out 'em an' dat's what counts.

(All this time TY *has been listening and observing. He has not shown any signs of approval or disapproval. He gets up from the chair, walks contemplatively around a little bit before he speaks)*

TY: *(Quietly)* Looks like if you keep this up, you'll be old man Wallace's number one overseer in no time.

FLET: *(Now straddles the chair, sits down, and throws up his hands in defense)* Naw, man, naw. Not me. De wages ain't high enough, and you can't get no overtime. Anyway, as soon as I get myself some wheels, I'm gonna be gettin' outter Greensville. I wus thinkin' 'bout Frisco till I heard 'bout you . . . *(Doesn't finish the sentence, but notices that he is not frightened of* TY *any longer. Pauses a little and goes on)* When yo' mama wrote us about what happened to you, I changed my mind. But today gettin' off de Greyhound bus and walkin' over here, I know I don't want to live in Frisco. *(TY laughs a knowing laugh.* FLET *goes on, pointing in the direction from where he has come)* You know dat little place over dere on uh . . . uh . . . Market and somethin' called de Blue Light? *(TY nods and smiles)* Well, I went in dere just to get myself a little cold drink. No sooner den I sits down, dis clown had his hand in my pocket fo' I did, *(disgustedly)* talkin' 'bout he so stoned he don't know which way is up. If I hadn't left my blade at home, he sho' wouldn'ta had no trouble findin' out which way wus down. And all these ho's right roun' *(Pointing again)* de corner dere. And what the hell is dat big old pink thing where all dem folks is livin' anyway?

TY: *(Obliges)* Folks call it the Pink Palace.

FLET: Shit—palace my ass—dat thing looks like San Quentin without de gun towers. And ho's and pimps all roun'. I must have counted five on one corner. Dere wus one fine young chick—couldn't been mo' den seventeen or eighteen at de mos'—dere she wus—dis White dude had stopped his little Datsun pick-up right on de corner. And dere she wus—standin' out dere on de streets, leanin' over in de truck, givin' dis guy a hand job with one hand and eatin' a hamburger with de other. De dude was laid back, man, grinnin' like a two-year-old baby in his crib.

TY: *(Inquiring, curious about* FLET's *understanding of what he'd observed)* You saw a lot on your way over here, huh, Fletch?

FLET: *(Rushes on, not listening to* TY, *not wanting to lose the spotlight)* But I will say one thing—I have to give it to de dudes roun' here for one thing *(He gets up from the chair, becoming more and more animated)* dey do know how to dress. Man, I ain't never seen so many super-flies in my whole life as I saw between de bus station and over here. But dere wus dis one pretty nigger. He came outter one of de little motels over dere. Man, he had on a purple suit dat would make yo' mouf water. It wus cut somethin' like your'n, *(Goes over to* TY *and brushes a tiny particle off the back shoulders of* TY's *jacket)* but de coat wus almost down to his knees. De sucker had on a wide-brimmed maroon hat *(Shows the size with his hands while speaking)* with a purple band. I mean de dude wus bad! And do you know what de cat wus drivin'?

TY: *(Answers, almost stern and hostile)* Yes! He was driving a black Bro-ham with chrome grill and gangster white walls.

FLET: *(Surprised)* Did you know de cat?

TY: Yes, his name is Carcinoma.

FLET: What?

TY: People around here call him Carcinoma.

FLET: Well, don't just let dem words just roll outter yo' mouf so easy. A *Bro-ham* ain't nothin' to be turnin' up yo' nose at. Dat sucker must be sittin' on a mint. I wouldn't mind comin' to Frisco if I could get in on somethin' like dat.

TY: Something like what, Fletcher?

FLET: I mean dis is de first nigger I ever seen with a special made Bro-ham. I ain't never seen but one Bro-ham in Greensville, and it wus bein' drove by one of dem fat-ass White politicians. So, I mean, dis Black cat, Carcinoma, must be doin' somethin' right.

TY: *(Matter-of-fact)* He sells dope and strings out women and puts them on the streets.

FLET: What?

TY: You heard me.

FLET: *(Collecting himself)* Well . . . I mean . . . I mean I could look past lot of things when I can get my hands on some money.

TY: *(Staring into vacant space)* Naw, man, you can't look past nothin'. 'Cause when you get round to tryin' to look past it, it just keeps staring you back in the face. You saw all that stuff on your way over here, didn't you? You would have to be a fool to try and look past all that.

FLET: Well I ain't no fool, and I ain't stupid, and I knowed a lot fo' I got up here. And one thing I know is dat you were tryin' to get yo' hands on some quick money when dey got you, wasn't you?

TY: *(Simply, nodding his head)* Yeah, yeah . . .

FLET: *(Goes on angrily)* Hell, what makes you think you so lily white pure? *(Getting angrier and remembering childhood days)* You always did think you wus so much better den everybody else, Tyrone. Even when we wus little you use to ack like dat. And in high school you use to laugh at me when we'd be together because I'd get scared when you would talk back to White folks. And now look what done happen to you. You even went and broke into de Black church and tried to steal de gubment food stamps. Dat prove you ain't got no sense. Dey shot you in de church and dey kil't yo' ass, didn't day? *(Hammers message home)* Ain't *nobody* never got away wid stealin' nothin' from de gubment. You ain't got *no* respeck fo' *nobody*: not White folks, de *po*-lice, de gubment, God, or de church.

(A second of reflective silence; then TY *begins with a little laugh. The impact of what* FLET *has said hits him harder and harder. His laughter builds to a point where his whole body is shaking with it)*

FLET: *(Pleased at finally saying something to get back at* TY, *but gets a little scared when he sees* TY *on the verge of becoming hysterical. Speaks in order to interrupt)* Well . . . well ain't I right? *(Waits intensely)*

TY: *(Cools down his laughing, coughs to clear his throat, then looks at* FLET *for a moment and bolts towards him.* FLET *is frightened and thinks that* T *is going to attack him.* TY *snatches* FLET'*s cap and puts it on.* FLET *starts to move backwards as* TY *moves forwards towards him.* TY *goes into his best down-home shuffling-nigger voice)* No suh, Mr. Wallace, suh. Y'all is wrong, suh, I mean, y'all is right, suh. Yes suh. I respecks y'all suh, right down to de las' bone in my body. Yes suh, y'all knows how to treat a nigger all right, suh. Yes suh, Mr. Wallace, suh, y'all might be a red-neck but y'all sho' ain't scared to give no nigger no credick when he can do de work. *(FLET is puzzled and still frightened, thinking that* TY *is going to attack him.* TY *stands at attention in front of* FLET *and salutes him in military fashion)* Yes suh, Cap'n Wallace. What y'all wants me to do now, suh? Y'all wants me to go ober dere and shoot down dem gooks. Yes suh. *(TY does a quick salute and about face.* FLET *is still astonished and speechless.* TY *goes over to center stage, gets into a crouched position, and pretends to spray down the "gooks" in military, machine-gun fashion while making the noise of the machine gun as he fires)* t-t-t-t-t-t- . . . *(TY then straightens up, brings the gun up to shoulder position, and marches in high-stepping, British goose-step fashion, back over to* FLET *who is now hypnotized and immobilized by* TY'*s actions.* TY *stands in front of* FLET *and salutes)* Mission completed, suh. What y'all wants me to do now, Colonel Wallace suh? Panama, suh? But dem's our little brown brothers down dere, suh. Oh, no suh. *(He quickly takes off his cap in an apologetic manner)* I ain't questionin' nothin' y'all done tol' me, suh. *(Puts cap back on and does an about-face. Repeats the same machine-gun action as before. Comes back to* FLET *with a little less enthusiasm this time. Salutes; comes to attention)* Yes suh, Gen'l Wallace, suh. Any further orders, suh? Af-ika, suh?! *(Jumps back in disbelief)* But Gen'l Wallace, suh, *(Shaking his head)* Af-ika, suh . . . . *(TY snatches his cap off again)* Oh no suh . . . yes suh . . . Af-ika, suh. Yes suh, Gen'l Wallace. Y'all kin trust us niggers, suh. *(Salutes and does an about face and goes into a frenzy of machine gun fire. While firing, he looks at* FLET *to see if* FLET *gets the message.* FLET *is still frustrated and frightened.* TY *gives up and comes an end of this pretense. He stops, blinks, looks at* FLET *again, and drops his hands in defeat, not pretending anymore. He stands up straight and in a defeated, low voice repeats the childhood rhyme that he and* FLET *made up)* Willis is so ugly—Willis is so po'—ain't go shine his shoes no mo' . . . *(Looks at* FLET *and gently tosses* FLET*'s cap back to him)*

FLET: *(When he catches his cap, he snaps back to reality, but he is still puzzled. Goes slowly and inquiringly over to* TY *and peers into* TY*'s face)* Tyrone, is you all right?

TY: *(Not looking at* FLET *but smoothing his clothes)* Yeah, yeah, I'm all right.

FLET: Den why you ackin' so crazy? *(No answer from* TY; FLET *goes on)* You know dem newspaper clippings yo' mama sent us said dat you wus usin' dope on yo' self. *(Pauses to see* TY*'s reaction)* Wus you puttin' dat shit in yo' veins, Tyrone? Is dat how come you ackin' so crazy?

TY: *(Honestly replying but angry at* FLET *for being taken in by the press)* No, man. I was clean. Even the coroner had to say that, man. *(Getting more angry)* And I quote: "The body is that of a well-developed, well-muscled, wiry, well-nourished, Black man with no abnormalities noted. *(Proud and angry)* The external surface and contour of the heart are normal. The four chambers and four valves are normal. *(Continues with angry sarcasm)* The consistency of the liver is firm, and there is no evidence of any foreign or synthetic substances present in the system." End quote. *(Now shouts at* FLET*)* And if you don't believe me . . .

FLET: *(Waving his hands)* Hey, man. Hey, man. I believe you. Hey, Tyrone, man—you wus my ace boon, man. *(Pleadingly)* You don't think I would come all de way up here to see somebody I didn't care about do you? I mean . . . you ain't go hold no grudges against me is you? You know what dey say—dat people have all kinds of powers after dey die. Say, man, say, Tyrone, you know I wouldn't say anything to hurt you . . .

TY: *(Breaking in)* Naw, Fletcher, *(Becoming less angry)* I wasn't thinking nothing like that. I know you did come all the way up here to see me, and that bus ride must have been long and made you tired, huh?

FLET: Naw, it wasn't nothin', Tyrone. Dem niggers at home didn't even think I was comin'. Dey didn't think I could get enough together to get up here and back. But I managed. I have to go back today though on the two-thirty. I got to be back home by Monday 'cause ol' man Wallace might put some of us to work on his place, and it takes me forty-eight hours to get back.

TY: *(Sympathetically)* Hey, Fletcher, I wish I had some bread to lay on you. But, I ain't got . . .

FLET: *(Cuts in emphatically)* Naw, naw, naw, no sweat. I wanted to do it. And hey look, if you had any coins, you would do best to be layin' dem on yo' mama so dat she won't be spendin' de rest of her nat'chal life payin' fo' dat white silk suit you got on dere, pretty boy.

TY: Yeah, when Mama found out that the state was going to bury me in my autopsy gown, she went out and borrowed everything she could to buy me this. I wish I had some way of paying her back. She didn't know that this was the worst thing of all she could have bought me.

FLET: *(Disgusted with* TY*)* Worst thing of all . . . . Boy, Tyrone, you ain't got no appreciation at all. Here yo' mama done gone out and got herself in debt just so you kin look good, and all you kin do is criticize. *(Goes over to* TY, *inspecting and admiring his suit)* Damn, man, if I had dis I could get me any gal in Greensville. I . . . *(Voice trails off here as he begins to get an idea)* Say, Tyrone, we 'bout the same size, ain't we?

TY: Yeah.

FLET: Well, I wus thinkin'—I mean . . . *(Hesitation now, not sure of how to go on)* well, I mean—I'm gonna be goin' to work for ol' man Wallace soon as I git back, and I wus thinkin' that I could maybe . . . *(Hesitating)* buy dis suit off you *(Rushes on now)* and send yo' mama de money as soon as I get it. Man, dat would take a whole lot off her mind.

TY: Naw, naw, Fletcher. This suit ain't nothin' . . .

FLET: *(Cutting in)* Nothin'! Man, you know how dem niggers' eyes will be stretchin' when I gits off dat bus wid somethin' like dis on.

TY: Fletcher, you don't need this suit, man. The suit you got on is plenty good enough for . . .

FLET: Come on, Tyrone. You know a nigger ain't nothin' but a drop in de bucket till he got a white suit on.

*(*TY *looks at* FLET. *for a moment then stares past him. Without words or expression* TY *slowly starts to undress.* FLET. *grins with anticipation and hastily starts to take off his clothes too. Both men undress down to their shorts, T-shirts and socks.* TY *places his clothes on the chair and* FLET, *in a haste, leaves his clothes in a heap on the floor.* TY *picks up* FLET*'s clothes and shoes and takes them over to the side where he begins dressing in an orderly fashion. But* FLET *makes a big ceremony out of putting on his first silk suit.* TY *pretends not to watch, but he is watching every move that* FLET *is making. The drums come up.* FLET *pulls on the yellow silk shirt; the feel of the material on his skin throws him into ecstasy. He buttons it with every care and rubs it down to a fit before he steps into the pants. He pulls the pants on, all the while trying without too much success to see his reflection somewhere in the room. He tucks his shirt*

in with every care, latches the belt around his tapered waist, and zips up his pants. He spins around again, trying to look at himself while beginning to behave more and more like a peacock with every piece he puts on. He bends over to put on the boots and is sure to straighten his pants and shirt again when he straightens up. He slides the white silk tie over his head, underneath his collar, and tightens it with refined skill. He takes the gold cuff links out of the breast pocket of the shirt where TY *has placed them, puts them into place, and admires them as though they were diamond rings on his fingers. He takes the gold tie clip out of his shirt pocket and clips his tie in place.* TY *stands fully dressed and waiting with cap in hand, watching* FLET *and just waiting.* FLET *by this time has become completely oblivious to* TY, *but* TY *still waits patiently. Finally* FLET *picks up the white silk coat, hold it at arms length, admiring it. Then he holds his cuffs and slips one arm and then the other in the jacket. At this point,* TY *folds his arms in a kind of shiver but does not intrude.* FLET *takes hold of his shirt cuffs and pulls them out so that his gold cuff links are showing. Then he wiggles his body a little to settle into the jacket and buttons it. He pulls at his shirt cuffs again and wiggles his shoulders as he tugs gently at the back bottom of his jacket in order to pull it into place. Now he is set—he knows he looks fine. The satisfactory grin on his face is revealing.* TY *looks on quietly but does not move.*

FLET: Well! Tyrone, what do you think? *(Does a little soft shoe step to the drum music and waits for* TY*'s approval)*

TY: *(Not really participating in* FLET*'s joy)* Fantastico! Fantastico!

FLET: *(While continuing to do a little show of a dance)* Man, the girls back in Greensville won't know what to do with me in dis. *(Shows off with a smooth dance, and* TY *applauds.* FLET *still dances but gets a little bit out of breath. Shouts at* TY *now while still dancing)* Man, all I need now is one of dem long white Bro-hams and I'd be fix fo' life, right Ty?

*(*TY *moves a little bit more into the picture as* FLET *begins to tire, slow down, and stop.* FLET *wipes the sweat from his brow with his right thumb and slings it away so as not to get any on his suit. He is breathless.* TY *hands* FLET *his black handkerchief from his breast coat pocket so that* FLET *can dry his face.* FLET, *still panting, takes the handkerchief and mops the sweat. He touches either side of his neck, being careful not to muss his collar. He wipes his hands, and he hands the handkerchief back to* TY. TY *notices the panting as it increases in* FLET*'s chest. But as far as* FLET *is concerned, he is just out of shape, and the little dance routine has winded him. The music goes out)*

FLET: *(Inquiring)* Hey, man, ain't dere no mirror . . . *(Breathes harder)* roun' here . . . where . . .

where I can . . . *(Panting)* see myself . . . before I go out? *(Pulls at his tie a little, still breathing hard)*

TY: *(Answering in a resigned voice and pointing)* Yeah. There's one in that little supply room back there.

*(*FLET *almost stumbles now, pulling at his tie, but still not wanting to muss himself. Still panting, he stumbles into the supply room. Organ music, "Nearer My God to Thee," comes up low. There is a loud scream.* TY *braces himself.* FLET *stumbles out of the supply room, his face ashy. He walks in an almost paralyzed way—stiff legs and back. He stares at* TY *and stretches his eyes as he gasps for speech)*

FLET: *(Pointing back at the supply room)* I could see . . . see death comin' in me. *(His clothes are feeling tight and are strangling, but he does not have enough strength to get out of them. He stumbles to the chair and holds on, feeling this horrifying thing enveloping him. Pleadingly)* Ty . . . Tyrone. *(He reaches out for* TY, *but* TY *does not move. There is almost a ghost-like stare on* TY*'s face)* Tyrone, dere's dis awful feeling of death all roun' me. *(He stares wildly around and stumbles into the chair. His body doubles forward, but he does not fall out of the chair. His heaving slows and finally stops. He is still—he is dead.* TY *walks over, bends down, and puts his hand on* FLET*'s shoulder.* FLET *sits up slowly. He stares straight ahead and then speaks to* TY *without expression or turning)* Why didn't you tell me, Tyrone. *(This is not so much a question as it is a statement)*

TY: 'Cause we all have to find it out for ourselves.

FLET: *(Turning towards* TY, *saying with revelation)* And I thought dere wus a whole lots of difference —I mean me being out dere and you being in here. *(Gives a little laugh, shakes his head, and looks longingly up at* TY*)*

TY: It really don't make no difference where we are, Fletcher. If the master wants you, he gon get you. You can find his crumbs and bait everywhere, even in the Black church. *(Gives a little cynical laugh)* I should know; I fell into the trap, didn't I? There don't seem to be no way of getting round him: If you lock up your front door to keep him out, he comes in the back; if you nail up both doors, he comes down the chimney; and if you plug up the chimney, he'll smoke you out. *(Gently takes* FLET *by the arm and assists him towards the embalming table.* FLET *goes willingly)* Come on, Fletcher. It's time to go.

(The organ music which has been playing now comes up as TY *helps* FLET *get up on the table and covers him from head to foot with the sheet. As* TY *puts on the cap and prepares to leave, the organ music goes down and continues at this low level. There is the sound of the telephone ringing in the front office.* TY *turns and leaves the room slowly. When he opens the*

door into the front office, the lights in the front office go up and the lights in the embalming room remain up. TY *leaves the door open as he walks towards the front door.* MR. FULLER, *in the front office, is talking on the phone)*

FULLER: *(As* TY, *whom* MR. FULLER *thinks is* FLET, *leaves)* Hey, Mr. Fletcher, have a good trip back to Texas! *(*TY *does not answer; he opens the door, leaves, and closes the door behind him. With his attention back to the phone)* Oh, no. No, Mr. Coroner. I was talking to a young man who came to view the remains of his friend. But just one minute, sir, and let me get my receiving book. *(Puts down the phone, goes to get the receiving book, and returns to the phone)* Yes, sir, Mr. Coroner, go ahead. *(Pause; continues in a serious voice)* Yes, Haight near Fillmore—at Al's Bar and Lounge. Yes, yes. *(Writing quickly)* How many? Yes, three you say . . . yes, I see . . . one woman and two men. I will have to have their home addresses as well for the record, sir. Yes, yes, well why don't we start with the woman . . . . Age 21 ; 3726 Fell Drive, San Francisco. Multiple stab wounds to the chest and abdomen. Name . . . LaTanya Simmons . . . . Okay, the second one . . . Donald Hardie . . . 23; 478 Rowling Heights, San Francisco. Two bullet wounds in the stomach. Are . . . are these wounds three-fifty-seven police magnum? Oh, I see, her boyfriend shot him . . . Saturday Night Special . . . I see . . . that's an easy job. And the third . . . oh, I see . . . this is the three-fifty-seven mag case . . . . The police got her boyfriend then. That can be messy, but you know we do good work. Name . . . Clifford Darnell Davis . . . age . . . 32; 829 Hampton Circle, San Francisco. What time should I be expecting them? Oh, I see. Oh, no, no—we'll be here. We stay open twenty-four hours a day on weekends. That's right. Just ring the bell in the back. Tell the driver to come up the side driveway. I'll be here.

Lights go down, Curtain goes down

Organ music goes out

SHARON STOCKARD MARTIN

I WAS BORN in Nashville, Tennessee and attended public schools in Tennessee, Florida, and Louisiana. I earned a B.A. from Bennington College, an M.A. from Southern University, and an M.F.A. in playwriting from the Yale School of Drama.

My interest in theatre began while I was a member of a children's theatre group at Tennessee A & I in Nashville. The Free Southern Theatre was organized during my adolescence in New Orleans, Louisiana. The theatre's successful wedding of social awareness and entertainment and its effectiveness so evident in the faces of members of the audience who had never witnessed live theatre before inspired my earlier writing attempts. I became a member of the FST Writer's Workshop, and my early plays became part of the FST touring repertoire.

Proper and Fine: Fanny Lou Hamer's Entourage, about two Black shoppers ignored by department store workers, and *Edifying Further Elaborations on the Mentality of a Chore,* a satirical look at a Black couple's attempt to adjust to the dashiki/afro/pseudo militancy and their own very basic and regretably ordinary feelings of love, were part of the 1979 and 1972 FST Touring Season.

Another New Orleans based Black theatre group, The Dashiki Theatre produced *Entertaining Innumerable Reflections on the Subject at Hand* in 1973. From 1973 until 1976, I was a student at the Yale School of Drama where I studied with such notables as Adrienne Kennedy, Jack Gelber, Thomas Babe, John Ford Noonan, and E.L. Doctorow. I was a Shubert Fellow and received the O'Neill Award and the C.B.S. Foundation Prize in Playwriting for the best student play in 1976.

I have been a member of the Ed Bullins' Black Theatre Workshop (1968-69), the FST Writers' Workshop (1970-73), the Frank Silvera Writers' Workshop (1973-76), the Congo Square Writers (1976-79), and the L.A. Actor's Theatre Playwright Workshop (1980). Two of my plays have been published: *Proper and Fine: Fanny Lou Hamer's Entourage* in *The Scholastic Book Series* on Black Literature for high school students, and *Canned Soul* in *Callaloo,* a literary magazine published at one time out of Tougaloo. Other experience includes elementary school teaching and employment as director of communications for the Urban League in New Orleans. I have an interest in writing for television.

While at Yale I wrote *Deep Heat,* a comedy about two couples madly in love with each other and their long lost pets; *Canned Soul,* a short comedy about two Whites expounding on the absence of the town's Black folks; and *The Moving Violation,* an absurd treatment of a family whose freedoms are systematically taken away. *Deep heat* had productions at Yale University, the harlem Performance Center, and at the Clinton Hill Repertory Company in Brooklyn. *Canned Soul* was part of a Yale Cabaret Production that later grew into *SOS, Baby Death, and Other Anxiety Pieces for the Contemporary American Stage,* produced and directed by the author at the Free Southern Theatre in 1977.

The Moving Violation received the J.F. Kennedy Center Black Playwright Award for the southeast region in 1979 and was produced by the Dashiki Project Theatre. A Dashiki Theatre press release describes the play thus: "It does not resort to accustomed protest or propagandistic diatribes, but poetically reveals human survival techniques and responses under a rigid authoritarian system or police state." Everyone in the play is divided into two categories: those who are free to move and those who are not. One group has last names ending in 'man' and the other in 'son.' It's as irrational a division as Black and White. The idea for this play stemmed from an incident in Baton Rouge in 1972 where some police or FBI were trying to get into a man's house. He didn't know what was going on and wouldn't let them in. They finally broke the door down and shot him, but it turned out he wasn't the man they were looking for. Still, they didn't apologize and blamed him for resisting arrest. The absurdity got to me, something about evil rationalizing itself."

THE MOVING VIOLATION

Sharon Stockard Martin

CASTING AND A NOTE ABOUT THE PLAY'S STYLE

The Moving Violation *is not a realistic play. An unexplained set of rules begins to govern the character* JACKSON *and the members of his family. These people have done nothing wrong but are being punished for what they are rather than what they've done. It is a situation reflected in the life around us and should be the basis of identification with the characters in the play.*

The author has taken the notion of race away from color and has created a new ethnicity based on the principles of progress and reactionism. It is a play about survival and how human excesses determine the quality of life.

JACKSON, *the head of the house, and his wife* DAWSON *appear to be rational enough; however,* DAWSON'*s brothers are all afflicted by obsessions which determine how they respond to the restrictions that befall them.*

EMERSON *is concerned with food to the exclusion of all other aspects of life.* WILLIAMSON *is social. He fits in. He converses. He must make others listen to him. He is a dancer, a rapper.* JOHNSON *is the youngest of the brothers. He has been sheltered by his sister. He is vulnerable, cerebral, lovesick.* ANDERSON *is a pseudo-intellectual. He must rationalize the surrounding realities even though they make no sense. He will not admit that he doesn't understand or has no control.* DIXON *is a woman whom* JOHNSON *has a crush on.*

Those in control are the OFFICERS *and* THE MAN WHO HANDLES INQUIRIES.

Casting choices affect the interpretation of the play. If the "family" is cast as one race and the oppressors another, the effect is different from the family being cast irregardless of race, which may broaden the meaning of the play.

ACT ONE

Scene 1

A Surprise Party, a dumb show seen through stuttering strobe lights. Assorted people, including DIXON, DAWSON, ANDERSON, EMERSON, JOHNSON, *and* WILLIAMSON *do all the standard things that go on at parties. There is the playfulness, the profiling, and the suspense. There is dancing and food, the rap, the games. A huge sign strung across the room reads, "Happy Birthday, Jackson." It is the home of the honoree, but when it becomes apparent that* JACKSON *will not arrive any time soon, the mood of the party changes to impatience and mischief. The cake is cut, the food is consumed. Guests give their apologies and leave.* ANDERSON *has been standing against a wall looking bored;* EMERSON *has been stuffing his face;* WILLIAMSON *has been partying back;* JOHNSON *has been looking at* DIXON *from a distance. As the party dissolves, all the principal characters fade into the background, the inner region of the*

living space. DIXON *leaves with the other guests. Only* DAWSON *remains, looking angy, tired, hurt. The strobe turns into a natural light as* JACKSON *unlocks the front door and enters the room.*

DAWSON: Where have you been?

JACKSON: I missed my stop.

DAW: You missed your what?

JACK: I must have fallen asleep.

JACK: I didn't mean to.

DAW: I put a lot of work into this.

JACK: Did I miss something?

DAW: You're late, you know?

JACK: I said I had trouble getting home.

DAW: That's not all the trouble you're going to have.

JACK: What's for dinner?

DAW: You mean what *was* for dinner?

JACK: Never mind. I'm not feeling well. All I need

is a glass of warm milk and some rest. (JACK *goes to the refrigerator, but is knocked out of the way by* EMER)

EMERSON: Howdy. What time do we eat?

JACK: What's he doing here?

DAW: Weekend company.

ANDERSON: Well, looka here.

WM: The man of the house has arrived.

AND: It's about time.

JACK: *(To* DAW) So, you plan to punish me with a plague of relatives, do you?

AND: Jackson, your choice of words is so harsh and unnecessarily cruel. We're here to cheer you up, to spread good tidings and other diseases.

WILLIAMSON: *(To* JACK) What are you staring at me for? Like what you see?

JACK: Those clothes look familiar—

WM: They ought to. They're yours. I hope you don't mind.

JACK: Think nothing of it. Help yourself.

WM: I intend to.

AND: So where is it tonight, Williamson? Clubs, discos, a cozy party for two or less?

WM: *(Straightening his tie, timing his turn)* All of them and not necessarily in that order. I'm open for company. Anyone? Dawson?

DAW: I have to clean up.

WM: Jackson's the one who needs to clean up his act. You kept us waiting, man. We had to start the party without you and now I plan to take it to the streets. Coming, sis?

DAW: Why don't you go with him, Anderson?

AND: If you ask me, dancing is an affliction of the nervous, much akin to a tic no longer localized. It takes a healthy, uncommon man to sit quietly in place and contemplate his navel. Isn't that right, Jackson?

JACK: Why don't you leave me alone.

AND: We're just trying to bring a little joy into your tired life. A personal favor to Dawson here.

JACK: All I want is a little peace and quiet.

DAW: He's been running around all day.

WM: And I plan on running around all night.

AND: *(To* WM) If you'd stop moving for a second and settle your brain, you'd think about what you're doing and realize how foolish it is to exert so much unnecessary movement. When you're through, you're in the very same place you started off in. I can't think of anything more futile and frustrating.

WM: No more unnecessary than never having gone anywhere at all, Anderson. You and Jackson are the only men on earth who're going to die having never lived.

AND: Wait a minute there, Williamson. Don't go putting deadhead and me in the same category.

I'm only conservative; he's inconsiderate. I dare anyone of you to show me any function worth the effort, and I will be the first to fulfill my share of the pushing and pulling, the picking up and the putting down. Until then, don't bother me with the circular exercises as they were, the mechanics, both trivial and mundane, of being alive.

WM: Well, hold on. Dancing, my dear brother Anderson, is the highest intellectual activity there is, the most complicated of any act, the culmination of all art. In the dance, I am not handicapped by *who* I am, but get over for that very reason. I'm not burdened by an object or a tool or a purpose to direct my energies toward. I don't have to strain myself with the weight of a book or experience fatigue trying to reach a certain destination by a certain time. In the dance, I don't have to think of some idea and wait for the materials to come together or the most opportune moment to affect it; or find myself in some muscular spasm and spend hours wondering why it ever happened or if it will ever happen again. In dance, my body and mind are perfectly coordinated. An idea actualized. I am the movement and the object of the movement. I am doing myself, for myself with no other stipulation or limitation than the strength of my own imagination. I am both the creator and the creation at once. So you see, Anderson, while you and Jackson look for salvation in these yellowed pages, in forgotten words and the spaces in between them, I find salvation in myself, in transcending myself, in becoming myself, making real concepts that are too abstract for even you to understand. *(To* JACK) Could you lend me some money, Jackson ole buddy. I'm somewhat short.

*(*AND *puts his book down.* WM *holds out his hand for money.* JACK *digs in his pocket for dollar bills.* WM *takes all of them)*

AND: For your information, Williamson, I don't even read. While my eyes are crossing the page, I am thinking of other things. I am continually amazed by the expenditure of so much effort put into filling so many pages with words that don't mean a damn thing when you put them all together. I only keep scanning these archaic pages in search of some reason for such an obvious waste of time. No. The answer won't be found in books. I'm convinced of that, if nothing else.

WM: *(Counting his bills)* So. There's not that much difference between us then.

AND: But thank God, there's space. *(Puts his book up between them)*

DAW: *(To* JACK) Well?

JACK: Well what?

DAW: Where have you been? I put a lot of energy

into this party and you weren't even here to enjoy it.

WM: Come on out with it, man.

AND: We don't have all day.

EMER: And cut it short. We break for a snack in fifteen minutes.

JACK: Do you really want to hear what I have to say?

AND: No.

DAW: Let him talk.

AND: But we don't have to listen.

EMER: And try to make it worth our while this time, huh?

(JOHNSON *enters, goes to the window, and looks out. He seems detached, preoccupied*)

JACK: I went to work this morning, like I always do—

EMER: I went to work, too; and, funny, that don't make me miss dinner.

JACK: They were all there outside the office waiting for me.

DAW: That was thoughtful of them.

JACK: They wanted to see if I was on time.

EMER: Were you?

JACK: I was early as a matter of fact. By several minutes.

AND: Good for you, ole boy.

WM: Hip. Hip.

JACK: I expected things to go as usual. The day before, I changed desks. I moved from the back of the office to another desk that has plenty of room and lots of light.

WM: Moving up in the world, eh, br'r?

DAW: How about the view. Tell me about the view.

JACK: I didn't have time to enjoy the view. Before I could step inside the door, they presented me with a cake for being the most punctual employee.

EMER: Did you bring me a piece?

DAW: Shh!

JACK: Then they took my gold watch.

DAW: It's better than giving you one. You're not ready to retire yet. You have your whole life ahead of you.

JACK: Then they had the nerve enough to ask me the time of day.

DAW: You told them, didn't you?

JACK: How could I? They had my watch.

DAW: But that's insubordination. You could be fired.

JACK: The card on the birthday cake not only contained the name of every trusty employee of the First National, past, present, and future, but several unidentified tear stains, smudge prints, lipstick marks, and a pink slip.

EMER: I didn't think it was showing. Promise me you won't look.

JACK: The company manager of our local office stopped by my desk while I was cleaning it out.

AND: At least he's neat about it.

DAW: You did speak, didn't you? It shows proper home training.

JACK: They were his tear stains on the card. He commended me on a job well done. He said I was the finest worker of any of the workers he's ever had and hadn't had. A pleasure to work with—

AND: At least the man was polite.

JACK: —he said he hated losing me—

AND: A likely story.

JACK: —and hadn't the slightest idea of who would replace me. As I offered him my shoulder, he expressed a fear that upon my departure, the whole operation would collapse and severe losses would be experienced in each of the two hundred branches here and around the world. He plans to commit suicide as soon as he's filed for bankruptcy.

DAW: Do you think I'll have time to run out and buy him a going away present.

JACK: What about me?

DAW: You'll have plenty of time to get one. I'm the one who has to go to work tomorrow, not you.

JACK: After he left, the five vice presidents and twenty-four supervisors from various sections on the floor, crowded around my desk with funny hats and streamers and proceeded to beat me within an inch of my life.

AND: They should have gotten closer.

JACK: When I no longer responded to their blows, having lost consciousness and ceasing to give them pleasure, they threw me out into the street in the path of oncoming lunchtime traffic.

EMER: Oh, God, I'm hungry!

JACK: A policeman came.

DAW: (*To* EMER) You can't have anymore.

JACK: I thanked him for rescuing me from the path of a five ton Mack truck.

EMER: (*To* DAW) Please. Just a little.

DAW: (*To* EMER) I have spoken.

JACK: I reached out my hand for assistance and salvation. A mere touch would cure the unfairness of the day and soothe my aching sensibilities, but his gloved hand didn't pull but pushed, shoving me and forcing me down with the force of five hundred Mack trucks onto the rough pavement below. Beating me again and again. Opening wounds that I though had long since been healed. Washing the street with the contriteness of my much recycled blood. (*Pause*)

AND: Why didn't he tell us he was going out for a little fun?

DAW: It couldn't have been as bad as all that. You must have done something to provoke it. Was your hair combed?

JACK: He said I was J-walking.

AND: Ah ha!

JOHNSON: His name does start with a J.

WM: So does yours, Johnson.

JACK: Walking in a standing zone.

JOHN: But weren't you lying down?

AND: That's just as bad. Having back and behind on a surface meant for feet—

DAW: As long as you didn't litter.

JACK: He kept beating me and beating me with his fists, his nightstick—

DAW: In broad daylight, too. The shame of it!

JACK: With the butt of his gun, his boots. And when they were finally worn away, he ran over me again and again with his motorcycle, returning to the gas pump six times for refills and a change of tires. Over and over, squeezing every dimension of my body into a single one. Not satisfied until he saw the sidewalk beneath me. Even then, he didn't stop, coming again and again, over and over, until he was more than sure that I was dead.

EMER: Life is like that sometimes.

AND: Baby didn't overexert himself, did he? I don't know why he can't work out in the gym like everybody else. Such an exhibitionist!

JACK: Later on, in the morgue—

WM: I'm gon' give you all one last chance. Now who wants to go?

JACK: When I blinked my eyes—

WM: How 'bout you, Emerson?

EMER: Will they serve food?

JACK: They took me to the stationhouse and put me in a lineup. I overheard that the Second National had been held up by four dwarfs and an albino gentleman. I was identified by an undisguised catatonic blind mute who swore on a stack of oral braille Bibles that I was the one. Separately and together. The robbers supposedly wore masks and fit my description exactly. Ten other people identified me including the dead clerk and the wife of the security guard who were both vacationing in South America at the time. Two vice presidents from the First National refused to verify my alibi, declining to reveal my whereabouts at the time of the crime, hiding out in the restroom, washing the blood from their own hands; and the company manager stepped in at the last moment and accused me of stealing his watch.

JOHN: You didn't take it, did you?

DAW: Of course, he didn't.

AND: Records like these follow you all the way through life and then some.

JACK: I tried to bribe them with chocolate bars, promissory notes and my college degree, but they ignored me, using my bail money to purchase time on T.V. to campaign for law and order. They found an abandoned prison and locked me up without food, water, clothes, and bowel movements for what must have been months. A few seconds later the judge sentenced me.

EMER: Never look a gift horse in the mouth. It's teeth may be full of holes.

JOHN: Did you get the chair?

JACK: Among other things. At the last minute, before my fourth death, I was given a reprieve by the appellate courts.

AND: I'll tell you what it is. It's this obsession with making progress, if you ask me.

JACK: The sentences were reduced to nine consecutive life terms, twenty-six accidental and unexplained deaths or sixteen electrocutions, whichever came first.

DAW: You mean you were given a choice?

EMER: See. Blessings do come disguised in affliction.

AND: A choice? Johnson never could make choices, You need to hear this, Johnson. Six can play this game.

EMER: I never had that problem.

AND: That's because whenever you were given a chance to choose between an apple and a pear, you took both of them and ate both of them before anybody knew what had happened.

WM: Did you hear the categories, Johnson?

JOHN: What categories?

EMER: Could you please repeat the question?

AND: I'll repeat the question: If you were given three oranges and a handful of hay, how could the chicken get to the other side of the road?

WM: That's not what he said. I wasn't even listening and neither were you.

AND: I was too. My ears were pointed toward the east.

WM: What he was saying was if *I* had two chickens. *I. I.*

AND: I thought he was talking about himself. My apologies.

WM: If *I* had two chickens and a handful of road, how would the orange get to the other side?

AND: Roll?

EMER: And better yet, which company will be given the contract to black top?

JOHN: Side of what?

AND: The side of the question, of course. Every question has two sides—the known and the unknown.

WM: And let's not be forgetting the question mark.

AND: Who's Mark? Is he one of your friends you've failed to introduce me to, bad boy!

DAW: You're forgetting the electrocutions!

WM: You mean the poor bird was electrocuted? I can think of much easier ways to get feathers for a Sunday hat.

JOHN: You mean to say that I'm going to have to carry a handful of feathers all the way to the bus stop. Can I wear gloves?

AND: Only if they're biodegradable.

EMER: Before we start the trip, can I get a quick bite?

(AND bites EMER's arm)

JACK: Stop!!!

EMER: What's wrong with him? I was the one Anderson bit. If anybody should be screaming, it should be me.

JACK: I don't know why all 'a you don't leave.

WM: I don't know it either. How 'bout you, Emerson?

EMER: No.

AND: I'm not familiar with the title. Has it been out long?

WM: It's not a book, it's a record that I used to do the Bus Stop to.

EMER: I was under the impression that you could afford a taxi. Hard times?

JOHN: Could I have the question just one more time?

AND: How about it, Jackson? You gonna be a sport for a change. Throw it at us one more time. Now what was it? Death by torture or abandonment?

EMER: Or perhaps both?

WM: Leave him alone. I'll tell you. If you stick your finger in gosling fat on the morning after Memorial Day—

EMER: Now wait a minute. That can't be right. Night comes after day, Memorial Day or not.

WM: You're missing the point.

AND: Could oranges have points that we cannot see?

JOHN: The seeds do.

EMER: The seeds do.

WM: Seeds do.

EMER: Seeds.

AND: *(Indicating JACK)* And if the orange is seed-less?

(The foursome break out laughing)

DAW: Leave him alone. He's had a hard day.

WM: Hard day. Hah!

AND: I don't know why you encourage him.

JACK: *(Still enraptured by his memory)* That would be the first time. I would be stopped no less than five times for reasons, reasons, none of which applied to me, each incident worse than the one that preceded it, each one more humiliating,

more devastating, more—

EMER: Spare us.

JACK: They put me in a hole, a deep dark one, that was so deep I couldn't even see the light that was shining above me and began to doubt altogether whether there had ever been one. I couldn't remember or see. And then they threw the dirt on.

AND: You call that dirt? Show him the ring around your tub, Emerson.

(EMER raises his shirt to reveal his flab. AND laughs)

WM: *(Yawning)* Is it over yet?

AND: Talk about all the running around. The useless expenditure of energy. The never really getting anyplace. The even if by chance you stumbled over your destination, the never having recognized it. The too busy moving, the keeping up. The not getting left behind.

EMER: That's achievement for you. It's the process, not the prize.

JACK: *(Agitated)* I'm going out.

DAW: But you just got here.

JACK: It makes no difference.

EMER: Ask him to go to the store. I'm hungry.

WM: I'm all out of smokes, too.

EMER: Where's my pocketbook. *(Looking under the rug)* I swept this morning.

DAW: I don't think you ought to—

JACK: Leave me alone.

EMER: And see if you can find some pickles. Dill. and some peaches. Nectarines are out of season. Anything for you, Johnny boy?

DAW: I wish you wouldn't act this way in front of our—

JACK: Our nothing. Your. They're yours.

AND: Whatever. Let's just get this joker out of here.

DAW: If we could just talk—

(JACK leaves, slams the door)

AND: Dawson, my sympathies. I had no idea.

EMER: Check your children before you have them. Identity crises are contagious.

JOHN: *(Suddenly reciting)* She's a brook, a waterfall, a cascade gently brushing up against my mind. She's rain that falls in sheets from the sky, warmed over and lightened by summer's quiet labor. She's a stream that flows, a river that winds, the constant tide playfully slapping the shore, a rainbow never having experienced the storm.

(AND, EMER, and DAW look at each other quizzically)

WM: Some woman he met at a party.

JOHN: I didn't meet her.

WM: *(Correcting himself)* Some woman he *saw* at the party.

AND: Are we talking about a girl or a half gallon of

bottled mineral water?

JOHN: I'm only thankful that she was there. She left me a letter.

AND: Ah ha! What's her name then?

JOHN: It was unsigned.

WM: Then it could have been sent by anybody.

EMER: He may have even sent it himself.

JOHN: But I know who sent it. It was her.

AND: How can you be sure? How can you know for sure?

JOHN: The way the words laid upon the page. The hands that wrote them. The mind that thought them. I'm going to ask her to marry me today.

AND: *(Sarcastically)* Listen to him.

WM: Good for you, ole Johnson, ole boy.

AND: What are you saying? You're going to ask a woman whom you've only seen, whom you've never spoken to a day in either of your lives to spend the rest of her life with you, not to mention yours. Ridiculous!

DAW: Leave him alone. He knows what he's doing. It even sounds romantic in a peculiar sort of way.

AND: All right. As long as he doesn't bring her here to live. We have close enough quarters.

EMER: But if she'd care to cook us a complimentary meal in honor of her rites of passage, I wouldn't see any harm in an occasional visit.

WM: *(Exiting with JOHN)* I don't know about the rest of you, but I'm ready to go. I got four on the floor. Two on the seat, and one under the hood. Come on, Johnson, stick with me and I'll make you a star.

JOHN: *(Singing offstage in a deep voice)* "Some enchanted evening. You may meet a stranger. Across a crowded room."

AND: Ah. Keep it to yourself.

(The door opens again. WM and JOHN come back inside looking stunned)

AND: My, that was quick. Don't say it. She rejected you. I could have saved you the trouble. And done it myself.

WM: The guard on duty told us to come back inside.

DAW: Guard! We don't have a guard!

JOHN: We do now.

DAW: What would a guard be doing here?

JOHN: The same thing guards do anywhere.

DAW: How long has he been there? How long will he be there?

JOHN: I don't know.

AND: He don't know nothin'. I'll find out. *(Goes to door)* See here, kind sir. Could you be decent enough to tell us what is the meaning of this. *(The door is slammed in his face)* I don't think a reaction of such a hostile nature was called for.

(AND holds his nose. JOHN goes to a window)

DAW: What's he doing now?

JOHN: He's reaching in his uniform for something.

EMER: Shield your faces. He's gonna shoot.

(Six letters fall through the slot to the floor)

AND: Bingo, Johnson. This must be your lucky day.

(JOHN picks up the letters, giving one to each person, keeping one for himself. EMER opens his letter with the enthusiasm of a starved man at his first meal)

EMER: *(Reading)* "John M. Emerson. You are hereby forbidden use of the sidewalks, the streets, alleys, roads, highways, public and private byways and thoroughfares of this town or any other town or collection of human wildlife. Signed, the citizen's council."

WM: *(Stumbling over words, assisted by JOHN, EMER, and AND)* "John M. Williamson. You are hereby forbidden use of the sidewalks, the streets, alleys, roads, highways, public and private byways and thoroughfares of this town or any other town or collection of human wildlife. Signed, the major." Uh, "mayor." What'll we do?

EMER: *(Checking his own letter)* Ah, you are so right. The mayor.

JOHN: *(Reading)* "John M. Johnson. You are hereby forbidden use of the sidewalks, the streets, alleys, roads, highways, the public and private byways and thoroughfares of this town or any other town or collection of human wildlife. Signed, the governor."

EMER *and* WM: *(Reviewing letters)* The . . . uh, governor.

(EMER, WM, and JOHN look from one to the other)

AND: *(Joking)* This must be *some* lady Johnson's trying to court. She'll stop at nothing short of official decrees and personal bodyguards to keep him away from her.

DAW: Why would she send the same message to Emerson and Williamson. They're not after her fancy.

AND: They may not be after her fancy, but that they're capable of being after her is plain as day. Neither of them's married.

WM: And neither are you.

AND: But I'm above that sort of sophomoric useless expenditure of energy that everyone else around here seems to be in such an abundance of. What kind of threat could I be to anybody? I don't write dirty letters to unattached women — like our boy Johnson here. I don't run around the streets and nightclubs in broad daylight dancing like a fool, tapping strange women on the shoulder and admiring their one-two, one-two, like mad marvel Williamson over there. And I don't promise to eat everybody out of house and home, like dark-meat-light-meat-it-really-doesn't-matter-I'll-take-both-come-lately Emerson over there. So what could anybody have to fear from me?

JOHN: Read your letter, Anderson.

WM: Yeah, read it.

EMER: My sentiments exactly.

(AND *looks at his envelope. He slowly unfolds it, quietly reading to himself.* WM *tries to read the letter, but* AND *tears it away from him, turning his back for a moment, but finally turning again to face them and reads with a sense of superior dignity and personal honor and esteem.*)

AND: (*Reading pompously*) "John M. Anderson." (*To the others*) It's P, not M. I'm a person; gender is not warranted here. (*Reads again*) "John P. Anderson. So there. You have hereby been forbidden from using the sidewalks, the streets, alleys, roads, highways, public and private byways and thoroughfares of this town, or any other town or collection of wildlife. Signed, the president. P.S. Stay off the grass." (*He folds the letter and puts it back in the envelope, placing it in a vest pocket next to his heart*) So there you have it. Surely you can see that my letter is different from yours, by the inclusion of the business concerning the peripheral vegetation, proving that my treatment is, in effect, preferential to yours. Besides, my letter was signed by the president, making it federal jurisdiction.

EMER: You were still given more restrictions than us.

AND: But more choices within that restriction; by having more areas forbidden to my shoes' soles and barefeet, I am given less choice to make about violating the law, thereby relieving myself of the burden of the same obligation to rebel that looms so highly in your own jaded eyes. (*He looks at his eyes in the mirror*)

EMER: (*Displacing* AND *at mirror, examining his mouth and teeth*) Hell, I don't have any need to break nobody's law. I can eat just as comfortably here as I can anywhere else. Besides, home-cookin' is best. Everybody knows that.

WM: (*Examining his own physique*) I can dance at home and get as much satisfaction as I can elsewhere. I'm here, ain't I?

JOHN: (*Examining picture of woman*) And I can still ask my intended to marry me through the mails. It's safer, anyway.

AND: How can you ask her anything when you don't even know her name!

EMER: Stop confusing the issue with irrelevant technicalities!

AND: These overt attempts to constrain my liberties can hardly be thought of as ridiculous technicalities in anybody's language.

WM: But the islanders of Samoa and Greenland are not the ones being kept from their streets.

EMER: They don't have streets in Singapore and Zanzibar; they have paths with thick undergrowth and icecapades respectfully.

WM: Call them what you will; they're bound to gain something in the translation.

JOHN: Which is more than we can say.

AND: The problem remains that we have been made prisoner to the house.

EMER: But at least, it's a big house.

JOHN: You're forgetting the curb.

AND: Quite precisely. The curbs have been made prisoner to this house also.

WM: What Johnson means is that there was a failure on the part of the planning committee to list curbs as restricted modes of travel.

(*Everyone reads his letter searchingly*)

AND: In such omissions lie our salvation.

EMER: (*Looking out the window*) The curbs are gone!

AND: Impossible. They were all here yesterday when I had to scrape dog excrement from my boots.

WM: Perhaps they were all taken by the same sort of fellow who delivered the letters.

EMER: For a cleaning and a good pressing.

JOHN: But would the postal service stoop to such adolescent preoccupations in order to pass the time?

WM: One must stoop to do anything to the curbs. There's no way around it.

AND: We still haven't answered the question of what we have done and why we have been chosen for this unprecedented experiment.

EMER: What experiment?

AND: This irrational grounding—

WM: We're not allowed on the ground either. It says so in the small print.

EMER: Call it what you will.

AND: Whatever the reason or the source, you can be sure to retrace the cause of this national disaster to the mysterious young water woman of Johnson's wet dreams who has surely peed on this particular parcel of personage.

DAW: It's not fair.

AND: If it had not been for this ordinance forbidding all single men to walk the streets of their own free will and recognizance, we would be able to go on our merry ways.

EMER: I thought you didn't have anyplace to go anyway.

AND: That's besides the point or the seeds. I'm talking about principle.

EMER: Did he get a letter too?

DAW: But Jackson and I got letters too, and we're not single.

AND: In whose eyes?

WM: Who cares! Open yours, Dawson.

DAW: *(Tears her envelope and reads the contents expectantly)* "Dawson P. Jackson—"

AND: *(Insulted)* See. They got her name right.

DAW: *(Reading)* "You are hereby forbidden use of the sidewalks, the streets, alleys, roads, highways, public and private byways and thoroughfares of this town or any other town or collection of human wildlife between the hours of two and six. Signed, God."

EMER: Of course. That's traffic hour.

WM: *(Correcting him)* Traffic hours.

AND: See. What did I tell you?

JOHN: I don't know.

WM: What does it prove?

EMER: It proves that she is only partially obstructed which is more than I can say at the moment. *(He belches and hits his chest with a closed fist)*

AND: It only proves that the woman in question is not a lesbian. It's obvious that she has nothing to fear from Dawson at certain hours. Congratulations.

JOHN: Perhaps all of us have letters with typographical errors and Dawson has the only true letter, the one all the rest of us should have.

WM: Two to six? Suppose there's a record sale between two and six?

DAW: But what does that prove?

AND: That the chicken and the orange that laid it are both freer than you or I.

DAW: That doesn't sound right.

WM: Much less maintain rightness in itself.

AND: Whether it's right or wrong makes no difference to me at this point. I will not be able to sleep tonight for worry about this unfair and unjust act which has been passed by both houses of congress and the old and new testaments. Not to mention Williamson tap dancing on the mattress. What'll we do?

EMER: Perhaps they merely want to wash the streets—

AND: And why should we allow Dawson to get wet?

EMER: Perhaps we should take it upon ourselves to forbid Dawson from going out on the streets at all. It's not safe.

WM: But there'll be no one out there save herself. What does she have to fear?

AND: Stampeding wild chickens and rabid oranges with fungus, both of which have a minimal regard for traffic regulations and human rights.

WM: Whatever this disconcerting limitation is, I'm sure it will pass like an illness—

EMER: Heartburn.

JOHN: Heartbreak.

AND: A heart attack.

DAW: Just about everything passes sooner or later, if you have the time to wait for it to.

EMER: Words well chosen. Food for thought. Now, let's eat.

Scene 2

On a separate space JACK *is seen walking with groceries in his arms. He is accosted by an* OFFICER *who slings him around, pushes him against a brick wall, and frisks him roughly.* JACK *turns to protest but is hit with a billy club. Another* OFFICER *runs in with weapon drawn, then several other run in. Soon* JACK *is surrounded by* OFFICERS, *each ready to shoot. The characters freeze, the scene goes to black. The scene comes back up.* JACK *is alone on stage.*

Black

Scene 3

Home.

AND: *(In a huff)* I refuse to stay in this house any longer. I cannot share quarters with a pig! I merely turn my back for a second to acknowledge the day, and when I face front again, my dinner is gone.

(EMER is hiccupping, drinking glass after glass of water for relief that does not come)

DAW: *(Putting on coat)* It's two. I'll go out and get some more food.

AND: That won't solve the problem. Emerson's bad enough, but Williamson insists on doing the Mash Potatoes in my mashed potates, doing the Fly on my fly, and doing the Bump against the dining room table, causing me to suffer contusions and the most unbelievable migraines imaginable every time I think about food. Want to pick my nose, but I'm afraid the suggestion will make him start the Boogie.

WM'S VOICE: Paarty! Paarrrrttttyyyy!!!!

AND: And if that's not enough, Johnson is over there crying his heart out, calling out women's names thinking that if he hits on the right one, she'll appear as if by magic. Scribbling letter after letter that he knows he can't mail and hogging up the line with calls that simply won't go through. And where is Jackson!

DAW: I don't know.

AND: It's all his fault. Men! Never around when

you need them.

DAW: While I'm out, I'll get some food—

AND: For Emerson.

DAW: A new record—

AND: For Williamson.

DAW: Stationery—

AND: For Johnson.

DAW: Books.

AND: For what? Who can read at a time like this!

DAW: What do you want?

AND: Freedom. And not the kind you get on sale.

JOHN: *(To DAW)* Mail these for me. And if you see her, tell her I love her.

(DAW *leaves. Sound of sirens in the distance. They get louder, then fade away*)

AND: How many are out today?

JOHN: Forty.

WM: Forty guards! God, there were only ten this morning. They must be using ditto paper!

JOHN: Williamson, they're towing away your car.

WM: *(Frantic)* The can't do that. I haven't finished making my payments yet. Stop! Thief! *(Starts to run to the door but is stopped by the* VOICE*)* It's custom-made.

VOICE ON MEGAPHONE: *(From outside)* Prisoners—

AND, JOHN, WM, EMER: Prisoners?

VOICE: The prisoners previously referred to will not be allowed to leave the room.

EMER: Is the kitchen considered a part of the room?

VOICE: They will be alloted one uniform stripped of fashion and fad.

WM: As long as it's in style.

VOICE: They will be given a daily diet of bread and water—

EMER: What! No more birthday cake!

VOICE: Denied visitors and mail service—

(JOHN *runs to the telephone, begins to dial furiously*)

JOHN: Hello. Hello. It's dead. *(He hangs up)*

EMER: Don't say that.

VOICE: —and must entertain themselves until such time when they will be served their sentence.

EMER: I'll have mine with chef's salad. Thank you.

WM: Sentences!

EMER: That's what he said.

JOHN: What are they talking about? Are we in jail?

AND: I suspect that this has something to do with Johnson's spelling and paragraph structure.

JOHN: I don't understand—

AND: What's there to understand. We're obviously being punished collectively for a crime that one of us, all of us, or none of us at all committed.

EMER: Perhaps it is merely a quarantine and we will be temporarily detained here until the world gets better.

WM: Maybe we hurt ourselves while performing some difficult step and we need to rest and recuperate while our spirits are healing.

JOHN: A blemish so small that even we cannot see it.

EMER: I did injure myself last summer at the county fair, come to think of it.

JOHN: I get blisters and callouses from excessive writing—

WM: I sometimes contract an occasional charlie horse or cramp.

JOHN: A blemish from birth. The mark made upon the earth from being born.

AND: A recessive trait that only shows itself in men.

WM: In some men.

EMER: In us for sure.

AND: Well, I for one won't stand for it.

WM: That's about *all* you *can* do at this point.

AND: I intend to talk to the priest about this unprecedented usurpation of human freedoms and responsibilities.

EMER: That's the spirit.

WM: You tell 'em.

JOHN: Does he make house calls?

AND: I'm sure it's all a mistake. They'll be on their knees apologizing to us before the day is over. *(Puts on women's garb)* Those of you who know me know that I am not a violent man. that I am quiet, soft spoken, humble, modest. That I would just as soon turn the other cheek and look the other way. But I am also the first to rally around duty when she calls, and having been bottled up in a corner is no way to spend the holiday season. We must learn to fight fire with fingernail polish. But above all, we must fight back with tooth and claw. Never allowing ourselves to lower our standards, but tightly holding on to them, hoisting them high above us like trophies won honorably before battle. *(Puts on hat, looks through his purse for loose change and keys)* I will take the Volkswagon parked next to the sink and abandoned by some insurance man from New Dehli.

JOHN: You're breaking the law, Anderson.

WM: Several.

AND: Who's to know it. You're not allowed to leave this house. Who're you gonna tell?

EMER: As long as I'm not asked.

AND: Such backwards thinking does not become you, Emerson.

WM: But it does become you, eh?

EMER: While you're out, pick up a Chinese cook. On second thought, never mind. Two hours later, and he'll only want to go out again.

AND: *(Barely able to walk in heels that don't fit and clothes that are too tight)* Goodbye. I'll be home before the last of the dew drops congeals on the futility of all our efforts.

(AND leaves. EMER chews. WM dances in place. JOHN looks out the window and sighs. DIXON passes the window en route to the door)

JOHN: *(Alarmed)* She's here.

EMER: Who?

JOHN: Her.

EMER: Where?

JOHN: There. And she's coming here.

WM: Who? Who?

EMER and JOHN: Her. Her.

JOHN: What'll I do?

EMER: Do?

WM: First we must recollect ourselves, stop stuttering. Then we should let her in.

JOHN: Why?

EMER: Why not?

WM: It's only customary. If a person is knocking on one side of a door, it stands to reason that that person wants someone on the other side.

JOHN: If the person knocking wanted something, the person knocking wouldn't knock.

EMER: The person knocking would use a key.

WM: In which case, the person knocking would be the person using the key.

EMER: If the person using the key has a key, why doesn't the person with the key use it?

(DIX knocks)

WM: Let her in. It's obvious that she wants someone, not something on this side of the door. One opens the door after it is knocked.

JOHN: And suppose *she* is wanted by someone on this side of the door?

EMER: In that case, perhaps we should open the door before it is knocked.

WM: But then we run the risk of opening the door before she has come. Now how would I look standing in the doorway in the middle of the night with nothing there?

EMER: Probably much like you do now. Only much more so.

WM: But does it make sense? Or serve anyone's purpose?

EMER: It exercises the door.

JOHN: It's safer. You can't get hurt that way.

EMER: Unless a stray bullet is being blown about in the wind.

WM: I say we open the door now.

EMER: And not a minute before.

JOHN: Or after.

WM: While.

EMER: Precisely. Open the door while she is knocking. That way we can find out whether she's carrying concealed weapons or merely a boxed lunch.

WM: Fool. If she's knocking, that means she can't be carrying anything at all.

EMER: Williamson, I'm surprised at you! There are many other variations besides the two-handed knock. She could be using any form or number of them, separately or in groups of two's.

JOHN: She could even be using her head.

WM: Which is more than you can say. *(DIX knocks)* Open the door.

JOHN: I can't. I don't know what to say.

WM: There's a slight chane that she will speak first. She's doing the wanting and has no way of knowing that you have wants too. No matter. Emerson will. He's an oral person. *(To EMER)* Talk to her. See what she wants. Find out what it is we must do, not not do, to regain our freedom. Whatever you do, don't provoke her. We have problems enough without bringing on a flood.

(DIX knocks again, more impatiently. EMER opens the door as she knocks, surprising her)

DIXON: Oh.

EMER: *(Congenially)* Hello.

DIX: I'm sorry if I'm disturbing you, but did I leave my purse here?

EMER: Here. Take mine.

DIX: Sir, I don't want to put upon you.

EMER: Put upon me. Put upon me.

DIX: But could I trouble you for a glass of water? It's so hot out there, and I don't think I'll make it to where I have to go without it.

EMER: Allow me.

(JOHN is pushed out with a pitcher and a glass. He pours the water into the glass and then lingers. WM pulls JOHN back. DIX drains the glass. EMER, WM, and JOHN watch intently)

DIX: That was good. It's so hot out there. Unseasonably so.

EMER: *(Drinking from the pitcher)* I can't imagine what's wrong. Perhaps a pinch of salt will do.

(DIX starts to leave. WM pushes JOHN out. JOHN pours more water in her glass. DIX forces herself to drink)

EMER: Stirring is good. It mixes the ingredients.

DIX: Then you are a chef. A travelling chef?

EMER: No, it is the food that travels. Not I. From the primary source to the pot to the plate to the mouth where I peck, nibble, bite, crunch, chew, munch, gnaw, and swallow. Once I assimilate and/or dispose of, the itinerary is satisfied. Completely predicated, executed, and timed. I pride myself with being on schedule though sometimes I must strain a bit at the stools. Would you care to get on board?

DIX: Thank you, but I'm on a diet.

EMER: But aren't we all.

DIX: *(Rising)* I have to go—

EMER: *(Stalling)* A small meal, a light repast, a little refreshmentation. Pot luck. A la carte. Dutch treat. Everyone for himself. Who knows? What starts as a casual picnic might develop under cheesecloth like mung seeds into a copious feast or finally a formal banquet. I'm not asking you to eat the whole goose. Only a wing or leg at the start. After it's been well seasoned, carefully dressed, and delicately trimmed, we will lower it so deliberately into its own personal utensil where it will be parboiled, steamed, coddled, then broiled, braised, browned, fried, roasted, barbequed, stewed, sautéed, fricasseed, pan-fried, or pressure-cooked until its own individual juices appear. The choice is yours.

DIX: No thank you. Not today.

EMER: I'm not a hard man to please. Perhaps you have simpler tastes. A basic baking with a single turn is not beneath my level of culinary maturation.

DIX: No, I—

EMER: What's wrong with you! I offer you the world from the viewpoint of a silver platter held high in the sturdy arms of a butler or personal maid, complete with matching dinnerware and crystal glassware, and you act as if the bird has not yet been thawed!

DIX: I told you. I'm not hungry!

EMER: But I am! And forced feeding has proven effective in similar circumstances.

(EMER *starts to ravage* DIX. JOHN *and* WM *come in to disengage them.* WM *forces* EMER *away)*

WM: Fool. I said rap, not rape!

JOHN: *(To DIX)* Are you all right?

EMER: *(Gnawing on celery)* I'll be fine in a moment.

JOHN: *(Still to DIX)* Are you hurt?

EMER: The buns were squeezed a bit during the delivery, but they'll do.

DIX: If I could just sit down for a bit.

JOHN: For as long as you like.

WM: *(To DIX)* Please excuse Emerson. He's always overdoing it. A bit overdone, as a matter of fact. You see, we've all been pent up here for quite a while. For such a while in fact that I don't even know if my running buddies are still running, much less walking—

DIX: If I could go somewhere. But it's like this everywhere.

JOHN: There are smelling salts. I could call an ambulance for legal aid.

WM: —I used to go down to the corner. Just to see what's happening. You know.

DIX: Everybody's always stopping me for something, usually something I don't want to give and more than likely don't even have.

JOHN: You could stay here. I'll admit it's not much

better than nothing.

WM: Everyone decked out. Dudes together. Mamas swinging they thing in my direction. Looking good. I say. Hey.

JOHN: Not a very big house, but large enough for everyone to have his own corner in an emergency.

WM: Yes indeed. Ummm hummm.

DIX: Get so fed up with it, you know. Say, "Look, mister," I tell 'em. "You know what you're asking is against the law" and they look at me right funny, pull in they clothes for a badge and show me that they are the law.

WM: Me on the corner checking it all out. I got eyes.

JOHN: Then there's the matter of love, honor, and obey. We can alternate. I fully believe in a staggered work week.

DIX: Say they gonna charge me with something, exactly what I'm refusing to do, if I don't comply. I say where can a girl go, and even if I knew where to go, how the hell am I going to get there?

JOHN: After awhile, when we get on our own four feet, we'll be able to move about and move out. I believe in one step at a time.

WM: I was standing on the corner last Tuesday night. Just got my clothes out of the cleaners. Pants pressed, creased sharp, hair conked and curled, manicure. Looking good, if I have to say so myself. We had a gig upstate. Wasn't nothing special, but it was work. Sonny had just gone to get the car, and I was just waiting. Sun was shining. It was a good day when one of them pulls up and comes over to me and asks me to identify myself. I say, "Yeah, man, that's me. I recognize myself." And he knocks me in the face and kicks me on the ground. Got my clothes all dirty and me wondering what I'm going to tell Sonny when I see him. Didn't have no more clean clothes, man. Me trying to keep from getting dirtier and him hitting me and kicking me, pushing me in the squad car saying, "Yeah, you the one all right. All a' y'all." Me saying, "Aww, man, I ain't done nothin.'" Him cursing me, calling in for reinforcements. They took me away. Kept me locked up for three days trying to find something to charge me with. When Sonny did come back, I was gone. We missed the gig. Ain't had nothing to do since either.

DIX: Want to call me a streetwalker. Just cause I walk on the street. I say, "Uh uh. No sir. Indeed not, I ain't." And they say, "If you combed your hair, wouldn't that make you a haircomber. If you ate cake, wouldn't that make you a cake-eater?" I didn't know what to say. Words have a way of making something be that never was.

JOHN: I can provide.

WM: Now, I ask you. What was I doing? When does it become a crime to look good!

JOHN: Then there's the matter of children, geographical relocation, life insurance, grandchildren, an adequate pension, a burial plot.

WM: Next thing I knew, here they were every night with the wagons carting everybody away like it was some kind of quota they had to fill. Everybody's on the list.

JOHN: I found the place. I did procure a key and I did inspect each room and I knew we would grow out of it with family and have to move, but what could be better to start off in?

DIX: Now they take out this ordinance and read it to me every chance they get about the restrictions telling women that they can use the street, that they must use the streets.

WM: Harrison . . . Sonny . . . Little Man . . .

JOHN: I'd say three at the most before we'd be forced to move.

WM: Dyson . . . Tyson . . . Broke J.C.'s back.

(The following two monologues, DIXON's and WILLIAMSON's, are spoken simultaneously)

DIX: Tell me I'm made to walk up and down form one end of the city to the next, looking for faces I don't want to see. My body is chilled from exposure, not covered so all can see my shame. My face is torn by the wind and rain and is quickly becoming unfamiliar to me, hard and ugly from the cruel sights it's forced to see. And there are no benches for me. No kind words. Only oaths. And it is only in the presence of he who is allowed to move can I be still. He can take me anywhere he wants to and do with me as he pleases, but I cannot move until he is more than finished with me and then he leaves me wherever I am and in whatever condition from which I must pull myself up and begin the walk again. But I'm not what they say I am. And where are all the men. Where are they to protect me? I'll tell you where they are. Standing around looking with their mouths hanging open and their feet stuck in the cement. They might as well not be there at all for the good they're doing me.

WM: Corner's not the same anymore. It's quiet and cold and empty as if the world had stopped . . . I stopped going over there. You know what I mean? Can't talk to yourself and be considered sane. Nothin' to do there anyway . . . . Saw Mason. Said What's happening. He said you got it. Say how's your wife and kids. Say his wife left him. Took the kids. Say looka here, we got to get together sometimes and talk. What you doing tonight? He say nothing. He say how 'bout you? Same here. I wasn't going to lie. Say, how about meeting me on the ole corner like old times. Tell some of the boys. Ole times. Good ole times. Hot dog! I went. Nigger ain't showed up. Cop came by and busted my head with a stick. I'm tired of being beaten down. They probably all inside. Waiting for the weather to change. Waiting for the time with nothing to do and women out to be seen and rapped to. Waiting to come out again to decorate the street with our finery and our style.

DIX *and* WM: *(Both monologues end at the same time with:)* Um hum.

JOHN: Life is an interminable series of upheavals, which is why we can't sit still.

DIX: It has been my singular purpose to slip through life attracting the least attention to myself. But if such is the case, why should I be here at all?

WM: Which is why I'm asking for things to be back the way there were.

JOHN: And though you may react violently to what I am saying, let's not confuse the reaction with the reactionary.

DIX: What do I want? Just what any woman gets—

WM: Not at once, but gradual.

JOHN: One step at a time. We needn't rush into any of it.

DIX: A husband, one, a family, a home—

JOHN: A constant movement toward progress, mutual understanding—

WM: A small gathering here, a hip word there, a feather boldly placed on the side of the cap. A cap carefully placed on the side of one's temple defying gravity, fitting snuggly without pressing down the hair . . .

DIX: —dirty clothes, day dreams—

JOHN: —decency, determination—

WM: —a condemned building along the way for deals, the barbeque joints, the unemployment lines, rent parties, homicide—

DIX: Time on my hands, not enough time, time and a half, the time of my life. But that's asking too much, so it seems.

JOHN: That time equals rate over distance is axiomatic.

WM: The all night dances. In the dark. Sweating bodies, close screaming minds that never speak. Where we close our eyes not to hear. Where we jam, tighter, louder, harder to express our pain and our lack and our anger and our excess, pouring out a massive joy, a dangerous gladness, euphoria released from a prison of days of little relief.

DIX: I just want to be happy for a little while.

JOHN: I just want to make you happy for a little while.

WM: We never hurt anyone except ourselves occasionally and now we don't even have that anymore.

JOHN: If you care to see my references—

WM: What do you want? A promise? A denial? An accessment? A conception?

(The following two monologues, DIXON's *and* JOHNSON's, *are spoken simultaneously)*

DIX: If you ask me, they're all leeches, braggart, drunkards, sloths. They're not clean. Don't ask them to wash anything but themselves and they don't half do that. Don't pick up after themselves. They yell. Curse. Love to order people around. Violent. Childbeaters. Wifebeaters. Never at home. Out gambling, lying, stealing, running around with other women, funny, wierd, wrong. All the time. Don't care about nobody's children. Don't even know what to do with one except start it coming. Inconsiderate, irresponsible. Good for nothing. Every last one of them. And I dare you to show me one's different, I'd jump in on it in a minute. I have nothing against marriage, you understand; it's what one ends up marrying. It's having no choice.

JOHN: I'm no leech. I can leave be. I don't drink, smoke, or sport bad habits. I am clean, inside and out. I even wash the tub. I do the wash, even the rinse cycle. I iron. I do do windows. I do not yell. I rarely raise my voice above a whisper. Can you hear me now? I am nonviolent. I will never raise a hand in your presence even for permission to leave the room. I don't hang out. I know enough to stay out of your way. I work hard. Constantly, I will be a good father. I love children. Others have told me so, though I have none of my own at the present time to the best of my knowledge. I will respect you as I respect all of womankind. I am considerate as I will be of your desires. I am tolerant, responsible, and understanding. I am exceptional. Please do not mind. Would you marry me!

WM: If you'd only tell me, I could perhaps do something about it; but you only offer the most obvious contempt and disregard as if you don't even hear what I am saying. And keep me guessing as to the source of the offense. And if it's our very persons that you dispise, unshackle our legs so that we can walk away. But it seems so unfair, so unnecessary, ridiculous that you require both our presence in our absence as if it feeds some plan, some divine disorder, as if by devaluing our lives, you have somehow put a premium on your own.

JOHN: Perhaps I've not done the right thing, said the right thing. Gone about this the wrong way.

If such is the case, would you deign to forgive me for whatever it is or was as the case may be. I know it's sudden, but unavoidably apparent.

WM: Tell me what it is, what I've done. What I so dangerously am!

DIX: I would pray, believe in something, anything, wear long dresses, hide my face behind some veil, confess, sacrifice to keep away the moments like these when I could just scream!

DIX, WM, and JOHN: Please!

JOHN: Oh! I beg your pardon.

WM: I seem to have gotten off the track. Now where was I?

DIX: I've completely forgotten about the time. I'd better go.

WM: If only I could go.

(DIX goes)

JOHN: Her eyes are tears trained not to fall. She's gone and I didn't say what I wanted.

WM: Patience. Patience.

JOHN: But patience implies—

WM: —relief—

JOHN: At some point.

WM: There will be none.

VOICE ON MEGAPHONE: The following persons have broken laws and have been punished. Billy Robinson, found between South Central and North Sixteenth walking his dog; Lionel Watson, mowing his lawn; Jason Lawson, born at four nineteen. Died four twenty.

JOHN: It only gets worse.

WM: Each day a new restriction, a more rigid demand, diminishing the meaning of our existence by halves and quarters. Each fractions of a vanishing reason.

JOHN: —and each day—

WM: —we endure—

JOHN: —in spite—

WM: —of conditions that are unendurable.

JOHN: How long can it go on?

WM: What is the infinity of the nothingness our lives are being reduced into? Will it somehow work itself up into another whole, complete, full—

JOHN: —overflowing—

WM: —with the realities we're missing now?

JOHN: Will the wrinkles in her face disappear and the smile come back into her eyes. The mold encrusting her face break into a million pieces, or the disappointments and total obliteration of our dreams cancel themselves out and present themselves to us in another chance. Patience—

WM: —expects—

JOHN: And I am slowly being taught—

WM: —to expect—

JOHN and WM: —nothing.

EMER: *(Poking his head out from kitchen)* Can I come out now? Is she gone?

WM: She was never here. Do you suppose she could have been deaf?

JOHN: We were like strangers passing in the night. She didn't even recognize me.

WM: She didn't even recognize herself. Perhaps she is blind.

EMER: Thank goodness we found out in time before I squandered this week's ration on an eight place setting.

WM: I don't know what the world is coming to when its villians don't even perceive themselves for what they are. Look at me. I would gladly reveal myself at any and all times for any reason to anybody upon proper identification of course and it is my hope that the rest could at least do the same.

JOHN: We were like two strangers passing in the night wrapped and shielded. And it was the light that came from the passing that was the connection that bound us together for an instant of a second. And in the darkness, the utter darkness, the two of us appeared as one, creating an illusion of eternity in the bliss of a joyful time.

EMER: Do you suppose she could have stolen anything while she was here? I'm missing a purpose and two reasons.

WM: Beats me.

EMER: But then, I'm always misplacing things.

WM: Fasting, was she?

EMER: A little too fast for my tastes.

JOHN: We were like two strangers passing in the night or two ice skaters pulled apart and drawn together by the forces all around; but for a second of an instant they touched ever so briefly before being torn apart again.

WM: Put it on paper, Johnson. There are no best seller's here.

JOHN: What keeps me from following her and begging her hand until she gives it to me?

WM: Could it be death?

EMER: Or a shortage of spare parts.

JOHN: We only live once.

EMER: And it is my intention to keep it that way.

(JOHN goes to the door, hesitates, leaves)

JOHN: *(Yelling after DIX)* Wait!

EMER *and* WM: *(To JOHN)* Wait!

(Gunfire starts. EMER and WM close the door quickly and stand against it)

WM: Johnson?

(Screams are heard. JOHN being shot. DIX reacting. Policemen yelling directions, clearing the streets. JOHN trying to get away, dragging himself on the pavement. EMER closes his eyes tightly. WM looks the other way. Sounds of heavier feet. JOHN beating on the door for help. Men's voices, curses)

VOICE: Clear the streets. Clear the streets. He's trying to go back to the house.

EMER: Do you hear something?

WM: What do you mean?

EMER: A knocking of some sorts. Perhaps we are wanted.

WM: Impossible! No one that we know can use the streets. It's against the law. Anyone that we know would use a key, if they lived here. And then they wouldn't be knocking. In which case, the person knocking would be the person using the key.

EMER: If the person using the key has a key, why doesn't the person use it?

WM: Perhaps his hands are full.

(Sirens. JOHN pleads at the door, calling their names. The approaching feet get louder)

EMER: And now it speaks. It knows our names. Could we be hearing things?

WM: Crime comes personalized nowadays. We needn't go out. It is delivered fresh to us. Don't be fooled.

EMER: Is it human? It sounds in distress?

WM: Some pathetic animal from some subtropic rainforest having overheard intelligent chatter enough to imitate it, now having fallen into a clever trap or one pursued by a larger beast of prey.

EMER: If it has religion, then it has nothing to worry about. It will be saved by divine intervention.

(The knocking continues, more frantic)

EMER: There is is again. *(To himself)* Be brave.

WM: Could it be your recurring indigestion. I do recall knockwurst on your weekend menu.

EMER: Yes, having taken a turn for the worst, perhaps we should open it and see.

WM: Fool! We have not the proper tools. Nor are we well scrubbed nor sterilized!

EMER: I mean the door!

WM: Wash it then!

EMER: Let it in!

WM: Let *what* in!

EMER: Whatever it is!

WM: And stand the chance of being bit?

(Voices distorted into loudspeakers, searchlight scanning the windows. Cars pulling in and stopping suddenly, sirens, crowds, dogs. The knocking changes to a weakened scratch. The voice a sob, then a wimper)

WM: Now how would I look standing in the doorway at the end of the day staring out into the light with everything there?

(EMER pushes WM aside. EMER attempts to open the door. The final shots ring out causing EMER and WM

to cease their struggle. The outside noises subside. We hear a woman crying, cars pulling away, and a deafening silence. Pause. The sound of a key in the lock. EMER *and* WM *are petrified.* JACK *enters like a man running for his life. He reaches the sofa and throws himself on it in exhaustion. Then to* OFFICER *and* DIXON. *Smoke rises from a discharged gun)*

OFFICER: Unmoving woman, why are you so still? Have you no sympathy for this injured man? Doesn't his condition arouse your feelings, your instinct to comfort? To aid? Or perhaps he is dead. Should we contact the next of kin or should we leave the body here to soak up the rain and prevent the formation of puddles and other collecting bodies of liquid. *(*DIX *is frozen. An expression of grief stamped without relief on her face. The* OFFICER *puts his hands on her)* Can you not speak, woman? Have you no feelings in your iced and rusty bones for this poor man here who lies at your feet and pretends to know you. Could he be mistaken? Could he be mistaking you with another woman of the streets, thinking you the one to relieve him of all the misery of his wretched life? If the dead cannot move you, perhaps the living can. I'll get your blood running so fast you won't be able to catch up with it. You'll thank me for it in the end and you'll forget.

(Tears fall down her stilled face. EMER *and* WM *watch.* EMER *covers his mouth;* WM *has a nervous twitch.* AND*'s Volkswagon pulls up without* AND *and idles quietly.* DAW *enters from the rear. She looks disheveled but pulls herself together and feigns good humor)*

DAW: I'm back.

EMER: *(Frightened)* Aghhh!

WM: *(Composed)* Ah, you're back We were worried about you. Tell us about your day.

DAW: What's there to tell. I've been out. That's all. Why are you so jumpy?

WM: We weren't expecting you that way. I mean, you know us well enough to use the front door.

EMER: But it's just as well. The front is covered with weeds. The flowers are knee deep in their khakis. Their artillery has completely destroyed my victory garden. The green tomatoes are stunted and shrivel on the pole.

WM: *(Preventing* DAW *from seeing)* Now. Now. Vegetables grow best unseen and in complete quiet and stark darkness. They are sensitive to the truth. Reality must be kept from them at all costs.

EMER: *(To* DAW*)* You look so tired. Why don't you go lie down and rest. Jackson, get up so Dawson can go to sleep.

JACK: *(Awakening and fearful)* They're after me.

DAW: Who's after you?

WM: No one's after him. He's high. Take it from

me. I know.

JACK: I didn't do it. I swear I didn't.

DAW: Do what?

WM: Move his desk from the darkness into the light.

EMER: Did you bring me anything to eat?

DAW: Where's Johnson?

WM: *(Quickly)* Johnson's not here.

DAW: Where is he?

WM: Johnson has escaped.

EMER: Don't blame Jackson. It's not his fault. I was sleeping at the time, wasn't I, Jackson?

WM: Jackson was the one sleeping, Emerson.

EMER: Precisely. I knew one of us was.

DAW: Then he's gone.

EMER: Yes.

WM: And so much the better off because of it.

JACK: I dreamt that Johnson was dead. As all of us are.

WM: Let's not be morbid, Jackson. Didn't you just hear me say that Johnson has escaped!

JACK: He was killed as we watched, and we did nothing to help him—

EMER: You're the one who had the dream so don't blame us.

WM: He said he would write us once he settled. He even suggested that he may even send for us, if we're good. There are snap shots that I seem to have misplaced—

DAW: Well, I should be glad for him.

EMER: Do.

DAW: But I'm not. There comes a time when they all have to leave. Time's not something you can hold on to. I just can't help wanting to.

EMER: The carcass of dead animals always made me ill. Remembering the sight at meals only serves to make me lose my appetite.

JACK: It happened slowly. Day after day. Drained of life.

WM: Bleeding is a well known remedy of some folk's ailments.

EMER: *(Holding his mouth)* I think I'm going to be sick.

DAW: As long as he's happy.

WM: I see no reason why he shouldn't be.

DAW: I can't wait to see the grandchildren.

EMER: You're not his mother.

DAW: I feel like it.

WM: At least he's gotten out.

EMER: Which is more than we can say.

JACK: We should feel guilt.

EMER: That's exactly what I feel.

WM: Jackson, stop tormenting us with your dreams. It's enough that we have an impending reality that we must deal with without these unsolicited extras. Can't you see our hands are full.

EMER: Our hands are tied.

JACK: Our hands are bloody.

AND: *(Offstage; from outside)* God! Is it Johnson dead?

DAW: What?

AND: *(Offstage)* Hello in there. Anybody there?

WM: *(Weakly)* Yes.

AND: *(Offstage)* As I was coming up the walk, I stepped in a puddle. When I stooped to scrape my soles, I noticed a striking resemblance to Johnson. Has someone called the police? Officer! Officer!

(AND reenters. We hear his noisy, uneven entrance from outside. He, too, is in shambles, as if a willing participant in an urban war. One of his heels has been broken off, stockings fall down around his ankles. His clothes are half torn off. His hat hangs to the side, barely anchored by a pin. Yet, through it all, he maintains a certain grotesque dignity and aloofness from the events that unfold around him.)

DAW: Johnson! *(Rushes to the front door and looks out in horror. She screams. JACK rushes to her, holding her, preventing her from going out, a restraint to comfort)* Oh, my God! *(She gets physically ill from what she sees)*

JACK: *(Forcing himself to see)* Good God, no! *(To WM and EMER)* How did this happen?

WM: Whoever's got the guns most likely's got the bullets too.

JACK: The guards!

DAW: But who are they protecting?

WM: I'll give you three guesses.

DAW: Surely not us.

EMER: Bingo.

(WM and EMER turn away. WM, to the record player, turning the volume full blast, pretending not to hear JACK, then putting on earphones. EMER looks in the refrigerator, hanging in the door longer than necessary, fanning himself with the door)

JACK: What could he have done to deserve being killed like that?

DAW: He was in love. Wouldn't hurt a fly.

JACK: I didn't know. I didn't know.

DAW: *(Accusingly)* You let them do this. You stood in here and did nothing. You let him go out there to die.

JACK: I wasn't even here.

DAW: Then you should have been.

JACK: You sent me out! I can't be in two places at the same time.

DAW: Who ever listens to me! I'm tired, Jackson. Just tell me what am I supposed to do? I saw his end the day he was born, and I pretended it wasn't there and looked the other way. But it stayed and each day grew until there was no way I could see anything without seeing it. He's your responsibility, they kept telling me. Take care of him. He's the last, the hope. I spend the better part of my life keeping him out of trouble, keeping him alive. Protecting him from the world. Keeping the world out, away. Protecting his smile, his innocence, his promise. Trying to sneak him through life unnoticed in clothes that would hide his age, in attitudes that would confuse his manhood. Stealing year after year. Praying for each new one. Giving thanks for each passing one. Knowing that old age was a dream for him and a curse for me, I dreamt it nightly. Prayed. Begged. One. Only. Just one more. The single solitary hope. Wishing. Take my own in exchange for a glimpse that alone would make it all worth the effort, that would make me smile. And I turn my back for a minute. Go out for grown men who can but can't or won't. Come back and it's all been torn down, each brick that I laid and every mile that I've walked with him, running ahead to see if the way was safe. And now he's gone and what do I have left? Not even the chance to lay him to rest for the last time!

JACK: We have each other at least . . .

EMER: Well, there's nothing we can do about it now. He had to have his way.

WM: Whether he's in here or out there makes no difference to him now.

DAW: For decency's sake!

EMER: Even she could do nothing about it if she lived in this town.

DAW: Go get it so we can weep over it. Curse over it. Tend to it. Whatever is done to bodies that are left and forgotten. Whatever we have to do to glorify what he could have been.

JACK: I set one foot on that road and they'll crucify me. And after they've shot me, who'll come and bring me back.

(Several OFFICERS break into the room with guns pointed at the family)

OFFICER: Everybody! Up against the goddamn wall!!

(Chaos within, all scrambling. Chairs are overturned, adornments broken. DAW is hysterical by this time. JACK tries to maintain calmness)

JACK: You can't come in here like this. Whatever happens on the street is one thing, but you will not come into my home. I won't let you violate this space.

OFF: *(Brushing JACK aside)* Search the premises!

JACK: I demand to know what you want.

OFF: Check the back rooms.

JACK: Tell me what you're looking for. *(He is pushed aside while OFFICERS continue to ramshakle the premises)*

(The second OFFICER looks at AND in drag who smiles seductively. Second OFFICER turns away.

DAW, *still grieving, runs to an* OFFICER *and beats him, struggling for his gun.*

DAW: You killed my brother. Killed him like a common dog in the street.

(She is knocked to the floor. JACK, *trying to protect all fronts at once, runs from the search being conducted in the rest of the house. An* OFFICER *begins to tear off* DAW's *clothes)*

OFF: A fighter, are you. You damn slut. Can't wait, can you.

JACK: My god. She's my wife.

SEC OFF: Suspect must be searched for hidden weapons.

JACK: *(Himself being searched, as well as* WM, EMER, *and* AND *most willingly)* Weapon? You see, my wife has undergone a severe shock. Her younger brother has been senselessly murdered. She was close to him. We all were. I think it might be appropriate to investigate that circumstance at this time. Those of us who live here are all victim to that crime. This is a time of mourning. Respect it. Please show some empathy, some compassion. I don't see the need to aggravate her grief. Please.

AND: You're wasting your breath, sweetie.

OFF: *(To other* OFFICER*)* Did you find anything?

SEC OFF: Not yet, sir.

OFF: Then take her in the back. I order you to find what you are looking for.

(DAW is dragged off screaming words of anger, fear, frustration. JACK *starts after her but is restrained by something within himself)*

JACK: My God. Can I still be dreaming. Then when will I awaken. Is this real. I can't allow it to be real. Wake me somebody. Please wake me, now.

AND: It don't get no realer than it be now. Smile, Jackson.

WM: Be cool, what ever you do. Just be cool.

(DAW screams loudly from offstage. Sounds of breaking, a beating and curses)

ONSTAGE OFF: *(To* JACK*)* You were talking to me, weren't you. I am listening.

JACK: *(To himself mostly)* I want to believe that you are here to help us. I will force myself to believe. We have been made victim to a grave injustice. Perhaps you are here to help us solve the crime and locate the person who slayed my brother-in-law and who detains my wife.

(DAW screams)

OFF: I do.

JACK: My wife. *(The commotion reaches a peak and then subsides. Weeping commences from offstage)* The hole ascends. The deep, dark one, so deep I can't see the light that should be shining above me and have begun to doubt altogether whether there

ever was one. And now the dirt.

OFF: Speak up. I can't hear you. You. The rest of you. Can you help him out. Who claims witness to the crime?

EMER: Oh, my brown gravy. Here it comes.

WM: *(Plugged into stereo with earphones)* What did you say? I can't hear you. Can you speak up a little louder?

EMER: *(Mouth full of food)* Mmurd em cjank meh dellik!

(Screams and the sound of things being broken offstage)

JACK: *(Starting toward backroom)* Officer, I think this outrageous activity has gone far enough—

OFF: *(Pointing gun in* JACK's *face)* It hasn't gone nearly far enough. We are here to be satisfied. You are here to provide the satisfaction.

DAW: *(Offstage)* Oh my God. Jackson. Help me. Please!

OFF: The story.

EMER: *(Sacrificial)* I-I-I was asleep at the time. I don't know nothin'.

WM: *He* was asleep at the time.

OFF: I was talking to him.

EMER: I'm telling you he was asleep. He don't know nothin'.

OFF: The whole time?

EMER: I was looking at the refrigerator. Williamson as listening to his music and he was asleep. We had no idea.

WM: The fool went and got his own self killed.

EMER: Got exactly what he deserved. You officers did your duty. We're blessed to have the finest think so much of us to keep us in our place like you done.

WM: I don't know what we woulda done. We're mighty grateful.

OFF: *(To* JACK*)* Do you agree with all this. *(*EMER *and* WM *shake their heads violently. Sounds from the other room.* AND *picks gun from an unaware* OFFICER's *holster and conceals it)* Wha'sa matta? You can't talk?

EMER: He talk all the time. Talk for the man, Jackson. I mean open your mouth and make some sound.

WM: At least smile for the man, Jackson.

JACK: I can talk.

OFF: But you won't talk, will you.

EMER: I'll never utter another solitary word. You have my word on that. My last word.

OFF: I'm talking to him. Will he talk?

EMER: He's showing you he won't talk by not talking now. He a quick one.

OFF: To anybody.

WM: Yes, sir. I mean, no sir.

EMER: Forever and a day.

(SEC OFF *reenters with* DAW *who is completely disheveled*)

OFF: Did you find any suspects in the back?

SEC OFF: Only her.

OFF: Arrest her then.

JACK: What's she done?

EMER *and* WM: Shhhh! Hush!

(SEC OFF *puts handcuffs on* DAW. JACK *starts toward her*)

OFF: Shoot them if they move. Read them their rights.

SEC OFF: They have none, sir.

OFF: I expect the premises to be cleared by Monday. If you are caught outside, you will be executed. (*To* SEC OFF) Double the guards.

VOICE: (*On megaphone from outside*) The following persons have broken laws and have been punished. Sara Benson, resisting arrest. Josuah Peterson, laughing in his home. Johnny Johnson, leaving his home. Under arrest, the woman Dixon. Under arrest, the woman Dawson. Under surveillance and house arrest, the family Anderson, Williamson, Emerson. And to be shot upon sight, the fugitive Jackson!

The last word echoes several times. A loud screeching noise drowns out the public address system. The four stand perfectly still as the scene ends.

ACT TWO

Scene I

A VOICE *over the loudspeaker rambles off a list of seemingly endless restrictions, violations, rules, including a repetition of past rules, and new ones such as only nonmovers can converse with nonmovers and that a daily interrogation will take place, that any and all questions must be answered, etc. . . . And then the list of the victims of the massive crackdown, always getting longer and longer. But the sound of the loudspeaker* VOICE *replaces specific words. The tone of authority supercedes precise wording making meaning, just as the four characters no longer need be reminded of the exact nature of their imprisonment. They have become what they are, replacing what they once were and determining that they will never be anything else—They believe in their subjugation. As the* VOICE *winds down, like a record turned off while the needle remains on the turntable, they seem to thaw out and go through the motions of being outraged and shocked over the strange turn of events.*

AND: Mounds of bodies lining the streets. The smell of rotting flesh, of stale purpose, and aborted ambition hung in the air like icicles.

WM: Unbelievable.

EMER: Can we not escape?

AND: Escape? And bring down all the wrath on earth for violating one of their sacred rules. We must obey and act within the perimeters of their demands. There are no two ways about it.

WM: It's not even a one way street. Not even a dead end. There's no beginning to it.

EMER: And no end.

JACK: God, can it be they're not just after our bodies, but our souls and our destiny as well.

WM: They're after *you*, buddy. We ain't done nothin'.

EMER: But did you see *him*?

AND: Who? What?

EMER: Help. Aid. Deliverance. Whatever its name is.

JACK: Some crime . . . a violation. But what have I done? The crime was not an act, but *any* act. The crime is not any act, but the ability to act. To make things different. To make anything different form the way it has to be.

EMER: Prevention, they say, is the anecdote of the law.

AND: I barely got home with my life. It's a jungle out there. People grabbing at you, offering you money, good times, security, a pension. Give me this, come to me, sweetie, go there with him . . . . And as I came up the walk, some gentleman of the law was dragging off some poor afflicted fellow by the name of Thompson, I think it was. The negligent fellow had allowed his toenails to grow unattended. Can you imagine that! When his crime was made conscious to him, he tried to make amends by biting away at his nails, passing the cuticles and nibbling all the way past his ankles, to the very nubs in despair. But it was too late. His crime had already been committed and detected. The damage was done. As a result of making the bloody mess and creating such a blatant disturbance to the balance of nature, the policemen commenced to beat him unmercifully, causing his head to pop off and roll away. They have pasted pictures of the renegade head in the post office and have offered a reward for its apprehension. And all around me, the most God awful stillness. The tides do not come and go, the sun does not set. I suspect the earth does not revolve if it is left to have its own way about it . . . . Long after the poor man's screams had trailed away, I was conscious of the most violent and obscene nothingness I'd ever experienced. (*A low sorrowful moan becoming defiance begins to rise from* JACK's *body. The end, or beginning of his refusal*)

AND: What's unsettling you, Jackson? You were

always the one with the well kept nails, both at the hands and feet.

JACK: (*Shouting out the window for dear life*) Goddammit! What do you want from us? You've taken everything. What else do you want?!

(*Gunfire welcomes* JACK's *outburst. The others pull him back*)

WM: The fool is trying to get us all killed with his homemade brand of courage. It's enough that he's a dead man himself without dragging the rest of us down with him.

EMER: I'll tell you what's wrong. He's starving to death, like I am. Deprivation brings this on a man.

(*A knock on the door*)

WM: Now you've gone and done it.

(JACK *answers the door. Standing at the threshold is a mild looking man who transmits with a certain impatience. It is the* MAN WHO HANDLES INQUIRIES)

MAN: Mr. Jackson?

JACK: Yes!

MAN: I've been sent here to help you. You have been requesting attention, have you not?

JACK: Yes!!

MAN: Then you must calm down. I can't help you if you are not willing to help me. And immediate attention is something we both desire. Is that not true? May I step in? (*He does*) I handle inquiries. What, sir, is your problem?

JACK: Tell us what's going on. Someone killed my brother. Someone took my wife away. And these strange new rules that keep us inside and threaten us with certain death—

MAN: (*Stopping his notetaking*) I can only handle one concern at a time. Overloading causes my circuits to blow, if you know what I mean. (JACK *smiles with the* MAN, *thinking it a joke*) Now, then, what do you want to know. Let's start at the beginning.

JACK: My brother-in-law.

MAN: And his name?

JACK: Johnson.

MAN: And your name?

JACK: Jackson. I thought I told you that.

MAN: Then you are inquiring into the death of Mr. Jackson Johnson.

JACK: No, his name is Johnson.

MAN: And you want to know—

JACK: Where he is.

MAN: Then he's probably wherever you left him.

JACK: He's dead.

MAN: Then there's nothing more to ask about him.

JACK: His body, sir.

MAN: Body? What could you possibly have in mind to do with a dead man's body? Are you some kind of pervert?

JACK: I want to bury it, sir.

MAN: For what?

JACK: Tradition, sir.

MAN: Throw him in a hole and pile the dirt on. You still won't be able to see him, and he'll still be quite alone.

JACK: Just knowing he's there will be a comfort, sir, to some of us.

MAN: Well, you have my permission to bury him then.

JACK: But, I don't have the body, sir.

MAN: Where is it?

JACK: I was hoping you'd be able to tell me that, sir. Your men carried it away.

MAN: My men. I have no men.

JACK: Some men.

MAN: But who? So you don't know where it is?

JACK: No, sir.

MAN: Then how in blazes do you know the party we're discussing is actually dead?

JACK: He was shot, sir.

MAN: With what?

JACK: A gun.

MAN: Registered?

JACK: I voted in the last election, sir.

MAN: And where is this gun?

JACK: They took it away, sir.

MAN: The blood?

JACK: It's been cleaned up, sir.

MAN: By whom?

JACK: I don't know, sir.

MAN: Sounds peculiar to me. You don't have the body. You don't even have the gun. There's no blood that we can see or even approximate. Where's your proof? Everyone knows that proof is the closest thing to reality we have.

JACK: But I saw it with my own eyes.

MAN: Do you wear glasses?

JACK: On occasion.

MAN: Were you wearing glasses on the date in discussion?

JACK: I can't remember.

MAN: You can't remember!

JACK: But I did see him shot.

MAN: You saw him while he was being shot or soon after?

JACK: After.

MAN: Then can it also be possible that you could not remember the incident but could remember the glasses you were or were not wearing?

JACK: I don't understand.

MAN: Now it's that you don't understand in addition to not being able to remember.

JACK: But I do remember. I was there.

MAN: Then perhaps you shot him yourself.

JACK: No!

MAN: This is all very confusing. You remember what you saw, but you don't remember what you saw with.

JACK: I saw with my eyes.

MAN: But your eyes aided or your eyes alone? The law thrives on details.

JACK: But—

MAN: And then, on top of it, you can't produce the body you're seeking to recover. The body is nine-tenths of the crime. If you don't have the body, you don't have the case.

JACK: If you'd—

MAN: It seems very clear to me that there was no crime committed here.

JACK: I didn't say the crime was here.

MAN: No shooting. No brother-in-law. And what's this about a wife?

JACK: They took her away.

MAN: *(Aggravated)* Who?

JACK: The policemen.

MAN: Which policemen?

JACK: I don't know.

MAN: Then they could have been anybody. Are you in the habit of letting your wife dally about with any john that passes by. *(JACK lunges at him. He is restrained by* WM *and* EMER*)* Our records show that you are not even married, Mr. Jackson. That you have chosen to take up with this collection of *(Pause)* men.

JACK: But I was married—

MAN: But not now?

JACK: Of course I am.

MAN: Then where is your wife, the alleged dead man's alleged sister?

JACK: She was taken from me.

MAN: You mean she left you. And the marriage as well. My dear sir. You are not married. You have no wife. No brother-in-law. Only this rather wretched existence that you have obviously chosen for yourself. My pities, sir. Had I known this bit of information I would not have wasted my time. For future reference, I would suggest that you order your facts and relationships carefully before attempting to petition the law. It is a foolish man who deals in intangibles. Your perception of reality is only subjective and at the moment less than that, hardly a substantial enough base upon which to challenge the apple-cart of justice. Good day. *(Leaves)*

JACK: *(Yells out the window)* I know what you're trying to do. Don't think I don't know. I am not confused; I know what's going on here. You're wrong. How you got the power to do this is beyond me, but you can't stay in power forever. You are wrong and I'll yell it at this window if

this is my only platform. I'll yell it until I'm hoarse and tired or until my voice has given completely out or until I am dead. And I'll yell. So loud and long. All day and all night. In that indistinguishable time. For all time. and after I am gone, there will be others to take my place. They will yell it from their windows and on the streets among you. Those of you there will start saying the words in spite of yourselves, and children will learn that truth before they learn your own words. All over the city. And if your power extends farther, we will yell it all over the country and all over the world if need be until you will bend to us, you will beg us to stop. Someone, somewhere will hear us, and they will join us. We will beat you. We will win.

Scene 2

DIX *is led to a jail cell. Her clothes are tattered. She is physically and emotionally spent. The* OFF *pulls at his pants and gloats.* DAW *also occupies the cell. She maintains an aloofness and a sense of dignity, yet she looks in horror at the body of* JOHN *which is draped over her cell. Scene fades to black.*

Scene 3

Lights up on the stealthy sillhouettes of EMER *and* WM, *badly dressed in women's clothing, preparing to leave through the back door. They approach the exit from different directions and collide in the doorway, scaring the wits out of each other.*

AND: *(Appearing from nowhere)* And where are you two going?

WM: I'm leaving the only way I know how. All the other options are closed to us.

EMER: *(Stuffing cotton in his brassiere)* What else can we do. I'm so hungry, I could eat a cow.

AND: Then pass the appetizers because you look like one.

JACK: Don't fool yourselves. There's no protection for anyone anymore. Especially women. They're populating our jails while we remain trapped at home.

AND: And can't even take care of ourselves. What a disgrace.

WM: What else can we do. I'm losing my mind.

JACK: We've got to organize. That's the only way. A few more hours and someone will respond to our cries. I'm sure of it.

AND: Fool. There's no God out there who will hear us. He's either stone deaf or tone deaf. Our walls are well insulated. Your pathetic cries are more for your own benefit than anyone else's.

JACK: But it's all we've got.

AND: Not quite. Seeing that we're the only ones left, we must somehow figure out the method to our survival before we are irreparably immobilized. If there's one thing I won't allow to happen, it's letting them destroy me. I'm quite capable of destroying myself. Thank you. Therefore, I have taken upon myself the burden of thought.

WM: What do you plan to do?

AND: We must first understand the nature of the enemy.

JACK: He has no nature. If he did, his own inhumanity would sicken him.

WM: That's right. He has no soul.

EMER: And surely no stomach.

AND: The enemy divides the world into halves— the movers and the nonmovers—those who have the privilege and those who do not. The question arises: How do we get the privilege?

EMER: Is it bigger than a breadbox?

AND: I have developed an intricate system of communication with forces aligned with the other side. I have learned that it is possible to bargain with the enemy. We must therefore learn to speak his language.

EMER: That shouldn't be too difficult, if we can purchase the records—

AND: The answer is currency. We must save up enough movements to get us out of here.

JACK: Purchase our freedom?

AND: A one-way ticket to old age.

WM: Anything. Anything to get out of this hell.

JACK: It won't work.

AND: Of course it will.

JACK: And where are we saving to go?

AND: To a small colony beyond the country's boundary for people like ourselves.

JACK: And who's to say that it will be any different?

EMER: Or not worse?

WM: It can't be worse. Where's your faith, man? *(To AND)* It's a good plan. Tell us what we have to do.

AND: We must analyze our lives and decide which activities are meaningless in the face of our ultimate goal—freedom. Which actions are unnecessary, and if not unnecessary, which actions we can do without. Scrimping and scrounging is not new to us. We have suffered before and under a lot worse circumstances. Turning your head, for example, is a goddamn waste of time. What good can come from turning our heads? We can see what's to either side. What fiendish monster is sneaking up behind us to grab us around the very

neck and choke the very life spirits from our bodies; ourselves, struggling and gasping uselessly until we fall numb and worse than dead to the floor below. *(EMER and WM have been twisting and turning their necks excessively to see if the threatening presence is indeed present)* And even though such a calamity would take us out of our misery and render this fanatic concern with emancipation quite redundant, for we would have no use for salvation at that point or any use for anything else for that matter except an undertaker perhaps because we would be quite utterly dead. But because we are all at home here in safe quarters with our doors bolted, our windows locked, and our shades drawn *(WM puts on his sunglasses, raises his collar)* keeping us in and everyone else out, we can see that the twisting and turning of one's neck to see someone who isn't even there is both a grossly monotonous and tiring habit to have. So, let us step to the side and turn all the way around if you have reason to question your safety. Let's do it, shall we? *(They do)* The same can be said of all joints and body parts that bend—knees, elbows, wrists, ankles—all are accommodations for the lazy. And we don't want that appellation hanging around our necks weighing us down to the ground. *(They shake their heads)* Then there's the matter of the winking of one's eye. We wink to others. It's a mode of communication saying to some pretty girl or man—"see you around, sweetie," or "you a real fine mama or poppa," or "I'll get to you later." Or in blinking both eyes simultaneously, saying something to the effect— "s'all right with me, brother"—or prompting others to action—"Go Head"—or annoyance— "you do that one more time and I'll break both your arms." Blinking, as a wink with two eyes is fondly called, is also an attempt to remove some foreign particle lodged somewhere on the ball of tissues. But then excessive blinking is also a flirtation, much akin to the wink, but this time feminine in gender and insidious in nature. All this body language—winking, blinking, nodding, fluttering, and hard glancing is both complicated and ambiguous. How many times have you heard of someone misreading a signal, for we have many illiterates among us these days and getting the wrong message is commonplace. As a result, homes have been broken up, people have died, others have been born. All because of a gesture that was better off not made, movements unspent: backs arched, knees left unbent, neck pointing straight ahead, eyes left conspicuously open or closed. These are the natural and correct positions for any body. Here in our house, we don't have to make signs to one another to be understood. There is no traffic here. The question remains "are we being understood or better still, do we understand ourselves?" The Indians sent smoke signals but ask yourselves—what did they do on a rainy day? We communicate with words. We say things like, "Open the door," "Close the door," "Leave it ajar," or "Fuck off," and "Would you scratch my back lower this time, a little lower. Umm." It's intelligent, to the point, and direct. There is no ambiguity here. For those of you with limited vocabularies, I have taken the initiative of ordering the complete set of dictionaries of every known language on earth for your leisurely perusal and disposal. Only you may not waste time turning the pages or moving your eyes across the page. That brings me to the mouth. The yawning, the puckering, the smuckering, the miscellaneous contortions all performed under the guise of discomfort. I will set the thermostat at sixty-eight degrees, and that's where it will stay. Useless conversation will also be eliminated. What do we have to say to each other? Hello? Goodbye? Get off my foot? When is dinner ready? There. I've said them all. Dawson has run away from home and taken the law with her. Therefore, there is no need for pleasantries. We don't care about each other. We hate each other. If you don't talk to me, I won't talk to you. I promise. That's only fair enough. Emerson, those useless treks to the refrigerator must be cut out.

EMER: I request the floor.

AND: You have it.

EMER: I make a motion that—

AND: You may most certainly not.

WM: I'd like to second the motion—

AND: Not on your life.

WM: You mean you don't adhere to parliamentary procedure?

AND: I have nothing against Parliament. I smoke them all the time; it's procedure which is out of order here. No, Emerson, there is no food in the refrigerator anyway. So why go there? And you, Williamson, no more dancing. No more pointless movement done for its own sake. We must take on a vow of silence, conserve our energies for the trying days and tiring nights ahead, painfully reexamine each and every activity from the broadest pantomime to the most miniscule stir, barely perceptible, rarely perceived. The very blood in our veins must not circulate without just cause. Our motions must be saved and stored away like pennies for a rainy day—a turn here, a twitch there. A shuffle, a snort. Because the storm clouds have descended upon us, and we must not do anything remotely human to weath-

er the storm, even if it kills us. Now, here are the coupons I picked up at the bank. They are divided into denominations of ones, fives, and tens. Major, minor, and moderate movements. Transfer your activities into this script. When we have a sufficient amount, I will redeem them for first class airplane tickets. When we go, we'll go in style.

WM: Well, all right.

JACK: What about Dawson?

AND: Dawson's salvation is entirely up to you. If we can save enough coupons between now and the time we leave, of course you can take her along. If we can bargain for her freedom, that is. The catch word is sacrifice.

EMER: My lips are sealed.

The unintelligible broadcast recommences as the scene fades into the next.

Scene 4

DAWSON *in jail. Alone.*

DAW: Dear Jackson.... How are you at home? Time passes slowly, but I use it to think of life as I once knew it. Our old daily routine is my timepiece. I measure my own idleness by things that I used to do at home, at work, with you. I concentrate on details—the texture of each fabric, the dimensions of each space, and I carefully measure the steps that I once took—the running to catch the bus each morning, the number of grains of sugar dropped in a cup of tea, the depth of each wrinkle on each forehead that I knew, the brilliance of your rare but always appreciated smile. I miss you .... And as I eat what passes for food, I am given to think of the feasts that we once had, the small meals that grew in significance with our age. As I shift to cushion the hardness of these concrete slabs, I relish the thought of your touch. That firmness envelopes me, and I am strangely content in this fleeing moment. But then, they reappear, those cold hands, those lifeless faces, and I turn inside out with an anger that echoes loudly throughout these cells and beats frantically at the deaf heavens. I no longer have a body. I gave it away long ago to keep from feeling the pain..... I hope things are going well .... There is so much to do. I feel that I should be doing something. I look around and see everything with a purpose, even the bars that keep me inside. A purpose! And if my own has been spent and I am left with none at all, then is my purpose now a nonpurpose that I must faithfully perform? I can't believe that centuries and generations have lived and died for this!.... They're coming to take away the words soon. I fear not remembering. Tomorrow, we will not be able to use verbs. They say they are dangerous tools in the hands of the oppressed. I thought I could salvage some and hide them somewhere for later use, but already today I am having trouble with the concepts. I know I've tried, but will I be able to try again? I know we're right, but I am afraid. What if their whimsy doesn't bring them around to the obvious and the necessary. If they continue their subjugation of our bodies, our minds, our generations because there's no one to stop them. I can't. You must..... You must know that any gesture from this much abused body of mine is a threat, a genuine threat to whatever they stand for. They stand over me and wait for my cries and when they do not come they are forced.... Let me say it once, whether I yell it as a curse or in a prayer, a whisper. Let me say it and let them hear it and it will be dragged down every street on the face of the earth, made to stand naked and shivering in some public place and whipped, spit upon, cursed, condemned, then set fire to. And while it screams in agony, for mercy, from them, for me, I beg forgiveness for ever having wanted it, thought it, dreamt it, known it. Today I cried for you...

Scene 5

AND: *(At the coupon box)* I can't believe it. The more I put in, the less I have.

EMER: *(Quite still)* Can there be a hole?

AND: Jackson, confide in me. A day has passed and I refrained from reading, from chess, from T.V. I've had no diversions, and I expect everyone to boast of the same. Last night, I slept like a log. I didn't even roll over, so determined was I to avoid superfluous locomotion.

JACK: I didn't sleep a wink. The music kept me awake.

AND: Music!

JACK: Jazz, funk, rhythmn and blues, disco. I thought I was dreaming, but then I realized that I couldn't be.

AND: What was it?

JACK: A party.

WM: *(Quickly)* A few close friends.

AND: How did they get in? Did we spring a leak?

JACK: Williamson gave away movement coupons.

WM: Only those that I worked for personally.

JACK: It was fare to get them here and back. Safe passage.

WM: Consider it a loan. It will be repaid.

AND: What! You have been filching coupons, pilfering salvation right under our semiconscious noses, in the very midsts, usurping our freedom and passing it on to others in quantities that only exacerbate and aggravate our collective last ditch efforts for emancipation. Was the need so great, the urge, the desire so overwhelming that you had to step out of line and display, completely gratuitously as it were, conspicuous and pointless dance? *(To himself mainly)* And To Give Our Freedom To Others When There Is Hardly Enough For Ourselves—

WM: Anderson, it was you, I believe, who said we must organize and form a Party.

AND: Jackson spoke those words, and now they come back to haunt us.

JACK: But there are different kinds of parties. I didn't mean this type.

AND: Why? Just tell me why.

WM: I needed exercise.

EMER: I feel so bad, not having prepared hors d'oeuvres.

AND: Let it go on record that Jackson and my own records have been wiped miraculously clean. Let that serve as an example. And you, Emerson, I saw you put something in your mouth. What is it? Spit it out. Spit it out.

EMER: It's nothing. Nothing.

AND: Let's have it.

EMER: But I'm hungry. I'll waste away.

AND: You're a traitor—

EMER: Yes. Yes.

AND: —a turncoat—

EMER: I do not deny it.

AND: —a turd!

EMER: If only I could, my life would be complete.

AND: The energy you spend reaching down and picking up, not to mention the opening and closing of one's favorite orifice, the biting, the chumping. Wasted motion that could have gone into our pot. How senseless, selfish, and stupid, You're forgetting the "cause," the goal that is drawing us forward because we cannot propel ourselves on our own. We are winding down, lowering the staff, liquidating, cashing in. And you. You! You measure your unthinking, self-centered actions against this grossly real situation we find ourselves in and ask yourself: Will it educate our children—

EMER: We don't have any.

AND: —will it build houses that will keep us warm?

EMER: It's summertime.

AND: Will it pay the utility bill, erect monuments to our sacrifice and personal industry? Will it win wars? Huh? Will it bring peace? Huh?

EMER: *(Quietly)* No.

AND: Of course not. It will do nothing, an end to itself. Movement incestuously turned inward and forgotten.

EMER: But I'm not eating any food. So what does it matter?

AND: Eating and chewing on a chair or rug is just as bad.

EMER: Please!

AND: Let me have it. *(EMER barely opens his mouth as AND sticks his fingers between EMER's teeth and pulls at a foreign object. A wad of chewing gum is stretched in a long line that AND pulls completely across the room. To WM)* And don't think I haven't been noticing your antics, Williamson. Those furtive gestures done in assumed privacy did not escape someone's alert eyelids. There are no women here, therefore there should be no women in your dreams. Keep your hands to your sides and keep them there. *(EMER lets go of the chewing gum which snaps like a huge rubberband, propelling AND offstage. Reenters, dusting himself off)* You must understand that there are well trod steps to liberation. We must change this law peaceably. Or else there will be chaos.

WM: Or else there would be happiness.

AND: Anarchist!

WM *and* EMER: Dictator!

AND: All right, you lazy bums. I'm being instructed to give you one last chance. If you think you can stand around and be charity cases, you're sadly mistaken, sorely mistaken. The world is tired of supporting you. Burdens. Both of you. Heavy. Lardlike. The grotesque fat rolling on you in monstrous waves like gelatin from meals paid for and delivered by hard-working tax-payers, working people who get up each morning and struggle on the job. They work at struggling which is more than you can say. Mind you, I didn't say that they accomplished anything. Some do. Others never do. But they all attempt. Try. Pull themselves up by their bootstraps. Some fly, others fall flat on their faces. But amid the applause and the jeers, they are egged on by an undying will to do. Go stand in the corner and forget about supper.

EMER: We already have.

JACK: *(To AND)* This is madness, Anderson.

AND: This is life, my dear half brother-in-law. A hard and frustrating one, but the only one we've got.

JACK: But is it worth it?

AND: A resounding yes.

JACK: We're like animals here, caged and desperate. Like horses that have been bred to run and now we're for some reason locked away for an indefinite time, but the urge is still in us. It'll always be there.

AND: I, too, have always been amused by horse races—the cool breeze, the leaves, the dust, the nervous energy, false starts,the gun. Shaking out their limbs, stretching those muscles, their bodies like rubber bands stretched to the very limit, needing only aim and the slightest prompting to be propelled into the farthest distance of anybody's imaginary track. And the gun sounds and they run. Run like the very devil himself got hold of them. Running for country, mother, running for freedom. Running for dear life itself. Running, knowing somebody goin' to win, the rest got to lose . . . I want you to guard them, Jackson. guard them with your life. Keep them in line. Punish them if you must. You understand our struggle here. You will be among the winners when this is over. I want you to believe that.

(An urgent knock at the door. JACK opens it a crack. DIX's face can be seen through the small space. Her voice is breathless and frightened)

DIX: May I come in?

AND: Who is she?

JACK: I don't know.

DIX: They know me in there. I've been here before.

WM: I recognize the voice.

EMER: It does sound vaguely familiar.

DIX: Please, I have escaped. Let me in. Only for a little while until I catch my breath and decide the way I have to go.

JACK: What am I supposed to do?

DIX: They're coming. They'll see me. I must get inside.

JACK: Anderson?

AND: *(Counting his coupons)* It's all up to you. Use your discretion. Just make certain it doesn't have a hole in it.

DIX: Please. For a short while.

JACK: What do you want?

DIX: A glass of water.

JACK: We have no water.

DIX: A place to lay my head.

EMER: Let her in.

WM: Keep her out.

JACK: Anderson?

AND: Toss a coin. Only don't bother me.

(DIX shoves her way in. WM, who has been barricading the door with his own body, is easily pushed aside, so weakened is he by this incarceration)

AND: The woman has the strength of an ox.

JACK: Perhaps she's our salvation.

WM: Let's be realistic. She couldn't even save herself, much less the rest of us.

JACK: She's escaped, hasn't she. And might be able to show us the way.

WM: I don't think she should stay. We're already in enough hot water without harboring this fugitive from justice.

EMER: She seems harmless enough.

WM: But do we know who she is or what she's done in the past? What she more than likely will do in the future.

DIX: A glass of water. A place to lay my head.

EMER: What's she saying?

AND: Probably delerious.

DIX: The water is restless. Communications established between the water that has come and the water that will come from one side of the wall to the other, establishes a bond of intent. And the wall weakens from an effort in concert.

EMER: Such a pretty little thing. So plump. So helpless.

DIX: The water comes, faster, heavier with more pressure and more appeal until that which has come loses patience and demands the moment when it too will flow through. The wall begins to crumble, losing all the faith it had in its prior strength, in its prior ability to contain. Its legacy of separating the hills from the valleys, the grass from the sand, of a body from another body, however different, of a body from a mind, of a mind from itself falters, releasing gradually from its grasp the foundation built upon the history of every wall that had ever been built and every liquid that had ever not been allowed to flow free. The wall crumbles and then it breaks down, allowing all manner of fluid to pass through, the oceans and the streams, the rivers and the ponds, waterfall indistinguishable from the raindrops, tears, sweat, waters all, mingled into the flood that will come forth, that must flow through. The waters run. They flow. It runs out covering everything, soaking mud, becoming bank, filling cups that have been turned over, craters once content in their barrenness, satisfied. And what it cannot fill, it will wash away, pushing aside hesitations, drowning doubts until the amalgamation is complete and a unity of analogous matter has covered the earth. Matter than can move or stand still, pour, rise, freeze hard, boil over, disappear before your very eyes and then fall again from places we cannot see. Matter that eludes our grasp and slips through the openings between fingers of outstretched hands, finally satisfying its own thirst, having denied itself for so long.

EMER: Let me take care of her. I'll be responsible.

WM: Fool. She betrayed us once. Whose to say she won't do it again.

JACK: I'll guard her.

EMER: No. I will. First, I'll wrap her in the softest blanket, then watch over her night and day. Trust me. I'll do a good job. (*He takes* DIX. *into another room*)

VOICE: (*On the megaphone*) Prisoners! (WM, AND, *and* JACK *are immediately attentive*) We have come to the end of the road. Two of you will go free. Decide among yourselves. The other two must die.

WM: But there are four of us.

AND: (*Correcting him*) Five.

WM: You're not counting her. Are you?

AND: Let's do this democratically. We can pull straws.

WM: No. Chance is too fair. (*Yelling to guards*) Take me. Williamson. Williamson and, uh, Emerson. (*To other room*) Come on, Emerson, baby. We got to book.

VOICE: Williamson! You may speak.

WM: (*Yelling*) Yes, Sir!

VOICE: Your talents have been discovered by scouts from Duluth. You have been offered a contract to consider. You have considered long enough. Sign here on the dotted line. Never mind. I'll sign for you. You may speak.

WM: What's it for?

VOICE: You will sing, dance, stand on your head, tell jokes, give benefits, give thanks, give concerts, recitals, take roasts, give toasts, take punches, take dives, play ball, play hooky, play every instrument in a one hundred piece orchestra all at the same time, juggle, ride horseback, hang from a trapeze, hang from a noose, tame the lions, the dogs, the heathens, receive pies in the face, slip on banana peels, read poetry, train poultry, write short stories, novels, epics, sing arias, perform blindfolded in plays, playing each role simultaneously and in full costume, eat fire, throw your voice, throw your back, throw knives and receive them, sing popular, classical, rock, roll, soul, blues, ballads, jazz, ragtime, country, folk, accapella, in all languages, do the Jig, Square Dance, Boogaloo, Twist, Indonesian Sword Dance, the Hula, Cakewalk, Minuet, Slow Drag, walk on water, live on air, and never die . . . plus other non-extras. You may speak.

WM: How many shows do I give daily?

VOICE: It's continuous. You may speak. (*Applause.* WM *is flattered.*)

WM: What do I get for it all?

AND: You'll get applause, admiration, friends, fame, fortune—with a small percentage going to me, of course—and occasional fatigue. You may speak, but make it short.

WM: What else do you do?

AND: I handle the books. You may speak.

WM: Can I see them?

AND: We don't want you to strain your eyes. The people must see you. Speak.

WM: That all sounds like hard work to me.

AND: Williamson, I'm surprised at you. You are not working. You are performing. There is a qualitative difference making all the difference in the world. Speak.

WM: When do I start?

AND: Right now.

WM: I'll have to find my tap shoes first.

AND: Don't worry 'bout a thing. I'll pack your trunk tomorrow. It'll be waiting for you backstage when you get there this afternoon.

JACK: Billy, think this thing through first.

AND: He doesn't have time.

WM: This is my big chance. I'll entertain them into submission.

JACK: Don't believe it.

WM: Hey! What's the matter with you. I told you I made up my mind. Whatever's out there is better than rotting slowly in this place nestled in between two fools.

JACK: What have they done to make this time any different. It's a trick. Anderson can't see these things, but I do.

WM: Man, I know what your problem is. You're jealous. I'm special. I've got something to give, something that they want, something they're willing to pay for. And what do you have. Nothing. So, get your hands offa me, will you, man. Please!

AND: Your chauffeured limousine is waiting. Can we?

WM: I'll send you tickets for opening night.

AND: Just remember to smile and the whole world smiles with you.

(WM leaves with top hat and cane)

VOICE: Emerson!

EMER: *(Appears at the doorway. He is bloated, having gained additional weight. His eyes are glassy. His senses have dulled. He moves slowly and with great effort. He is bursting at the seams like a man on the verge of a belch)* Did someone call?

AND: Oh, merciful heavens!

JACK: Where's the girl?

EMER: *(Vague)* Girl? I don't remember a girl?

JACK: *(Looking into the other room)* She's gone!

EMER: *(Quickly)* Oh, her. She's escaped.

AND: Don't believe him. Emerson knows what happened to the girl. Tell us the truth, putty.

EMER: *(Drowsily)* I told you. She has escaped.

JACK: It's possible. She did it before.

AND: Do you think we're all fools. Emerson has eaten her. Look at him.

EMER: It's this severe starvation which has caused

me to swell. I am dying. Of hunger.

AND: *(To JACK.)* He killed her and consumed her flesh.

EMER: No, I didn't.

JACK: Which is the truth?

VOICE: Emerson. What is your decision. Your response. You must respond. Respond.

AND: Pull yourself together, Jackson. This is no time to show our emotionalism. We must keep our heads. The man said that two of us would survive. Williamson is gone.

JACK: But can we trust them. Dare we?

AND: Williamson is free. Free. Think of it. Now who will be second. The girl is dead. Is Emerson worthy of freedom? Or should he be punished. *(Shows JACK. a gun and places it before him)*

JACK: I don't know.

EMER: I can't move. I don't deserve to live. I hate myself. Punish me.

VOICE: Respond. Respond!

AND: Think, Jackson. Think of the humiliation. The pain you have suffered. Think of the others. Dawson, Johnson. Think of the girl. The helpless creature who sought safety here, who escaped into the jaws of death. Torn apart with his teeth. Seeing herself eaten alive. Think, Jackson. Think of it.

EMER: I am hungry. A crust of bread. A sip of wine. Kill me and let me dine.

VOICE: Emerson, we are awaiting your decision.

JACK: No.

AND: Take the gun, Jackson. Take the gun.

JACK: We are not animals. I am not a murderer.

AND: But you must.

JACK: I can't.

AND: You will.

JACK: I won't.

AND: Must I do everything myself?

(EMER has begun to disrupt the house, eating everything in sight, no longer able to contain his voracious hunger. He turns on himself and attempts to tear a huge patch from his body, but the puncture causes him to explode, like a hot balloon pricked by a pin)

VOICE: Emerson!

AND: *(Changing his voice)* I'll be right out. *(To himself)* If I cannot move, then let me move someplace where I can remain motionless in comfort. On a sandy beach with a brilliant blue sky to match my mind without clouds and a sun that warms just enough without overheating. Let me watch the sky and the sea, also of a stunning blue, the sea with no trace of gray or waves and wrinkles, but massaging lapping, flowing, back and forth over my body. A straw hat covering my face, a towel underneath, sand between my toes, a tall, cool glass in my hand. Wind rustling the leaves of a book in the background. Peace.

(The following two monologues, those of the VOICE *and* AND, *are spoken simultaneously)*

VOICE: Emerson, you are a strong and healthy individual. You have been appointed to alternate activity duty. You must keep the wheels of the world moving in the stead of man, while he will be given all the credit, naturally. In exchange for your labor, you will be given all the food you can eat and drugs and alcohol every weekend to keep yourself from thinking about and fully comprehending your miserable lot. If this arrangement is found unsuitable, you will be given a transfer and/or gun with which to kill yourself. Of course, your body will be left to the Harvard Medical School for study.

AND: *(While speaking, goes to the box, takes out all coupons, sorts them, and stuffs them in his pockets and suitcase as he packs his other belongings)* I say go. Go I say. Be what they want you to be but be it your way. In comfort. In wealth. In style. Go. Have a go at it. Make a go of it. On the go. Going about. Going after. Going against. Go ahead. Go ahead of. Go all out. Go aloft. Go along. Alone. Along with. Go around. Go around. Go around in circles. Go as one pleases. Go away. Far away. As far away from. Get away with. Go back. Go back on. Go back over. Go back to. Go. Go down, Moses, way out of Egypt land. Go for. Go in. Go in for. Go into. Go it. Go it. Go to it. Go to town. Go all the way. Go.

VOICE: The remaining prisoners, come out with your hands up. If you move, we will shoot!

AND: Listen to them. Sound pretty serious, don't they?

JACK: They're surrounding the building.

AND: Let them. I have these. *(He holds up thick bundles of movement coupons)* I would give you some, but I need all the protection I can get.

JACK: Look, Anderson. Let's be reasonable about this. If we combine our energies, we can make it. We have to survive. There's no one else left.

AND: *(He has snapped. He takes inventory, runs about packing a suitcase, attaches a party hat to his head. He is insane)* Let me run now. Hop aboard. One-way ticket. Passport. Shots. Currency. Map. Binoculars. Autograph book. Package deal.

OFF: *(Offstage)* He is an extremely dangerous and demented man. Extra precautions must be taken to keep his activities in check. Call in as many reinforcements as you think you may need. Two or three billion is not enough.

JACK: What do they want with me! I have repudiated my past life. I have restricted my present life as much as humanly possible. I check myself daily. I measure my steps, I cut down on all unnecessary movement. I barely breathe, if it is the air we must preserve. I try not to think, if it is the prevailing brand of order that we must somehow maintain. But there must be some reciprocity. What is it willing to do for me? I move in spite of myself as if it is only natural to go ahead. It happens when I am not thinking. My mind does wander in spite of itself. To be any more still, I would have to be dead.

OFF: Recruit, if you have to. Offer money, favors, sex. The man is armed. He has a brain.

AND: Perhaps you have lucked on the trail of the solution yourself. Race. Gallop. Strut. Lockstep. One-two. Slow march. Half step. Goose step. Quick quick. Double march. Double time. Half time. Overtime. CP Time. Move.

JACK: Kill myself?

AND: I couldn't have constructed a more exacting terminology if I had spoken myself.

JACK: Why should I have to punish myself any more than I already am?

AND: Someone has to.

OFF: We will need both land and air details. Put the Coast Guard on alert. Call in the National Guard. Supply deodorant.

JACK: What are you saying? Why won't you listen to me? They're out there preparing to kill us!

AND: Then perhaps go for an airing. Scramble, scrabble, monopoly, bid whist, go fish, grovel, go on hands and knees, on all fours, worm along, steal along, steal away to Jesus, tippy-toe. It's obvious that the only way you are going to survive this rearrangement of meaning is to give into it. If you had given into it long before this, I wouldn't have had this unpleasant mess to deal with today.

OFF: Deputize all available citizens. Put free guns in cereal boxes.

JACK: Then I'd be dead already.

AND: Precisely. Then all your troubles would be over and I would not have had to go this terrible distance for nothing! Take a walk, take one's constitutional, take a stretch, stretch the legs. I'd say it's about time, beat one's way, thumb a ride, bum a ride. Here's two bits. Buy yourself a cup of coffee.

JACK: Anderson! You don't seem to understand. We can't do anything. No moves. No words. They keep us from going, then they say that we are lazy; or they let us go, then keep us from coming in. They say we are content because we never complain. We don't complain because we are forbidden from it also. And tomorrow we will be completely muted. The next day and the next, we will be blinded to keep us from seeing their own injustices while they pretend them necessary; and soon after, our unfeeling bodies will be detached from our heads that no longer think, and we will be used as fertilizer for the flowers whose sweet fragrances you sniff daily.

OFF: Say that he killed the Christ. And document it.

AND: Let's not get carried away.

OFF: If you see any signs of life, fire without reservation. Give it all you've got. Bullets, slingshots, knives, bombs, slander. Bring his family here. All that he has. If he has none, bring anyone distantly related—friends, acquaintances—anyone who has heard of him, anyone whose name is the same, whose name sounds like his, anyone with a name with any of the letters found in his name. Whose alphabet is the same. Or different. Or exists. Or doesn't. They are traitors and must be dealt with accordingly. Hang them. Shoot them. Torture them with fire and water. Coax him, lure, tease him, only *get him* He struggles still.

AND: Allll right, Jackson. Calm down. What is it now that you want? Is it food? Are you getting enough to drink? Is it Dawson? Should we try to send out feelers to locate her body for you? What is it you want, man! Get gone. Beat it. Make one's self scarce. One thing. Can you narrow it down to one thing. Preferably something tangible and within reasonable costs.

JACK: My life!

OFF: Cover all possible and conceivable areas of entrance. Lock the doors. Bolt them. Chain them. Board up all the windows. With wood and bricks. Remove all air from the vicinity. Then ask him to come out nicely.

JACK: That's all I want! One small, lonely, pointless life.* Just the chance to keep it. Just the chance to live it. Our life! Yours and mine! We're the only ones left.

AND: Jackson, Jackson. I think you have asked for a wee bit too much this time. Won't you reconsider? A car with a chauffeur for an hour or two?

JACK: I haven't asked for anything that I don't already have.

OFF: And if he comes out, fill him full of holes.

AND: That's the point. I could see cigarettes or dirty pictures, or maybe, if it could be arranged, a plane flight to see the grave of your dear mother. It could be arranged. Believe me. I know the right people. But this? Jackson. It's unchangeable, immutable, constant, reverseless, nonreturnable, intransmutable, indestructable, incorruptible, deathless. Listen to me. Think about it. *Is death really that so god awful bad?* The pain won't last long. Then it will all be over. Forever. No cares, worries, responsibilities. You won't have

to take out the garbage. Soon, not long after, you will be forgiven. For everything. You will be proclaimed a national hero of sorts. Awards will be presented to your memory. Posthumously, of course. Tears, buckets of them will be shed for you by perfect strangers. The television will have covered your funeral and played back exerpts on the eleven p.m. news. Holidays will be proclaimed to commemorate your deathday and children will be let out of school early to ponder over and write reports on the significance of your life. Year after year. Books will be written about you. Movies released. Streets will be renamed in your honor. Parents will name their children after you. Why go through so much trouble to clear your name when your death can do it so much better. Inextinguishable. Infinite. Everlasting, Eternal. *(Hands* JACK *a book)* Here, you can have this. It's yours anyway. Where I'm going I won't be needing it. Where I'm gong everyone is illiterate. All they understand is this. *(He holds up coupons)* The way it should be.

JACK: Haven't you been listening to anything I've said. It's about our life!

OFF: If he shows signs of life and dreams of freedom, install barbed wire around the building, the block, the city, the state, the nation, and run electricty through it. Dig a moat. Put sharks and piranha in the drinking waters.

AND: *(To* JACK*)* Fool, turn me aloose.

JACK: Have you no compassion.

AND: You're only making it hard on yourself. They would have been so lenient on you. I'm convinced of that. But I see that you will settle only for the greatest torture imaginable. Now! If you will excuse me. *(He takes a breath, waves a white handkerchief in one hand and a bundle of movement coupons in the other, then gathers his luggage to leave)* No, it's over. Wish me luck. *(He sticks his head out the door)* Ah! Escape! Deliverance! Good riddance! Disengagement! Liberation! Goddammit, Free!!

(As AND *steps outside, he is mowed down by the* OFFICERS, *then is fired upon several times after his fall.* JACK *takes the gun and commences to return the fire, causing the* OFFICERS *to return their attention to him)*

JACK: Break the clocks and let time stand still. Take the motors and the machines. The gadgets that you turn. The gadgets that turn you. Stop the hand that waves, that caresses, that beacons. That saves. And deny it. Forbid it. Chain the feet and the minds that control them. And when all is sufficiently quiet, start the fire. Shoot everything that moves, anything that has moved. Anything that looks like its going to move. Destroy also the places they have been. Take their memories and dreams to where our fears and treachery do reside. Take the wheels. The words. The books, and all that has ever been written in them. The ideas and the imagination, take everything. Tear down the world if we must get to the point where there is nothing. No movement. All progress reversed and erased. When we will find ourselves back at the beginning, before the beginning, before there was a beginning. Before the race, the running, the walking, the crawling, the creeping, the budge, the stir, a flicker of hope, of possibility.

SEC OFFICER: *(Appearing in the doorway)* Freeze! Drop your gun and come out with your hands up!

> *(JACK shoots the OFF, who falls to the floor. JACK goes over to him and takes his gun. The SEC OFF, who has rushed into the room, trains his gun on JACK)*

SEC OFF: Reach for the moon, boy, and don't brings your hands down till you've caught it. *(To dead OFF)* Get on up, Mike. This here is no time to be asleepin' on the job. You're setting a bad example. *(The dead OFF does not move)* Mike?

JACK: He's not asleep.

SEC OFF: Not asleep? What else can he be doing?

JACK: He was shot. One of those damn non-movers shot him while his back was turned, but I punished him by waiting until his back was turned and then I shot him.

SEC OFF: Who?

JACK: There; over there. *(Indicating EMER)*

OFF: Are there any others?

JACK: Not here, sir. They're all dead. *(SEC OFF looks at OFF's body quizzically)* We must keep moving. We mustn't linger too long. Sentiment is deadly.

SEC OFF: I reckon you're right.

JACK: I suggest that we check the house next door. I'm sure I saw movement inside.

OFF: Good idea. Coming, man?

JACK: Right away. You go ahead. *(Repeats his words, this time whispered, even spit out, with rancor and threat. JACK trains his gun at the departing OFF and shoots. He picks up the OFF's gun)*

VOICE: *(On the megaphone)* Captain. Captain. You all right in there. Need some reinforcements?

> *(JACK picks up the megaphone)*

JACK: Yeah.

VOICE: How many. Ten. A hundred?

JACK: Just one. Send in one for now.

JACKSON *trains his gun at the entrance as the lights dim.*

End

CLIFFORD MASON

I HAVE BEEN WRITING for the stage for twenty years to the month, as of July, 1980. In that time I have completed seven full length plays, two one acts, and there are three other titles that are in various stages of completion.

My basic approach to writing a play is to begin by leaving it alone. It will come when it will come. Some are written in solitude, some in the midst of domestic chaos, some with a well thought out theme that is consciously applied to the work as it progresses, and some with simply an idea, or a place or an emotion as the initial impetus. Some are planned in advance and never get written, and some are not even suspected of being in any form of gestation until they are about to come forth.

But in all that I do, I leave the imagination unfettered by the facts of history or present reality. And I let the life force of the play exist for itself and not as a substitute for thwarted dreams that belong to other realities.

Clifford Mason
October 20, 1980

Mr. Mason's articles have appeared in many publications such as in the Sunday Drama Section of the *The New York Times* and in *Black World*. His play *Gabriel* is published in *Black Drama Anthology,* edited by Woodie King and Ron Milner (New American Library, 1972). Mr. Mason has appeared on television, was host of his own radio show on WBAI, and has written a weekly column for *The Long Island Weekly Voice.* Secondary level teaching experience includes teaching at Manhattanville College of the Sacred Heart and at the New Brunswick campus of Rutgers University.

THE VERANDAH

Clifford Mason

CHARACTERS

FATHER SWABY: *A solicitor, late 60s.*

MOTHER SWABY: *His second wife of thirty years, 50s.*

TREVOR: FATHER SWABY*'s oldest son, a high school teacher in his late 30s-early 40s.*

JOSEPHS: SWABY*'s neighbor to the right, late 50s.*

CYNTHIA: SWABY*'s daughter, in her mid-20s.*

BERTIE: *The younger son, late 20s.*

MONICA CHIN QUEE: TREVOR*'s mistress, early 30s, Chinese.*

MRS. JOHNSON: *The housekeeper, late 70s.*

GLORIA: *The maid for the front of the house, late 20s.*

ADC: SWABY*'s life-long male servant, late 80s.*

FAIZUL PABOOSINGH: CYNTHIA*'s man at the gate, East Indian.*

A PLAY IN FIVE SCENES

Scene 1

Sunday evening on the front verandah. 18³/4 Lady Musgrave Road on the Liguanea Plain in St. Andrew, Jamaica, West Indies, 1939. TREVOR *is sitting on the front verandah, reading the newspaper and drinking tea.* GLORIA *comes out in cap and apron and pours some more for him and adds milk and sugar and leaves before he looks up or says anything. He turns the page and folds it out, continuing a story from page one.* FATHER SWABY *comes out with his scissors and gloves and watering can. He eyes* TREVOR *closely, smells the tea in the pot, and makes a disapproving sound.*

FATHER SWABY: Humph. Orange pekoe, bought from the Chinaman.

TREVOR: I drink what they give me.

FATHER S: I happen to grow the best mint in St. Andrew. Why for heavens sake won't you drink that instead of this lye.

TREVOR: I drink what they give me. (*Takes a sip, still reading*)

FATHER S: (*Goes to the edge of the verandah, right, and pulls a leaf of mint from his potted plant*) Here, smell this. Just smell it.

TREVOR: (*Stops reading to smell it*) Excellent aroma, but I couldn't possibly drink it.

FATHER S: And why not?

TREVOR: Because of the milk.

FATHER S: What has the milk got to do with it?

TREVOR: Everything. You see, your mint is all well and good by itself, but mix it with milk and what have you got? An absolutely insipid concoction.

FATHER S: So don't mix it with milk.

TREVOR: Don't be absurd. What is the four o'clock tea ritual without milk? Nothing. No, one does have to have milk in one's tea at four o'clock. Even if it is almost six.

FATHER S: If one is the sort of one who is so proper that he has to out-English the English, then one has to. But if one were a different one from that one, then one might learn to be proud of what grows in one's own country and what one has come from and therefore what one is, which is (*Spells it*) J-A-M-A-I-C-A-N and not English. That is, if one were actually a whole one instead of only half of one, as one obviously is. Does one understand?

TREVOR: Yes, Father. (*Back to his paper*) I see your point, of course. By the way, your English roses haven't done well this year, have they?

FATHER S: England had nothing to do with the growing of my roses.

TREVOR: Are you sure?

FATHER S: As sure as I have to be.

TREVOR: I would have thought that a solicitor needed to be more particular about his facts than that.

156

FATHER S: There are facts that are of interest to a man and then there are obscure bits of petty detail that fascinate boys.

TREVOR: You're so clever, father. You should have been a barrister.

FATHER S: Why? Do they make any money? They get a case maybe twice a year and then only if I give them one.

TREVOR: You or someone else.

FATHER S: It's obvious that I was speaking generically. One does understand that, doesn't one?

(Just then the band concert at Hope Gardens begins with the band playing, "God Save the King." It's heard as in a distance)

TREVOR: The band concert at Hope is just beginning. They're playing "God Save the King."

FATHER S: Then why don't you stand at attention and salute, for Christ's sake.

(MOTHER SWABY comes out. FATHER S takes one look at her and goes down into the garden, after making a deprecating sound at her)

MOTHER SWABY: And how are you this evening, Trevor?

TREVOR: Fine, Mater, and yourself.

MOTHER S: Oh, it's such a lovely evening. I feel absolutely exhilarated.

TREVOR: Yes, there's a good breeze coming from the mountain.

MOTHER S: And they're playing "God Save the King."

TREVOR: Yes. The guango tree looks bigger than ever.

MOTHER S: And the lignum vitae is as strong as a rock.

TREVOR: But Father's roses haven't done well.

MOTHER S: No, poor dear. But his mint, on the other hand . . .

TREVOR: Ah, his mint! It fills the air with an aroma that is absolutely pungent, almost pulchritudinously sensual. It literally carooms about like an elfin in a dance.

MOTHER S: My dear, I don't understand a word you're saying. You know I didn't have your advantages as a child.

TREVOR: Yes, that's why Father treats you so dreadfully, because you're a tradesman's daughter.

MOTHER S: Yes, it's your mother he really loved. She was so beautiful and delicate, like one of his pink roses. I used to see her when she was a young girl. She'd pass by our house in the horse and buggy.

TREVOR: When did my mother pass by your house, ever, even in a horse and buggy?

MOTHER S: Oh, that was only once a month, when she'd go to town to visit the Campbells.

TREVOR: Oh, of course, the Campbells.

MOTHER S: Shall I get you more tea, this seems to have gotten cold.

(As she picks up the pot, FATHER S comes back up from the garden)

FATHER S: Let the servants do the fetching and carrying, for God's sake. That's what they're there for! You can take a bitch out of the country, but you can't take the country out of the bitch.

MOTHER S: Yes, dear, of course. Any tea for you?

FATHER S: No. Rum and water and no ice.

MOTHER S: The way you always take it, you mean.

FATHER S: Yes, yes.

TREVOR: But I thought Sealy said you weren't to drink.

MOTHER S: Oh, he isn't to, but your father's lived this long in spite of the doctor, so there's no reason why he can't continue to do so until it kills him. You must remember, your father's done his living, all of it. He's been a war hero, a sports hero, an American adventurer, a colonial student in London, and a successful lawyer. He's seen it all and he's done it all.

FATHER S: *(Settling himself down)* Including the women, I've done them too, don't forget that.

MOTHER S: *(Takes up the teapot again)* Since I'm going in anyway, I might just as well take the tea. *(Exits)*

FATHER S: Well, what're the cricket scores?

TREVOR: From England?

FATHER S: No, from Hawaii. Of course from England, where else?

TREVOR: *(Without looking)* They beat Australia again. Means that they've kept the Ashes.

FATHER S: Phhhh. They'd never play us.

TREVOR: Even if they did, they'd never play you for the Ashes.

FATHER S: Of course not, because they know we'd give them a proper thrashing.

TREVOR: With your weekend cricketers against their professionals who do nothing else seven days a week but play cricket and have been playing it against world class competition for as long as there's been a game to play, since they invented it.

FATHER S: So what! I could lick the whole lot with half a team of good Jamaicans.

TREVOR: Oh, you mean if a man is black then he's twice as good as anyone else.

FATHER S: Anyone!

TREVOR: Especially an Englishman.

FATHER S: Especially! *(GLORIA comes out with fresh tea)* Where's my rum?

GLORIA: Mrs. Swaby bringing it, sar.

FATHER S: Well, see that she does and hurry up about it.

GLORIA: Yes, sar. *(She exits)*

TREVOR: Aren't you worried, really. Don't forget, your father died of sclerosis of the liver.

FATHER S: That's a lie. My father died while he was humping the maid.

TREVOR: He did not.

FATHER S: He did so. Were you there?

TREVOR: Don't tell me you were.

FATHER S: Anyway, it doesn't matter how he died.

TREVOR: Suppose he'd died a hero, wouldn't that have mattered?

FATHER S: Any poor fish can die a hero. What does it take to show off for a few minutes before you die? Nothing. If you're dying anyway, you know damn well you won't have to do it for long, so any pipsqueak can pull it off.

TREVOR: There's a stillness at Appomattox.

FATHER S: Why?

TREVOR: I don't know.

FATHER S: What the hell are you talking about?

TREVOR: Appomattox, in America. It's where Lee surrendered to Grant after he'd lost the Civil War.

FATHER S: What do you know about America?

TREVOR: Nothing, really, but it seems like a fascinating country.

FATHER S: Well, it isn't, take my word for it.

TREVOR: When they call a black man a Negro in America, do they mean any black man or only a black black man.

FATHER S: They don't know what they mean.

TREVOR: Oh, oh. Here comes Josephs.

FATHER S: What the hell does that bastard want.

TREVOR: I don't know, but if you're going to have a row, I'll go for a walk.

FATHER S: No, stay, for God's sake. That's the only thing that will keep me from stabbing him with the garden scissors. *(JOSEPHS comes up onto the verandah from stage right)* My dear Josephs, how are you? *(Big smile)*

JOSEPHS: What a way some a we can sound English though. "My dear Josephs, how are you?" I'm fine, my deah Swaby, and how are you? And you, my deah Trevor? "Fine," you say, then I say I'm glad to hear it, my deah boy. And I'm fine too. *(Pretends to have a mustache, which he twirls)* And now that we're all fine, I say that's jolly good, jolly good. *(Waits a beat)* Shall I take a chair? I think so, rawther, don't I? *(Sits, crossing his legs and grinning at the two of them)*

FATHER S: Isn't it enough that I've let you into my neighborhood. Do I have to put up with your pestering on top of it?

JOSEPHS: Oh, is your neighborhood. I never knew that. I thought it was government neighborhood that belong to whosoever could afford to live in it. I know you don't own the road or the water, or my property what I pay good money for. You own the street light? Huh? Or the sidewalk, or what? I think firs' thing a mornin' we have to go to Kingston & St. Andrew Corporation and make them know that this is not Lady Musgrave Road, St. Andrew Parish, but is Swaby Heights and him one own the whole a it and everything that run through it, around it, under it, and over and in it.

FATHER S: I don't have to own anything except this verandah and what's on it. And I don't have to associate with anyone on my verandah that I don't want to.

TREVOR: Now, Father, Mr. Josephs is our neighbor to the right and we must be polite to him. After all, we're polite to the MacPhersons and they're our neighbors to the left. So why can't we be polite to the Josephs.

FATHER S: There are no Josephs, there is just one Josephs. That didn't come out right, somehow.

JOSEPHS: Him don't like me 'cause I'm not cousin to the Campbells like the MacPhersons. I'm not cousins to anybody. I don't even know where my name came from. My mother was a poor, ignorant, black woman from St. Elizabeth, God rest her soul. Couldn't even read and write.

FATHER S: Oh. And can you read and write?

JOSEPHS: Not what you could call real readin' and writin'. But I do have ten thousand pounds in the Bank of Nova Scotia.

FATHER S: And do they let you come in through the front door when you want to get any of it, or do you have to go around the back and pass a bag through a window. *(Laughs at his own joke)*

JOSEPHS: No, man, them let me in through the front. Of course now when I reach the cashier and she turn up her nose and ask for all kind a identification and I gi' her everything: bank book, proof of residence, birth certificate, report card, everything, just to draw out my own money. And she still get up and go check with the Englishman. Him come back and him look pon me good. And the two a them go back again and whisper some more. Then she come back again and say I must write my name a second time and mek she see. So, I write it again. Them check that against the card them have in the file. All the while, them steady a look pon me good. And is not till a little ole white woman who I did a piece a work for once pass and say, "Good mornin', Mr. Josephs," that them give me my money. And is only ten pounds I did want.

FATHER S: Well, they have to be sure that they're dealing with the right party. After all, they were just trying to protect your money. *(MOTHER S comes out with a tray with rum and ice and glasses on it)*

Well, it's about time.

JOSEPHS: Hello, Mistress Swaby.

MOTHER S: Hello, Mr. Josephs. I heard your voice so I brought an extra glass. I know Mr. Swaby doesn't like to drink alone.

FATHER S: That's a damned lie. When have you ever heard me say that I didn't like to drink alone—when? I love to drink alone. I just love it.

TREVOR: No, you don't, you're always drinking with the MacPhersons.

FATHER S: What the hell have they got to do with it?

JOSEPHS: Is all right. If him don't want me to have a drink from him bottle, I can do without. I have plenty of bottle at home.

MOTHER S: Oh, you mustn't take Mr. Swaby seriously, Mr. Josephs. That's just his way. He doesn't really mean anything by it.

FATHER S: Who says I don't mean anything by it. Who? What's the matter around here? Can't I talk for myself. Don't I have a mouth and a tongue? Well, don't I?

MOTHER S: *(She has poured two drinks and added water to* FATHER S's *during this)* Yes, dear.

FATHER S: You're damn right I do. And I say I do mean anything by it.

MOTHER S: Yes, dear. Of course you do.

JOSEPHS: Then you don't want anybody to drink with you?

FATHER S: No!

TREVOR: Too bad, I was just about to have one.

FATHER S: I didn't say you couldn't have one. Did I say he couldn't have one, did I?

MOTHER S: No, dear, you didn't.

TREVOR: Then what's the fuss all about?

JOSEPHS: Indeed. Uh, no water for me.

(FATHER S just makes an anguished sound)

MOTHER S: Why, Mr. Josephs, do you really take your rum straight. My father used to drink it that way too. I've always admired a man who could drink his rum straight.

FATHER S: Oh you have, have you? *(Throws his rum away and slams his glass down)* Pour!

MOTHER S: Yes, dear. *(Pours)*

FATHER S: *(Swills it down)* Is that all it takes to get your admiration?

JOSEPHS: But stop. First you throw good, good rum, what you ask fuh, on you roses, . . .

FATHER S: What the hell business is it of yours what I throw on my roses!

JOSEPHS: . . . then you get your darling wife to give you more rum, and you swallow that down like is water. Bad for your liver, if you drink too fast, you know, old man.

FATHER S: *(Apoplectic)* I don't give a rass about my liver!

MOTHER S: But you should, dear, you should.

TREVOR: Well, cheers.

JOSEPHS: Cheers!

MOTHER S: *(Taking a drink too)* Cheers!

FATHER S: And since when did you start drinking in public?

MOTHER S: Oh, it's all right, dear. Mr. Josephs is like one of the family.

FATHER S: *(Spitting out a fresh drink)* What! What! Wha, wha . . . wha . . . *(Starts stuttering)*

TREVOR: Careful, Father, you'll get apoplectic.

FATHER S: I am apoplectic!

CYNTHIA: *(Comes out from the house singing "The Mikado")* "The flowers that bloom in the spring, tra, la, bring promise of merry sunshine, as we gaily dance and we sing, tra, la, of flowers that bloom in the spring. And that's what we mean when we say or we sing, tra, la,la,la,la,la, tra, la,la,la,la,lah." *(Then she disappears down the steps and off the front lawn, stage right)*

MOTHER S: Dinner will be served promptly at six, dear, mind you're back by then.

(CYNTHIA is heard "tra, la,la,la,la"-ing as she goes off, doing it almost as in a response)

JOSEPHS: What a fine voice she has.

FATHER S: *(Sulking)* How do you know she's got a fine voice?

JOSEPHS: I just heard it, didn't I?

TREVOR: She's practicing, actually.

JOSEPHS: What for?

FATHER S: What difference does it make?

MOTHER S: Oh, Mr. Swaby, you're such a tease. She's in the pantomime. They're doing "The Mikado" from Gilbert & Sullivan. Isn't it wonderful.

JOSEPHS: And that's one of the songs she's going to sing?

MOTHER S: Yes.

JOSEPHS: What a shame.

FATHER S: What a shame what?

JOSEPHS: That a fine looking black girl like that can't sing a rukun bine or a nice calypso or whatever instead of some white man's song.

FATHER S: And what's wrong with a white man's song? Doesn't he have just as much right to write a song as anyone else?

JOSEPHS: Oh I don't say he don't have a right to write it. It's just a shame she have to sing it.

FATHER S: Why is it a shame? If it's a good song, then why shouldn't she sing it?

MOTHER S: *(Starting off a little strong for her and then getting quiet at "dear")* When did you get so pro-British, dear.

FATHER S: I'm not pro-British!

JOSEPHS: You sure don't sound like it.

TREVOR: You mustn't be too hard on Father, Mr.

Josephs. He tries to hate the Englishman, but he just can't quite manage it.

JOSEPHS: Yes, I know what you mean. It's a pity, too, when you come right down to it because he's such a fine, upstanding black man, all in all.

FATHER S: *(To JOSEPHS)* Why are you making excuses to him for? He's the worst black Englishman alive. All day long he sits up there in that college and lectures about Shakespeare and Goldsmith and Sheridan and the rest of that rotten lot. I spend all my time trying to make him realize he was born in Kingston and not Stratford on Avon.

JOSEPHS: Shame on you. You shouldn't talk about your own flesh and blood like that.

MOTHER S: Have another drink, dear.

FATHER S: You got to hell! The lot of you, just go to hell! *(Gets up and stalks into the garden and begins watering his lawn)*

TREVOR: He loves to water his own garden. Busha can do everything else, but Father won't let him water the garden.

MOTHER S: *(Sits beside JOSEPHS)* Have another drink, Mr. Josephs.

JOSEPHS: Thank you, Mistress Swaby, don't mind if I do.

MOTHER S: And you, Trevor?

TREVOR: Why not?

MOTHER S: And one for me. *(They all drink again)*

JOSEPHS: *(After a slight pause)* Where's your other son, Mistress Swaby, the one that's really yours. I haven't seen him around lately.

MOTHER S: Oh you mustn't say that, Mr. Josephs. Trevor is as dear to me as if he were my very own.

JOSEPHS: Oh, I have nothing against Trevor. He's a fine and generous man. Very upstanding and well educated. A credit to you and to everyone. But there's nothing like your own, you know, Mrs. Swaby. Your own should come first. Blood before anything else I always say.

TREVOR: And what about me? My blood's dead. At least half of it is. The other half is watering the lawn. And Cynthia and Bertie are just that, only half blood. Does that mean that I must be only half loved?

JOSEPHS: Of course not. You must find a woman of your own and start your own tree growing. Then you will be the patriarch. Whatever comes from you will be your blood and yours alone. Remember, "God bless the child who's got his own."

TREVOR: It's not blood that makes the difference, Mr. Josephs.

JOSEPHS: Not blood alone, mind you. But blood with something else. Familiarity, having the same things in common, living together, sharing life's pleasures as well as life's pain.

TREVOR: The old brutalize their young, brothers kill each other off, sisters try to marry the same man, and one family takes a blood oath to destroy the other. And as for familiarity, about the only thing we're sure of is that it breeds contempt.

JOSEPHS: Oh, I don't know. Take Mistress Swaby and me for instance. We're both poor people from the country, members of the lower classes, you might say. She goes and marries an upper-crust like your father and it's all right because she's what you call lower middle. Not too too lower, but not too much middle either. But me, now. I'm definitely not in the middle any way at all. I'm bottom, bottom. But we both come from the same part of the Bush, so that means that we know one another, like family, like blood. Your father, while I respect him, will never know her the way I know her. Never. Don't care how long he lives.

TREVOR: I really should get up and leave you two alone, but since Father is not going to go farther than eye shot of you and since dinner is almost ready anyway, you'll forgive me if I stay and share your little rendezvous.

MOTHER S: Of course, dear. Mr. Josephs doesn't mind. He's fond of you. He's just told you that. *(She touches JOSEPHS' hand)*

TREVOR: Careful, he's looking this way.

MOTHER S: *(Turns out)* And here comes Monica. Now you won't be left out, dear.

TREVOR: Yes, I'll just got to the gate and meet her. *(Exits front towards the gate)*

GLORIA: *(Comes out)* When you want dinner served, ma'am?

MOTHER S: Go see if Mr. Bertie is ready to come down.

GLORIA: Him in him room asleep.

MOTHER S: Then wake him.

GLORIA: You mean I must go in him room when him one in there?

MOTHER S: Yes, of course, he won't bite you. And wake Mistress Johnson too.

GLORIA: Yes, ma'am. *(Goes back inside)*

JOSEPHS: Why won't you leave this man and marry me, Mistress Swaby?

MOTHER S: Because I'm already married.

JOSEPHS: So you want to be with me, not him.

MOTHER S: I am with you, Mr. Josephs.

JOSEPHS: I don't mean like this. I mean all the time.

MOTHER S: I couldn't do that to Mr. Swaby.

JOSEPHS: That bastard. All he does is mistreat you. He just have you around so he can cuss you, that's all. He's still in love with that yellow gal he married over four hundred and four years ago.

MOTHER S: Thirty-five.

JOSEPHS: What difference does it make?

ADC: *(Comes out looking for* FATHER SWABY*)* Evening, Mrs.

MOTHER S: Evening, ADC.

ADC: You want me to do anything for you, sir, before dinner?

MOTHER S: That isn't Mr. Swaby, ADC. It's Mr. Josephs.

ADC: Eh! And how come him sitting in Mastah's chair and you next to him. I don't think I like that. I don't think him goin' to like that either. Where him is?

MOTHER S: Where he usually is before dinner.

ADC: Oh. Then I better bring him another rum 'fore him start sneezing.

MOTHER S: Oh I don't think so, ADC. It's not chilly this evening. Why don't you just go back to your room and lie down a bit, if you're tired.

ADC: But I'm not tired.

MOTHER S: Then you can get your supper from cook if you want to.

ADC: What! Eat before he does?! I would never do that.

MOTHER S: Well, you don't have to stand there as if you're at attention.

ADC: Yes, I do.

MOTHER S: Why?

ADC: *(Edges towards her)* Him! I can't leave you alone with him.

MOTHER S: But Mr. Josephs is our neighbor. He's a friend of the family.

ADC: I thought the MacPhersons were our neighbors.

MOTHER S: That's to the left.

JOSEPHS: I'm to the right.

ADC: I thought that place was empty.

MOTHER S: It was six months ago.

ADC: That's not a long time, six months.

JOSEPHS: I guess not, mastah. Not to you anyway.

ADC: But stop. You're out of order, calling me mastah. There's only one man can call me mastah, and that is my mastah. And you are not he.

JOSEPHS: Beg your pardon!

ADC: You don't have to beg my pardon about anything.

MOTHER S: Now, now, ADC, that's enough. *(*MRS. JOHNSON *comes out)* Why Mistress Johnson, I see Gloria woke you up.

MRS. JOHNSON: She did not. She's been upstairs in your son's room ever since you sent her in to wake me. People think I don't know what goes on, but I do. I may be old, but I'm no fool.

MOTHER S: *(Looking out)* Now where are Trevor and Monica going off to. They're turning out of

the gate. I thought he said he was just going to meet her.

JOSEPHS: They probably want to be alone for just a little while. When two people are in love, Mistress Swaby, the most important thing in the whole world is to be alone together. Can you understand that?

MRS. J: Oh she understands it all right. Dirty gal. Never could keep her away from the men. I don't know why Swaby married you in the first place. He knew you weren't a virgin. Everybody knew. You didn't fool him, you dirty little slut.

MOTHER S: Yes, Mistress Johnson. It's a chill, why don't you go in and get a shawl.

MRS. J: And leave you two out here to get into mischief. I will not. ADC, get my shawl.

ADC: Can't, I'm standing guard.

MRS. J: Bertie's upstairs with the maid, by now he's probably got her clothes off. You're on the front verandah, of all places, entertaining your man friend with your husband not ten feet away. Trevor's gone off with his Chinese wench, and Cynthia's somewhere behind a bush with, god only knows who. And I'm left all alone with no one to choose from but ADC who doesn't have a tooth left in his head and Busha, who never looked at anything that didn't grow green leaves in his whole life. And you expect me to worry about the chill.

MOTHER S: Yes, Mistress Johnson. I'm going to send you back to the country if you don't behave yourself. You can't work anymore anyway, so what good are you?

JOSEPHS: Where abouts in the country are you from, Mother Johnson?

MRS. J: I don't talk to anyone who's darker than I am.

JOSEPHS: Yes, ma'am. Where's she from?

MOTHER S: Moneague.

JOSEPHS: You're from Moneague too, aren't you?

MOTHER S: No, Ewarton.

JOSEPHS: I could have sworn you told me Moneague.

MOTHER S: Well, I didn't. I should know where I'm from, shouldn't I?

JOSEPHS: Of course.

MRS. J: She's a liar. She's always been a liar. Always. Even when she was a little girl she lied.

JOSEPHS: Have you known her ever since then, Mother Johnson?

MRS. J: I've know her ever since she was born.

JOSEPHS: Did you know her mother?

MRS. J: Of course I did, you idiot.

MOTHER S: I think it's time we all went in.

MRS. J: Why, you getting a chill!

MOTHER S: Yes, it's suddenly gotten damp and it's

getting late. The band's stopped playing.

ADC: Oh, was the band playing today?

MRS. J: Yes, you idiot. It's Sunday. The band always plays on Sunday.

ADC: I remember when they would only allow white men to play in the band.

MOTHER S: That was a long time ago, ADC.

ADC: Oh not so long ago. Do they let black men play in the band now, Mistress?

MOTHER S: Yes, ADC. Even the conductor is black sometimes.

ADC: Oh that's wonderful. My father would have loved that. He always wanted to play the trumpet. But he had bad front teeth. Couldn't get a good sound. You know you had to have good front teeth in those days to get a good sound.

JOSEPHS: You still do, old man.

ADC: I guess so. Why do white men have such good front teeth?

(JOSEPHS and MOTHER S exchange a look that indicates the less said the better)

MOTHER S: Trevor and Monica are coming back.

MRS. J: He probably smells of sperm.

MOTHER S: I doubt it, Mistress Johnson. Hello.

TREVOR: *(Offstage)* Hello.

(Both TREVOR and MONICA come up onto the verandah)

MONICA: Good evening, everybody.

MOTHER S: Good evening, my dear. Enjoy your walk?

MONICA: Yes, but I would have enjoyed it more if it had been longer.

MRS. J: Of course you would, you wench. You're the type who always wants it longer.

MOTHER S: When is your father going to give the hose to Busha so we can get started with dinner. I'm starving.

TREVOR: He wouldn't talk to me when I passed him either time. Seems as if he thinks I took Mr. Josephs's side against him. Called me an ingrate.

JOSEPHS: Sorry about that, son. You want me to go talk to him.

TREVOR: No, he'll be all right. Let's go in.

MOTHER S: Yes, let's. Won't you join us for dinner, Mr. Josephs. I hate the thought of anyone eating dinner alone. It's so sad.

JOSEPHS: Oh, I'm not alone. I've got the sound of happy laughter coming from here to keep me company.

MONICA: Don't you have any family, Mr. Josephs?

JOSEPHS: No. Only my mother before she died.

MONICA: And you never married?

JOSEPHS: No, never.

MONICA: A man should have a family, Mr. Josephs, start his own line.

TREVOR: Grow his own tree.

MONICA: *(Agreeing with TREVOR eagerly)* Yes!

JOSEPHS: I know. But I never found her. At least if I did, it was always the wrong time or the wrong place.

MONICA: But there must be somebody in the whole wide world for you.

JOSEPHS: For me the world isn't so wide. No wider than the street I live on and the people I've come to know in these my years of tranquility.

MOTHER S: Come in, Mr. Josephs, please!

MRS. J: You'd better watch out, it could be his last supper. *(She cackles)*

FATHER S: *(Comes up)* Well, that's that. Are we all ready to eat?

MOTHER S: Yes, dear. We've been trying to get Mr. Josephs to join us for dinner.

FATHER S: Where's Cynthia? Didn't you tell her not to dally.

TREVOR: Here she comes.

FATHER S: ADC.

ADC: *(Snaps to attention)* Sar!

FATHER S: Get me another pair of shoes. These are soaking wet.

ADC: Then I'm relieved of duty?

FATHER S: What the hell are you talking about?

MOTHER S: Nothing, dear. Yes, ADC, you're relieved.

ADC: Hup, faaace; hup, two. HUP! *(He exits marching)*

FATHER S: Monica, my dear. *(Extends his arm. She takes it)* Mistress Johnson.

MRS. J: *(Jumps up with glee)* Well, it's about time you took some notice of me. *(Laughs as she takes the other arm)*

FATHER S: Let's go in. Gloria!

GLORIA: *(From inside)* Sar!

FATHER S: You may make the announcement.

GLORIA: *(Still inside)* Yes, sar. "Dinner is served."

FATHER S: *(On his way in)* Bertie!

BERTIE: Coming!

(FATHER S and the two women go in)

MOTHER S: *(Hesitates)* Oh, Mr. Josephs, won't you please join us.

JOSEPHS: *(Gets up)* No, I'll just stand here awhile and catch the last light before I go across. The crickets have started.

TREVOR: Come, Mater, darling. *(The clock starts up)* It's seven o'clock.

MOTHER S: Yes.

(MOTHER S takes TREVOR's arm, looks back at JOSEPHS, and they both go in. JOSEPHS stands looking at the last light)

MOTHER S: *(Heard calling from inside)* Cynthia!

(CYNTHIA, offstage, is heard singing, "The flowers that bloom in the spring . . ." as JOSEPHS goes offstage right)

Scene 2

Two hours later. The family has finished dinner, and the sound of gay laughter can be heard as the drinking and the eating ends. FATHER S*'s voice rings out loudly:* "Somebody put on some music. Gloria! Where is that girl?" GLORIA *replies:* "Sar?" "Put on that island boy calypso." "It's not here, sar." "Well, where the rass is it?" "Miss Cynthia lend it to a friend, sar." CYNTHIA *and* BERTIE *have come out by this time to get away from the din. She's dressed as she was before in a simple frock that fits her well without being unseemly.* BERTIE *is tall and handsome and reedily well built. He's dressed in white with a cricket sweater on.* FATHER S' *voice is heard again:* "All right, then put on Linstead Market." GLORIA: "Yes, sar." CYNTHIA *and* BERTIE *exchange looks of 'Oh, no, not that again,' as they try to get some air.* CYNTHIA *flops down in a chair and* BERTIE *stands. Linstead Market starts up.*

BERTIE: Did you see all the rum he drank?

CYNTHIA: What do you mean, drank.

BERTIE: Is still drinking.

CYNTHIA: Drinkum, drankam, drankarium.

BERTIE: Your Latin is worse than my French.

CYNTHIA: Oh what the hell. *(Jumps up and starts swinging to the music)* Come on, Bertie, let's dance.

BERTIE: Can't. I have to practice my stroke. *(Begins doing his cricket moves, making the appropriate sounds)* Fore leg; gully; slips; a four! a six!!

(While BERTIE *does this, to the rhythm of the music,* CYNTHIA *continues dancing. They begin to laugh and work together. She does a step, and he hits a stroke. They improvise and are beginning to really have fun when they hear* FATHER S *coming and stop. He enters with* MRS. J *and a bottle in one arm and* MONICA *in the other. He enters laughing.* MRS. J *laughs with him. He sees that* CYNTHIA *isn't dancing)*

FATHER S: What's the matter? Why aren't you dancing?

CYNTHIA: I thought you disapproved of dancing on Sunday on the front verandah.

(The music has stopped by this time)

FATHER S: Who said I disapproved of it? Who? Bertie, I ask you as a cricketer and a gentleman, did you ever hear me once say I disapproved of dancing on Sunday on the front verandah?

BERTIE: Yes.

FATHER S: See. I knew old Bertram wouldn't let me down. Good lad. *(Touches him affectionately behind the neck)* Stout lad. *(To* CYNTHIA*)* Well!

CYNTHIA: Well, what?

FATHER S: Well, why don't you dance, for heaven's sake?

CYNTHIA: And what would the MacPhersons say?

FATHER S: The MacPhersons can kiss my rass! *(*MRS. J *goes into peals of laughter)* What's the matter with you?

MRS. J: The MacPhersons, they heard you. *(Starts laughing again)* You can get sued, you know, for using that word. It could cost you ten pounds.

FATHER S: Who gives a rass. Besides, I'm the solicitor. Anybody does any suing, it'll be me. Who do they think they are anyway. Goddamn English snobs. They're not even English, they're goddamn Scots. *(Goes stage left and yells)* You're a no good, goddamn, firking Scotsman, MacPherson, and you can suck my socks, you white bastard. This is my country. Mine, do you hear me. And anything I do in it is my business. And you and the Kind and the Governor and the whole lot can go to hell! I said rass and I'll say it again. Rass, rass, and more rass. You want ten pounds, I'll give you ten pounds. *(Before anyone can react, he's gone inside the house and comes back out with a gun)* Here's ten pounds for you, you bugger. You set one foot inside my gate, laddie, and I'll give you what I gave the Russians in the Crimea. Do you hear me, MacPherson?

BERTIE: I think he heard you.

FATHER S: What'd you say, lad?

BERTIE: I said, I think he heard you.

*(*TREVOR *and* MOTHER S *come out)*

TREVOR: Who heard what?

BERTIE: MacPherson. I think he heard Father.

MOTHER S: Oh he heard him all right. He'd have to be dead not to hear him.

FATHER S: Well, if he's not dead, I can soon fix that.

MOTHER S: Yes, dear. *(She takes the gun)* Bertie, put this away, please. And tell Gloria to play the record again so Cynthia can dance for your father. You know how much he enjoys seeing Cynthia dance. *(*BERTIE *takes the gun from her and goes in)* Sit down, dear, and catch your breath. You must be absolutely exhausted from the splendid display of ferociousness.

FATHER S: *(Shrugging her off)* Don't try to butter me up. I saw you sucking up to the black bastard, Josephs, while I was watering the garden.

MOTHER S: How sweet of you, darling, to be jealous after all these years.

FATHER S: I'm not jealous.

MOTHER S: Of course not. Well, Monica, my dear, and how is your father?

FATHER S: He's Chinese, isn't he, so how should he be?

(The record starts up again)

MOTHER S: Cynthia, there's the music, dear.

CYNTHIA: You mean I have to dance alone.

MOTHER S: Of course not. Trevor will dance with you.

CYNTHIA: Trevor can't dance.

FATHER S: I'll dance with you.

CYNTHIA: Oh, Father, you're such a good dancer too, when you're sober.

FATHER S: Who says I'm not sober? Who? Bertie, am I not sober? *(Gets up and does a few absurd steps)*

MOTHER S: Bravo, dear. That was first rate, even if you aren't sober.

FATHER S: *(Sits, out of breath)* I'm only drunk when I want to be. Isn't that right, Gladys?

MOTHER S: Of course it is, dear.

FATHER S: Well, go on, dance.

MONICA: I'll dance with you.

CYNTHIA: Two girls.

MONICA: None of the men in my family can dance either. I always end up dancing with a cousin or a friend.

CYNTHIA: I know what you mean. But Bertie can dance.

MRS. J: Yes, Bertie. *(Calling for him)* Bertie!

FATHER S: Leave him alone, he's humping the maid. *(Exits, staggering)*

MOTHER S: Have a good sleep, dear. Well, continue.

(CYNTHIA and MONICA dance again)

CYNTHIA: Is it like that with you, too, Monica? The men always having all the fun and the women having to pretend that they'd die from shame if they lost their virginity?

MONICA: No, we Chinese are more practical than that. We accept what the world is. And act accordingly. A women was born to mate with a man, whatever else she may have been born for. And we just do it, that's all. Life's really quite simple if you know what it is you have to do and just do it.

MOTHER S: But wouldn't your father be terribly upset if you bore a child our of wedlock?

MRS. J: Your father wasn't upset!

(MOTHER S turns off the musci)

MONICA: It would be silly to go around having children all over the place, of course. But if it's the child of the man you love, then wedlock or no wedlock, you're not worth much if you're afraid of that. What's life for, if not to be the mother of the children of the man you love. Even if he breaks your heart, deserts you, proves unworthy in the end. Still, if you're not woman enough to take the chance, they you're no woman at all.

CYNTHIA: Well, Trevor, ole boy, and what have you got to say for yourself.

MONICA: Trevor knows how I feel. And I'm not pressing him into anything. God knows it's difficult enough living in this colonial nightmare

being black. But at least the black can play cricket and go into politics and put on plays, even if most of the ones who do are light skinned. But to be Chinese, that's really asking for trouble. We can't even show our face outside of our grocery stores without someone sneering. And even if we can buy and sell everyone else, that doesn't mean a damn. Our money's not worth a brass farthing when it comes to getting us any social self-respect. Any impoverished Englishman can come down here, and two seconds after he has a few pounds in the bank, he's treated like the Prince of Wales. Yet if he went back to London, they wouldn't let him cross Piccadilly Circus after midnight. We have to keep to our grubby little shops and make sure that the windows are always closed as if we were still the indentured servants we were a hundred years ago.

MRS. J: A hundred years ago we were slaves.

TREVOR: A hundred and seven years ago.

CYNTHIA: Does it matter?

MRS. J: I remember when they used to tie the servant girls to a tree and beat them until they drew blood. And nobody said anything about it.

TREVOR: Mother Johnson, they still do.

MRS. J: Wouldn't know, it's been a long time since I left the country.

TREVOR: I don't really remember my mother, but she was so beautiful and fair, like a delicate flower. I was only five years old when she died. Father says she played the piano beautifully and had a voice like a nightingale. The first woman I ever loved, and I lost her. And I've been a little lonelier ever since.

MOTHER S: I'm sorry, Trevor. I've tried to be a mother to you.

CYNTHIA: You still didn't answer Mother's question, Monica.

MONICA: My father wouldn't care what I did with any man, as long as the man was Chinese.

TREVOR: It's time I took you home.

MONICA: Yes.

MOTHER S: You want to call a taxi, dear. *(A statement)*

TREVOR: No, we'll walk to Cross Roads, and I'll get one there. Don't wait up for me, dear.

MOTHER S: Mind you don't take a chill, it's turning cooler.

TREVOR: I'm fine.

CYNTHIA: Next time, let's dance. It beats sitting around.

MONICA: Next time.

(MONICA and TREVOR exit. BERTIE enters)

MOTHER S: If you spoil that girl or make her pregnant, she'll have to be discharged and sent back to the country. The child will never be able to set foot in your father's house, and she'll have to find a man from her own class who'll not only take her in but your seed as well.

BERTIE: I couldn't, of course, have any real feeling for her.

MOTHER S: Such as what?

BERTIE: Such as a man has for a woman.

MOTHER S: Oh you can have all the feelings you want, as long as that's all they are, feelings, not fact, not reality, not something that the world can look at.

BERTIE: I could move out and keep her, as a maid of course.

MOTHER S: And what would your wife say?

BERTIE: But I haven't a wife.

MOTHER S: When you get one.

BERTIE: Must I get one?

MOTHER S: It doesn't matter whether you do or not, does it?

CYNTHIA: What Mother's trying to say is that you can't live in two worlds at the same time. You want to play cricket and you expect Father to support you while you're doing it, then you must go out with girls of your own class. It's all right to sleep with the maid as long as you get out of bed when it's all over.

BERTIE: And what about you? Who do you sleep with?

MOTHER S: We're not discussing Cynthia, we're discussing you, my dear. Mind you don't indulge yourself too much.

BERTIE: But if I can't do what I want, be with whom I want, then what's the point of anything.

MRS. J: Your mother's only trying to spare you, boy. You try to make a life with that girl and there won't be a place on this whole island where either of you can find peace. In the end you'll hate her because you loved her and because you had to pay such a terrible price just for love.

MOTHER S: And believe me, love isn't worth it.

BERTIE: You two sound as if you've been through this before.

MRS. J: We have.

BERTIE: Well, I haven't. I'm a man, not a boy, and I'm going to live my life, not your history. *(Just then someone is heard whistling "Love Letters")* Hmmmm. He rides a bicycle with clever lights attached to the wheel. I can't make him out though. Does he come from the right class? Does he make more than two pounds a week? Does his family own or rent? Is he civil service? Is the address respectable? Does he dress like an Americans? Is he very dark or just enough so it doesn't matter? Does he have straight hair?

CYNTHIA: Poor Bertie. You're bitter. But your fight's not with me. *(Gets up from the steps and moves out onto the front lawn)*

MOTHER S: Where are you going, dear?

CYNTHIA: Just to the front gate. I won't be long.

MOTHER S: You know, of course, that it's quite unseemly for a young lady to stand at her own front gate after dark.

CYNTHIA: *(As she goes out)* Yes, mother, I know. But sometimes the unseemly is the necessary.

BERTIE: Think I'll go to Cross Roads and hit a few.

MRS. J: You mean you haven't had enough cricket for one night?

BERTIE: Billiards, not cricket. And don't wait up for me.

MOTHER S: Yes, dear. And mind you don't get a chill.

(BERTIE follows out behind CYNTHIA)

MOTHER S: Those two will be the death of me.

MRS. J: Pity they're not like Trevor, sensible about these things. Knows the way of the world. Think he and the Chinese girl will ever set up shop?

MOTHER S: Never. Nobody wants it, not the Chinese, not us.

MRS. J: And what about your own children?

MOTHER S: I do the best I can.

MRS. J: I thought I taught you better than that.

MOTHER S: Meaning what?

MRS. J: Meaning that whatever you do isn't good enough unless you get the job done.

MOTHER S: That was a different time.

(FATHER S comes to the doorway unnoticed by the two of them)

MRS. J: Was it?

MOTHER S: Yes, it was. Mr. Swaby was a young bull in heat who'd just lost his half-white princess. He'd had enough of delicate flowers. He wanted a woman who had the strength to bear him children, run his house, and save his money.

MRS. J: And he got all of that?

MOTHER S: He did.

FATHER S: Did I?

MOTHER S: I didn't know you were up, dear.

FATHER S: *(Mimicking her)* "You didn't know I was up, dear." You two have tricked me from the very beginning with your vile country cunning. Well, I'll teach you both a lesson you won't soon forget. *(To MRS. J)* You get your backside back to the country, Mistress. See how that suits you. And you, my dear, dear wife. You can do with just one maid instead of three. See how you manage then. I'll shame you before the world, let them all know what I think of you, you common tradesman's daughter, you, you . . . servant girl! So I was a bull in heat, was I. Well, I'm still a bull in heat, and I have been among strangers ever since I left my father's house. *(Stalks back inside.*

They are silent for a beat)

MRS. J: *(Whispering)* Think he means it?

MOTHER S: Now he does. Who knows how he'll feel in the morning.

MRS. J: It's all right for you to be calm, you don't have to go back to St. Elizabeth.

MOTHER S: Neither do you. You can sleep in one of the empty maid's rooms. It'll be a week before he finds out you're there. It was probably just the rum talking anyway.

FATHER S: *(Looks out of one of the windows)* And don't think it's just the rum talking either, because it isn't. *(Then he disappears from view again)*

MRS. J: Any more bright ideas?

MOTHER S: Yes, as a matter of fact I just had a very bright idea.

MRS. J: What?

MOTHER S: *(Starts rocking)* Never you mind. Anyway, it might do you good to go back to the country. You'll live longer there.

MRS. J: Who the hell wants to live long at my age. I just don't want to miss any of the action in the few years I've got left, that's all.

MOTHER S: Yes, Mother.

MRS. J: Besides, I, I.... What'd you call me? *(Very touched)* You haven't called me that in years. I'd almost begun to believe I wasn't. I'd been a servant for so long. I understood why you didn't in the early days when we first moved to Kingston. You were ashamed of me, the way I looked and talked. But as I got more used to the city ways, I thought one day before I died I'd be able to be my daughter's mother in her own house. Just once before I died. And you never even used the word, not even when the two of us were alone.

MOTHER S: *(Getting up)* Think I'll take some supper over to Mr. Josephs. Poor dear, living alone like that. I'm sure he eats poorly.

MRS. J: Are you crazy? Suppose he's still up? *(Indicating FATHER S)*

MOTHER S: *(Going inside)* Whatever do you mean? It's just a friendly gesture, nothing more.

MRS. J: *(Getting up and following her)* You're serious.

MOTHER S: *(Offstage)* I am, I am.

MRS. J: I tell you it's madness. If he's still up, then he'll really sack the servants and send me packing.

MOTHER S: Why don't you go see if he is or not, if it worries you so.

MRS. J: I'm all in a sweat. *(Comes back down)* I don't know what to make of this. I don't know what you're up to.

MOTHER S: *(Has come back out by now with a plate of food in a porcelain container)* It'll only be a short while. Do go to bed.

MRS. J: I will not! I'm going to sit right here until you're back inside that gate.

MOTHER S: But I'm not going through the gate. I'm going over the fence.

MRS. J: Over the fence! She's gone mad. I know it. I just know it. Absolutely cracked.

(MOTHER S has left the playing area by this time, exiting stage right as did JOSEPHS and humming "September Song" as she does so..."For it's a long, long while, from May to December, and the days grow short, when you reach December.")*

MRS. J: *(Sits and rocks back and forth vigorously, saying nothing but looking up constantly as if she expected FATHER S to come out or MOTHER S to return. She finally gives up on both, grunts, and sits back, folding her arms. Then she suddenly stops, sits up, and a light comes into her eyes. She starts to smile and then bursts into a loud peal of laughter)* Yes, that's a really bright idea!

Scene 3

Several hours later. As the lights come up, voice on the radio is heard announcing a program: "This is Zed Q I Kingston. From now until two AM we present moonlight & roses, a program of late night music to take you past the witching hour. Tonight we salute John McCormack, the great Irish tenor, with selections from his most memorable performances. Included in this first hour will be 'Sonny Boy,' 'Three O'Clock in the Morning,' 'Marcheta,' 'Lover Come Back to Me,' 'Rose Marie,' and 'Love Me and I'll Live Forever.' We begin with 'You Forgot to Remember' and two favorites from the World War, 'The Rose of Picardy' and 'Keep the Home Fires Burning.'" *The voice stops and "You Forgot to Remember" is heard.* FATHER S *comes out with his gun. He's polishing it. He's quite sober now and very ominous. He checks it. Fires a shot. Reloads and puts it away. He takes out his pipe and sits in the rocking chair, waiting. "You Forgot to Remember" comes to an end. He goes inside and turns off the radio. He comes back out and relights his pipe when* TREVOR *comes up from the front.*

FATHER S: Well, did you satisfy the wench?

TREVOR: More important, did she satisfy me.

FATHER S: Did she?

TREVOR: Do you really have to know?

FATHER S: Not especially.

TREVOR: *(As he sits)* What're you doing up at this hour?

FATHER S: I'm waiting for someone.

TREVOR: Who?

FATHER S: My wife!

TREVOR: *(Taken aback, he doesn't answer right away)* You mean she finally got up the nerve to actually go to him.

FATHER S: You sound as if you admire her for it.

TREVOR: But I do!

FATHER S: You ungrateful bastard. You mean you'd take her side against mine, your own flesh and blood, after all I've done for you. I should have put you out the way my father put me out. Then you'd have had a sense of loyalty. Then maybe you'd have know the meaning of respect.

TREVOR: You mean you respected him.

FATHER S: In my way I did.

TREVOR: You wouldn't even go to the funeral.

FATHER S: Of course not. The bastard cheated me out of my inheritance and then took all the money I'd saved from the war to feed the rest of them and maintain himself in country squire splendor. I could have been a barrister if he hadn't robbed me. My own father. And now you turn and stab me in the back when I need you most. The only one who's ever cared for me is Bertie.

TREVOR: Bertie despises you.

FATHER S: He does not.

TREVOR: It's Cynthia who loves you.

FATHER S: Of course she does. She's a woman, isn't she? She's supposed to love me.

TREVOR: And what does that mean?

FATHER S: It means it doesn't count if it's a woman.

TREVOR: Why not?

FATHER S: Because all they do all day long is go around loving and crying and cleaning and the rest of it. What was it Dostoevski said? "There isn't a man who can stoop so low that he won't find either a woman or a dog to love him."

TREVOR: Well, the quote's not quite right, but I get the point. Anyway, how long has she been over there?

FATHER S: All night.

TREVOR: Must be enjoying herself.

FATHER S: I'll thank you to keep a civil tongue in your head. *(Goes back inside and turns on the radio. "Keep the Home Fires Burning" is just coming on. He comes out tarum te dumming)*

TREVOR: That's just what you need to get the blood up.

FATHER S: "they were summoned from the hillside, they were called in from the mountains. And their country found them ready when they gave the call for men. Keep the home fires burning . . ."

(Just then MOTHER S comes toward the verandah from JOSEPHS')

TREVOR: Here comes Mater now.

FATHER S: *(Goes back in, switches off the radio, and* returns to stand with his hands behind his back as if he were a school master) Well, mistress—*(As she comes up)* what have you to say for yourself?

MOTHER S: Why dear, you're up and it's gotten so chilly. Didn't the drinking bother you. You did have an awful lot, you know.

FATHER S: That's hardly the point, madam.

MOTHER S: *(Sitting)* What is the point, dear?

FATHER S: You and that low class quashie bastard who isn't good enough to suck my socks, that's the point.

MOTHER S: Oh you mean poor Mr. Josephs. You're right, dear. He definitely isn't good enough to even suck your socks.

FATHER S: Very clever. And just what were the two of you doing all this time. It's only past midnight, and I went in before nine.

MOTHER S: I know, dear. And I'm amazed at your stamina. To be up and about only three hours later, not even three. You're really in first class shape for a man of your age. That's really splendid, darling, really.

FATHER S: I'm not talking about that! I'm talking about you and that . . . Josephs.

MOTHER S: What about us, dear?

FATHER S: That's what I'm trying to find out, what about you!

TREVOR: Why don't you just tell him and get it over with.

FATHER S: Tell me what?

TREVOR: What everyone else has known for months.

FATHER S: Which is what?

TREVOR: That Mater and Mr. Josephs are very fond of each other. Very fond, indeed. As a matter of fact, they're probably in love.

MOTHER S: Oh Trevor, you will have your little joke, won't you. *(Smiles, embarrassed)*

FATHER S: *(Pacing)* Is this true? Well, madam, I'm waiting.

MOTHER S: Well, dear, to be perfectly honest with you, I used your threat to send Mother back to St. Elizabeth as an excuse for . . .

FATHER S: Shhh. . . . For god's sake, don't call her that, not here on the front verandah. Suppose MacPherson heard you.

TREVOR: Then you'd really be scandalized, wouldn't you?

FATHER S: I would not. It's just that, well, it's none of his business, that's all.

MOTHER S: I'm sorry, dear. You know that I've always kept my word never to refer to her as my mother ever—since we brought her from the country.

FATHER S: Just see that you continue to do so.

MOTHER S: Yes, dear. *(There's a pause)*

FATHER S: Well, go on.

MOTHER S: Yes, dear. Mr. Josephs has agreed to let mother, Mistress Johnson, stay with him for as long as she wants.

FATHER S: Are you mad?! I'd be disgraced. It's absolutely out of the question.

MOTHER S: Well, I'm sorry, dear, but you see, Mr. Josephs has already said yes. And, all in all, I think it's a splendid idea. It actually makes everything quite simple. He won't mind what I call her over there. In fact, he wants me to call her "Mother." Says it's only right.

FATHER S: I don't give a damn what he says. I tell you, she's not going and that's all there is to it. She won't have to go back to St. Elizabeth after all. She can stay on if you promise not to see Josephs again.

MOTHER S: Oh dear. It's so awkward. You see, it's already been agreed to.

FATHER S: What's been agreed to? What're you talking about?

TREVOR: I think she's leaving you, Father.

FATHER S: *(Uncomprehending)* Who's leaving me?

TREVOR: Your wife, Gladys. She's going to live with Josephs, and she's taking her mother with her.

FATHER S: What! What! Are you mad?! You! You'd do that to me! After all I've given you all these years. This house in a respectable upper class neighborhood, my name, the servants, the car for going to the market on weekends, everything, everything that a woman, any woman could have ever hoped to want and ... and ... *(Catches his breath)* this is how you repay me.

MOTHER S: I know. I'm being ungrateful, shamefully so.

FATHER S: Well, just as long as you admit it. Then we can forget this ever happened and go back to things as they were. I ... I'll forgive you. *(Holds up his hand as she is about to say something)* No, it's all right. I know I shouldn't, but I've always had a soft spot for you, Gladys, you know that. Let's say no more about it. Sometimes things just happen, that's all. But life goes on. We're only human after all. But that man! That scoundrel, that, that ... yard boy from Muccuh must never set foot in my house again!

MOTHER S: Oh dear, dear, dear Keith. How awful it's going to be for you being alone again after all these years, with no one but Trevor to grumble with and maybe ADC occasionally.

FATHER S: *(Very frightened)* Gladys, what are you saying?

MOTHER S: I'm sorry, dear. I didn't want to hurt you. When I went over to see Mr. Josephs earlier, I'd only intended to make an evening of it and no more. I know it's shameless of me. I admit that. And you have every right to think poorly of me. Every right. And they'll agree with you, dear, all of them. Especially the MacPhersons. They'll say you were wronged and that you're well rid of me.

FATHER S: I don't care about the MacPhersons. It's you I care about.

MOTHER S: Oh that's so dear of you, really dear. But you see, it's too late. It seems as if Mr. Josephs has made me feel happy again, the way you used to. But, of course, for us the moments of real joy only came when we were alone. You were always just a little ashamed of me in the world. But I forgave you for it. I knew how courageous it was of you to have married beneath your class and face the contempt of your whole family the way you did. They all turned against you, all of them. But you stood up to them, every one. Told them the time would come when they'd beg for an invitation to your house and you'd see them on their knees grovelling before they'd get it. I was so proud of you for that.

TREVOR: He wasn't standing up for you, it was his own ego that he was protecting.

FATHER S: It's not true.

MOTHER S: Of course it isn't, dear. Trevor was always like that, too hard on you, on all of us, especially on himself.

FATHER S: Gladys, please ...

MOTHER S: Oh dear, oh dear. Don't, Keith. I couldn't bear it if you begged or cried. I couldn't. Please don't. It will only make it worse. But you must understand, I've made up my mind. With Mr. Josephs I won't feel like a servant in my own house. And it's so wonderful to be able to say that after all these years.

FATHER S: I won't give you a divorce, ever.

MOTHER S: I know, dear. And it's all right. I'm perfectly willing to live in sin.

FATHER S: Gladys, I'll change. You'll see. I'll be kind. We'll go out, to the cinema, concerts at Hope. I'll even take you to the Governor's Ball next year. Gladys, oh, Gladys. *(Sits and sobs)*

MOTHER S: I'm sorry, dear, but you see, the bloom's gone from the rose, as they say, and all we have left are dried leaves. So pretty when the air is crisp, but so piteous when the noonday sun of all the days of our years have turned them to dust. I'm going in to get my things. I'll have taken all I want long before the first light. You can inspect the lot. If there's anything there, anything at all that you don't feel I have a right to, just tell me and I'll put it back. If you wish, you can even have the dress I'm wearing. Mr. Josephs is quite prepared to take me as I am, without a stitch. As a matter of fact, I rather suspect he'd prefer it that way. He has quite enough money to buy me anything I'll ever need. By his own account he's quite well off. In fact, he has more money than you, dear. Much more. *(Goes in)*

FATHER S: *(Sits in a stupor. TREVOR gets up and goes over to a table and gets him some water. FATHER S gulps it down with both hands and gets up, shaken. He holds his head as he stumbles. TREVOR helps him to regain his balance. He comes down into the garden. TREVOR watches him from the verandah steps)* So it's come to all this. All the years of hunger and pain. Hunger for a wife I never even knew, for a chance to wear the wig and argue a case before the high court. My ambition, my fate, my empty life, what a pitiful waste. Oh Trevor, my son, what did I do to deserve it. Oh, my god. And I never loved her, never. But I love *her* now. *(Turns to TREVOR)* Don't you see? Now that she's going, I actually love her. It's the truth. I can feel it. My breath is so short. I . . . O can't breathe. *(Struggles with his collar. TREVOR goes down and helps him)* What is the mystery with us that makes this possible? I see her now as I saw her then, as clear as a vision, beautiful. And each year she grew stronger in my mind's eye until she became a tyranny. *(Grabs his temples in pain)* And the fantasy became fact. And reality a fiction. Don't you see, I never loved your mother! How could I have. I never even knew her. She was a child. I adored her as you would an icon of old. But the flesh and blood of it never existed. It was only Gladys, no one else but Gladys. I knew it and I despised myself for it and tormented her for my guilt. And because she was a servant woman's daughter and I was always a little ashamed of the blackness in me, I made her life a living hell.

TREVOR: Then you deserve this.

FATHER S: I know. *(Gets up resolutely)* I'll go in to her now and beg her again, on my knees if I have to. I have no shame anymore. No shame or pride. I've wallowed in it for so long that it's become a vile and despicable thing to me. Take away a man's pride and you don't destroy the man, you liberate him from his vanity.

(TREVOR goes back up onto the verandah and sits in FATHER S' chair. He lights up a reefer and begins inhaling strongly from the outset in order to get a quick effect. He has the stage to himself for a brief moment, and he has just begun to relax when BERTIE comes up from the front)

BERTIE: What the rass are you doing smoking ganga on the front verandah?

TREVOR: Why not, there's no one to know the difference.

BERTIE: Don't be a simpleton. That stuff smells up the place. It'll be days before the air is fit to breathe again.

TREVOR: Rubbish. Besides, it's good for the ivy, helps its color.

BERTIE: It does not.

TREVOR: You stick to your rum and I'll stick to my weed.

BERTIE: There's no comparison. Besides, rum is legal.

TREVOR: So was slavery once. *(Gets up, still smoking)* You should know that your mother's gone to live with Josephs.

BERTIE: Marvelous! That means I can sleep with Gloria all night long without anyone bothering me.

TREVOR: You bastard!

BERTIE: Tut, tut. Temper, temper. *(Goes to door)*

TREVOR: Don't you ever think of anything else besides humping the maid.

BERTIE: Other than cricket, you mean? No, why should I? Besides, it's good for the ivy. *(Goes in laughing)*

(TREVOR lights up another reefer and is walking around puffing. Finally, he goes down into the garden and sits on the bench with his head down, still smoking, when CYNTHIA comes on from the front)

CYNTHIA: What're you doing sitting out here all alone smoking ganga at two o'clock in the morning.

TREVOR: That's what I'm doing out here, sitting all alone smoking ganga at two o'clock in the morning.

CYNTHIA: Is something wrong?

TREVOR: A lot's happened, how much of it is wrong, I don't know.

CYNTHIA: What's happened?

TREVOR: Your mother's left. She's taken up with Josephs, gone to live with him.

CYNTHIA: Why I think that's marvelous. Now I can bring Faizul to the house.

TREVOR: And that's all it means to you. Don't you care about them? About him?

CYNTHIA: Father's treated her dreadfully for years. Serves him right.

TREVOR: He's a broken man, nevertheless.

CYNTHIA: Father? Don't be ridiculous. Why, in a day he'll have gotten over it and gone wenching with the boys.

TREVOR: You don't understand. It's not the same thing. A man needs a home.

CYNTHIA: Well, isn't that just too bad. Men, ugh. I hate them all. They need you to make a home for them, and as soon as you do, they run off and leave you to your knitting. You want to be faithful, but they don't. So what do you get for your love, your loyalty, the fact that you care? A pair of underpants that has another woman's smell on them.

TREVOR: I had a dream last night that frightened me. I was alone in a green field. It was early afternoon. The sun was still high. I was warm and snug in the grass, resting. I was at peace. And then suddenly I felt the presence of a huge thing behind me. It kept growing and growing. It had hard crusty skin and large unblinking eyes, and long, pointed, yellow teeth that protruded from every pore of its hideous shape. I could feel the sound of its terrible being inside me pounding and pounding away at me until its beat became my beat. Then suddenly it stopped breathing. It never moved. But it was getting bigger and bigger. I was afraid to look at it, but I knew I had to. I knew that only if I looked in the face of the terrible thing could I live. I was trembling, the way I am now. I stood up and turned slowly, showing no fear. And when I looked, there was nothing there but a tree. A little nondescript tree. I was so relieved, I cried for joy. And that's when I saw myself as an infant lying on my naked back at the foot of the little tree. But even though I was crying as loudly as a child can, I couldn't hear a sound I was making. I cried and cried and cried until I convulsed and began to bleed from the mouth. And then I stopped crying. I stopped everything. the child who was father to the man could cry no more. but the man himself was drowning in his own tears.

(CYNTHIA *just looks at him helplessly as the lights fade*)

Scene 4

Six days later. It's Sunday evening around seven-thirty. The light is just fading. CYNTHIA, FAIZUL, TREVOR, *and* MONICA *are on the verandah dancing to "Love Letters." Both couples are completely engrossed in themselves. When the record ends, a noise is heard coming from the house, as if something had been knocked over. Then the sound of loud voices as in an argument, then more furniture being knocked over. Finally a scream.* BERTIE *stalks out angrily. He stops momentarily to look sneeringly at* FAIZUL *and then passes into the garden. He kicks over a chair as he does so and says . . .*

BERTIE: That's damn rubbish.

GLORIA: (*Comes out*) Please excuse me. (*Passes going out, following* BERTIE)

TREVOR: (*Picks up the chair*) So much for the well-bred middle class. (FAIZUL *and* MONICA *sit*) Well, Cynthia—(*He sits too*) Aren't you going to offer your guests anything to drink?

CYNTHIA: I thought I needed your permission first.

TREVOR: (*Going along*) Well, you've got it.

CYNTHIA: Well, thank you. Faizul?

FAIZUL: Rum, thank you.

CYNTHIA: Monica?

MONICA: Scotch.

CYNTHIA: And what does the substitute master of the house wish?

TREVOR: Rum, thank you, my dear Cynthia.

CYNTHIA: (*Goes about serving excessively. Puts down coasters and glasses, pours, serves ice, etc., talking as she does so*) One for you and one for you and one for you.

TREVOR: You must excuse Bertie, Mr. Paboo-singh. He's usually not so rude to company. But he's not himself tonight. Problems of a personal nature.

CYNTHIA: Which means he wants the maid to come on the front verandah and dance with him. But of course she won't. She knows that if Father ever found out, she'd be sacked.

FAIZUL: And where is solicitor Swaby. I thought I'd have the privilege of meeting him.

TREVOR: He's out for the evening, gone into town, Mr. Paboosingh. I'm afraid you'll have to settle for second best privilege.

FAIZUL: Can't you call me "Faizul"? It's not British, I know, but it shouldn't be that hard for you to say.

TREVOR: Faizul, of course.

(BERTIE *comes back up, dragging* GLORIA *by the hand. She's crying and hiding her face*)

BERTIE: Now I want you to sit in that chair. (GLORIA, *still crying, sits covering her face with her hands.* BERTIE *puts liquor in a glass and throws in an ice cube*) Now take this. (*She doesn't respond*) Take it, damn you. (*He grabs her by the hair, pulls her head back and forces the glass into her hand. She takes it. Satisfied, he takes a drink and sits also*) That's better. Well, let's all relax. (*Looks around*) Cheers!

TREVOR: Yes, of course, cheers.

BERTIE: (*To* FAIZUL) I don't think we've met.

TREVOR: This is Mr. Paboosingh, Mr. Faizul Paboosingh. And this is our own dear, sweet, Bertie. The younger son. A cricketer and a gentleman. His father's favorite.

BERTIE: Where do you live?

FAIZUL: Does it matter?

BERTIE: Of course it matters. You can tell who a man is by one of four things: where he went to school, what sort of work he does, how much money he's got, and where he lives.

CYNTHIA: And does he have to get a passing grade in all four, three out of four, or will just two do?

BERTIE: (*To* GLORIA) Will you stop snivelling and drink up.

CYNTHIA: Will you stop torturing the girl. Gloria, you may go in if you wish.

BERTIE: She may not go in if she wishes. If Trevor's Chinese girlfriend and your East Indian boyfriend can sit on the front verandah, then she can.

TREVOR: She can if she wants to. But as it is now, no one's able to even talk with her whimpering and hiding her face.

(GLORIA gets up and rushes inside, crying and ashamed)

BERTIE: *(Getting belligerent)* And just who the rass are you to order people about? Don't pull that big brother rass with me. Only one man can be the master in a house at one time. And he's not dead yet. And when he does die, I'm not so sure that it'll be you who'll take over.

TREVOR: *(Stands)* And just what do you expect to accomplish by acting like a yard boy in front of everyone? Are you suggesting that you're going to physically enforce your will, or are you just showing off for the guests?

CYNTHIA: Whatever he's doing, I wish he'd stop it.

BERTIE: The whole lot of you can go rot. *(At the door)* But let me tell both of you this. When he dies, things will be different around here. If they're not, then I'll burn the damn place to the fucking ground.

TREVOR: *(Sitting)* Petulant boy, empty-headed jackass, indolent, self-indulgent puppy, maid impregnator.

BERTIE: Well, at least I'm man enough to do that, which is more than I can say for you. School teacher, phhhhhh. Women's work. I have nothing but contempt for you, every damn one of you. *(Exits inside)*

TREVOR: *(Getting up again)* Another drink, Faizul?

FAIZUL: Yes.

TREVOR: Monica?

MONICA: I'm fine.

TREVOR: Relax, Cynthia. They'll be at it again in no time, and we won't hear a word from either of them for the rest of the evening.

FAIZUL: He seems serious about her.

TREVOR: Maybe he is. Who knows. It's been known to happen.

FAIZUL: I've never heard of it happening. *(To MONICA)* Have you?

MONICA: No. Oh, they keep a lot of them. But that's all.

FAIZUL: Right. But he sounds as if he wants to live with her, here.

TREVOR: He does, doesn't he.

CYNTHIA: You think he means it?

TREVOR: I doubt it.

(Just then GLORIA is heard screaming and crying . . . "Bertie, Bertie, lawd god, somebody help me!")

FAIZUL: Shouldn't we do something?

TREVOR: We are doing something. By ignoring it, we're allowing them to work it out between them.

(GLORIA starts screaming again)

CYNTHIA: *(Gets up)* Well, I'm going in and stop it.

FAIZUL: Should I come with you?

CYNTHIA: No, you'd better stay here. *(Goes in)*

TREVOR: *(Changing the mood)* I wonder how many men have died in France, since the beginning, I mean. *(Both FAIZUL and MONICA look at him as if he's just said the most absurd thing in the world)* My life is just like that, my life, one man's. Compared to the hundreds of millions of men who have all died in one huge bloody spot on the battlefields of France, my death would hardly seem to matter. And yet, it is always the single death that saddens us most. In four years of fighting in the World War, between one and a half to two million men died in France alone. And that was just one war. But such a fact will never make us weep or feel the everlasting pain of true suffering. Kill a child or a bird or make some poor, witless fellow suffer with no means to relieve his plight, and our compassion rushes forth like a flood. Does that mean that my life means more than the lives of two million men? Not to me, of course, but to man the thinker, the literate, self-determining being.

FAIZUL: As an example of what man is and stands for, it might.

TREVOR: Then how can we ever let such a precious gift languish unfulfilled like the dry rot of unused clothes? If one life can mean so much to the whole world and mean even more to the man whose life it is, then how can we ever let it suffer destruction? I have probably lived more years than I have years left to live. And so, much of what I have left undone will be undone still, after I'm gone. So I have misused my life, let it atrophy. And in my own way I too have died in France without ever having been there. But the deaths in France are history. And their meaning is the meaning of history. I am life. Still capable of giving meaning in a way that history will never understand. Even after all my disuse.

MONICA: And what do you determine from that?

TREVOR: Nothing. Because the life in us does not depend on what we do without life. It takes its meaning from the simple fact of its existence. My life will be what it will be simply because it is a life. And nothing that I say or do has anything to do with that.

FAIZUL: Do you really believe that?

MONICA: Yes, he does.

FAIZUL: Then you believe that you have nothing to say about what happens to your life?

MONICA: Yes, he does.

FAIZUL: I disagree. You're the only one who has anything to say about it. And I say to waste a life, any life, for any reason, is sinful because it's the most precious thing we have. I mean, what's more important—to understand life's meaning or to participate in its discovery?

MONICA: And how much can you understand if you don't participate?

TREVOR: Yes, but you know, you see. You understand anyway.

FAIZUL: You think you do.

TREVOR: But you do. And even if you turn off the understanding and just do to the point of making doing a tyranny, it doesn't change anything. It will all fill out differently, perhaps, but in the end it will have been the same as if you had never taken one step to fight the indolence.

MONICA: *(Gets up)* And yet a single life touches so many other lives or can touch them, if given half a chance. If only you'd love me as much as you love history, even if you did nothing about it but let it happen. Then maybe I too could live. Instead, I'm forced to become old clothes.

TREVOR: It doesn't matter. None of it matters. Maybe the successes and failures are sharper if there is more reality and less thought, but nothing really happens to change any of it from what it essentially is.

MONICA: Not true. All of it changes, all of it. The hate, the love, the faith, the loss of faith. Bertie understands that. His world may be a limited one, but at least he's decided to live it, now, here, this minute. There is probably more love, more human understanding in every vicious blow that he gives that poor, unfortunate girl than there is in all of your being. I must go now. It's getting late.

TREVOR: *(Gets up)* I'll walk you to the gate.

MONICA: No need. I drove Daddy's car, and it's just down the road. Good night. *(To FAIZUL)* No, don't get up. I'm not a lady so there's no need to treat me like one. I'm just an indentured servant pretending that I'm something else. There was a time in China when they broke a woman's feet so she couldn't run away from a man she didn't want. My feet aren't broken, and what do I do, spend all my time running after a man who doesn't want me. *(Exits)*

TREVOR: *(Comes back)* Can I get you another drink?

FAIZUL: No, I've had enough.

TREVOR: *(Puts down his glass and sits, lighting up a stick of ganga)* Do you indulge?

FAIZUL: Not usually, but it has a great smell to it. I suppose I could take a few puffs just so you don't have to smoke alone.

TREVOR: *(Sincerely)* How kind of you. *(Hands him the reefer.* FAIZUL, *not knowing how, puffs too hard and quickly hands it back, but he doesn't cough, just gets a little choked)*

FAIZUL: *(Trying not to gasp)* Thanks.

(TREVOR takes it and just drags quietly)

CYNTHIA: *(Comes out)* Where's Monica?

TREVOR: She left.

CYNTHIA: What do you mean, she left?

TREVOR: That's what I mean, she left.

CYNTHIA: And you let her go alone?

TREVOR: Why not? She's in her father's car. What harm can come to her there. And since I'm already home, what's the point in going all the way down into Kingston only to have to turn around and come back again?

CYNTHIA: Well, if you don't know, I certainly can't tell you.

FAIZUL: It seems as if your brother believes it's more important to try to understand life than it is to live it.

CYNTHIA: He's always believed that, poor fool.

TREVOR: *(To CYNTHIA)* And you, of course, don't need to understand anything. You're just one mad liver who can't wait to get started.

CYNTHIA: Wait? Who's waiting? I'm getting out of here tonight.

TREVOR: I see. Mater's little move over the fence certainly opened the floodgates, didn't it?

CYNTHIA: So what if it did.

TREVOR: And are you two going to set up shop, as they say, or just live in sin?

CYNTHIA: What difference does it make? *(To FAIZUL)* Come on, let's go. *(She picks up her bag which she had brought back with her.* FAIZUL *takes it)* You see, my dear, dear Trevor, life's happening all around you, and still you do nothing but sit and think. Before you know it, you'll be sixty. *(Goes to him and they embrace.* FAIZUL *shakes his hand)* Ta, ta, and take care of yourself, won't you.

TREVOR: I will. Be good.

(CYNTHIA and FAIZUL pass into the garden. She calls back to him from there . . .)

CYNTHIA: You'd better put something on or you'll catch a chill.

TREVOR: *(Smiles at her)* Don't worry, bye.

(They are heard replying "Bye." TREVOR *stands there for a moment looking out. Then he goes in and puts on the radio. A Strauss waltz plays for about ten seconds. Then the announcer's voice is heard again. "This is Zed Q I, Kingston. We now bring you our regular Sunday night service. Tonight, the Reverend . . ."* TREVOR, *who had come out and sat*

down during the waltz, gets up at this, annoyed, and goes back in. "...Joseph Farquarson from the North Street Congregational Church will..." TREVOR *cuts off the radio. He comes back out a second time and sits again. He lights up a reefer, takes a few puffs, when* FATHER S *is heard coming through the gate, a little drunk and singing, "Keep the Home Fires Burning.")*

FATHER S: "They were summoned from the hillside, they were called in from the glen. And the country found them ready, at the stirring call for men." *(As he gets to the first chorus, he's at the steps. He sees* TREVOR *and stops abruptly)* Oh, it's you. I just saw some slut getting into a car with a lower class East Indian. Even had the brass to carry her bloody suitcase with her. If she were my daughter, I'd beat her until I made her bleed!

TREVOR: Didn't know you had a daughter.

FATHER S: Very funny. *(Sits in a chair, none too steadily)*

TREVOR: What's her name?

FATHER S: What's whose name?

TREVOR: Your daughter. You say you have a daughter, so what's her name?

FATHER S: Of course I know her name. Damn rubbish. Why shouldn't I know it. Where's my pipe?

TREVOR: You left it over there.

FATHER S: Oh *(Gets up and stumbles to a table, picks it up, and comes back and puts some tobacco in it.* TREVOR *gives him a light and then sits again. There's a pause. He mumbles as if he's irritated at* TREVOR *for forcing him to remember* CYNTHIA's *name)*

TREVOR: Well?

FATHER S: Well, what?

TREVOR: Did it come to you yet.

FATHER S: Will you stop badgering me, damn you. What do you think I am, a village idiot! Her name's.... Well, it's what it's always been, of course. Which is what it should be. It's a fine name. I ought to know. After all, I picked it out. Gladys, that's it. Gladys...no, that's her mother's name. Gladys. Hmmmmmm. It's been almost a week since Gladys left me.

TREVOR: Six days exactly. *(Changing the topic)* Well, how was it?

FATHER S: How was what?

TREVOR: Your first night out.

FATHER S: Horrible. All the old girls have gone. Gone, I tell you. Fancy that, the damn whores aren't there anymore.

TREVOR: Sounds like an excellent title for a poem.

FATHER S: What does?

TREVOR: The whores aren't there anymore.

FATHER S: *(Starts laughing)* Brilliant, old chap. Absolutely first rate. I've never liked you, but you are a clever bastard. I've always given you that.

You're a clever, clever bastard. The whores aren't there anymore. *(Laughs again)* How do you think them up?

TREVOR: As you say, I'm clever.

FATHER S: Hmmmmmm, yes. Reminds me of a whore I knew once. But if I tell that story, I'll get sad. And I don't want to get sad. It'll make me cry. I'll think of Gladys and I'll cry.

TREVOR: Well, tell me a happy story. Wasn't there a fat one that used to be your favorite.

FATHER S: Cynthia, that was her name.

TREVOR: Your daughter's, you mean.

FATHER S: No, the whore's. *(Starts laughing)* Fat Cynthia, that was her name. She was one big laugh from the time you hit the place until they put you out. *(Gets quiet again)* But she wasn't good at it.

TREVOR: Then why'd you like her so much?

FATHER S: Because she was so much fun. Not like this lot. Young twits. I should have the whole bunch arrested. They're breaking the law, after all.

TREVOR: That they are.

FATHER S: But fat Cynthia and her group have all left.

TREVOR: What happened to them?

FATHER S: Got married, went into a different business, bought property in the country, joined the church. Who knows.

TREVOR: And what did Cynthia do?

FATHER S: She's dead. Happened last month. I went to the funeral.

TREVOR: *(In earnest)* Did you?

FATHER S: Yes. Poor thing. Fat covered her heart, and she just stopped laughing. Cynthia always said she couldn't live if she couldn't laugh.

TREVOR: Well, it seems to be a time for losing your women.

FATHER S: I wish you'd show some damn respect around here! First thing in the morning we'll draw up a new contract. You'll pay me three guineas a week for your room and board instead of two.

TREVOR: Up a whole guinea! *(In mock dismay)* How awful. I'll have to cut down on my smoking.

FATHER S: Damn weed. It's illegal, you know.

TREVOR: No.

FATHER S: Yes. And I'm an officer of the court. I should arrest you right here and now.

TREVOR: You should.

FATHER S: Well, never mind. I'd never harm you, old chap, you know that. You want to smoke the blasted thing, smoke it. It's little enough to comfort you in your waning years. Poor fellow. To have to go to bed with a Chinese every night. How awful for you. How bloody awful. They had one of them down there, but I'd never go near her.

TREVOR: Why?

FATHER S: It's those eyes. I just can't get used to those eyes.

TREVOR: It grows on you.

FATHER S: Like everything else, I suppose.

TREVOR: Yes, like everything else.

FATHER S: Well, I'm going to sell the place.

TREVOR: That'll show her.

FATHER S: She has nothing to do with it. It's my place, and I can sell it if I like without there being anything more to it than that. I'm bored with it, that's all. Tired and bored. Besides, the neighborhood's changing. They're letting all sorts of trash move in. If I don't sell now, I won't be able to get a tenth of what I paid for it.

TREVOR: So it's the money and the neighbors who're driving you out.

FATHER S: Yes.

TREVOR: I don't see MacPherson worrying about his money.

FATHER S: Damn MacPherson! What do I care what MacPherson does! *(He gets up)* Are you there, MacPherson? Are you, you Scottish bastard. Don't sham with me, blast you. I know you can hear me. And I say, I don't give a rass what you do. Not one goddamn rass! *(To TREVOR)* Besides, he's white, so he'll get a good price no matter what. *(Sits)* Someday I'm going to kill him. *(Said quietly, almost to himself)*

TREVOR: Kill MacPherson, whatever for?

FATHER S: Because he needs killing.

TREVOR: Why, for heaven's sake?

FATHER S: He's been a thorn in my side ever since he moved in. Always pretending that he's a little friendlier than he really is. Always smiling a little more than he really has to. Taking time to stop by the fence and ask how my roses are. As if he gives a damn. Firking hypocrite. I'll show him. I'll get out the trusty MI and I'll blast him to bloody hell.

TREVOR: The way you did the Bosch in the World War.

FATHER S: I wasn't in the World War. I was in the Boer War. Damn you, can't you remember anything. They let everyone in the World War, even Americans.

TREVOR: And were you in the Crimean War too?

FATHER S: Of course.

TREVOR: Not possible. You're not that old.

FATHER S: I'm old enough. "They were summoned from the hillside, they were called in from the plain. And their country found them ready, at the stirring call for men. Let no tears add to their hardship, as the soldiers pass along. And though your heart is breaking, let it sing this cheery song."

TREVOR: I've never heard you sing it sadly before.

FATHER S: *(Begins to break down)* Oh god, oh god, oh god!

TREVOR: *(Gets up)* If you're going to start your snivelling, then I'm leaving.

FATHER S: No, don't go. I won't cry.

TREVOR: Want a drink?

FATHER S: Yes, a drink.

TREVOR: *(Fixes one, no ice, for FATHER S only)* Cynthia's left.

FATHER S: Good riddance. Let them all leave, all of them. Who needs them? Not me. I've never needed them, any of them. Let the whole bloody lot get out, vacate the premises. *(He's up and breathing hard)* I did it before and I can do it again. I have my work, my roses, and my wenches at Cross Roads, so who cares if they leave. Who cares! I've spent my whole life thinking only of my family, and what do I have to show for it! Nothing! Deserted in my dotage. Left, like an old toothless horse to just wither away and die, with no one to comfort me, no one. Bertie doesn't care about anything but his bat and balls, and you don't care about anything whatever.

TREVOR: *(Very hurt)* You've always got ADC.

FATHER S: Is he still alive? I thought he died years ago. I died years ago. Years and years and years ago. A long, long time way in the past, when the world was a different place and I was someone else. Good god, how did it all get lost. How? If only I could go back to the one spot in time when I let it all slip by me. I, I remember a time when I was young, not just in body, but inside, in the heart beat, in the feel of it. And then, quite suddenly, I was old. The body was still young, there was still vigor, a zest for living, ambition, greed, lust, hunger. Everything was all still there and yet I was old. I knew, knew as well as I've ever known anything, that I would never be surprised again. And I never was.

TREVOR: Yes, of course.

(TREVOR goes inside and shoots himself. FATHER S jumps out of his chair, almost as if he had been shot, at the sound of the gun going off)

Scene 5

Sometime later. MOTHER S is sitting on JOSEPHS' verandah, stage left. She is quietly sipping tea and seems very much alone. MRS. J comes out and takes a seat opposite her. She's snapping beans in a small wicker basket that's lined with a linen cloth. They look at each other before anything is said.

MRS. J: Well!

MOTHER S: Well! *(Then nothing)*

MRS. J: Do you know what's going on over there?

MOTHER S: *(As if bored with it all)* What's going on?

MRS. J: Bertie's moved Gloria into the house. That's what's going on.

MOTHER S: Has he?

MRS. J: Is that all you can say? *(Imitates her removed manner)* "Has he?" Don't you have any shame.

MOTHER S: No, Mother, none whatsoever.

MRS. J: Well, I think it's disgusting.

MOTHER S: Yes, Mother, I'm sure you do.

MRS. J: *(In a reflective mood)* Poor Swaby, with Trevor gone and those two running amuck, he has no one left to talk to except ADC. *(MOTHER S doesn't answer. Probing)* He did love you, you know. In his way. *(MOTHER S still doesn't answer. Finally hitting her hard, although she means it)* Well, I'm going back to Black River.

MOTHER S: You're doing what?!

MRS. J: I'm going back to Black River.

MOTHER S: Why stop at Black River, why not go all the way back to Balaclava?

MRS. J: Because I remember Black River and Black River remembers me.

MOTHER S: Who's left in Black River that remembers you?

MRS. J: I don't need *anyone* in Black River to remember me. I remember myself. I remember the little children going to school, and I remember my garden and my green and yellow yams and the rich, black earth. And I'm going back to it all.

MOTHER S: Why?

MRS. J: Why not? There's nothing left here for me anymore.

MOTHER S: *(Hurt)* How can you say that?

MRS. J: Easily.

MOTHER S: Mother!

MRS. J: Well it's ture, isn't it? You and Josephs, it's all so dull. The two of you acting like Bertie and Gloria all the time. And when you've finished, he goes to sleep and you come out here and drink tea. At least Swaby knew how to laugh and dance and have fun.

MOTHER S: Have you forgotten how he threw you out the night I left him?

MRS. J: Don't try to blame it on me. You left him because you wanted to.

MOTHER S: I'm not trying to blame anything on you.

MRS. J: Anyway, you deserve to be left alone with his nibbs. *(She indicates that she's talking about JOSEPHS by sticking out her lips and making a sucking sound)* Swaby's all alone so why shouldn't you be. It's only fair . . . *(Changing)* Poor Trevor. He was all alone too. So all alone and lonely. That's how it all got started, everyone was lonely. That's how you ended up over here. And that's why Cynthia ran off with the first man who came along. She didn't want to get married. Don't tell me she

wanted to get married because I know better.

MOTHER S: She may not have wanted to, but she did.

MRS. J: They won't last a year.

MOTHER S: *(Almost ruefully)* And then again, they may last forever.

MRS. J: When is Monica's wedding?

MOTHER S: Next Sunday.

MRS. J: Are you going?

MOTHER S: No.

MRS. J: Weren't you invited?

MOTHER S: Yes, I was invited.

MRS. J: Marrying one of her own, I bet.

MOTHER S: Yes.

MRS. J: Well, at least the family'll be happy.

MOTHER S: Which doesn't do Monica much good.

MRS. J: No, she'll never love anyone the way she loved Trevor.

MOTHER S: Never. *(There is a pause)* When are you leaving?

MRS. J: Tomorrow or the next day or the day after that. Who knows? But one fine morning you'll wake up and I won't be there. And what about you?

MOTHER S: What about me?

MRS. J: Will you go back?

MOTHER S: No, Mother, I won't go back.

MRS. J: Why not?

MOTHER S: Because there's nothing to go back to. All my green yams have grown yellow with age. My garden is covered with weeds, and my black earth has turned porous and brown.

MRS. J: But maybe if you tried. If you gave it one more chance.

MOTHER S: *(Gets up)* I spent thirty-five years doing that, remember?

(MRS. J doesn't answer)

JOSEPHS: *(Offstage; his voice is heard calling from inside)* Oh, Mrs. Swaby. Mrs. Swaby.

(MOTHER S and MRS. J look at each other. MOTHER S hesitates and then answers him)

MOTHER S: Coming, Mr. Josephs.

(She goes in as the lights fade on that portion of the stage and come up on FATHER S sitting in his garden. He's in the heat of a conversation with himself. The effect is as if it's been going on for some time. He feels his rage very earnestly)

FATHER S: Not an officer. Not an officer. What! Me, Percival Augustus Horatius Ignatius Swaby, not an officer, indeed. Rupert, Rupert. Come here, blast you, you ignorant savage. You lower class West Indian. You no good, black, belly crawler. Rupert! *(ADC comes out)* Look at me! How dare you, how dare you say I'm not a officer and a gentleman. I'll have you know I've worn the King's colors. Not even MacPherson can say that. *(He gets no response from ADC who doesn't know what's going on)* Well, I'm talking to you, Rupert, don't you hear me?

ADC: Yes, I hear you.

FATHER S: Then answer me!

ADC: What was the question?

FATHER S: *(Exasperated)* The question was "How can you say that I'm not an officer and a gentleman?"

ADC: *(Answering with no difficulty)* Easy.

FATHER S: What! What! You mean you're actually going to deny me my commission to my face!

ADC: No, I'd never do that.

FATHER S: Well then?

ADC: Well then what?

FATHER S: How can you say I wasn't an officer.

ADC: I didn't say it, you did.

FATHER S: Aha, then you admit that I was an officer.

ADC: No, you was a corporal. The Englishman was the officer. And every time you saw him you snapped to and said, *(Imitates the manner)* "Yes, sahr." I was just a belly crawler, like you always say, what they call a Gunga Din.

FATHER S: *(Affecting a manner)* Kipling, you say.

ADC: No, I don't say 'cause I don't know anything about Kipling. Who he?

FATHER S: *(He recites the quatrain pompously)*
"Din! Din! Din!
You Lazarushian-leather Gunga Din!
Tho' I've belted you an' flayed you,
By the livin' Gawd that made you,
You're a better man than I am, Gunga Din."
(Then he beings to break down) Do you hear that, Rupert, you're a better man than I am. *(Starts laughing and crying at the same time)*

ADC: *(Confused, not knowing what to make of it)* You all right . . . sah?

FATHER S: Oh Rupert, it's been a long life, hasn't it? Longer than most.

ADC: Yes, it's been long all right.

FATHER S: How long would you say?

ADC: Oh, I forgot.

FATHER S: Think, Rupert, it's important.

ADC: Well, let's see. I was in the Boer War from the very beginning, and I was already forty years old. Then World War I come around and that's when they formed the first West Indian regiment, and you joined up and got your stripe. I couldn't even carry a gun. All they'd let me carry was water. But you not only got to fight, you got your stripe too.

FATHER S: Oh Rupert, you remember! *(He's crying from joy)*

ADC: I remember.

FATHER S: Good Rupert. And we'll always be together, Rupert, won't we? Say we'll always be together. Say it, please.

ADC: Yes, we'll always be together.

FATHER S: Till we die. Say "till we die," Rupert.

ADC: *(Indulging him)* Till we die.

FATHER S: *(Changing quickly as he looks around)* But we'll never die, will we? You know we will never die. You know it, don't you. Don't you? Don't you?

ADC: Yes, yes.

FATHER S: You mustn't even think it ever. You must think only of the long years ahead, years that will just be ours together, the two of us. just the way it was in the old days.

ADC: There ain't too many of them left. Not for me, anyway.

FATHER S: Oh my god, Rupert. *(Quickly covers ADC's mouth with his hand)* You mustn't say that. I won't let you. You're young and strong and in your prime. You'll outlive us all. Do you hear me, Rupert!

ADC: *(Finally getting the hand off and trying to calm him)* Yes, yes, I hear you.

FATHER S: *(Placated)* Good, good. The days are longer now, Rupert. Not shorter. *(Getting resolute)* And the longer they are, the stronger we must be. We must fight, Rupert, and stand tall, Rupert, stand tall. *(Gets up quickly)* I said, stand tall!

ADC: *(Not wanting to oblige)* Please, can't we do it in the morning.

FATHER S: Quiet in the ranks. Teenshun!

ADC: *(Going along reluctantly)* Sah. *(Comes to attention)*

FATHER S: 'Bout fahce! *(ADC turns around)* Forward march! *(ADC starts marching)* Halt! *(ADC stops)* Left turn! *(ADC turns left)* Satnd easy! *(ADC stands easy)* Now then, repeat after me, "We will never die, we will never die."
(ADC picks it up on the third time)

ADC and FATHER S: *(Together)* We will never die. *(The fourth time is the strongest)* We will never die.

FATHER S: *(Falls down as he says the fifth one strongly)* We will never die.

ADC: *(Repeats it the fifth time after FATHER S. But by now he's lost his enthusiasm)* We will never die. *(Helps FATHER S to the bench as he says it the last time)*

FATHER S: *(Looks up at ADC with a desperate plea, and then out)* Oh my god!

End

CARLTON & BARBARA MOLETTE

DURING THE PAST twenty years, the theatrical team of Barbara and Carlton Molette has amassed a myriad of dramatic credits including more than 150 stage productions. Both were awarded graduate degrees in theatre from Florida State University; Carlton has a Ph.D. and Barbara has an M.F.A.

Born in Pine Bluff, Arkansas, Carlton has theatrical credits as producer, director, designer, publicist, technician, and actor. He has worked with a number of theatrical groups including the Negro Ensemble Company, the Des Moines Community Playhouse, and the University of Michigan Theatre Program. In addition to teaching courses in playwrighting, theatre history, and costume design, Barbara has served as consultant for a number of television workshops and is one of the foremost authorities on stage makeup for Black performers. "Makeup for Black Actors," a filmstrip, is available through Paramount Theatrical Supplies in New York City. Both Carlton and Barbara are presently employed by Texas Southern University in Houston where he is Dean of the School of Communications and she is an assistant professor. They are the parents of two children, Carla and Andrea.

The duo has collaborated on major productions including *Rosallee Pritchett* (1970) which was first performed by the Morehouse Spelman Players and later staged off-Broadway by the Negro Ensemble Company; *Doctor B.S. Black* (1972), a musical play first performed by the Atlanta University Summer Theatre; *Booji* (1971), revised and produced as a video tape by KPRC and at Texas Southern University in 1978; and *Noah's Ark,* first performed in 1974 by the Morehouse Spelman Players.

Barbara is listed in *Who's Who of American Women* and Carlton is listed in *Who's Who in the South and Southwest.* Both have received a number of professional and academic awards. As presentors of research papers exploring the gamut of issues and concerns associated with American theatre, the Molettes have presented a number of papers for the American Theatre Association and the United States Institute for Theatre Technology. "Bibliography of Afro-American Theatre" —an on-going project initiated in 1965—is a

collaborative work with over 3,000 listings of plays by Afro-Americans and published materials about Afro-American theatre.

Both Barbara and Carlton are members of the Dramatists Guild, the American Theatre Association, the National Association of Dramatic and Speech Arts, and the United States Institute for Theatre Technology.

Recently, Carlton's professional concerns have been principally aimed at the development of the School of Communications at Texas Southern University. His fund raising efforts have resulted in Radio Station KTSU-FM being on the air at more than 18kw. He is still working on the acquisition of film and video production equipment and the development of a professional theatre company on campus.

Barbara, as an educator, is concerned with developing competent and creative scriptwriters. She is formulating a course that uses psychocybernetics and music to enable students to write stress free. She is currently serving on the editorial board for the Technical Theatre Course Guide sponsored by the United States Institute for Theatre Technology.

NOAH'S ARK

Carlton & Barbara Molette

CHARACTERS
(In order of appearance)

NOAH THOMPSON: *College professor in his 40s*
GLADYS THOMPSON: NOAH's *wife, in her 40s*
RUTH THOMPSON: *wife of* ADAM, *in her 40s*
ADAM THOMPSON: NOAH's *brother, in his 40s*
ESTHER AKIWOWO: *Nigerian economist/writer in her late 30s*
VALERY LAWSON: *College professor in her early 30s*
DANIEL THOMPSON: NOAH's *and* GLADYS's *son,*
college student in his early 20s

ACT ONE

Scene 1

Early Sunday afternoon in the home of NOAH *and* GLADYS THOMPSON, *and their son,* DANIEL. *The scene is the family room. It is raining, and we see* NOAH *running back and forth carrying stuff in from the patio that he was going to use in barbequing. The T.V. set is on. A bad movie is on the T.V.* GLADYS *is not in the room at the moment. She left to get some wig spray.* DANIEL *is not at home.*

NOAH: *(Goes toward the kitchen)* Gladys! *(Notices T.V. set)* Gladys!!! *(No answer. He moves away from kitchen)* Where is that woman?! *(He stops and screams)* Gladys! Where the hell are you?

GLADYS: *(She is right behind him as she quietly speaks)* I'm right here, Noah. You don't have to yell.

NOAH: *(Still tending to scream)* Why did you switch channels?! *(More quietly)* You knew I was watching the football game.

GLADYS: How could you be watching T.V. when you weren't even in the room?

NOAH: You're always turning off my football game!

GLADYS: You were outside! You couldn't even hear the game out there!

NOAH: Well, do you mind if I switch back? *(As he switches channels on the T.V.)*

GLADYS: Not if you're gonna watch the game . . . what we need is another T.V. set around here.

NOAH: *(Goes to the bar, gets a drink, sits to watch the game on television)* Maybe Daniel could fix one up for you. Lord knows, he has enough spare parts in the basement to build three or four T.V. sets.

GLADYS: I don't want to bother him—he's got enough work to do for other people that he's getting paid to do.

NOAH: I'm going to ask him as a favor to his daddy to build his momma a T.V. set.

GLADYS: Oh, leave the boy alone. We're just going to have to work out a schedule.

NOAH: The schedule is simple—the only thing I ever watch is the football games on Sunday. You can watch those grade B movies any time you want to —except on Sunday afternoons.

GLADYS: All I'm asking is that you *watch* the football game after you turn it on.

NOAH: I will, if you quit switching channels on me.

GLADYS: Is the barbeque in the oven?

NOAH: Yeah, I sure hope those ribs don't dry out.

GLADYS: All you have to do is add some water and cover them with tin foil. I'll go do that right now. O.K?

NOAH: I'll do it myself. I don't want you messing with my ribs. *(He starts out, remembers the football game, comes back)* On second thought, you go ahead and fix the barbeque. I don't want you messing with the T.V. set either.

GLADYS: Make up your mind Professor Thompson. *(Exits)*

(Sound track of football announcer. RUTH *comes in*

patio door with newspaper on her head and covered dish of sweet potato pie. NOAH *is fixing himself a drink)*

RUTH: You-hoo, Noah!! Can you get the door for me?

NOAH: Sorry, Ruth, here let me take that from you. *(Sniffs)*

RUTH: Watch it, the pie's still pretty hot.

NOAH: Uhmm Uh—sweet potato pie.

RUTH: Where's Gladys?

NOAH: She's in the kitchen. You only brought one pie? Aren't the rest of y'all having any?

RUTH: That pie is for all of us, Noah! I didn't have enough butter to make one just for you.

NOAH: Ruth, honey, I sho' do like your sweet potato pies. How much butter do you need? You need some sweet potatoes, too?

RUTH: Well, like the old colored lady said, "I puts in uh whole lotsa butter, uh whole lotsa eggs, uh whole lotsa sugar, and just uh little bit uh taters."

(RUTH laughs, NOAH does not. Throughout the sequence the football game is on and we hear commentary on the game intermittently)

NOAH: Was that supposed to be a joke? Let me take this pie on out to the kitchen before I decide to eat the whole thing right here.

RUTH: *(Takes the pie out to the kitchen)* Oh no you don't. I'm not trusting you with this pie. *(Exit)*

(ADAM comes in without knocking. NOAH is watching television)

ADAM: I need to have a conference with the man upstairs and tell him to turn off the faucet.

NOAH: Did you preach a good sermon this morning, my brother?

ADAM: You would know that if you ever came to church. Had 'em layin in the aisles, as usual.

NOAH: What do I need to got to church for—when I have to listen to you preach the *same* sermon, while you drinking *my* liquor, sitting in *my* easy chair, and keeping *me* from listening to the football game.

ADAM: But it's the fellowship, man. It's the fellowship. When you hear the melodious blending of the voices of the senior choir, the junior choir, and the gospel chorus, you know you're listening to the sound of angels and that you sitting next to god.

NOAH: Ah, Reverend, what can I get you to drink?

ADAM: Just a little preacher's punch. *(Sits)* That's an olive that's been sprinkled with vermouth and baptized in gin.

NOAH: Didn't you tell those people this morning that that was the devil's drink?

ADAM: You're right, Noah; that is the devil's drink. I guess you better hold the olive.

NOAH: That's what I say about jackleg preachers.

ADAM: *(Gets up to "preach" the word)* My brother .... You know that statue where Booker T. Washington is raising the cloak of ignorance from the Black man? Well, Booker T. Washington has been trying for all these years to remove the cloak of ignorance that still covers you. And what are you doing to help? You taking that ignorance and just spreading it all around like you know what you talking about.

NOAH: See! That's why I don't go to church! I have to listen to you preach all the time, anyhow! And if I'm still under that cloak of ignorance, so are you. We both went to the same schools. And, if I recall correctly, I made better grades than you did.

ADAM: Yeah, but I said, "Booker T. get that cloak of ignorance away from me."

NOAH: And without cracking a book, *all* that ignorance just vanished, huh?

ADAM: I also prayed real hard.

NOAH: Man, you better take this drink before I baptize you with it.

(GLADYS and RUTH enter from the kitchen)

GLADYS: Hi Adam, I didn't know you were here.

NOAH: You mean to say you missed chapter one of today's sermon?

GLADYS: Noah, Clinton Frazier just called and said he had started over here but he couldn't get out of his driveway.

NOAH: What's the matter?

GLADYS: His front yard has turned into a lake. You know, his house sits down in a valley. A really bad place to put a house. But what would an English teacher know about buying a house?

RUTH: I think the house is kinda cute, myself.

GLADYS: *(Mumbles)* Oh, it's horrible.

ADAM: I know I missed him at Sunday School this morning. He hasn't missed his Sunday School class in years.

RUTH: Come to think of it, Mother Frazier wasn't in her regular seat in church this morning. I need to call her and see if she needs anything. I know she'll be getting bored if she isn't able to get out soon. That woman really gets about, for her age.

GLADYS: Clinton said he won't be able to get his car out of the driveway for days. Noah, are you watching the football game?

NOAH: No, I was listening to you, but I don't want to turn off the football game, either.

GLADYS: Well, would you mind turning it down, then?

NOAH: I can't keep up with the score if I can't hear the T.V.

RUTH: Where's Danny? I haven't seen him lately.

GLADYS: Oh, he's been staying busy.

NOAH: So busy, we haven't seen too much of him ourselves.

RUTH: Studying, huh?

NOAH: That's what he needs to be doing, but I doubt that he is. He has to keep his grade point average above a B so he won't be drafted.

ADAM: Has Danny heard from the draft board again?

NOAH: Not really. Not since he went down for the physical.

GLADYS: It seems to me that there are enough folks to send to war without sending Danny. I know that sounds unpatriotic, but I didn't go through childbirth pains just to have my son sent off to Africa to fight a war.

NOAH: Gladys, no need to get upset about it; it doesn't do any good. *(Gets up, goes to the bar)* They haven't sent for Danny yet; and they probably won't be sending for him any time soon.

GLADYS: I just get mad whenever the thought crosses my mind.

NOAH: The thing that's really got me worried is the concentration camps.

ADAM: Oh, they won't go that far.

NOAH: They did it to the Japanese in World War II, and they'll do it to us now. And furthermore, Reverend Thompson, they'll do it in the name of God, Justice, and Patriotism.

ADAM: But not in that order, I hope.

(Doorbell rings)

GLADYS: Saved by the bell! I'll get it. *(Goes to answer door)*

RUTH: Noah, while you're up, fix me a little bourbon and sweet soda.

ADAM: Do you think you should drink anything on top of those pills you're taking?

RUTH: Just one little bourbon and soda isn't going to do me any harm.

NOAH: What kinds of pills are they, Ruth?

RUTH: Oh, just hormones. Adam calls them my sex pills.

ADAM: They sure as hell make you easier to live with. And I think you get sexier and sexier every day.

RUTH: They also help me to tolerate you, Reverend Thompson.

ADAM: *(Gets up to do his "comedy routine")* Before Ruth was taking those pills, it was "It's burning up in here. Open the window, Adam." And just as soon as I'd get the window open, it was, "Close the window, Adam. It's freezing in here." You better hope Gladys is on those pills when she starts going through the change.

NOAH: I'll pay special heed to your advice, Dr. Thompson. Any other little tidbits you have to offer for marital bliss?

ADAM: You can't tell a professor nothing. Trying to teach you a little sex education and you're getting sarcastic.

NOAH: But Reverend Thompson, sex education is not your field. Unless of course, all those rumors about you and the good sisters of the church are true. 'Cause if they are, you are one of the world's leading authorities on sex education. Here's your bourbon and soda, Ruth. Enjoy it in good health.

RUTH: *(Sarcastically, but not taking his remark seriously)* Thanks a lot, Noah.

(GLADYS enters accompanied by ESTHER AKIWOWO, Nigerian author. ESTHER's outward appearance is quite British. NOAH speaks to her and she speaks to NOAH during GLADYS's speech)

GLADYS: We're all back here. It's much more informal. We had planned to have the barbeque outdoors, but it's been raining so and we didn't think it was going to let up anytime soon.

NOAH: Hello, Esther.

ESTHER: How do you do.

GLADYS: Esther, this is Noah's brother, Reverend Adam Thompson and his wife, Ruth. This is Dr. Esther Akiwowo.

RUTH: How are you? Noah gave us one of your articles to read. Certainly was interesting.

ESTHER: Thank you, Mrs. Thompson. I'm very pleased to meet you.

(ESTHER extends her hand and shakes hands with both ADAM and RUTH)

ADAM: I've been looking forward to talking to you, Dr. Akiwowo. Noah is quite a disciple of yours.

ESTHER: Please call me Esther.

ADAM: Well, I hope you don't call me Reverend Thompson. Now, since we are all gathered together—You know what Paul said?

NOAH: *(Sits)* Here we go again! Another sermon.

GLADYS: Which Paul?

ADAM: The only Paul who counts.

NOAH: Yes, and you don't need to tell us again.

ESTHER: *(To GLADYS)* What did Paul say?

GLADYS: *(Shrugs)* I really don't know, Esther, but I'm sure the theologian there will enlighten us.

ADAM: *(Preaches while NOAH agonizes aloud)* The Apostle Paul, in his . . . letter to the Corinthians, said . . .

RUTH: Anyway, Esther, do you bring us any news of the motherland?

ESTHER: I'm afraid it's not very good news.

NOAH: Before we get into that. Can I get you a drink, Esther?

ESTHER: Yes, thank you. A little whiskey and soda.

NOAH: That's scotch and soda for you plebians, Adam.

ADAM: Esther, quick say something! Noah's getting ready to give another lecture. *(NOAH goes to fix ESTHER a drink)* By the way, from the sound of that article, you must really be homesick.

ESTHER: Homesick? Which article are you referring to?

ADAM: The one where you lambasted the United States. You really gave it to us.

NOAH: What "us"?

ADAM: I meant "them," professor.

ESTHER: But what do you mean by "homesick"?

ADAM: That article sounds as if you're trying to shorten your visit to America.

ESTHER: I'm only expounding a theory. And, there *is* freedom of speech here.

ADAM: Well, we are all in the habit of *saying* that we have freedom of speech.

GLADYS: You are quite courageous to say what you did in print.

ESTHER: I sincerely believe that most wars of aggression are fought for natural resources. In this case, the United States has been fighting for oil resources for the past twenty-five years. The United States involvement with Asia was to secure petroleum resources. Before that, it was rubber in the Philippines; and in the Carribean it was sugar, and also tobacco.

NOAH: Here's your drink, Esther.

ESTHER: Oh, thank you.

NOAH: What other reason would Teddy Roosevelt and the Rough Riders have to be in Cuba?

ESTHER: The civil war in the United States was also fought for a resource—human labor. By controlling the world's resources, the United States maintains power. Very simple, really, By the way, this theory also applies to other countries as well. The only reason I'm singling out the United States is that they are attacking my country.

GLADYS: I guess the United States wants to make sure that a country they consider backward . . .

NOAH: *(Interrupts)* Meaning non-White . . .

GLADYS: *(Continues)* Doesn't have anything that's vital to the American economy that they could withhold.

NOAH: The way that we are using up the resources in this country . . .

ADAM: What do you mean "we"?! I don't use up no more than my fair share.

RUTH: I doubt that us Black folks ever get our fair share of anything.

NOAH: As I was saying, the way that White folks waste the resources of this country, new sources have to be found.

ESTHER: The truth of the matter is that Nigeria has some of the largest oil fields in Africa. They still remain largely untapped. There have been all sorts of atrocities committed to obtain rights to these oil fields.

RUTH: But why start a war? Why don't the oil companies just lease the land?

ESTHER: That's the problem. Traditionally, ownership of land in Nigeria, and most parts of Africa, didn't work the way it does in the United States. The land was there for whoever needed it to grow food on or hunt food. So the easiest way for the oil companies to acquire the land is to run the people off. Just as the European colonists did with the Indians in this country.

ADAM: I am just standing here listening to you and thinking—White folks ain't no more Christianized now than they were one hundred years ago.

RUTH: Or two hundred years ago, either.

NOAH: Or two thousand years ago, for that matter.

ESTHER: The little aid that was sent over to help people living in the Sahel was just enough to create confusion.

NOAH: I read that there were riots over who was going to get what little food there was.

ADAM: *(To ESTHER)* Are you saying that no aid would have been better than what was sent.

NOAH: No, Adam. What she's saying is that America could have and should have done more.

ADAM: Oh, I don't doubt that.

ESTHER: People were killed by soldiers just because they were trying to get something to eat.

GLADYS: It seems to me, with all the money that gets spent on research, that something could have been done to provide water for the Sahel.

ADAM: There you go, asking the federal government to play god, as if they don't play god enough already.

GLADYS: I'm not asking them to play god, just to use my tax money where it would do some poor people some good for once. I figure if the United States can build an outpost on the moon . . .

ADAM: How do you know they really have that outpost on the moon?

GLADYS: I'm not going to debate that point with you now. Let's just say that they have the technology to do it.

RUTH: I wouldn't be surprised if those White folks have discovered oil on the moon. Or better yet . . .

GLADYS: What about those moon rocks?

RUTH: That's just what I was going to say. Does anybody know what those moon rocks are good for?

NOAH: If they do know, you'll be the last to find out.

GLADYS: And all this crazy weather we've been having . . . the bigger the space rockets get, the crazier the weather gets.

ESTHER: My country should have been so fortunate to have as much rain as you're having now.

ADAM: I'll take your problem up with my boss.

RUTH: Stop kidding, Adam. This is very serious.

ADAM: I hope that your articles and speeches are not being taken too seriously by the government.

GLADYS: The only reason she wouldn't be taken seriously is that she is not only Black and a woman, but she also comes from a "developing country." Black women are not supposed to have any theories on economics especially on an international scale. So they'll figure that nobody's paying any attention to her—not even other Black women.

(NOAH *stands, lectures—the others are obviously bored by his lecture—except for* ESTHER—*she has not heard it before; the others have*)

NOAH: The White boys are at it again. By allowing the Sahara to continue its southward movement, communities and whole nations are killed without firing a gun and the greedy imperialists can move in and take over the resource without any trouble. Don't think for a moment that Russia and the U.S. are really at odds. They are together. Both sides are being controlled by the same people.

RUTH: What people?

ADAM: Ruth, you're encouraging him!

NOAH: People who have international wealth. They control the industries all over the world. They are concerned with maintaining their industrial complexes by controlling natural resources. The people who are really in power have no allegiance to any country.

RUTH: Isn't that just speculation?

ADAM: Oh, Ruth! Here we go again!

NOAH: There's nothing wrong with speculation, but that is not exactly what I'm doing. I'm analyzing the facts and coming up with conclusions that I think are valid.

ADAM: You?! Analyzing? You'd be better off praying for a divine vision.

RUTH: Noah, that sounds so farfetched—you mean to tell me that a group of men . . .

NOAH: A very small group . . .

RUTH: What you're saying is that these men already govern the world.

NOAH: They do!!

ADAM: Professor Thompson, may I please have another drink? Your lecture is awfully dry.

GLADYS: (*Takes his glass en route to the bar*) What are you drinking, Adam?

RUTH: What does he always drink? When he gets to heaven he will have a stem glass for a halo.

GLADYS: Don't mind them, Esther. They only carry on this way in front of people that they really like and trust.

ESTHER: (*To* GLADYS *with considerable warmth, considering her Britishness*) I am very glad I had the opportunity to come to a Black university. I have felt rather like one of the community. So many of my countrymen have told me that they felt completely alien in the White universities.

RUTH: How long are you planning to stay?

ESTHER: Just one semester. Then, I'll take a two-month tour to visit some of the major universities.

GLADYS: We're rather fortunate to get Esther. There's really a big demand for her to lecture.

ESTHER: I'm really looking forward to working with the young people. Back home, I have been spending most of my time researching and writing.

ADAM: Gladys, when are we going to eat?

RUTH: See! That's why Black folks can't make progress in this world. All you ever worry about is eating and drinking.

ADAM: (*Starts toward* RUTH) No, there is one other thing that us Black folks worry about.

(*Doorbell rings*)

RUTH: Saved by the bell.

GLADYS: Let me go see who this is. I'll check on the dinner in a minute, Adam. (GLADYS *exits*)

RUTH: Noah, what I can't understand is why doesn't somebody stop them.

ADAM: That's his cue for another lecture!

NOAH: Who's to stop them. They are above the law of any one country.

ADAM: (*Deliberately changing the subject*) Esther, where did you get your degree?

ESTHER: I went to the London School of Economics.

(GLADYS *enters with* DR. VALERY LAWSON)

ADAM: Um Humm . . . . How did you manage to survive that London weather?

VALERY: Doctor T!!!

NOAH: (*Seeing* VALERY *wearing the latest Black hairstyle. Her clothes are very Africanesque*) Valery Lawson! You're the one who started calling me that, aren't you? Just the other day one of the students called me Doctor Thompson, and someone else said, "Man, don't call him that, call him Doctor T."

VALERY: Yeah, I christened you two, Dr. and Mizzus T. That was to distinguish between you and Reverend and Mizzus Thompson.

GLADYS: You always did seem like one of the family.

VALERY: Dr. T., you were the best teacher I ever had. We sure could use you up there.

NOAH: Congratulations, Doctor Lawson. You see we keep up with our students.

RUTH: Well, blow me down, you don't seem like the same little Valery. Where are you now?

GLADYS: Pardon me, Dr. Esther Akiwowo, this is Dr. Valery Lawson. She was one of Noah's students and used to babysit for us.

ESTHER: How do you do.

ADAM: One of the best Sunday School teachers we ever had.

VALERY: I've really missed you all. I was reading an article about one of the children who used to be in my Sunday School class. He's an executive with some big firm now. Really makes me feel ancient.

GLADYS: Dr. Akiwowo is a visiting professor this year in the Economics Department.

ESTHER: Please, call me Esther.

VALERY: Yes, I have been hearing quite a bit about you lately. All very complimentary.

NOAH: Have a seat, Valery. Can I get you a drink?

VALERY: Yes, thank you. Could I have a glass of white wine?

GLADYS: That's okay, Noah, I'll get it. It's in the refrigerator. *(Exits)*

NOAH: So, Doctor Lawson, where are you working now?

VALERY: That sounds so funny.

NOAH: What?!

VALERY: You calling me "Dr. Lawson." *(NOAH smiles quietly)* Anyway, I'm at the University of the Midwest. We're on holiday leave, and I hadn't been home for quite a while . . .

NOAH: *(Sits)* How long have you been there?

VALERY: This is my first year.

ADAM: Do they have many Blacks on the faculty?

VALERY: Well, we have seven now. I'm the first Black woman, though.

ADAM: I guess all those big schools in the midwest are looking for Black faculty members now?

VALERY: Well, not really.

NOAH: Man, haven't you heard? Niggers is obsolete!

ADAM: I'm trying to carry on an intelligent conversation with Doctor Lawson here, and you insist upon . . .

NOAH: You? Carry on an intelligent conversation? I just can't keep up with all these new developments!

ADAM: Noah, will you please make up your mind! You are the one who is always complaining about *"them"* stealing all of our best young minds while they have got them up there in graduate school.

NOAH: My very own brother, you are slow. Man, that was five years ago. I know you don't keep up with the latest styles in clothes, but you *need* to check out the new styles in oppressed minorities. I'm telling you, my brother, you are out of

fashion. This season the fashionable oppressed minority is the Eskimo, last season it was women —White women, that is—and Orientals, I *told* you, Niggers is obsolete! *(ADAM walks away)* Doctor Lawson here got that job at the University of the Midwest because she is a qualified *woman* who just happens to be Black. Valery, when were those Black *men* hired up there?

VALERY: They must have all been hired around 1969, 1970, I think. They've all been there since the year one, practically.

NOAH: See!! All those token jobs that used to be reserved for Black men go to White women, Orientals and now Eskimos! Anything to keep a Black man out of a job!

VALERY: But that does create some employment opportunity for Black women, too.

NOAH: Right!! As maids for all those White women who are getting the good jobs.

(NOAH sits; watches T.V.; ADAM watches over his shoulder)

ADAM: Black folks ought to have their own businesses and employ their own people so we wouldn't always be begging White folks for jobs.

NOAH: Watch out folks! Reverend Thompson is getting ready to pass the collection plate!

GLADYS: *(Enters)* Here's your drink Valery. I just *love* that outfit you're wearing!

VALERY: Thanks, Mrs. T. How's the dress shop doing? I know you still carry the best looking clothes in town.

NOAH: I keep telling her to get rid of that place. She's working herself to death and the government takes all the profit.

GLADYS: But I enjoy doing it, Noah.

NOAH: Valery, the only reason she keeps the shop open is to avoid being classified as a housewife on her "C" card.

GLADYS: As I said, Valery, I enjoy running the dress shop. We do the best we can, under the new guidelines.

VALERY: New guidelines?

GLADYS: Yeah, we're classified as a class "D" retailer, so we can't keep much of an inventory. I have to make most of the clothes myself, so we only keep the place open in the afternoons.

VALERY: Your dress shop is a real institution around here, Mrs. T. Remember the time that Danny pulled all those dresses down off the rack. By the way, where is Danny?

GLADYS: He left here early this morning. He ought to be home soon.

VALERY: I can hardly believe he's in college now. And he decided to go to school here? What is he majoring in?

GLADYS: Engineering. Electronics engineering.

He left here without his raincoat, and will you look at that weather out there!

RUTH: By the way, is Danny through fixing that little old black and white T.V. set of ours?

GLADYS: I don't think he is, Ruth. Soaking wet . . . I know he is . . .

RUTH: Well, I gave it to him over two months ago. I wouldn't be concerned about it, but we're not allowed another T.V. set on our "C" card so I figured we'd better get that one fixed.

NOAH: The protectors of our economy figured that a preacher ought to have more important things to do than to watch T.V.

ESTHER: You keep mentioning a "C" card. What is a "C" card?

RUTH: It's a consumer card. It's what we use now instead of money. You have to have one in order to buy anything!

ESTHER: Anything?!

NOAH: Even a toothpick!

ESTHER: But, what are they for?

NOAH: It's big brother's way of controlling our lives. In addition to being outrageous, they are also unconstitutional, for whatever that's worth.

VALERY: I think they've been rather beneficial.

RUTH: What! How can you say that?

ADAM: Where in the name of all the heavenly hosts do a handful of White men get the wisdom to decide what I can buy and what I can't.

VALERY: It's been a big help in curbing the inflationary spiral.

NOAH: You don't really believe that, do you?

ADAM: I didn't realize that the "inflationary spiral" had been curbed.

VALERY: Consumer cards allow the government to control supply and demand.

ADAM: I can see it now. Your president is gonna have all the "Please Curb Your Dog" signs taken down and replaced by signs that read "*Please Curb Your Inflationary Spiral.*"

ESTHER: How do these consumer cards work?

NOAH: Well, first, all personal data is programmed into a computer. Then, you are classified according to income, professional status, age, and so forth.

ADAM: "And so forth" means *race,* Esther.

NOAH: From that information, they determine what type of food you are allowed to puchase, what type of car, clothes, furniture, books, everything. All consumer items are coded; and according to your consumer card index, you may or may not buy any given item.

RUTH: Wasn't it your George Orwell that predicted something like this?

ESTHER: What do you mean "*My* George Orwell?"

RUTH: Well, he was British and your country is a member of the British Commonwealth, so I naturally thought that . . .

ESTHER: *(Laughs, more at herself than at* RUTH*)* You know I used to think of myself as being very British. But I don't anymore.

VALERY: Personally, I think the consumer cards are a good idea. At least they keep people on welfare from owning Cadillacs and color T.V. sets.

GLADYS: You mean to say that you are willing to give up your personal freedom just to keep somebody on welfare from owning a Cadillac.

NOAH: If people want to take what little money they have and spend it on a Cadillac, they ought to have the right to make that choice.

RUTH: But, they also keep me from getting another television set.

NOAH: Valery, I thought I taught you better than that.

ADAM: Don't be so hard on the girl, Noah.

VALERY: I don't mind my tax money going to help somebody blind or crippled, but I do mind my tax money being wasted on frivolity.

NOAH: *(Goes to* VALERY*)* Oh, Frivolity? Well, what about the other ninety-six percent of your tax money? The part that's being spent on non-frivolous things like . . . bombs to kill our Black brothers in Africa.

VALERY: But that's in our national interest.

NOAH: What do you mean "our" national interest?

RUTH: Come on, Valery, surely you don't believe everything you read in the newspapers?

VALERY: Of course I don't believe everything I read in the newspapers.

RUTH: You need to talk to Esther.

GLADYS: Anyone need to . . . freshen their drinks.

NOAH: Wait a minute, Valery. I take it you're not putting us on?

VALERY: No Doctor T., I'm not putting you on. I've been studying the welfare problem a long time. You know I wrote my dissertation on that subject. I came to the conclusion that if Black people treated money with more respect, they wouldn't be on welfare. These consumer cards are the best things that could happen to poor people—because now they can't spend money on junk. They have to buy food for their families instead of throwing it away. People who are that fiscally irresponsible need to be controlled.

NOAH: Valery, you know that welfare isn't something that's just given to poor people . . . a lot of millionaires get welfare, in fact, that's how most of them got to be millionaires. I'm not gonna start on that because that's another lecture.

ADAM: Amen, brother.

NOAH: Valery, you've lost something somewhere

along the way. I guess it's your sense of charity or . . . . You are wrong. However, to conserve the last little vestige of freedom that I have, I'll defend your right to say what you believe. And, with that, I'm going to watch the last three minutes of the football game.

GLADYS: Can you stay for dinner, Valery?

VALERY: No, Mrs. T., Mother is having some relatives over for dinner. Some people I've never seen that are from my mother's hometown.

GLADYS: Well, you can't blame her for wanting to show you off. After all, you're quite a celebrity around here. Tell your mother hello for me. I plan on calling her real soon.

VALERY: Well, I guess I'd better get on back home and help Mother with the dinner. I just dropped by to say hello. Nice meeting you, Esther.

ESTHER: It's my pleasure, Valery.

RUTH: It's been good seeing you again, Valery.

ADAM: Next time you're in town, come on over to your old Sunday School class and see what we're doing.

VALERY: I'll do that, Reverend Thompson.

GLADYS: Come back over before you leave if you have the time.

VALERY: I will. I do want to see Danny before I leave. We might get back by tomorrow afternoon. I'm going to surprise Mother and take her shopping downtown.

GLADYS: Honey, I wouldn't do that if I were you. We don't shop downtown anymore.

RUTH: It's like an armed camp down there. They've got barbed wire up all around to keep a close check on who comes and goes. And they search your packages.

GLADYS: I haven't been downtown in over five years.

VALERY: Why?

RUTH: It's to keep the niggers from stealing downtown. I ain't going nowhere I got to be searched . . .

ADAM: You got searched when you went to Jamaica.

RUTH: That was before my political consciousness was raised.

ADAM: Your *political consciousness* gets raised and lowered like the American flag!

GLADYS: The last time I was downtown it took me almost an hour to get from the store to my car, which was in a parking lot next to the store. I was afraid to take the steps down to the parking level —I saw men with runny noses eyeing me. Little boys with empty bags under their arms walking in and out of the store.

RUTH: Gladys saw her first Black streaker.

GLADYS: Streaker nothing—he was a pervert.

ADAM: White men streak and Black men expose themselves—that's what Gladys told the parking lot attendant.

VALERY: You told on a Black brother!

GLADYS: When I'm threatened—color don't mean a thing. He jumps right out in front of my car almost—with his pants down! Lord—he was so pathetic looking.

RUTH: What little shopping I do now, I do it at a mall. Downtown is infested with dope addicts and perverts!

VALERY: Thanks for the warning. I hope Mother hasn't been going downtown by herself.

GLADYS: I bet if you ask her, she'll tell you the same thing we did.

VALERY: Well, I'll try to get back over. Got to go now.

GLADYS: Noah, Valery is leaving.

NOAH: *(Slowly turns away from the T.V.)* Come on back home. I think you need us as much as we need you.

VALERY: I'll keep that in mind.

(VALERY and GLADYS exit)

GLADYS: Danny's going to be so mad he missed you.

(NOAH turns up sound on T.V. football game. The following conversation is over the football game)

RUTH: That poor child. She just doesn't seem like the same little Valery that used to go to school here.

ESTHER: I guess our elders thought we were a little bit mixed up too when we were younger.

RUTH: Young or old, something just happens to Black folks after they've been living around White folks for a while . . . . It seems like they just lose their common sense, or something.

ESTHER: Maybe they start believing in the same things White folks believe in.

RUTH: Like I said, they lose their common sense.

GLADYS: *(Enters)* Dinner ought to be ready by now. You all come on out to the kitchen. We'll do it buffet style. Then, take your plates on into the dining room. I have the table set up in there.

RUTH: Can I help you do anything?

GLADYS: No thanks, just come on and get your plate. *(Exits)*

ADAM: Esther, you haven't tasted anything like the ribs Noah cooks. What's your secret, Noah?

NOAH: I been telling you for years, Brother; you don't hold your mouth right.

RUTH: What Noah is saying is that you talk too much.

(RUTH and ESTHER exit)

NOAH: If you had helped Papa when he cooked, you would know how to barbeque ribs. But not you, you were too busy dodging work. A slothful man shall come to no good end.

ADAM: Aw, Noah, don't try to quote the Bible on me. *(Exits)*

GLADYS: *(Enters)* Go on and get your plate, Adam. *(NOAH goes over and turns off T.V. set)* It's been raining steady all day and Danny's been gone without a raincoat. Noah, I'm so worried about him.

NOAH: He's a grown man. He ought to have sense enough to be in somewhere out of the rain.

GLADYS: It's not the rain.

NOAH: What is it then?

GLADYS: I'm worried about Danny being drafted.

NOAH: Danny is smart enough to keep a B average.

GLADYS: I know he can keep a B average. I'm worried about him being drafted in spite of his grades.

NOAH: Daniel won't be drafted.

GLADYS: How can you be so sure.

NOAH: I'm sure. We better go get something to eat. When Adam eats at our house, he acts like food isn't rationed anymore.

GLADYS: *(Wistfully)* Will you look at all that rain out there?

(Sound of laughter from kitchen)

NOAH: Sounds like Adam told another preacher joke. Let's go see what's going on.

GLADYS: I need to save a plate of ribs for Danny.

(GLADYS then starts out to the kitchen as the lights fade out)

Scene 2

The barbeque is over and it is still raining. NOAH *and* GLADYS *are sitting in the family room. Some kind of Black music is playing. Something that is somber and melancholy.* NOAH *is rubbing his shoulder.*

GLADYS: *(Winces)* I think I ate too much at dinner. That barbeque sure was good, though.

NOAH: You hardly ate any. Are you okay?

GLADYS: It's nothing serious; I just shouldn't have eaten those onions, that's all.

NOAH: You want me to get you something?

GLADYS: No, I'm okay. You just relax. *(She starts to rub NOAH's shoulder)*

NOAH: Every time it rains, my shoulder acts up. Rub up around my neck, too . . . I think I'll sleep with the hot pad on my shoulder . . . . Hmmmm . . . that feels good. I hope it stops raining soon; I don't know how long my old war injury can take it.

GLADYS: War injury? What war were you in?

NOAH: The battle of the United States Post Office.

GLADYS: That part of our life seems so far away.

NOAH: I remember those years quite vividly. And, I have this shoulder to remind me. Carrying that mail pouch for two years, five months and sixteen days was worse than carrying a rifle. I've done more than my share of service to my country.

GLADYS: At least at the end of the day you did have me to come home to.

NOAH: Now, you're right about that . . . at least I did have a fine, good looking woman . . .

(He reaches for her behind the chair as DANNY comes in hurriedly on his way to his bedroom. He is taking off his shirt which is soaking wet)

GLADYS: Daniel, where have you been? Get outta those clothes before you catch pneumonia.

DANNY: Oh, hi folks. *(Sits down and takes off shoes)*

GLADYS: Look at you, just dripping wet. Noah, I thought you said he would have enough sense to be in out of the rain.

NOAH: *(Sarcastically to DANNY)* That's what I said. Obviously, I was mistaken.

GLADYS: You look like you've been swimming with all your clothes on. It's going to take me a week to dry these shoes out. Where have you been?

(DANNY gets up and starts out)

NOAH: Let the boy get dry first.

DANNY: I was at Helen's.

NOAH: Doesn't Helen's place have a roof on it?

(DANNY exits)

GLADYS: Go get outta those wet pants. Put your bathrobe on. It's hanging on the hook behind your bedroom door. I washed it yesterday. *(To NOAH)* He did say he was at Helen's, didn't he?

NOAH: Yes, he did.

GLADYS: Well, Helen called here three or four times this evening looking for him. He was supposed to have taken her someplace.

NOAH: Maybe he was at Helen's earlier.

GLADYS: No, I don't think he was. That's not the impression I got from her on the phone. And that really doesn't make sense, anyway. Where has he been to come in soaking wet?

NOAH: I don't know. Why don't you ask him?

GLADYS: I was planning to ask him just as soon as he gets dry.

NOAH: Well, I don't know. Maybe you shouldn't ask him.

GLADYS: But you just said . . .

NOAH: I know what I just said. But you know what I meant.

GLADYS: Yeah, I know what you meant, but I'm still planning to ask him about it.

DANNY: *(Enters)* Ask him about what?

GLADYS: About where you've been all day.

DANNY: I told you . . .

GLADYS: Helen has called here five or six times looking for you, Danny.

DANNY: She has?!

GLADYS: Yes, she has!!

NOAH: Were you at Helen's?

DANNY: Daddy . . . I . . .

NOAH: All that question requires is a simple yes or no.

DANNY: But, it's not that simple.

NOAH: Can't you answer the question.

DANNY: I can . . . but then, well . . . I can't . . .

NOAH: Where have you been then?

DANNY: Please don't ask me that!

NOAH: I respect your right to privacy and all that . . . but your mother has been worried about you.

GLADYS: Maybe it's not that important, Noah.

NOAH: What's important now is that Danny has lied to us.

DANNY: Daddy, I'm doing it for your own protection.

NOAH: My own protection from what?

DANNY: I can't tell you.

NOAH: Why???

DANNY: So if anybody asks you about what I'm doing, you can honestly tell them that you don't know.

NOAH: What "them"? Who will we have to tell, Danny?

GLADYS: Noah, you said we ought to respect his privacy.

NOAH: But ignorance won't protect anybody from anything.

DANNY: But, if you honestly don't have any information to give them, they won't have any reason to bother you.

NOAH: What *they?* What are you involved in?

DANNY: *They!!!* You know, the government!

NOAH: Surely you don't think our real innocence is going to keep us safe from Big Brother? You can't protect us by not telling us what you're doing. If you get caught, we'll be implicated, and there will be nothing you can do about it . . . . It will be out of your hands. We'll all be able to do a better job of protecting ourselves if we know what we're up against.

GLADYS: Danny . . . your father is right, you know.

DANNY: *(Takes a deep breath)* Okay, we're running a radio station.

GLADYS: Well, what's wrong with running a radio station?

DANNY: *(Goes to GLADYS)* It's a bootleg station.

GLADYS: Bootleg?!

DANNY: We don't have a license or a frequency assigned to us. We just operate on a low fre-quency FM band. You can also pick up our radio broadcast on the television set by turning to channel six.

GLADYS: But why?

DANNY: Somebody has to keep Black people informed.

NOAH: How long have you been doing this?

DANNY: About a year now. You do listen to the broadcast, don't you?

NOAH: Most of the time . . . doing a good job. But, I didn't know you had . . .

(DANNY smiles)

GLADYS: That must be very risky?

DANNY: It is, but it is worth it. Did you hear our broadcast tonight?

NOAH: No, we've been too worried about you.

DANNY: Well, tonight the broadcast was about the "neighborhood centers" that are going to be set up. This is another way the government is going to be able to keep tabs on Black people.

GLADYS: *(Sarcastically)* I haven't heard anything about that on the news.

DANNY: Of course not, Momma. Do you think the government is going to anounce, "Listen, Black people, we're getting ready to set up neighborhood spies." There are gonna be people paid to do nothing but sit and watch who leaves and who comes into the neighborhood . . . and all in the name of community service.

GLADYS: Black folks are gonna spy on other Black folks for the White folks.

NOAH: That's nothing new. Been going on for years. By the way, I did hear the broadcast about the banks.

GLADYS: *(Gets up, goes to DANNY)* Noah kept saying all that night that the first thing he wanted to do the next morning was to take all of our money out of the bank and buy service coins. I had never heard of "service coins" before.

NOAH: Son, I had been keeping up with the stock market and the interest rates. So, I knew you all were on the right track and your information couldn't be too far from the truth.

DANNY: You got the coins?

NOAH: Yeah, I bought gold and silver. I gave them to Adam for safe keeping. So, in case anything ever happens to us, see Adam about what's coming to you.

GLADYS: I'm really sorry for the poor Black folks that couldn't get their money out of the bank in time. Those poor souls that had worked so hard all their lives to save a little bit of money and then have the government tell them that they couldn't have the money when they wanted to get it out of the bank.

NOAH: Adam was telling me that after that broadcast some of his church members gave him their money for safe keeping.

DANNY: I guess they figured that they might as well trust a Black preacher as a White banker.

GLADYS: I still don't understand how you got so wet making a radio broadcast.

DANNY: We have to keep moving the transmitter from place to place so they don't find us. Part of my job is to set up and dismantle the transmitter.

NOAH: That must be why on some nights the signal is so weak I can hardly pick it up, and other nights it just about blasts me out of my chair. I wondered what was going on.

GLADYS: Oh, Lord. . . . I bet you haven't had a bite to eat all day. I saved a plate of ribs for you. Let me go get it out of the oven. *(Exits)*

DANNY: Hey, Momma, can I have a beer with those ribs?

NOAH: How many other people are involved in these broadcasts?

DANNY: Just two other people are actually involved in the transmission operation. And, as far as I know, you and Momma are the only other people who even know who is running the station. The people who get the information and write the copy don't even know who we are, and we don't know who they are.

NOAH: You need to be real careful . . .

DANNY: I know . . . I will be.

NOAH: I don't think you do know.

DANNY: What do you mean?

NOAH: Mr. Hemsley called me.

DANNY: What was the draft board doing calling you? I'm keeping my grades up in school.

NOAH: Mr. Hemsley offered what he called an insurance policy. He wants me to pay him ten thousand dollars in gold coins to keep you out of the army.

DANNY: Don't do it! He can't keep me out if they decide to take me.

NOAH: I'm afraid you're right.

DANNY: You haven't told Momma, have you?

NOAH: No.

DANNY: Well, don't. She'll want to pay him off—and it won't do any good.

NOAH: If I thought he could really guarantee that you wouldn't be inducted, I'd pay him in a minute. But the problem is that if I don't pay him, he probably *can* guarantee that you *will* be inducted right away. So, we've got to get you outta here before they put you in the army.

GLADYS: *(Enters)* Army. . . . What about the army? *(Winces again)*

NOAH: Nothing. I was just asking Danny about his grades. Are you okay, Gladys?

GLADYS: Yes, here's your barbeque, Danny.

Would you mind getting your beer? I think I'm gonna sit down a minute.

DANNY: Hey, please sit, Momma. I don't think I've ever heard you say you wanted to sit down before.

GLADYS: I guess this indigestion has gotten the better of me.

NOAH: The way you've been acting the last few days. I think it is more than indigestion.

GLADYS: I thought nobody noticed. I tried not to let it show.

NOAH: I know. Look, why don't I take you to the emergency clinic right now?

GLADYS: I hate to go to the emergency clinic. If I were really sick, I'd be dead before I saw a doctor. Sometimes I believe that people who work in emergency rooms take a course in how to walk slow and take forever to do anything.

DANNY: If they waited on you real quickly—you would think that the only thing they had to do was to wait on patients.

GLADYS: Noah, I'm going to the clinic first thing tomorrow morning.

NOAH: You're not saying that just to put me off are you?

GLADYS: I promise—I'm going. Danny, did Noah tell you Valery came by?

DANNY: Valery who?

GLADYS: Valery Lawson. She used to babysit with you.

DANNY: Yeah, I remember . . . . She used to bring those classical records over and put them on. I always had to sit and listen to those classical records the whole time she was here. I've hated her and classical music ever since.

GLADYS: I didn't know that. She always seemed like a fine person to me.

DANNY: I think Daddy was taken with her because she always made good grades on his exams.

NOAH: Just goes to show you that making "A's" on exams doesn't have anything to do with common sense.

GLADYS: She said that she wanted to see you before she left.

DANNY: Did she say what she wanted?

GLADYS: No, she didn't. I guess nothing really . . . except to see you.

DANNY: Just as well, I don't have a thing to say to her.

GLADYS: Neither does your daddy.

NOAH: Can we talk about something a little more pleasant? Like . . . are there anymore ribs left, Gladys?

GLADYS: No, Danny's finishing off the last of the ribs.

NOAH: I ought to know better than to expect leftovers after Reverend Thompson gets through eating.

GLADYS: By the way, Danny, Ruth wants her T.V. set fixed. She asked about it today.

DANNY: I'm going to fix it as soon as I get a chance.

GLADYS: She said you've had it almost two months.

DANNY: I haven't had time. Tell Aunt Ruth I'll fix it first chance I get. I've just been so busy with the transmitter . . .

GLADYS: Next time you go messing with that transmitter wear your raincoat, will you?

DANNY: I will . . . if it's raining.

GLADYS: That's what I meant.

NOAH: Danny, you need to take the time and fix Ruth's T.V. set.

DANNY: Okay, I will . . . in fact, I'll go downstairs and work on it right now.

GLADYS: Danny, you never did get your beer, did you? I'll get it now.

DANNY: Sit still, Momma . . .

GLADYS: That's okay, I'm up. *(Exits)*

NOAH: I believe there's some lumber piled in front of your work bench.

DANNY: Lumber? What you gonna do? Build yourself an Ark.

NOAH: The way it's raining out there, maybe I ought to.

DANNY: I thought you were supposed to build the Ark before it started raining.

NOAH: With the price of lumber today, I couldn't afford to build a decent sized row boat. I'm finally going to put up those shelves to store all my books and papers.

DANNY: *(As he exits)* I'll go on down and move the lumber, then. Where do you want me to put it?

NOAH: *(Follows him toward the door)* Stack it over against the back wall! That's where I'm going to put the shelves.

GLADYS: *(Offstage)* We're out of beer.

NOAH: Danny is downstairs. Bring me a glass of water, will you?

GLADYS: You want anything else?

NOAH: No, just a glass of water.

DANNY: Hey! There's water all over the place! It's flooded down there!!! I'm going out to the garage to see if I can rig some kind of a pump or something.

NOAH: Gladys, the basement's flooded! Bring the mop! *(Exits)*

GLADYS: *(Comes on stage on way to basement with mop in hand)* I'm coming! The bucket's downstairs. I didn't think it was raining hard enough to flood.

Blackout

ACT TWO

Scene 1

Next mid-morning. GLADYS *and* RUTH *are in the family room.* RUTH *is being fitted for a new dress that* GLADYS *is making.*

GLADYS: Just water everywhere. It seemed like the more I mopped, the more water there was. I thought we'd never get through.

RUTH: I bet Noah remembers to close the windows from now on.

GLADYS: Danny said he should be able to salvage your T.V. set. It's got to dry out first. All of Noah's papers got wet. All those years of work . . . I told him he should have had another copy somewhere else. Now he's got them spread out all over the house trying to dry them out. I told him all that stuff is never going to dry out while it's still raining outside. Sometimes he listens . . . and then again . . . I told him, "It's just like trying to dry clothes in the house when it's raining outside. They never really get dry." But you know Professor Thompson . . . can't tell him a thing.

RUTH: Ouch!

GLADYS: Sorry Ruth. I'm having a tough time concentrating this afternoon.

RUTH: Is something the matter?

GLADYS: Not really. That is, if there's nothing the matter with being over forty and pregnant.

RUTH: Gladys!! Since when?

GLADYS: I'm a month gone.

RUTH: What does Noah think?

GLADYS: I haven't told him yet? I called his office, but he was in class.

RUTH: Oh, Gladys . . . that is so beautiful.

GLADYS: I'm not sure I can cope with another child this late in life.

RUTH: Oh, I wished it had been me. Gladys, you can cope. Look how well you brought up Danny.

GLADYS: I was looking forward to Danny getting married and bringing my grandchildren over for me to babysit. Now it looks like I'll be asking Danny to babysit for me.

RUTH: Gladys, why don't we put this dress aside. I can wear something else. Adam claims I've got enough clothes to stock a department store, anyway.

GLADYS: I'm not an invalid just because I'm having a baby. Nothing doing. Besides, I need the exercise. Let's see . . . back up a little. I still don't like the way that neckline's fitting. Maybe a couple of darts right here.

RUTH: I think it looks all right like it is.

GLADYS: I don't want you looking tacky . . . folks will be saying "That dress sure looks home-made." There's a difference between homemade and custom made. I want you to be the best dressed woman at that banquet . . . so you can tell everybody where you got your outfit. You're the best advertisement I have for the dress shop. But, if you go out in a tacky looking dress just one time . . .

RUTH: Gladys, you're so talented. I wish I could sew.

GLADYS: Oh, you could, it just takes a little time and patience.

RUTH: But, I could never do it like you do. I hope this rain lets up by tomorrow night. I sure don't want to get this dress wet going to that banquet.

GLADYS: You can get out of the dress now. Come back after work and let me try it on you again. I wish it would stop raining. Noah's shoulder was bothering him again last night. I know it must really hurt him in this damp weather, it always does.

RUTH: Thanks for making me a dress on such short notice. I try to cooperate with the women at church, but sometimes I think they expect me to do the impossible.

GLADYS: I don't mind helping you out. And you know you'll feel guilty if you don't go to the banquet. After all, you are the pastor's wife.

RUTH: Sometimes, I get tired of being the pastor's wife. Every church program that gets scheduled and some that are just thrown together at the last minute . . . I'm expected to be there.

GLADYS: While you got that dress on, I'll go ahead and mark the hem.

RUTH: It's not that I mind working. Lord knows, I put enough energy and time into the church day care center. But what I'm talking about is all this ceremonial stuff. I'm just not up to the spectacle of a room full of well-fed people eating cold peas and cold mashed potatoes just to have an excuse to pass out some plaques.

GLADYS: But Ruth, people have to feel rewarded.

RUTH: I know they do, but it seems to me that doing a good deed and knowing that you did it well ought to be reward enough.

GLADYS: But it's not enough.

RUTH: Besides, the people who get the awards are usually not the ones who did the real work, anyhow.

GLADYS: Yeah, I guess so.

RUTH: I just don't feel like babysitting with a bunch of fifty-year-old matrons when I've got a day care center full of two- and three-year-olds who can't do for themselves. And some of the parents too . . . I've got mothers who are going to have to quit their jobs.

GLADYS: Have to quit work? . . . Why???

RUTH: Their consumer indexes have been re-evaluated. Free day care expenses have been taken off their consumer cards so they can't use our day care center anymore. Imagine a woman, who has tried to help herself by training and getting a job, only to be told that her job places her in a higher consumer category. Now she makes too much to live in public housing and get free day care for her children. But she still doesn't have a high enough consumer index to afford private housing and private day care. So she has to quit her job and stay on welfare.

GLADYS: Sounds like a conspiracy to me. After all, if there are no people on welfare, then there's no need for social workers.

(Doorbell rings)

RUTH: It's not the social workers. It's people who make the policies that the social workers have to carry out. *(Already on the way out)*

GLADYS: Wait a minute, Ruth. Let me get the door. *(Exits)*

RUTH: Okay.

(Fiddles with dress. "Models" for herself in the mirror. GLADYS and ADAM enter)

ADAM: Where's Noah?

RUTH: What are you doing here this time of day?

ADAM: Noah asked me to meet him here.

GLADYS: Did he say what he wanted?

ADAM: I think I better wait and let Noah explain.

GLADYS: Explain what?

ADAM: I don't have all the details, and I don't want to upset you unnecessarily.

RUTH: Adam, don't sound so ominous! You're beginning to scare me.

GLADYS: Maybe I ought to call Noah again.

ADAM: I think he was leaving the office when he called me.

GLADYS: Well, I wish he would hurry up.

RUTH: I'm going to go ahead and get out of this dress now. *(Exits)*

GLADYS: Okay, I'm through for now. What's wrong, Adam?

ADAM: Don't get upset. Everything may be all right by now.

NOAH: *(Enters)* Gladys?

GLADYS: Noah, did you get my call? What's wrong?

NOAH: Is Danny here?

GLADYS: No, doesn't he have a lab this morning?

NOAH: He wasn't in the lab. Has he called?

GLADYS: No, he hasn't. Noah, what's wrong?

NOAH: I'll tell you in just a minute.

ADAM: I made all the phone calls.

NOAH: I just hope they haven't taken Danny yet.

GLADYS: What they? Taken Danny where?

NOAH: Today . . . in my class . . . my class . . . two officials came in and took students out of my class.

GLADYS: For what?

NOAH: To put them in the army. The government is rounding up Black students and putting them in the army. At least they said they were putting them in the army.

GLADYS: Oh, my God!

NOAH: Now, hold on a minute. I don't know what they're doing—but I'm trying to find out.

GLADYS: Did you talk to president Woodard about this?

NOAH: I couldn't. He's out of town.

ADAM: Everytime something goes wrong at this college, the president is out of town. I'm glad my boss doesn't desert me like that.

NOAH: Adam, quit joking.

ADAM: I'm serious! He probably keeps a plane ticket in his desk drawer just so he can leave town whenever there's a problem on campus.

GLADYS: He probably couldn't do anything about it anyway.

NOAH: Yes he could! He could tell those damn army people that they can't come into our classrooms dragging our young men off to fight. No sanctity left in this world, anywhere.

ADAM: If they get away with that, they'll be dragging folks out of the churches next.

NOAH: It's got to stop.

GLADYS: I just hope they haven't taken Danny.

NOAH: If they don't have him now, I'm going to make damned sure they don't get another chance.

ADAM: I brought the gold coins. Are you going to pay off Hemsley?

GLADYS: Pay off Hemsley . . . for what?

ADAM: To keep Danny out of the army.

GLADYS: Noah, what is Adam talking about? Oh, wait a minute. Hemsley is over the draft board . . . . Oh, no! Why didn't you tell me.

ADAM: Never could stand anybody with eyes real close together.

NOAH: Gladys, I didn't want to upset you.

GLADYS: I am upset!!!

NOAH: You were sick, and I didn't want you to worry.

GLADYS: Are you going to pay off Hemsley?

NOAH: No, I'm not.

GLADYS: Oh, please. Pay him . . . pay him . . . Noah.

NOAH: It won't do any good.

GLADYS: Why not? It'll keep Danny safe.

NOAH: He can't guarantee Danny's safety. Just

calm down, honey. I've got it all taken care of.

ADAM: Well, what's the gold for, then.

NOAH: Danny.

GLADYS: Danny? What can he do with the gold?

(RUTH enters)

NOAH: He's taking it with him.

GLADYS: Where?

RUTH: What?

NOAH: Out of the country.

GLADYS: How? You know they won't let anyone leave the country who's draft age.

ADAM: I contacted some church people in the Caribbean. They said they will help us if we can just get Danny over there.

(The two couples carry on two separate conversations simultaneously)

GLADYS: I wonder where he is now.

ADAM: The problem is going to be getting Danny out of the country.

RUTH: The officials have probably stopped giving Black people visas to leave the country, whether they're draft age or not.

ADAM: This is slavery all over again.

NOAH: *(To GLADYS while ADAM and RUTH are talking to each other)* Did you see a doctor?

GLADYS: Yeah, I'm fine.

NOAH: Did you find out what was wrong with you?

GLADYS: Nothing serious . . . don't you worry. *(GLADYS and RUTH exchange glances. GLADYS gets everyone's attention with)* Why don't I fix some sandwiches. I bet nobody's had any lunch.

RUTH: Here, let me help you, Gladys.

ADAM: Anymore of that barbeque left?

NOAH: Are you kidding? Reverend Thompson was here for dinner yesterday.

ADAM: I didn't eat that much!

NOAH: I'm getting ready to make you earn your board. Adam, you still pretty handy with a hammer?

ADAM: I guess so. I haven't tried my hand at it lately, but . . .

NOAH: Roll up your sleeves and come down to the basement with me.

GLADYS: You're not getting ready to work on those shelves while our son is being kidnapped?

NOAH: Call me just as soon as Danny comes in.

ADAM: What the hell are you getting ready to do, Noah?

NOAH: I'm gonna go build me an ark!!

Blackout

Scene 2

Later that same evening, GLADYS *is sitting on the sofa sewing* DANNY*'s jacket.* NOAH *is in the basement, hammering and sawing. We hear the sound effects.* GLADYS *is singing to herself softly.* DANNY *walks in.*

DANNY: Momma, where's Daddy?

GLADYS: *(Drops sewing and runs over to him)* Oh, Danny. We've been so worried. Where have you been? We thought they had taken you.

DANNY: Worried? Who's doing all that hammering in the basement?

GLADYS: Your daddy's in the basement. Go get out of those wet clothes. You just won't listen, will you. *(GLADYS goes to basement door and yells down for NOAH)* Noah!!! Danny's here. Come on up!

NOAH: *(Offstage)* I can't hear you!! *(Sawing stops)*

GLADYS: I said Danny's here!! *(To DANNY as he exits)* Go on and put on some dry clothes. A grown man . . . coming in here wet again.

NOAH: *(Enters)* Boy, where in the hell have . . . Danny? Where did he go?

GLADYS: He went to change clothes . . . . Soaking wet again. Are you sure we're doing the right thing?

NOAH: This is the only way.

GLADYS: How much longer before you're finished?

NOAH: I don't have too much more.

GLADYS: Noah, what's happening to us? I used to think I knew where things were headed . . . we used to make plans . . . but what can you plan for now? There's nothing to hold on to . . . nothing is stable. All those years of working and saving and planning . . .

NOAH: Gladys, Danny is a grown man now. In a few months he would have graduated and moved away anyway.

GLADYS: Yes, but he would have gotten a good job, settled down, gotten married . . . we may not ever get to see him again, Noah.

NOAH: He'll only be a few hundred miles away.

GLADYS: But he can't ever come back. There's no way, no hope.

NOAH: There is hope. If I didn't believe that . . . well anyway . . . there's still some hope.

GLADYS: Noah, what would you say if . . .

(DANNY enters. NOAH sees him)

NOAH: Where have you been?

DANNY: I went to electronics lab this morning, and when I found out what happened, I just got away from there as fast as I could.

NOAH: Why didn't you tell me, or somebody, where you were going?

GLADYS: We were so afraid that you had been taken by the officers.

DANNY: We've been broadcasting all day. Trying to warn people about what's going on.

GLADYS: You should've called home and let us know that you were all right.

NOAH: We need to get you out of the country.

DANNY: *(He is completely taken aback; recovers . . .)* Leave he country? I can't do that.

GLADYS: You could be picked up and sent to Africa to fight in this war, and we wouldn't even know what had happened to you.

DANNY: But I'm needed here. Who's going to run the radio station if I leave?

NOAH: Sometimes the situation dictates that you just get the hell out.

GLADYS: We don't want you to get picked up.

DANNY: I don't want to be picked up either. But I've got to risk it. I've got too much to do here.

NOAH: But you can be more valuable if you get away.

DANNY: Daddy, I put all that equipment together with junk. The other guys couldn't stay on the air for a week if I wasn't around to keep that transmitter working.

NOAH: Danny, do you know what you're doing? You're ego tripping, that's what. You're more interested in turning Danny Thompson into a dead hero than you are in the success of the movement. You're just worried about somebody saying you got scared and ran. Danny, Black people have always known that their first responsibility was survival. Nobody had to tell us that; we just knew. So if you have to run away in order to survive, you run, boy.

DANNY: They haven't caught us yet. Maybe they never will.

NOAH: You know better than that. If you didn't know that it was only a matter of time before they caught you, why were you so worried about your mother and me knowing about the radio station? If they never catch you, they won't ever bother us.

DANNY: Yeah, I guess you're right. You know, the real reason I never worried much about going to the army is because I figured I'd get caught with that transmitter long before they got around to drafting me.

NOAH: Danny, any cause that's worth dying for is worth living for, too. Survival, Danny. Get away; stay alive; and then you choose the battlefield.

DANNY: But where? How and . . . ?

NOAH: Adam has contacted a group that has a training center on an island in the Caribbean. They need people with your skills. And they have some resources . . . not a lot . . . but I'll bet they can get you the materials to build a transmitter that'll reach a lot more people than the one you've got now.

DANNY: What do you think, Momma?

GLADYS: *(Still is not sure)* I think you ought to go, Danny.

DANNY: But...what's going to happen to you and Daddy?

GLADYS: Nothing. We'll keep on going. Just like we've been doing.

NOAH: If you get away, with your energy and creativity, you'll find a way for us to survive too.

DANNY: Daddy, you're preaching. You sound just like Uncle Adam. How are you going to get me out of the country. I can't just go out to the airport and get on a plane.

NOAH: No, no...you can't.

DANNY: Well, how?!

NOAH: In a box.

DANNY: A box?!

NOAH: I've just about finished building you one.

DANNY: How in the world...?

NOAH: It's been done before, Henry Brown got his freedom from slavery by shipping himself to the north in a box.

DANNY: You two are incredible. I think I'm being revolutionary and you come up with something that sounds so, so, so fantastic...it will probably work.

NOAH: Of course it'll work. Worked in the past ...it'll work now, and for the same reason... White folks think we're stupid! Let 'em keep on thinking that, son—it's our ace in the hole!

DANNY: When do I get to see this...box?

NOAH: In a minute. Gladys, you finished sewing those coins in the jacket?

GLADYS: Just about. *(She goes to the sofa, gets the jacket, takes it to DANNY)*

DANNY: What are the coins for?

NOAH: You got gold coins in your jacket to buy what you need.

DANNY: I thought this was your savings.

NOAH: I'm not giving you all of them. But you're going to need something to get you started, and you can spend those gold coins anywhere. I hope that jacket isn't too heavy for you.

DANNY: It's a lot heavier than a "C" card. You know, I remember when we used to have that green paper for money, and you could buy anything you wanted to buy.

NOAH: Well, you could buy anything you had enough of that green paper money to buy.

GLADYS: We're putting some water in plastic bags, and some high protein food.

NOAH: You're being shipped air freight as a piece of church statuary. We've marked "fragile—religious art" all over the box. Even put it on with a stencil to make it look more official.

DANNY: I hope you've got some arrows pointing this side up.

NOAH: I do...probably won't do any good, though. It's going to be a rough ride.

GLADYS: But the inside of the box is padded, so you won't get hurt.

DANNY: I still don't like the idea of running away.

GLADYS: You can't help the cause very much if you're in jail or in the army...or dead.

DANNY: What about all the others? I'm going off and leaving everybody else behind to fight.

NOAH: Daniel, I promise you, I'll help others get away too. Now if I don't hurry up and get this box finished, you might not have the chance to get away. Gladys, call Adam and tell him it's all set.

DANNY: Wait a minute, Momma. I still haven't said I would go.

GLADYS: Danny...

DANNY: I'll tell you what I'll do. When we go out to broadcast tonight, I'll turn the whole thing over to the others. I'll just go along as an observer. If everything works out, I leave in the morning. If not, I stay.

NOAH: What can we say?

DANNY: Okay, show me this box.

NOAH: I call it my ark. Noah's Ark! Son, I'm going to sail you to higher ground.

Fast fadeout

Scene 3

GLADYS *and* RUTH *are onstage waiting for* NOAH *and* ADAM *to return from the airport.* GLADYS *is really worried. She is trying to make light of the situation.*

GLADYS: Lord, you should have seen him.... Danny looked like something from outer space. Noah rigged an oxygen tank...

RUTH: Oxygen tank...?

GLADYS: The one Danny used when he was scuba diving. He had to have air to breathe....Well anyway, then Noah tucked water bags around him.

RUTH: Water bags...?!

GLADYS: For drinking and to help cushion him.

RUTH: Danny must have looked a sight.

GLADYS: Noah even put insulation in the box so Danny couldn't get cold.

RUTH: Could he hear you talking after he was in the box?

GLADYS: Just a little. We had to practically scream, though.

RUTH: Was he standing up or lying down?

GLADYS: Sitting down. *(Goes to look outside)*

RUTH: Sitting down . . . ?

GLADYS: I wonder what's taking them so long?

RUTH: Adam said that he was going to stop by the telegraph office to send a telegram. The church people are supposed to meet the plane.

GLADYS: It's sure taking them a long time to get back.

RUTH: This rain we're having is probably slowing them down. *(GLADYS goes to look at the rain through the patio door)* Adam wasn't too sure that old station wagon was going to get started. You know, that station wagon hasn't been driven in over a year. We just had to quit driving it after they cut our gas allotment.

GLADYS: *(Goes back to hemming the dress)* It's a good thing you all kept that car because the box wouldn't fit in any of these little cars we're driving now.

RUTH: Even the extra allotment of gas we get because Adam's a minister won't fill up that station wagon.

GLADYS: I'm sure Noah will repay Adam for the gas.

RUTH: Oh, I'm not asking you to pay for gas, Gladys. I'm just so thankful we had the car and could do it. In fact, I don't see how you can sit there and sew on that dress for me after all you've been through today.

GLADYS: I know Danny will be able to make it. Ruth, he looked so silly and yet so pathetic. This whole business is just unreal.

RUTH: It's going to be hard to get used to the fact that Danny won't be around. What are you going to say when people start asking about him? Especially, Hemsley from the draft board.

GLADYS: He's not here. I don't know where he is or when he will be back.

RUTH: Those army officials are going to get suspicious, though.

GLADYS: I'm sure they will. You know, Ruth, I hope this baby will be a girl so I won't have to go through this again.

RUTH: Gladys, by that time those folks will be sending women off to war.

GLADYS: I just don't understand folks that take better care of their dogs than they do their children—and . . . and call themselves civilized!

RUTH: What did Noah say when you told him?

GLADYS: I still haven't had a chance yet. I didn't want to add to the confusion while we were trying to get Danny off.

RUTH: You better tell him soon.

GLADYS: I will, I will—just as soon as I get a chance.

(NOAH and ADAM enter. Both have on clerical collars with crosses on chains)

NOAH: Gladys?

GLADYS: In here, Noah. Is Danny okay?

NOAH: The plane should be landing in a couple of hours.

ADAM: Who would question such respectable looking colored gentlemen? *(Goes over to bar and starts fixing a drink)*

NOAH: Yes thank you, I'll have one too, Adam.

ADAM: Coming right up, *Reverend* Thompson.

RUTH: Noah, you could pass for a real preacher in that collar.

ADAM: Yes, we just walked right in, told the baggage clerk we had a parcel that was very heavy . . .

NOAH: . . . and fragile, and that we needed some help. I told him that it had been blessed and was an important piece of church art. Then he made a crack to Adam about the church taking money from the poor to spend on art.

ADAM: That just goes to show how much White folks know about Black churches.

NOAH: It was all we could do to keep a straight face.

GLADYS: Did you send the telegram?

NOAH: Stopped and sent the telegram.

GLADYS: I hope it gets there in time.

NOAH: Danny should be okay, even if he does have to sit in a mail room for a couple of hours.

GLADYS: Well, at least we won't have to worry about Danny getting into trouble with the police again.

RUTH: Again?! I didn't know Danny was having trouble with the police.

ADAM: For once Ruth doesn't know all your business.

GLADYS: I thought I told you. I had intended to. Well, he wasn't really in *trouble*. I mean, he didn't do anything *illegal* or anything. He ordered some fried chicken at this restaurant downtown. *(Pause)* Well, he complained to the waitress about the chicken, that's all. He said the chicken was, well, rare in the middle. Have you ever heard of anybody serving half-raw chicken?

ADAM: White folks like it half-raw.

NOAH: You *claim* to be a Christian—and you're making a blanket statement about a whole race of people.

ADAM: If you had to go to their damned brotherhood banquets all the time and try to *eat* that cold, half-raw chicken, you'd be a little bitter yourself. *(Admiring DANNY's behavior)* Besides, that's not quite all Danny said. He asked the waitress how they cooked their chicken. And she said it was a genuine "soul food" recipe—they pan fried it in lard. Well, Danny must have gotten a little loud.

NOAH: He takes after his uncle.

ADAM: *(Enjoying the story)* He said, "Lard! Woman, the only thing lard is good for is keeping pigs warm in the winter time!" There were two White policemen in the restaurant, and they thought Danny was talking about them. Actually, he was talking about them, but he told them that he only meant that hogs use their excess fat for insulation from the cold and that lard is made from pork fat.

NOAH: Lies like his uncle too.

ADAM: That's not lying, that's survival!

RUTH: Well, what did they do to him.

NOAH: They just issued a warning citation, that's all.

GLADYS: That was enough.

RUTH: I'm really going to miss him.

NOAH: I might as well hang on to this collar, Adam, I have a feeling I'm going to be needing this . . .

ADAM: You're going to quit spreading ignorance and preach the good news.

NOAH: No, I'm going to be sending a lot of Christian art to the Caribbean.

RUTH: If you send too many statues, the government is going to suspect you of something.

NOAH: I'll do it for as long as I can . . . I can't just sit by and watch others suffer. I promised that I would get as many out as I could.

ADAM: *(Takes GLADYS, then NOAH a drink)* Never let it be said that you did more than me.

NOAH: I was counting on using that gas guzzler of yours.

GLADYS: Noah, we need to repay Adam for the extra gas we used today.

ADAM: I put five gallons of gas in the car today, so you owe me a fifth of liquor.

NOAH: Fine, now that's your last drink outta my bottle for the day.

ADAM: Don't you know that the Lord loveth a cheerful giver.

NOAH: That doesn't have anything to do with you sitting here drinking all my liquor.

ADAM: I'm insulted. *(Starts out)* I'm going to leave . . . talking to a man of the cloth like that.

NOAH: Anyone can wear a turned around collar. Take one of those fifths out of the bottom cabinet, and drink your own liquor.

ADAM: *(Goes and sits in chair)* Because I feel so insulted, I think I'm going to stay and have another drink . . . of your liquor.

RUTH: I think you need to go home and drink your own liquor!

ADAM: Huh? What are you talking about?

RUTH: *(Attempts to be confidential)* Noah and Gladys need to be alone.

ADAM: At their age!

NOAH: Hypocrite!!—You're older than I am!

ADAM: Shhh . . . don't tell the whole world.

NOAH: Come on Adam, get your lazy ass out of my chair and let's go downstairs and start building another box.

ADAM: If this keeps up, I'm gonna join the carpenter's union.

NOAH: You aren't that good!

ADAM: Better than no help at all.

NOAH: That's what you think.

ADAM: That's what I know.

NOAH: Now, how do you know?

ADAM: Divine revelation.

Blackout

OWA

Photo by Roger Christiansen

I MET OWA during The Negro Ensemble Company's 1974-75 season when he came to join our Playwrights Workshop. That he had natural talent was immediately evident, and no attempt was made to change his raw, almost tribal style and make him conform to standard playwriting techniques. That he had been inspired by the playwright Oyamo was but another plus in his favor.

Owa has grown immeasurably since he came to the NEC. Recognition by The Eugene O'Neill Playwrights Conference is but one attestation to this.

The play here, *Transitions for a Mime Poem* [directed in a staged reading by Kalima, with Gylan Kane and Loretta Greene, and moderated by Townsend Brewster] is taken from his *Study in Transcendence,* one of four written while a member of the NEC Workshop under the collective title, *The Soledad Tetrad.* The others are: *A Short Piece for a Naked Tale (A Study in Chaos); That All Depends on How the Drop Falls (A Study in Direction)* and *Rejections (A Study in Development).* Owa tells me that it is "based on the metaphysical system of *solar-tetragramation.*" However, its inclusion in this anthology says more eloquently than he—for his plays are an eloquent, but powerful spokesman—or I, why he has to be regarded as one of this country's most potent writers. I am not alone in my prediction that he will be an influence on writers to come.

Steve Carter, Dramaturg
Negro Ensemble Company
St. Marks Place, New York City

Owa has done work as a photojournalist in East Afrika and Europe. Some of his additional credits include productions at La Mama ETC, Urban Arts Corps, Brooklyn College, City University of New York, Hudson Valley Freedom Theatre, Bijou Theatre, and Eugene O'Neill National Playwrights Conference. He was the first Rockefeller Writer-in-Residence at the Frank Silvera Writers Workshop in Harlem, U.S.A.

There are many stories that could be told about *Transitions for a Mime Poem;* Pamela Poitier made her debut on the New York stage in this play, and many other wonderful people have worked with it. There are also a fair share of horror stories too. However, the most important thing is the play was written a living memorial to George and Jonathan Jackson and the Soledad Brothers.

THE SOLEDAD TETRAD, PART II:
TRANSITIONS FOR A MIME POEM

Owa

to my Dandy Dada and my Mummy O-live

CHARACTERS

A MAN
A WOMAN

SOME NOTES FROM THE AUTHOR

Transitions for a Mime Poem *is a play that relies very much in the main on the body language of the players; mime is the devise used to explain and explore the inner mechanism of human patterns and behavior in terms of ongoing life. The poetry is intended here as the medium of exchange, through which we might obtain the most poignant human expression in its more spiritual sense, at times grandiose and high flown as well as well spoken, while on the other hand, simplistic yet deeply personal. The songs attempt to convey, through Afro-Jazz Ballad and Afro-American Gospel technique, the purest expression of human faith in the intrinsic goodness of man's destiny and ultimate hope.*

Music as a pastiche could be of extreme value in setting of tone and mood for the piece in terms of its production values. The attitude of the play lends itself quite freely in its ritual tempo and dialogical cadence to the smooth and ethereal atmosphere of Afro-Jazz composition, perhaps finding its sublimest inspiration to the accompaniment of the more traditional instruments in the Oriental and Afrikan repertoire such as the gator-horn; the tabla, shakare, talking drum, marimba, and thumb-piano, to name a few. Conventional Western instruments like the violin and the horn or flute can be of use too, even sticks, glass jars with water and rubber tubing can find a place, creating the sounds that would help to underline the play in a holistic approach.

Though there is no provision in the script for a defined "set" as such—the creative use of masks hanging like mobiles could be used by the players as an aid to transitions in the production.

In regards to the actual text of the play from the viewpoint of the actor, much of it can be considered subtextual. The preparation for character understanding and, hence, development would start in the personality creation, *beginning with the essential components of the "anima" and "animus"—of* the respective characters. *I am indeed talking about the "cycology" of the archetypes, by which I mean to say, the cycle of idea, attitude and mood constructions that swells to the emotional wave-front, producing the characters' impulses, compulsions, reactions and responses. Those aforementioned considerations apply to the characters' animal and spiritual natures.*

A line may not necessarily express a "truth" for the character, so much so as it reflects a position that is more subjective in its dependence on the objective exchange of human interaction. Moreover, the "true" response may find exposure in the character's posture vis-à-vis one another and the situational determinants.

These factors must not, however, allow themselves to obscure the many bonding elements of what is "real" and what is "really felt" by the characters. For the elements sometimes mesh and at times confront and conflict with the characters' own personal sense of self and condition.

A PLAY IN ONE ACT FOR MIME, DANCE, AND VOICE

Setting: Bare; a black house

Sound: Overture—shakare/violin

Voice:
La-il la-ha—il la hu
La-il la-ha—il la hu
La-il la-ha—il la hu
La-il la
La-il la
La-il la
Ha—il la
Ha—il la
Ha—il la
Ha—il la—il La-il la
il la il la il la il la
Hu-la-il la ha—il la hu
La-il la-ha—il la hu il
la hu.

Sound: Gong—Gong—Gong—Gong

Lights: A warm orange wash emerges like the new day sun, revealing s.l., the MAN—*pushing against an invisible wall. As he strains, the Shakare is a furious rattle— He relaxes—He pushes and strains again— He relaxes, resigned to the fixity of the wall in bewildered vexation —Only for a moment though —He palms the air as if he were in an invisible glass box, a stifling enclosure of terrifying containment. . . . In an attempt to defy the authorative finality of box/wall, he attacks the illusion violently, and with equal violence the wall repulses his efforts and sends him reeling along a corridor of multidimensional walls u.s.c., where he freezes, again contained.*

The WOMAN *in freeze pushing against her own wall repeats the same action as her male counterpart. She ends up d.s.r.*

WOMAN: He sits like a pre-historic myth in a cave—
MAN: As the sounds of giant motors roar with their horse-powered screams
　　(Sounds)
　　　Screams—
　　　　(Sounds)
　　　　　Screams—
And Crashes in the Darkness Outside . . .

WOMAN: As if they were frightful beast—
　　Howling
　　Howling
　　Howling
　　Monstrous Howling for Blood!
　　　　And i think to myself—

MAN:	WOMAN:
All the while	All the while
i don't live here	i don't live here
i don't feel	i don't feel
i belong here	i belong here
i sure don't!	i sure don't!

　　(Sound: tabla—simulates the human heartbeat for sixty seconds; violin—contrapuntal screech)
MAN: Change—i hunger for change! . . . Looking for change—Waiting for change . . . *(Beat)* Hoping for change . . . . Being changed. Seeing change. To give a completely different form. To alter, vary, modify, transform and transmute— Transitions, the change of one thing to another.
　　(Both tabla and violin compete in cacophony)
MAN: I Am Changes—I Am The Revolutionary —I Said I Am The Revolutionary!!!
　　(The WOMAN *cartwheels x and crashes into the wall)*
WOMAN: —So is a wheel, sugar!
　　(Sound: One funky blast of the brass—silence)
MAN: You just violated my rights to public—
WOMAN: —nuisance . . . . Perhaps?
MAN: What about the wall?
WOMAN: The wall was here before you came.
MAN: And, i take it, will be here after i'm gone.
WOMAN: It's really very simple. We'll just have to deal with it.
MAN: This is an urgent situation that requires an urgent reaction!
WOMAN: Response—Not reaction—Response. We both want change. An alteration that varies an already modified situation that will constantly transform itself—That calls for a response!
MAN: You respond if you want to—I'll react!
WOMAN: And how far will that get you?
MAN: As far as you let me go with it.
WOMAN: I beg your pardon?
MAN: I believe in taking what i hafta—And giving back what *you* can. *(He grabs her, he kisses her long and hungry with a lusty love of life)* They usta call me the kissing bandit.
WOMAN: —You musta been robbin' em blind! . . . For starters, how do you do—
MAN: —the things that i do—Fine, and you?

WOMAN: Somehow i feel just a little bit strange. Perhaps if we were a little more familiar.

MAN: To one another?

WOMAN: That's a possibility you can't rule out.

MAN: Rule it out!

WOMAN: Why?

MAN: I am the soldier. There is very little room for familiarity, except with my weapon of course.

WOMAN: At least to thine own self be true.

MAN: Now what could cause you to say that?

WOMAN: Oh never mind—There seems to be a wall here.

MAN: Please, i want to know what you're about. Things like that. Maybe there is a little-bitty room for familiarity?

WOMAN: I'm searching for a point of conscious awareness. *Something real!!*—Human contact . . .

MAN: When you find it—let me know. Human contact, does not compute—Does not seem to follow.

WOMAN: You're impossible!

MAN: Where are you from?

WOMAN: That's a good question.

MAN: I'm part of the landscape.

WOMAN: Really?

MAN: Sure, i came over on a cruise. I'm one of the older members of the community.

WOMAN: You mean like the Mayflower and stuff?

MAN: Gee, i never thought of it like that. But i guess you could say that there were plenty of job openings in the neighborhood—y'know what i mean?

WOMAN: And you stayed?

MAN: *(Shackled, wide leg position, hands x o'head)* No—i was kept!

WOMAN: I know a lot about being kept.

MAN: You mean like hungry in the soul, ignorant in the mind and fearful in the heart?

WOMAN: Something like that. Maybe not in that order.

MAN: What do you mean not in that order?

WOMAN: People have different kinds of experiences—Priorities. One person's microbe is another's yogurt.

MAN: You sound as if you think you know what you're talking about.

WOMAN: My aren't we touchy—Why shouldn't i—I mean, why shouldn't i know what i'm talking about?

MAN: What do you know that i don't know?

WOMAN: All i know is what i feel.

MAN: You may not know anything—What you feel—Can you see a river of blood that flows slow and thick through a jungle of pain, where it meets a vast sea of blinding light?

WOMAN: Only because i don't have eyes right?—

Now you wait just—

MAN: —No!—You wait a minute. Don't tell me anything about your feelings or nuthin' else for that matter.

WOMAN: Why?

MAN: Because i don't have feelings—For nuthin' or nobody!

WOMAN: Talking to you is like talking to a wall.

MAN: *(Silence)*

WOMAN: We want change, agreed?

MAN: Agreed.

WOMAN: What about the wall?

MAN: . . . Well, what about the wall?

WOMAN: Thinking like that is what got you in here.

MAN: I really don't know how i got in here. But i am getting out.

WOMAN: Oh yeah?

MAN: Oh yeah.

WOMAN: Have you got a plan?

MAN: Have i got a plan?—Have i got a plan?—Yeah but it's secret.

WOMAN: Most plans are.

MAN: Listen, i don't need you to hassle my mind—You understand. Just raise and quick!

WOMAN: What an awful state of mind. What are you afraid of?

MAN: I am afraid of nothing. Fear is feeling. I said i don't have feelings. Fear is a feeling. I don't have feelings. Therefore i am afraid of nothing.

WOMAN: You must be dead?

MAN: Or dying . . . *(Calling her, wanting her to listen)* Too slow to be dead . . . too much alive to die. *(He twirls into a Hathra mode)*

WOMAN: What do you call yourself doing. What kind of foolishness is that?

MAN: I am not to be considered foolish. This is a high and Holy manner in which to communicate with the Atom of all existence.

WOMAN: Just what are you doing?

MAN: *(With the accent of an ancient Indian Holy man)* Seeking Nirvana.

WOMAN: And what are you going to do for an encore?

MAN: A resurrection. What else?

WOMAN: You're the one going through the changes.

MAN: A turn for the worst. A turn for the better. An exercise in futility.

WOMAN: I think we better make a doorway to one another. I pray to God we can.

MAN: There is nothing to pray to or for.

WOMAN: I don't understand you. A moment ago you were in a high and Holy state—Seeking Nirvana. There is a Creator. The Creator is our only hope.

MAN: Who created this? *(He slaps the wall)*—I ask myself, who created this? And i think about Hell.

WOMAN: Hell is a very sick illusion created by very sick minds for very sick needs.

MAN: Hell is a cruel joke. Where some miserable Devil laughs at the idiots who don't know the difference between a hole in the ground and reality—Well i do!—I'm right here right now. And the pain tells me; this is Hell. The torment is Hell. The pain is Hell. The pain is real.

WOMAN: Did you say pain?

MAN: I said pain.

WOMAN: Pain is a feeling. To know pain, one must feel. Pain is the most telling of human feeling.

MAN: An oversight, so sue me. I want to find a way out of here.

WOMAN: If you got out. . . . Would you know what you were getting into?

MAN: Getting out is a pursuit. There is an echo somewhere in the recesses of my soul that screams—Pursuit!

WOMAN: Pursuit. Pursuing me. . . . Yesss, that's it —Don't you see? Happiness is an object in this livelong life. An object of pursuit.

MAN: Where is it?

WOMAN: Tell me about it?

MAN: Tell you about pursuit or happiness?—You must be joking. You have to be joking. You just have to be.

WOMAN: No joke—And you better get your thing together, fella.

MAN: And you better have a more respectful attitude. Anyway, who are you?

WOMAN: Gee, i thought you'd never ask.

MAN: I'm asking—Who are you?

WOMAN: Some think, just an endless hole. A hairy pit, soaking up fluid memories like the thirsty desert cactus. With needles of crystalized fire. A warm giving comfort. I am flashing eyes. A revealing mouth. A tummy round as apples, crisscrossed with the baleful tracks of stretch marks. The road of life for the newborn traveller. I am the land of thunder in the cloudless sky. In the realm of the red light district, where the sun is a misshapen womb that bleeds quicksilver cords of eternity, winding its way to the broad avenues of despair or destiny.

MAN: I'm sorry i asked.

WOMAN: I am a woman. That's who i am—I am a woman. The truth—

MAN: —The truth is the truth!

WOMAN: And nothing else but! And the truth in this case—I am a woman.

MAN: The truth being truth, if you say you are a woman, then i guess you are a woman.

WOMAN: And nothing else but.

MAN: Well i don't know. If you wish to press the issue, it is a fact, you are a woman. But for the truth of it—

WOMAN: —C'mon now, you just said—

MAN: You don't need to remind me of what i just said. That's the trouble with the world today— Always and forever quoting!

WOMAN: All right, all right. Just so long as we understand that the truth is the truth.

MAN: I just said that.

WOMAN: Wel-l-l-l, i do have a question.

MAN: As long as it ain't a repeat.

WOMAN: You just said that the truth is the truth—

MAN: I did and i also said no repeats.

WOMAN: How can it be anything else—The truth —That is?

MAN: There is no truth in this world—That is the only truth as such. There is fact, and once recognized as such it becomes knowledge; and when it is applied knowledge, it becomes our only salvation.

WOMAN: That's a fact?

MAN: Exactly.

WOMAN: I'm not sure i understand fully.

MAN: Simple—I am me and you are you and those are the facts.

WOMAN: What are the facts concerning this wall?

MAN: It is there.

WOMAN: I know that. I know the wall is there.

MAN: There where?

WOMAN: *(She demonstrates)* There.

MAN: Can you see it?

WOMAN: That does not mean it is not there.

MAN: *(He demonstrates)* Or here . . . . That is the fact of the wall.

WOMAN: I think i like you. You seem so wise and knowing.

MAN: I think i like you too. You seem so understanding.

WOMAN: There is a need, if i could get closer to you. Feel what you're about.

MAN: I don't really know if any two human beings can get any closer.

WOMAN: I think we have a relationship. There is so much to give.

MAN: What is there to give?

WOMAN: Why do you ask?

MAN: Because there is nothing to give. Perhaps even less to share. Anyway, i'd like to know, can i take you out sometime?

WOMAN: Anytime you like.

(He bows, she curtsies. Heavenly dance music, something warm and cuddly as they do the cheek to cheek. The music stops, fading low and away)

MAN: Come to me.

WOMAN: Now? . . . Yes, now.

MAN: I need you . . . I need you so very much.

WOMAN: I have so much to give. Love me.

(The lights turn a deep red)

MAN: I fear of loving. I fear of feeling. Yet i need you. Your love. Lest i walk in the way of some error, some grief.

WOMAN: *(The lights go down)* Try to love. Please, our salvation depends on the love. *(A spot on her)* . . . You can touch me. Like the light of the sun. I open like a radiant morning glory, each petal folding back, laying bare the interior. Where you can reach inside and touch me. I think you are.

MAN: *(Red lights up again)* I am i think. Is that reality?—Maybe yes—maybe no. But you must admit, it is logical. Though there is urgent doubt that still there is nothing to give.

WOMAN: Give yourself a chance.

MAN: Where i come from chances are taken not given.

WOMAN: That is probably the problem.

MAN: What problem?

WOMAN: Everything is left to chance.

MAN: No chance of problems. Are you trying to make problems?

WOMAN: No.

MAN: No what?

WOMAN: No, i am not trying to make problems.

MAN: No problems—good! *(He falls asleep. She cradles his head in her lap)*

WOMAN: Well, how many times can i ask: What is he like? *(Laughter)* Selfish, insensitive, even childish—Well he needn't be. He should be about himself. Yet willing to take time out from himself. . . . To give to those around him. With me, he could take more than time out for himself. He could invest himself with me—Something he said about sharing. He can give!—Hoping his giving will please me. Giving simply because he enjoys being a part of my life. He is giving because he is generous and romantic. And the pay-off—He is receiving from me when he is giving. . . . I got it!!

MAN: Wha-wha?

WOMAN: I Got It!!

MAN: You got what, woman?

WOMAN: A Key—We Can Feel Our Way Out!!

MAN: Yeah!—Just think it. If you think of its no longer being there.

(They both begin to crawl along the wall)

WOMAN: It's no longer there and no guilt.

MAN: Guilt!—Did you commit something?

WOMAN: Only myself.

MAN: Good start. Jolly good start. The joint!

WOMAN: Oh i feel so happy—Like when i was a little girl and today is my birthday or daddy was coming home. I am happy.

MAN: Will you marry me?

WOMAN: Will i marry you—Ohhh. *(She bursts into sobs)*

MAN: Hey-hey, i didn't mean to make you unhappy i—

WOMAN: Oh you silly man—i am happy—i'm so happy i could cry.

MAN: ???—Yeah right.

WOMAN: Well?

MAN: Huh?

WOMAN: You said you wanted to marry me.

MAN: Oh—I take thee to wife.

WOMAN: And i take thee to husband.

MAN: Form, what lovely form.

WOMAN: Content, what meaningful content.

MAN: Blessed is the lamb—

WOMAN: —that ends up in the stewpot!

MAN: What shall he be?

WOMAN: She will be a queen.

MAN: A king.

WOMAN: A queen.

MAN: A king.

WOMAN: A queen.

MAN: He must far outstrip his potential and extend beyond the boundary of his limitations. Oh Lord, send me a king.

WOMAN: She must rise to the full splendor of her beauty and walk in the way of wisdom. Oh Isis, send me a queen.

MAN: My son, oh my son; the standard that all others shall seek to rise to.

WOMAN: My daughter, my precious gem of a daughter; that all others are gracious to kneel before.

MAN: Freedom—

WOMAN: —is choice.

MAN: My son must be free.

WOMAN: My daughter must have a choice.

MAN:	WOMAN:
That's why a king.	That's why a queen.

(She flings her dance skirt over her head and it becomes a suggestion of the eternal shroud, enveloping the living pain of childbirth. Her mutterings in tongues, her screams of sharp, ever-deepening labored agony become the hypnotic magnetism for him in a dance of intense ecstasy. The man upright in fetal position, as if to make prayer after the fashion of the East—Born to worship, in a slow rise, hands in praise to the Sun . . .)

MAN: Mama—Mama—Ma?

WOMAN: Oh my baby son.

MAN: Mama—Ma—Ma.

WOMAN: What a strong voice. What a strong man he will be.

MAN: Ma—Why is this wall here? What does it

do—What is it for? There is mystery—Ma?

WOMAN: Touch is a beautiful feeling. Let me touch you.

MAN: Ma, this wall—This wall, Ma. Will there be pain? There is mystery.

WOMAN: There will always be pain. There will always be joy. For they are both but simple illusions. I name you —Shamek

MAN: Shamek—I like that name. Shamek.

WOMAN: To you it will mean King of the Holy City. A city without walls, without brick or mortar. Your soul is the Holy City and you are its king, Shamek.

MAN: And what are the duties of the king in the city of the soul?

WOMAN: To rule with discretion. To judge with deliberation. To tax in moderation. To love the Lord of Creation.

MAN: The Lord of Creation?

WOMAN: The Sun.

MAN: The Sun?

WOMAN: The Lord of Creation.

MAN: Is there nothing above the Sun?

WOMAN: Only the Father. And to love the Sun is to love the Father. Every day is a testament of the Father's love for the Sun. There is no gold brighter than the Ray of the Sun in the morning of the new day. The Universe is redeemed in the Glory of the Light of the Sun. The resurrection of the Earth from the death of Night is possible only through the Sun. I am your Mother, your Earth.

WOMAN:	MAN:
Wommm.	You are my tree.
Wommm.	Rooted, steadfast in all
Wommm.	Divinity.
Wommm.	The Master of Harmony.
Pied Piper of–	irresistible melodies that
draws the children–	of the Light to the edge
of a new horizon–	Mother, the Sun loves you.

MAN: My daughter. My dear sweet daughter.

WOMAN: I am what they say i do.

MAN: For what reason?

WOMAN: Father, there is no reason without pain.

MAN: Daughter, there is no pain without reason.

WOMAN: The word is—

MAN: —the word is not the thing, daughter.

WOMAN: Then there is no word for it.

MAN: Shamekka, Queen of the City of the Soul is there a word for the thing that you do?

WOMAN: I am that that i am and i do what i do.

MAN: As your father, can i believe that?

WOMAN: I am Shamekka, Queen of the City of the Soul. As the Father is above the Sun—So likewise will the Daughter be below the Mother. I would have you believe that is much better than this.

MAN: There is much marvel to behold—That better than this.

WOMAN: I have questions placed before me. I seek my answer in you.

MAN: The question?

WOMAN: Can i be gay?

MAN: The answer, only in spirit.

WOMAN: The spirit moves.

MAN: I will tell you a story, Shamekka . . . This ol' world is Roman 'round about the globe. Russian into something old, something new—Pisces sending Jus'us, the fisherman over the Neptune Blue. And many a lot were cast by the catchers upon the trident spike—A grim image indeed.

Three points on the ocean Atlantean
A triangular middle passage
Where the carps delight
With molecule reason
To fling a body below

The briny deep of Dawoud's
Never so Bible black
As the Dark Age
When the light 'twas cast
Out

A demon dance of sugar coated souls
As slow as crude molass
Greed
Half-lie
And ignorance

Those most unholy Trinity
That correlates this Tragedy
And heads took part
From the very start
In foul and evil deed

Blood
Mayhem
Their despicable creed
Noble souls better fettered
Than freed

Riches
Power
And Glory
Increase their might
The Orb aghast in stricken fright

Till the Galaxy
And upon the Throne of the Lord
They do indeed
With upstarts heart
Fix their sight

Justice bowed in rattling chain
As Commerce in her fortune gain
Great men
In greater error
Rush upon us
The times when babes
Their hair bleached white
In terror at the assault
Of the flesh against
The ramparts of the Soul
And Mankind would hurl
Down into the dungeon of desire
And bound with fetid cord
Of lowered emotions
The lofty perogatives
Of so Kingy a race
In modern time
The pulsated drum
And sensuous lyric
Do conspire to pepper
The blood in hot steamy mist
That cloud the vision

And banish to dormant plane
The chaste
While mixing seed
Egg and spit
In Hellish waste

Never a good nor wise Father
Would implore the child
Whom or how to love
That being a private province
Of which property must remain
Inviolate

Yet as to the nature of Love
My station does permit me
To relate

All the world's gain is wrought
By love of Love
So too all the World's loss
Be purchased by love of Hate

You see, Love can be a sword
With double edge
That cuts quick and slow alike

For when we set our view
To see Love in sight
Of contentment and happiness
For oneself
Have we not likeness of
The robber's oath
To take and fill our pockets
With the wealth of another?

Love is the eternal magic
That radiates from the within
To the without
In that share has Love triumphant
Over human lust
And Earthly dust

Your Mother has birthed you
With the greatest Love of all
Choice in will
You are free to drink of carnal swill
As well as climb atop
Life's highest hill

From the gift of P'tah
Are we given two eyes
One to see the Abysmal
The other to see
The light

In summary let me say
'Tis a little of this
And a little of that.

WOMAN: That's that.
MAN: Let us reason together my sister.
WOMAN: Wha's happenin' brotha luv?
MAN: Let me bind up the wounds my sister.
WOMAN: Brotha, where are you?
MAN: Are you she, sista?
WOMAN: Come . . .
MAN: Kummmm?
WOMAN: I am not she, my brotha.
MAN: Where is she?
WOMAN: She went thataway!
MAN: Who?
WOMAN: Justice.
MAN: When was she here last?
WOMAN: When there was power and glory.
MAN: What happened?
WOMAN: She took it with her—Can you dig that?
MAN: Will she return?
WOMAN: She might—it won't.
MAN: In that case—
WOMAN: In case of what?
MAN: A case of this or that huh?
WOMAN: The general purpose of the this or that
    principle is to balance through design an error in
    one element which may be negative by an equal
    but opposite error which is positive.
MAN: I'm afraid i don't understand.
WOMAN: I'm afraid you don't understand.
MAN: You don't say?
WOMAN: I do say—Now listen to me. I have a
    statement to make.
MAN: *(With amorous intent again)* Can it wait?

WOMAN: Weight broke the wagon down.

MAN: Then you better hurry up.

WOMAN: Be it known by these presents—

MAN: Presents—What presents?

WOMAN: I state my case. *(There is absolute chaos. The sounds of mechanized warfare drones and screams)* It looks like we need a hero, brotha!

MAN: Are you in the habit of repeating yourself?

WOMAN: It looks like we need a hero, brotha.

MAN: *(Silence)*

WOMAN: I said it looks like we need a hero, brotha.

MAN: How much does it pay?

WOMAN: All you can take, brotha.

MAN: I'll take it!—And i'll take it sum mo'—I'll take it and i'll take it again—I'll take it!!! *(The din stops as abruptly as it started. He continues with the harrangue)* I'll take it—Do ya' hear me—I'll take it and take it some!! *(Silence—embarrassed silence)* . . .

WOMAN: Excuse me. Are you all right?

MAN: Mam, ah say, a hero is always a'right. And you can betcha gold medal on that!

WOMAN: Well about this wall?

MAN: Who are you?

WOMAN: I am you.

MAN: I don't understand that. If you are me, then who am i?

WOMAN: You are the light by which i am seen. *(Lights to silhouette)*

MAN: You are a shadow.

WOMAN: If i am a shadow, then you are the Phantom.

MAN: If you ask me—Everything here is a Phantom—the wall—you.

WOMAN: I am your shadow, you are my Phantom. In the doorway of life you are the deviation of light.

MAN: The deviation of light?

WOMAN: Light waves are assumed to travel in a straight line. A body will stop the wave of light in direct proportion to its mass, creating the Phantom outline of that body. There is little light where the shadow falls.

MAN: —Phantoms—Shadows?

WOMAN: —The shadow is the mark of the Phantom. Therefore, you are the light by which i am seen. However you see yourself, so you will see me.

MAN: Where am i?

WOMAN: At the center of gravity in inner space.

MAN: Can you tell me what that means?

WOMAN: At the center of gravity, all things are fixed in their relation to you. All things rotate on your great axis. Turning on the poles in the universe of your own creation.
(Sings)
In inner space you'll find your place
So you better get going
Get going!
Don't let it be said
You spent your time in bed
Where you dallied
When you should've sallied
Into that beautiful place
Known as your inner space
(Speaks)
That's where you want to be.

MAN: *(Sings)*
Yeah—Yeah—Yeah—Yeah
That's where i wanna be
That's where i oughta be
That's where i better be
If anyone should look for me
That's where i'm gonna be
Yeah—Yeah—Yeah—Yeah
(Speaks)
Where i can really be free. My own inner space.

WOMAN: There are no walls that can hold you in that place. You can stay there as long as you want to, as long as you have to or longer than you need to. You must always remember that.

MAN: To me, a place like inner space is somewhere i need to go to get in touch with the me i always wanted to know. I can explore a new landscape and make some real discoveries. A place i can call home.

WOMAN:
I stand at the threshold of the dawning
   of a new age.
As the sounds of many rushing waters
Hum a sweet song in my heart
And as i move off into the future
With careful certain steps
I can feel the warm caress
Of the sun as it kisses
My Soul

MAN: And all the while
I think to myself

MAN:	WOMAN:
I do live here	I do live here
I feel that i belong	I feel that i belong
I sure do . . .	I sure do . . .

Black

CRYSTAL RHODES

"I DIDN'T LIKE the first play I wrote, so I decided to try again, and I came up with this one," says Crystal V. Rhodes, author of the one act play, *The Trip*. Since that time she has written two more plays, all comedies, but *The Trip* will always be special to her. "It was the first of my plays to be produced. It was the first time that I actually heard "my" words being spoken on stage. It was thrilling."

Crystal is a native of Indianapolis, Indiana, and now resides in California. A graduate of Indiana University, she holds a Master's degree in Sociology from Atlanta University and spent several years employed in the areas of counseling and social work before pursuing writing as a career. "I wanted to be a writer, and eventually I got tired of doing something other than what I really wanted to do with my life. I had always written . . . short stories . . . articles, everything I could write, and I had always been good at it, but somewhere along the way I had lost the desire to really promote my writing talent and to see where that talent could take me."

Eventually, stifled by a boring job and encouraged by family and friends, she revived her writing skills, packed her bags, and moved westward to California. She chose California because her ultimate goal is to write for television. "The television medium has a lot of influence on Black children, and I feel that it's important that the images of Black people on television be shaped by the people who know them best, Black writers."

In working toward this goal, the author has realized her ambition to some extent. Her play, *The Trip,* has been video taped for presentation on cable television in the Bay Area. "I produced the show. I've learned all that I could about the television medium since I moved west. By not only writing, but producing my own work, as a writer I retain artistic control, and that's important."

Presently the prolific author is working on several more plays and teleplays and is in the process of completing a book. She hopes to produce even more of her works for television in the future.

THE TRIP

Crystal Rhodes

NIKKI: *An introverted personality, she wants to be more dominant but must develop her assertiveness. She has been dominated all of her life by personalities much stronger than her own. In situations of crisis, however, she displays leadership abilities unrecognized by her peers.*

VICTORIA: *Fairly assertive at times and is often the mediator when disagreements arise between her companions. She displays leadership abilities and is not easily dominated by others.*

JO ANNE: *A chronic complainer, she is a totally negative personality. She is argumentative, aggressive to a fault, demanding, and self-centered. She is basically an insecure individual and harbors feelings of jealousy towards her companions.*

GINNY: *A leader, she is aggressive, sure of herself, and assertive. She serves as the dominant personality among her companions. She rejects feelings of defeat, but displays a lack of self-confidence when faced with a crisis situation.*

Setting: The interior of a car. Four chairs sit in the center of the stage facing the audience. Two chairs sit side by side; two chairs sit behind them, positioned so that the occupants can be seen by the audience. The chairs are occupied by the young women. Each one is dressed casually in blue jeans and T-shirt. Luggage is stacked up behind the women in the back two chairs.

A PLAY IN ONE ACT

Scene 1

The three passengers are waving goodbye to the city of Chicago as they head toward a California vacation. GINNY is driving; NIKKI sits beside her; JO ANNE sits behind NIKKI, and VICTORIA sits behind GINNY.

WOMEN: *(Unison)* Goodbye Chicago. Goodbye . . . Goodbye.

NIKKI: Goodbye State Street!

VICTORIA: Goodbye Lake Michigan!

JO ANNE: Good Riddance!

GINNY: California sunshine here we come!!

VICT: Hallelujah!!

NIKKI: I can't wait!

GINNY: I don't know, I'm going to miss the Windy City for these two weeks.

JO ANNE: Sure Ginny, you're a swinging single in the big city. I'm an old married woman. My thrills are few and far between.

VICT: Old married woman! Jo Anne, you and Charles have been married for eighteen months. Don't tell me it's over already??

JO ANNE: Believe me Victoria, if I hadn't been looking forward to this trip for so long, I'd be in bed right now, and I wouldn't be by myself.

GINNY: Well alright!
(Everyone laughs)

VICT: I still can't believe we're going. Fifteen years ago we said we were going to do this and now, look at us, we're actually on our way.

NIKKI: A lot of time's passed. We'll all be thirty years old this year. It took a long time, but we got ourselves together. Good lord, today I feel like that fourteen year old freshman that Ginny took pity on and befriended.

GINNY: Aw girl, be for real.

VICT: Don't feel bad Nikki, at least your mother didn't force your friendship on the three of you like mine did. I've never been so embarassed in my life. She just pushed me on poor Ginny; I thought Ginny's mother would change telephone numbers, Mama called her so much.

JO ANNE: Your mother's a social climber. She wanted you to rub elbows with the idle rich.

NIKKI: Who's rich?

JO ANNE: You and Ginny.

GINNY: Girl, you know we're not rich!

JO ANNE: Come on Ginny! the Hyde Park area of Chicago is a long way from the State street housing projects where Victoria and I came from.

VICT: Aw, that's water under the bridge. I sure don't want to remember those days. We've come a long way since then.

JO ANNE: Thank God! Sometimes I sit in our apartment and look out over the lake and I just want to drop down on my knees and say thank you... thank you Lord for taking me out of the projects!

VICT: I heard that! Mama almost killed herself trying to move us out of those projects. I will always be grateful.

GINNY: Hey, stop it now! We said we weren't going to look back. We've been planning this trip for months and we're finally on our way. This is our first vacation together since we've known each other; let's talk about good things. *(Turns to NIKKI)* How many hours to St. Louis?

(NIKKI looks at the map carefully, tracing the distance as she does so)

NIKKI: We're here... this far from Chicago. We've got about an hour... maybe an hour and a half to go.

JO ANNE: *(Groans)* We should have started earlier. It'll be ten o'clock at night before we get there. I told you Ginny, we should have left sooner.

VICT: O.K. JoAnne, I know what you're thinking. Go on, blame me. It's my fault we started late. We shouldn't have stopped by my mama's house.

JO ANNE: You've got to admit, your mother can talk.

VICT: If I hadn't stopped by and seen that woman, she would have made my life hell when I got back to Chicago!

GINNY: Don't worry about it Vic, we're just a little behind schedule. No big deal. Do the three of you want to stop and get something to eat before we reach St. Louis or should we eat when we get there? *(There is no response))* Well? What do you want to do?

NIKKI: I don't know.

VICT: Whatever the group decides.

JO ANNE: We should have brought some food with us. I told you that, Ginny. It wouldn't be a problem if you had listened to me.

GINNY: *(Agitated)* Well we didn't bring anything, Jo Anne, except some junk food, so what do you want to do? *(Once more there is no response. Disgusted)* Nikki, look in my purse and give me a stick of gum.

(NIKKI opens the purse on the seat next to GINNY, takes a piece of gum out, unwraps it and hands it to GINNY. GINNY sticks the gum into her mouth)

GINNY: Anybody else want some?

(The response is negative. VICTORIA reaches into the back of the car and gets a bag of potato chips. Sitting back in her seat, she opens the bag)

VICT: I'm glad you rented a station wagon, Nikki, we need the room for all this junk we brought. Especially you, Jo Anne. We told you to pack lightly and bring one suitcase. Look at all of this stuff, and your suitcase must weigh a ton!

JO ANNE: Well I just have a lot of stuff, that's all. I can't help it.

VICT: Well we're not helping you carry that junk.

JO ANNE: I won't ask you to. *(Reaches for the potato chip bag)* Give me some of those. I hope I don't starve to death before we reach St. Louis.

(GINNY makes a face at this last statement and begins to smack on her gum loudly. There is a period of silence in the car as the other women become aware of the noise GINNY is making. JO ANNE looks at GINNY and frowns; she exchanges glances with VICTORIA who gives GINNY a puzzled look. NIKKI gives GINNY a quick sideward glance, while GINNY remains unaware of the looks of disapproval her companions are giving her)

VICT: Nikki, turn the radio on; let's see if we can still get Chicago or something... anything.

(NIKKI fiddles with the radio knobs. There is no sound. She continues to fumble with the knobs. The others look concerned. JO ANNE, annoyed with the lack of results, leans across the seat, crowding GINNY, to fumble with the radio herself)

GINNY: Jo Anne!!

JO ANNE: *(Ignoring GINNY)* You're not doing it right, Nikki; let me try it.

JO ANNE: *(Fumbles with the knobs. Again there is no sound)* What's wrong with this thing?

VICT: Must be broken.

(JO ANNE bangs on the radio in frustration)

GINNY: Obviously it's broken, Jo Anne; that's not going to do any good.

JO ANNE: *(Leans back in her seat in disgust)* I don't believe it! I just don't believe it!!Nikki, didn't you check the radio when you picked the car up? How can we drive all the way across the country with no radio?

NIKKI: I... I didn't know. I...

JO ANNE: This is ridiculous! How far are we from Chicago? Let's take this car back! Now!!

VICT: Be for real, Jo Anne! You're the one complaining about us leaving late. If we go back now, we'll really be behind schedule. We can get it taken care of in L.A.

JO ANNE: Well I'd rather get to California one day later than have to drive across half the wheat fields in American with no music!! Who's for turning back?

GINNY: No way!

VICT: Not hardly!

NIKKI: I'm sorry about the radio, Jo Anne, but it seems like a waste of gas and time to turn back.

(JO ANNE *slumps in her seat, muttering to herself. She reaches into the potato chip bag, grabs a handful, stuffs them into her mouth and munches them ferociously.* GINNY's *gum smacking has subsided, and the silence is now interrupted by* JO ANNE *as she begins to suck her teeth.* GINNY *notices it first and frowns as she looks at* JO ANNE *through the rear view mirror.* NIKKI *then* VICTORIA *begin to notice the sound. Each looks annoyed. The lights dim denoting a passage of time. When the lights come back up. The four women are sitting quietly in their seats.*)

VICT: St. Louis, fifteen miles. Thank Goodness! (*Glances at her watch*) We made pretty good time. How you doing up there, Ginny?

GINNY: Fine, I can make it. Nikki, do you remember which route to take to the motel?

NIKKI: Yeah, just stay on this highway. You can see the sign from the road. It's going to seem funny going back there again. That's where Norman and I stayed when we were here for a conference of his. We were happy then. Who could have guessed we'd ever separate.

JO ANNE: Honey, you're better off without that turkey. He's been a turd since high school.

VICT: Jo Anne!!

JO ANNE: Well it's true! Nikki knows it's true! Norman was a player in high school, and he just kept right on playing when he graduated and they got married.

NIKKI: I didn't find out about his playing around until later. I loved Norman. He was the only boyfriend I ever had.

GINNY: Norman's a nice guy. He's just got his ways, that's all . . . strange ways, but they're his ways.

NIKKI: Nobody really understands Norman. He's always been ambitious. He's obsessed with the idea of success. He has a hang up because he had such a hard time as a kid, and he felt that my parents thought he wasn't good enough for me. They never did care for him, especially my father.

GINNY: He almost had a heart attack when you dropped out of college to help put Norman through. He begged me to talk to you. I really felt sorry for him.

NIKKI: I know. Mama said he used to pray that I'd leave Norman. I guess his prayers were answered . . . it took ten years, but, it looks like we're heading for a divorce.

VICT: Well, take it from me, separation is hard enough, but that divorce can be a killer. I thought I would die if I didn't get my freedom from Harry, but when it happened I was depressed for months. I still don't know why. I didn't even love Harry by the time we busted up. I guess I was just use to having him around.

JO ANNE: I don't believe that! You treated that man terrible . . . throwin' his stuff out in the snow . . . changin' the locks on the door.

VICT: I did him a favor. I probably saved his life 'cause I was mad enough to kill him when he acted a fool with me.

GINNY: That's cold, Victoria. Anyway, you didn't love Harry the way Nikki loves Norman, and you know it. You were only married to him a year.

VICT: The roughest year of my life.

NIKKI: I don't love Norman anymore.

JO ANNE: Sure Nikki, and it don't snow in Chicago in the winter time. You always were a fool for that man. You put him through school, obeyed his every order. He treated you like a slave. Hell, I would've eliminated him a long time ago . . . no loss at all.

GINNY: Jo Anne, you oughta quit it. How do you know Charles is not another Norman? I'm sure he's not perfect.

JO ANNE: Honey, I have Charley in line; believe me, he's no Norman. I don't play that.

(*Her companions look skeptical*)

NIKKI: Hey, that's the motel! There's the sign, The Wayward Inn, over there. Take the next exit, Ginny.

(GINNY *turns the wheel toward the exit. Parking the car, she turns it off, and the four of them sit stunned as they stare upward at the motel*)

JO ANNE: This is it?

VICT: This crummy joint?

GINNY: I'm scared to get outta the car.

NIKKI: This can't be . . . it looks like it . . . it has the same name . . . but . . .

JO ANNE: How long ago was it when you were here, Nikki?

NIKKI: Five years . . . but . . . I didn't think it would have changed this much.

VICT: I don't want to go in there.

JO ANNE: Me either!

GINNY: We really don't have a choice. The town is booked solid because of the big convention, remember.

JO ANNE: Well I can understand why this one's not

full. Those dudes in the lobby look like Alcatraz rejects.

GINNY: *(Swallows hard)* Well, let's go in. If we can make it through the lobby without getting raped or robbed, maybe we'll luck up and make it to our room alive.

VICT: I hope the door has a lock.

JO ANNE: I hope the room has a door.

The four women open their car doors slowly as they look around suspiciously. Closing the doors, they walk back to the back of the car and take their suitcases out. JO ANNE *struggles with hers. Huddled together, they inch across the stage as they look around from side to side fearfully. They exit. Lights out.*

Scene 2

As the lights go up, JO ANNE *is driving.* GINNY *sits beside her.* NIKKI *sits behind the driver and* VICTORIA *sits beside* NIKKI. GINNY *is reading the map.*

JO ANNE: Thank God that motel last night in Denver wasn't as raunchy as the one in St. Louis. At least I didn't have to sit up all night in fear for my life.

NIKKI: I said I was sorry about that motel, Jo Anne.

GINNY: It's not your fault, Nikki, you didn't build the motel.

VICT: Yeah, anyway, it wasn't that bad, sleeping in shifts, I mean. We got plenty of sleep in that stretch between St. Louis and Denver.

GINNY: I'll say, that was the most boring ride I've had in my life. Reminded me of the time we drove to that stupid camp in Indiana.

NIKKI: Oh no! I'd forgotten all about that! How old were we? Sixteen? We had the nerve to call ourselves counselors. I almost died trapped in those woods for three months.

VICT: I could stand the weeds and bushes, but the kids almost drove me crazy. They must've pulled every trick in the book on me.

NIKKI: At least they did have some respect for us. They used to call me Miss Nicole. I've always liked being called Nicole. I always asked you. . . .

JO ANNE: Aw girl, you don't look like a Nicole, you look like a Nikki!

GINNY: What possessed us to take those jobs anyway? We must've been crazy!

VICT: I took it for the money.

JO ANNE: That's for sure. If it hadn't been for the money, I would've packed up and left a week after we got there.

VICT: After that summer I decided to be childless forever.

GINNY: You're not by yourself.

NIKKI: Oh, I don't know. I don't think the kids were that bad. I always wanted children, but Norman . . .

JO ANNE: Forget Norman! I wish Charles would tell me I couldn't have any kids. Why didn't Norman get a vasectomy? Why did you have to get your tubes tied? Now you're up a creek without a paddle, and he's laying around Chicago overpopulating.

NIKKI: I never thought Norman and I would split up. I really thought we'd be together until death us do part. I really did.

GINNY: That's what we were led to believe with all of those fairy tales that were read to us when we were kids. The only reality in life is that everything must change and we've got to accept those changes. That's why I change boyfriends every two years. Two years . . . three . . . that's tops! If no committment is made by then it's over jack; hit the road. I'm getting ready to get rid of Bill as soon as I get back home.

VICT: Get rid of him! That fine hunk of man. The two of you have been living together for three years! Didn't he just get a promotion to the executive suite? I wouldn't let all that money slip through my fingers for nothing. If you don't want him, I'll take him!!

(The others laugh)

GINNY: Well you can have him. I'm tired of the changes he's been putting me through. Bill's so snobbish now it's pitiful. He used to be a real down to earth person, but now he's a walking status symbol. I sent him out for some beer the other night, and he came back with a six pack of Perrier water. Water! I've got my lips set for some beer, and the man brings home water!!! Hell, I had water in the faucet. Here he comes talking about "we're going to get some class in this place." The man's got to go.

VICT: Well Bill is used to nice things. He is a doctor's son.

GINNY: Well he'll need the good doctor when I get through with him.

JO ANNE: I'm glad my Charles is different. He's nothing like Norman or Harry or Bill. He's just about perfect.

VICT: Humph. I never made the mistake of thinking that Harry was perfect. He was an ass when I met him and a bigger ass when I threw him out.

GINNY: Why did you marry him anyway? I never understood it. Here you are the first woman manager of the Windy City Loan Company and here he is a little nobody. You always were smarter than him.

VICT: I married Harry to get out of my mother's

house. I would've married King Kong to get away from her . . . come to think of it, I did marry him. Anyway Ginny, I didn't exactly have men falling all over me like you did. After they met my mother, they usually didn't come back. He did. I should have known something was wrong when he got along with her. If I hadn't been such a coward and let Mama scare me so bad about living alone, I would have moved out by myself, then I wouldn't have taken such a desperate step as marriage. Lord knows my apartment is as expensive as hell and it's a struggle to keep going, but I'm not falling for her tricks anymore if I can help it. She's doing everything she can to get me back home now.

NIKKI: Well I'm determined not to go back home. My father is giving me a hard time, but I've made it so far in these four months by myself and I'm holding out.

JO ANNE: I don't blame you. Your father's a tyrant. He always did scare me. Norman's just like him too, bossy as hell. I dare Charles to try and boss me around the way Norman bossed you.

NIKKI: Well Norman means well, he just . . .

VICT: They all mean well, Nikki, but anybody will take advantage of you and say anything they want to you if you let them. You have to learn to speak up for yourself.

GINNY: I agree with Vic. You have to speak up for yourself sometimes, Nikki. How could you become the District Manager for the largest chain of boutiques in Chicago without speaking up?

JO ANNE: Some people are good in business, but losers in their personal lives. Take me, for instance. The three of you thought I was crazy when I took that job as a secretary after I graduated from college. But I knew what I was doing. I worked my way up to a position as an executive legal secretary and made as much money as the rest of you and then landed a well to do lawyer to boot. I turned this potential loser into a winner. Some people know how, others don't.

GINNY: *(Teasing)* Congratulations, Jo Anne; let me commend you on your fortitude. I think I'll write your life story and see if I can get backing for a production. It could be a movie of the week, prime time. I'm sure the nation is interested in your story. It'll get great ratings.

VICT: Yeah Jo Anne, maybe Ginny can get you a spot on her talk show. You'll be a star then, an even bigger success story than you are now.

JO ANNE: Very funny, you two are really a riot. *(Pause)* Hey Ginny, check the map. Are you sure we're on the right road? I don't see any other cars around, and this road is beginning to look awfully rough.

(Everyone looks out of their window in concern. GINNY *checks the map and traces the route with her finger)*

NIKKI: This road is narrow too, and I don't see any guard rails.

VICT: How high up are we? It sure looks like a long way down. Look at the tops of those trees. Look . . . snow . . . a mountain stream . . . wow!

GINNY: We're on the right route. This is the fastest route to Highway 80. This connects Denver to Salt Lake City. I guess we could have taken State Road 25 to 80, but this is supposed to be a state highway too.

JO ANNE: Look at this road! This is primitive! We're on the top of a mountain. Here's a sign coming up. How high are we?

(They each strain to see the upcoming sign)

VICT: Eleven . . . eleven thousand feet.

JO ANNE: Eleven thousand feet!! Oh damn!! I'm turning this baby around. We're too high up.

GINNY: Turning around! Are you crazy!!! Where the hell are you going to turn the car around? The mountain's on one side and there's an eleven thousand foot drop on the other! You better drive this sucker and drive it like you've never driven before!

JO ANNE: *(Hysterical)* Drive it? Drive? I've never driven on the highway before in my life! Oh my god! We're climbing higher! Look at that sign, eleven thousand three hundred feet! Oh my god!

VICT: *(Shouts)* Never driven on the highway before!! What do you mean you've never driven on the highway? Why didn't you say something before we left Chicago or while we were planning the trip??!!

GINNY: I bet you better drive this car, Jo Anne, and stop acting like a fool!

JO ANNE: I can't! I can't! *(Whines)* You drive, Ginny. I'll stop and you drive.

VICT: Don't stop! Don't stop! Look how far up we are and still climbing. If we fall off the road they'll never find us in all those trees. Oh Lord!

GINNY: There's no place to stop! Drive this car!

NIKKI: *(Leans forward and begins to talk to* JO ANNE *calmly)* Jo Anne, you can do it. Don't think you can't. You know how determined you can be when you really want something, so I know that you're not going to let a little mountain stop you now. Just stay calm and check the gears. Are you in low? If you're not, then put it in low.

GINNY: Twelve thousand feet!! Oh Shit!!

*(*JO ANNE *grips the wheel tightly, in terror, but she does as she is instructed.* VICTORIA *looks out of the window, her eyes wide with fear)*

VICT: Don't get too close, Jo Anne, you're too close to the edge, move over . . . move over!

GINNY: *(Equally as fearful as her companions, begins to pray loudly)* Oh Lord, I swear I'll go to church for four weeks straight if you get us out of this!

NIKKI: Just steer straight and don't let anything or anyone bother you. You're doing great.

VICT: Fourteen thousand feet! Fourteen thousand feet! We're up here with the angels!!!

GINNY: *(Louder)* Six weeks, Lord... six weeks. I swear this sinner will spend six solid Sundays in Church!!!

NIKKI: You're doing great, Jo Anne, just beautifully. Keep it up.

JO ANNE: There's a scenic view sign! The scenic view is only one mile away! I'm turning off! I'm turning off! Somebody else take the wheel!

VICT: O.K. turn off, but don't get close to the edge. We're still high up.

(JO ANNE turns the car off the road. The four women slump back in their seats simultaneously. They give sighs of relief)

GINNY: Thank you, Lord.

VICT: Amen.

JO ANNE: Who in the hell drew this route? Who in the hell tried to kill me?

NIKKI: Triple A drew the route.

JO ANNE: Well they'll get a piece of my mind when I get back home.

GINNY: Come on, let's get off this mountain. Whose turn is it to drive?

VICT: Mine.

JO ANNE: Well come on, let's go. *(JO ANNE hurries from the driver's seat and rushes around the car to the back where VICTORIA is sitting. VICTORIA gets out of the car reluctantly)* Hurry up!

VICT: I'm hurrying! I'm hurrying!

(JO ANNE jumps into the car while VICTORIA walks around car to the driver's side and slides in behind the wheel)

NIKKI: Victoria, I'll take your turn if you want me to.

VICT: No... no I'll do it, just hand me a cigarette out of my purse. I'm gonna need a drag of something for this. From the looks of that road, it's straight down all the way.

(NIKKI hands VICTORIA her purse from the back. VICTORIA digs into it, withdraws a cigarette, and lights it shakily. She takes a long, slow draw and exhales. GINNY coughs and glances at VICTORIA in disgust. All three passengers roll their windows down and glare at VICTORIA. Unaware of their discomfort, she takes another puff and starts the car. She pulls the car onto the road as the ohers hang out of their windows and wave the smoke out of the car)

NIKKI: *(Coughing)* Remember, Vic, take the car out of second going downhill and don't ride the brake.

(VICTORIA nods, changes gears, then putting her foot down on the gas pedal hard, she leans forward on the wheel as if imitating a race car driver as she races down the mountain)

GINNY: Slow down Vic! Slow down!

JO ANNE: Step on the brake! Step on the brake!

NIKKI: No! Don't ride the brake! Don't ride the brake!

VICT: Shut up, everybody! We're getting down this mountain, *today!!!*

(The lights dim denoting a passage of time. The lights come back up. VICTORIA is still driving. She is calm now. Her companions, however, sit huddled in their respective places against the car doors, still shaken.)

JO ANNE: I'm glad I'm alive to tell my grandchildren how I flew down a mountain.

VICT: I got you down, didn't I?

GINNY: Thanks a lot, Victoria. I almost had a heart attack.

VICT: Well why didn't you drive the car then? I didn't hear you volunteering, just praying.

GINNY: Don't knock it if you haven't tried it.

JO ANNE: You know you haven't been to church in years, Ginny. How many weeks did you promise?

GINNY: Six.

NIKKI: Oh oh, I'll have to see this for myself.

GINNY: I'm going to go! I really am! I just didn't say when I was going to start.

NIKKI: Girl, you better not play with God like that.

JO ANNE: Especially when you've got to go through this damn desert for Lord knows how long, and without a radio I might add.

GINNY: Jo Anne, would you please lay off of the radio. I'm tired of hearing about it.

JO ANNE: Well excuse me. Can I help it if I enjoy some form of entertainment when I'm stuck out in the middle of nowhere.

GINNY: Well why don't you just hum.

JO ANNE: My... my, aren't we testy. *(She reaches into the back of the car and brings out a box of cookies. She pops one in her mouth, eats it and begins to suck her teeth. The others tense up)* I sure hope this car makes it through the desert. Do we have enough gas? Did the man at the gas station check the water and oil?

VICT: Will you stop being so negative. This is a brand new station wagon. It only had three thousand miles on it when we got it.

JO ANNE: Well there's more than three thousand miles on it now. Climbing that mountain might have hurt it.

GINNY: Oh be quiet, Jo Anne; the car's O.K. Hand me my purse, will you? I need some gum.

(The others look dismayed as JO ANNE reaches for the purse. She glances at GINNY, who is looking out of

her window and reaches into GINNY's *purse.* VICTORIA *observes* JO ANNE *through the rear view mirror as* JO ANNE *takes the gum out of the purse and puts it into her pocket. She hands the purse to* GINNY. GINNY *digs in her purse frantically looking for the gum)*

GINNY: Where is that gum. I was sure I had two sticks of gum left. I'm positive about it. Where the hell is it?

(As she continues to go through her purse, NIKKI, JO ANNE, *and* VICTORIA *stifle their giggles)*

VICT: Maybe you lost the gum back at the filling station when you went in your purse.

GINNY: I guess I did. It's not in here. Anybody else have any? *(Her companions respond in the negative, smiling gratefully)* Oh well, I'll get some when we stop again.

(The others groan. There is a moment of silence which is interrupted by JO ANNE *who begins to suck her teeth)*

VICT: You know, Jo Anne, in all these years I've known you I never noticed that you sucked your teeth.

JO ANNE: *(Surprised)* I do?? Hmm, I never noticed it either. I forgot to bring my dental floss. I must be doing it unconsciously. I hate that little goop that gets there in between your teeth. *(Demonstrates)* You know, those little pieces of food that get stuck up there and just drive you crazy. You know what I mean?

GINNY: Yeah, we know. Why don't you buy some floss when we stop in the next big town and do us all a big favor.

JO ANNE: I'll do that, Ginny, if you'll do me a favor and . . .

NIKKI: Jo Anne! Ginny! Please, stop fussing!

VICT: Yeah, why don't you look on the map, Jo Anne, and see where we are.

JO ANNE: *(Snatches the map up and studies it)* We're a couple of miles outside of Wendover, Utah in the middle of nowhere, without a radio. For all we know, we might be the only people left on earth.

GINNY: Well we don't have a radio, Jo Anne, so why don't you shut up about it! I'm tired of hearing your mouth.

JO ANNE: I'm not choked up about hearing your mouth either, Ginny. Everytime you open it another order comes out. You always did act like you knew everything.

GINNY: *(Turning to* JO ANNE*)* I beg your pardon.

JO ANNE: You've always been bossy. Ever since we were kids you've had to have your way about everything. Quite frankly, I never did like that superior attitude of yours.

GINNY: It's not hard to feel superior to you, Jo Anne. If it hadn't been for me you never would

have made it through high school, you never were heavy in the smarts department, and everybody knows how you got through college.

JO ANNE: And exactly what do you mean by that?

NIKKI: Hey, come on. Cut it out. We've got almost a week and a half to be together, come on now.

JO ANNE: No, she's got something to say, let her say it.

VICT: Oh the hell, I don't feel like hearing all this crap. We've got five miles to go until we reach the next town, and I'm tired. The two of you can fuss later, right now look for a vacancy sign on a motel so we can all get some rest.

(JO ANNE and GINNY glare at each other, their anger festering.)

JO ANNE: I've got to pee.

VICT: Ah, can't you hold it until we get to Wendover? It'll just be a few minutes more.

JO ANNE: No I cannot. Now stop this car Victoria, and let me out near some bushes or something!

GINNY: You must have kidney failure, Jo Anne. You've left piss every ten miles from Illinois to Utah.

JO ANNE: Stop this car, Victoria!!!

(VICTORIA pulls off of the highway angrily. JO ANNE jumps out of the car, slamming the door behind her)

NIKKI: There's some bushes over there, Jo Anne.

GINNY: And hurry up.

(JO ANNE exits. The others sit in the car waiting)

VICT: I hope the sun cooks her butt.

(Her companions giggle. Offstage a scream is heard, and JO ANNE rushes back onto the stage, carrying one shoe and limping. The others look concerned)

NIKKI: What happened, Jo Anne?

JO ANNE: I stepped in it!! I stepped in some cow shit!! Right over there . . . right by those bushes!

(The three women in the car begin to laugh hysterically while JO ANNE cleans off her shoe then gets back into the car. VICTORIA pulls back onto the road)

JO ANNE: I don't think it's funny. I ruined a good pair of shoes.

NIKKI: Oh Jo Anne, where's your sense of humor?

GINNY: How do you know it was cow shit?

JO ANNE: As big as it was it had to be. I know cow shit when I see it.

GINNY: Oh? I thought you'd be more familiar with bullshit.

JO ANNE: Ginny, if you say . . .

VICT: Ginny! Jo Anne! Pleasssssseee!

NIKKI: Thank goodness, we're in Wendover. There's a vacancy sign, over there to your right, Vic.

VICT: O.K., I see it.

JO ANNE: You're not going in there are you? It's a dump.

VICT: It won't be the first dump we've slept in, or have you forgotten St. Louis?

JO ANNE: I tried to.

(VICTORIA pulls the car into the parking lot and turns off the ignition)

JO ANNE: If we are going to go in *there*, I'd prefer that we get two separate rooms, and I don't want Ginny as my roommate.

GINNY: Listen, honey, the feeling is mutual. I'd rather sleep in the car than in the same room with you.

VICT: *(Impatient)* If you two want to get separate rooms, go right ahead. I've been through hell today and I'm tired, and I plan on sleeping in a bed, in a room, in that motel, tonight.

NIKKI: Right on!

(NIKKI and VICTORIA get out of the car and exit. JO ANNE and GINNY continue to sit, eyeing each other on occasion with hostility. A few moments later NIKKI and VICTORIA return to the car. NIKKI goes to GINNY's window and knocks on it. GINNY rolls the window down)

NIKKI: We're in room 2-A on the first floor, straight through the lobby.

Neither woman replies. NIKKI *looks at* VICTORIA, *who shrugs, and both of them exit.* GINNY *and* JO ANNE *continue to sit in silence. Then* GINNY *slowly opens the car door and gets out of the car. She slams the door behind her, glares once again at* JO ANNE, *goes back to the back of the car and gets her suitcase. And with one last defiant exchange of gestures between* GINNY *and* JO ANNE, GINNY *exits. Lights out.*

Scene 3

As the lights go up, NIKKI *is driving.* JO ANNE *sits beside her in the front seat.* VICTORIA *sits behind* JO ANNE, *and* GINNY *sits behind* NIKKI. *The tension is at its height, and their attitudes reflect this.*

JO ANNE: Whose idea was it to wear halters and shorts in San Francisco?

NIKKI: *(Defensive)* How did I know it wasn't hot in San Francisco!!

JO ANNE: I just know I'm gonna catch pneumonia. I've never been so cold in my life. I would have dropped dead if I had to climb one more hill!

GINNY: *(Mutters)* In that case, maybe we should have stayed longer.

JO ANNE: *(Turns to* GINNY *angrily)* Ginny . . .

VICT: *(Shouts)* I can't stand it! I just can't stand it! Will you two stop it; both of you are getting on my nerves. I just started my period and I don't need this aggravation!

(VICTORIA takes a cigarette out of her purse and lights it shakily. Taking a long draw, she exhales. Her companions roll their windows down simultaneously. JO ANNE *waves the smoke out of the car, then begins to suck on her teeth.* GINNY *smacks on her gum.* NIKKI *becomes irritated)*

NIKKI: How far is it to L.A., Jo Anne?

JO ANNE: *(Checks the map)* We just left Santa Barbara . . . now we're about one hundred miles from L.A. We'll be there soon.

NIKKI: It won't be soon enough for me. I can't wait.

JO ANNE: So that's the reason that you're driving so fast. Why don't you slow down and save a life, mine.

VICT: It's her ticket if she gets caught, not yours, Jo Anne; she's comfortable, so let her alone.

JO ANNE: Since you brought the subject of comfort up, Victoria, don't you think it's about time that you had some consideration for the rest of us and lay off of those cigarettes so we can all breathe a little?

VICT: Really?? I didn't know you felt that way about my smoking. But yours is the only voice I seem to hear objecting. Nikki? Ginny? *(Neither of the women respond as they shift in their seats uncomfortably)* Ginny, is my smoking bothering you?

GINNY: *(Hesitant)* Well Vic, you know I never did smoke . .

VICT: *(Interrupts)* Nikki? Do you feel the same way?

NIKKI: Uh huh.

VICT: *(Puts her cigarette out angrily)* You'd think that my best friends would have said something to me about this sooner. If my smoking bothered you, all you had to do was tell me.

GINNY: Aw Victoria, don't sound so hurt. It's just that closed up in this car on such a long trip . . . well, it's kind of hard to take . . . you know.

VICT: Yeah, I know, Ginny, just like your gum chewing; Smack, Smack, Smack, Chomp, Chomp, Chomp. I can identify with your feelings very well.

*(JO ANNE *and* NIKKI *laugh.* GINNY *bristles)*

GINNY: I see . . . yes . . . I see. So that's why my gum has been disappearing so mysteriously in the last few days. Yeah, I understand now. Nobody had the nerve to ask me politely not to chew the gum. Instead, somebody . . . *(Eyes* VICTORIA, *then* JO ANNE*)* steals my gum, like a child would and hides it. Very clever . . . immature, but clever.

JO ANNE: Ah calm down, Ginny. Hell, you could've busted our eardrums with that noise. Between choking to death on Vic's smoke and going deaf behind your gum chewing, I'm surprised we've made it this far.

GINNY: Humph, you've done your little bit to add

to the symphony of sound, Jo Anne. *(She beings to suck her teeth)* Does that sound familiar?

(JO ANNE says nothing as she stares out of the window, furious. The situation is potentially explosive as NIKKI increases her speed, stepping harder on the gas pedal. JO ANNE turns to NIKKI nervously)

JO ANNE: Nikki, will you slow this crate down, for God's sake!!!

NIKKI: Fuck you, Jo Anne.

(There is a collective gasp as her companions sit stunned)

JO ANNE: What did you say?

NIKKI: You heard what I said.

VICT: I don't believe it! I just don't believe it!! Miss Take Anything finally speaks up. After all these years, she finally speaks up!!

JO ANNE: *(Amused)* Nikki, Little Miss Perfect . . . Miss Goody Two Shoes curses. She actually curses. I knew the truth would come out. I knew you weren't as perfect as you always pretended to be.

NIKKI: I never pretended to be perfect, Jo Anne. The simple fact of the matter is that you were always such a bitch that you made everybody around you look good.

(GINNY and VICTORIA convulse in laughter)

JO ANNE: *(Angry)* If I made you look good Nikki, then I was doing you a favor.

GINNY: *(Snickering)* Jo Anne, why don't you . . .

NIKKI: Be quiet, Ginny; I can handle this. For once in your life stop taking up for me. Stop butting in. I'm capable of taking care of myself.

GINNY: *(Hurt)* Well I just wanted to help.

NIKKI: I know you wanted to help, but sometimes you go too far. You're always defending me against somebody, then you turn right around and boss me around yourself. I'm tired of it. Stop butting into my life.

VICT: That's really gratitude for you. Ginny always was there for you, Nikki. You never had the guts to stand up for yourself . . . always creeping around like some ghost, scared of your own shadow. You're afraid of your father, afraid of Norman . . . afraid of everybody. You wouldn't even have the job you have now if it hadn't been for Ginny talking you into taking those promotions. There you were ready and willing to live in Norman's shadow and continuing to be a dumb Miss Nobody.

NIKKI: Listen who's talking about being afraid, Miss Mama's Baby of 1902! You won't even go to the toilet unless she tells you to. You're always bragging about how you threw Harold out! You know damn well your mother picked him out for you and told you when to get rid of him. The poor man probably was more than happy to

leave. Between you and your mother, his life must've been hell!

JO ANNE: *(To NIKKI)* I'm certain living with Victoria had to be hell for poor Harry, especially with a mother like hers.

VICT: *(Controlled fury)* I could respect your observations about my private life, Nikki, if they didn't come from a woman who was stupid enough to let the biggest woman chaser in Chicago talk her into getting her tubes tied. As for your two cents worth, Jo Anne, I do not appreciate you talking about my mother, and there is no way that I would ever listen to a thing you would have to say anyway. Everybody who went to college with you knows where your brains lie . . . and it's not between your ears.

(JO ANNE whirls completely around in her seat, enraged, as she faces VICTORIA. NIKKI leans forward in her seat, stepping on the gas even harder as she vents her anger)

JO ANNE: I oughta kick your ass.

VICT: Then you'd better go get some help 'cause I don't think you're woman enough to handle the job.

NIKKI: Victoria, you're a liar!!! Norman didn't make me do a thing I didn't want to do. Tell her, Ginny!!

GINNY: Me? . . . You want me to butt in . . . are you kidding? And you, Jo Anne, I don't know why you're acting so indignant. You know Victoria's telling the truth. You screwed your way from State Street to Lake Shore Drive, nonstop.

JO ANNE: *(Turns to GINNY)* You're not exactly a virgin yourself, Ginny. You know something, you've been on my case since we left Chicago, and i'm sick of it. As a matter of fact, I'm sick of you. Big bad, Ginny . . . cute Ginny . . . smart Ginny . . . popular Ginny. People always made me feel like I should have gotten down on my knees and kissed your feet cause you took this poor little girl from the projects into your precious inner circle of silly friends. I always knew you felt that you were better than me, and I swore to myself that I'd make it in this life even if I had to use you or anybody else to do it. Now I have make it . . . living right there on Lake Shore Drive where I swore I would be . . . right there with you and your stuck up little Billy boy, and you . . . *(Points to GINNY)* you can't stand it. It eats you up inside.

GINNY: Frankly, my dear, I don't give a damn. I'm sure lots of whores live on Lake Shore Drive.

(JO ANNE tries to leap into the back seat, going for GINNY's throat. She bumps against NIKKI, who fights to control the wheel of the car. VICTORIA attempts to break up the ensuing fight as squeals and

obscenities fill the air)

NIKKI: Damn it, stop! Stop it! You trying to kill us??

(NIKKI pulls the car off of the road, cuts off the ignition, and helps VICTORIA pull the two women apart. She pulls a crumpled JO ANNE back into the front seat, while a frazzled VICTORIA holds GINNY, equally rumpled, in the back seat. JO ANNE jerks loose from NIKKI's grip on her.

JO ANNE: Let go of me.

NIKKI: *(Shouts)* We are now in the Los Angeles city limits. We've got two choices. Either we complete this trip in peace or we turn this car around and go back home, *now!*

GINNY: Are you kidding! Do you think I would go another mile with that . . . *(Points to JO ANNE)*

JO ANNE: The feeling's mutual, baby!!!

VICTORIA: I've got a better idea. Hand me that L.A. map, Nikki, I'm gonna find a route to the airport and you can drop me off there. I can't stand another minute of this madness.

GINNY: Sounds good to me, I'm going with you.

JO ANNE: Oh, no you don't. I'm not getting stuck here with her. *(Indicates NIKKI)*

NIKKI: Well you can get the hell out of the car now for all I care!!

JO ANNE: The hell I will; I helped pay for this car and I plan on staying in it as long as everybody else!

NIKKI: That won't be long!!! *(Starts the car)* The map won't be necessary, Victoria. I've already studied it and I know how to get to the airport. I'm not as *dumb* as all of you seem to think I am. *(She pulls into traffic so suddenly that the others are tossed around in the car)*

JO ANNE: Hey watch it, what are you trying to do, kill me!!??

NIKKI: Don't tempt me.

(NIKKI drives with a vengeance as each woman keeps a look out for the airport exit)

GINNY: There's the sign, three more miles, over there!

NIKKI: I can read, Ginny, thank you.

VICT: This really amazes me, after all of these years of growing up with someone, sharing secrets, sharing experiences, practically sharing you life, you think you know your friends and you don't really know them at all. Life can pull some cruel jokes.

JO ANNE: Yeah, and our so-called friendship is the cruelest joke of them all. Here's TWA, you can let me off here. *(Pause)* Hey, you're passing it!

NIKKI: I fly United!!

GINNY: You? Fly? What about the car? It's in your name.

NIKKI: Hertz will take care of it.

(NIKKI pulls the car over and stops. Taking the key out of the ignition, she bolts from the car, followed by JO ANNE. As VICTORIA opens her car door, it hits JO ANNE who falls back stunned)

JO ANNE: You hit me with that car door on purpose!!!

(VICTORIA ignores her as she and JO ANNE join GINNY and NIKKI at the back of the car. NIKKI pitches the luggage to the ground as she gets her own bag)

GINNY: Watch it, Nikki!! That's my stuff you're throwing around.

(VICTORIA and JO ANNE go into the back of the car for their things at the same time, bumping and elbowing each other viciously. Grabbing the same bag, they grapple over it)

VICT: That's my bag!! Let go!

(JO ANNE lets go as VICTORIA is tugging, and VICTORIA loses her balance. JO ANNE chuckles in triumph as she reaches for her own suitcases. VICTORIA swings her bag at JO ANNE, who dodges it successfully. As this is happening, NIKKI starts to exit, then turns back toward the others before she leaves the stage)

NIKKI: One more thing, for fifteen years I've begged the three of you to call me Nicole. Well I'm not begging anymore. My name is Nicole and don't you call me Nikki again, *ever!!!* *(She exits)*

VICT: *(Calls after her)* Don't worry, I won't call you period! Come on, Ginny, let's walk down to American Airlines.

GINNY: All right. I wouldn't ride United or TWA if someone paid me!

(The two women start toward the exit)

JO ANNE: Thank God, I won't have to ride on the same plane. I'm going to call Charley, I can't wait to get home.

(GINNY and VICTORIA stop, grin at each other, and turn back to JO ANNE)

GINNY: Oh, Jo Anne, when you get back to Chicago you'd better take a cab to 4305 Smith Street, apartment 11-A. Charley will probably be sleeping there tonight . . . that is if United Airlines is faster than TWA.

(GINNY and VICTORIA exit laughing loudly. JO ANNE stands rooted for a minute, looking puzzled and muttering to herself)

JO ANNE: 4305 Smith Street . . . 4305 Smith Street . . . *(She gasps)* 4305 Smith Street . . . that's Nikki's place!!!! *(Laden with her overweight luggage, she rushes toward the exit which NIKKI has taken)* Nikki! You bitch!!! *(She exits)*

Lights out

LOUIS RIVERS

LOU RIVERS, WHO WAS BORN in Savannah, Georgia, on September 18, 1922, attended the Savannah public schools, and in 1946 graduated from Savannah State College with a Bachelor's Degree in English. During his high school and college years, he wrote poetry, plays, short stories, and essays, and was duly recognized as a student with "great literary promise." It was also during these years that he was most active as a youth leader in the N.A.A.C.P. and Youth Association for Community Betterment.

Recognized and respected as a youth leader, Lou received additional acclaim as winner of awards in local and statewide writing contests. He was an honor student for four years at Savannah State College, and he served as a feature writer and editor-in-chief of the college literary periodical, the *Georgia State Herald*. He also served as president of the college's Little Theatre Movement. Each year he won the distinction of being voted the best actor in a play on campus.

From 1946 to 1949, Lou worked as a language arts teacher at Center High School in Waycross, Georgia, where he organized and conducted a Black community theatre and was influential in bringing Black professional theater companies to Waycross. The Little Theatre group put on seasons of plays and musicals including some of Lou's earlier efforts at playwriting.

Lou Rivers maintains, however, that his first professional introduction to playwriting came in 1949 when Father Hartke at Catholic University in Washington, D.C., gave him his first scholarship to study theater. The scholarship had come as a result of intercessions of Sister Mary Julie at Rosary College, River Forest, Illinois, who had read a play Lou had adapted from a short story by Paul Laurence Dunbar.

"It was at Catholic University that my love for theater deepened," Lou says, "and I began to understand theater as an art form—its development, its purpose, and tremendous possibilities." He loves to boast that his first teacher in playwriting was Walter Kerr, "who opened up to me a whole new beautiful world."

When Lou Rivers returned to his teaching at Center High School in Waycross, he became more divided than ever between developing himself as a teacher and that of a playwright. After many conferences and soul analyses, he discovered he could combine the two; so, he was off to acquire a Master of Arts in dramatic arts at New York University.

From 1951 to 1958, with his newly-earned degree, Lou Rivers taught speech and drama at West Virginia State College, Southern University, and Tougaloo College. On these campuses, he became well-known as a teacher of speech and composition, as well as director, drama coach, and playwright. He also planned and helped to organize, direct, and coordinate community theatre groups in West Virginia, Kentucky, Louisiana, and Mississippi. It was during this time that he also worked with the Committee for Negroes in the Arts and studied with Howard DaSilva and Brett Warren in New York City.

In 1958, Lou left Tougaloo College to study playwriting under John Gassner at Yale University on a John Jay Whitney Creative Writing Fellowship. During this time, he also studied playwriting with Elmer Rice at New York University. He also became the drama coach for Voices, Inc., a Manhattan-based Black company of professional actors, singers, and dancers telling of the Black experience through dramatic art forms.

In studying Lou Rivers' career, one would find a fine intertwining of academia and theater. "Like most writers," he says, "I too want to write 'masterpieces,' be recognized and celebrated for them, and be classified as a 'great' playwright who increases, through his contribution, the development of understanding and appreciation of the human animal." That same ideal holds for Lou's being an educator. "To reach both objectives is the ultimate," Lou declares.

Presently, Lou is associate professor of Writing and Speech at New York City Community College, Brooklyn. He holds a Ph.D. in Administration and Supervision from Fordham University, and he is a member of Kappa Delta Pi and Phi Delta Kappa. "I am the husband of a lovely wife, Ligia Sanchez Rivers, and the father of three beautiful daughters, Luisa, Liana, Loria, and a handsome son, Leigh."

Some of Lou Rivers' other plays are: *Seeking; Purple Passage; The Scabs; Mr. Randolph Brown; The Making of a Saint; The Ghosts; Monologues for Black Actors; Black Talk from a Barber Shop; The Witness; Bouquet for Lorraine; Madam Odum; This Piece of Land; Papa for Jimmy Jr.; Crabs in a Bucket;* and *Spiritual Rock Incident at Christmastime,* a musical. His play, *This Piece of Land,* appears in *The Best Short Plays of* 1977, edited by Stanley Richards.

MORE BREAD AND THE CIRCUS

Louis Rivers

CAST OF CHARACTERS
(*10 Black men; 6 White men; 3 Black women*)

LESTER DENEGAL: *Black man in his early 40s*

MR. THOMAS JEFFERSON: *Black man in his late 60s*

CHARLIE BAD BOY GILLISON: *Black man in his late 60s*

MR. PRIESTER: *White mailman*

MR. GEORGE: *Black man in his 50s*

MR. COTTEL: *White man in his early 30s*

BOBBY: *Black man in his 40s*

REDD: *Black man in his early 50s*

JAKE: *Black man in his early 40s*

SONNY: *Black man, 19 years old*

DAVID: *Black man, 19 years old*

MOE: *White man, 19 years old*

AL: *Black man, 19 years old*

MR. FOXX: *White man*

DETECTIVE: *White man*

POLICEMAN: *White man*

HELEN GREEN: *Black woman in her late 40s*

IDA: *Black woman in her middle 60s*

VIOLA DENEGAL: *Black woman in her late 30s*

Time: Hot early summer morning, 1938
Place: Harlem, New York City

A PLAY IN ONE ACT

Scene: An exterior-interior setting. The exterior is the end corner of a Harlem street. It begins downstage right with only the end corner of a tired old brick apartment building showing. Most of the building is hidden offstage. Beginning upstage right and moving left is the front of a brownstone brick building containing two identical adjacent stoops with two heavy front doors and a common flight of stairs that connect with the pavement. There's a window right of the first front door.

The interior is the second half of the stage, adjacent to the first. For vision of the audience, almost all wall interior has been removed, and the audience can clearly see that the interior is a much lived-in living room. Up center is a doorway that leads into the center hall that leads upstairs to a small room which holds a single bed; a dresser holding a Negro history book, the size of a large family Bible; a chair and a table, a window over the bed; and a door leading to a coat closet.

The downstairs hall also leads to the downstairs living room. There's a battered upright piano with large stacks of sheet music on top of it. Downstage is a round table surrounded by chairs, a sofa, a floor lamp, a phonograph, and a radio, the newest thing in the room. Downstage left is a door that leads off into other parts of the apartment.

Discovered: LESTER, wearing his checkered cap and chewing on a cigar butt, sits alone on the top step of the stoop. He reads the newspaper. Somewhere in a nearby apartment a radio plays: A singer sings "God Bless America." Presently HELEN GREEN appears in the window. She busily waters her potted plants in the window.

MRS. GREEN: *(Discovering LES)* Hi there, Lester!

LESTER: *(Looking up)* Good mornin, Mrs. Green.

MRS. G: How's the world treating you?

LES: Oh, about the same I suppose.

MRS. G: As if I didn't know. *(Listens to the singing)*

LES: According to the papers here, we need two things to get us out of trouble. More bread, and I see the Ringling Bros. Circus is coming to town. *(Turns the pages)*

MRS. G: *(Giggles)* I always liked the circus, and it's for damn sure, we could use more bread. We could use a few porkchops to go with the bread, eh Lester?

LES: We ain't gonna be able to stay out of this war too much longer—I can see that. Hitler done declared Austria is a part of Germany.

MRS. G: Well, the war might just make things bet-

221

ter, Lester. At least when there is war, our folks do get work. That's for damn sure. How's Viola?

LES: She's all right.

MRS. G: Still sleeping?

LES: Yeah. We played the club until three this morning. The League of Nations ain't worth the time they meet. Just like they didn't do nothin for Ethiopia when Mussolini stormed in there and took Ethiopia, they ain't go do nothin about Austria neither.

MRS. G: Only God hisself can figure out the crazy things White folks do—Or don't do.

LES: But then they might do something after all. Austria is White. Ethiopia is Black. Don't make too much difference though how they knock us Blacks off, do it?

MRS. G: No, it don't.

LES: It's either in war—Or they let us starve to death.

MRS. G: Besides, Lester, we all know what the Bible says about wars. There will be wars, until Judgment Day. *(Cautiously)* Didn't Sonny come home again last night? Lester?

LES: *(Presently)* No—It's been a week he ain't been back.

MRS. G: Ain't you worried? He could be in some kind of trouble.

LES: He ain't in no trouble. He knows how to look after himself. Sent word he'd be here sometimes today. Since he finished high school, he thinks he knows all the answers. He thinks he's just as grown up as me or Vi. He's smart. We's dumb, but I'm gonna show him a thing or two—you betcha!

MRS. G: Only yesterday, old Lady Ida was telling Mr. Jefferson and us Sonny told her he had run away from home for good—that is after you and him had real bad words.

LES: He's all right. *(Pensively)* Today, young people ain't like we was when we was coming up.

MRS. G: That's for damn sure. Sonny was always such a nice kid. I expected he'd go on to college and make a man of himself.

LES: He will! I ain't given up on Sonny. He'll do it. It's just that—well, it's that White crowd he's got himself mixed up with. That's the trouble.

MRS. G: Always the Whites, ain't it? It's a shame. . . . You and Viola tried so hard . . . . Old Lady Ida says that crowd of his is a bunch of dirty communists from Russia.

LES: Don't listen to Ida. She don't know what she's talkin about. She don't half the time get things exactly right no more since she had her breakdown. Sonny ain't against America if that's what you mean. He's against *war,* and he ought to be! After all, it ain't us old ones they's gonna

shuffle off to war. It's his crowd.

MRS. G: That's for damn sure. *(Giggles)* Lord, the war takes all the good men and leaves us women with broken down models for lovers, huh? How do you like that? *(Cackles. MR. GEORGE, the super, carrying an old trashcan, enters from the first door. On seeing MR. GEO)* Lester, don't you smell stink in the air? *(MR. GEO hesitates)* There he is, the biggest *asskisser* in Harlem, an old Uncle Tom. Farthead! I'm keeping a pot of boiling water on my stove so as I can scald your natural ass—Dirty motherfucker! *(MR. GEO exits up the street)* I'm gonna get you or my name ain't Helen Green! That's for sure. Ain't that bastard something, telling the court I couldn'ta fallen down those steps as if he was there to see it.

(MR. JEFFERSON carrying a checkerboard and checkers and MR. GILLISON carrying two pillows enter through the first door)

MR. JEFFERSON: *(Entering)* Good morning, Mrs. Green.

MRS. G: Good morning, Mr. Jefferson—and you, Mr. Gillison?

MR. GILLISON: Fine, thank you, fine.

MR. J: How are you, Mr. Lester?

LES: O.K. Mr. Jefferson—and you?

MR. J: Beyond the petty annoyance that life deals us, I have no major complaints.

LES: Good enough.

MRS. G: They didn't find your check. Did they?

MR. J: No, Mrs. Green. They didn't. I'm afraid the check is not really lost. It has been stolen. *(MR. GIL adjusts pillows on the steps for them to sit down)* When I went down to the post office several days ago, I convinced them of that fact. *(Sits to arrange the checkerboard. MR. GIL helps)*

MR. GIL: *(Selecting checkers)* All right, governor. You take the reds. Today, I'm gonna beat you every game.

MR. J: *(Arranging checkers on the board)* And if you do, Mr. Gillison, what does it all add up to in the end, eh? I beat you a game. You beat me a game. You're the winner, and I'm the loser—Or I'm the winner and you're the loser. What's the difference?

MR. GIL: *(Moving a checker)* Your move. *(The game begins)*

MR. J: *(To all in general)* I insisted on speaking directly to the Postmaster General. Oh, they tried to put me by, but I was adamant—so when I got to speak to the general—I said to him— "General, I wish you would indulge yourself a little with me in a bit of sound reasoning. Now for the last three years except for once—just once —when we had that terrible snow storm, my check has come on time, each month. My son is dutiful about putting it into the mail so I may receive it on time, have it cashed, and be prepared to pay my rental and other bills that come due at the first of the month.

MR. GIL: *(Referring to the checkerboard)* That's a king now. Crown him.

MR. J: As each time in the past, I came down on the first of the month to receive my mail. I looked for my check. It was not there. On the second day I checked my mail and again it was not there. On the third day I then confronted the postman who had the audacity to tell me he had given me the check in person. I said to him, "Sir, I am in complete charge of all my mental faculties, and if you had given me the check, I would certainly know it. He said he remembered clearly that I had asked him to give me the check because I was on my way to do my marketing.

MR. GIL: Because you're old—

MR. J: Mr. Gillison, I don't consider myself to be a young man if that's what you mean. But neither do I consider myself to be old.

MR. GIL: What I'm saying is that the mailman he thinks you're old, and because you're old, he thinks you're also a fool. I don't have to tell you, governor, about what age do to some people. Now the mailman figger he's got hisself a fool in you. He go take your check, pocket the money, and make like he gave it to you because he know you don't remember too well anymore.

MR. J: If he's done that in the past, then he's done it once too often. This time he will be brought to justice.

MR. GIL: What will they do to him?

MR. J: Well, first, they must catch him at his crime. They have laid a trap for him, and we will all hear about it soon enough. *(MRS. G, hopping on crutches and carrying the newspaper and a pillow under her arm, enters through the first door. To MRS. G)* Do you need any assistance, Mrs. Green?

MRS. G: No, you all go right on with your game. I can manage. *(With much maneuvering she gets settled on the top steps. She spreads her paper to read)* Hey, you all, I need me a good number. Since my last big hit, all my money is just about gone. *(Reading the paper)* Old Sam Bo here says 574. Bad Boy, what you think? 574 got a chance?

MR. GIL: Not a chance. The next big winner is going to be a triple—333.

MRS. G: 333? Say, Lester? What number you got going for you?

LES: Tell, Mrs. Green, and you put a jinx on it.

MRS. G: *(Giggles)* Lord, ain't that the truth? Maybe that's why I can't git another hit.

MR. GIL: Speaking of jinx! My fourth wife was just that.

MRS. G: Bad Boy, leave that poor woman alone. You done told more lies on that poor dead woman than the Law allows. Let your wife rest in peace.

MR. GIL: Why, that woman could jinx Lincoln's face right off'n a penny without the bank even suspecting it. And that ain't no lie. *(To MR. J)* Your move. *(MR. J studies the board)* Ask anybody in Savannah, Georgia who remembers me. They'll tell you—I was a successful businessman with all three of my wives. I sold ice, wood, parched peanuts. On Saturday nights, I sold fried fish and homebrew. Everything went good until I married that fourth woman, and then I started my streak of bad luck—and that bad luck has stuck with me until this very day.

MRS. G: That poor woman didn't have nothin to do with it. Bad luck lives with all Black people, Bad Boy.

MR. GIL: Like hell you preach! Ain't nobody's gonna tell me different about that woman when I lived with her. I know the truth. Didn't matter what I did, what I said, bad luck, bad luck, bad luck—all because of Gertrude Gordon. When I was married to them other three, never once did I have a fire in my business. As soon as I married her, I had three fires—the last one burned me to the ground—every blessed thing I owned. Besides, them white folks wouldn't give me no insurance.

MRS. G: The trouble with Black men, Bad Boy, is you all don't appreciate a good Black woman when you all get one. I know I did everything but kiss Mr. Green's ass to get along with him, and in the end—what happened? He left me for some old no-good slut down there on 110th street. The bitch can't even speak English, and yet he left me for *her!*

MR. GIL: If I come across a woman I might consider to be the fifth, she ain't go be nothin like Gertrude Gordon, I'll tell you that.

MRS. G: What I don't understand about you, Bad Boy, is how come you outlived all your four wives. Women's supposed to outlive men. At least, that's what they tell me.

MR. GIL: I took care of myself. That's why. I didn't hump myself to death.

MRS. G: I got my suspicion about a man who outlived four wives.

MR. GIL: What suspicion?

MRS. G: *(Cackles)* I ain't telling. Lord, I sure ain't telling.

(MR. GIL pauses. MR. J brings his attention back to the game)

LES: Mrs. Green? What's the court going to do about your legs?

MRS. G: Not a damn thing, Lester. And do you know why, Lester? Cause I couldn't get a single Black man in this building to stand up behind me. The super testified against me. Ain't that something? His own kind! He told the Court that I was trying to get something for nothing. Now you all remember last year when the plaster fell and hit me on my head?

MR. GIL: I wasn't there to see it.

MRS. G: No one was there to see it.

MR. GIL: You told us about it.

MRS. G: Why would I lie about it if it wasn't true?

MR. J: Mrs. Green, in a court of Law you cannot submit hearsay evidence. We were not there. We did not see the accident.

MRS. G: You saw my head, didn't you? How you all think I got it busted. The doctor said I had a "concussion."

MR. J: Nevertheless, it was still hearsay. We did not see the accident.

MRS. G: Ain't that some shit? I guess you all didn't see the rug torn on those steps either.

MR. J: We saw the rug torn all right.

MR. GIL: What we didn't see was when you fell.

MR. J: And I don't see how you could have tripped over where the rug was torn, Mrs. Green.

MRS. G: Don't matter whether you can see it or not, Mr. Jefferson. It happened. Don't you call me no liar.

MR. J: Well, as I told the lawyer, I personally did not see the accident. I also told him I have never seen you drunk, and I haven't. But he pointed out to me, I cannot say you were not drunk since I was not there at the time of the accident.

MRS. G: Both of those lawyers was full of shit. Since mine didn't win my case, I'm gonna see how he's going to get paid. You know, Mr. Jefferson, school teacher or not, a lot of you all got a lot to learn. Now you all don't like Amos and Andy cause the White man has got your number with Amos and Andy. This house is full of Amos and Andies, and that's for damn sure.

MR. J: Mrs. Green, I have never shirked my responsibility of speaking up for the race when I considered it the proper thing to do.

MR. GIL: Ain't no White man ever made no coward of me either. Ask anybody who know me from Savannah. They'll tell you I'd as quick as go up the side of a White man's head as a Black man's if he gave me cause to. Why most of the time I spent on the chain gang bustin rocks was for whippin White men.

(BOBBY and REDD enter from up the street. On seeing them, LES rises)

MRS. G: You all can say what you all wants to— But not until Black people stick together as a people, nothing is going to change for none of us. All we will git is shit.

MR. J: I'm afraid, Mrs. Green, that is precisely what we are getting—and much too much of it for any good.

BOBBY: Hi Les! Good morning, you all!

(The others return greetings)

LES: *(To BOBBY and REDD)* You all come on in.

(They enter into the house through the second door. Lights fade down on the exterior, up on the living room)

BOBBY: *(Entering the living room)* Les—*(With his arms raised for mercy)* I plead guilty. I throw myself on the mercy of the court.

LES: What else is new, Bobby?

BOBBY: I ain't denying the fact that you got a right to be mad. As I told Redd here, I know you ain't been feeling good about your son, and I guess I put you guys in a hole, but as Redd said he told you, I've been having problems, man—real problems.

LES: We all have real problems—less bread and less porkchops. So, Bobby? What do you want from me?

BOBBY: *(Bowing)* Mercy, your honor, mercy! Les, I ain't perfect.

LES: No man is.

REDD: Les, I told him to come to you, talk to you face-to-face like a man should.

BOBBY: Les, I know—

LES: Who said Bobby was a man? *(Loudly)* You know what, Bobby? Look, I've heard all this before. Ain't no sense in going on with this. I've made up my mind. Bobby, you can find yourself another group.

BOBBY: Les, I know.

LES: You know what, Bobby? What do you know? That you ain't shown up at the club for the last three weeks? That you took those arrangements we was depending on, said you'd give them to us the next night—That was a month ago?

BOBBY: I got those arrangements, Les. I did them.

LES: So what good will they do us if you have them? Do you know you've been fired from the restaurant?

BOBBY: The restaurant, Les, I don't care about the restaurant.

LES: You don't care about nothing. The restaurant is just one of the things you don't care about, Bobby. You don't care about anything or anybody but yourself.

BOBBY: I ain't no waiter, Les.

LES: You ain't no musician either, Bobby. To tell you the truth, Bobby, you ain't nothin but a poor excuse for a man.

BOBBY: I guess I got it coming to me.

REDD: Les, I think if you let him explain, he can convince you why he ain't been showing up at the club. It's true—he's been having trouble.

LES: We all have trouble, Redd. Bobby ain't no different from the rest of us. Shit!

REDD: No. Les, he's different. Les, he has been sick. I talked with Bea.

LES: And that's another thing, this goddamn Bea! This woman you're giving Maggie and your three children a hard time for. Why, Bobby? In God's name why? You can't take care of one house! How in the hell are you going to take care of two?

BOBBY: Les, I don't take care of Bea. That's it. Bea takes care of me. That's the difference between Bea and Maggie. Bea *helps* me. Now, no matter how you look on me—I ain't go let you or nobody else put Bea down. Bea's been a damn good woman to me.

LES: *Me, me, me!*

BOBBY: If it wasn't for Bea, I wouldn't be here now.

LES: Bobby, just leave my house. Go on! I just can't stand to look at you.

REDD: Les, you gotta hear him out.

LES: I ain't gotta do a goddamn thing I don't want to. Ain't Maggie been a good woman to him, huh? *(To BOBBY)* You pump her full of fuckin babies, and now you're gonna stand there and tell me that Maggie ain't been a good woman to you?

BOBBY: I didn't say that.

LES: You didn't say that!

REDD: Lester, Bobby's been sick—real sick.

LES: Redd, stop being Bobby's *mammy*. Bobby is sick—and so am I—sick of Bobby—riding for free.

REDD: It ain't just started—

LES: You damn right it ain't.

REDD: I mean his sickness.

LES: It started the day Bobby was born. Bobby is sorry-assed with no fuckin sense of responsibility.

REDD: Les—

LES: With no sense of responsibility!

BOBBY: Les, it ain't no sense trying to talk to you, when you're like this.

LES: *(To BOBBY)* When last did you see Maggie and the children, huh? When? Do you know how they are eating?

BOBBY: They're eating, Les.

LES: How in the hell do you know? When last did you give Maggie money for the children?

BOBBY: Redd told me you'd given them my pay.

LES: You—you—your pay? Redd told you—Your pay for doing what, nigger? You ain't blowed a

note in a goddamn horn for the last three weeks. What in the hell am I supposed to be paying you for?

BOBBY: You never said I was fired.

LES: I'm saying it now, Bobby. You are fired. Goddammit fired! *(To REDD)* Didn't you tell him? That is what I told you to tell him. He's fired.

REDD: Les, I'm trying to tell you the man been sick. *(To BOBBY)* Tell the man, Bobby. Tell 'em. *(BOBBY hesitates)* Tell the man!

LES: I'm all ears, Bobby. Tell me. Tell me. About your heart palpitations, your bad kidney, your asthma. Tell me.

BOBBY: Look! You know our business—

LES: Bobby, get the hell on out of here.

REDD: Les—

LES: Redd, I know what he's going to tell me. I ain't no fool. He's been on stuff!

REDD: Les—

LES: Well, Bobby?

BOBBY: Les, I'm clean now. So help me God, I'm clean now. I beat it.

LES: In my fuckin band! You know what I told you when you first came to me.

REDD: Les, listen!

LES: All of you! I told you—if I caught anybody on that shit—you're out—

BOBBY: That's what I'm trying to tell you, Les.

LES: Tell me what? That next week you're on again.

BOBBY: No, I'm trying to tell you. Bea helped me, Les. I'm better. I'm over the hill, man. So help me, God, Les. My mind's clear. See, *(Holds out his hand)* I'm steady—

LES: So you're right for another group. With me you are through, Bobby. Through.

REDD: Les—

LES: He's through, Redd. Do you think I'm a damn fool? Didn't you know why Detective Mooney and Sullivan's been hugging our band? They're on to you, Bobby, Goddamn you. They're on to *you!*

BOBBY: Les—

LES: Get out of here, Bobby. Redd, get him out of *here.*

REDD: Les, give the man a chance. *(Buffering* BOBBY*)* Les—listen to me. Listen, now he didn't come before 'cause he had to get himself straightened out. And he has, Les. He has. Now he first came to me, told me his troubles. I told him no way was you going to let him off unless he got himself right. Les, he went cold turkey. Les, do you know what that mean?

LES: It means the band can do without Bobby. I want no connection with dope in my band.

REDD: Les, take a damn good look at him. He's a *colored* man. Now, if we don't help one another, who else will, huh? He's got to work, Les. He's got the children.

LES: He's got Maggie and the children!

REDD: Maggie and the children! And they've got to eat. They've got to have a roof over their heads.

BOBBY: I ain't going back to Maggie. It's all over between us.

REDD: *(To BOBBY)* You and Maggie will work it out! Les, are you hearing me? Are you listening—to me? To what's deep inside of you? Les—This could be Sonny—your own son—standing there. Would you want him turned away? *(Presently)* Give him the same chance you'd give your own son. That's all I'm asking. Give the man a chance.

LES: *(Presently. To BOBBY)* You say you want to do the right thing? Then do the right thing by Maggie and your three girls.

BOBBY: Les, you don't understand.

LES: I understand that if you're going to work in my band, you're going to take care of Maggie and your three girls.

BOBBY: Then I don't work in your band, Les!

LES: Then you don't work, Bobby, not in my band—and I'm going to put the word out on you.

REDD: Les—

BOBBY: What are you, Les? Mussolini? Hitler? Franco?

REDD: He's Lester, Bobby, and he's giving you another chance. Don't ruin it.

BOBBY: *(Trembling)* He don't understand. Maggie will wreck *me*. She's already ruined my life—and I oughta have a few things to say about my own life.

REDD: Bobby, cool off—cool off! Les, I'll talk to Bobby.

LES: You do that. You talk to him. *(He angrily exits into the room off left)*

BOBBY: *(Trembling)* Look, Redd! Les ain't my daddy. I don't have to take this kind of shit from him. I've got—

REDD: To stop talking and do some thinking. Come on. I'll go with you to Maggie.

BOBBY: *(Trembles more)* To Maggie? No, I ain't—You don't understand.

REDD: She's just another woman. Maybe she's willing to give you up to Bea. Let's go talk to her.

BOBBY: Redd, I ain't going to Maggie. I'm getting sick. I'm getting all sick inside again.

REDD: Come on. Let's get out of here.

BOBBY: Redd, I ain't gonna make it if I go back to Maggie. I swear I ain't gonna make it. I tell you I'm getting sick. I need something.

REDD: Come on. Come on.

(BOBBY and REDD exit to the street. Lights fade down on the living room and up on the street as they exit up the street with REDD's arm around BOBBY's shoulder. The mailman, MR. PRIESTER, enters up the street. LES reenters the living room. He's having second thoughts. He starts for the front door. Then he stops. He paces thoughtfully before he sits heavily at the piano. He's a troubled man. Presently he touches the piano keys with one finger. He continues in deep thought)

MRS. G: *(On seeing the mailman)* Here comes the mailman.

MR. GIL: Just when *nature* is calling me to go to the bathroom. Will be right back, governor. *(He exits through the first front door)*

MR. J: *(To MRS. G)* Mr. Gillison doesn't want to be a witness to my confrontations with the postman.

MRS. G: *(Adjusts herself in anticipation)* Give him hell, Mr. Jefferson. Afterall, he stole your check your *son* sent to you. These White folks are something else!

MR. PRIESTER: *(Ascending the steps of the first stoop. Cheerfully)* Good morning . . .

MRS. G: Good morning!

MR. J: For some of us, it *is* a good morning, sir, I suppose? For others, there's some doubt.

MR. P: *(Moving up the stairs)* Sir, it's like that the whole world over.

MRS. G: Before you go inside, Mr. Priester, this man wants to know about his check.

MR. P: *(Stops)* Please—I don't want to get into any more arguments about his check.

MRS. G: Lord—what you say! You don't want to get into—It's your job, Mr. Priester, to give this man satisfaction. We are taxpayers! It's *his* check.

MR. P: As I've told the gentleman before, I don't know anything more about his check than what I've told him. My job is to deliver the mail. That's all it is—and I delivered him his check.

MR. J: That is the lie under question, sir. Did you or did you not deliver the check? That is the rub of the question, sir.

MR. P: The rub? The rub? I delivered the check.

MRS. G: If you delivered it, when was it stolen? In your investigation, did you find anything about the check? It's got to show up somewhere.

MR. P: Do you mean, did the post office find anything about his check? If the post office has, it has not informed me, and I doubt that it *will*. It will, however, no doubt, inform the gentleman of the check *if* and *when* it learns more about the check.

MRS. G: Even when the check was stolen?

MR. P: Lady, a stolen check has no value unless it is cashed. Now according to the gentleman's claim, the check was stolen—

MR. J: And it was!

MR. P: Then I still advise you, sir, put a stop payment on the check. It will not be of any service to anyone if you do.

MR. J: You can rest assured that the proper steps have been taken, sir. What I'm finding most complex, however, is to fathom your audacious persistence in relating that you did deliver the check to me personally.

(MR. GEORGE *and* MR. COTTEL *enter from up the street.* MR. GEORGE *carries a police club*)

MR. P: Sir, I did! I cannot help it if you—Look, when we get older, we tend to forget.

MR. J: (Agitated) Sir, that is a *lie*. I am in *full* charge of my mental faculties. I say *you* never delivered that check.

MR. P: If you say, sir. (Starts, then back again) I remember, sir, on the morning I delivered the check, you were standing there in the doorway. You said you were waiting for me because you were on your way to buy groceries . . .

MR. J: (More agitated) Sir, I said *that* is a lie!

MR. P: As I said, I don't want to argue with you about it. (Goes into the house)

MRS. G: (On seeing MR. GEO and MR. C) Look what's coming! The rat with his louse!

MR. J: (Agitated) I can fully understand why some men revert to physical violence. That man is a *liar* and a *thief!* He needs to be compelled by force to tell the truth.

MRS. G: (For the sake of MR. C and MR. GEO) Jesus, have mercy! It sure does stink. (To MR. J) Mr. Jefferson, do you think it's some dead rats behind the walls? O-o-o-o-e-e-ee—God, does it smell!

(MR. C and MR. GEO go to the second door, ring the bell. LES answers it)

MR. C: (To LES) Good morning, Lester.

LES: Good morning, Mr. Cottel. Just a minute. (LES goes back into living room and gets an envelope from the top of the piano. In the meantime, MRS. G continues)

MRS. G: Could it be bad breath I smell? Eating White folks' garbage?

MR. J: Madam!

MRS. G: All muscles and no brains! And it's against the law for anybody to carry a police club unless he is a policeman. I asked my lawyer about that. Muscles for brains! No guts! Yellow-belly! I'm going to the police precinct and find out if some people have licenses to have police clubs? (MR. GEO mumbles to MR. C. To MR. GEO) Did you say something to me?

MR. C: (To MRS. G) He was speaking to me. (MR. GEO slaps the club threateningly against the palm of his hand)

MRS. G: He knows better than to open his god-

damn mouth to me . . . I ain't got no respect for a coward. . . . One of these days, a real man is gonna take that club from you and make you eat it.

(MR. GEO and MRS. G angrily stare at each other. LES breaks it by counting the money to MR. GEO as MR. C writes a receipt)

LES: (As he counts the money) We are still waiting for you to fix that leak under the kitchen sink—and I told you the last time that something is wrong with the frigerdaire. (MR. C is writing the receipt) And the water pressure in the bathroom is still too low. When you go to the bathroom, you've got to pour buckets of water into the toilet to make it flush. . . . And it's time for you to paint the apartment again, Mr. Cottel.

MR. C: We'll take care of it.

LES: That's what you said last month, Mr. Cottel, and the month before that.

MR. C: We'll take care of it, Lester. Rome was not built in a day. It takes money to do all these things, and money is not what I'm getting from you people down here. A lot of excuses, yes— money, no!

LES: That's what you say, Mr. Cottel, but when I can't pay you on time, you don't seem too ready to wait on me. How many eviction notices you done served me over the years?

MR. C: I have waited for you, Lester, many times. If you don't like it here, you don't have to stay, you know.

(MR. P comes from the first house and exits up the street)

MR. J: (Calling behind MR. P) You will be found out, sir! (Without turning around, MR. P waves him "good-bye") You are fooling with the business of your Federal government.

MRS. G: What is the super supposed to do—if he ain't supposed to fix broken steps and torn rugs? I almost broke my neck on those goddamn steps.

MR. C: Last year it was your *head.* You're accident prone.

MRS. G: And this day, it's gonna be your ass if you start with me, Mr. Cottel.

MR. C: Don't threaten me, Helen. I won't take that from you. (Comes to MR. J) You've got your rent?

MR. J: Sir, my rental is sent to you each month through the mail.

(MR. C starts up the stairs followed by MR. GEO)

MRS. G: I've got my rent.

MR. C: You keep it. All I want from you, Helen Green, is my apartment. I want you out of here. You have until the end of this month, and if you're not out by then, the sheriff will come and put you out.

MRS. G: That's the day hell will freeze over, Mr. Cottel. We'll see about that. (Struggles to get up)

All I want from you or that Black sucker behind you is one wrong move so I can "salivate" your asses.

(MR. C and MR. GEO exit into the house. MRS. G on crutches follows)

LES: *(Calling to MRS. G)* Take it easy, Mrs. Green. Take it easy. The law is on their side.

(MR. J, mumbling, gathers up the checkers and board and follows into the house. LES hesitates then enters again into the living room. Lights fade down on the stoop and up on the living room. IDA, tightly wrapped in a winter coat, hat, and gloves, enters into the living room from off left. She carries a suitcase. Her pace is slow but determined. She sings, "I'm on my way to the Promised Land")

IDA: *(On seeing LES)* Les, don't try to stop me. If you don't wanna go, don't hinder me. I'm on my way, praise the Lord! Unless you all repent, you all will perish. Luke, thirteenth chapter, third verse.

LES: Ida, let's not start that bullshit again. Now, you've been warned. *(Calls)* Vi! Vi!

IDA: Les, he said "they who have done good shall come forth unto resurrection of life." *(Moves out of LES's reach)* "Go down, tell old Pharoah to let my people go. It's my message saith the Lord." On my dying bed, I promised him I'd go into the valleys and on the mountain tops if he blessed me back to health.

LES: Ida, it's going to be at least ninety degress in the shade today. Now in heaven's name, girl, tell me, where are you going all wrapped up in that overcoat?

IDA: I'm on my way to New Orleans, Les, where I'm needed.

LES: *(Calling)* Vi!

IDA: I'm not afraid, for no evil can harm me. I am a woman who fears the Lord.

LES: *(Stops IDA)* Ida, listen to me. *(Calls)* Vi!

VI: *(Off)* Yes, Les! What is it?

LES: *(Studies IDA's face. Then draws her to him tenderly. He struggles to hold back his tears)* Ida, honey, Ida—*(Gets control)* T'ain't nobody waiting in New Orleans for you. *(Calls)* Vi, come get Ida!

VI: *(Off)* Mamma—

IDA: Cousin Elizabeth and the children are there, Les, waiting for me. I know.

LES: Ida, you don't know nothing. Your cousin Elizabeth is *dead*. She died ten years ago. Don't you remember?

IDA: No!

LES: Ida, cut out the bullshit! Her oldest daughter, Drucilla, is in Chicago, and Evelyn is a nurse living in Savannah. Don't you remember? *(Calls)* Vi—

IDA: Les, you're trying to keep me here against

God's will. That's a sin, son! We shall have many good things if we *fear* God. Now you obey him. It was God who told me to go to the children in New Orleans.

(Carrying his guitar, JAKE enters the exterior from up the street. He stops to muffle a fit of coughing)

LES: *(Taking off IDA's hat)* Ida, we love you, girl, and we don't want anything bad to happen to you. Now you gotta listen to us. You've been sick. *(He hugs her tightly. Presently)* You've got to stop running away. You know what they told you the last time.

(As JAKE climbs the steps for the second door, MR. GEO and MR. COTTEL exit from the first door and exit up the street)

IDA: God told me to go to New Orleans to watch over Elizabeth and the children. God showed me Elizabeth is not well. Les, she needs me.

LES: Ida, that's a lot of bullshit. Cut it out. Elizabeth is dcad! Ida, that judge told you if they catch you on the streets again they're going to lock you up, honey, and it ain't gonna be *nothin* we can do to get you out—

VI: *(Enters, holding a bottle of beer and dressed in a fading kimono)* Mamma, what's you up to now? Are you going to send me to the crazy house?

IDA: *(Mildly resisting LES as he tries to take off her coat)* This house is full of sin, and I'll run away again ever chance I git. *(JAKE enters the hall. He has another fit of coughing)* The sisters in the church are going to help me get away.

VI: They are going to help land you in jail again. Is that what you want?

LES: Take it easy, Vi!

JAKE: Good mornin, all.

LES: Hi, Jake.

IDA: Go into the whole world and preach the gospel to every creature. Mark, sixteenth chapter, fifteenth verse.

VI: Come on, Mamma. *(Gathers up IDA's coat, hat, and suitcase)*

JAKE: I tried to get here before Mr. Cottel. I saw him and Mr. George on my way in. Did Sonny come yet?

LES: Don't worry about Mr. Cottel. I had the rent.

JAKE: No—No—I'm not worried. It's just—I've got mine, Les. *(Goes into his pocket. Brings out a set of crumpled loose dollar bills. He busies himself straightening out the bills and counting them)* Grace had one hell of a house party last night. (VI *is angrily staring at LES who is consciously avoiding the confrontation)*

IDA: Be not conformed to this world. Oh, sweet Jesus, give me strength to do thy work.

LES: Jake, we can take care of that later.

JAKE: No, no, no. I've got it, Les. Let me give it to you while I've got it. *(Busy with the money)* Did our boy come home?

LES: No. *(Everybody stops)*

IDA: *(Presently)* Grace be to you, and peace from God our Father and from our Lord, Jesus Christ. *(VI ushers IDA off. VI returns with a new bottle of beer)*

JAKE: I've got good news for Sonny. I was talkin to Mr. Rabinowitz—and he said he is sure he can get Sonny a scholarship at either Morehouse College or at Morris Brown. I don't think you need to borrow money.

VI: We borrow money to buy horns, not to educate Sonny.

(She and LES exchange angry expressions as she gulps down some beer. JAKE has a fit of coughing. VI is deeply distressed by it. After the fit, JAKE, LES, and VI, pause awkwardly. JAKE extends the money to LES. MR. J and MR. GIL return to the stoop with their checkerboard and pillow. They set up their boards as the interior scene continues)

JAKE: I told Mr. Rabinowitz I would talk to Sonny. Those are two of the best colleges in the country, white or black. *(Presently)* Take the money, Les.

LES: *(Taking the money reluctantly)* Jake, I—

JAKE: Don't worry about it. You know me. When I've got it, I pay. If I don't have it, I say so. Right?

LES: Right!

JAKE: I'm excited about how Mr. Rabinowitz can help Sonny. *(Another fit of coughing)* Looks like I'm trying to catch pneumonia dead in the middle of summer.

LES: You'd better get some sleep, man. You can't play all night and talk all day.

JAKE: *(Embarrassed by his coughing)* Yeah—*(He's tired)* I've got another job lined up for tonight—You're right. I'd better get some sleep. When Sonny comes, call me. He promised me—he'd come today. I'll talk to him—tell him the good news . . . *(Slowly exits up the staircase into his bedroom. He pauses—lays down his guitar and quietly lies, face down, across the bed. LES watches JAKE's exit)*

VI: Why did you take his rent?

LES: I'll handle this in my own way, Vi.

VI: Yeah, by that time, we'll all be dead. *(Sits at the table)* Everybody and everything comes before your family, right Les?

LES: He *is* my family. *(Paces aimlessly)*

VI: He is your *friend*, Les. We are your family, me and Sonny, and blood is thicker than water, Les!

LES: I don't want to talk about it.

VI: No, you don't want to talk about it, Les. You don't want to talk about anything I want. I want Jake out of my house. That's what I want. I'm not going to expose myself—

LES: You don't have to expose yourself!

VI: We are all exposing ourselves.

LES: Keep your voice down.

VI: We have one bathroom. When we're not here, I don't know where he goes, what dishes he uses. I can't keep on rewashing dishes in cooking soda everyday.

LES: Vi—

VI: Jake has tubeculosis, Les. He's got it.

LES: You don't know that.

VI: Les, I know that, and you do too. Now, goddammit, Les, I know how you feel about Jake.

LES: Don't you curse at me! No you don't.

VI: Les, you love Jake.

LES: *(Nods)* I love him. He's been like a brother to me all my life. He's more than just a friend—

VI: I know that, Les. And, Les, I love Jake too. I swear to God I love him, and when I hear him up there coughing his lungs out in the middle of the morning . . . I know how it hurts you. You don't fool me. You're not sleeping either. But, Les, he's got to go before he passes his T.B. to all of us. He'll listen to you, Les. Get him to go to the sanitarium.

LES: That's like telling him to go into some damn alleyway and die . . .

VI: The sanitarium is better than keeping him *here* and killing us all off, Les—

LES: I said I'll talk to him, and I will. *(Starts off)*

VI: Today, Les! You give him back his rent. You tell him he's got to go.

LES: *(Pauses at the door)* Yeah, I'll tell him . . . and in the meantime who's going to tell you, Vi? To knock off the drinking? . . .

VI: I drink a couple bottles of beer.

LES: A couple?

VI: Les, don't take it out on me. I'm not blaming you—but somehow, we have not managed things well at all—Where are all our dreams for Sonny? We said he was going to college—He was going to be a doctor.

LES: Sonny is only nineteen years old. There's time . . .

VI: That's what you said when he was twelve! Why can't we borrow the money?

LES: Borrow the money on *what*? Borrow the money from who?

VI: Les, if you really want to send Sonny to College, you can do it. I know you, and I know when you want to do something, Les, you do it . . .

LES: I want to stop you from becoming a lush. Tell me how to do that.

(He exits beyond the living room. VI stares at the bottle, bows her head on the table and quietly weeps. JAKE has a short period of coughing—then lies quietly again. The lights fade down on the living room and up on the exterior. MRS. G comes to the window with

a large plate of food. *She sits at the window and begins to eat)*

MRS. G: *(With mouthful)* I'm going downtown and get me another lawyer. I offered Cottel my rent and he refused to take it. You are my witness, Mr. Jefferson. Now I know that's against the law.

MR. J: Madam! Do you need to sit in the window to eat your food?

MRS. G: *(Chewing hurriedly)* I'm in my own *goddamn* window . . .

MR. J: Madam, it is bad taste, and it casts an aspersion on the entire Black race.

MRS. G: Cast a what?! I don't have a patio, Mr. Jefferson, or a piazza. I have my window, so let me eat in my window until my patio comes along.

MR. J: It is *uncouth!*

MRS. G: It's what? You and your big words! You watch what you say to me, Mr. Jefferson. Oh, to hell with you, man! You ain't seen nothing yet. *(She leaves the window with her food)*

MR. GIL: *(To MR. J)* Don't you get into *nothin* with that woman. What is she up to?

MR. J: She's the kind of woman that could get a man into a world of trouble.

MRS. G: *(Comes to the stoop with her food)* I think I'll sit out here on my patio and eat my dinner. Now let's see who's going to take my damn draws down and spank my behind.

MR. J: Mr. Gillison, we will go into the house. We can finish the game in a proper environment.

MRS. G: *(Cackles)* You two are something else! If you all wasn't so old, I'd be suspicious about what's going on between you.

(The two men exit into the house. The DETECTIVE and POLICEMAN enter from up the street. In the distance the radio plays, "God Bless America." They quietly talk to MRS. G, showing her papers, etc. While they talk to her, SONNY, MOE, DAVID, and AL enter up the street carrying books. The DETECTIVE and POLICEMAN go into the first house. MRS. G is agitated, curious, perplexed)

SONNY: *(Arriving)* Hello, Mrs. Green.

MRS. G: Hello, Sonny!

(The others greet her. She mumbles her greetings and watches them exit through the second door. Once they're beyond the door, the lights fade down on the exterior and up on the interior)

SONNY: *(Pauses at the entrance with his friends as he discovers VI. Presently)* Vi—Vi, it's me, Sonny.

VI: *(Slowly realizing it is SONNY)* Sonny—I— *(Rises. Delighted, embarrassed. Calls)* Les! Les, Sonny is home. *(JAKE hears, sits erect on the bed. Starts, falls back into a fit of muffled coughing)*

SONNY: *(Presently)* These are three of my com-

rades. David. You know him.

DAVID: *(Enthusiastically)* Hi, Mrs. Denegal.

VI: David! Hello. . . . You fellows, come in. . . . Sit down, please. Let me get you something. *(Starts)*

SONNY: No, Vi! We want nothing. *(Presently)* Vi, this is Al.

AL: Hello, Mrs. Denegal.

(VI nods)

SONNY: And this is Moe.

VI: Moe! *(MOE nods. Calls)* Les! Les, Sonny's home. You all excuse me, please. I didn't know Sonny was bringing company. I must get on some decent clothes.

SONNY: No, Vi! *(VI stops)* You don't have to get dressed to please us. If you are comfortable like you are, that's all that matters, Vi! *(The others agree)*

VI: Well, I'm not comfortable this way, Sonny. You know—I don't want your friends to think—

SONNY: *(Impatient)* My friends think you don't need to apologize, Vi! *(SONNY moves about the room)*

VI: *(Presently)* I guess Les fell asleep. He must have laid down. He hasn't been to bed since we got in . . . *(Starts)* I'll get him. *(JAKE sits silently on the bed)*

SONNY: No, Vi! *(VI stops)* Let Les sleep. It will be easier . . .

VI: He wants to see you, Sonny.

SONNY: *(Shrugs indiffernece)* Vi, are you afraid to talk to me without Les?

VI: No!—Why—That's silly. It's just—the real reason he hadn't gone to bed was because—when Jake told him he'd found you and you promised you'd come home today—

SONNY: Vi, I promised Uncle Jake I'd come today to get a few of my personal things.

VI: What personal things, Sonny—

SONNY: Vi, I don't want to have another fight with Les! *(Moves impatiently about the room)*

VI: But you don't understand Les!

SONNY: Nor with you! *(Continues to move about the room. He's torn)* Vi, how's Grandmama?

VI: She's *all right* . . . *(Presently)* No, the truth is, Sonny, she's getting *worse.* *(Gesticulating)* She gets things all mixed up. Her real mind's gone. . . . But it's Jake who's got good news for you—about a scholarship to Morehouse or Morris Brown College. . . . *(Presently)* Are you eating like you should, Sonny? You look tired . . . Sonny, go to college, and if you don't like it—then—

SONNY: *(More irritation)* Vi, I'm not going to college. Please, let's not start that all over again. Try to understand what I've been telling you. *(AL crosses to SONNY as a restraining gesture)* College has only one purpose, and that is to make me a willing pawn of the capitalistic system. *(LES enters. He was sleeping. There's an awkward pause)* Hi, Les! *(JAKE is off the bed)*

LES: Hello, Sonny! So, you've come home again? Good! You look all right. Who are your friends?

SONNY: These are my comrades, David, Al, and Moe. *(They greet LES as "Mr. Denegal." He nods his greetings)* I've come to get a few of my personal things.

LES: Welcome! Get whatever you think you want. If you want the piano, take that too. *(Presently)* Did you feel you had to bring bodyguards to protect yourself from us?

VI: Les—

SONNY: Les, I don't want to fight with you!

LES: Who's fighting? Sonny, I don't want to fight with you either. I'm glad you've come back. But is it asking too much of my only son to tell me why he couldn't come home—alone—after the way he left? Didn't Jake tell you we wanted you back? We want you back! Is that so bad? Half those things I said to you was—well, I was angry —and when a man gets angry, he says a lot of the wrong things . . .

VI: Les has a sharp tongue, Sonny, but he—has a good heart! Sonny, you know that.

SONNY: Les, my comrades came with me because I asked them to.

LES: Your friends are welcome here. This is your home too. You know that.

SONNY: I thought they might help me to explain to you what the whole class struggle is all about. That is if you want to hear.

VI: Les, listen to them. It can't hurt.

(JAKE has another fit)

LES: *(Sits. Presently)* Gentlemen, I'm all ears.

SONNY: It's about survival, Les!

LES: Whose survival, Sonny? Yours? Theirs? Mine?

AL: The working class, sir! . . . We're members of the working class . . .

MOE: We're struggling against the oppression of the ruling class, Mr. Denegal. Comrade Lenin said, the working class has nothing to lose but their chains. Workers of the World must organize and struggle against all forms of oppression.

LES: I see, Whites are already organized against us Blacks. I don't need no Lenin to tell me that the Whites are born organized against us.

SONNY: Les—

DAVID: It's more than just that, Mr. Denegal. True, we must fight against White chauvinism, all forms of it, because it is White chauvinism that continues to poison the minds of many White workers.

AL: But it's more than just gentiles against Jews and anti-Catholics against Catholics . . .

LES: I know a lot of White workers who ain't above lynching *me*—and only because of one thing—my skin is *black*.

AL: True. And we must rid the working class of them.

LES: How?

AL: *(Intense anger)* Shoot them!

LES: Shoot them?

MOE: If we have to!

LES: With guns?

MOE: When the revolution comes—

(LES's and VI's alarm stops him)

AL: *(Presently)* Comrade Lenin and Stalin said we must rid ourselves of all oppressors whether they be capitalists or members of the working class.

SONNY: Les! It's what I've been trying to tell you!

LES: *(Angrily)* You ain't never told me nothing about killing nobody. What the hell are you talking about?

VI: *(Sits next to LES)* Not about shooting people, Sonny!

SONNY: It's not about that. It's not as simple as Les makes it. We must first educate the working class. Look! We've brought you some books you gotta read before you can really understand. *(Collects books from others and places them on the table)* What I've been trying to tell you is—school is not what you all think it is at all. It's just another supra structure of the capitalistic economic structure such as the police . . . insane asylum . . . the relief . . .

LES: *(Thumbing pages of a book)* I don't want to live no place where there ain't no school or police to protect us.

MOE: As you surely must have realized, Mr. Denegal, the exploitation of the working class is sending the sons of workers off to fight imperialistic wars. Your *son* . . .

DAVID: Wars that further enslave us, members of the working class. We will not go to war to make profits for capitalists.

VI: *(Presently)* Wars are bad. . . . Killing and crippling people . . .

DAVID: Working people, Mrs. Denegal! Capitalism cannot survive unless it has its wars. It is the wars of the imperialists that will destroy Europe.

MOE: The world if we allow it. We won't allow it.

AL: Mrs. Denegal, read these books. If you think the correct way a worker should, you will see that you are a Black woman and are doubly oppressed by the capitalistic system. *(Selects one of the books on the table)* Here's one. You should read this one written by one of our Black woman comrades. *(Gives the book to VI who is hesitant to take it)* It is an education in itself. As comrade Jones says first as a member of the Black nation

. . . and secondly as a woman, . . . you are doubly oppressed.

SONNY: *(Crowding in on* VI*)* Read it, Vi. You'll see you don't have a chance under capitalism.

LES: Wait! Wait a minute, not so fast! Don't you fellows believe in America no more?

SONNY: *(Impatient)* That's not the point!

LES: Then what in hell is the point?

AL: We do believe in America, Mr. Denegal. That's why we struggle.

MOE: *(Closing in)* That's exactly why we must fight our oppressors, because capitalists around the world are united. We must believe in an international revolution of all oppressed people that will free not only America but the world of oppressed people!

DAVID: *(To the others who agree)* Comrade Stalin says let the woking classes of the world unite!

LES: Then, it is more than just this country? It sounds to me like Hitler and that other crazy man in Italy.

DAVID: Hitler? No—Socialism is not Nazism.

LES: I see no damn difference.

MOE: We're Marxists, not facists.

SONNY: *(Enthusiastically)* It's the revolution of the whole wide world of oppressed people, Les!

DAVID: We must organize the oppressed peoples of Africa, Asia, Europe . . .

LES: I thought you all pledge you all's allegiance to the flag of the United States of America. I thought schools taught you all to believe in American democracy.

SONNY: We do believe in democracy—in socialistic democracy—

DAVID: Not in capitalism, Mr. Denegal.

AL: A democracy of the people and for the people.

DAVID: A socialistic democracy, Mr. Denegal. We find nothing wrong believing that, fighting for it, dying for it if it's necessary.

LES: Dying for it?

AL: We really believe in real freedoms of democracy, Mr. Denegal! Do we really have freedom of speech, freedom to pursue happiness? Did you read what they did to the union organizers down in Pennsylvania?

LES: *(Rises)* Cut the bullshit out. Cut it out!

*(*JAKE *sits again on the bed)*

VI: Les!

LES: Don't *Les* me!

SONNY: Don't be ignorant all your life, Les!

LES: What the hell is this? Who the hell are you mouthing to me about freedom and workers of the world? Your goddamn mother's milk ain't dried around your fuckin mouths yet.

VI: Les, don't!

LES: I'm no child. I'm a *man.* What kind of work has any of you done?

MOE: I'm a member of Local Thirty-nine—

LES: You're a member of what? You're a member of *nothing!* And if you all's examples of being educated, then I'm glad I'm ignorant.

SONNY: I told them you wouldn't listen. You were *born oppressed* and you will *die oppressed.* You *love being oppressed.*

LES: I won't listen to a lot of bullshit if that's what you mean. You've never worked a day in your life, Sonny.

SONNY: But you have, Les! You've worked all your life, and you ain't got *nothing* to show for it.

LES: We sacrificed so's you could get to school, get an education.

SONNY: I went to school. Do I have any more than you have? I want to go to Harvard, Les! Can you send me to Harvard or Yale?

LES: You don't need to go there to make a man of yourself. You can stay right here and be a *man.*

SONNY: Yeah—stay here and be a *man* like *you,* eh Les? I'll be like *you.*

LES: You come in here telling me about school being like a jail.

SONNY: *(Yells)* It is a jail! It's the capitalists' institution of keeping me oppressed.

VI: Sonny!

LES: *(To* SONNY*)* Yell at me again, and I'll knock your goddamn teeth down your throat. *(*SONNY *grabs a vase)* What are you going to do with that vase?

SONNY: I'm going to protect myself, Les!

LES: You raise a vase to me? *(Starts for* SONNY. VI *intercepts. The others push* SONNY *out.* VI *is torn between* SONNY *and* LES. JAKE *comes to the stairwell)*

VI: No, Les—Please, Les—Sonny! Sonny, don't go! Sonny. *(Follows him to the exterior)* Sonny! *(Calls after* SONNY*)* Sonny! Sonny—

LES: *(In the doorway)* Let him go! He'll *learn.* . . . Let him learn the goddamn *hard* way—*(Goes back into the living room)*

JAKE: Les, I'll talk to him. I'll go to him . . .

(As SONNY *and the others exit down the street,* MR. FOXX, *the insurance man, enters from up the street.* MRS. G *sees* MR. FOXX *and is torn between* SONNY *and the others leaving and* MR. FOXX *approaching.* VI *returns to the hall)*

JAKE: Vi—

VI: Jake—what's the use? What's the use?

JAKE: What can I do to help? I'm sure I can do *something.* Sonny believes in me.

VI: Leave my house, Jake! That's how you can help. Leave my house and spare us all from catching T.B.

LES: Damn you, Vi! What are you talking about?

VI: Show me you're a man, Les. Tell Jake he's got

to move. Tell him!

LES: You start telling me what to do!

VI: You drive Sonny out—but Jake—That's a different story.

JAKE: Vi, if you all want me to move, I'll move.

LES: Don't listen to her. *(To JAKE)* You'll stay here as long as you want to. I'm still the man in my house. *(VI looks from LES to JAKE)* It's all that goddamn drinking Vi's taking to lately.

VI: *(Tearfully)* What's the use! What's the use, Jake? *(Exits beyond the living room)*

JAKE: *(Presently)* Go to her, Les! You and me can talk later.... Sonny is the soul of her life.... She's hurting, Les, deep down...

LES: Jake—

JAKE: Don't worry about me!... You go to her. *(Presently JAKE exits up the stairwell into his room. LES crosses to the stairwell to look up the stairwell. JAKE sits dejectedly on the bed. The lights fade down on the interior and up on the exterior. Lights fade upon the exterior. MR. FOXX, the insurance man, sits opposite to MRS. G on a step below her. Radio in the nearby building plays Ella Fitzgerald singing "A Tisket, a Tasket")*

MR. FOXX: *(With his handkerchief wipes his brow)* Helen, how are you doing?

(LES exits downstairs beyond the living room)

MRS. G: I hope you ain't gonna tell me what I think you gonna tell me, Mr. Foxx. You got my check?

MR. F: Helen, my mother's sister, Aunt Sadie, had a colored maid who used to say—"You can't squeeze blood out of a turnip." *(JAKE rises, gets an empty suitcase from the closet, and begins to pack his clothes)* And when I was a kid, I didn't know what in the hell she meant. I thought anybody in her right mind would know wasn't no blood in a turnip.

MRS. G: If the insurance company don't pay me, I'm gonna sue them.

MR. F: They got three lawyers to every one you can afford. They claim they paid you for the last accident—that is when the plaster fell on your head!

MRS. G: It was an accident—just as this one was— me tripping on that ripped rug on the steps.

MR. F: I told them, Helen, but they said the first claim was doubtful too. I said I know this woman. Helen Green is a fine, honest, upright Christian woman. If she says she tripped, she *tripped*. She ain't lying.

MRS. G: That's for damn sure. Besides, they ain't doing me no favor. That money is mine. I pay that insurance every week.

MR. F: I told them. Not once have you been lapsed, I told them. That ought to mean something, I said. But, Helen, the company was ada-

mant. My bosses say, "No." They won't pay you unless you can give them more proof it was an accident.

MRS. G: We'll see what the Law says about that.

MR. F: That insurance policy reads that the company will take sides with the court's decision.

MRS. G: They would! I wouldn't be surprised if I learned that the landlord paid them off too. *(The DETECTIVE and POLICEMAN escort MR. GIL through the first front door)* Hey, what's going on? *(MR. F rises to permit the men to pass)* Charlie Bad Boy, you being arrested? What for? What's the charges?

DETEC: *(Calling back)* Forgery! Among other things—*(They exit up the street. MRS. G rises to watch them)*

MRS. G: Lord, have mercy! What they arresting him for? *(MR. JEFFERSON enters from the first door)* Mr. Jefferson, what's going on? What did Bad Boy do?

MR. J: I am on my way to the NAACP. Mr. Gillison will need a competent lawyer to defend him.

MRS. G: What did he do?

MR. J: It's not what he did. It's what they claimed he did.

MRS. G: Who claimed he did what?

MR. J: The Post Office is claiming he stole my check and forged my name.

MRS. G: Charlie Bad Boy! Do, Jesus!

MR. J: As you can very well understand, they aim to protect the real culprit in this crime, the mailman. *(He exits up the street)*

MRS. G: Lord, do have mercy! *(To MR. FOXX)* I know Bad Boy's neices. I'd better get down there on 119th street and let them know he's been arrested. This is something else! Mr. Foxx, you tell that company I'm suing them.

(She exits through the front door. Presently, MR. FOXX exits up the street. The lights fade down on the exterior and up on the interior. LES enters the living room and slowly ascends the stairwell. He knocks on the door. JAKE opens it, and LES enters. As the scene develops between JAKE and LES, IDA, dressed in her ovecoat, hat, and gloves and carrying her suitcase, tips through the living room and out of the door, down the steps and up the street, singing "I'm on my way...." The music playing on the radio is "Gold Mine in the Sky." The lights fade down in the living room and up more in the bedroom)

JAKE: *(To LES as he enters)* Is Vi all right?

LES: She'll live, if that's what you mean. *(LES sees the suitcase. Looks to JAKE for an answer)*

JAKE: *(Presently)* She's right, Les. It ain't fair.

LES: She ain't no damn doctor. How does she know what's wrong with you? Don't you see— She's looking for somebody to blame.

JAKE: *(Packing several last pieces of clothing)* She wants to be sure, Les. If I ain't got consumption—

LES: Some colds hang on like that, Jake. Don't you remember when I had that summer cold—

JAKE: No, I'm sick. It's not because of what Vi said. . . . I had already made up my mind—

LES: To do what?

JAKE: Go to the island.

LES: Jake—*(JAKE locks his suitcase)*

JAKE: If I'm to get well—That's the only place.

LES: Don't go there, Jake! Do you know anybody who's gone to the island and has come back—

JAKE: *(Presently)* Les, I'm not afraid of dying. Besides, Les, I'm *tired.*

LES: Because of the—

JAKE: No! More, more. It's like being at the circus, Les, and riding the carousel. After a while you want to get off. You've got to get off. *(Gets his guitar)* Remember when we were boys and the Ringling Bros. Circus came to town, the biggest circus in the whole wide world!

LES: I remember.

JAKE: Remember how we hauled water all day Sunday for the elephants while our parents thought we was in church.

LES: Me, you, Thomas, Frank, Leroy.

JAKE: We hauled water—

LES: And more water . . .

JAKE: The elephants just couldn't drink enough.

LES: We loved the circus! We went early in the morning before the circus opened up and stayed all day until it closed. Our parents thought we was in school.

JAKE: Yeah—

LES: We used to get our behinds whipped too for doing that.

JAKE: But we did it again and again. It was the loud music . . .

LES: And the clowns!

JAKE: And bright colors . . . pretty women . . . people laughin. . . . They forgot the miseries. . . . Les, they were happy. I've always thought about that.

LES: The Ringling Bros. Circus is coming to New York, Jake. I read of it in today's paper. Stay. You and I can take it in *this* time . . .

JAKE: *(Presently)* We waterd those elephants all day

—for a pass that allowed us only to enter the big tent and ride the carousel—as many times as we wanted to.

LES: *(Remembering)* And we sure rode the hell out of that carousel. We used to ride it and ride it and ride it . . .

JAKE: But, Les, we always got off exactly where we got on! *(Presently)* It was a ride, Les, that took us nowhere . . . *(Strapping his suitcase)* You and I have loved each other like brothers we never had. . . . We planned together. . . . We dreamed . . . *(He's incapable of going on.* LES *crosses to* JAKE *who is struggling to abort his tears.* LES *places a hand on* JAKE'*s shoulder)* I'll write. . . . Let you know my ward number . . . *(Gains control)* Sonny is going to be all right. . . . He's trying, Les, trying to find answers . . . trying to make the triangles equal. *(Lifts his suitcase and guitar)* You stay here. . . . Make it easy for me . . . *(He has a short fit of coughing)*

LES: Oh, God—Jake, *(Embraces* JAKE *tightly and sobs bitterly)* I'm losing everything I love. . . . I've tried. . . . Oh, God, how I've tried . . .

JAKE: *(Consoling* LES*)* It will be all right, Les. It will be all right.

LES: Sonny is ashamed of me!

JAKE: We've got to keep on thinking about the *rights* in this life . . . always keep *looking* and thinking about the rights—somewhere just behind or in front or under the wrongs. . . .

(Presently pulls away gently from LES *and, with his suitcase and guitar, exits hurriedly down the steps out the front door, and up the street, stopping briefly to end a fit of coughing. Presently,* LES *wipes his eyes, gets control of himself, and moves pensively around the room. In the meantime,* MRS. G *enters through the first front door on crutches and exits up the street. Presently,* LES, *still in a pensive mood, leaves the room, comes down to the living room. Presently, he picks up one of the books on the table. He thumbs through the pages. He begins to read and closes the book sharply. He moves to the stoop. He looks up and down the street. The radio is playing "God Bless America." He sits on a step. Presently, he rises, goes back into the living room, picks up the book, hesitates, then takes the book to the stoop where he sits on a step and begins to read it, at first cautiously. As he begins to deepen his interest in the book, the lights fade, signaling the end of the play)*

The curtain closes

TED SHINE

TED SHINE WAS BORN in Baton Rouge, Louisiana and raised in Dallas, Texas. His interest in theatre began when, at a very young age, his father would take him to see popular entertainers and touring companies that came to Dallas. In elementary school he began to write skits for classroom programs, and by the time he reached high school, he was assisting with theatrical productions. At Howard University Mr. Shine majored in drama, studying with Owen Dodson. At the University of Iowa, where he received his Master's degree, his instructors were William Reardon and Oscar Brockett. Mr. Shine has worked at the internationally famous Karamu House and has taught and directed drama at Dillard University, Howard University, and at Prairie View A&M University where he is current head of the department.

His plays, which have been produced all over the country and on television, include: *Morning, Noon and Night; Baker's End; Contribution; Comeback after the Fire; Shoes; Herbert the Third; Idabel's Fortune; Sho is Hot in the Cotton Patch;* and *Packard.*

Ted Shine's play, *Contribution,* appears in *Black Drama Anthology,* edited by William Brasmer and Dominick Consolo (Charles E. Merrill Publishing Co., Columbus, Ohio, 1970). Mr. Shine collaborated with James V. Hatch on the publication, *Black Theatre USA: 45 Plays by Black-Americans 1847-1974* (The Free Press, Division of Macmillan, 1974).

THE WOMAN WHO WAS
TAMPERED WITH IN YOUTH

Ted Shine

CHARACTERS

MISS ALBA RUCKER   MISS ELVIRA SIMPSON
MAN—BILLY BOB SMITH

Setting: MISS ALBA RUCKER's *parlor. Furnished with ancient pieces from the 20s and 30s: a sofa, chair, end table, coffee table, and a floor lamp. A cupboard rests against the right wall. A door, stage left, leads outside the house into the front yard. Another door, up right, leads into the other rooms of the house. Conspicuously, on the upstage wall is a photograph of* ALBA *as girl of 13. It is faded now.*

A PLAY IN ONE ACT

At Rise: ALBA *sits in the overstuffed chair sipping properly from a tea cup. Although she is 69, she appears to be the picture of health. Seated uncomfortably on the sofa is* MISS SIMPSON, *a conservative school teacher in her late 40s.* ALBA *takes a sip from her cup, then studies* MISS SIMPSON *for a moment.* MISS SIMPSON *clears her throat, forces a smile. After a moment:*

ALBA: I'm what you call a self-made woman, Miss-what's-your-name. Learned to manage the little money I got 'holt to. This here house is bought and paid for, and I ain't hard pressed for cash. Aside from my pension, I gets social security—and I bought bonds during the war. Noooooooo, ma'am, when I put that room-for-rent ad in the *Chronicle* it was out of the goodness of my heart—

MISS SIMPSON: Miss Rucker—

ALBA: I can pick 'n choose the type of person I want in that room. Pick 'n choose. I said, "Room for rent to an upright Christian woman." Four men done called here this mornin'. I said, "No drinkin' and no smokin'." One woman said she didn't drink nor smoke, but she did take company. I said, "What kinda company?" She says, "Men friends." I said, "Not in my house you don't."

MISS SIMPSON: I have few men friends to speak

of—none who'd come calling. I don't smoke or drink. I won't wash my stockings and leave them hanging all over the bathroom. I'm...a...a person who stays to herself mostly.

ALBA: Me. too, child. I'm set in my ways. *(She looks at* MISS SIMPSON *for a moment)* Lord, how am I gonna manage with somebody else messin' round in my kitchen?

MISS SIMPSON: I usually eat at school—

ALBA: Rummaging through my things?

MISS SIMPSON: Miss Rucker, I value my privacy just as much as you value yours.

ALBA: Where did you say you're living now?

MISS SIMPSON: I've had a room at the YWCA for sixteen years.

ALBA: How come you want to move?

MISS SIMPSON: The atmosphere there has... changed—just like the times. There are a lot of ...younger girls there now. They...play those record players all during the night and day. I can hardly sleep.

ALBA: You say you don't entertain friends?

MISS SIMPSON: No, Miss Rucker, I don't.

ALBA: You ever been married?

MISS SIMPSON: *(Embarrassed)* Er...no...

ALBA: Well you needn't feel bad. I ain't neither— and I'm one woman who's proud of the fack! See that *pitcher* of me up yonder on that wall? *(*MISS

SIMPSON *nods)* I was not what you might call an unattractive girl. I was cute if I must say so myself. Innocent. Pure. *(She reflects on this for a second)* Then—

MISS SIMPSON: What?!

ALBA: Ol' R.B. Kemp was close to ninety. Usta press pennies into my palm 'n give me roses. So you know, Miss-er-what-ever-your-name-is—

MISS SIMPSON: Simpson. Elvira Simpson.

ALBA: He tried to *touch* me once! Come into my room and tried to put his hands on me!

MISS SIMPSON: Oh!

ALBA: Snuck up to me while I was asleep in the nighttime. I screamed and my papa come running with his shotgun. The only reason he didn't kill R.B. was 'cause that ol' man already had one foot in the grave!

MISS SIMPSON: How tragic . . . but . . . I've never seemed to appeal to men for some reason . . .

ALBA: We *all* appeal to 'em, honey. They got what you call "animal instincts." That means they *blind* to appearance—not sayin' you're not an attractive woman—

MISS SIMPSON: Well . . . I've never seemed to appeal to that instinct in men.

ALBA: You sorry 'bout it?

MISS SIMPSON: Life is too short for sorry, Miss Rucker! I keep myself *busy—occupied*. I teach my classes, make my lesson plans, read novels, and occasionally write poetry. My life is full—complete—happy!

ALBA: *(Grunts)* The rent's eighteen-fifty a week.

MISS SIMPSON: I'll take it.

ALBA: Without even seeing it?

MISS SIMPSON: I'm sure it will be perfectly satisfactory.

ALBA: The rent's due in advance.

MISS SIMPSON: I'll pay for the month by check if that's alright with you?

ALBA: Suit yourself.

MISS SIMPSON: *(Removes check from purse and proceeds to write)* Your first name?

ALBA: Alba. A-L-B-A. It means "high." I looked it up once in the dictionary. Reckon that's how come folks usta consider me stuck up—'cause my name meant "high" up. 'N it fit me like a perfect shoe. I was always untouchable. Ol' Billy Bob Smith, who lived down the street from us after my papa died, just doted on me. Couldn't stand him, 'n didn't bite my tongue tellin' him either. He just grinned 'n said, "ice melts when hot." Well, you can believe this was one block of ice that he didn't melt!

MISS SIMPSON: Remarkable. *(She presents the check)*

ALBA: *(Doesn't quite know how to accept this and decides not to confront it)* When you plan to move in?

MISS SIMPSON: Tonight, if you don't mind.

ALBA: I don't furnish linen.

MISS SIMPSON: I have my own.

ALBA: *(As* MISS SIMPSON *starts for the door)* Here's your key, but you don't need one. I never lock my door.

MISS SIMPSON: Is that safe? I mean—

ALBA: The only thing a thief could get in here is *me*, child! Ha! Ha!

MISS SIMPSON: But I'll be here. *(They look at each other for a moment)* I've got fine silver and books of value—

ALBA: Who you reckon's gonna steal a book?

MISS SIMPSON: Just the same—

ALBA: Wonder how come I happen to think of ol' Billy Bob Smith after all these years? I wasn't nothin' but a girl when it happened.

MISS SIMPSON: *(Pretending to be bored)* When *what* happened?

ALBA: There ain't but two men that I've ever had a feelin' for, Miss-what-ever-your-name-is—my papa and Jesus.

MISS SIMPSON: All of us girls are attached to our fathers, so they say.

ALBA: And Jesus.

MISS SIMPSON: Yes . . . some of us . . . maybe. *(At door)* And my name is—

ALBA: You told me, Miss Simpson.

MISS SIMPSON: Then why do you—

ALBA: Since you're gonna be living here with me now, I'm gonna tell you my innermost secret.

MISS SIMPSON: That's not necessary.

ALBA: I was tampered with once.

MISS SIMPSON: What?

ALBA: Molested! A man raped me!

MISS SIMPSON: No!

ALBA: That's how come—

MISS SIMPSON: Miss Rucker, I appreciate your confidence, but—

ALBA: Know who it was?

MISS SIMPSON: No! Of course not.

ALBA: *Him!*

MISS SIMPSON: What *him*, Miss Rucker?

ALBA: Ol' Billy Bob Smith! He overpowered me out on Fishtrap Road in the broad daylight behind the Three Sixes sign! Four o'clock p.m. on this very day—fifty-seven years ago. I was wearing that dress I'm wearin' up yonder in that pitcher. Wasn't but thirteen.

MISS SIMPSON: Shame! How old was he?

ALBA: Fourteen or fifteen, I reckon.

MISS SIMPSON: No wonder you're so anti-man! No wonder you never got married. I'm sorry, Miss Rucker. Shame. Shame on that man! Was he sent to jail?

ALBA: He run off and nobody seen him since. Jesus

musta swept him right off the face of this earth. Sister Jenkins say she heard tell of him bein' out west leadin' a reformed life. Say she heard he was married 'n had churren, but Jesus wouldn't allow such a tainted man to exist. He tore that beautiful dress up yonder offa me, Miss Simpson, and after he had pleasured hisself—he didn't even apologize.

MISS SIMPSON: Maybe that tragic event was your blessing in disguise.

ALBA: What do you mean?

MISS SIMPSON: Look at the progress you've made. You've bought and paid for this home. You're an independent woman—a secure woman. Lots of married women can't say that.

ALBA: No, I reckon you're right.

MISS SIMPSON: I'll . . . get my things and be back shortly.

ALBA: Suit yourself. *(MISS SIMPSON exits. Once she is outside, ALBA rushes to the door and yells out)* I don't talk a lot, Miss-er—Simpson, but— *(The door of an automobile is heard slamming. The engine starts, and the car moves off)* but—I—I . . . reckon I needs somebody to talk to now 'n then. *(She picks up her cup. It is empty. She crosses to the cabinet and removes a bottle of sherry, pours a stiff drink, then crosses to the photograph on the wall)* I *was* a beauty in them days. Innocent. Unspoiled. Then—! The *dog!* Pantin' over me! His hot breath steamin' into my ear! His sweat droppin' onto my body. The devil's hands squeezin' me like the day was endin' then and there. Lord, I hope maggots feasted on his rotting corpse. Oh, yes I do! I hope red ants nibbled his eyeballs. I hope bluejays plucked his hair out strand by strand 'n he had headaches until he died! *(She takes a long drink from her cup)* Why can't people let beauty be? When my zinnias bloom it's always a boy-child that plucks 'em to stick into the hand of some innocent girl-child what don't know what's happenin' 'til its too late. Lord—and Sister Jenkin's got the nerve to talk about love. Say she loved her man 'cause he sweet talked her into believin' *he* was in love with *her.* She wasn't in love with ol' Ezra—she just wanted a "Mrs." before her name. There's more'n that to life. Like Miss Simpson say, "I'm a secure woman." I done made progress on my own and in my own way. Lord knows it wasn't easy, but I done it—and I'm better off'n many a married woman I know around here. *(There is a knock at the door. ALBA is startled momentarily. She hastily places her cup on the table, then composes herself)* Who is it? *(There is no answer. She crosses over to the door)*

VOICE: *(Outside)* Can I come in?

ALBA: If you lookin' for a room, I don't rent to men! Besides, it's already let.

VOICE: I'm lookin' for peace-a-mind.

ALBA: If you need peace-a-mind, you oughta get on your knees 'n go to Jesus.

VOICE: Don't know 'im.

ALBA: Well, brother, I sho don't want you hangin' round my door! Now you "split," as they say—else I'm gonna get on my telephone and call John Law.

VOICE: I don't mean you no harm.

ALBA: Don't I know you?

VOICE: I know *you.*

ALBA: What's your name?

VOICE: Lemme in.

ALBA: I ain't no Salvation Army.
(The door opens, and an ancient little man enters. ALBA is seemingly frightened. He is frail and about 71 or 72. He appears ill)

MAN: How come you don't lock your screen?

ALBA: I didn't invite you inside. My home ain't opened to strangers. What you want?

MAN: *(Crosses to chair and sits)* Just to rest my weary bones for a spell 'n maybe get some peace-a-mind.

ALBA: I tol' you, Mr.-what-ever-your-name-is—to go to Jesus! *(She looks at him)* Don't I know you? Where you come from?

MAN: Out wes'.

ALBA: How come you bust in here and sit in my chair?

MAN: Alba—

ALBA: What you doin' callin' me "Alba"?! Don't no man call me that—don't *nobody* call me that!

MAN: You never got married, huh?

ALBA: You don't bus' into my house astin' me questions 'n I don't know you. I'm gonna call the police—*(She crosses to the phone)*

MAN: Alba. Alba . . .

ALBA: *(Who has picked up the phone, suddenly puts it down)* Didn't you hear what I said? You don't bus' into a lady's home—Don't you know I could have a pistol?

MAN: You wasn't ever the kinda woman to mess wif no pistol.

ALBA: Who in the world—?

MAN: Ain't you looked at me close?

ALBA: Yes, I've looked—

MAN: You ain't looked close enough. Come mere, baby—

ALBA: Now you listen here!

MAN: You ain't changed none, is you?

ALBA: What you mean?

MAN: Still miss high and mighty, but didn't I tell you once—no matter how cold you pretended to be—

ALBA: *(She shrieks softly, stunned)* Jesus! You! *(He

smiles) I thought I had prayed you right into the depths of hell, damned your no-good soul!

MAN: Still hate me?

ALBA: Like fire hates water! I have a strong notion to call the police right this minute 'n have you arrested for tamperin' with a young girl who was underage!

MAN: That was years ago—

ALBA: I still carry the scar!

MAN: So do I.

ALBA: Where'd you go anyway?

MAN: I just run, that's all. Was scared.

ALBA: I didn't even tell my mama what happened, just begged Jesus not to let me be with child—and he answered my prayers.

MAN: He didn't answer mine. I wanted to marry you, Alba, but—

ALBA: *What?*

MAN: I knew that you never woulda . . . after—

ALBA: Did I have a choice after what you had done? What kinda girl did you think I was?

MAN: I was scared.

ALBA: So was I! *(She picks up her cup and takes a drink. The cup is empty. She crosses to cabinet and pours herself a sherry)*

MAN: You a wino now?

ALBA: A wino is somebody who looks like you! This here is *sherry*. *(Pause)* What happened to you anyhow? You look a mess.

MAN: I been . . . sick.

ALBA: I can see that. *(Takes a sip)* Sister Jenkins say she heard you went to California.

MAN: You been checkin' up on me?

ALBA: No! But if I coulda found out where you was, I woulda had you arrested 'n sent to the pen.

MAN: Would you-a-done that to me, baby?

ALBA: What you think?

MAN: I reckon you woulda. *(Pause)* You didn't tell your mama, huh?

ALBA: I didn't want to shame her like I was shamed!

MAN: I left here runnin' 'n I run right into the hell fire.

ALBA: Thank Jesus—'cause that's what I was prayin' for!

MAN: Ended up in L.A., you know. Married an ol' gal out yonda that I didn't care nothin' 'bout. Usta pretend she was you.

ALBA: *(Grunts)* How many churren yawl have?

MAN: Four.

ALBA: I heard it was two.

MAN: Was, but two died at birth. Now I ain't got nobody 'n nothin' but me. Bob Junior died in the war 'n Joan Denise—well, she got mixed up in dope 'n kilt herself wiffa overdose.

ALBA: The father's sins passed on to the churren.

MAN: You know that ain't so.

ALBA: Ain't you the proof?

MAN: You been sufferin' for your papa 'cause he sinned?

ALBA: My papa was a proud family man.

MAN: I tried to be, but my heart wasn't in it.

ALBA: How could it after what you done to me?

MAN: I loved you, Alba. I wanted to ask you to marry me, but you was so high 'n mighty—I couldn't even touch the hem-a-your-garment.

ALBA: So you just ripped it offa me!

MAN: I . . . couldn't help myself, Alba. I was a young boy—

ALBA: You was blue-black steel! Chest stickin' out from here to yonder. Muscles in your arms lookin' like they was just frightin' to bust outta them shirts you usta wear. You sho was a *cocky* boy —*too* proud of yourself—and for no reason a'tall. What did you have to offer to any young woman 'round here? You didn't have nothin' to offer nobody. I always knowed you wouldn't amount to nothin'. How you have the nerve to come back here after all these years?

MAN: A pretty woman like you 'n never got married.

ALBA: If I had wanted to get maried, I reckon I coulda!

MAN: Waitin' for me, huh?

ALBA: Ha! Ha! Don't make me laugh!

MAN: *(Smiling)* Know why I come back?

ALBA: Don't know and don't care.

MAN: Somethin' tol' me you was still alive.

ALBA: Somebody tell you I own this house? Somebody gave you the impression I'd let you—or any man take advantage of my security?

MAN: No, Alba.

ALBA: Go back to that woman of yourn out in California—if she'll have you. Go anywhere, Billy Bob Smith, just *leave*.

MAN: She's dead.

ALBA: Oh. *(Pause)* Well, what she seen in you to begin with I'll never know.

MAN: I reckon she seen what you seen—this blue-black steel body—what was all I had to offer then like you say.

ALBA: Is *that* what you thought *I* wanted?

MAN: I didn't know what you wanted. All I know is I give you all I had to offer.

ALBA: How can you molest somebody against their will then say it was a present?

MAN: Alba . . . don't . . .

ALBA: Didn't I tell you "don't" on this very day fifty-seven years ago? Remember? That pretty little Alba Rucker you see up yonder in that pitcher died that day.

MAN: Maybe I ain't got no business bein' here, but

you got to know that when what happened happened, it was 'cause it had to happen. *I loved you.* I loved you, Alba, 'n I ain't loved no other woman sinct.

ALBA: Man, you makin' my blood boil.

MAN: Ain't never in all these years forgot you, baby—

ALBA: How in the hell can you walk into my house after all these years 'n tell me you loved me when you walked away leavin' me there cryin' and hurt? How dare you come into my house 'n have the nerve to say you still love me!

MAN: I come back to repent like the Bible say—to make amends. I'm willin' to marry you, Alba. We can spend the remainder of our ol' age together.

ALBA: I look desperate or somethin', man? You must be outta your mind—*senile.*

MAN: Ah, baby—

ALBA: I don't see no baby in here!

MAN: You know what I'm talkin' 'bout, mama. *(He grabs her arm and pulls her toward him)*

ALBA: And I ain't your mama!

MAN: We can get married 'n I can get a job—

ALBA: You so frail I doubt if you can lift a spoon. You're sick 'n you lookin' for somebody to take care of you, but if you think it's me, you got another think comin'. I didn't work all my life to end up buryin' a no count man!

MAN: I get a little social security.

ALBA: So do I! *(He crosses to cabinet, gets sherry, downs a long swig. She looks at him for a moment)* If I recall correctly, you had been drinkin' that day—

MAN: *(Nods)* Sherry.

ALBA: Did I offer you a drink?

MAN: Ah, baby—I'm gonna get well, then things'll be groovy.

ALBA: My name is *Miss* Rucker.

MAN: You gon' always be Alba to me.

ALBA: What you mean "groovy?" You-a-old worn out man!

MAN: You only as old as you wanna be.

ALBA: Old as you look 'n act!

MAN: You make me frisky like a puppy. There's still a few sparks, I reckon, left near this kindlin'.

ALBA: Ashes you mean!

MAN: *(Drinks)* Right on. *(She looks at him)* That's the way we talk in L. A. *(She grunts. He looks at her picture)* Shooooo was a fine gal! Like angel food cake.

ALBA: 'N you was the devil. *(Pause)* So you back to apologize?

MAN: I wuz, but not no more. *(She looks at him sharply)* You was the cause of what happened anyway. Dressin' up real cute 'n all. Smellin' like vanilla. Them big eyes just flashin' 'n you walkin'

like the sunshine 'n just as cold as snow. *Temptation Alba.* That's what we usta call you.

ALBA: Temptation?! I was innocent—a child. You was the one! Never buttonin' your shirt—skin naked to the world. Always managed to be out of breath so your chest would heave up 'n down. Them ol' muscles in your stomach lookin' like a washboard.

MAN: See! You noticed me.

ALBA: Who could help noticin' you, Billy Bob? You was so disgustin'.

MAN: *(He laughs, pleased)* Ah, baby—

ALBA: I was walkin' home from my auntie's house. Mindin' my own business.

MAN: I seen you goin' over there. I waited over by Jerico Bridge 'til you started home—I was just gon try 'n talk to you. Ask you to be my gal, but—

ALBA: You hid in the woods off Fishtrap Road—

MAN: I stepped out, but you looked so scared—

ALBA: *I was.*

MAN: I wasn't no bear. I just wanted to—

ALBA: "Melt my ice?"

MAN: Naw . . . !

ALBA: *(Crosses to sofa where he stands)* You had your hand over my mouth like this. *(She places her hand over his mouth. He groans)* Then you told me, "I been watchin' you." You ran your free hand through my hair like *this. (He groans as she runs her hand through his scarce hair)* I was too scared to even try 'n fight you off. You pushed me to the ground. *(She forces him onto the sofa)* You was like a ton of blue-black steel. Pantin' in my ear like an ol' dog. I told you—

MAN: *(Breathing deeply)* "Please . . . Alba . . ."

ALBA: I squirmed—like you squirmin' now—tryin' to free myself, but you wouldn't turn me loose. No! You kissed me on the neck—right here—*(She kisses his neck. He groans)* Then you nibbled on my neck . . . my cheeks . . . my nose . . . my eyes—like an animal. *(She demonstrates. He moans, exhausted).*

MAN: Alba . . . I been . . . sick . . .

ALBA: You kissed my forehead. Circled my face with your kisses, breathin' hard, Billy Bob, like you doin' now. You was like a ton of blue-black steel—

MAN: *(Suffering)* Look at me, Alba . . .

ALBA: That's what you said, "Look at me, Alba—" *(He turns away as she leans back and looks at him)* When I turned away, you took your hand and turned my face around—*made me look at you! (She turns his face to her)*

MAN: *(On the verge of tears)* Please . . . been real sick . . . heart condition . . .

ALBA: You put your lips on *mine!* I tried to turn

away, but—*(She grabs his head with her hands, then kisses him passionately on the lips. He struggles to get away from her, but he is too weak and she is too strong. He ultimately gives in, and they kiss passionately for a moment. After a moment she releases him. Pause)* Yes. That's the way it was. But age done made you weak 'n soft like a powder puff. When you bit my neck back yonder you had teeth like piano keys—now you ain't nothin' but mostly gums.

MAN: I . . . been . . . sick . . .

ALBA: After you kissed me—I could taste what you'd been drinkin'! I sampled all kinda wines during my lifetime 'til I finally come upon that sweet taste again—*sherry. (She kisses him again)* Remember it?

MAN: Please . . .

ALBA: You ain't even a slight resemblance to what you usta be. All of your ol' huff 'n puff's done turned to air.

MAN: Gotta . . . go . . .

ALBA: You ripped that dress offa me! Exposed me —naked to the world. *(She rips his shirt off)*. Tellin' me—

MAN: Baby, I love you, but—

ALBA: *I believed you*—for a minute, but then—I told Mama that a girl called me "nigger" 'n we had a fight—that's how come my dress was torn.

MAN: I . . . cried along side the T & P railroad tracks outside Longview all that night—thinkin' 'bout you.

ALBA: I soaked Mama's feather pillow with so many tears it wouldn't fluff up no more.

MAN: Tears for me?

ALBA: Tears for *me.*

MAN: I come back here to tell you that you was my first woman—no matter what the circumstance.

ALBA: You run—

MAN: I . . . just want to say . . . I'm sorry . . .

ALBA: That don't mend no life.

MAN: Ain't no old life gonna be mended once it's old.

ALBA: You say when you get well . . . you-a-be "groovy—"?

MAN: In time . . .

ALBA: Time's short—

MAN: That's how come—

ALBA: You think I oughta make a fool outta myself carin' for you?

MAN: I didn't come here to depend on you, Alba.

ALBA: You oughtn'ta come here a'tall! *(Pause)* Still got that same bay rum smell to your body.

MAN: You smell like tea cakes.

ALBA: Ah, man, hush!

MAN: Well you do, baby.

ALBA: I baked some today.

MAN: From scratch? I mean . . . they wasn't outta

one of them ready-mix boxes, was they?

ALBA: I always make my cakes from scratch.

MAN: Maybe . . .

ALBA: What?

MAN: We can start from scratch—

ALBA: Maybe we could—if you was still blueblack steel, but them days is long gone.

MAN: In time I'll—

ALBA: I'm just kiddin' you, honey. I got what I want in life at this stage of the game. All I'm waitin' on now is for Jesus to come and sweep me away in his arms.

MAN: I ain't got no beard, but—maybe—don't get me wrong—maybe I can be your Jesus.

ALBA: That don't even make me mad it's so ridiculous!

MAN: Alba?

ALBA: What?

MAN: I apologize . . .

ALBA: You said that, but it's fifty-seven years too late.

MAN: I-a-go then . . . *(He crosses slowly toward door; stops)* Alba?

ALBA: What?!

MAN: *(Looks at her for a second)* Nothin', I don't reckon.

ALBA: Then bye!

MAN: Bye . . . *(He exits)*

ALBA: *(She stands for a moment staring at the door)* He . . . he didn't even kiss me goodbye! *(She crosses to her teacup and lifts it)* As if I'da kissed him! He's just like ol' R. B. Kemp now—old 'n weary —only *he* ain't ninety. Lord, but he was a dandy young man once. Poor Billy Bob. Suffered and come to that after all these years—*over me.* He said he *loved* me. I oughta call him back! Shoot. We don't even *know* each other. We ain't got nothin' in common—never had nothin' in common. But, Lord, I've thought about that man. Billy Bob, baby, you done been in my dreams—nightly. I lied to that Simpson woman. I loved more'n my papa and Jesus. Billy Bob, baby, I loved you. Not that skeleton what walked into my house just then, but the you what . . . tampered with me. The only thing that ain't changed about you is your lips 'n your eyes. Your lips still taste like sherry, 'n your eyes—Jesus, that sweet man's eyes! He said he loved me! Didn't I always know he did? Didn't I always know it? Billy Bob, I love you too! *(She crosses to the door)* I oughta go out yonder after him, but . . . I just *can't.* What would Sister Jenkins think? Besides, he'd die on me 'n I'd be stuck with a funeral. I'd dress him in a pink shirt and I wouldn't button it! I'd make the undertaker fix his face with a smile! Just think . . . he come back . . . after all these years . . . on the anniversary of our—

MISS SIMPSON: *(Running into the house)* Miss Rucker! You've got to help me! Call an ambulance. There's an old man outside in the street—looks like a wino or something. I think he's dying!

(ALBA shrieks softly, stunned. She rushes from the room with MISS SIMPSON following)

ALBA: *(Offstage)* Help me bring him inside!

MISS SIMPSON: Into your house?

ALBA: You help me, gal!

(The WOMEN enter with the MAN. He is not dead, merely weak, exhausted. They assist him to sofa)

MAN: I . . . fell . . . down . . .

MISS SIMPSON: *(Seeing him for the first time, she is immediately attracted to him)* Poor thing!

ALBA: We all fall down one time or another.

MAN: I'll . . . be . . . alright . . .

ALBA: I know you'll be.

MISS SIMPSON: You just rest here on this sofa. I'll warm you some soup.

ALBA: Say what?

MISS SIMPSON: This poor man reminds me of—well, he has features like someone who was once very dear to me—

ALBA: *(Looks at her sharply)* I'll fix him some soup. Home made soup with a bone in it.

MISS SIMPSON: You should have a blanket over you, mister. Your chest is out—Look at this man's chest, Miss Rucker, it's all exposed to the world. I have a blanket outside. I'll get it and my Vick's salve—your chest needs massaging.

ALBA: I got a quilt right here!

MAN: Yawl . . . needn't carry on so . . .

MISS SIMPSON: Oh, I don't mind—! I . . . mean . . .

ALBA: You got your things outside, Miss-what-cha-ma-call-er?

MISS SIMPSON: Simpson! Yes, in my car.

ALBA: Well, here, you take your check and go on back to the "Y."

MISS SIMPSON: What?

ALBA: He needs that room more'n you do.

MISS SIMPSON: I can sleep on the sofa until—

ALBA: Three's a crowd!

MISS SIMPSON: What? *(She looks at ALBA and the MAN)* You mean . . . you? . . .

ALBA: *He* was the *him* who melted the ice.

MISS SIMPSON: *(Offended)* And you—?!

ALBA: Yes!

MISS SIMPSON: I thought that this was a decent home.

ALBA: Maybe it will be now.

(MISS SIMPSON looks at her a bit angry and envious, but not wanting to admit either. She turns and hastily exits from the room)

MAN: Suppose I die, Alba—

ALBA: Shoot, Billy Bob! When you get through eatin' my fine food; when I get through fattening you up—why you'll bury me! Billy Bob Smith, you're still blue-black—and you're gonna be steel again.

MAN: Right on, mama.

ALBA: Right on then—as we say *here* too!

They look at each other for a moment, then laugh. She crosses to him, sits beside him on the edge of the sofa. They embrace.

Curtain

THELMA JACKSON STILES

THELMA JACKSON STILES, an Oakland, California resident, has worked for many years as a writer with industry. Born in Monroe, Louisiana, she arrived in California at the age of three with her parents; attended public schools in Oakland and Hayward; and, after graduating from the University of California at Berkeley with a B.A. in English in 1961, traveled to Hartford, Connecticut, where she lived with relatives and worked as a copywriter with the department store chain, Sage-Allen and Company.

Over the years, she has also worked as a high school teacher, a writer with the training department of Wells Fargo Bank's head office in San Francisco, a faculty member of California State University at Hayward, and as a technical editor with Physics International Co. of San Leandro, California. She is married and the mother of two teenage daughters, Pamela and Ashley.

Stiles began writing fiction in 1969 after joining the San Francisco Black Writers Workshop. There, she met such talented playwrights as Fred Hudson, now president of the Frederick Douglass Creative Arts Center in New York City, and the late Buriel Clay II, one of the leaders of the community arts movement in San Francisco. "The process of writing," claims Stiles, "is a form of therapy for me. Life can be painful—painfully funny or sad. When I write, I suppose I'm able to order things a bit more to my liking, something I rather enjoy."

No One Man Show, the first and only play that she has written, was first presented by the San Francisco Black Writers Workshop in 1971. Wrote the late Paine Knickerbocker, drama critic for many years with the San Francisco Chronicle, of the workshop production of *No One Man Show:* "This black domestic comedy is witty, deft, and has shrewdly drawn characters." In the Spring of 1972, B&B Experimental Theater, a little theater company led by director Mary Booker, thought enough of *No One Man Show* to raise a large sum of money to present the vehicle for a limited run at a top, legitimate theater showcase: the On Broadway. Over the years, the On Broadway in San Francisco has been one of the leading homes for professional theater productions, especially of traveling companies of Broadway hits such as *No Place to Be Somebody.* Since that time, B&B has launched several productions of *No One Man Show* in Oakland and San Francisco and at local colleges.

In addition to her play, Stiles has written several nonfiction articles and short stories. Two of her stories, "Juanita" and "In Light of What Has Happened," have appeared in *Essence,* and several articles have appeared in *Essence, Players, The California Monthly* (U.C. Berkeley's alumni magazine), and in Bay Area newspapers.

NO ONE MAN SHOW

Thelma Jackson Stiles

CHARACTERS

RUBY MacINTYRE   JAMES PHILLIPS
YOLANDA MacINTYRE   MORRIS TADEMY
DONALD MacINTYRE   REGINALD HARDING
T.J.

Time: *The early 70s*
Place: *The city—Out West*

A PLAY IN ONE ACT

Scene: A young man is sleeping on the couch in the living room of a modestly furnished apartment. A young woman, struggling with a suitcase, enters the living room from a hallway that leads to the apartment's two bedrooms. She glances at her watch then begins pacing. A beat passes. She stares at the suitcase as if it is a foreign object, walks quickly to the living room closet, carefully places the suitcase inside, and quietly closes the door to the closet.

 She leans against the door, breathes deeply, then walks over to the kitchen area. She sits down at the kitchen table. She sighs, obviously relieved. Seconds pass. She looks in the direction of the closet, looks away, looks again at the closet. Finally, shrugging her shoulders, she rises, tiptoes over to the closet, opens the door, and retrieves the suitcase.

 She is once again pacing the floor and alternately glancing at her wristwatch when she hears a sound that comes from the direction of the living room couch. Gathering courage, she walks slowly and cautiously over to the area. When she spots the young man asleep on the couch, she sighs in relief. Placing her suitcase near the couch, she hovers over him.

YOLANDA: *(Whispering)* T.J.! Wake up.

T.J.: *(Singing in his sleep)* Home...home on the range...

YOL: Sshhh....Wake up. Please. We have to talk.

T.J.: And the deer...and the antelope playyy...

YOL: *(Pulls back after getting a whiff of his breath)* Good grief...

T.J.: Where seldom is heard...

YOL: Get up right now. *(She pauses, waiting. A beat passes)* Get up, I tell you!

T.J.: And the skies are not some 'um some 'um all dayyy...

YOL: *(Threateningly)* All right...I'll pinch you. I'm not playing....*(He continues singing. Exasperated,* YOL *grabs him by the shoulders and shakes him silly)* Wake up, I said. Get up, you silly drunkard.

T.J.: *(Dazed, he struggles out of her arms and once again reclines on the couch)* Home, home on the range...

YOL: *(Sighs. A beat passes. Her brow knits devilishly)* Tee—Jayyy. There's a girl in here...and she's naked. *(Though still dazed,* T.J. *sits up. He is quietly and sweetly alert. He shakes his head as if to clear his thoughts)*

YOL: *(Anxiously)* Oh, T.J.! T.J.! Where—Why did you do this to me? Why did you have to pick last night to run out and start drinking? *(Dejectedly, she plops down next to* T.J. *on the couch)*

T.J.: Huh? Where is she? Flaselle?

YOL: Every night of the week, you're here drawing. And painting. And meditating. And the one night I really need you! *(Tries to strike him with her fist, but he manages to grab it)*

T.J.: Whoa. Hey. Shloo...shloo...sslow down. What's going on?

YOL: None of this would have happened if you'd been here. It's all your fault. Where were you? Where have you been all night? *(*T.J. *tries to remember, but his head is too heavy for his neck, and the living room is swirling. He moans)* Out drinking, I gather. While I'm sitting up till the early hours of the morning, waiting to talk to you. Drinking! You. Of all people.

T.J.: *(Shaking his head and sighing)* Out...drinking....Yeah, Littlebit...sipping....Sitting in the bar...sipping...and feeling like a rat...

YOL: While I'm sitting in your bedroom...waiting...feeling like a—a reject.

T.J.: *(Wearily)* Sitting and sipping....Sipping...and sitting.*(Brightening)* When hey! I spot this big, fine thing. This wonderful female specimen. The woman of my dreams...

YOL: Nobody home but me. On a big Friday night, I get to stay home.

T.J.: To make a long story *(Burps)*—'scuse me—short...there she was...my dream...in the back, sharing a booth with her buddies....And they're fussing away about the Giants' record. *(He stands with effort, sways unsteadily, pretends he's swinging his bat at a slow breaking curve)* And then Flaselle—that's her name—she spots me over in the corner watching her! Heyyyy! And fireworks, Yolannnnda! Fireworks!!!

YOL: ...all by myself. All because of Reginald's wife! Would you believe she made him take her out last night? How do you like that? What's the use of having a boyfriend if he has to take his wife out every Friday and Saturday night instead of you?

T.J.: *(Dreamily)* Yesss...I can see her now. She jumps up, puts her hands on her big, fine hips and yells "I don't care what nobody say. I *still* digs the Three W's—Willie Kirkland, Willie McCovey. And Willie Mays." *(Laughs)*

YOL: T.J., did you hear anything I just said?

T.J.: *(Dreamily)* Later that night at *her* place, Flaselle gave me the Three W's batting averages ...and told me mine was better. *(Smiles slyly, plops down on the couch, and sits there nodding and grinning, pleased as hell)*

YOL: T.J.? T.J., listen to me. Reginald's on his way. He'll be here any minute. By the time he walks in here, I want to be sure I'm doing the right thing. When I called him this morning, I was pretty sure and all. But now....*(Stands, begins pacing)* He's late naturally. Niggahs are always late. He's *(Glances at her watch)*—twenty minutes late! T.J., you know how I make up my mind one minute and then change it the next? You know how I am. I can't help it...T.J.?*(T.J. is still thinking about Flaselle.* YOL *touches his shoulder. He looks up at her)* I need your advice.

T.J.: Huh?

YOL: I said! I need your advice. I need your help about something.

T.J.: Help?

YOL: Yes!!! *(T.J.'s eyes grow dull. Wearily, he stretches out on the couch and turns on his side)* Don't! Wait. Don't go back to sleep!

T.J.: Got to. Beat...whipped.

YOL: Come on, T.J. Please. You see, I think maybe I did something really silly this morning.

T.J.: *(Struggling to sit up)* Yolanda Faye...you do something silly just about every morning.

YOL: O.K. O.K., please. Just listen for a minute.

T.J.: Yolanda, I'm tired. I need some sleep. Gotta rest my loins.

YOL: O.K. O.K. But before you go back to sleep just tell me one little thing.

T.J.: Let's talk later. I'm not feeling so hot.

YOL: *(Whining, bleary-eyed)* Later's too late. Oh, T.J. I was so lonely last night. Even Ruby was out. The whole world was out. And I was feeling sorry for myself. And I got mad. And I got on the phone early this morning....And I called Reginald's house and talked to him. And then his wife, she picked up the phone. And...well...

T.J.: I'm bushed...wasted.

YOL: Reginald warned me never to call his home. But I said "Tough! I'm calling," and so I did. So There! *(Suddenly hysterical)* T.J., I'm scared. What am I doing? I'm scared...

T.J.: *(Yawns)* Poor baby.

YOL: Then you'll help me?

T.J.: *(Jumping to his feet, suddenly quite sober)* Now wait! Did I say I would? Did I say anything about helping you?

YOL: I don't believe this. You always help me. You always give me advice. Even when I don't need it. (T.J. *staggers towards the hallway)* That's right, Cousin. Turn your back on your favorite Littlebit. Just like you did last night. There I was... deserted in my hour of greatest need.

T.J.: *(Turning to face her)* Aw, come on Yolanda. How was I to know your hour of greatest need would come while I was sitting at the bar in the Starlite? Besides, Sweetheart, you don't want me to advise you. You want me to tell you what to do. *(She smiles, nodding her head in agreement. He nods his head up and down and then from side to side)*

YOL: *(Frowning)* Are you angry with me about something?

T.J.: No, I'm not angry with you about something. I just feel it's time to figure things out for yourself. Somebody's always doing for you, Yolanda. People are always making decisions for you. Yet you're practically grown. You're seventeen. A freshman in college. You're intelligent. Very intelligent. You can make it. Take my advice. No! Strike that. Don't take my advice. Look, let me put it this way. Certain people should stop depending on other people. Certain people should learn to be independent, think for themselves. Herself.

YOL: You aren't making any sense.

T.J.: On the contrary. I'm making plenty of sense. Look at me. I didn't have anyone doing for me when I was young. But I managed. I learned to fend for myself. Clothe and feed myself. Make a few bucks. Find shelter. I've been on my own since I was nine. And liking it, too. You see, when you start out on your own at the age of seven, like me . . . uh . . . that is . . . at the age of nine (YOL *gives an exasperated sigh*)—don't smirk now—you learn to appreciate life more fully. To savor every moment. To live every second to the hilt. Did I ever tell you I was a scuba diver at thirteen? Didn't know that did ya? I worked the slopes at Stowe by the time I was fifteen. I traveled clear cross the world on a freighter by the time I was twenty. I tell you, I've been a janitor. A cowboy. A runner. A short order cook. Sold insurance, shoes, encyclopedias, you name it. I've been living life, unafraid. Ready for whatever comes my way.

YOL: T.J. . . .

T.J.: Why, I tell you, learning early to be independent gives you an advantage, Yolanda. And I'm a good example of what I'm talking bout. You see, I'm a free spirit, doing what I want to do. My life is free and easy. Like a—

YOL *and* T.J.: —brook trickling downstream.

(RUBY *enters hallway, walking sleepily and quietly along, stretching*)

YOL: I know, I know, T.J. Enough of this. I mean it. Reginald's on his way. (*Shrieking*) And I don't know what to do!

(RUBY *is startled, freezes for a beat, listens, then pulls back out of sight of* T.J. *and* YOL, *and continues listening, unobserved by them.*)

T.J.: (*Very coolly*) I'm sorry. But I have nothing more to say, Yolanda. (*Crying,* YOL *throws her arms around* T.J. *He hesitates then pats her on the back*) Yolanda Faye. Please. Please. No more advice. Please. (*She cries a bit louder.* T.J. *sighs. Then brightening, he walks her towards the kitchen table*) Unless . . .

YOL: (*Breaking away and looking hopeful*) Yes?

T.J.: Unless, of course, you have a "friend" who needs advice . . .

YOL: I need advice. Not my friend. Me, Yolanda. Remember? Your favorite cousin? Your Littlebit?

T.J.: Like I said, Yolanda. Tell me about this problem your "friend" has. (*Exasperated,* YOL *observes him coolly for a beat*) Come on. Come on now.

YOL: (*A beat passes*) O.K. O.K., you win. O.K., my friend, uh, she has this problem.

T.J.: Yes? Go on.

(RUBY *sneaks forward a few paces, then crosses her*

arms and listens intently at the same time that T.J. *crosses his arms and begins listening intently*)

YOL: Uh, she goes with this guy by the name of—

T.J.: No names, please. I don't want to know any of the particulars. You-have-a-friend-who-has-a-problem-she-goes-with-this-guy—please continue.

YOL: (*Sighs*) Well, this guy, he's on his way over to my "friend's" house to take her out for the day, uh, to make up for the fact he didn't get to take her out last night. And so. And so, anyway, he thinks he's taking her out for the day, right? But actually my friend is really planning to have her bag packed and move in with the guy (*Angrily*) because she's tired of having to sneak around with him. And besides, she's sick of having to sit home on weekends while he's out with his wife.

T.J.: And? So? What's the problem?

YOL: So . . . my friend—T.J., this is stupid!

T.J.: Go on, girl!

YOL: My friend is thinking that if she shacks with the guy for a while, gives him a chance to know the spiritual side of her instead of just the, uh, the other . . . uh . . .

T.J.: Fleshy side?

YOL: No! You know! Anyway, *then* maybe he'll do the right thing.

T.J.: The right thing being?

YOL: Dump his wife!

T.J.: I see.

YOL: But then again, I'm not—I mean, my friend's not so sure her boyfriend *will* do the right thing. And anyway, even if he does, if she shacks with him, maybe he won't ever marry her. Maybe he'll like things just as they are. What do you think, T.J.? What do you think she should do? Do you think she should leave home for her boyfriend?

T.J.: Well . . . all of this is a bit tawdry, I have to admit. But not so terribly difficult. You see, Yolanda, the trick is to try to simplify one's life. You just tell your friend to stop worrying about what she's going to get from her man and what he's going to do for her. She's got to follow her feelings. Stop all that scheming and planning and second guessing. You see, if she wants to live a full life, she'll have to take some risks, learn to strip away the nonessentials. She'll have to strip away her family. And strip away her friends and all her other protectors and security—

YOL: (*Remembering, glancing towards the hallway*) Could you keep it down, please?

T.J.: She's gotta strip away her concern for clothes and all the finery that keeps her in debt. And strip away the parties and other childish things. She's gotta peel. Hah! And strip. Hah!! Till she gets down. Deep down. Hah! Till she gets deep down bottom—to you!...Uh, her...uh, whoever. Yes! She has to forget about plans. Forget about money. Forget about wedding bells. Forget about the future. And live!

RUBY: *(Entering living room)* Tell it, Brother!

T.J.: Have to, Sister! I have—

YOL *and* T.J.: Ruby!!

RUBY: In the flesh...

YOL: What...why you up so early? It's Saturday. *(Sneaks a glance at her suitcase, tries to ease over to hide it from RUBY's view)*

RUBY: *(Spotting the suitcase, she walks towards the couch)* Gimme that! *(Flings the suitcase into the hallway. YOL grimaces, hearing the suitcase bounce on the floor. T.J. tries to tiptoe out of the line of fire)* So! What do you have to say for yourself, Mr. James?

YOL: I paid thirty dollars for that suitcase you just banged around, Ruby.

RUBY: *You* paid?!

T.J.: Don't antagonize the woman, Yolanda. She's acting crazy enough as it is.

RUBY: I'm acting crazy. Hah! That does it. I want you outta here. 'Fore the week's out. I have had it!

T.J.: What's wrong? Have I done anything wrong? If so, I humbly apologize, Ruby.

RUBY: I don't wanna hear that Who-Shot-John. Look! Did you or did you not stand here just now and encourage my sister to run away from her family? To strip us away like so much trash?

T.J.: *(Worried)* I didn't mean it that way. Naw. That's not what *I* said.

RUBY: Then who said it? Stepin Fetchit? *(Sighs)* And after I went out of my way to warn you. Didn't I warn you? Plus, didn't you give me your word?

T.J.: *(Grimacing)* Well...

RUBY: Don't you "well" me. Just yesterday you stood right here in this room—Terrence Milhaus James—and gave me your word.

T.J.: Aw Ruby. You come in on the tail end of the conversation and still expect to understand? *(Glances furtively at YOL and then once again addresses RUBY)* I didn't do what you thinking.

RUBY: Niggah, hush. Yes you did. I heard you. Yesterday morning, before I went to work, you stood right here in this room while Yolanda was still asleep and promised me! And what do I hear coming out of your mouth just a minute ago?

YOL: Promised you what, Ruby?

RUBY: Hush, Yolanda.

T.J.: Yes, shut up Littlebit. This is between your sister and me.

RUBY: Don't be telling my sister to shut up. *(To YOL)* Just yesterday, I told T.J. here I'd think about letting him stay with us another six months or so if he'd promise me just one thing...that he—

T.J.: ...O.K. O.K. *(Sighs, paces, deliberates, glances guiltily at YOL)* Ruby told me you'd been threatening to move out and get a place with Reginald. She told me I could stick around if... if I promised to keep my two cents out of your love life...in case you asked me what to do. *(YOL's eyes grow wide with disbelief. RUBY smiles smugly)* Come on, Littlebit. It didn't seem like so big a thing. After all, I figure you're grown. You shouldn't have to come running to me for help. *(He staggers into kitchen, searches in cabinet for medicine for his hangover, plops a tablet into a glass of water and watches the tablet sizzle)*

YOL: *(Angrily to T.J.)* You!! *(To RUBY)* And you! I should have known you'd try something. Make him do something like this.

RUBY: I didn't make him do anything.

YOL: Yes you did. I know you, Ruby. You're a dictator. A selfish, interfering dictator.

RUBY: Selfish? You're calling *me* "selfish"? *(Imitating YOL)* "Ruby, I'm crazy bout the Dynamic's latest. Gotta have it. I'll pay you back. Ruby, maybe you're right. Maybe I should go to junior college. Can you get me the money for books?" It's Ruby I need this and Ruby I need that. And, furthermore, who is it pays for all those bills you rack up at that dumb boutique you so crazy bout? I'll tell you. Old selfish dictator me!

YOL: I don't care what you say. T.J. has as much right to help me as anybody else. Oh, I'm sick of all of you, anyway. Where is that man? Where is he?

RUBY: If you talking bout Reginald, you better hope he's miles away from here. And stays miles away—if he knows what's good for him.

YOL: Ruby, I'm seventeen years old!

RUBY: And dumb as you wanna be. *(To T.J.)* Thanks to you always filling her mind with that trash you call philosophy. Do you want this child to run out here and marry that skinny fool? That pimp?

YOL: Pimp? Reginald? Reginald Harding?

RUBY: That's right. Pimp. P-I-M-P.

YOL: That's a monstrous lie. Reginald is...he's like a...a business consultant.

RUBY: Pimp. Business consultant. What's the difference?

YOL: He has his own business cards. Does that sound like a pimp? *(T.J. hurriedly drinks his medicine, places the glass on the counter and leans over the sink, resting)* Oh Reginald. Hurry. Please come take me away from this...this madhouse. From these nuts. I know you'll walk in that door any minute. *(She paces)*

RUBY: He may walk in, Sugah, but he'll have to crawl out. *(YOL rushes over to the telephone on the kitchen wall and dials a number)* And bet not let Donald see him. If I go in that bedroom and get your brother, he'll come out here and reduce your Mr. Reginald Harding to peat moss. *(To T.J.)* And as for you— *(T.J. bristles, ready to run. But RUBY sways, suddenly off-balance. Recovering, she moves towards the kitchen table, perches on the edge of the table and breathes deeply)*

T.J.: *(Alarmed)* Ruby, what is it? You look kinda . . . ashy. *(Approaches RUBY)*

RUBY: *(Breathes deeply, shakes her head as if to clear her thoughts)* Must be crazy letting you two upset me like this.

YOL: *(Angrily hanging up the receiver)* No answer! What's going on over there?

T.J.: No lie. You look absolutely gray.

RUBY: Just shut up, T.J. I'm sicka you. Sicka fussing at people. Sicka trying to get folks to do the right thing—especially these kids. They bout to worry me to death.

RUBY: *(Looking dejectedly at YOL, who is pacing in the kitchen)* Look at her. Got grown too damn quick. Didn't used to act this ugly. No indeed. Things used to be different. Nice. Truly nice. Ask anybody.

RUBY: *(Sighs)* Yolanda, why can't you act like you used to? Huh? You hear me, girl?

YOL: *(Wanting to be disagreeable)* What?!

RUBY: You remember?

YOL: Remember what?

RUBY: How things used to be? When you was little?

YOL: No!

RUBY: Yes you do. *(To T.J.)* She remembers, all right. *(To YOL)* I used to dress you up real pretty. You was so sweet. I used to braid your hair into long, thick plaits . . . and dress you in pinafores so wide you could hardly get through the door. Then off we'd go. You, me and Donald. To the movies. To the zoo. To the ball game. To the—

YOL: —to Sunday School. Eleven a.m. church service. Sunday afternoon fellowship. Sunday evening prayer meeting. Oh, we had grand times . . . at church. It was church, church, church.

RUBY: Best place for you, far as I was concerned. Plenty of good people. Concerned about our welfare. *They knew* I was struggling. Yes Lord. They knew! You remember Sister Reeves? That old sister that used to sit up front with us every Sunday? Whenever things got hard and I'd get depressed, Sister Reeves would whisper, "Just trust in the Lord, Ruby. He may not come when you call Him. But He's *always* on time."

YOL: Yes yes yes.

RUBY: *(Chuckling)* Remember the time Reeves got happy and her fist went flying into Brother Gaines's mouth?

YOL: *(Triumphantly)* I remember! That was the day you fell asleep during the sermon.

RUBY: Girl, I wasn't asleep. I was just resting my eyes.

YOL: You were snoring, Ruby. And Reverend Bell asked us to stop you. I was right there . . . . I heard it all.

RUBY: *(Sighs, ignoring YOL)* Ohhh, I'm tired, you know? And there's something I'm supposed to do today. Got up early to do it. But can't remember what it is . . .

T.J.: *(Pacifying her)* Yes, anyone can see that you're overworked, Ruby.

YOL: *(To T.J.)* If she is, it's her own fault. She's always meddling. *(To RUBY)* You worry about everybody's business. You're always taking over. Maybe if you'd stay out of things, you wouldn't be so exhausted and irritable all the time.

RUBY: Maybe you're right, Yolanda. But let me tell you one thing. Before Mu'deah passed, I promised her I'd take care of you and Donald. And I'm gonna do *just that*.

T.J.: Even if you end up having a nervous breakdown? *(RUBY nods her head up and down grimly)* Does that make any sense?

RUBY: Plenty to me. Now hush and get out of my face. You have upset me enough today. Breaking your promise like that. And not twenty-four hours later. I oughta kick your lazy behind.

T.J.: You don't mean it! Ruby, hey! You misinterpreted my words. There's no justification for getting nasty. Yolanda and I were just discussing what amounted to a hypothetical situation.

RUBY: And you're just a "hypo—" whatever liar. Every time you come stay with us, it's something new. The time before, you had this child joining some group that claims the world is going to end on the fifth of January—only the fools keep changing the year.

T.J.: *(Sheepishly)* Well . . .

RUBY: And last week. Just last week you tell her to change her major. Now what is Yolanda supposed to do with a B.A. in . . . in Meta—Metaphysics, that's it! They don't teach Metaphysics in no grammar school—cause I checked! Anyway, Yolanda can't even pronounce the word, much less teach it. I know one thing, she betta—

YOL: *(Interrupting RUBY, YOL begins demonstrating her skill in pronouncing the word, speaking it faster and faster)* Me—ta—physics. Meta-physics. Meta-physics. Metasific. Metasifics.

RUBY: *(Triumphantly to* T.J.*)* See?! See what I mean? Now listen to me. I got plans for this child. My sister is gonna get herself a degree in education and teach school. Then later, maybe she can go for a Master's degree so she can make her some—

RUBY *and* YOL: —big money!

RUBY: *(To* YOL*)* That's right. Big money.

YOL: Money money money.

RUBY: Try living without it.

YOL: "Go to college, Yolanda, so you can make a good salary."

RUBY: Can you think of a better reason to go? Why you think people struggle to get in these colleges and all?

YOL: This may come as a surprise, Ruby, but some people go so they can learn something about the world. And some people, they go because they want a challenging career or profession. They want to see if they're smart enough to be a social worker or a college professor or . . . or . . .

RUBY: And why do you suppose they want to learn them "challenging professions"? So they can be poor the rest of they lives? Uh uh. It all comes down to M-O-N-E-Y. They going to school so they can get lots of that green stuff and don't you forget it. And, furthermore, speaking of green stuff, how much do you suppose that Negro, Reginald Harding, clears in a week?

YOL: You can't be serious. I'd never ask him something like that! Anyway, I'm not concerned about his paycheck. I'm concerned about his inner qualities—his personality, his spirit. As far as I'm concerned, Reginald has a lot of fine qualities.

RUBY: And from what I hear, they're all below his waistline . . . . Now listen, I can't be bothered bout Reginald's spiritual qualities. How much does the man make? That's the question!

YOL: Ruby, Reginald Harding could be the world's most insensitive individual, but if he had a job and a big savings account, you'd urge me to marry him. Just so I'd have someone to support me.

RUBY: Better him supporting you than the other way around. Is that what you want? Cause if you not careful who you take up with, that's exactly what's gonna happen. *You'll* be supporting *him.*

YOL: And what's so terrible about that?

RUBY: *(Wincing)* Lord Lord Lord Lord *Lord!* *(To* T.J.*)* You put that idea in her head, didn't you? Who else but a parasite who sits around the place shucking and jiving while his women folk go off to work everyday?

T.J.: But Ruby, you know I'm selling my paintings. And my poetry. I mean, they're bound to sell! I'm no parasite. I resent that!

RUBY: *(Ignoring him)* Listen carefully, Yolanda. I'm not out here hitting it everyday because it's fun. And I'm not sending you to college for you to get out here and support some no-count loser. While your behind's in school, you better find yourself somebody with some backbone so you won't have to get out and slave the rest of your life like me and Mu'deah. Sure. You can teach for a while. To help out your man. Say, two, three years. But then you retire. Stay home and take care of the kids till they grown. You hear? Now, you're lucky. Me, I never had no choices. Or can't you get that through your thick head? Do you know how long I been working? *(A beat passes)* Since I been breathing, that's how long. Calluses on my hands. Bunions on my feet. An ulcer starting up. You name it, I got it. And that ain't the half of it. I don't even want to talk about my problems with the folks at work. You see, Yolanda, I don't want this kind of life for you. Or Donald. And that's why I say your behind had better concentrate on finishing college.

YOL: Listen to yourself! You're planning my life for me.

RUBY: Better me than T.J. You accept his advice and you'll end up pregnant, poor, and pissed.

T.J.: Come on, Ruby. Ease up. Give her a little space. Maybe then she'll come to the same conclusions as you about what's important. Maybe then she'll stay home.

YOL: No way!

RUBY: *(To* T.J.*)* She's not going anywhere.

YOL: Oh yes I am.

RUBY: *(To* YOL*)* If anybody's going, it's T.J.

T.J.: Aw, Ruby, no!

RUBY: No?! Is this ten-seventy-five Hayes, T.J.? Apartment G? The place where *I* pay all the rent?

T.J.: Yes—well—I'm going to contribute to the rent as soon as—

RUBY: Yes . . . well . . . I'm gonna . . . nothing, Niggah. This is *my* apartment. And I want you to vacate the premises, cousin or no cousin.

T.J.: You're not being fair, Ruby. You should let me explain what I was attempting to accomplish during my conversation with Yolanda. I was simply trying to show her, by example, how to make her own decisions. *(Turns and appeals to* YOL, *who ignores him.)* Right, Yolanda? Yolanda?

RUBY: Don't try and drag her in on your lie. You got caught, that's all. Inside a week, you pack your clothes—if you got any—and git! I won't have you messing with Yolanda's mind any more. I don't care if you *are* family. How can anybody that's been on this earth as long as you be so simple-minded? "Forget about plans. Follow your feelings. Forget about money." Hah! Forget about money and your behind will starve to death.

T.J.: *(Pompously)* If only you had the right attitude about life. If you weren't such a striver. If only you could accept life as it is, as it manifests itself, we could be kindred souls. We could live here together in this apartment in peace. For then you'd be able to understand where I'm coming from. Ruby, we're not gods. We are God's instruments, and He alone orders our lives, sends pleasure and pestilence and trials and tribulations and solitude and pain and love. And our duty, our mission in life, is to accept His works. His plans for us. That's what I do. And this is what you could learn to do from me. Look, Cuz. I'm not such a terrible person. Honest. I'm not out to exploit you. Really. You know, I have very simple tastes. Very simple needs.

RUBY: And a very simple mind. Don't forget that.

T.J.: I tell you, Ruby, all I really need to be happy —if that is what He wants for me—is the wind. The snow. The rain . . .

RUBY: *(Aside)* I'll take central heating, any day.

T.J.: . . . a bicycle ride through the park.

RUBY: Give me a big car and plenty money for gas.

T.J.: . . . love, joy. Sweet solitude.

RUBY: Give me a split level house with a master bedroom big as a basketball court, lots of storage space for all the clothes I'm planning to get me, a white shag rug on the floor, a stereo set, a color television—See how different we are, T.J.?—A mink coat. A diamond ring—

YOL: *(Still pacing)* Mink? Oh Ruby! You're hopelessly bourgeoise.

RUBY: Not "hopelessly," Yolanda. End-less-ly!

T.J.: You really need help, Ruby. I pity you.

RUBY: *(To herself)* He pities me. *(To T.J.)* Get out of here. Get out!

T.J.: Wait a minute, now . . .

RUBY: Out! Today! I mean it!

YOL: Good grief! Listen to her! She's sick. A real sicko!

RUBY: Get out! Now! Get out! Out!

(T.J. backs towards and inside the living room closet as RUBY moves forward menacingly. As the closet door slams shut, DONALD rushes from the hallway and into the living room. He's dressed in shirt and trousers but is barefoot. A tie is draped around his neck)

DONALD: Hey! Take it easy. Be cool. *(Yawns)* I'm up. I'm up. No need to be shouting. I'm up.

RUBY: *(Trying to pry open the closet door)* You come on outta there, you poor excuse for a man. You coward. I want you out now.

YOL: Donald, what in the world are you mumbling about? What's wrong with you?

DON: Nothing's wrong with me. Ruby yelled for me to get up. Thas' all.

RUBY: *(Hands on hips, shouting towards the ceiling)* Come out, you pinhead!

(DON stares at RUBY, a puzzled expression on his face)

YOL: *(To DON)* She didn't say "get up." She said "get out."

DON: Out? Ruby wants me to get out?

(YOL shakes her head in disgust, while pacing)

RUBY: I'll burn this closet down. With you in it! I mean it. I'll smoke you out!

DON: Ruby?

RUBY: Damn it, what?

DON: Hey! Damn it to you, too. Damn it to everybody.

YOL: That's what I say. This place is a madhouse.

DON: You don't need to be yelling at me, Ruby. I don't 'preciate that. I'm nobody's child.

RUBY: *(To DON)* Can't you see I'm busy? *(To T.J.)* You got ten seconds. Yolanda, hand me some matches.

(YOL ignores the command, continues pacing)

T.J.: *(From the closet)* Aw Ruby. You must be crazy.

DON: Who is that?! That T.J. in there?

RUBY: *(Winking viciously at DON)* Not for long.

DON: Hey, forget him. We gotta talk business, Ruby. You know. We gotta talk about . . . *(Glances furtively at YOL)* about—you know.

RUBY: *(Distractedly, still trying to open the door)* What, what?

DON: *(Menacingly)* I'm trying to tell you! We got to talk about . . . about you know what. About today. To-day. You dig?

RUBY: Today. Today? *(Suddenly alarmed)* Today! Ohhh . . . no . . . . It's today? It's time? You ready? *(Begins frantically inspecting DON's attire as he finishes stuffing his shirt into his pants. He grabs the tie draped around his neck and begins wrapping it. RUBY watches him for a second then grabs the tie from him and begins wrapping it for him)*

DON: I thought you was yelling at me to get outta bed.

RUBY: I was yelling at T.J.

DON: Do I look all right?

RUBY: Fine. So far, so good.

DON: What was all the hollering bout? Why's T.J. in the closet?

RUBY: Cause I'm hot with him. That niggah told Yolanda to run off from here and get together with that fool, Reginald Harding. And then tried to make me into a liar. Says I misunderstood him. Anyway, I told him to get himself out of my apartment today! But he acts like he's gonna do what he damn well pleases.

DON: *(Disgusted)* Oh wow . . .

RUBY: *(Pulls* DON *back as he attempts to walk towards the closet, finishes wrapping* DON's *tie, steps back to admire her handiwork, then glances at* YOL*)* Stood right here and told that child to run off and live with the man.

DON: *(To* YOL*)* Reginald's married. You know that, doncha?

YOL: So? He can go and get himself unmarried—after we've lived together for a while. And then *we'll* get married. That's no big thing, Donald.

DON: So you thinking *then* he's gonna turn around and get married again? To you?*(He turns around and walks over to the closet and pulls on the door; when he discovers he can't pry it open, he begins a tug of war with* T.J.*)*

YOL: Look, Donald. I happen to know I'll make Reginald a very good wife. I'll be fresh and pretty for him when he gets home from work each evening.

RUBY: What work?

YOL: I'll cook him all kinds of special meals. . . . I'll—

RUBY: Leave him a sink full of dishes to wash, like you do round here. Girl, you don't have no idea what marriage is all about. You too young to remember them battles Mu'deah and Daddy used to have—up to the day he passed. Don't you realize marriage is more than wearing nice dresses and cooking up a storm? Do you know what's gonna happen when your man don't have the money to buy you them pretty trinkets and fancy food you talking about? When he don't have the money to buy you food, period? Do you understand how hurt and humiliated he's gonna feel when he can't even keep a roof over your head? Do you know what's gonna happen then? I'll tell you. All that love you counting on will just shrivel up and die.

(DON pulls hard; the door flies open; he grabs T.J.'s *arm and twists it)*

YOL: Ruby MacIntyre, all you ever think about is problems.

T.J.: Owwww. Man, stop. Stop, Donald!

RUBY: No, all I think about is reality. I face the cold, hard facts. And it's about time you did the same.

T.J.: *(To* YOL *and* RUBY*)* He's killing me.

RUBY: Good!

DON: *(To* T.J.*)* Hey! Listen to me. You do what Ruby tells you. You hear? I don't care if you *are* older than me. . . . Now . . . I gotta finish dressing. And I bet not hear no more mess outta you. *(He releases* T.J. *and then reluctantly enters the hallway)*

RUBY: *(To* YOL*)* Just look at your cousin here. He's another example of somebody who can't face the facts. Who cannot, for the life of him, face reality.

T.J.: *(Shaking his arm, the one that* DON *has just finished twisting)* Aw, come on Ruby. Get off my case.

YOL: *(Sighing)* I can't deal with any more of this. *(Enters hallway)*

T.J.: Hell! Everybody faces reality. Mine is just different from yours. That's all. You're concerned about things like keeping a good credit rating and getting a promotion to G.S. whatever. But I feel different. I figure all this is just an illusion. This is a dream world we're passing through, you know what I mean? You understand where I'm coming from? *(RUBY gives him a cold, lingering stare)* You see, reality, Ruby, is nothing but your own personal little world. Your own creation. A place where you can escape. It's nothing more than a retreat. And it has nothing to do with paying the dentist on time or the department store or working hard to get a promotion. No! To me, reality is being. Accepting. Enjoying. Living in harmony with the universe.

RUBY: Oh, T.J., don't try and tell *me* what it is. I *know* what it is. I've lived it. Would you like to know what it is? Huh? It's being around two people who love one another and seeing their love smothered day by day. By rent bills and medical bills and food bills and you name it. It's seeing that love turn into something ugly, turn into a painful little thing can't nobody revive. Hah! Reality, T.J.? It's the tenth of the month. *(DON enters the living room; this time he is also wearing his suit coat and shoes. He eyes* T.J. *suspiciously, fidgets with his tie, listens)* It's a hard life out there, Mr. James. And we don't have time for sitting in some corner nodding or daydreaming or pretending we one with nature. Life is a struggle and I'm out here wrestling with it. That's my life. And that was my mother's life too. And her mother's. They all had to struggle right long with the men for us to make it. Else we wouldn't be here now.

T.J.: Ahhhh. Survival. Is that it?

RUBY: That's it. Unless you in favor of early death.

DON: *(Fidgeting with his tie, a bit uncomfortable in his suit)* I don't know, Ruby. Wow. Sometimes I wonder what's so great about survival. . . . Course, I'm not for dying, either. But sometimes I think—Hey! I'd rather die, go down fighting, then spend the rest of my life like this. And then, the next thing, I think about dying . . . bout being dead. *(He shudders)*

T.J.: *(Excited, pleased)* That's the point, Donald. It all comes to the same thing, the same end. What difference does it make whether or not somebody struggles? You see, you have to ask yourself, what does all this struggling accomplish? And the answer? Well look around this neighborhood. You still have your same old bitter, frustrated men hanging out on the block. Same old abandoned women, starved for affection, looking around for the husbands and boyfriends who still keep slipping in and out of their lives. You got your eight year old junkies and hipsters and your teenagers running round robbing and beating old folks, stealing their social security checks and radios and black and white television sets. Ruby, there are things you must learn to accept, things you will never change. But oh no. Here you are. You and your kind. Tired, lonely women who spend generations scrubbing other people's kitchens, and robbing Peter to pay Paul, sacrificing so that everybody else in the family can go out and do the Philly Dog on Saturday night. Is that what you women are struggling for? "Here you are, folks. Get your piecemeal survival!" Get wise, Cousin. Better stop all this struggling and sacrificing and accept things. Stop trying to control life. Flow with it. *(His hands imitate the rippling motion of a stream. DON looks at his wristwatch)* Flow . . . with it.

RUBY: Hush. Please, T.J. Your words are tumbling around in my head like clothes in a dryer. Please. I stayed up all night, working on them dashikis for the 'sociation. And I tell you, right now I need peace and quiet more than I need an argument from you. *(Sighs dramatically. A beat passes while she stands there, looking drained)* And after staying up working all night, still couldn't sleep.

T.J.: That's another thing. Do—

DON: —Ruby, it's time. You said we should get there bout fifteen minutes early.

T.J.: As I was saying . . . do you think that group of yours appreciates all the work you take upon yourself?

DON: *(Impatiently)* Still running your mouth, huh T.J.? Trying to worm your way back in. Well forget it. Ruby told you she wants you out and that's that.

RUBY: No sleep. Too much on my mind, I guess. Can't remember what, though.

DON: Ruby, we gonna have to be going now.

RUBY: Go?

DON: Yeah! You know!

RUBY: *(Confused; a beat passes)* . . . that's right. Gotta go. *(DON walks over to the living room closet, opens the door, searches inside, and finds a coat; returns*

to RUBY *and helps her put it on)* Just kept lying there, wide awake, thinking. Worrying I guess. Bout everything and nothing.

DON: —Ruby!! Look! It's time to split!

RUBY: *(To herself)* Probably just gas.

T.J.: *(To RUBY)* Are you going out? Didn't you say you were tired? Don't you need to rest?

DON: Hey, Big Mouth. She'll be all right. Keep outta this.

RUBY: *(Suddenly clearheaded)* Yes, T.J. Don't be pretending like you're so concerned about my health. If you are, it's only because you're wondering where your next meal is coming from. You oughta be ashamed. Sitting round here, depending on a woman. You go on now and get packed. Don't think I've changed my mind. And let me tell you one thing. I don't—*(DON throws up his hands in defeat, sighs audibly and heads for the front door. RUBY notices him as he walks away)* Donald?

DON: *(Pauses for a beat; turning to face RUBY, he considers the concerned look on her face then shrugs his shoulders)* Well, come on then! *(Relieved, she hurries into the hallway)*

T.J.: Hmmm . . . I guess that's that. *(Walks around the living room, collecting papers and books of poetry and sketch pads, etc. while DON glares at him)*

RUBY: *(Returning with her purse and checking its contents)* Now, when we get there, pretend we're not together. You can walk in a little ahead of me . . .

DON: *(Walking slowly towards the front door with RUBY)* Yeah, yeah, yeah. Be cool. O.K.?

RUBY: *(Still examining her purse)* And when he gives you a seat, I'll grab the chair across from you, near the partition. And listen carefully. I know this man. He thinks he's slick. If I nod once, that means you're not interested. And if I raise my eyebrows like this—*(Raises her eyebrows)* —that means to ask for more money. And when I cross my legs, that means it's time to talk about benefits. Insurance and medical coverage and—

DON: *(Angrily)*—Will you come on?!

RUBY: One more thing. If I clear my throat, that means it's time to talk about opportunities for promotion. You don't want to be a counselor to them little hard head boys forever.

DON: *(Embarrassed)* Hey! Let's talk about it on the way over. O.K.? *(Opening the front door)*

T.J.: *(Aside)* I do believe Donald is going to a job interview and taking his big sister along.

DON: *(Whirling around to face T.J.)* I heard you. I heard what you said, T.J. Look. If you still here when I get back, it's gonna be me and you.

(While DON stands at the opened door and glares at T.J., two men tap lightly on the door, then nod at DON as they ease past him. Smiling, they greet RUBY and enter the living room. YOL rushes into the living

room, sighs angrily on discovering that REGINALD *still hasn't arrived. She runs to the phone and dials a number)*

RUBY: Phillips?! Morris?! What you all doing here? Sure picked a bad time to drop by.

PHILLIPS: Drop by?

DON: *(To the visitors)* Yeah. So, hi and goodbye! *(Tries to pull* RUBY *out the front door)* Let's go.

PHIL: Don't tell me you forgot, Ruby!

RUBY: *(Pausing, remembering)* That's right! I sure 'nuf did. 'Til just this moment. *(Gloomily)* I tell you . . . it's always something.

DON: *(Pulling on* RUBY's *arm)* The time's flying.

RUBY: *(To* PHILLIPS *and* MORRIS*)* Look, I'm sorry. Y'all make yourselves at home. Have to rush. Be right back.

PHIL: But Ruby.

RUBY: *(Turning to face him)* Huh?

*(*DON*, really angry now, stares at the ceiling)*

PHIL: We have to start immediately. This has turned into an emergency.

RUBY: *(Glancing at* PHIL *and then at* DON *and then at* PHIL*)* Phillips, I'll be right back . . .

PHIL: I'm serious, Ruby.

*(*YOL *slams the receiver down and stalks towards the hallway)*

PHIL: *(Startled)* Oh. Hello, Yolanda. I haven't seen yo—

*(*YOL *enters the hallway in a huff and disappears)*

MORRIS: Wow. Yolanda act like she going through the change.

PHIL: *(Recovering)* Donald, I'm sorry to interrupt your plans. It looks like you're in a big hurry. Wish we could all be accommodated . . .

T.J.: *(Ironic tone)* So do I . . . so do I.

PHIL: *(Noticing* T.J.*)* Hello! Are you? Yes—you must be Ruby's cousin. I've been hearing a lot about you. Ruby tells me you're quite an artist. I'm James Phillips. And this is my assistant, Morris Tademy. *(Gestures towards* MOR; *the three men shake hands)*

T.J.: Welcome to the domicile of the MacIntyres.

MOR: *(To* PHIL*)* Welcome to the what?

T.J.: To the home of the MacIntyres.

MOR: Yeah, right ownnn. I been here befoe. *(Steps to the side and takes a long, hard look at* T.J.*)* Hey. You know, you look kinda familiar, Brother. You hang around with Rufus? Rufus Atkin?

T.J.: No.

MOR: Oh . . . . What you say your name was?

T.J.: T.J.

MOR: Oh . . . . What do that stand for?

T.J.: Terrence James. Terrence Milhaus James.

*(*DON*, completely disgusted, grabs* RUBY *around the shoulders and marches her to the front door)*

PHIL: I'm telling you now, Ruby . . . we're facing

a tight deadline here. . . . I'd like you to stay so we can start *now*.

RUBY: *(Turns around slowly to face* PHIL; DON *leans his elbow against the wall next to the front door and leans his head wearily against his arm in despair and moans)* I don't plan to be gone long. Just thirty minutes. At the most.

PHIL: *(Sternly)* We don't have thirty minutes or even one minute to spare. Even now we're cutting into our time.

*(*DON *moans louder)*

MOR: *(Approaching* DON*)* You acting kinda shaky, too, Bro'. What's with you and Yolanda?

RUBY: *(Sighing)* Donald, walk on round. And don't worry. I'll be there by the time you get called. I'll run on around after we start this meeting. Right, Phillips?

PHIL: Huh! I can see nobody called you, Ruby . . .

RUBY: *(Patting* DON *on the shoulder)* See? I'll be right there. I promise. In bout ten minutes.

PHIL: Ruby . . .

DON: *(Pulling away from her)* Leave me lone. You all have destroyed my confidence. Now I'm sweating. And nervous. *(Holds out his hands; they're trembling)*

PHIL: Ruby . . .

RUBY: *(To* DON*)* Oh Boy! Go on! Stop acting silly and get on round there. Fore you make me angry. *(*DON *leaves, still sulking.* RUBY *hollers out the front door)* In ten minutes. I'll be there. I promise. *(Closes the door, turns and claps her hands)* Let's get started.

PHIL: I think we have a problem, Ruby.

RUBY: Now what? *(Takes off her coat, throws coat and purse in closet)*

MOR: *(Watching* T.J., *who is still busy collecting his paints and paintings)* Hey, Phillips. I seen this dude somewhere befoe. *(Snaps his fingers)* I know! You the guy what was in the Starlite last night. *(To* PHIL*)* You know! The one kept acting up with old big mouth Flaselle.

PHIL: *(Ignoring* MOR*)* I can see Reecie didn't call you this morning. He was supposed to tell you bout the change in the agenda for today's special meeting.

RUBY: Nobody called me. I gotta phone right by my bed . . .

PHIL: *(Angrily)* Signals crossed again. *(Shrugs his shoulders)* I hate to tell you this, especially after all the work I heard you and Mattie did last night . . .

RUBY: Phillips, I'm in a hurry . . .

MOR: *(To* PHIL*)* You remember this guy! At the club. This is the guy what was talking all the trash to old big mouth Flaselle. And loud, too. *(To* T.J.*)* Wasn't you in the Starlite last night?

T.J.: I was there Friday night.

MOR: *(Thinks for a second, puzzled)* Yeah. Right ownn! Last night! Just like I said!

PHIL: Pipe down, Morris. Ruby, we need you to help finish the dashikis. I told Reecie to call you. And I also told him and the others not to come because, frankly, they wouldn't be much help. They argue too much. And right now we got to produce. We gotta finish the hems on these things by noon, in time for the initiation ceremony. With you helping, I know we'll make the deadline. We need to sew the hems and sleeves. All right? Will you help?

RUBY: Dog-gone it. Will you listen to this?! I worked on those tops till three this morning. Drafted the patterns. Helped Mattie cut everything out and helped her sew 'em. And from what I understand, Gladys was supposed to do all the hemming.

PHIL: That's the problem. Gladys and her daughter were supposed to drop by Mattie's this morning to pick up the dashikis. But they didn't show. And when I called Gladys's house, her husband wouldn't let me talk to her.

RUBY: Why not?

PHIL: *(Sheepishly)* He says he's tired of her spending all her free time with the Association.... Anyway. Mattie is on her way out of town right about now. So that leaves Morris. And me. And you, I'm hoping.

T.J.: *(Still gathering his junk and piling it now in one spot)* No rest for the weary, uh Ruby?

RUBY: *(Aside, while watching T.J.)* Why is this man still messing with me?

MOR: *(Still thinking about last night)* He bothering you, too, Ruby? Wow. He was carrying on the same way last night. Got on my natural born nerves.

PHIL: Keep out of this, Morris. Remember, you're a guest in this home.

MOR: Same stuff he pulled at the club. I'm trying to talk to the people bout the movement and he's at the bar, messing with Flaselle. Ruint my whole gig.

PHIL: Morris, we do not have time to discuss what happened last night. There are more important matters at stake he—

MOR: —I'm trying to talk some sense to some of them boo-shie types and doing fine till that big sister starts stealing my thing right out from under me. And all because she's showing off for this here dude. Hey! I had 'em. They was with me, you know? They was all bout to join the 'sociation.

T.J.: He had them all right. "We gotta join hands, and we gotta love one another." That how it went down, Morris?

MOR: You heard me.

T.J.: "But if y'all ain't with us, you must be against us. So, hey! Everybody for the movement, y'all sit over there and wear your dashikis and your naturals and be proud, be bad! And the rest of y'all—you Toms—stay right where you are and go right on wearing your Brooks Brothers and your quo vadis and jive, processed hair cuts. And dig on this. We gonna get ours before you cats get yours. Cause, hey! We some righteous, right-on brothers and sisters . . . and *you* cats ain't shit." *(A beat passes;* T.J. *points at* MOR*) That* was his "Call to Unity" speech.

MOR: *(Laughs; a beat passes)* Ain't that a bitch? Yeah! When I calls 'em, I calls 'em like I sees 'em.

T.J.: Well, you're calling them wrong, Morris. You got to love everybody, recruit everybody. The sinner and the saved. The cop. The janitor. The maid. The businessman. The housewife. The pimp. The prostitute. The artist. The—

MOR: Hey, Man! How you supposed to go round loving everybody? There some people out there hate you, Man. On sight!

RUBY: We not gonna have no pimps joining the 'sociation.

PHIL: Goddamn! I've attended a lot of meetings in my time. But this one . . . *(Shakes his head from side to side)*

T.J.: High class, low class, no class. You have to care about everybody. You have to celebrate life and love. Share your blessings with everyone . . . *(Glancing knowingly at* RUBY*)* even with streetwalkers—and pimps.

MOR: *(To* RUBY*)* What's with this dude?

RUBY: I said! We don't need any pimps in the 'sociation. As long as I'm an officer in this group, there ain't gonna be no people like Reginald Harding joining up.

MOR: Who, Reginald? Reginald Harding? I know old Reggie. *(Laughs. A beat passes. He's suddenly serious)* How come he can't join?

T.J.: Yes, how come, Ruby? Reginald's human. He's going to keel over and die one day, just like the rest of us.

RUBY: *(To herself)* I don't want to hear about it. I see him out there, always messing round, joking with the women folk insteada taking care of business. Unless that is his business. Oh I tell you! And here he is messing with Yolanda. Well, if he steps inside here and tries to walk off with my sister, I just don't know. May the good Lord keep me from violence.

PHIL: Ruby, come on and call the meeting to order.

RUBY: All right. Will this damn meeting come to order? *(To* PHIL*)* O.K.?

PHIL: Fine. If that's how you want to do it. Good! I don't have time to play games either. First order of business. Are you going to fix the hems on the dashikis? Yes or no?

RUBY: In other words, now I'm supposed to kill myself over those tops, right? And yet I stood right here and heard Morris say you two were at the Starlite last night, while I was working my behind off.

PHIL: Just a minute. Wait. Woman, you know I try every weekend to get you to join me for dinner or a drink. But you never want to go. Every time I ask, it's "I don't have time for no foolishness. I don't have time for no bars." So don't throw that in my face. If you want to fight, Ruby, fight fair. *(Looks at her sternly)*

RUBY: How many?

PHIL: Twelve.

RUBY: You mean nobody's done any? All twelve?

PHIL: I don't want you to do them all. I just want you to help. Morris and I. We can do about three apiece.

MOR: Not me. Uh uh. I ain't doing nobody's sewing.

RUBY: I just don't know. I worked hard last night. And I'm tired. Didn't get no sleep. And I can't stay here long, anyway. Donald's expecting me. I can't finish much in—*(Looks at her wristwatch)*—seven minutes. Because I'm gonna have to leave here by then.

PHIL: Well . . . I suppose we'll have to pin them up with straight pins . . . . Although . . . wait a minute. We'll talk to Mrs. Humphries. Ask her to help us. She's a little senile, but she's always asking us to let her help out. Says she likes the company. Likes being around young people. Let's go! *(Beckoning to MOR)*

RUBY: *(Genuinely alarmed)* Mrs. Humphries? Do you actually think that woman can help you? Do you actually think she can make a decent slip stitch and sew quick enough? Why her hands are all crippled, poor thing. Don't be bothering that poor old woman. *(Looking around)* Where are they? I'll go on and sew a couple. Probably save myself some work in the long run. *(Surprised, PHIL recovers, then signals to MOR, who opens the front door and rushes out without closing it)* I wouldn't want to have to rip out everything she sewed and then do it all over again later on. That would be twice as much work for me in the long run. Now, let's see . . . after I finish one or two tops, I'll run on over to Settlement House and sit in on the interview, while you and Morris work on yours. Then I'll rush on back and finish up the rest of mine. Shouldn't take too long. Donald's interview shouldn't go over fifteen, twenty minutes. That's

about how long he usually keeps them. . . . Where are they?

PHIL: Morris went to get them. They're in the trunk of the car. *(Walks over to kitchen window and looks out)*

RUBY: *(Searches in kitchen drawers)* Let's see . . . . Think I'm out of black. But brown will do.

PHIL: Now, you're sure this isn't going to inconvenience you?

RUBY: What do you mean? Of course this will "inconvenience" me.

PHIL: *(Turning around to face RUBY)* I'm not forcing you to do this, Miss Priss. I'm sure Mrs. Humphries would be more than willing to help. I'll go give her a call right now.

RUBY: Just hush, Phillips. *(Rushes around, gathering scissors and thread and packages of straight pins from several kitchen drawers and places everything on the kitchen table)*

T.J.: *(Enters the living room, arms filled with paintings and drawing pads. He adds these items to the pile already assembled in the living room)* Hurry hurry rush rush.

RUBY: Shut up and keep packing. Clear out all your junk. And be sure and get all those rags that you call clothes out of the bathroom hamper.

T.J.: Ruby, must you always ridicule my possessions? It just so happens I have quite a few clothes. Clothes you haven't even seen.

RUBY: *(Searching through sewing items)* T.J., what you have in the way of clothes could be packed in a lunch bag. *(PHIL clears his voice, looks uncomfortable)* I'm sorry, Phillips. But T.J. is such a fool. He likes to give advice. Foolish advice. That's why he has to leave. Today.

T.J.: Phillips, I want you to know that I didn't do anything to merit getting thrown out of this apartment. I just want to set the record straight.

PHIL: That's all right, T.J. I'd rather not hear about your family matters. I'm sure you and Ruby will work things out.

MOR: *(Entering with a pile of dashikis in his arms and closing door with his foot)* Hey, y'all. Guess who I just saw trying to park his caddie?

(YOL rushes out, suitcase in hand, and begins pacing)

MOR: Yolanda! I saw you. I saw you hanging out yore window, yelling to ole lover boy and waving and carrying on. Wow, Ruby. You mean to say you let your baby sistuh hang around with Reginald? Ooo-whew! If I had me a sistuh—

RUBY: *(Mumbling)* Somebody better stop him. I'll call the cops! I swear! She's still a minor. He betta not try and leave here with her. *(Angrily grabs the dashikis from MOR and throws them over the couch, selects one to work on, walks to the kitchen table and paces, dashiki in hand)*

YOL: That man! He was so busy eyeballing those women, he could barely park. . . . I don't know what I see in him . . . *(Places her suitcase on the floor, folds her arms)*

MOR: Look at Yolanda. All excited. Ain't love grand, y'all?

YOL: He's just pitiful. He isn't worth it . . .

RUBY: *(Glances hopefully at YOL)* Maybe she's finally coming to her senses . . .

    (T.J. puts more junk in his pile then walks over and consoles YOL, taking her in his arms)

YOL: Oh, T.J., what should I do?

RUBY: *(Dejectedly)* Maybe she's not.

T.J.: Yolanda . . . Littlebit . . . *(He nuzzles her ear affectionately)* I'm sorry. I'm sorry I made that deal with Ruby. I want you to know I felt real bad about it. I compromised. I admit it. But don't you. Don't you compromise. Follow your feelings, Yolanda. You'll be all right if you do. *(Kisses her cheek then walks over to his junk pile and begins inspecting it)* I've been following my feelings since I was *(Pause)* four years old. And it hasn't hurt me one bit.

YOL: *(Runs to kitchen window, looks out, turns around, alarmed)* He's coming up the stairs.

MOR: How else he gonna get here? Ain't no elevator. *(Walks to the window and looks out)* There he is—Hey. He stopping. He just standing there . . . hahahah . . . talking to a couple foxes! *(YOL stares daggers at MOR)* Well that's what it look like to me.

RUBY: *(To YOL)* You see? See what I mean? *(Drops the dashiki.* PHIL *retrieves it and watches her, a concerned look on his face)*

RUBY: *(To YOL)* Baby, you don't know what you want out of life, yet. Listen. One day you'll be able to make it on your own. But you not ready yet. Right now you have to find something meaningful to work towards. Some goal in life. You too young to know what's really important. You can't just go chasing after one thing and then the other . . . changing your mind from day to day. *(Begins pacing)*

YOL: *(Returns to kitchen window, looks out)* Why don't they leave him alone? Why don't they stop throwing themselves at him?

MOR: Seem like it's the other way around, to me.

PHIL: All right. That does it! Morris, sit down and sew! Morris! *(A beat passes. Finally, reluctantly,* MOR *returns to his chair. He grabs a dashiki. He sews.* PHIL, *dashiki in hand, hovers over* MOR. *Together they sew, with* PHIL *establishing a verbal military tempo for each stitch. In other words, a stitch in time . . .)* Sew! Two, three, four. Sew! Two, three, four. Sew . . .

MOR: *(Sewing)* Don't be rushing me, Phillips. I ain't getting paid for no sewing.

PHIL: Sew, damnit! Good . . . good.

RUBY: *(To YOL)* Don't let yourself get sidetracked by some fool. You gotta reach high.

T.J.: No. That's not how it is.

RUBY: Shut up!

T.J.: Don't reach high, Yolanda. Get high. Off of life. Off of people. Live each day like it's your last. Because it may be just that. You see, Yolanda, people like Ruby are always planning, always talking about tomorrow. How things are going to be better tomorrow. And what they do is end up squandering their todays. Their best years . . . their best hours—gone forever. And so what if their dreams and plans occasionally come true? Nothing changes, really. The sun still rises. The seasons still come and go, bringing the same old catastrophes and pleasures. And at night men still lie awake, worrying about dying. You understand where I'm coming from? Believe me, Yolanda. Whether you plan and struggle or not. It all comes to the same end.

MOR: *(To T.J.)* Hey, what you talking bout, man? Here I am trying to sew this mess and you over there hollering bout the sun and shit.

    (A knock on the front door; RUBY *stops in her tracks;* MOR *pushes his chair back, jumps to his feet and rushes towards the door)*

MOR: I'll get it.

PHIL: Morris, get back here.

MOR: *(Retreats, picks up his dashiki and stares at door while trying to sew.* T.J. *continues collecting his junk. A beat passes while* RUBY, PHIL, YOL *and* MOR *stare at the door. Slowly, almost reluctantly,* YOL *walks to the front door. She opens it)*

YOL: *(Shyly, as short, roly-poly, balding* REGINALD *enters)* Hi . . .

    (T.J. looks up from his task, smiles faintly, then resumes his work)

REGINALD: Hello, Baby! *(Hugs* YOL, *kisses her warmly and then gently holds her at arms length and looks her over fondly)* I should really be hot with you . . . but . . . . that's my Yolanda, my little girl! Hmm. You're a pretty thang.

    (Relieved, YOL *snuggles against him;* REG *brushes his lips against hers. They sway in one another's arms.* RUBY *turns her back on them and begins pacing)*

MOR: Ahem . . . . Hello, Reginald . . .

REG: Say?! Morris!

MOR: What's been happenin', Reggie?

REG: Me and you, Man. Me and you. *(Noticing* PHIL *and* T.J.*)* Hello . . . . Hey, T.J.

T.J.: Hello, Reggie. And good luck.

REG: Good luck?

PHIL: *(Walking over, he shakes hands with* REG*)* Pleasure. I'm James Phillips. And I see you already know Morris, my assistant.

REG: *(Smiling)* Oh yeah. Long time!

MOR: Say, Reggie. When you gonna join the 'sociation?

REG: Give me a break, Home. I just got in the door. I'll get round to it one day. When I get some time.

MOR: *(Breaking into a slow, wide lascivious grin)* Yeah, we all know how busy you keep. *(He looks around and smiles wickedly at* YOL*)*

YOL: *(Pulls* REG *to one side)* Well?

REG: Well, what?

YOL: What took you so long, Sugah Bear?

REG: *(Chuckling)* I knew you'd bring that up . . .

YOL: *(Stomping her foot)* Reginald!

REG: *(Softly to* YOL*)* O.K., Baby, O.K. I'm sorry bout being late. But Clarice gave me a hard time after you called. We really got into it. Lawd, that woman can punch! You know you ought not a done that, doncha? Course the harms been done. *(Shrugs his shoulders)* Everything's gonna turn out O.K., though. Maybe it's for the best. I don't think we gonna have too many problems. Plus, it'll give Clarice a chance to see how tough it can get out there when you on your own.

YOL: What are you talking about, Reginald? What problems?

RUBY: You can talk to your Mr. Harding all you want, Yolanda . . .

REG: *(Cheerfully)* Hello! You must be, uh, are you Ruby?

RUBY: *(Ignoring his question)* . . . but he's leaving this apartment by himself.

MOR: Yeah, Reggie. You in for it, Man. You in big trouble.

(PHIL gives MOR *the "evil eye." Very quickly,* MOR *gets busy sewing)*

REG: Ruby?

(RUBY ignores REG *and continues pacing)*

YOL: Sssh. Don't say anything to her. Let's just go. *(Pulls* REG*'s sleeve)*

RUBY: Well, Mr. Harding. Just how you expecting to support my sister, an ex-wife and them five kids I heard you got?

REG: What?! What ex-wife? Who you been talking to? I don't . . . *(Spots* YOL *as she stoops to pick up her suitcase.* YOL *draws closer to him and places her suitcase at his feet.* T.J. *appears, grabs more of his junk and disappears into the hallway while* REG *observes* YOL*, a knowing expression on his face. A beat passes)* Baby, can I talk to you a sec? *(Yanking* YOL *aside before she can respond)* What you up to?

YOL: I'm tired, Sugah Bear. I'm tired of sneaking around to your friend's place. I'm tired of being left out of things on the weekend because of Clarice. Let's find an apartment of our own. And

later we can get married.

(REG shakes his head solemnly from side to side)

MOR: Oooo! I wouldn't let her tell me what to do, Reggie, if I was you. Hey, she got a big mouth, if you ask me.

YOL: You shut up, Morris.

MOR: See what I mean?! She something else.

(PHIL, exasperated, takes a dashiki and tosses it over MOR*'s head.* MOR*, grabbing the dashiki from his head, continues listening to the heated argument between* YOL *and* REG*)*

REG: Baby . . . Yolanda. Come on, now. You know I'm not gon leave Clarice. I told you that right from the jump. I can't marry you girl . . . *(YOL bristles)* leastwise not now. Maybe sometime in the future I might feel different bout Clarice and thangs. . . . Anyway the situation is bad enough already without you bringing up this marriage crap. Now look! Let me explain something. And don't go getting no big ideas . . . O.K. You can come stay with me. That's cool. *(YOL throws her arms around his neck and squeals for joy)* But just for a while. *(YOL is puzzled, draws back)* That's right. For a while . . . till things get straightened out.

YOL: But why not for good?

REG: Impossible. I told you not to get no big ideas. You understand?

YOL: T. J. always says nothing's impossible if you really want to do something.

REG: Tell T. J. talk is cheap.

MOR: That's right! Talk to her, Reggie! I'd slap her down if it was me. That's what's wrong with us nowadays. Take too much lip from these bigmouth women.

PHIL: *(Stares at* MOR *in horror)* Morris, sometimes you talk like a plain and simple fool. We're here in Ruby's place . . . begging her to help us on this project . . . and you turn around and insult her sex.

MOR: Sex ain't got nothing to do with it. I'm talking bout men and women.

(PHIL sighs and continues sewing)

YOL: I'm moving in with you, Reginald. For good. I mean it.

REG: *(Pulling her into the hallway)* Come in here.

MOR: Right ownnnn!

RUBY: *(Still pacing)* My baby sister's bout to run off from here and make the biggest mistake of her life. *(PHIL walks towards her to console her.* RUBY *waves him away)* I spend all these years looking after her, worrying bout her and Donald . . . trying to keep the both of them outta trouble. A hard-headed girl and a . . . . . . *(Beat passes)* Oh oh.

PHIL: What is it?

RUBY: *(Rushes to the front closet, opens the door, grabs*

her purse and coat, rushes to front door, opens the door just as DON *is entering)* Outta my way! *(She rushes out, slamming the door shut as she leaves.* DON *turns and watches the front door. A beat passes. The front door flies open, revealing a shocked, out-of-breath* RUBY) . . . Donald . . .

DON: Don't worry bout it. It ain't important.

RUBY: I got to sewing and . . . fussing with T. J. and then . . . the next thing I knew . . .

DON: I said. Don't worry bout it. I figured I wasn't gonna get it anyway. Me and this guy, he drove us over. They told him the same thing—turned us away. Said we didn't have no experience. Now, where was we supposed to get it? Huh?

RUBY: *(Hurt)* Ohhh. I tell you! Ohhh. *(Giving* PHIL *a dirty look then once again facing* DON) Well did you talk to Johnson? The one that knows me?

DON: He's the one said he couldn't interview me. Said he didn't know why you signed me up for an interview in the first place, knowing I don't have no experience. Said it would be a waste of his time and mine. Cause I wouldn't get hired. So . . . *(Shrugs)* We drove on back.

RUBY: Donald, Donald, Donald. I'm sorry. I was trying to get there. Honest to God. Maybe if I'da been there . . .

DON: *(Sarcastically)*—I woulda got the job. Yeah, I know all about it. *(RUBY tries to touch him; he pulls away)* Don't do that. *(She tries once again to touch him, but he pulls back and lifts his hand as if to strike her.* PHIL *appears alarmed. Haltingly and guiltily,* DON *lowers his hand)* I told you not to bother me.

MOR: *(Aside, while sewing)* Right ownnn!

RUBY: Don't bother you? Look, boy! I'm the one diapered your behind and defended you and fed and clothed you. Yes I *will* bother you. What is your problem, anyway? Can't you even sound grown and intelligent enough to get your foot in the door? You tell 'em what they want to hear, if you have to. But you get the job! That's what it's all about. Lord! Here you are nineteen and don't even know the first thing about how to go about getting a decent job.

DON: Yeah, it's sad, huh?

RUBY: Damn sad.

DON: Yeah, damn sad. Yeah, well you the one raised me. Seems like you shoulda been able to do better. Yeah. But here I am. The world's oldest delivery boy. Today shoulda been my chance . . .

RUBY: You acting like I planned it this way. I didn't plan for you not to get the job. I didn't mean for it to happen this way.

DON: Oh?

RUBY: Oh? What's that supposed to mean?

DON: *(Genuinely confused)* I don't know, myself. Look. Just leave me lone. *(Pauses, suddenly pen-sive)* Ruby, do me a favor. . . . Stop and ask yourself something. Just ask yourself . . .

RUBY: Ask myself what?

DON: I know you been trying, Ruby. I know it's been hard for you, raising us and all. But . . .

RUBY: But what?

DON: *(A beat passes)* What I'm saying is . . . well . . . Ruby, we ain't done nothing. You do it all. You so used to doing for us, sometimes it seems like you don't really want us to do for ourselves. *(RUBY appears stunned. She stares at* DON *for a beat and shakes her head from side to side.* DON, *guiltily)* I mean . . . that's how it seems to me . . . sometimes. *(RUBY walks over to the kitchen window and leans wearily against the kitchen sink, her back to the others.* REG *and* YOL *return as* DON *walks dejectedly past them and disappears into the hallway)*

REG: *(To* YOL) That's tough. I don't care what you say, Baby. That's how it's got to be for the time being.

YOL: But I thought we'd get our own apartment.

REG: And who's supposed to take care of my kids?

YOL: That wife of yours! Why did she have to leave them with *you?* Why didn't she take them with *her?*

REG: Over my dead body! Ain't *nobody* taking *my* kids. They my life. Now listen. Since you the one started this mess by calling up, you the one gonna help straighten things out. Till Clarice gets back. Come on. Cheer up, Baby. Might turn out to be fun. *(Picks up* YOL's *suitcase)*

MOR: *(Still sewing)* They leaving, Ruby! Hey! Ruby, they leaving. What you gon do?

PHIL: Morris! It seems you are never satisfied until you have people at each other's throats. *(PHIL walks over to* RUBY *and puts his arm around her shoulders)*

MOR: Aw, Phillips, Man. That was really cold. I ain't like that . . .

PHIL: *(To* RUBY) I don't want you to feel that you have to do anything. You understand? Come on. You don't look good. Go rest. Morris and I will finish what we can and that'll have to do.

RUBY: Me. . . . *I* am the problem, he tells me . . .

REG: *(Walks to the front door.* YOL *appears wary)* Baby?

MOR: *(Glancing guiltily at* PHIL) I wouldn't let my sister walk out of here with Reginald Harding if I was you, Ruby.

REG: *(Testily)* Say, Morris. One minute you for me . . . trying to get me to join your group. And the next minute you talking against me. Whose side you on, anyway?

PHIL: *(Still observing* RUBY) Mr. Harding, there's only one side that Morris is for. And that's the side of the argument.

(YOL reluctantly joins REG at the door, turns, glances expectantly at RUBY)

MOR: Ruby, they—

PHIL: Quiet!

MOR: *(Meekly)*—leaving.

RUBY: *(Angrily)* Well, I'll be damn if *I'm* the problem! I'll be damn if *I'm* to blame. After all I've done *(Pauses, a revelation)* . . . for them . . . *(A beat passes; she sighs as if confirming the truth of DON's accusation; PHIL embraces her)*

YOL: *(Shrugs her shoulders in a huff)* Let's get out of this place. I hate it.

(YOL and REG leave the apartment)

RUBY: *(Laughs nervously, stares at the ceiling)* Why, any fool can see what a good job I did with my sister . . . *(Fighting tears, she breaks away from PHIL's embrace, walks to the window, and looks out. T.J. enters with two large, battered, overstuffed suitcases)* Spoilt! That's her! The girl is spoilt as the day is long.

T.J.: Well . . . so long, everybody. I'll send for my other things when I get settled. Bye, Phillips. Nice meeting you. Morris, goodbye. Where's Yolanda? Don't tell me she left without saying goodbye.

MOR: She left, all right. And Ruby just stood there.

T.J.: No!

MOR: If I'm lying, I'm flying.

T.J.: Well . . . good. Good for both of them . . . for Yolanda *and* Ruby. Wish I could have said goodbye, though.

PHIL: *(Joining RUBY at the window and putting his arm around her shoulders once again)* Come on, Miss Priss . . .

RUBY: What a mess, Lord. What a mess.

PHIL: *(Walks RUBY towards the hallway)* Time for you to get to bed and get some rest. Don't worry about anything. Just think about yourself for a while.

MOR: Phillips, where y'all going?

PHIL: Where does it look like?

MOR: Well, do it take the two of y'all to put her to bed? She can't make it in there by herself? Don't think you gon leave me the only one out here working. Well? Y'all just gon stand around and not do nothing? Ruby, you gon help finish these dashikis?

T.J.: Hear, hear! Get your piecemeal survival!

RUBY: *(Smiles faintly. PHIL sees her smile. Encouraged, he massages her shoulders. She closes her eyes)*

MOR: *(To T.J.)* Cool it, Man. We tryna conduct business.

RUBY: . . . Piecemeal survival . . .

T.J.: Get it now . . .

MOR: *(To T.J.)* You wanna know something? Of everybody here, you got the biggest mouth of all.

(DON enters, walks into the kitchen, opens a can of soda, and begins drinking it)

PHIL: T.J. has a big mouth? Morris, if you'd give yours a rest, we might still have a chance to finish this project.

MOR: Hey! Not without Ruby! Look. If Ruby don't come on back over here and help out, then we men gonna have to finish everything by ourself.

DON: So?

MOR: What you mean, "so"?

DON: So, what's wrong with "we men"? Do for yourself for a change.

MOR: Look who's talking bout "do for yourself." Hey! I don't see you doing nothing. I don't see you bending over no needle, tryna push a piece a string through a hole you can't even see.

DON: Aw. Gimme one of them things! *(Grabs a dashiki from the couch)* Where's the needles and the thread? (MOR *points to the middle of the kitchen table.* DON *walks over, picks up package of needles, selects one, picks up a spool of thread, examines the dashiki)* Which is the right side?

MOR: Boy. Don't you know nothing?

(DON laughs)

PHIL: *(Turns to RUBY)* Come on. I'm relieving you of your duties, Miss Priss. *(He is leading RUBY to the hallway, when the front door flies open and YOL enters. Everyone turns and stares at her)*

YOL: If he thinks I'm going to drop out of school for a month or two and spend my time washing dishes and washing and drying clothes and cooking for five kids . . . *(Suitcase in hand, she walks jauntily towards the hallway, pauses awkwardly in front of RUBY and PHIL, eases past them, and then disappears into the hallway. RUBY remains sternfaced)*

RUBY: Just like I said . . . the girl is—

RUBY, PHIL *and* MOR: . . . spoilt as the day is long . . .

MOR: And got a big mouth . . .

RUBY *and* PHIL: Right ownnn!

T.J.: *(Encouraged by laughter, sheepishly standing around, balancing two large suitcases)* Ah . . . Ruby . . . ?

RUBY: *(Sighs dramatically, expectantly)* Yes, T.J. . . .

T.J.: Do you . . . you don't suppose Yolanda is back for good, do you?

RUBY: I hope so. But . . . it's up to her, really.

T.J.: Yes . . . but for all practical purposes . . . I mean, it looks like everything's O.K. again . . . ?

RUBY: *(Pleasantly)* I don't know . . . maybe so, T.J. Who knows. . . . I certainly don't. *(A beat passes)* Well? Go on . . . spit it out . . .

T.J.: Now, Ruby, don't get me wrong. I'm prepared to leave, if that's still what you want. And I'm prepared to take care of myself as I've been doing for all these years. Besides, I've got this friend Flaselle who digs me. Course, she drinks. And smokes. . . . And I believe the body is a temple. But I could stay with her if I want. Yet . . . it's just . . . it's just that I like the ambience of this place.

MOR: *(To DON)* He like the who? *(To T.J.)* Man, speak English. Like everybody else do!

T.J.: And you and Yolanda and Donald—you all are my only kin. And I know I'm going to miss you. Cause . . . *(Pompously)* I love you all. . . . And . . . and you understand where I'm coming from, Ruby?

RUBY: *(Smiling)* I'll expect $75 a month in rent, payable the first Friday of each month. And $10 each week for your food.

T.J.: Fine, if you'll make that $65 a month for rent and $5 weekly for food.

RUBY: Better yet, let's raise it to $80 a month and $15 a week for food.

T.J.: *(Frantic)* O.K. O.K. O.K.! Like you said the first time . . . $75 for rent and $10 for food.

RUBY: A week. $10 a *week* for food.

T.J.: Right. $10 a week for food.

RUBY: *(Walking towards the hallway)* Deal!

MOR: *(To RUBY)* Hey, come on back. Ain't you gon work on these dashikis? This ain't no one man show!

RUBY: Morris, for once in your life, you're right. Tah, tah! *(She waves goodbye and enters hallway and disappears)*

PHIL: *(Calling to RUBY)* May I join you? For a minute?

(RUBY's hand reaches out and pulls PHIL into the hallway)

MOR: Look. Somebody else better get in here and help. I ain't jiving. Where's Yolanda? *(He jumps up and runs over to the hallway)* Come on outta there, Yolanda. We ain't finishing all this by ourself. Bring your lazy self on out here, girl.

DON: That's right. Come on out here, now, Sistuh Deah. And let's get this over with.

MOR: Did you hear your brother? You betta do what he say, 'fore he go up side your head . . .

YOL: *(Making a lot of noise as she enters the living room)* What do you want, Morris? Please stop yelling. I'm trying to do my homework.

DON: *(Aside)* After I finish helping y'all, I'ma go out here and find my own job. Myself!

MOR: *(To T.J., who has been busy replacing his junk)* You too! Come on. Yeah, you! *(MOR grabs several dashikis from the couch)*

T.J.: *(Joining YOL and DON at the kitchen table)* I don't know. Sewing . . . it doesn't quite fit in with my way of doing things, my interests. I've got to get busy and sell some of my paintings. Got to come up with my part of the rent money. Then later . . .

MOR: *(Joining everybody at the table)* Hey, first things first. We got a deadline to meet. So everybody shut up and sew. *(He throws a dashiki to Yolanda and one to T.J.)*

(YOL and T.J. examine the dashikis reluctantly)

DON: Don't be telling me to shut up, Morris. I ain't nobody's child.

MOR: I don't care whose child you are. I'm giving the orders now. I'm the head niggah in charge. And I say everybody shut up and sew.

REST: *(Sewing)* Yeah, well . . . I don't care if you the last niggah in charge. . . . So?! . . . Be cool. . . . That doesn't give you the right to talk to me like. . . . How can I give up my paintings? My paintings are me!

End

JACQUES WAKEFIELD

Photo by George West

JACQUES WAKEFIELD, BORN IN NEWPORT NEWS, Virginia, was brought a babe in arms to New York (Rockaway Beach, Queens). At fourteen years of age he and his family (mother and eight children) moved to the community of Harlem. "Because of the abrupt transition from a 'White' community to a 'Black' one, I am fortunate to have some of the best of both worlds with a balanced insight into the American racial circumstance."

Jacques' artistic interests derived from his concern for the Black community and America during the late '60s. He appeared as an actor in the first major network televised shows dedicated to educating the public to the cultural and political mores of Black Americans (*Black Heritage, Positively Black, Soul, C.B.S. Repertory Theatre*). It was suggested by established artists in the Harlem community that Jacques write. As a further development, he was published in some of the major publications of the day: *Black Fire*, edited by Imamu Amiri Baraka; *We Speak as Liberators: Young Black Poets*, edited by Orde Coombs; *Journal of Black Poetry*, edited by Larry Neal; and a short story in *360 Degrees of Blacknus Comin' at You*, edited by Sonia Sanchez.

"I participated in any cultural activity that pertained to establishing an equilibrium towards an American ideal. I went so far as to quit high school to study in the Shomberg Library in Harlem. Soon after, I was drafted into the Army. I was not the best soldier I could have been if the times were different, though my expectations of myself were more than the military understood and a little out of context. I completed my high school education in the Army, but I didn't complete the Army."

As a self-exiled American in America Jacques heard about the Brooklyn College Scholars Program in English. He was accepted. Before earning a B.A. in theatre, Jacques starred in a co-produced film, *Moja: The Last American* (winner of first prize, Brooklyn College Film Festival, and runner-up in the Black American Film Festival). As well as being published in most all campus magazines Jacques began writing a play, *The Poet and His Wife,* which he completed after graduation, and it is now a film that is proving to be a novel contribution to the art-film world.

"After the dust clears from the slap on the wrist given us in the '70s for our activities in the '60s, things will be seen in their true light, and I feel, unfortunately, but logically so, Black persons will be responsible for their own shortcomings in the '80s. They, especially the Black Middle Class, can't put all the blame on 'Whitey,' though they're trying to provoke the 'poor' Black to do so. The strategy by which the Black middle class intends to use the 'poor' Blacks to tap into the money resources for 'race issues,' direct or indirect, is what I'm keeping my eye on. What I didn't understand when I was younger, and why I gave freely without exploiting my own talents, is that 'poverty is not vice.' The idea that it is is a way class monopolists put one guiltily on the defensive, and it distracts from the important things in life, like finding out what are the important things in life."

Jacques has directed and coordinated several theatre programs and has taught courses in drama. Now working on a full length play, he states, "I've been having some difficulty with this work. I'm trying to give it a breath of fresh air. I'm trying to incorporate a 'realistic' theme with a so-called ancient form. I need time and patience. It's breathing. Soon, it'll speak."

PERCEPTUAL MOVEMENT

Jacques Wakefield

CHARACTERS

BLACK MAN IN WHITE FACE: *Dressed in tails, no shirt, sneakers, 40-ish. Precise mannerisms, arrogant, boisterous. He wears an admiral's hat and medals on his jacket.*

BLACK MAN: *Dressed in tee shirt and overalls. Mid-20s.*

BLACK WOMAN IN WHITE FACE: *Meek though not timid when speaking, 40-ish, dressed in an evening gown, has a rose in her hair.*

CLOWN 1

CLOWN 2

JUGGLER

ACROBAT

Time: Present

Place: Large living room. Two walls, one wall has a large clock on it, the other, a window. There is clothing dispersed on a sofa and a chair. Luggage. There is a golf cart, a toy box with a Raggedy Ann doll atop it. A writing table, a phone.

A PLAY IN ONE ACT

The sound of war can be heard ever so faintly throughout the entire play. The COUPLE *is in the process of moving. There is a* BLACK MAN *sitting in the room; he is writing, crossing out, rewriting, considering, reconsidering. The* WOMAN IN WHITE FACE *goes to wall, reaches with some effort for the clock. Takes it from wall, shakes it, listens, looks at it, looks at audience, throws clock out of the window. Walks back to packing, stretches, yawns, pats man in white face on buttocks. He in turn slaps her on the buttocks, she returns same action. They begin to make a hilarious game of it. They stop abruptly.*

W. F. WOMAN: He's a poet. A mercantile mechanic of words. Wants a colored revolution. A rainbow rebellion. His words are afterthoughts to the reign of, as he calls them, "the first," "shall be the last" he said. Spoke to him Thursday in the History Department of a most prominent University. He cried, actually wept the next morning, repenting, repeating explicit radical rhetoric to his patrons. Now, for heavens sake, there's no getting rid of him, he's become popular and has reason to be feared.

BLACK MAN: *(Standing abruptly)* I've heard miracle men, gibberish, jargon, jive, jibe in the motion of the ocean. American's notion of revolution did not serve me any purpose. *(Pleads to the heavens)* Oh ancestors on whom I place my fate, faith, to whom on cue I return to you from uncertained manifest destinies, to you my masterpieces I reveal. *(Sits down to writing)*

W. F. MAN: The course, of course, is money. He says he has credit on history, a reason for grievances, a reason to stop the consumption of time, he meddles into the private thoughts of civilization. His race races and erases every possible good we attempt to equal their eyes to our vision. I've had quite enough my good man! *(Turning to* W. F. WOMAN*)* Shall we spank him or confine him to the word! The makings of a trouble maker I say, unbecoming to his genetic structure, then again, words will suffice. *(Screams)* Primitive! Barbarian! Fool! Flunky! Funky! *(Turns to* WOMAN, *gets down on one knee, holds her hand)* Oh dear, Oh me, it is so fair, as you are in a covered wagon. *(Kisses her hand, gets up and goes to the golf cart and begins to putt a ball in a highly stylized fashion)*

W. F. WOMAN: Even he said that. We don't even mean what we say. We don't even say what we mean. This is without exception the light years of Negroes with reason, or reasonably light

Negroes, or Negroes with light. (Pause) I do speak well, (Holds herself) I used to speak well. Deep as a well. I'd goosh with feeling, with overwhelming emotion to my credit cards, til' I . . . I . . . I, Oh yeah a yeah drowned in my own . . . own . . . tearsssssssssss!!! (Big finish, arms spread wide, long pause) Oh well, (Beginning to pack again) tomorrow's another day, anyway there's nothing to do, a war is all the time, (We hear the sound of war outside) all the time in the world. (Screams) All The Time In The World! (Pause, she is despondent, then in a sustained whisper) What do you think about that, nigger? There, in the beginning was the word!

BLACK MAN: I don't think very much of it. It'll leave a deep impression on me, I know.

W. F. WOMAN: (In an outrage) Don't you dare speak to your mother like that! Remember, when I call you nigger, it's a love you'll never, you'll never know. When the cold winds come over the channels, there is warmth in my bosom embrace. Grace is the means to success, humility to the power of chess, and guns. My God! Do you hear them? Sun, Son? I'll protect you. Won't you? (Looks to W. F. MAN)

W. F. MAN: Yes. All the time in the world. By the way, what time is it?

W. F. WOMAN: It's nearly summer. (Yodels) Just as we thought. Oh, summer a nocturnal element, warmth. Warmth, no fear of the cold unpredictability of your futures. You do imagine much, but boys will be boys, boys will be men, you will be like a man, you will be like a father, you will be like that, and even more like that. (We hear the sound of war. COUPLE cup their hands to their ears, listening)

BLACK MAN: I wondered at pity for humankind in my drunken pompousness. Nevertheless the English dawdled prosperity to their lost American children. Aha! It's coming back to me . . . yes (Writing) yes . . . yes . . . indeedy . . . let me see now, ummmm . . . yes, I got it . . . I have got it! (Writes) Yes . . . confusion, compliance, conformity, exactly. See?! See? See?

W. F. MAN: He talks of revelations, of mornings, let's stick those words down his crummy throat. Ethnic slick sit sick shit! (Waving his arms frantically in the air) Get him away from our baby. He'll press the button and none of us will see the dark of day. (Begins stalking, foot soldier style in the vicinity of the BLACK MAN) Rat-a-tat-tat. The generation will humble you! You nihilistic trouble maker, wake up and spend some blood! (Rips BLACK MAN's shirt off) There. Europe lives. (Puts on dark glasses, woman rushes over to him, gives him a cane; he wobbles and stumbles, making horse riding sounds and commands) Whoaa, hey there boy, whoaa, whoaa! It's the place of holy men. I know it's over there. (Takes off glasses, begins to march in time, singing "Over there," then, he begins to pack again, and pats WOMAN on the buttocks) I know it must be so. It's standard mustard be so. (There is a long pause, the COUPLE is packing. They pat one another on the ass, giggling; BLACK MAN is writing, then speaks)

BLACK MAN: Damn double standards, lies, lackey living, low-life loafers. Left-over learning, palsied palates, miniscule minds, begging buyers, users and tryers, nought to nothing!

W. F. WOMAN: Projection! Projection!

W. F. MAN: Oh, glory to the pace of the race! Individuals make mischief and disgrace! Why rock the boat, is the question, why rock the boat?

BLACK MAN: What is cultural pluralism?

W. F. WOMAN: Oh no, you mustn't. We must protect our best foot forward. Forward is the key. The passing age must make its mark. Must mark its age on the brow of your horizons. Darling, are we making progress, or . . . no I still hear it. It's time to project. I'm sure he'll understand.

W. F. MAN: Yes, it's tea time, you two timing titillating toe tapper!

BLACK MAN: Projection. This is revolting indeed.

W. F. MAN: You assimilated asshole, leave the Queen alone. Your language is indeed dead, jungle bunny. Speak silence in your ignorance.

BLACK MAN: And what do you know of royalty? Robinson Crusoe is your last hope to subjugate me. Surely Western Man at his apex. Mere myth, (Looks to the heavens) Oh American spirit, whose spirit has claimed mine. What reasons do my father's fathers give for me to be reborn of you?

W. F. WOMAN: Myth you say? You pirate of pilgrims. Myth? What? My Raggedy Ann? (Rushes to Raggedy Ann doll, embracing it desperately)

W. F. MAN: The course, of course, is money!

BLACK MAN: While I am the deviant, the deception to the rule. Among words and the thoughts of great men who never belonged in my situation. Men who pondered on my history and smirk in great white beards. Aha! At the pagan pogopogo pooped deck of their sinking vessel. Their presences are sails, the winds that carry the seeds of my seasoned mind.

W. F. MAN: Unheard of. Simply preposterous!

W. F. WOMAN: No Alamo? No Civil War?! No doodah doodah? No nigger dirges? Pre-posterous! History is your master and control. Defeat! Defunct! Demystification!

W. F. MAN: Why, no sell outs? Sit ins, Daughters of the American Revolution? What? No loose noose in the back of your mind? Preposterous!

BLACK MAN: The children are Mile's tones, no, milestones to the future. I'm getting there. *(Sits down to write)*

W. F. MAN: You're going nowhere fast and getting there. Bring it home, home.

BLACK MAN: Mine eyes have seen the gory!

W. F. WOMAN: That's glory, bastard, glory! *(Distressed)* He thinks of little things, he has a little mind, very limited, very narrow, very unfunny. We must pack, we must leave.

W. F. MAN: Where to, might I ask? Our truth isn't marching on anymore, says he.

W. F. WOMAN: Our last hope, we must leave this place.

W. F. MAN: What about him? *(Points an extended arm at BLACK MAN)*

W. F. WOMAN: Well? What about Rastus? Oh dear, can't we afford to be indifferent?

W. F. MAN: I guess so. *(Looks at door, then back at W. F. WOMAN)* Shall we? *(Offers his arm. They start to exit. BLACK MAN jumps up)*

BLACK MAN: So the wind is the determiner of sorts!

W. F. MAN: Stop it! The world is watching! We must make the world safe!...*(He is interrupted by the phone ringing. BLACK MAN answers it. COUPLE is watching, they back off, embracing each other)*

BLACK MAN: Hello, Hello, yes... this is projection ... yes... I'd like to report someone who has got it... yes uh huh... good, thank you. *(Hangs up)*

W. F. WOMAN: Have you actually got it, huuummmmmmm? A nigger Christ ohhhhhhh. *(Places head in clasped hands)* Is that it?

W. F. MAN: What a way to go... golly... geeee.
(There is a brisk knock at the door. COUPLE straightens up. They look at door with eager but restrained

anticipation. *Where the sound of war was faintly heard, now we hear circus music. The door opens slowly. Enter* CLOWNS, *carrying a cassette recording of war sounds.* JUGGLER *enters,* ACROBAT *tumbles in)*

CLOWN 1: Welcome. Welcome to the sixties. Welcome to the seventies, the fifties, welcome!

JUGGLER: And nineties, and forties, welcome, and the nineteen twenties too, welcome!
(COUPLE slowly moves toward the door as CLOWNS, JUGGLER and ACROBAT coax them along)

ACROBAT: Yes, welcome to the thirties, fifties, sixties, etc., do move along.
(CLOWNS and JUGGLER and ACROBAT are to do what clowns and such do while COUPLE is moving out one step at a time, looking forward, procession like, looking in the distance. Light should shine through open door on COUPLE, as if sunlight. COUPLE should begin to mumble, and repeat the years that the CLOWN and JUGGLER mentioned. Confetti should be thrown at COUPLE by CLOWN 2 as if it were rice at a wedding. There is a loud roar of a crowd for seconds when COUPLE make their complete exit. All sounds subside. Pause. W. F. WOMAN reenters, exhausted)

W. F. WOMAN: Oh dear, I forgot to give what all there is to give. My love. *(Takes a heart from her breast, offers it to BLACK MAN, collapses. W. F. MAN rushes in, kneels down to pick her up)*

W. F. MAN: Oh, honey? *(Calls to outside, lifts WOMAN)* Hey there!! Wait there!! We're coming!! We're coming!! *(Exits)*

BLACK MAN *returns to writing, crossing out, considering, reconsidering. Finally he rips paper. Pulls drawer of table open, smears whiteface on, stands, does tableau of exiting to door.*

Black

LEONA NICHOLAS WELCH

I WAS BORN July 13, 1942. Making my way in on the tail end of a war bears no significance to my being. Personally, I am a peace-loving, "I'm-touchin'-you-world" kind of person, very often living up to the demands of creativity, sensitivity, and homebodiedness expected of one born under the sign of Cancer. I have a deep-down-inside-of-me need for self-expression. My husband, James, and our six children are my first true expressions. My writing is my second, and my teaching, both as English teacher and creative writing consultant, are my third. I have now exposed my life lines to you.

My mother and father, John and Aline Nicholas, both southern born and bred, both starched and ironed Catholics, and both obviously of very strong creative veins (untapped to the world) offered me all three inheritances. There were nine of us children, and I must stop here and now and inform the world that I have known and still do know LOVE.

And now I write. I write plays, poetry, songs, essays, and few forms that I probably made up myself. I write Black. I write colors and no colors. I write woman. I write tears and laughs. I write waterfalls, rocks, butterflys, and blood. But underneath it all, I write love. And when did it all begin? The magic number is seven. In seventh grade I got all A's on my essays and compositions. In highschool I was praised highly for my use of "excellent grammar." In my first year of college I received one special comment scribbled in the margin that read, "I like your individuality of approach." That did it. I then vowed loyalty to my pen. It is a sacred affair. It is a passion.

In 1971, ten years after high school graduation, my first book of poems, entitled *Black Gibraltar,* was published by Leswing Press of San Rafael. Since then I have had poems published in various magazines and anthologies. I have sat in the audience on a natural high and watched the performance of my first play *Black Through the Lookin' Glass,* and I anticipate the performance of *Hands in the Mirror* soon. *Hands in the Mirror* grew out of my love, respect, and concern for old people, particularly for old Black women. There is a sacred, hollowed ground resting in the hands of old Black women, hands extending from hearts and wisdom-packed minds, hands being salve for bleeding hearts, hands being pillars for soul-searching earthquakes, and hands being shelter from storms, all here in America. It is high time we all stood up and cheer old black women. It is time we paid tribute to the doings of these hands. It is time we did their dance. Here is my cheer, my tribute. Within these pages, I do my dance—to them.

Leona Nicholas Welch

HANDS IN THE MIRROR

Leona Nicholas Welch

PERFORMERS

COMMENTATOR/READER
DANCERS:
  FIRST WOMAN: *Knowing and Caring*
  SECOND WOMAN: *Birthin'*
  THIRD WOMAN: *Tired Old Woman*
  FOURTH WOMAN: *The Cookin' Pot*
  FIFTH WOMAN: *Sunday Mo'nin'*
  SIXTH WOMAN: *Prayerful Exuberance*
  SEVENTH WOMAN: *Wisdom, Age, and Loneliness*
  CHURCH GOERS: *Brief appearance of a small group (four or five)*

Note: Music is distinct when COMMENTATOR *and* DANCER *first begin, grows quiet and fades out during recitation and dance, picks up at end of recitation, continues until blackout and exit.*

Option 1: One PERFORMER *may dance ALL parts, or* DANCERS *may be changed as written; same goes for the* COMMENTATOR.

Option 2: Dances may be extended for continuation of mood after the comments (poems) are completed; parts of poems may be repeated for same effect.

Dance/poem opens on a stage empty with the exception of a mirror tall enough to show complete form. On the walls are a variety of pictures of old black women which depict segments of the poems. The mirror serves as a focal point for dancers from which the theme of the dances are moved. The lighting is dim. The only instrument to which the DANCERS *move is a flute, an oboe, an alto sax, or an occasional drum, whichever instrument best creates a solemn and serious mood. Generally* DANCERS *will move out in a continuous flow, with one or two indicated exceptions. There are seven segments to the drama, seven poems, each representing an area of life in which the hands of an old black woman is being portrayed.* DANCERS *must make their hands the focal point of their dances. Curtain is held until completion of the drama. Blackouts may be used at the end of each segment.*

A DRAMATIC DANCE/POEM

Prologue

A distant flute is heard as COMMENTATOR *moves onto stage. She is a young woman and moves with reverence. Spotlight follows her as she talks and moves about the stage, moving her eyes deliberately from audience to pictures of the women on the walls.*

COMMENTATOR: This is a dance/poem, a moving poem, a poetic expression written as a tribute to old black women everywhere. This is their lost poem, the poem that got caught in the brambles the day before the harvest, the poem that became the tears after the crop was lost. This is the poem, the black woman poem that was misplaced in the shuffle up the hill to work and back down to soak two tired, lonely feet. This is the poem that moved with the spirit from wooden pulpit to the top of a nodding head and a constant and rhythmic "amen." This poem has touched many-a soft milk-chocolate, tiny smiles and cupped them in its hands. This poem has glided in soundless doe-

268

like fashion through open fields, tapped its feet in light-hearted exuberance, and held its breath at the edge of a million hopes. This poem is energy, dark and rich. This poem is motion, as it is sound. Hear this beautiful old black woman poem whose meter and beat could have been the anxiety beat of a heart birthing a black child on a cold, rainy night in an Alabama backwoods. This poem remembers the hands that started the breath, and it remembers the breath. *(Pauses, moves toward pictures in reverence. Extends a hand toward pictures. Spotlight on pictures. Speaks in a louder and more emphatic voice)* This is their poem, old black women. This is *(Faces audience)* their dance, the dance whose movements waited and waited until the right day got here, waited too long, and became tired before they recognized the right to be movements in their own rhythms. *(Swirls back to face pictures again. Emphatic gesture of the arm)* THIS IS THEIR DANCE, their swirls and twirls of joy, knowing a new day, a new dollar, and a new strength for daring. This *(Slows up, almost quiet)* is their dance, slow, stretching, turning, yearning, giving, living as love moves inside and reaches itself outwards to those in their world. The dance and the poem are one with the woman. *(Moves closer to audience, facing them directly)* It is a tear dropped in the dark, a smile crossed with the sun, a psalm whispered at the edge of a precipice, a cry shouted on a meteor, streaking from clay to cloud. This is LOVE. This is a love dance of age, a love dance of black, a dance of woman. *(Turns again toward pictures, swirls with joy, extends hands toward pictures. Sound of flute picks up again)* Take this offering *in* your hands, this offering *of* your hands, in its solemnity and sincerity, and dance, *(Swirls with joy)* now to the rhythm of your own souls. *(Holds out hands, cupped toward pictures. Spotlight picks up hands and pictures)* Take this offering and move at the pace of your own joy, knowing back the love that you gave out. *(Moves closer to pictures, hands still extended)* Take this offering now, and move, as your hands have moved across the wrinkled brow of a heavy world and sweetened its bitter sweat. Let this offering sweeten the sweat of your own brow . . . *(Twirls)* DANCE OLD BLACK WOMAN and speak your poem to us now, let us hear *(Backing off toward audience, half facing them)* the rhythms of your long, too long hushed soul. *(Faces pictures with hand extended)* DANCE.

Blackout

Poem of Knowing and Caring

At the sound of distant music, the FIRST WOMAN *moves out in slight dance movements before the mirror. The* COMMENTATOR *is standing in the shadows on stage, out of the way of* DANCER, *who does a full dance of knowing and caring while recitation is going on.*

COMMENTATOR: She knew. She knew when I snuck in through the back door, after he drove off, after I snuck in, putting my foot between the screen and the door facing to snuff out the screeching hinge, she knew I had a tear in my eye, so she quietly flicked off her lamp light and crawled under the quilt. She knew just when to give me my own moments of pain, when I needed them to myself. *(DANCER dances off to side of stage, freezes; spotlight on COMMENTATOR who moves up a few steps closer, focusing on pictures on the wall as she reads several lines)* She knew that when the last salty tear had rolled down my face onto my white chiffon dress, to my brand new silk stockings and landed, tap, on the linoleum, and when I had slipped into the bathroom, she knew when she heard the water running that it was cold, and I was making a desperate splash to wash out the red in my eyes. She knew, just as she knew which corner of the bureau drawer she'd have to stick her hand into in the dark to get her Anacin bottle, just as she knew which day and which hour the sparrows would reappear on the back fence; she knew my private tears. In her mind and in her heart, she held me to her bosom, 'cause she knew that in a minute or two I'd be sitting there in the pitch black room in her favorite and only straw rocker with the sunken seat. *(COMMENTATOR moves back, spotlight picks up dancer, who moves back to the mirror and continues dancing while recitation is continued)* She knew I'd come in and pretend to be interested in how many Mason Jars she'd filled with figs and peas today, and that she'd pretend to be interested with me, that we'd both build up the importance of getting the new venetian blinds strung tomorrow, but it didn't matter 'cause we both knew that she'd already kissed my hair and placed her oily mahogany hands aginst my tear-stained face and said without opening her mouth, "It's gon' be alright chile, come mo'nin', just you wait, come mo'nin', just you wait." She knew that I had heard what she had not mouthed, and felt what she had not stirred a muscle to touch. We both knew that there in the silent unmoved night, she had already touched away most of the pain. *(Both COMMENTATOR and DANCER pause, freeze; spotlight on pictures, silence for ten seconds; both continue)* O God, how she knew that I could feel her damp hands touching my mind there in the dark, her hands, counting the beads one at a time, counting in resolved whispers, "Hail Mary . . . Hail Mary . . . Hail Mary, . . . " ten for me, ten for her arthritis, ten for somebody worse off than both of us, and so on and so on till every bead had been counted and the tarnished cross kissed three times. "It's gon' be alright, chile." She knew that come morning the back door would *(DANCER does full swing; COMMENTATOR becomes enthused)* swing open wide and full, and my half trembling smile would be full grown and sitting on top of the new day sun, full grown smile, and me . . . *(Pause in dancing and reading for just a second)* she knew that I'd be a bit closer to being full grown myself *(Slight pause in dancing and reading; DANCER moves toward pictures, extends hands towards them)* She knew.

Blackout

Segment 2
Poem of Birthin'

At the sound of distant music, the SECOND WOMAN *moves out in slight dance movements before the mirror. The* COMMENTATOR *stands in shadows out of the way of* DANCER, *who does FULL dance of giving birth and preparing to give birth while recitation is going on.*

COMMENTATOR: The rain was pouring down faster than the wind could whip. Lightning flashing against the house, flashing across the room, across her belly, belly big and heavy, heaving in birthing pains, hard and fast as the rain and the lightning. "Won't be no mid-wife out tonight, not before it lets up a bit anyway." Grandmama's in the room with her, watching like a mother lion peering at the door of the cave, keeping an eye on her cubs. It is grandmama watching and counting the minutes in her mind, knowing just when it's time, pacing the floor in a way that no one knows it's a pace and that she's counting the time. "Huh, did it befo', Lawd willin', gon do it agin. Birthin' pains gittin' stronga. Po' chile in misery, takin' it real good tho'. It's a might bit harder for her this time than befo'. Don't 'spect she got two of 'em comin' this time. Lawd don't 'spect she do." *(DANCER moves off to side and freezes, spotlight on reader who moves up toward pictures)* Hot water boiling faster than the rain pouring, louder than the thunder clapping over the roof. Grandmama turned it down low and started in pacing the floor, pacing like nobody'll know. Grandmama's

hands at her side, ready, just in case the lightning beats out the mid-wife, just in case. Hands, olive and sturdy, puff veins showing through smooth wrinkles on top, ready just in case. *(DANCER moves in again;* COMMENTATOR *fades out, then continues)* Grandmama's hands moving across the floor in a birthin' time rhythm, moving slow and steady in a pace can't nobody tell about. Rain harder, thunder getting angry and loud. Lightning flashing across her belly, belly tighter than a conga drum, she groaning, doubling up, tightening fist in a mercy cry . . . *(Dance stronger)* "Lawd . . . Lawd . . . Lawd." That's the word. Grandmama's hands, smooth wrinkles on top, moving fast and steady. *(Dance ends with* DANCER *in a birthin' position)*

Blackout

Segment 3
Poem for a Tired Old Woman

At the sound of distant music, the THIRD WOMAN *moves out in slight dance movements before the mirror. The* COMMENTATOR *stands in shadows, on stage, out of the way of* DANCER, *who does FULL dance of a tired old woman while recitation is going on. No interruptions of* DANCER *during this segment.*

COMMENTATOR: Sun beatin' down on the pavement, pork-chop-fryin' hot. Sun beatin' down on a gray kinked head. She wore her overcoat this morning when she left to do her shopping. "Never can tell when it might turn off cool, 'sides a fool always carries his . . . ." Brown paper bag in her arms, too heavy to tote along with the coat. She keeps the coat on her already heavy back in spite of the sun. "Got to get this shoppin' done." Heavy coal black hands, thin and boned, clutching the sides of the bag, reaching 'cross the vegetable bin, long fingers tugging at the collard leaf, making sure. Heavy coal black hands tugging at the side of the bag, pointing 'cross the meat counter. "That on' there, best hock you got." Gray kinked head trudging under the sun. "Got to get this shoppin' done. Make some hambone soup for Bro' Jenkins. Check came yesterday. Three chops, grits, Maxwell House coffee. Coat getting heavier. Keep it on in spite of the sun. . . . "Got to git this shoppin' done." *(Slight pause-freeze—for change of tempo and rhythm. Continues;* COMMENTATOR *has moved closer to audience)*
Old black woman trudging down the street,
heavy brown paper bag, sore tired feet . . .
covered a million years times ten million more,

lived a million lifetimes trudging to and fro.
Head rag tied over gray kinked head,
back bent, draggin' on, heart full of lead.
What is she totin' in that big brown bag?
 (Attention on DANCER*)*
A TON OF BITTER BLACK BREAD for
 every year she's had.
Tired old woman,
weary in yo' soul,
lay yo' paper bag down,
let 'cho tale be told.
 *(*COMMENTATOR *is silent while* DANCER *does a*
 full minute dance of tired and old. Recitation con-
 tinues)
What is she totin' in that big brown bag?
A TON OF BITTER BLACK BREAD for
 every year she's had.
 (Dance goes on while COMMENTATOR *moves to*
 background)
Tired old woman, weary in yo' soul,'lay yo'
paper bag down,
let 'cho tale be told.

Blackout

Segment 4
Poem of the Cookin' Pot

At the sound of the music, the FOURTH WOMAN *moves*
out in slight dance movements before the mirror. The
COMMENTATOR *stands in shadows on stage out of the*
way of DANCER, *who does full dance of cooking rhythms*
while recitation is going on.

COMMENTATOR: Black eye pea juice simmering
 on the back eye of the stove, yellow corn bubbling in the boiling pot, chicken frying hot in the
 black cast iron fryer, smell of Grandma's kitchen
 tickling my nose and teasing me alive, waking
 me up in the middle of a heated summer day.
 Bubbling, simmering vapors drifting out
 through the back window where I doze waiting
 for the call... "Y'all c'mon now." Her hands
 moving faster than a yellow jacket from honeysuckle to honeysuckle. Her hands, stirring gravy,
 gravy-brown hands, a sea captain on the steer,
 whippin' up a storm in the kitchen. Fingers,
 long, skinny, kneading dough, a masseuse in a
 biscuit parlor, kneading it to health. *(*DANCER
 freezes right where she is, light on COMMENTATOR,
 beneath the pictures) An orchestra, two hands,
 blending in harmony of taste. Maestro syncretiz-
 ing flavors to the tune of boiling pots. Long
 fingers skipping over floured pork chops, sliding

across yellow corn ears, thumping at the edge of
 pots. Melodies of a cookin' pot teasing my ears,
 waking me in the middle of a hot summer day.
 Hisses and bubbles bouncing keyboard-like on
 the breeze, drum majoring out the back door
 where I wait for a call... "I said y'all c'mon
 now." *(Dancing resumed, focus on* DANCER*)* Her
 hands moving faster than a yellow jacket in a
 honeysuckle vine, her hands stirring gravy,
 gravy brown hands, stirring up a melody for my
 hungry ears and nose, gravy brown hands making songs for the cookin' pot....
  rag time keys
  jazz time peas
  hot jazz simmering under my nose
  humming under my tongue
   waking me up....
Her hands, stirring gravy, gravy-brown hands
 moving faster than a yellow jacket in a honeysuckle vine, stirring up a melody for my soul.

Blackout

Segment 5
Poem on a Sunday Morning
(for my Baptist Friends)

Change: DANCER *does not move on right away, music*
begins, lights come up on COMMENTATOR *at edge of*
stage, the only instance in which background cast is used,
pointing out the utter importance of religion in the lives of
blacks, especially these women; also meant to break the
monotony brought on by regularity. Flute stops and
church music is heard faintly in background. Dim light on
a small pew of church goers at back right of stage)

COMMENTATOR: I stood at the door of her room,
 watching her as she painstakingly shoved the last
 button of her jacket through the hole, stuck a
 small switch from the peach tree in her purse (for
 me if I got 'figity' in church), and gave her white
 pearl hatpin one final easy tap to be sure it was in
 right, looked over at me with a "now-you-mind-
 what-I-said" look, and motioned me out the
 door with her black patent leather pocket book.
  *(*FIFTH WOMAN *dances on before mirror, toward*
 CHURCH GOERS, *and back to center of stage where*
 she does her dance of Sunday Morning. COM-
 MENTATOR *recites, church music soft in background)*
COMMENTATOR: Sunday morning, and the world
 was another whole different color now. The
 blues from "Sattidy" night have turned to gold
 and purple, 'cause praising the Lord is a mighty
 royal affair. No sir, no church no where, for no
 reason could boast of the Royal Crown and Dixie

Peach heads, and the vaselined legs. No church no where, for no reason able to boast of a more proud Usher Board and blue gaberdine suit deacon bench like ours. No church could out rock, out shake, or out "amen" ours on Sunday morning, no church, no where, for no reason. *(Pause, mood change to quiet and reflective)* I sit on the inside of the pew next to her and watch her out the side of my eye. I could close my eyes though, and tell you exactly what she be doing. I can see her hands, color of the maple dining room table in our house, and just as plump and round as the table legs, hands sticking out from under her arms where she had them folded. Her short, fat, dining room table leg hands just be patting her side from under her arm, and her short, fat right foot be thumping on the floor as the choir claps and sings. She never patted her left foot 'cause it sometimes hurt a lot and got stiff on her, but I could see how even her left foot sometimes wanted to pat a little too, but it never did work up a real pat, just twitched a bit now and then like it wanted to pat some. I keep my eyes on her hand 'cause that way I know that she won't be reaching for the peach switch in her pocketbook if I drop my tithe nickel four times. Now and then the hand would jerk from under the arm, and I'm just about to jump off my seat, but all she did with it was clap four or five times, and back under her arm it went. *(DANCER dances off while COMMENTATOR, at edge of stage, talks on to audience)* I would sit Sunday after Sunday and watch this ritual, watch her short, fat, thumpy round hand tap, tap under the arm, clap, clap, back again, tap, tap until the final benediction was asked *(DANCER pacing the floor for variety)* and it was time to be kissed by everybody at the back door, and then go home. And O, Yes, when I was asked later what the preacher had spoke on that morning, all I could think of was her hands, that right-sided one, patting and clapping, and I would stand there looking ready to run or pretend like I was going to answer *(Starts walking toward exit)* in a minute, but all I could remember was her hand.

Blackout

Segment 6
Poem of Prayerful Exuberance

Lights come up on the SIXTH WOMAN *on knees as music swells. This time a drum beat joins in the rhythm.* WOMAN *has her hands folded and her head down in dance fashion. Drum stops, flute fades into background.* WOMAN *begins to move into dance of prayerful exuberance as* COMMENTATOR *moves on in recitation)*

COMMENTATOR: Lawd, I'm heh on my knees now b'fo ya with tears of joy streamin' down my face! 'Cause, Lawd, you done come down heh and gived me a helpin' hand. You done showed me a better way. You done gived me a better day, and I'm on my knees a-thankin' ya. My heart is a-jumpin' ot my bosom, and my feets wants to move all around fo' ya, Lawd. Alleluia, Jesus, I'm cryin' tears a' joy for ya, Lawd, 'cause you done sent me back my son. He come home from the wa', and all he's a-missin' is a foot. My heart is a-jumpin' ot my bosom, Lawd, 'cause my baby boy is back, back where he b'long, and one foot gone, next to a whole life, ain't too much to scrape about. *(DANCER and COMMENTATOR both quiet tone)* And Lawd, you done gived Mary Louise a baby girl, after she tried three times and los'em all. Glad I talked to you 'bout her. *(DANCER does a pace motion)* Don't mind these tears none, Lawd, 'cause they gon' come a rain, gon' fill that there wash tub full, and, Lawd, I ain't gon' feel no shame. Alleluia, you done come through like I tole 'em you would. *(DANCER picks up pace, rhythm)* My heart is a-jumpin' ot my bosom and I don't wanna hold it back. *(DANCER spreads arm in speculative fashion)* Now there's co'n and peas, and 'tatoes in the field, and squash, and the peach trees doin' fine agin this year. Praise yo', Lawd! *(DANCER on knees)* Hattie's youngun gone and got right b'fo yo' eyes. He don't fight and cuss and steal like he use ta, only 'cause you touched him, and I'm mighty glad you came. Alleluia, my heart is a-jumpin' ot my bosom with gladness of ya, Lawd, and I'm heh b'fo ya on my knees! *(DANCER arises, exuberant)* Thank you fo' Sis 'Tildas rheumatism actin' alright heh lately. Lawd, heh, take this heh washtub-a-tears. *(Stretches arms wide and dramatically)* I say take this heh washtub–a–tears and po' down your joy on me till I can't stand no mo'—till I drown in yo' goodness, Lawd. *(Sound of drum; flute distinct,* DANCER *on floor, huddled, head down, overcome with joy and thankfulness)*

My boy is home
MY BOY IS HOME
    (DANCER wipes away tears)
One foot ain't too much to ask.
My boy is home, Lawd. We got
peas and co'n. Sis Tilda doin' just fine.
    (DANCER rocks her body)
I'm tremblin' b'fo yo' goodness, Lawd. *(All music stops)* Heh, *(Holding out arms)* take this heh washtub–a–tears. . . .

Blackout

Segment 7
Poem of Wisdom, Age, and Loneliness

Scene opens on the empty stage, lights dim, spotlight slowly follows faces of women on the walls. No music for first ten seconds, gradually flute begins, gets louder and louder. Figure of SEVENTH WOMAN *moves in, jumps and leaps from picture to picture, pausing briefly before each. She dances offstage. Music quiets to a solemn flute if any at all.* COMMENTATOR *appears at edge of stage, speaks to audience while spotlight moves in reflective manner about stage, from speaker to pictures in circular motions.*

COMMENTATOR: We stand in the backyard, or mostly just sit in her quiet, dim, age-decorated room. Listening to her, I ask (not of her, but of life): Is loneliness a fair price to pay for age?
  Is loneliness a going price?
  Is loneliness a fair price to pay
    for having lived well
    for having worked hard
    for having chopped too much cotton
    for having buried two sons?
As we talk, I can see her life revolving *(Spotlight revolves)* before me, there in that quiet dim snuff-scented room, there among the thirty pictures of little black children tucked in one worn wooden frame on the wall, middle-aged men in zoot suits, and a Jesus Christ calendar in the middle of it all. There over the torn plastic table cloth and the one-knobbed bureau, over the sunken seat of the cushioned rocker, the enamel chipped spittoon . . . each sudden spurt of snuff is a mark of defiance, refusing to pay the price, determined to "live and let live," determined to keep up the love pact between her and my one year old son, and he her assurance not to pay the price. *(*DANCER *moves in, spotlight picks her up. She goes into a reflective dance as* COMMENTATOR *continues)*
  Is loneliness a fair price to ask?
  Need she sign for such a bargain?
  Where will she mark her X?
  Who returns revenue for "living and letting live"?
  How high are the interest rates on loneliness?
    High as a welfare check
    a state-bought box of snuff
    white organdy curtains over torn window shades
    High as a bathtub washing machine,
    High as a cup of hot coffee sipped
    each morning from a chipped china saucer?
  How far is the bargain center for age-brewed, highly fermented loneliness?
    As far as the corner meat store,

the eye doctor's, or the front door mail slot?
  How does one collect . . .
  By cleaning out the dresser drawers and counting up mixed-matched stocking, burial insurance receipts and hair pins, by adjusting the hearing aid now and then, winding the alarm clock and cleaning out the dresser drawers again?
What are the colors of loneliness?
Hers come in black only, a most expensive kind.
  (Pause in dancing and reciting, pace is slowed)
As we talk in the evening-tinted room, I can see the many shades of black, different shades for every year, but hers *(Spotlight revolves)* always in black . . . *(*COMMENTATOR *turns to leave. As she says these last words, she turns and points toward pictures on wall,* DANCER *swirls at the words and faces pictures)* And The Beauty And Nature Of Growing Old Is Punishable By Life Imprisonment?????

Blackout

Conclusion

Lights come up on all DANCERS *standing in a dance freeze position, each a different position, with backs to audience, facing pictures. Spotlight captures them. The flute is heard in the distance and is gradually joined by a drum, slow beat, then faster.* WOMEN *come alive and begin to dance as* COMMENTATOR *begins to recite; music fades out.*

COMMENTATOR: We have danced the poems lost in the bramble, and have offered you *(All arms outstretched to pictures; dance goes on)* space to feel your own rhythms, to unstiffen your souls, and move to the sound of the wind blowing through your minds. Tough yet tender, often untaught yet always wise, you move in our world and sweeten the sweat of our brows . . . *(*DANCERS *move off, each pausing for a second before mirror.* COMMENTATOR *moves toward pictures, spotlight on them, flute heard faintly in background)* Old Black Woman, keep your dance going and your poems flowing, and keep us, your children, knowing that you are moving, that you are moving *(*COMMENTATOR *moves toward exit)* that you are moving . . .

Complete darkness on stage for ten seconds; spotlight goes from mirror to wall-pictures; flute solemnly heard in distance, fades out.

Curtain

RICHARD WESLEY

MY DEVELOPMENT AS A WRITER can be attributed primarily to four individuals: Professor Owen Dodson and Professor Ted Shine, then at Howard University, and to Bob MacBeth and Ed Bullins at the now-defunct New Lafayette Theatre in Harlem. Everything I have learned as a writer I first learned from them. Subsequent years have only served to reinforce what they taught me.

All of my work is rooted in Black culture, for this is the "soil" from which I sprang. I reject the notion that to become "universal," I must write about subjects other than Black people. This seems to imply that African people have no traits, mores, or values with which the rest of humanity can identify. Obviously, such an attitude is patently racist and therefore something to be ignored by me. The same pressures, pains, joys, and happiness that exist in other cultures can be found in the Black experience. I choose to recount these experiences in my plays, thereby allowing me to deal with the specifics of African life in America and with the commonality of the human experience.

There is also a solid political foundation to my work in that I view myself as an African nationalist—that is, I adhere philosophically to the teachings of Booker T. Washington, Monroe Trotter, Marcus Garvey, the Honorable Elijah Muhammad, and Malcolm X. I believe in the development of powerful economic and cultural institutions within the community equal with, and independent of, "outside influences." These institutions will serve the purpose of constantly addressing themselves to the needs of the community, irrespective of "New Deal Liberalism" on the part of the majority, or of "benign neglect" when the majority population is in *that* mood. I am in favor of African-American participation in the future of Africa and, as such, consider myself a Pan-Africanist.

I believe that the concept of "art for art's sake" has no place in the Black Arts community. All art should be functional, collective, and committing. It should move people to change, as Baraka once said. Art should teach and inspire. Artists are the "sensors" of the community. Through our work, we must seek to make the community aware of situations "when things fall apart," so that the community can begin to decide on what corrective measures must be taken to remedy a negative situation. I have tried to do this in all my plays, and to a large extent, I have succeeded.

In *The Sirens*, we have Mavis, who, no longer seeing the beauty in herself and the *worth* of herself, punishes herself by becoming a prostitute; degrading her body because deep down she feels she somehow "deserves it." There is Pepper, who wants to get off "the block" and start over again, because if she doesn't, she may die on "those mean streets." And Betty, the young teenager, who is still trying to find her way to love and happiness.

All of these women are searching for some form of self-definition, and at the crux of the dilemma are men. Each of them defines themselves through their relationship with men. In the end, it is their failure to understand this which creates a grand dream world for each to hide in one way or an other: Mavis asserts herself by saying, "fuck it" to the rest of the world as she defiantly stays "in the life," determined to make it on her own. Pepper runs off into a marriage which holds only the slimmest of promises and which requires her to make all the sacrifices, and Betty revels in the promise of a marriage to a boy who still has not fully comprehended the complexities of manhood.

The Sirens demands that men and women think seriously of redefining the sexual role-playing that is going on. What is at stake is the very core of the Black Nation itself. For, as we all know, a nation is only as strong as the men and women who inhabit it.

Richard Wesley
May 13, 1980

Richard Wesley was born in Newark, New Jersey in 1945. He received his B.F.A. at Howard University in 1967. His plays, produced in New York, include: *The Black Terror* (1971); *Gettin' It Together* (1972); *Strike Heaven on the Face* (1973); *Goin' Thru Changes* (1974); *The Past Is the Past* (1974); *The Sirens* (1976); *The Last Street Play*—aka: *The Mighty Gents* (1977). He is the author of two motion pictures which were produced and directed by Sidney Poitier: *Uptown Saturday Night* (1974) and *Let's Do It Again* (1975). Mr. Wesley is the recipient of several playwriting awards, and he has lectured on Black art, theatre, and films at Manhattanville College, the African-American Institute at Wesleyan University, and at Manhattan Community College in New York City. He is currently on the Board of Directors of the Frank Silvera Writers' Workshop in Harlem and of the Theatre of Universal Images in Newark, New Jersey.

THE SIRENS

Richard Wesley

CHARACTERS

MAVIS: *Age 29. Lonely; resigned to it.*
DUANE: *Age 31. Ambitious.*
BETTY: *Age 17. High school girl with dreams of romance.*

BOBBY: *Age 17. Stone youngblood.*
PEPPER: *Age 28. A woman trying to survive the best way she can.*
JOHN 1
JOHN 2

Time: The present   *Place: Newark, New Jersey*

Production Note: This play is meant to be performed on a large bare stage with only a minimum of suggested sets to designate a given location. The intent here is that the actors bring the "reality" onstage with them so that the combination of acting, lights, and suggestive sets create the illusion of reality.

Property List: (1) Onstage: couch; bed; rug; coffee table; lamp post; lamp; night stand; wine bottle and glass; magazine; dresser; telephones; cigarettes and matches. (2) Offstage: basketball; package containing dress; bottle of soda. (3) Personal: PEPPER—purse containing cigarettes, knife, & straight razor; BOBBY—folding money; MAVIS—purse with brown case, matches; JOHN 1—folding money.

A PLAY IN FIVE SCENES

Scene 1

Lights up on a street corner somewhere in Newark. It is very late at night. The smell of cooking food from a nearby "greasy spoon" permeates the air. Two men saunter across the stage, both fairly inebriated. One turns his back and urinates while the other stands humming a tune to himself. They continue walking and talking about nothing. R&B music blares from a distant speaker and the two men dance a few drunken steps as they move offstage. The stage is now empty except for the music and the smell. Suddenly, noises are heard. Shouts, footsteps. PEPPER rushes onstage.

PEPPER: Quick, Mavis, in here!

(MAVIS comes rushing onstage and both duck inside a doorway. The headlights of a police car flash across the stage, then go away. The two women come out)

MAVIS: See, now? I thought them suckers was gettin' paid to be cool.

PEPPER: They must be new on this beat, or somethin'.

MAVIS: Yea. See, they still cruisin'. If they was the regular ones they woulda been inside the house gettin' their taste right now. The jive punks.

PEPPER: It's gettin' almost as bad over here as it was in New York. Well, no matter, I'm cuttin' alla this loose someday, anyway.

MAVIS: Yea, sure, honey. Tell Mavis anything.

PEPPER: It's the truth. I'm gettin' too old for this. Besides, these johns around here ain't hittin' on nothin'. Broke-ass nigguhs.

MAVIS: Hard times, you know?

PEPPER: Yea. There was a time when I could hit these dudes out here for twenty—twenty-five dollars. No more.

MAVIS: Wage and price controls, honey. Ain'tcha heard?

PEPPER: That don't break no ice with me. I need some big bucks, honey. *(Shivers)* Have mercy! It's

277

cold as hell out here an' I ain't wore no drawers.

MAVIS: *(Smiling)* Well, who's fault is that?

PEPPER: Shoot, later for you, whore. *(Both laugh)*

MAVIS: I hope there's some money to be made out here tonight. I don't wanna be out here freezin' my ass off for nothin'.

PEPPER: Maybe your truck driver friend will come by an' make it all worthwhile.

MAVIS: That man's gettin' to be a pain, chile. Wants me to marry him.

PEPPER: Shoot, why don't you?

MAVIS: Ain't nothin' he can do for me. 'Sides, I like my independence. Can't no man tell me what to do. But he is kinda nice, though. Nicer than most of the johns that come around here. Got a cigarette?

PEPPER: Yea. *(Reaches into her purse and gives a cigarette to MAVIS. MAVIS takes it and lights up)*

MAVIS: Thanks.

PEPPER: You hear from your job?

MAVIS: Not yet.

PEPPER: How long you been laid off, now?

MAVIS: Almost a month.

PEPPER: You gon' go back if they call you?

MAVIS: Prob'ly. *(Both laugh)*

PEPPER: You makin' more money out here than you ever did in that factory.

MAVIS: *(Begins to shiver)* God, where the hell all the tricks at? It's way too cold out here.

PEPPER: You better believe it. It get too cold, I'm gon' go in. That's one of the advantages of bein' an outlaw. Over in New York, when I had a pimp, he used to make me stay out no matter how cold it got. There was a time with him that was so bad that I almost committed suicide.

MAVIS: Suicide? Pepper, you outa your mind?

PEPPER: *(Laughs uneasily)* Yea, I know. But I was young and stupid, then. Today, a nigguh put his hand on me, I'll put a pot of hot grease in his face so fast he won't know what happened. *(Looking offstage)* Hey.

MAVIS: *(Looking off also)* Yea, I see him. You want him?

PEPPER: You can have him. I'm gon' see what's happening in the bar. *(Enter JOHN. He looks at the two women)*

MAVIS: Well, You like what you see?

JOHN: Maybe.

PEPPER: See you later, honey.

MAVIS: Okay. *(PEPPER exits)* Well, mister?

JOHN: What if she was the one I like?

MAVIS: Well, hey, you got legs. Go on after her.

JOHN: No need. One box is just like any other. C'mon.

MAVIS: That's fifteen dollars for me an' three for the room.

JOHN: Fifteen?! I could buy a pair of kicks for that kinda money.

MAVIS: Well, I ain't no shoes, motherfuckah.

JOHN: Forget it.

MAVIS: *(Conciliatory)* Hey, wait a minute. Don't go away mad. Look, how much you got? *(Moves close to him)* How's ten for me and three for the room?

JOHN: *(Looks at MAVIS as though he were inspecting a slab of meat)* Yea, I can live with that.

MAVIS: Solid. C'mon, then.

(They exit. Lights fade on the street corner and pick up on MAVIS' apartment. A slow blues plays on a stereo in the living room, while offstage we hear soft moans. An alarm clock suddenly goes off. Then, we hear sounds of scurrying about. We hear offstage voices)

BETTY: Oh shit, there goes the clock. Get dressed, Bobby.

BOBBY: How soon 'fore your aunt get here?

BETTY: About twenty minutes. C'mon, we got plenty of time. That's why I set the clock.

(BETTY and BOBBY come rushing onstage adjusting their clothing and picking up wine bottles and food scattered on the table. Soon, they are finished)

BOBBY: I guess I'd better go. Your aunt would never understand if she caught me in here. She'd swear we was doin' somethin'.

BETTY: *(Embracing BOBBY)* Oh, baby. You so good to me. I'm yours forever.

BOBBY: *(Pulling free)* Hey, baby, lighten up. I got to go. *(Moves to the door as BETTY follows him)* You gonna be at the game tomorrow?

BETTY: Who y'all playin'?

BOBBY: East Side.

BETTY: Y'all gonna win?

BOBBY: 'Course. Watchu think?

BETTY: Bobby, do you love me?

BOBBY: Sure, baby. Ain't I your man?

BETTY: I ain't so sure.

BOBBY: Whatchu mean by that?

BETTY: All you ever want is whatchu can get.

BOBBY: Betty, is that what you think of me? Here I am, just got finished layin' up with you in your aunt's house all night an' her daughter sleep in the next room. I'm takin' a chance on gettin' *caught*, just to be with you an' you think I'm usin' you. Wow, what kinda jive is that?

BETTY: You don't never take me nowhere, like you ashamed to be seen with me.

BOBBY: I ain't got no money.

BETTY: Parks is free.

BOBBY: It's too cold to be walkin' through somebody's park. Besides, sweet thing, a park ain't good enough for a princess like you.

BETTY: It was good enough for Sheila.

BOBBY: What about Sheila?

BETTY: You took her to the park. You took her to the Continental Ballroom an' to the Five Kings, an' even to New York. Only place you ever take me is to the goddamn couch!

BOBBY: Where you here lies like those?

BETTY: (Angrily) They ain't hardly no lies!!

BOBBY: (Grabbing BETTY's arm) Bitch, I know you ain't been spyin' on me.

BETTY: Then you admit you been goin' out on me.

BOBBY: Hey, why I gotta answer any questions from you? You ain't got no claim on me.

BETTY: Solid. So, maybe tomorrow me an' Franklin Johnson will get a good thing goin'.

BOBBY: I catch you 'round that nigguh and' I'll walk in both your asses. You my woman an' I don't play that.

BETTY: Oh, it's alright for you an' Sheila—

BOBBY: (Interrupting) Ain't nothin' between me an' Sheila. I had to take her out. See, me an' the fellas had this bet 'cause Sheila was playin' hard to get an' so we had this bet to see who could rap heaviest to her an' take her out an' I won. Hey, she don't mean nothin' to me. You the only mamma for me, baby.

BETTY: You ain't lyin', Bobby?

BOBBY: Baby, I'd never lie to you.

BETTY: Please don't, Bobby, You know I couldn't stand it.

BOBBY: You the only one for me, baby. (They kiss)

BETTY: It's always nice when I'm with you, Bobby.

BOBBY: It's nice when I m with you, too, baby.

BETTY: Mama an' Daddy always be fightin' so much. It's like I don't even exist sometime. I like being held. I feel so safe.

BOBBY: (Uneasy) Wow, baby. Uh . . . er . . . hey, look, I got to go.

BETTY: We still got a little time. You can stay a little longer.

BOBBY: No . . . uh . . . I'd better get goin'. My mother's already on my case about bein' out late so much.

BETTY: I'll see ya at the game tomorrow.

BOBBY: The first points I score'll be dedicated to you, Betty.

BETTY: Really?

BOBBY: I promise. Look, I gotta go. Take it easy. Hear. (BOBBY *kisses her and rushes out as the music continues to play.* BETTY *goes back and sits on the couch as lights fade on her part of the stage to very low but not quite out. Lights come up full on another part of the stage where we see* BOBBY *in a phone booth somewhere. Lights also come up dimly on the street corner where* MAVIS *and* JOHN I *part company, and she stands alone shivering waiting for her next customer.* BOBBY *in the phone booth, laughing)* Yea, Eddie! Yea! I got her in the bed, man. A real bed. Huh?

Oh, it was good, man. Damn right. You got more freedom than on a couch. Yeah. I bet I'm one of the first guys in our gang to get a girl in the bed. Yea, I'm a man, now. That's right. (Laughs) Yea, man, we *nekked.* No clothes, at all. If I'm lyin', I'm flyin'. Oh man, she was moanin' an' groanin' an' all kinds of fantastic shit. Oooweee! Man, I musta got about seven nuts. Yea! I ain't lyin'. I couldn't help it. That was some good stuff. (Laughs) You ain't foolin', man. Well, you know our names: "The Get Overs." (Laughs) Aw, it was easy as hell. These broads go for anything you tell 'em. Sheila or Betty, they all the same. It ain't nothin' for me to rap my way into a broad's drawers, man. (Laughs) If you were here, I'd slap you five, my man. Man, I got Betty's nose so wide open, I could drive a Mack truck through. Huh? Oh, yea, sure. You can rap to her when I get through. Just like with Sheila.

(Lights fade to black on everyone and then come up on MAVIS's *apartment.* BETTY *has just finished cleaning up the apartment and is now reading)*

MAVIS: Hi.

BETTY: Hi.

MAVIS: Whatchu doin' up so late, honey?

BETTY: Couldn't get to sleep.

MAVIS: Uh-uh, Well, you have enough to eat?

BETTY: Yea, but you shouldna fixed so much food, Aunt Mavis. (Smiling) Can't nobody eat all the food you cook.

MAVIS: I like to cook. It can be tiring sometimes, but most times it relaxes me. Keeps my mind off my troubles.

BETTY: Will you teach me to cook like you, someday?

MAVIS: What's wrong with your mama?

BETTY: She ain't got no time. Too much mess goin' on in our house.

MAVIS: My brother an' your mother. Don't seem like they ever gon' get it together. He still drivin' that cab?

BETTY: Yeah, an' when he ain't drivin' for his boss, he schemin' on gettin' a coupla cabs of his own. He stay so busy tryin' to get money, he sometimes be out the house all week long. That's when him an' mama get to fightin'.

MAVIS: Yea, that's a familiar story, honey.

BETTY: Daddy be scared there ain't gonna be enough money in the house, so he tryin' to get as much as he can. He scared we might have to go on welfare like the folks next door. Boy, when he found out about them it seemed like he just changed. Mama scared he gon' work himself to death.

MAVIS: That's 'cause she don't understand. Our family was on welfare for the longest time. Your grandfather couldn't get no jobs an' finally he left the house so Mama could get on the relief. He an' mama used to have to meet in a friend's apartment or spend a night somewhere else in case the welfare inspectors came snoopin' around. Your father hated those days. He got his first job when he was thirteen an' ain't stopped since. The house changed when your father stopped laughin' like he used to.

BETTY: Maybe if I told Mama she'd understand more.

MAVIS: Don't you tell your mama nothin', you hear me? Your father find out I told you that story he'll beat the black off both of us.

BETTY: Okay.

MAVIS: My little girl sleep all right?

BETTY: Delores? Like a log. I swear, that child can "z" more than anybody I know.

MAVIS: Takes after her daddy. I remember he used to sleep so soundly 'til sometime you'd think he was dead.

BETTY: You ever hear from him?

MAVIS: No. Don't want to, neither.

BETTY: Yea, sure.

MAVIS: I mean it. Honey, the worst thing you can do is take a nigguh back after he has messed over you, 'cause then you've givin him license to do the same thing over again and again.

BETTY: Don't you haveta start trustin' at some point? I mean, if you love a man—

MAVIS: (Interrupting) Love? Is that in the dictionary? (Yawns) Girl, if you don't get your buns in bed, you had better. You got to go to school tomorrow. I'm sorry I had to even ask you, but your grandmother just had to go down South so I had to find me another baby-sitter. I just hope your classes don't suffer tomorrow 'cause of this.

BETTY: Don't worry. Say, when you comin' off this night shift, anyway? You been on it the longest time.

MAVIS: Don't know an' I don't care, either. I'm makin' good money, girl. Go on to bed, now.

BETTY: (Rising, yawning) Okay. See you, Aunt Mavis. (Exits)

(Lights come up on MAVIS standing alone. The light should be a spot lighting an area large enough for her to move about in during her monologue)

MAVIS: I'm old. I feel old. I look old. Old before my time. Why? How did it happen? Can't say that I really care that much. I dunno. I feel so empty inside. Wasn't always like that. No. There was a time when I used to laugh and joke and play and just plain act wild like I ain't had no sense. They used to call me loud Mavis when I was in high school. Mama used to say wouldn't no man marry me 'cause my mouth was so big. But I loved life and I loved to party and wear bright dresses and just plain be myself. I felt beautiful. Beautiful. And every day was the summertime for me. I used to party for days, then. Knew all the latest steps and all the hit songs by heart. Couldn't nothin' get me down. Not this raggedy-ass town or summa the raggedy-ass people in it. I still don't know what happened. Why everything just suddenly dried up for me . . . me an' Duane used to be so happy. Just outa high school, both workin' an' makin' money. Doin' it to death. (Laughs) Then I got pregnant an' we didn't party that much anymore. An' the money started goin' elsewhere an' suddenly me an' Duane had to grow up an' when we did Duane started actin' funny. Talked about nothin' but money. An' we didn't make love no more an' I started puttin' on weight an' Duane's face started to change. An' suddenly, Mama looked old, an' nothin' seemed to be the same. It was like I was caught in some kinda quicksand and the more I wiggled the deeper I plunged down. Lord have mercy. What's happened to me? That's all I wanna know? So now, I'm an old woman an' Duane is gone an' I don't laugh no more an' I don't care no more. I wish . . . (MAVIS does not finish the sentence)

Scene 2

The following day. BOBBY *and* BETTY *are on a street corner just after the basketball game against East Side High.*

BETTY: Sorry y'all lost.

BOBBY: Aw, those chumps got lucky as hell. That number forty musta travelled at least sixty times in the game and the ref didn't call it once. We gonna get 'em next time, just you watch.

BETTY: I was really proud of you. You did good. I was so happy when you scored your first basket 'cause of what you said last night.

BOBBY: (His mind elsewhere) I just hope losin' to East Side don't hurt my chances of gettin' into the County Tournament. Scouts from summa the big time colleges will be there. It'll be my big chance.

BETTY: Everybody was impressed with the way you played, Bobby. I betcha that East Side coach wished he had you.

BOBBY: Boy, if I can just make all-county, I got a chance. I'll get offers from all over.

BETTY: Did you hear me screamin' your name every time you got the ball?

BOBBY: I got to try to score at least twenty-five points a game. Can't nobody miss me then. I'll be able to cut this raggedy town loose.

BETTY: Bobby, I'm talkin' to you.

BOBBY: Yea, I hear ya, baby. That's nice.

BETTY: What?

BOBBY: What you said.

BETTY: What did I say?

BOBBY: Un . . . uh . . . er . . . c'mon, let's go.

BETTY: Bobby?

BOBBY: Yea.

BETTY: Why do you ignore me all the time?

BOBBY: I don't ignore you.

BETTY: Yes you do. I thought you said you loved me.

BOBBY: Of course I love you. Really.

BETTY: You tryin' to make a fool outa me?

BOBBY: Oh, wow.

BETTY: You know your friend Eddie tried to hit on me today.

BOBBY: Eddie? C'mon.

BETTY: In the cafeteria. Kept followin' me around. When I told him about you he talked like you didn't care if he rapped or not.

BOBBY: I'll talk to Eddie, okay?

BETTY: Did you say anything to him about me?

BOBBY: Betty, be serious.

BETTY: I *am* serious. Eddie ain't never even looked at me before today. He always kept his distance 'cause he knew I was your women. Now, suddenly he's on me like white on rice.

BOBBY: Look, I said I'd talk to him.

BETTY: Same thing happened to Sheila when she was goin' with you. No one within a hundred miles of that broad. Then suddenly, every nigguh in the school was tryin' to pull her. What's your job? To break all the girls in?

(BOBBY slaps her)

BOBBY: Fuck it. I don't need to listen to this kinda bullshit min' from a dizzy bitch like you. Later. *(Exits in a huff)*

BETTY: *(Crying)* Bobby, wait. I'm sorry. I didn't mean it. I was mad. Bobby, don't do this to me. Bobby. Bobby. *(Rushes off after BOBBY as the light fade. Lights up on the street)*

PEPPER: Yea honey, someday I'm gon' cut alla this loose. Got to for my looks are gone an' I'm shootin' up to keep from goin' crazy. Know what I mean?

MAVIS: Yea.

PEPPER: These men out here are freaks, Mavis. Gettin' so you take your life in your hands just to go in a room with 'em. If I could just save the money I make.

MAVIS: Hmpf. What would you do with it? Take a trip to the Bahamas, or somethin'?

PEPPER: Maybe. Look, I'm twenty-nine years old. I'm out here competin' with high school girls, so how much time I got left? You know these men.

They go for young flesh.

MAVIS: That ain't no news.

PEPPER: You ain't no spring chicken, either, "granny." You five years older than me.

MAVIS: I'll make out. I been hustlin' one way or another all my life. If I got to do somethin' else, I'll do it. Later for it.

PEPPER: I hear the girls over in New York are holdin' johns up.

MAVIS: Them bitches is crazy. That's why I got my ass from over there.

PEPPER: Yea, I'm gonna get out. Just go away somewhere an' meet a man an' make some babies.

MAVIS: Pepper, be serious. You a whore. The kinda okey-doke you runnin' down only happens in the movies.

PEPPER: I'll make it happen.

MAVIS: How many men have you laid down with since you been on the block? You got any idea what your box must look like? Hell, ain't no man in his right mind gonna marry you.

PEPPER: *(Hurt)* Oh, wow, Mavis. What's the matter with you?

MAVIS: Change of life. Okay?

PEPPER: No, it's not okay. Who you think you are talkin' to me like that? Just cause some man messed over your life don't be takin' it out on my dreams. Shit.

MAVIS: That ain't got nothin' to do with it. I just ain't got no time for people who refuse to deal with reality.

PEPPER: Reality is tellin' me to get my bootie off this corner. Times are changin', honey. These new broads and these johns ain't got nothin' to do with what we was about when we first came out here. Our day is past, Mavis.

MAVIS: Oh, broad, you don't even know what you talkin' about.

PEPPER: Don't I? Look up an' down these streets. Look at these people. They gettin' desperate. Nigguhs is broker now than ever before. I read that the suicide rate for Blacks is up and the life expectancy rate is down. More nigguhs is dyin' of cancer an' heart attacks an' high blood pressure than ever before.

MAVIS: You read all this?

PEPPER: You damn right. Our people are goin' crazy an' we gettin' old an' sick an' tired. So how much importance can a coupla whores on a street corner have?

MAVIS: *(Walking away from PEPPER)* Don't tell me I ain't important. Don't take that away from me, too.

PEPPER: Huh?

MAVIS: Oh . . . uh . . . nothin'. I didn't say anything.

PEPPER: Oh. *(Pause)* Tell you one thing, though.

You lucky. You got that truck driver. I wish there was somebody who would come my way. Hell, Pepper'd be long gone. You a fool not to marry that dude.

MAVIS: Maybe. But the man don't interest me. No man does.

PEPPER: He still got your nose, huh?

MAVIS: Who?

PEPPER: Duane.

MAVIS: Shit.

PEPPER: What would you do if he came back?

MAVIS: Duane ain't comin' back. (Quietly) Never.

PEPPER: But what if he does? Would you take him back?

MAVIS: Hell, no.

PEPPER: Then you the one who's refusin' to deal with reality. (JOHN 2 enters) Excuse me. (To JOHN 2) Hey, baby, you goin' out tonight? (PEPPER walks toward him) You ain't got much time, Mavis. This corner don't belong to us no more.

Lights dim as PEPPER *and* JOHN 2 *go off together with* MAVIS *watching.*

Scene 3

BETTY: (On the phone) Hello? Hi, it's me, Betty. Yea. Bobby, I'm sorry about what I said. I was mad . . . well, you act like you don't care no more and Bobby you mean so much to me . . . well, boys act so jive all the time, a girl takes a big chance lettin' herself feel like I do . . . I know you got your heart set on makin' all-county an' all-state an' gettin' to college, but you don't have to walk all over me to do it . . . yea, that's how I feel. What? Patience. It's hard to be patient with somebody like you, Bobby. No, wait; don't hang up. Please. Let's talk. No, we *don't* always talk. You're always tryin' to do it to me every chance you get. You seldom talk. An' usually when you do you talk about yourself. Bobby? . . . Of course I understand about gettin' the athletic scholarship, but that's not what I'm talkin' about. I'm talkin' about you an' me. What's so funny . . . yes, you *were* laughing. Bobby you ain't no damn good. You know that? . . . That's right. I love you an' I've given myself up to you. Don't that mean nothin' to you? . . . Oh, you're grateful. Thanks a lot . . . what? . . . Well, if you don't know what else you're supposed to say don't look to me to tell you . . . whatchu s'posed to *do*? Bobby, you can kiss my ass! (She slams the phone down and sits fighting back tears) All I want is to be happy . . . and safe from bein' hurt alla time. Is that so much to ask? I want someone I can believe in. Someone

who loves me. That's all. It's startin' already. I can feel myself gettin' tense an' angry all the time. Like Mommy an' Daddy. I don't wanna be like that, but sometimes it seem like there ain't gonna be any other way.

(*Lights come full up as* MAVIS *enters and sees* BETTY *near the phone*)

MAVIS: Hi, Betty. (BETTY *mumbles an answer*) How'd your day go? Oh, I picked you up somethin' at Bamberger's. Hope you like it. Here. (*Hands* BETTY *a package*)

BETTY: (*Opening package*) A dress. Oh, wow, Aunt Mavis, this is very beautiful.

MAVIS: Yea, next time your boyfriend comes to take you out, you can have somethin' outa sight to dazzle him with.

BETTY: Yea . . . next time.

MAVIS: I get any calls?

BETTY: No. You work tonight?

MAVIS: No, I'm too tired. So, I took the night off. Called in sick.

BETTY: Yea, you need to stay home an' rest. You don't never seem to get no days off.

MAVIS: I need the money. Work as much as I can.

BETTY: You shoulda stuck to singin' in the clubs on weekends. You were very popular.

MAVIS: And very broke.

BETTY: You could work during the week and sing on the weekends. You'd be rich. You'd pull at least two hundred dollars a week from both gigs.

MAVIS: (*Chuckles*) I don't mean to make fun of you, honey. But two hundred dollars a week.

(*The lights pick up* BOBBY *in another area of the stage as we see* BETTY *sitting*)

BOBBY: (*On phone*) Man, Eddie, I'm gonna put my foot up that broad's behind, I swear. What do hammers want from dudes? I told her from the giddyup that I didn't want no entanglements. Hey, what I look like tied down to one broad . . . no, well later for it, man. I'm gonna go on to college somewhere, then come out an' get me a job as an architect, just like I always planned. Make me some big bucks an' leave dizzy broads like her behind forever . . . yea, these chicks think their box is some kinda sacred ornament. Yea . . . hey, that's what I say, too. Look, a box is made to be opened, right? An' if I got the right key is that my fault? (*Laughs*) No, man, I ain't takin' her back. I learned from my uncle that a woman hates a man who begs. He said any time a woman sees any signs of softness or weakness in a man she use him, 'cause she ain't got no respect for him. I ain't never gonna forget that . . . yea, that's right. Next time Betty sees me, I'll be hirin' her as a maid to clean up my apartment. Yea. (*Laughs*) Look man, I gotta split. I'm late for practice . . . .

Okay, later on, my man.

(BOBBY *hangs up then looks at the phone for a long time. On the other side of the stage we can still see* BETTY. BOBBY *picks up the phone and dials.* BETTY'*s phone rings*)

BETTY: Hello?

BOBBY: (*Starts to say something but gets cold feet. Instead, he disguises his voice*) Uh . . . er . . . ah— sorry, wrong number. (*Hangs up*)

(*Lights fade on* BOBBY *as he moves slowly and sadly offstage*)

MAVIS: Lord! (*Laughs again*) Child, the things your old aunt could tell you. You hungry? I got some meat in the refrigerator.

BETTY: Naw, I ain't hungry. An' Aunt Mavis, you shouldn't eat so much anyway. One of these days you gonna lose your figure.

MAVIS: It don't matter that much to me. What I got to look attractive for?

BETTY: Why you say that?

MAVIS: Oh, I don't know. Just the way I feel, I guess.

BETTY: Oh. (*Pause*) Aunt Mavis, why are boys so hard to get along with?

MAVIS: 'Cause they can't be trusted.

BETTY: There must be some.

MAVIS: Nope. Nary one. Listen to the voice of experience, honey.

BETTY: But—

MAVIS: Men are born hustlers. Gettin', possessin', keepin', reachin'. That's all they're about. A woman is just another commodity. She goes good with penthouses and Cadillacs.

BETTY: My father's not like that.

MAVIS: Yea, maybe he ain't. Sorry.

BETTY: There must be some way out.

MAVIS: The trouble with young girls is they dream too much. Best you wake up and deal with the real world, Betty. (*Lights change to pick up* PEPPER *and* JOHN I *sitting on a bed together after having conducted a "business transaction"*) Relationships between men and women is mostly physical, 'cause that's the only way men been taught to deal. When you understand that, you can begin to learn how to handle nigguhs.

PEPPER: Was I good to you, Daddy?

JOHN I: You was all right.

PEPPER: Then that means every time you come 'round here you gonna look for me, is that right?

BETTY: I don't believe you.

JOHN I: Pussy is pussy. If you be around, I'll look you up.

MAVIS: All right, don't listen to me. But hard heads make soft behinds.

PEPPER: Man, you can't be serious. Good as I am, you can't possibly be interested in summa these other broads around here.

BETTY: I don't wanna spend my life bein' hurt.

JOHN I: Any time I got the money, any one of you broads will do.

PEPPER: Damn, ain't you the cold one?

MAVIS: Yea, baby, yea.

JOHN I: Not cold, just practical.

PEPPER: Okay, Mr. Practical Motherfuckah. I'll see you next time you come around.

JOHN I: Solid, baby, later.

(*Lights out on* PEPPER *and* JOHN I)

MAVIS: A man will walk into your life, take everything you got to give, then split. Like it don't mean nothin'.

BETTY: Why?

MAVIS: Why do fish swim in the sea?

BETTY: Well, it ain't gonna be like that with me.

MAVIS: I used to be determined like that. Just like you. But that didn't stop Duane from splittin'. Woke up one mornin' an' found a note an' some money. Nigguh said he had to find himself; had to get himself together before he could truly be righteous to me an' Delores. So, he split. Left me an' Delores by ourselves an' left some money on the night table like I was his whore, or somethin'. As if that money made his leavin' all right. (*During the preceding speech by* MAVIS *lights pick up* DUANE *u., rising from a bed, dressing, and leaving as a woman sleeps*) Shit, this is gettin' depressin'. I'm gonna go lie down for a while. I'll see you later. Be sure an' lock the door when you go out.

BETTY: Uh-huh.

MAVIS *goes off to another part of the stage and stands silently a moment. She reaches into her purse and removes the brown case and stares at it.* BETTY *sits alone on the couch, listening to soft blues as lights slowly fade on both women.*

Scene 4

A spot comes up on BOBBY *alone, his foot propped up on a basketball and a fistfull of dollars in his hand.*

BOBBY: Alla my life women have been tellin' me what to do. I been surrounded by women. My mama and my grandmama raised me. In fact, *both* my grandmamas. They shared me on alternatin' weekends whenever Mama wanted to go out an' party. My aunts used to hug and kiss me and tell me how I was such a cute little boy an' how I was gonna break so many hearts when I got to be a man. They used to talk about it as though it was a badge of honor. They all used to spoil me an' cater to me an' everything. That is until they got into one of their sour moods about men. Then, they'd change. Mama stopped spankin' me when I was real young 'cause one day she found out that she wasn't spankin' me so much 'cause I did somethin' bad as 'cause I looked so much like my father. Once, when I was nine, my Aunt Alma was givin' me a bath an' my other aunt an' another woman was in the room an' they was talkin'. An' my aunt took me outa the tub to dry me off. An' for the briefest second. I could feel alla them women's eyes on me. I knew they was lookin' 'caused I was nekked, but I didn't care 'cause it was mostly family and the neighbor knew me since I was a baby. But it was the look they gave me. It was different and then I knew. They was admirin' me. It was like I could hear them thinkin' that there was no doubt that I was gonna be a lover. I was developin' muscles . . . *everywhere*. It was the first time I ever felt a woman's eyes on me in that way. An' it scared me. It was like I was bein' sized up for the kill. They seemed to be more strict with me after that. Always bossin' me around. An' the teachers in school. More women. Seemed like from one end of the day to the other, all I could hear was women's voices. Got so I was able to tune them out whenever I wanted to. I got out onto the streets where there were men and I stayed there even though I knew it used to hurt Mama so. But I had to be there. I had to know who I was, what I was. Mama could teach me to be good, and she could teach me to have discipline an' she could teach me to love. But she couldn't teach me to be a man, an' the streets seemed to be the only place where I was gonna learn. Then, the girls in school started their clutchin' an' whinin'. Tryin' possess me before I could even possess myself. Ain't no woman gonna possess me . . . *ever*. I'm tired of women wantin' in on my life. I wish they'd just give me a chance to realize my own dreams. If they could just wait for me. Wait for me to do the things I got to do. Everything would be so cool, then.

(BOBBY continues counting the money as the lights go down on him and come up on MAVIS and PEPPER standing on the street corner)

PEPPER: Your truck driver friend was by the other day.

MAVIS: Yea, I heard.

PEPPER: He was lookin' for you. Had a gift.

MAVIS: No kiddin'? What was it?

PEPPER: I dunno. He had it all wrapped up. 'Sides, it wasn't nunna my business.

MAVIS: Well, well, well . . . gifts. Hmmmm. Guess I better stick around. I need some additions to my wardrobe.

PEPPER: Thought you didn't wanna be bothered with him.

MAVIS: This is business, baby.

PEPPER: Girl, you'd better snatch that man.

MAVIS: No, tell you what: You snatch him, if you can.

PEPPER: What makes you think I can't?

MAVIS: Nothin'. You the one with all the theories an' ideas about old whores on the block. Let's see if you can't pull this nigguh. *(Laughs)* Fat chance, stale as your pussy is, girl.

PEPPER: One of these days you gon' go too far in your teasin', Mavis.

MAVIS: Look, don't you understand? That ol' truckdriver see somethin' in us that ain't really there. All we really is is forbidden fruit. Once he's had his fill he'll go back to that old biddie he always been with.

PEPPER: Ain't nothin' real far as you're concerned, but for me he's a way out an' a way for me to hold my life together. If you don't want him, then hey—

MAVIS: Like I said, the nigguh's all yours.

PEPPER: Don't be doin' me no favors.

MAVIS: That truckdriver ain't hardly no favor. He's prob'ly the best you can do . . . how long you think it's goin' be before that truckdriver decides you ain't right for him? 'Specially when he start thinkin' about alla them men who've had you before him.

PEPPER: I can be loved!!

MAVIS: Loved! Pepper be serious.

PEPPER: I can be loved, Mavis. You ain't got no right to be talkin' to me like this. I had a beautiful relationship once!

MAVIS: You a "ho" . . .

PEPPER: Not forever . . .

MAVIS: . . . just like me, Pepper . . .

PEPPER: . . . I'm a woman . . .

MAVIS: . . . you're a piece of flesh and you can be bought and sold every day of the week.

PEPPER: Just keep it up, hear?

MAVIS: "Meet a man and make some babies," ha! Your body's so scrambled inside you'll be lucky if you even manage to get pregnant, much less *have a baby*.

PEPPER: *(Slaps MAVIS, knocking her a few steps backward)* No!!!

MAVIS: *(Angrily)* Who the hell you think you slappin' on?

PEPPER: You keep away from me, you hear! *(MAVIS angrily starts toward PEPPER, when PEPPER pulls a knife from her purse and swings wildly at MAVIS, causing MAVIS to back away. PEPPER cries uncontrollably)* Dontchu come near me, no more, Mavis. You keep away from me. I don't need to take this kinda shit from you. I hate you. I hate you. I hate . . . I . . . I . . . *(Turns and runs off)* Goddammit! Goddammit!

MAVIS: *(Shouting after* PEPPER*)* Your tears don't break no ice with me, Pepper! You still no better than me. So, later for you jive dreams, broad. You hear me?! You still just like the rest of the broads out here. *(*MAVIS *is quiet for a moment. Speaking to herself)* Pepper? Pepper? Pepper, come back. I didn't mean it. *Pepper.*

(Lights fade as MAVIS *stands alone looking off in direction* PEPPER *has run. Lights come up on* MAVIS*'s apartment as* BETTY *sits alone on couch reading, and* DUANE *comes to the door and knocks.* BETTY *answers)*

DUANE: Hello, is Mavis here?

BETTY: No. She didn't get home from work yet.

DUANE: Oh, I see. Well, can I come in and wait?

BETTY: Sorry. She don't allow nobody in the house when she ain't home.

DUANE: Well, I ain't exactly nobody. Is Delores home?

BETTY: Yea, but she sleep.

DUANE: Let's see, she just had her tenth birthday three weeks ago, didn't she?

BETTY: Who are you, the police or somebody?

DUANE: No, no days like that. I'm Duane Carter.

BETTY: *(Stepping back)* Oh, wow. Ain't this a blip?

(Lights fade to blackness. In the darkness there is a loud scream, almost a wail. Light comes up on PEPPER, *sitting alone with a bottle of cheap wine and a glass. A husky-voiced blues singer of the Etta James variety is heard on a nearby record player singing a baleful tune.* PEPPER *has been crying; screams again, then laughs)*

PEPPER: Whew! Thanks, I needed that. *(Laughs)* The girl gon' do it tonight. Yea! *(Takes a straight razor from her purse)* I'm tired of these four walls an' this city an' this broke down, twenty-eight year old, goin' on sixty-eight year old body that ain't never had a chance to be nothin' 'cept what it is. Yea, I'm gon' do it *tonight.* An' I won't be laughed at or ignored or hurt by blind nigguhs who don't love me or care about me . . . *no more!* That's right! *(Starts to cry)* 'Cause Pepper gon' die tonight. An' I'm gon' lock all the windows an' lock the door an' let the smell of my dead carcass funk this place up. Yea, that's right. An' when men come to get my body, it'll be one of the few times since I been on this earth that any man has touched my body for free!!! *(Laughs. Then grows silent and sits thinking. She reaches for the bottle of wine and unsteadily pours herself another drink)* Pepper, girl, you better leave this stuff alone 'fore you wet your drawers. *(Chuckles)* Yea, just as the last bit of life oozes outa me all my muscles relax an' I pee on myself. An' that's how they find me. I wonder if they would laugh. They probably would. That's all I need. Be just my luck. Yea, be just my luck! *(Starts to cry again)* You a wrong broad, Mavis. I thought you was my friend. I thought you understood me. I can be loved. Yea. Somebody loved me once. That's right! Someone touched me once. For free. Yea, an' I felt good inside like 'Retha and Etta James be talkin' about on they records. Frankie was good to me, real good. Our times together were wonderful. I felt like I was alive, an' all the people who called me ugly an' all the men who walked all over me on they way to pretty women and fancy dreams just disappeared outa my life forever! An' I didn't care about what Frankie was or what anybody said about us, or how my mama cried an' carried on. Frankie loved me an' cared for me and treated me right. And when I was with Frankie I didn't never have to be out on that block. I loved Frankie . . . and she loved me. She wasn't afraid to touch me. She treated me like I was worthwhile. Somethin' no one else ever did. I didn't wanna fall in love with her, but I couldn't help it. It ain't that easy for me to be alone that much. But man, she split, too. That jive butch walked out on me. Left me for some high school broad in New York. What's wrong with me? I'm just a helpless, stupid 'ho'. I couldn't even keep a butch. Now, you know *that's* helpless. So, I'm gon' do it tonight, y'all! 'Cause I'm tired an' I'm ugly an' I'm . . . alone. *(Picks up the bottle of wine. Looks at it a long time, then wipes her lips with the back of her hand)* Later For My Drawers!!!! *(She starts wailing uncontrollably and guzzles the wine straight out of the bottle. She puts it down, quickly picks up the razor and slashes at her wrist, but just as she is about to pierce her skin with the razor, she hesitates and pulls the razor away. She repeats this several times. Then, she nicks herself ever so slightly with the razor. Having done this, she steels herself for one last attempt. Still crying, she raises the razor and aims it toward her wrist. Suddenly, the razor is lowered, and we notice that her sobs have turned to a kind of forlorn laughter, both at and with herself. Looks directly up into the light)* Shit, I ain't crazy.

Scene 5

Lights come up on DUANE *sitting alone in the living room listening to music when* MAVIS *enters. It is some hours later.*

DUANE: Hi.

*(*MAVIS *stares at* DUANE *a long time saying nothing.* DUANE *rises, goes to her, takes her in his arms, and attempts to kiss her. She turns her face so that he is only able to kiss her on the cheek and pushes herself clear of him)*

MAVIS: Well, this damn sure is a surprise.

DUANE: I knew it would be. Wow, you don't look like you hardly changed at all.

MAVIS: You been waitin' long?

DUANE: Coupla hours, I guess. Looked in on Delores. She's sure growin' into one beautiful little mama.

MAVIS: Yea. In a coupla more years, she'll be just ripe for pickin'.

DUANE: So . . . uh . . . how you been?

MAVIS: All right. Makin' a livin'.

DUANE: Yea, you got a pretty nice place here.

MAVIS: It beats Ferry Street. Remember them days?

DUANE: Yea.

(Both fall into an uneasy silence)

MAVIS: Um . . . well, can I fix you a drink?

DUANE: No, I don't think so.

MAVIS: Still the health freak, huh? No drinkin' an' smokin'.

DUANE: Can't break old habits, baby.

MAVIS: Well, how about some food? You look thin. I remember you used to be a husky dude.

DUANE: Went on a diet an' I stopped eatin' meat, too. I feel a hundred times better.

MAVIS: Oh.

DUANE: Lemme have a cold drink like a soda, if you got it. That'll hold me. (MAVIS *goes off and returns with a soda.* DUANE *takes it)* Thanks. *(Sips)* This is good. *(Pause)*

MAVIS: Duane . . . why are you here?

DUANE: *(Caught off guard)* For you and Delores.

MAVIS: Why?

DUANE: Why you think, baby?

MAVIS: Ten years you been outa my life. Now, you just gon' come on the set an' act like you only been on an overnight trip.

DUANE: Don't be that way, Mavis. This ain't easy.

MAVIS: Shit. I should hope not.

DUANE: There ain't nothin' here for you, Mavis. Not a damn thing.

MAVIS: A doctor wants to marry me.

DUANE: You gonna do it?

MAVIS: I dunno maybe. He been mighty good to me.

DUANE: Where the hell you ever meet a doctor?

MAVIS: *(Tensely)* Whatchu mean by that?

DUANE: Nothin'.

MAVIS: I met him at church.

DUANE: You still go to church?

MAVIS: *(Lying thru her teeth)* Occasionally.

DUANE: Yea, I remember you in the old days. You used to sing in the choir and help organize the outings. The Perfect Little Angel.

MAVIS: That was a long time ago.

DUANE: High school days.

MAVIS: Uh-huh. The happiest time of my life.

DUANE: My greatest ambition then was to make all-state in basketball.

MAVIS: And get between the legs of every girl in sight.

DUANE: *(Laughing)* Oh, wow, baby, why you wanna take me there?

MAVIS: 'Cause it's true.

DUANE: Maybe. But I've changed now.

MAVIS: Nigguhs don't change.

DUANE: Why don't you give yourself a chance to find out?

MAVIS: Duane, I found out all I needed to know from you ten years ago.

DUANE: I was a *boy,* then.

MAVIS: You was man enough to ask me to marry you. Man enough to make a baby.

DUANE: And boy enough to have failed you, baby. That's why I'm tryin' to come back if you would only let me.

MAVIS: You know what it's like to walk down the street for two weeks lyin' to everybody, tellin' 'em that you went down South to visit some relatives 'cause I couldn't face the fact that you left me? You ever sit in a welfare office and watch those pinched up face bitches ask you about your personal life and like you ain't shit? Huh? You got any idea what livin' on a food stamp is like, Duane? Let you come back?! Shit! You can crawl the hell on back to where you came from for all I care. I had to feed Delores by myself on chump change when your little pint-sized checks stopped comin'. You ever see a child goin' to school hungry day after day after day an' knowin' ain't nothin' you can do about it?

DUANE: And what good would it have done for me to have stayed around? I wasn't doin' nothin'. My job wasn't payin'. You got better care from the city than you ever got from me.

MAVIS: But I was happy with you, Duane. Didn't nothin' else count.

DUANE: That's the way you saw it, baby. I saw it differently.

MAVIS: And now look at the result.

DUANE: Look, I finally got that music thing together. I got my own group an' I'm doin' real well playin' gigs around the country. We tour with all the big names and we get lots of recording dates. I got money now, baby. Alla the things I couldn't give you before I can give you now. That's why I'm back.

MAVIS: Forget it, Duane. Hey, why don't you send us a check every now and then. Like you used to do. Remember?

DUANE: Mavis? . . .

MAVIS: So where you livin' now?

DUANE: Atlanta.

MAVIS: No kiddin'? I hear it's real nice down there.

DUANE: Yea, it's a beautiful place. 'Course the rest of Georgia's kind of a drag.

MAVIS: What're the women like? I hear they're real man-getters.

DUANE: They got a lotta Southern charm an' they really know how to work them roots on the man they want.

MAVIS: How come ain't nunna them got you?

DUANE: I was too busy. I had work to do.

MAVIS: Well, at least I ain't the only woman you've fucked over with that line.

DUANE: I was tryin' to get my thing together to get back to you, Mavis. My leavin' an' stayin' away ain't never had nothin' to do with no other woman. *(MAVIS says nothing)*

MAVIS: So . . . you a big time musician, now? Shoulda' known you'd be somethin' with that horn someday.

DUANE: I ain't no John Coltrane, but I can handle myself pretty good.

MAVIS: No kiddin'. You need a singer in your group?

DUANE: Oh, you a singer now.

MAVIS: I've done a few clubs around here on the weekends. Did pretty good, too.

DUANE: Well, sorry Mavis. I can get a singer any time. What I need is a wife.

MAVIS: Hey, I thought I had steered us clear of that conversation.

DUANE: It's too important to be covered over by small talk.

MAVIS: Duane, I'm free. My life is my own. I do what I want, go where I want, and be what I want to be. I ain't givin' it all up.

DUANE: I ain't askin' you to give up nothin'. I'm askin' you to come back to Atlanta with me.

MAVIS: You know, Duane, sometimes I get these flashes of rage. Like I wanna hurt people. For no reason other than to see them hurt like I been hurtin' alla this time. You don't want me back, man. You don't even know me.

DUANE: I been waitin' ten years to be together enough to deserve you, baby. I don't hear a word you sayin'.

MAVIS: No. I ain't goin' back.

DUANE: Whatchu gonna do, spend the rest of your life strugglin' to make ends meet? And for what? To satisfy some jive notion of false pride. Damn, Mavis, be serious.

MAVIS: Whatever I am an' whatever I'm gonna be couldna' never happened if it hadn't been for you, my man.

DUANE: Wow. Okay, so alla your misery is my fault. But I ain't denyin' it. I been insistin' on it ever since I got here. Okay, but look around, baby. You got this crowded little four room crib an' maybe you payin' about $150 a month for it. So what? What the hell is that? I betcha you scuffle to make that rent. An' that overcrowded school down the street? Is that where Delores goes? Is that where you sendin' my daughter to school? How many clothes she got? You got any credit cards anywhere? If she get sick can you afford the hospital bills? When you walk in a store do motherfuckahs fall all over themselves to wait on you 'cause you somebody? No! So, whatchu tellin' me, actin' all sanctimonious an' shit. Hey, just where the hell do you think you're comin' from with me? Duane Carter. Duane *Carter!* You mention that name anywhere in the music business and people go crazy 'cause I'm one of the best side men there is. Go look on the back of your record albums over there and check out the personnel. That "D. Carter" you see is me, baby. I play the best clubs in the top cities in the country. Down in Atlanta I'm a personal friend of everybody that's anybody. You understand? Don't a week go by that I ain't pullin' in big bucks. Hey, look at me, woman! I ain't no wayward nigguh who just happened to make good because he hit the number. I spent ten years of my life buildin' somethin' that's gonna last. It may sound like pie-in-the-sky to you, but I ain't jivin'. Mavis, I can offer you the world 'cause I can *give* you the world.

MAVIS: Yea. You givin' me everything but yourself. That's why I know can't nothin' be real between us.

DUANE: Then, don't forgive me. Hate me. But just come back. Everything I got is yours. What we had has always been real for me, Mavis.

MAVIS: That why you left me an' Delores?

DUANE: Look, I couldn't do nothin' here. I was stiflin'. Workin' as a short order cook, an' knowin' all the time I was better than that. Knowin' all the time I was a young man who had the talent to be *somebody.* I couldn't see bringin' Delores up like we was brought up. But you. All you wanted was security. Nothin' else. To hell with my dreams and ambitions.

MAVIS: Security can mean a lot to a woman who ain't never had none.

DUANE: Just one word of encouragement from you was all I needed. That job wasn't no good for me.

MAVIS: You was makin' good money. Why should I have to give that up for somethin' I wasn't even sure could work.

DUANE: You coulda at least give me a chance.

MAVIS: I couldn't *afford* to. I was happier than I ever coulda imagined. I couldn't throw alla that away for a pipe dream.

DUANE: Except now you see it wasn't no pipe dream.

MAVIS: Yea . . . now, I see.

DUANE: Baby, I had to have more than what we had then. I knew I had to grow up, I knew I had to provide for you, I knew I had to be somebody, or die. I tried to make you understand, but you wouldn't listen.

MAVIS: It was a beautiful time for us, despite the hassles.

DUANE: It was hell for me. I don't never wanna see those days again. But now, I'm satisfied, 'cause I got everything I went after.

MAVIS: Yea, but you lost me, Duane, 'cause where I'm at today don't even include you.

DUANE: You really mean that, don't you?

MAVIS: You had no choices? Well, neither do I.

DUANE: At least live there, baby.

MAVIS: You know that it wouldn't work out.

DUANE: Then, ain't no reason for me to stay around here. *(Rises to leave)*

MAVIS: It's late, Duane. Why don't you spend the night an' drive back tomorrow? The sun'll be up an' you'll be fresh. Besides, you can see Delores.

DUANE: Thanks, but I'll be all right. It's best that I split. Seein' Delores woulda been nice, but, well . . . it would just make things worse, you know? Sides, Mavis, I don't dig sleepin' in no strange beds.

MAVIS: *(Without emotion)* I can send Delores down to see you on summa the holidays an' durin' the summers.

DUANE: I'll keep a lookout for her.

MAVIS: She oughta enjoy herself. By the way, you got any other kids?

DUANE: Yea. A son in Baltimore.

MAVIS: Oh. *(Smiles)* Well, maybe someday you can take Delores to see him. She's always wanted a brother or sister. *(Lights a cigarette and begins to smoke.* DUANE *stands watching her a long time)*

DUANE: Baby—

MAVIS: Goodbye, Duane.

(DUANE goes out without a word as MAVIS continues sitting on the sofa staring straight ahead. A spot picks up BETTY in another part of the stage)

BETTY: Aunt Mavis! Aunt Mavis! Bobby gave me his fraternity ring an' he says I'm gonna be his forever. He said when he gets outa school he's gonna come back an' marry me. We're gonna be so happy. You'll see. I love him so much. We gonna have lotsa kids an' Bobby's gonna work hard an' make everything sweet for us. Everything's gonna work out. You'll see. You'll see.

(Light fades on BETTY and picks up on PEPPER)

PEPPER: I told you! I told you I'd be offa this block. Me an' your truckdriver friend's gon' hook up. That's right! Live with it, broad. Look at that ring. Coulda been your ring, but it's mine now. An' I'm gonna be a good wife to him, too, 'cause I got everything to lose.

(Light fades on PEPPER as MAVIS continues sitting, although her face now reflects loneliness, bitterness, and resignation. She rises, slips off her dress, and tosses it casually away from her. The cigarette dangles from her lips as she saunters across the stage to a bed and falls upon it and lies still almost as though dead. JOHN I stands near the bed adjusting his clothing as though in the final stages of dressing. He reaches into his pocket and tosses some money on the bed. It lands near MAVIS who makes the barest of moves to pick it up. JOHN I looks at MAVIS a moment then exits without a word. MAVIS simply lies still, then slowly rises and rolls the money into a tiny roll, places one leg on a chair, and with her back to the audience inserts the money into her vagina. Lights come up on BETTY and PEPPER who stand at opposite ends of the stage. MAVIS stands tired and worn as though the years of what she has been doing have finally caught up with her. BETTY and PEPPER begin to laugh)

MAVIS: Fuck it!!! *(Breaks into laughter and then tears)* You can all kiss my ass!!!

Blackness

KENNETH ALAN WESSON

KEN WESSON WAS BORN and reared in the San Francisco Bay Area where he completed all of his education, including undergraduate and graduate work in psychology at the University of California at Berkeley. Since then he has worked at Stanford Research Institute as an Educational Consultant and has taught at San Jose State University, Foothill College, San Jose City College, and Santa Clara Valley Medical Center. Presently, he is working with Laidlaw Brothers Publishing Company, the education division of Doubleday Publishing Company, Inc.

Miss Cegenation was written in 1971 originally as a lengthy poem. So much filled his imagination about the details that "I couldn't help being obsessed with what the story told," remembers Wesson. "The more I pondered on the possibilities of the visual imagery, the more I was certain that it had to be put in dramatic form." Most history has been seen only from one perspective, *Miss Cegenation* approaches the same events but from a fresh new point of view.

Biographical reviews of Wesson appear in the first and second editions of *Who's Who Among Black Americans* as well as *Who's Who in the West*, 1980-81 edition.

Another play by K. Alan Wesson is presently in the works and should be completed in late 1980. "This one to me illustrates the growth and changes in my perception over the last ten years. No difference in maturity or the like but rather new dimensions of the same *"Miss Cegenation"* man.

MISS CEGENATION

Kenneth Alan Wesson

CHARACTERS

MR. CHARLIE: *The owner and "Master" of the plantation*

"MISS" ANN: MR. CHARLIE'*s wife*

MISS SCARLET: *The elder daughter of* CHARLIE *and* ANN

MISS JANE: *The younger daughter*

UNCLE TOM: *Butler, house watchman, etc.*

WILLA MAE: *Cook maid, etc. for the "Big House"*

ZERO: *One of the field workers*

JIM: *Another of the plantation hands*

THE SHERIFF: *The constable of the town*

A MAN: *A man in town*

TYLER: *A visiting soldier*

miscegenation: (mǐs'ǐ jə nā'shən), n. 1. mixture of races by sexual union. 2. interbreeding between differences. [f. L. *miscere*, MIX + *genus*, race +-ATION]

The Story of "Miss Cegenation"

The American taboo of miscegenation,
Began right here on this plantation.
'Bout eight score years ago, or so,
With a story I'm sure not all of you know.

There was nappy-head Willa Mae, ol' "honey chil','
She was boisterous, and voluptuous, and untamably wild.

Mr. Charlie was there as the head of the place,
White suit, hat, and shoes, and a sheet-white face.

His painted-up ol' lady, Miss Ann was her name,
Had two "Snow White"-like daughters who looked just the same.

One was little Miss Scarlet, she was really cool,
She was Virginia's Virgin, so thought a town of po' fools.

Then the other whose name was sweet Miss Jane,
When someone would say "black man," she'd go insane.
She was the purist of all young Southern daughters,
About the birds and the bees, well, the parents hadn't taught her.

In the field there was a slave named Black Jim,
Mr. Charlie had told his daughters, "beware of him."

Another slave named Zero was Charlie's pride and joy,
When they'd go to town he'd boast, "That there's Zero . . . ma boy."

As usual there was a house-nigger named Tom,
No one was warned of him, "Why, he can do no harm,"
Said Charlie, he'd assure the wife and daughters if he'd go
Into town—but listen, little did he know!
That while Charlie was in town doing business at the store,
Tom was at home, upstairs, takin' care of even more!
(That is why in all the pictures all bent over he is shown,
He was bent over for some reasons heretofore unknown.)

Late at night and sometimes even frequently in the day,
Mr. Charlie would slip out to visit Willa Mae.
He'd catch her on the hay, in the garden, on the wagon,
Then he'd retreat to the mansion real tired, tail a' draggin'.

But while Charlie had ol' Willa Mae up against the willow,
Tom had Miss Ann on Charlie's sheets and brand new pillow!
About the same time they all heard a scream of pain,
It was ol' Jim out in the meadow perched atop our sweet Miss Jane.

Quietly to the basement stole big Zero and Miss Scarlet,
Who turned out to be Zero's pert and private harlot.

But at dinner they'd all talk about those "repulsive
beasts,"
Though each knew what he'd do after meal, and all did
hurriedly eat.
They all spilled food quite purposely to hurry and get
dinner over,
And Mr. Charlie soon thereafter had Willa Mae out on
the clover.

Ol' Jim complained of all the hay that he had to pitch,
Though in his mind he knew the chore would easily be
switched,
To fun and games up in the loft,
As he signaled with a cough.

"Work's piled up on me, jes' more and more."
Although his name was Zero, he really knew the score.
Seems that while he and Miss Scarlet out in the field
would lie,
He taught her 'rithmetic and how to . . . multiply.

Miss Jane who at dinner would usually go at least two
rounds,
Hadn't eaten much of lately, but was putting on the
pounds.
When she told ol' Jimmy, he did tremble and a' shake,
Just by watching him you'd think it was the results of two
earthquakes.

But that dumb, dumb, dummy, yes that foolish poor
Miss Ann,
Claimed that she'd been raped by a "raper" from the
wicked town San Fran'.
Mr. Charlie said "why didn't you call for Tom, he
would have helped?"
And in anger he began to beat her with his alligator belt.
As he hit her with the belt, and then next the buckle,
From the closet came a loud and most hideous muffled
chuckle.
Mr. Charlie heard this and to the closet then he ran,
Ripping the door open, there stood Tom with shoe in
hand.
Miss Ann thought, "Oh, Lord, he's caught us, what
now will he do?"
But Uncle Tom just walked off grinning saying, "Well,
Ize finally found dat shoe."
Charlie turned back asking, "Must you tell me such a
lie?"
Miss Ann answered, "Well, I thought I'd give the ol'
San Fran' trick a try.
Would you believe it's immaculate conception, or maybe
it's even yours, dear."

"No, 'cause you ain't no goddamn Virgin Mary, and I
ain't slept with you in years.
Oh, yeah, maybe it is mine, honey, 'cause when we was
havin' that bad weather,
I remember that we did sleep a night or two together.
That was funny how you tried to play that scare trick on
daddy-o,
Why sho' that is my child in your belly." (But little did
he know!)

Miss Jane claimed it was a fellow who'd seen the family a
month before,
But he had gone off and gotten killed while fighting in the
war.

Miss Scarlet cried "immaculate conception," but was
terribly confused,
When she heard that the "conception" story had been
already used.
So she "remembered" that it had been the preacher's son,
Thus she married him, and that's when things begun.

See, Mr. Charlie himself even began reflecting,
When he noticed that Willa Mae, too, was soon
expecting.
But ol' Mr. Charlie, well he really didn't care,
He'd just say it was Jim's, and one more slave he could
bear.

Then came June twenty-second, the end of spring,
They all had noticed precisely one perplexing thing.
Why Willa Mae's baby had Charlie's youthful face,
when compared to the picture in the frame.
And Scarlet's baby had Zero's muscular build and his
color, hmmmm, almost the same.
Miss Ann's baby was the cutest kid in town,
Though he "sorta resembled Tom," and his skin was
"kinda brown."
But Miss Jane's baby, oh, do you remember ol' Black
Jim?
Yeah, that particular baby sorta "looks like him."

Here is where the story actually commences,
There were just "too damn many coincidences"
Three babies all had the "Charlie" noses and eyes, and a
mole on each left hand,
And they all had a luscious little cinnamon tan.
But the question was asked and instigated,
"Were all these children somehow related?"
But the supposed baby of Charlie and "Miss" Ann
Didn't have the tell-tale mole on his small left hand!

Now Charlie began to really suspect the "San Fran'
Raper,"
As he figured it out now with his pencil on some paper,

"That my kid should have had a mole on his left paw,
Or I ain't the dad or she ain't the ma.

"Miss Scarlet's baby, now what makes him so brown?
Why her husband's ghost-white, and there's so much
    shade in this town.
And Jane's soldier who died, too was pastey white,
Her child is brown, too, ummm . . . something just ain't
    right!
But Miss Ann's kid really looks like old Uncle Tom,"
(I ain't spreadin' no gossip, and I mean no harm.)
"And Scarlet's kid sorta looks like Zero,
I've figured it out!" (Boy, what a hero.
I tell you something and I really mean this,
Ain't Mr. Charlie truly one hell of a genius?)
"Now, Scarlet's kid is Zero's; Ann's Tom's; Jane's
    Jim's; and Willa's mine,"
(We knew that all along, but thanks a million, Charles
    Einstein!)

"So my grandkids both are darkies, and my sons are both
    the same,
And they all sort of resemble, so I'll give them all my
    name.
They're the handsomest boys in the whole damn county,
'Cept for thct "furriner," the Canadian mounty,
And the word will get back here real soon,
Whether or not he's an "octaroon!"

So, that's how come some of us are so light,
Those with bronze tans and those passing for white.
That's really the story of this entire nation,
But this particular story is from a Virginia plantation.
So don't be too prejudiced and try not to hate each other,
For all you know you might be my twice-removed
    brother!

The moral of the story is easily seen,
Now, sleep with your own, or take off your genes!

ACT ONE

Scene 1

MR. CHARLIE, dressed all in white from head to toe,
enters from the right with cigar in mouth.

MR. CHARLIE: Ann! . . . Ann! . . . Where arh you,
gal?
MISS ANN: (Enters at left, fixing hair and clothes) Why
. . . why, hello, honey!
CHARLIE: Where's Tom? Tell him to come here. I
want him to go fetch Zero. I got to go into town,
to take care of some real important business.
ANN: I don't know where he is, darlin'.
UNCLE TOM: (Enters from left, adjusting his belt and
buttoning his coat) Hey Massa, whatchu say, baby?
How's ever'thang?
CHARLIE: (Raising his voice) Don't talk to me like
that! Now, I've told you about that befo', Tom!
Don't talk to me like that!
TOM: I'm sorry, Mr. Charlie, I guess I'm still ex-
cited . . . er . . . I mean so excited . . . to . . . ah . . .
to see ya, massa . . . suh. I'm real sorry, suh.
CHARLIE: (Feeling guilty and somewhat apologetic)
Well, Tom, alright. (Pause) Hey, go fetch Zero,
I'm late. 'Spozed to be in town 'bout now, business is waiting, now go, boy!
TOM: O.K., O.K. (Exiting. Aside) . . . damn . . .
hold your water . . . "Chuck!"
CHARLIE: (To ANN) That boy sho' gets uppity
sometimes. I wonder what's gotten into him lately. He used to jump when I spoke. Now he does
what I say but he acts so damn . . . ree-luctant
about it. Like he got something better ta do, or

like he's got some real important business to tend
to. Why, the next time . . . (Interrupted by ANN)
ANN: Now Charles. You gotta try to understand
the nigra. He's a very sensitive creature. Tom
tries to please you 'specially, dear. Why just befo'
you came in he was tellin' me how much he likes
you, tries to please you, respects you . . . (Interrupted by CHARLIE)
CHARLIE: I thought you didn't know where he
was when I first asked you?
ANN: I . . . I . . . I mean . . . . Just, just this morning
he was saying that.
CHARLIE: I suspect something, Ann. (Pause, ANN
looks embarrassed) I suspect you is protecting him
sometimes. That's why the boy is so bad sometimes, honey! You can't treat them so nice, dear.
The nigra won't be of no use to nobody if he
don't know how to act. 'Specially when his master is around. He's gotta know his place, and you
can't show him much respect if you 'spect him to
stay in it. Why, if you be too nice, he'll be 'spectin'
special favors. He might even attack you . . . sex-
ually!! (ANN looks surprised and frightened and backs
off shaking her head) And "Daddy" knows how
much you are afraid of those black bucks. But . . .
I guess you really don't have to be too scared of
ol' Tom, he respects me too much, just like you
said . . . . But some of the rest of them . . . look
out! Well, anyway, though Tom is pretty harmless, be careful. There's a bit of the beast lurking
in all of them you know!
ANN: I had no idea, honey! I guess you are right,
but Tom?? (Laughing) Why I doubt if Tom even

knows what sex is. He's...(TOM *enters with* ZERO. *Hearing part of what* ANN *said, his mouth drops open in surprise. To* CHARLIE) Oh, oh, here they are, dear.

CHARLIE: *(Aside to* ANN) Watch this, dear. *(To* TOM) Tom, er, um, can you tell me what "sex" is?

TOM: Well.... Well, I think it comes just befo' "sebben," massa!

CHARLIE: *(Laughing and looking at* ANN) See! (TOM *turns to* ZERO *and they slap hands behind* TOM's *back)* Well, boys, I want you to go into town with me, Zero. Tom, you stay here and look after the place till I get back.

TOM: *(With a smile)* I will, sir.

CHARLIE: *(Aside to* TOM, *so as not to let* ANN *hear)* Ann's kinda scared of you but try to look after her while I'm out, but don't be around her too much, on account of she's kinda 'fraid of you, you know? *(To* ANN) Well Ann, me and Zero is goin' now. Tom will mind the house so you just rest yourself and go lay down or something till I get back, honey.

ANN: I will, I'll go do that right now. (CHARLIE *turns around and exits with* ZERO. ANN *looks back and shouts)* See ya later, honey. Don't you all worry about me, I'll be just fine.

CHARLIE: *(Shouts from outside)* Might be late for dinner, but I'll try to hurry, dear. Don't you all worry 'bout me neither.

ANN *exits to the left.* TOM *looks both ways and follows.*

Scene 2

CHARLIE *and* ZERO *are standing out back.*

CHARLIE: Oh my back is killin' me. Sho' is hot today. I sure am tired, Zero. I don't think I'll go to town today. Boy, that Ann can really be a bothersome little woman sometimes, always worryin' about me. Always buttin' in...

ZERO: You tellin' me! *(Shaking his head)*

CHARLIE: What?

ZERO: Oh, oh, nothing.

CHARLIE: I think maybe I'll just slip out back somewhere and sit under a tree and rest myself. You know Master is startin' to grow a little old already, huh, Zero?

ZERO: Yes, suh...I mean, no suh. You is in just as good shape as you was twenty years ago from what I hear, Chuck, er, Massa.

CHARLIE: Well, how am I goin' to make Ann think I went to town if the buggy doesn't pass the house? She's gonna know I didn't go, hmmmm ...what'll I do, Zero? If I could only get her to think I went into town by the buggy passing the front of the house.

ZERO: Hold it! Hold it, Massa! I got it, I got it!

CHARLIE: *(Trying to act surprised)* What is it, Zero? What is it? Tell me, son!

ZERO: I can drive the buggy past the front of the house, like I usually do, and make Miss Ann think that you is goin' into town when she sees it goin' by the verandah.

CHARLIE: Excellent, Zero! What a good plan! How did you ever think of that? Very good, Zero! *(Shaking his hand)* Hey, listen, the buggy should be passing the front about now. So you just go on into town part way and then you can just screw around if you want to, then come on back around supper time. You're a fine boy, Zero!...And a credit to your race!

ZERO: *(Shyly)* Ah, thank ya, Massa....Uh, what race is I'm runnin'? *(Looking confused)*

(ANN *and* TOM *peeking out the window)*

ANN: There goes the buggy, Tommy.

TOM: *(Singing)* So long, Massa.

Looking at each other, TOM *pulls the shade, as he winks out the window.*

Scene 3

ZERO, *remembering the "Massa's" order, goes part way into town, stops to think, and then ventures into town despite "Chuck's" plan. After entering town,* ZERO *stops and ties the buggy. He begins walking out on the boardwalk where he sees the* SHERIFF. ZERO *immediately does an about-face and heads back for the buggy in one devil of a hurry.*

SHERIFF: Hey, boy! Come back here, you ol' darkie! (ZERO *keeps on rushing toward the buggy, trying to figure out what to do while he's making haste. Then suddenly he turns around)* That's better boy! (ZERO *turns back around again and moves towards the buggy. The* SHERIFF *shoots at the buggy to scare* ZERO. ZERO *turns around, looking the* SHERIFF *dead in the eye)*

ZERO: Now you hold on a minute, sheriff!! First, you possess the audacity to endeavor to intimidate me! Preceding such, you employed titles denigrating to my dignity and exhibited your conspicious absence of the minutest expressions of social decor!

SHERIFF: *(Puzzled)* What?...*(Weakly)* what?...

ZERO: And furthermore, upon my entrance to the metropolitan section of this community, you incessantly put forth such remarks in the presence of my proprietor, Mr. Charlie Jackson!

SHERIFF: *(Again weakly)* . . . why, I . . . I . . .

ZERO: You "I, I" nothing! You consistently fabricate deceptive descriptions of my activities when near town or upon my presence therein! Your intense stupidity and your colossal existential absurdity, demonstrated by your persistence to prevaricate due to your intellectual perversity must cease and desist, immmmmmediately!! Boy!!

SHERIFF: *(To audience)* . . . What'd he say? . . . 'zat English . . . ??

ZERO: Did you hear me or is it of necessity that I repeat myself?!

SHERIFF: *(To audience)* Hmmm . . . I think I understood . . . part of that! *(To ZERO)* No, you don't necessity to repeat yourself! *(To audience)* Told him, huh? *(To ZERO)* I know what you said! The "pervacities" of this here town been botherin' you! And, Zero, ma boy, if they keep it up, they sho' gonna get 'rested!! I'll see to that, mista Zero!! Them rascals . . . disturbing the peace again!

ZERO: *(Looking at audience and pointing back to the SHERIFF with his thumb, winks. To SHERIFF)* Yes, see that you do! And by the way, your breath smells and you need a bath desperately! Upon the next occasion whereby I . . . *(Interrupted by the SHERIFF)*

SHERIFF: O.K., O.K.! I'll take care of ever'thang, 'rat now, suh. Jest hold on *(Pleadingly)* please, Mista Zero, I ain't never done nothin' to you! Why is it you gotta pick on *me* today! There is plenty of other people in the town to pick on, why *me??* Mista Zero, Suh??

ZERO: Perhaps, I did pick on you a bit, but you started by shooting at the buggy attempting to frighten me . . . *(Interrupted by the SHERIFF)*

SHERIFF: No, no, Mista Zero!! 'Twasn't like that a' t'all. I thought I heard someone behin' your buggy and, and I tried to shoot him, honest, Mista Zero, honest!! *(With handkechief in hand, about to cry)* Ize tellin' the truth! Ize tellin' the truth!

ZERO: *(Condescendingly)* Now, now, sherriff! You don't have to lie to Mr. Zero. He's a friend. You can always tell me the truth. You were just playing a game. Now, Mr. Zero even plays games on people too sometimes. But you must know when they're in a proper mood or not before you begin the game.

(SHERIFF, weeping uncontrollably, like a child who has told the truth and is still being punished. ZERO puts his hand on the SHERIFF's shoulder, leads him to a bench, sits him down, pats him on the back to comfort him. A MAN comes along and looks at the situation quite puzzled)

MAN: *(To ZERO)* What's wrong with the sheriff?

ZERO: Oh, well, his aunt from Kansas died, and I just came to bring word.

MAN: Oh, sorry to hear that.

(SHERIFF still crying)

ZERO: Please, we'd better leave him alone . . . in this moment of grief.

MAN: Yeah, maybe so. *(Looking at the SHERIFF in disbelief)* Yeah. *(Walks off in one direction, ZERO takes off in the other. ZERO's cheeks are puffed up with laughter. He finally gets to the buggy, coolly walks to the other side, and falls to the ground kicking and laughing)*

ZERO: *(Ha, ha)* . . . Oh the sheriff . . . *(Ha, ha)* Oh, that guy kills me . . . *(Ha, ha. Continues laughing for a while, picks himself up and gets ready to leave, talking to himself)* I guess we Black folks really gotta try to understand the Whites. He's a very sensitive creature!!

ACT TWO

Scene 1

CHARLIE: *(Walking out back calling in a whisper)* Willa? . . . Willa? . . . Willa? Oh, Willa, mama? Gosh, I wonder where that nigra gal is? Willa? . . . Willa, is you hidin' from me? . . .

WILLA MAE: *(To audience)* No, but it's a good idea! *(To CHARLIE)* Oh, Charles, it's so nice of you to come *(To audience)* out back *(To CHARLIE)* to visit me! I am dee-lighted. Why I haven't seen you since . . . early this morning, it was.

CHARLIE: Ahh, cut it out, Willa, chile.

WILLA: *(To audience)* Willa, chile?

CHARLIE: Yeah, it has been a long time, sweet mama.

WILLA: *(To audience)* Sweet mama?

CHARLIE: Guess what I did? I told Zero to ride the buggy into town part way, as if I had gone ma' self, so as to make Ann think that I had gone on account of some real impo'tant business.

WILLA: Oh, again? Don't you think she's on up to that one by now?

CHARLIE: Oh, no! I know jest how to say it each time to make her think I'm saying something new.

WILLA: *(Unconvinced)* Oh, yeah!

CHARLIE: Yeah, ain't I pretty smart? I've been tellin' her this story for the past 'leven years now and she ain't asked no questions yet. She *must* believe me or she wouldn't let me go out jest like that. She loves me and doesn't like me to go out too much, 'cause I have to leave her with Tom, and he makes her kinda nervous and jumpy, she scared that he's gonna try somethin' 'cause I ain't around. He's a nice buck, er, guy, I mean, but still she gets jumpy when I say that I'm leaving or something. Acts like she's got ants in her pants or somethin'... ha, ha, ha, ha, ha,... *(Pauses with a suspicious look on his face)* uh, Willa Mae, how come you ain't laughing? That was a joke, wasn't that funny? Do you suspect that she, I mean Ann, got a lover hidden somewhere in the house? Oh, I'm talking foolish now. I know there isn't a man on this side of the Mississippi that is as good as I am... is there?

WILLA: Well... I hate to lie...

CHARLIE: What did you say?

WILLA: I said, no, but they try; yeah, that's what I said. *(At this point, ZERO is startled as he sees CHARLIE and WILLA. Not because they are together, but because CHARLIE almost sees him and SCARLET, and SCARLET almost sees CHARLIE and WILLA. WILLA grabs CHARLIE and kisses him as ZERO and SCARLET pass by. ZERO puts his hands over SCARLET's eyes as if they are playing some game. SCARLET laughs and ZERO quickly puts his hands over her mouth and says "shh" as if silence is part of the game, too)* Yes, Charlie, you are irresistible.

(SCARLET and ZERO get passed CHARLIE and WILLA and proceed about five yards from them, stop, and SCARLET pulls out a book from under her petticoats)

SCARLET: Here it is, Zero. This is the one we had back at college. I still don't understand it. Our teacher said that even he didn't quite "comprehardy" it... *(Interrupted by ZERO)*

ZERO: Comprehend, comprehend it.

SCARLET: Yeah, that's it, that's the word. Anyway he didn't know what it was about. Matter a'fact nobody did.

ZERO: No one did, Scarlet, no one.

SCARLET: Yeah, that's what I already said. Listen Zero, if you's so smart, why aren't you going to college 'stead of me?

ZERO: 'Cause they don't let black folk go to those ol' lily-white colleges and besides, you do seem to need it a little more than I do.

SCARLET: *(Shocked)* O.K., I'm sorry.

ZERO: You're sorry, "sir"! Here I am trying to get you through college and you can't even express a little respect for the assistance that I provide for you? Well, let's just go back to the house.

SCARLET: No, Zero, I'm sorry, er, sir. I've just been a little irritable lately. *(Pause, they both smile, and he begins to turn the pages)*

ZERO: O.K., what was the "hard part" that you've been complaining about?

SCARLET: Right here. Where Lady MacBeth keeps washing her hands, there's some term for it...

ZERO: Yes, obsession-compulsion.

SCARLET: Huh?

ZERO: An obsession is when you continually think of the same thing, hours on end.

SCARLET: You mean like me thinking of you?

ZERO: Uh... yeah, and compulsion is when you keep on doing the same thing.

SCARLET: You mean like us meeting out here all the time?

ZERO: Well, yes, ummm... no, well, sort of.

SCARLET: *(Yawns seductively)* Oh, I'm sleepy.

ZERO: Oh, cut it out!

SCARLET: Zero, all I did up there was to think of you and of all the things we could have done during my "extracuticle" activities time.

ZERO: No, no. You mean your extracurricular, extracurricular, my dear.

SCARLET puts her arms around him and pulls him to a prone position along side of her.

Scene 2

JANE and TYLER, a soldier, standing in the living room, are talking. TYLER is a friend of the family and has come by for a visit. JIM sees the two together and is a bit jealous of TYLER)

JANE: Well, Tyler, tell me about the soldierin' that you've been doin'. I'll bet it's a lot of fun.

TYLER: No, Jane. It isn't. It's a pretty big deal. I've been doing secret work for the government and it can get pretty close sometimes. It's not just the ol' run-of-the-mill kind of stuff that any ol' person could do, like that buck there. Why he couldn't stand up to the pressures that we have to. You've really got to be tough. *(Flexes a muscle in his coat sleeve, and JIM walks by, laughs, and as he passes by, he slaps JANE on the bottom)*

JANE: Ohhhh!

TYLER: What?

JANE: All I said was "Ohh." *(As if it was a response to the "muscle")*

TYLER: Yeah, it was in France, the southern part, where I've been the past few years. Doing intelligence work for the Feds. It's extremely hard stuff, takes a whole bunch of brains, you know?

JIM: Excuse me but I couldn't hep but to hear what you was all talkin' 'bout. You says that you been to Europe, and to France? That sho' is in'erestin'. Did you ever see Marseilles?

TYLER: Marseilles, why sho' I saw him! He sho' is a nice guy. Little bitty short fella. We met him at a real fancy restaurant. "Marcy's" his nickname, you know? Say, boy, do you know him?

JIM: Come to think of it I don't know him, on

account of Marseilles ain't a him. Marseilles is a place and not a "little bitty fella."

TYLER: Oh, oh . . . uh . . . yeah, that Marseilles. That one? Why sho' I remember that Marseilles.

JIM: *(Sarcastically)* Yes, yes, that one!

TYLER: What business is it of yours if he's a man or a city? Why you ol' smart alecky coon. *(To JANE)* Who is that guy, anyway? He thinks he knows something, boy!

JANE: Jim, why don't you leave us please.

JIM: Yas, m'am. *(Passes by JANE, slaps her again)*

JANE: Ohhh!

TYLER: What did you say?

JANE: I just said "Ohh."

TYLER: Yeah, you've been "ohhing" a little too much lately! Like everytime he walks by you!

JIM: *(Skipping out)* Ohh . . . ohhh . . . ohhh . . . ohhh . . .

CHARLIE: *(Enters, acts surprised to see TYLER)* There you is, boy. Why, I was just looking for you. Hiddy, Tyler, I haven't seen you in a coon's age. Say, how's the army life treatin' you? They say it's real tough now.

TYLER: Yeah, sir!! It's tough alright. I've been in . . . uh, . . . Marseilles most of the time . . . doing spy work. Real scary business.

CHARLIE: Why? Is there going to be another war?

TYLER: Oh, no. It's just the kind of stuff you read in books. There ain't gonna be no wars, I don't reckon. But we've got to keep an eye on those sneaky, lying, Frenchmen. No telling what they is up to. Nigras is hard enough to trust, but a Frenchman is worse!

CHARLIE: Gosh, that does sound like impo'tant goin's-on. You says that the French is sneakier than the nigras? That couldn't be true. Why the nigra is about the most untrustworthy being on the face of God's earth. Every time I go into town I just get so scared that some big black buck is gonna attack my wife and daughters. Oh, I jest have to hurry back, jest to check on 'em to see if they's O.K. Coons is liars and two-faced; I can't seem to even trust ol' Tom, and he's one of the faithful nigras . . . but like I was tellin' ma wife earlier today, there's a bit of the beast lurking in all them nigras, so none of them is to be trusted. They'll be sleeping with our women next if we don't look out, I was jest talking to Willa, er, Ann, about the nigras rights as slaves. There is things that they's spozed to do and things they ain't, and . . .

JANE: Oh, Daddy, I don't think Tyler wants to hear any of your politicking today. He's just down here for a couple of hours.

CHARLIE: Well, I guess I got a little carried away. But you're aware of how sensitive I am about these nigras and the problems that they is creatin' for us white folks.

TYLER: Yeah, they should send them all back to Africa. Every last cotton-pickin' one of them nigras. If it was up to me . . .

CHARLIE: Yeah, they should send *nearly* all of them back to Africa. *(Sheepishly)* They all don't have to go, do they? We should be spared our cooks at least, don't you think, Tyler?

TYLER: No, for the good of the country and the safety of white womanhood, they all have to go.

CHARLIE: Now you wait jest one gol'darn minute, Tyler. You can't jest take our slaves from us and leave us like that; why, that's, uh, er, uh . . .

JANE: Un-con-stee-tuu-shanal.

CHARLIE: Yeah, that's what it ain't or what it is, or anyway you guys cain't do it to us, you jest cain't!

TYLER: I didn't say we were going to do it, I just said I would do it if it was up to me.

CHARLIE: Well, then it's a good thing you ain't in charge!

JANE: Yeah, it is a good thing you ain't in charge. *(TYLER and CHARLIE both turn and look at her suspiciously, look back at each other and then at her again. JANE looking almost as if she is about to admit something)* I was jest tryin' to agree with you, Daddy, that's all.

Scene 3

In the living room, the entire family gathered around listening to TYLER tell of war heroics. They have just finished dinner and are quite relaxed.

TYLER: So, there were Indians on the left of me, and on the right of me, and Indians to the rear of me, and Indians ahead of me! I was trapped!!

(While TYLER is telling the story CHARLIE nudges ANN as if he doubts the story that TYLER is telling. ANN gives a nod of certainty, signifying that the tale is indeed true. CHARLIE looks astonished and turns back to listen, even more attentively than ever before. Meanwhile JIM and JANE are making eyes at each other. SCARLET is yawning and keeps dozing off but is awakened each time TYLER raises his voice dramatically as he comes to the "interesting" parts of the stories. WILLA MAE stands off in the corner moving around so as not to fall asleep)

TOM: What did you do then, Mr. Tyler?

TYLER: I did what any red-blooded American soldier would do . . . I ran, as fast as I could, I ran. My horse fell over dead of exhaustion and I ran some more!

ANN: How brave!

TYLER: You betcha.

JIM: 'Scuse me again, Mr. Tyler, but I didn't know there was Indians in France.

TYLER: Oh...uhh...they...was...uh...they was French-Indians, just like you have French-Canadians, they was French-Indians, you see?

JIM: Oh, yeah, French-Indians, yeah, now that I is heard of. (JIM *looks over at* TOM, *smiles and winks.* TOM *winks back and nods*)

ZERO: Oh, please, Mr. Tyler, go on wit' dat story. It sho' is a good 'n.

TYLER: (*To* JANE *who is sitting next to him*) The nigras like these kinda stories, do they? (JANE *nods in agreement*) Well, like I done said once before, I was surrounded by Indians.

JIM: French-Indians.

TYLER: Yeah, surrounded by French-Indians, and I had to leave ma horse 'cause the ride was too hard on the ol' beast. Then the Indians—the French ones—was chasing me. Me on foot and them on bareback.

SCARLET: Did they catch you?

TYLER: Fat chance I'd be here now if they had!

TOM: That sho' was some runnin' you done did there, Mr. Tyler.

TYLER: Yeah, boy, it sure was.

JANE: You must be awfully fast.

TYLER: I sure am. Out-ran all them Indians and their horses, too!

ZERO: I sure wish that I could have seen that race.

TYLER: Oh, it wasn't nothing. I run that fast all the time.

JIM: Do you really, suh?

TYLER: I told you boys I do, now how many times do I have to say it?

ZERO: I've got an idea! Since Mr. Tyler says that he does this all the time, then why don't you show us all now. We all sho' would like to see that speed. (*Everyone begins cheering* TYLER, *telling him how much they'd love to see him in action*)

TYLER: Well, I just got finished eating and . . .

ZERO: Then we'll make it a short race!

TYLER: Really, boys, I'm a little tired.

JIM: Then we'll wait till morning!

TYLER: I've got to leave before then!

TOM: Well then, that leaves only today. It's settled!

WILLA: That gonna be *some* runnin'.

ANN: I think you boys are just making fun of Tyler 'cause you fellas don't believe him. Well, everybody else believes him, right? (*All of the Whites nod in agreement, and all the Blacks shake their heads indicating that they don't quite believe him*) Well, all that matters is that he told the truth, whether anyone believes him or not.

JIM: Well, I'm sorry, but the kinda runnin' he talkin' 'bout I ain't never seen, and I just wants to see it once befo' I dies. I guess I'll just go on out

back and pitch that hay that I was plannin' on havin' done by dis evenin'. I best go now. (*Takes about three steps, stops, coughs and looks at* JANE *who smiles. When* CHARLIE *and* ANN *look her way the smile quickly vanishes.* JIM *exits*)

ZERO: Yesss, there is some things that Ize 'spozed to do, too. I hope that is alright wit'chu, Mr. Charlie and Miss Ann. (*Takes about three steps and turns, looks under his arm and winks back at* SCARLET, *who does likewise*)

WILLA: I guess I'll jest mozy on out back. (*Smiles at* CHARLIE, *who smiles back.* ANN *catches the proceeding and looks at* CHARLIE *as if to ask "what's going on?"* CHARLIE *straightens up in his chair and clears his voice as if he didn't know anything was going on*)

TOM: There is a lot of cleaning to get done befo' morning. I'll get started on it right now. I'll start on the upstairs. (*Turns and does a little shuffle and winks back at* ANN, *who gives him a disguised wave*)

JANE: I'm getting a bit tired myself, no offense, Captain Tyler. I did miss my dessert. I'll go have something now. Ummm . . . yes, that's it, pickles and ice cream. (*Walks off and all say in unison with* ANN) Pickles and ice cream???

ANN: I'm tired, too. It has been enjoyable, Mr. Tyler. Do come again. I believe I'll retire to my room for the evening. (*Leaves to go upstairs*)

CHARLIE: I think I'll just wander out yonder and take myself a stroll, maybe catch a bit of fresh air before turning in tonight. (*Exits*)

SCARLET: It is getting late, I must be going now. Good evening, Mr. Tyler.

(*All have left, and Mr.—or "Captain," if you please—* TYLER *is alone in the living room and somehow gets the hint to leave*)

TYLER: (*Sniffing under his armpits*) I wonder what made them all fly outa here so fast? Hope it wasn't on account o' me or nothin' I said. (*Opens the door and exits solo, shaking his head*)

ACT THREE

Scene 1

JIM *is walking through the house when he is stopped by a "pssst." He turns to see* JANE *in a corner. She beckons him to come towards her. He looks both ways and does so. She places her forefinger to her lips in a "be-quiet" fashion. She looks both ways and then points to her stomach. He raises both hands in puzzlement. She points to him and then back to herself, then at her stomach, and* JIM *gets the message.* JIM *begins to rotate and vibrate as if being electrocuted*)

JIM: No, no, no, no, I, I, I, I, no, I, no, I, yi, yi,

nononono . . .

(JIM shaking his head still. JANE turns sideways so as to make certain that she convinces him that she is expecting. JIM grabs her and tries to push her stomach in. She screams and he puts his hand over her mouth, lets go, and both race out of the house. SCARLET enters to see what the scream was all about, and at the same time so does ZERO. She looks both ways, beckons ZERO to follow her to one of the corners of the room. He does and she grabs his hand and places it on her belly. He smiles and obliges, even rubs it a bit and smiles again. She stops him and takes his hand and places it in various spots on the stomach so as to let him find out for himself. He likes it and joins in with the other hand. She shakes her head, puts her own hand on her stomach, then out one inch, then two inches, then three, next puts both hands at their opposite elbows and pretends to rock an imaginary baby. ZERO gets the message and claps his hands and pats her on the back as if to congratualte her. But she spoils everything by pointing to herself and then at him and then goes through the rocking scene again. ZERO doesn't believe it and stands with his mouth wide open and with his eyes staring at her, his body completely motionless. She continues to make gestures to him, none of which he picks up. He still stands in the same rigid position. CHARLIE enters, SCARLET sneaks out the back. CHARLIE begins talking to himself)

CHARLIE: Oh my goodness! Not Willa Mae; oh, no! What am I gonna tell Ann. She'll kill me if she finds out. And after all that talkin' I've been doin' about the virtues of segregation—even though I never once said anything about "nighttime integration"—Oh, she'll kill me. What I gonna do Andy, what I gonna do?! *(Looks around, sees ZERO, and is surprised. To audience)* Did he hear me? *(To ZERO)* Zero, boy, don't tell nobody what you just heard me say, I'm beggin' you, boy. Please, Zero, I'll give you Saturday evenings off, I'll buy you chicken on Sundays, I'll give you my woolen pants in the winter; oh Zero, Zero, Zero, . . . Zero? Zero? What's wrong, boy? Oh, say it's yours, Zero, please, boy? *(CHARLIE gets on his knees. ZERO beginning to come to)*

ZERO: *(Hazily)* No, no, I can't, no, massa, it ain't mine, honest. I didn't do it, massa, no, 'twasn't me, no, no, no, 'twasn't me.

CHARLIE: Oh, please say it's yours.

ZERO: No, cain't say it's mine, massa, you'll kill me.

CHARLIE: No, I won't, Zero, I promise.

ZERO: No, massa, you ain't kept a promise yet, and I know you sho' ain't gonna keep this'n'.

CHARLIE: I will.

ZERO: You won't.

CHARLIE: I will.

ZERO: You won't.

CHARLIE: *(Screaming)* I willlllllllll!!

ZERO: You'll hang me.

CHARLIE: Ann'll shoot me.

ZERO: Ann'll shoot you???

CHARLIE: Yeah.

ZERO: Why'll she shoot you?

CHARLIE: 'Cause it's my baby! That's why!

ZERO: Your baby?? Why, you . . . you . . . child molester.

CHARLIE: Yes, I did it, I guess you shouldn't take the blame. *(Hanging his head shamedly)*

ZERO: You did it?

CHARLIE: Yes, me, I'm so ashamed now.

ZERO: Wow! You oughta be ashamed, I'm getting out of here, you old pervert!

CHARLIE: *(Goes to ANN's room and stands outside her door)* Ann? . . . Ann? I got something that I got to talk to you about, dearest darling. *(Waits awhile, hears a great deal of noise in the room)* Ann? Is you alright?

ANN: *(Opening the door dramatically, excited)* Charles, Charles, I've been raped! I've been raped! I've been raped by a rapist from San Francisco!

CHARLIE: How'd you know he was from San Fran'?

ANN: He left his card!

CHARLIE: Quick, I'll catch him!!

ANN: No, don't even try to catch him!

CHARLIE: Why?

ANN: He's long gone by now!

CHARLIE: Then I'll grab "Lightnin'," my fastest horse.

ANN: No, you can't catch him, it won't do any good. He was riding "Captain Tyler," and you know how fast Tyler is!

CHARLIE: Uhmm, yeah, I guess you're right! Why didn't you call for Tom, to get some help?

ANN: He didn't need any help.

CHARLIE: No, I mean for Tom to help *you*. *(They hear some bumbling noise in the closet)* What's that? He's still here, the San Fran' raper hasn't left!

ANN: You mean he's here?

(CHARLIE rips open the door and there is TOM, and in his hand is a shoe)

TOM: Miss Ann, Ize finally found dat shoe you been tellin' me to get for you; yep, here it is. I'll go get it cleaned up right now!

CHARLIE: Tom was right there and he didn't help you? . . . *(Pause)* Ann, are you sure you're tellin' me the truth? I don't know if I want to believe that story.

ANN: Well, I thought I'd give the ol' San Fran' trick a try. No harm done. I know what it is—it's "immaculate conception!" I'm gonna have another Jesus. That's it, Charles!

CHARLIE: The San Fran' raper, and now the "Virgin Mary." Come on, Ann, is you expecting or something?

ANN: Yes, and it's yours dear! We've waited this long to have our third child.

CHARLIE: Hold on there "Virgin Mary," I ain't slept with you in years. What is this, a relapse or something?

ANN: Oh, that's right. *(Scratching her head pensively)*

CHARLIE: Hey, come to think of it I did spend a night or two with you when we was havin' that big storm and you was scared and Tom had a bad case of pneumonia and was confined to his bed out back. Why sho' that's my baby you is carrying. Why did you try to play that ol' trick on daddy-o?

ANN: *(Shrugs her shoulders, turns, and wipes her forehead in relief)* I was gonna surprise you, Charles; I was gonna surprise you.

SCARLET: *(Rushes into the room)* Immaculate contraption! Immaculate contraption!

CHARLIE: It's immaculate "conception," and your ma already used that one.

SCARLET: Oh . . . *(Pause)* It was the preacher's son, yeah, that's it—the preacher's son! He's the one that done it to me. I'm going to have his baby! *(Begins to cry hysterically)*

CHARLIE: Here, here, Scarlet. Don't cry. I'll see to it that he marries you. There won't be no illegitimate goin's-on around here or my name ain't Charlie Johnson, er Jackson! Charlie Jackson!

Scene 2

Many months later. They all are sitting around playing with their newly born sons.

JANE: Well, isn't he cute, my first child.

SCARLET: He sure is. My little one isn't so bad himself, now is he?

ANN: Look at your new brother, girls. He's a handsome little fella already.

JANE: Scarlet's baby sure is dark.

SCARLET: So is yours, Mother.

ANN: So is your's Jane.

JANE: It's just the lighting in this room.

SCARLET: *(Looking at her baby)* It must be the lighting in all the rooms we go into, honey.

JANE: Hey, look. My baby has a mole on his left hand right here, just like the mole on my hand.

SCARLET: Well, I'll be. My baby has the same mole on his hand, too. I have one on mine, too, just like Pa's. Pa's is one that you sure can't miss.

Does your baby have one, too, Ma?

ANN: Well, er, yes, but it won't show for a while.

SCARLET: If he's gonna have one it'll show now if ever at all.

ANN: Oh, it will? Oh!

JANE: He must or he's not you and Daddy's baby. Or not yours, or not Pa's.

ANN: Why, of course this is our baby. Just because he didn't come out like carbon copies doesn't mean he's not our baby. Send you to college and you come back doubting the words of your own mother!

SCARLET: Jane, if you won't be offended, can I ask you something?

JANE: Well, let me ask you something, too.

SCARLET: Jane, we all know that your kid's father is the late Mr. Tyler, but can you give account for how come he's so dark? Why, Mr. Tyler scared me the first time I saw him. He looked as if he'd recently stepped out of a coffin, he was so white!

JANE: Well, Scarlet, will you tell me why your little Harry looks so much like Zero?

SCARLET: Why, I never!

JANE: You never! You must have, or he wouldn't look like him!

SCARLET: Are you trying to start some kind of scandal about me?

JANE: You must admit that they do sorta resemble.

ANN: That is right. *(Looking surprised)*

SCARLET: Mother. How could you agree to such a thing about your own daughter? An' besides, little Samuel does look a little bit like Tom you must agree.

ANN: How dare you speak to your mother like that!

JANE: She is right, Mother.

ANN: You have certainly got your nerve. Why Issac more than a little favors Jim.

JANE: Jim who?

SCARLET: *(Sarcastically)* Oh, Jim who? *(Pause)* Have you seen Willa's baby?

They all sit quietly looking at their own babies and then the others. Eventually they leave one by one.

Scene 3

CHARLIE *is at a blackboard with a desk in front of him. He has pencils and papers on the desk to figure out the genetic problems, and then he transfers them to the blackboard.* JIM, TOM, *and* ZERO *are outside the window watching* CHARLIE.

CHARLIE: Now, if I'm Scarlet's father and she has a kid, then the kid should be as much like her as she is like me. So, if I have a mole on my hand, then her kids and she, too, don't have no business not havin' a mole on theirs. And they do have the moles. But how come the baby is so dark? *(Outside,* TOM *and* JIM *turn slowly to look at* ZERO. ZERO *looks guilty and smiles, eyes pointed towards the heavens)* I ain't no "Anthrop-o-logist," but I know something here just ain't right. I'm beginning to suspect other parties' involvement.

JIM: Go get 'em, Sherlock Holmes! We'll give you three guesses.

CHARLIE: *(Drawing on the blackboard)* Now here's me, and I have a kid, and we both have moles on our hands and we both is white. Then she up and marries a fella who ain't got a mole, but he still is white. How does he and she have kid with my mole, but with brown skin, too?

TOM: Well, let's see.

CHARLIE: She and the preacher's son live on the shady part of town, so the kid ain't pickin' up no suntan. This sure is a "dyy-lemma."

ZERO: "Dilemma," Charles, "dilemma."

CHARLIE: Looks like I'm gonna have to include all possible parties. That baby is too dark for those two. There must be someone who I ain't considering and I oughta. I figured it out!

JIM: Very good.

TOM: Atta boy, Chuck!

CHARLIE: It ain't Scarlet's baby. The preacher's boy pulled a terrible and mean trick on my daughter and made her think that this is her baby when he and some nigra lady is the responsible parties.

ZERO: Oh, Chuck. And you were so close. Don't give up yet, it takes time. Rome wasn't built in a day!

JIM: And he won't figure it out in one day either!

CHARLIE: Scarlet's baby has a cute little smile on his little cinnamon face, kinda reminds me of Zero.

*(*TOM *and* JIM *slap hands and point at* ZERO, *who isn't laughing)*

TOM: Yay for Charlie, he finally got one. *(Turning back to* ZERO*)* Isn't Mr. Charlie truly one hell of a genius?

ZERO: One down and two to go!

CHARLIE: Well, that one is all but solved, Zero and that preacher's son is related!

TOM: Oh, no, you've got to try harder!

CHARLIE: And I guess that accounts for the way Zero and the baby look alike!

ZERO: *(Wiping his forehead)* Swhuuu . . .

CHARLIE: Or maybe it was Zero. Yep, ol' Zero hisself could have done it. All by hisself, he could've. Without lettin' anybody know, he could've done it without tellin' me, his master.

TOM: Uhh, oh . . .

CHARLIE: Scarlet's baby is Zero's!

JIM: Great goin', Charlie! I knew you had it in ya!

CHARLIE: So that's the story. Zero and Scarlet must have had somethin' goin' on that they wouldn't tell. Well, I found out and that's just as good now.

JIM: Go, wizard, go!

CHARLIE: And now about Jane's kid. I'll be darned for the sake of mercy if that kid is Zero's, too. I think that the whole Southern way of life is goin' to pot. I can't even turn ma back for one night without the bucks "miss-ceg-e-natin'" with nice, clean, wholesome, goody-two-shoein', white womanhood. Just wait till I get my hands on one of them, I'll tear him from limb to limb. *(ZERO and Company are outside laughing)* I know there is something suspicious lookin' about Jane's dark son-of-a-gun. There's gotta be an end put to this race mixin' stuff, there's got to. I'm so sick and tired of these nigras and all of . . .

WILLA: *(Enters the room)* Massa Charlie, suh, I couldn't help but to overhear what you all was sayin' 'bout the "nigra bucks" always carryin' on with ol' white broads, I mean "your" women. But why is it that you've never said one word about your power to exploit me for all that I am humanly worth.

CHARLIE: That's different.

WILLA: Yeah, it's always different when the colored folks is gettin' the short end of any deal. It's always different.

CHARLIE: Willa, I'm warnin' you. I'm up to here with you niggers and all of your garbage. Now get the hell out of here befo' you really have somethin' to complain about!

WILLA: So full of threats, but so void of power. It's in your Bible, Chuck, check it out.

CHARLIE: Why you nigger-bitch.

WILLA: You watch your tongue, white man; I haven't done nothin' to you! Yet . . .

CHARLIE: Are you tryin' to threaten me?

WILLA: No, but it's a good idea.

CHARLIE: A good idea, huh? Oh, may I ask what it is that a mammy like you thinks is so good that I'm goin' to . . .

WILLA: One guess.

CHARLIE: What?

WILLA: I said one guess. Try it, Chuck.

CHARLIE: You know my name.

WILLA: I said Chuck and Chuck it is. Anyway, Miss Ann might like to know a few things the fool should've figured out by now.

CHARLIE: You wouldn't.

WILLA: Try me!

CHARLIE: You try her. Who is she gonna believe,

me or you?

WILLA: It'll be interesting to find out.

CHARLIE: Just try it!

WILLA: Your wish is my command, massa. *(Bowing)*

CHARLIE: Willa, get a hold of yourself. You wouldn't go tellin' that kind of story to ma wife would ya, really, darlin'?

WILLA: Later! *(Walks towards the door)*

CHARLIE: Willa, please don't. *(WILLA exits through the door, slams it before CHARLIE reaches it)* Oh, no, Ann will . . . . Oh, no. *(Rushes out and comes right back with a rope. Mumbling as he ties a hangman's noose. Once completed he throws one end over one of the overhead beams, places the noose around his neck. ZERO, JIM, and TOM are cheering him on)* Well, all I can say is that I've tried all of these years to please my God and my country. I've lived up to what I have preached, occasionally. And now betrayed by one of my faithful nigras. Is there any justice for a white man in these troubled times? I think not. With these partin' words I leave in hope that the nigra problem will be solved one day. I've done all I can to help, but there seems to be little use in my efforts. I go now to God's White Heaven. *(CHARLIE jumps off the desk, but the rope doesn't catch, and he falls on his seat on the floor. As he does, ANN enters)*

ANN: Charles!

CHARLIE: Don't believe a word of it, the nigra's lying through her teeth. Nigger's is always lying, just to cause friction in the families of the very persons who work hardest to keep them alive. That Willa's the biggest liar of them all. I know what she told ya. Just before she told ya, she came in here and told me if I wouldn't have an affair with her, she'd tell you that we had anyway. You know how much they lie! I refused and that's why she told you all of that nonsense. Oh, they're a lying bunch, Ann. I've had to put up with threats like this befo', but halleluja, I didn't give in to the nigra pressures. Most of the Southern gents have given in, but not your faithful Charles Jackson. I've remained true to the last offer.

ANN: What are you talking about?

CHARLIE: About all of that junk that Willa just told ya.

ANN: What? I haven't seen her all day.

CHARLIE: Huh?

ANN: I haven't seen Willa all day today.

CHARLIE: *(Taking off the noose)* Ohh. Haven't seen her all day, huh? Ohh.

ANN: Charlie, is there something that you wanted to tell me?

CHARLIE: No, no, m'am, dear.

ANN: Charles?

CHARLIE: Didn't wanna tell ya nothin', nothin', nothin', uh, uh, no.

ANN: Then what was all that you were saying just a minute ago. About you and Willa.

CHARLIE: Oh, nothin'. Honest darlin'. From the heart of a true Southern gentleman, I'm tellin' the whole truth, so help me God. *(Raises his right hand)*

ANN: Charles, why do you look so guilty?

CHARLIE: Huh?

ANN: *(Mimicking CHARLIE)* Huh? You heard me.

CHARLIE: Are you sayin' that you don't believe me?

ANN: Do you?

CHARLIE: Now Ann, it's been a rough day for me. I'm a little touchy now. Don't make me mad.

ANN: Then will you just answer one question?

CHARLIE: Ann, cut it out, I told ya!

ANN: Charles?

(CHARLIE slaps her, and they begin fighting. Eventually he throws her on the floor. As he does, WILLA opens the door and walks in)

WILLA: Miss Ann, are you alright?

(CHARLIE turns his back on both of them)

ANN: Yeah.

(WILLA helps ANN up. ANN walks over to CHARLIE's desk, pulls open one of the drawers, and takes out a pistol)

CHARLIE: *(Turns around)* Now, Ann, I didn't mean to be so rough with you, but you doubted my word. *(ANN stands up now with the pistol showing. CHARLIE is surprised)* Ann, now put that thing away. It was all a mistake. I thought that Willa had gone off and told you some lies. Like I said befo', you know how much the nigra lies.

ANN: Yes, I know how much the nigra lies! *(Shoots CHARLIE in the stomach)* I also know how much the white man lies, too. The nigger may lie, but never, ever, ever as much as the white man, Charles, never. *(WILLA backs out the front door. ANN takes the gun, wipes it on her dress, and places it in CHARLIE's hand)* Never quite as much as good white folks, they got a lot of catching up to do, Charles. *(ANN exits. The SHERIFF walks in a few minutes later)*

SHERIFF: Suicide!

ANN: *(Reenters)* Yes, sheriff, suicide. *(Pretending to cry)*

SHERIFF: Did anyone see it?

ANN: I don't know, Maybe Jim, Willa, or . . . *(Interrupted)*

SHERIFF: No use in askin' one of the nigras. You know how much they lie.

The SHERIFF *stands over the body, turns towards* ANN. *He signals her to come towards him. She does, and he whispers into her ear. She stares at him, though not surprised, backs towards the door and opens it. She exits. The* SHERIFF *stands over* CHARLIE.

Curtain

ANITA JANE WILLIAMS

ANITA JANE WILLIAMS IS A GRADUATE of San Francisco State University with a Master's degree in elementary education and counseling psychology, and received her B.A. degree in sociology and anthropology. She wrote her first play at the age of sixteen for a Community Center in Houston, Texas, where she was born. In highschool she studied theatre arts and appeared in several school plays. While studying playwriting in Ernest White's course at San Francisco State University Extension, she wrote the comedy, *A Christmas Story*, a play loosely based on a true family incident. The play was produced with great success by the Black Repertory Group in Berkeley, California.

Ms. Williams, who has done radio broadcasting, has appeared on local television. (She is a music enthusiast, and because of this great love for music was selected as a contestant on "Name That Tune." This experience offered insight into "behind the scenes" television.) Ms. Williams studied voice at the San Francisco Conservatory of Music. Her interests in music include classics, jazz, and blues, and she has compiled research tracing Black music from slavery to modern day rhythm and blues.

"I was raised with two grandmothers," Ms. Williams tells us about the history of her play. "My mother died when I was nine. So I learned a lot about old people. These experiences have helped me to become more sensitive to the needs of older persons." Ms. Williams thinks that the theatre is a place where the plight of old people can be brought closer to the understanding of youth. "It is important for youth to see the impact of grandparents upon family relationships and imperative that older people see themselves as viable and contributing members of society. My play is a tragicomic look into the situations of older citizens."

Future goals in playwriting include more children's theater. "My next play will focus on situations to help children establish clear values and interests so that they will be able to recognize and understand their choices in decision making."

A CHRISTMAS STORY

Anita Jane Williams

CAST OF CHARACTERS

MARIE FREEMAN: *A precocious yet charming and alive 10-year-old.*
NIKKI FREEMAN: MARIE's *mother; thoughtful and compromising.*
GEORGE FREEMAN: MARIE's *father; rather witty though chauvinistic.*

GEORGIA FREEMAN: MARIE's *paternal grandmother, whom* MARIE *calls "Grandma"; now frail and senile, but once worldly and alive.*
ELLA ROSS: MARIE's *maternal grandmother, whom* MARIE *calls "Granny"; strong in stature and mind; alive, though somewhat embittered, yet religious.*

Time: Christmas Eve and morning, the present.

Place: The Freeman's home; a Black middle-class family in a large American city.

Setting: A split stage. Stage left is GEORGIA FREEMAN's *bedroom, which is rather cluttered. Stage right is the kitchen, which is extremely neat.*

A PLAY IN ONE ACT

Scene 1

The kitchen. GEORGE *and* NIKKI *are sipping egg nog at the table. It is late night, Christmas Eve.*

GEORGE: At last a moment alone. I bet this is the first Christmas Eve we've had all the presents wrapped and under the tree before midnight.

NIKKI: I'm glad we didn't have to put anything together for Marie. Thank goodness she only wanted a doll and clothes.

GEORGE: You know, I'm looking forward to seeing the whole family together. It's been a long time.

NIKKI: I hope everything will turn out all right. Twenty people for dinner scares me!

GEORGE: Don't worry. This might be the greatest reunion of all time.

NIKKI: I just keep getting this feeling of potential disaster. Like not enough chairs, not enough food . . .

GEORGE: Think positively. Everything is planned down to a tee. What could go wrong?

NIKKI: That's why I'm so apprehensive. We're too organized. Remember, if anything can go wrong, it will.

GEORGE: *(Reassuringly)* Relax, Nikki. *(Pauses and thinks as if trying to change the subject)* What did you get me for Christmas?

NIKKI: *(Snapping her fingers)* That's what *can* go wrong. Suppose your family won't like the presents we got them? Your brother Tom is a religious fanatic. You know how he always complains about the material side of Christmas. You'd think he was a monk.

GEORGE: Nikki, you've got a one-track mind. What am I going to do with you. *(Pauses and sips)* How about a little brandy in this egg nog?

NIKKI: If there's any left. You know your mother takes her regular midnight strolls through the kitchen. *(Goes to the cabinet)*

GEORGE: Are you saying *my* mother has been nipping in the still. Your mother lives here too.

NIKKI: George! You know my mother doesn't drink.

GEORGE: Well, how do you know my mother is drinking the brandy. You got some kinda surveillance setup around here, spying on my mamma.

NIKKI: Of course not, Geroge. *(Pouring a little brandy into the cups)* Yesterday this bottle was full. Now it's half gone. See! *(Shows him the bottle)*

GEORGE: You could be imagining things. Alcohol has a tendency to evaporate at the darnedest times.

NIKKI: Especially where your mother is concerned.

GEORGE: Now, that's what could ruin a family reunion.

NIKKI: What?

GEORGE: You and Ella teaming up against my mother. *(Points to GEORGIA's room)*

NIKKI: George, you know I don't team up with anyone against Georgia. *(Glances towards GEORGIA's door)*

GEORGE: Just because she's getting up in age . . . she's still as spry as ever.

NIKKI: You mean *sly* as ever.

GEORGE: There you go. At it again.

NIKKI: *(Seriously)* George, after Christmas we should consider the future of Grandma Freeman. She's getting rather forgetful.

GEORGE: Her future is right here with us. I'm not sending my mom to one of those old folks farms. *(Moves to GEORGIA's door)*

NIKKI: I'm not talking about that. She needs to get involved with people her own age. In one of those senior citizens programs. There are a lot around.

GEORGE: You're right about that. Now, all we have to do is convince her that she is a senior citizen. She thinks she's as young as Marie.

NIKKI: Yeah, I know.

GEORGE: We must make some plans for her. Someday we will both be old.

NIKKI: If we survive this Christmas.

GEORGE: *(Looks at his watch)* It's past twelve, so Merry Christmas, baby.

NIKKI: Merry Christmas, George. *(They kiss)*

GEORGE: Let's call this Christmas Eve a night.

NIKKI: Let's.

GEORGE: Should we take a last minute check of today's events?

NIKKI: I think everything is under control. Let's see. Marie's polished the silver. *(Points to the table)* The presents are all wrapped and under the tree. Oh, there's just one other thing.

GEORGE: What's that?

NIKKI: *(Opening the refrigerator)* The turkey has to thaw out before we can cook it. *(Places the turkey on the counter)*

GEORGE: Ah, there's nothing better than a house on Christmas morning smelling of evergreen, chestnuts roasting, and the aroma of a turkey baking in the oven. *(They exit)*

Lights fade

Scene 2

GEORGIA FREEMAN, *dressed in a robe and slippers, comes out of her bedroom and into the kitchen. She sings softly, a blues tune. At times she is heard talking to herself. The lights fade to black in her bedroom. The lights in the kitchen come up. The polished silverware is lying on the table. She is carrying a knitted sack or laundry bag. She proceeds to stuff the sack with the silver. Still singing and mumbling, she looks at the turkey wrapped in plastic, thawing in a flat pan on the counter. She moves to it and gently touches it, draws her hand back quickly. She returns to the table, picks up the sack, and takes it into her room. Lights dim in the kitchen, bedroom is lighted. She pulls out the bottom drawer of the chest and stuffs the sack in it. She rumbles around the room, finds a small blanket, and reenters the kitchen. She approaches the turkey.*

GEORGIA: *(Talking to the turkey in a child-like voice)* Here you are, my little baby, my lost little baby. *(Touching it)* You're so cold. Oh, you'll catch pneumonia. I'd better wrap you up good.

(Goes about diligently wrapping the turkey in cup towels, then wraps the blanket around it like a baby. She carries it back to her room. She sits in the rocker and begins to sing "Rock-a-bye Baby." After awhile she gets up and looks around for something to put the "baby" in. She finally decides to put it in the bottom of a laundry basket. She fills the basket with towels, then carefully places a sheet over the basket and tucks it in neatly. The basket gives the appearance of freshly laundered clothes. She sits in her rocker and looks out the window. Lights fade to black. The kitchen lights come up. ELLA, the other grandmother, enters the kitchen through the door at stage right which adjoins the dining room. She is fully dressed, neatly. She sings a Christmas carol as she goes about putting on an apron and making coffee. As she approaches the counter and sees the pan, now minus the turkey, she stops singing and exclaims . . .)

ELLA: Oh, my God, the turkey! *(Goes about the kitchen looking in the refrigerator, oven, cabinets for the turkey. She goes to the door and calls)* Nikki, come down here! *(Closes the door. Shaking her head, she says)* My Lord, my Lord!

NIKKI: *(Enters the kitchen)* What is it, Mamma?

ELLA: *(Seriously)* The turkey's disappeared.

NIKKI: *(Disbelieving)* What! Come on, Mamma, it's Christmas morning. Stop playing around. I took the turkey out to thaw last night.

ELLA: I'm not playing. It's gone now. And we have twenty guests to feed today. Who ever heard of a turkey dinner without the turkey?

NIKKI: My God! I don't believe this. How can a twenty-five pound turkey just walk away. I mean it was dead and frozen—stiff. Did you look . . .

ELLA: I looked everywhere a turkey ought to be. *(Goes over and sits at the table)*

NIKKI: *(Pouring two cups of coffee)* Mamma, have a cup of coffee and let's figure this out. *(Goes to the table with the cups and sits down)*

ELLA: Nikki, I never heard of such a thing. A turkey disappearing. *(Noticing the missing silver)* I told Marie to polish the silver last night. That child's lazy.

NIKKI: Mamma, she did polish the silver. It was here last night!

ELLA: *(Moving towards door)* Marie, come here. *(Returns to the table)* We'll find out.

MARIE: *(Coming through the door)* Yes, Granny.

ELLA: *(Commandingly)* I told you to polish the silver and leave it on the table.

MARIE: And I did, Granny. It's right over here on, on . . . *(Sees that it's not there)* It's not here, but this is where I left the silver last night.

NIKKI: *(Shaking her head)* You mean the silver got up and walked away too!

MARIE: Mom, is something else missing also?

NIKKI: Yes, the Christmas turkey.

MARIE: *(Surprised)* The what? The turkey?

ELLA: That's right, child. The turkey. And now it looks like we'll be eatin' mashed potatoes with our fingers. *(Throws up her hands)* Lord in heaven, first the turkey, now the silver. What next?

MARIE: Maybe Daddy put the silver back in the dining room. I'll go look. *(Exits stage right)*

NIKKI: *(To ELLA)* Did some kind of burglar come in and take our turkey and silver?

ELLA: *(Disgusted)* I dont' think so, Nikki. I just don't know. But it looks like an inside job to me.

MARIE: *(Reentering the kitchen)* The silver is not in the dining room. *(Spreading her hands)* Unless someone is playing a trick, Santa Claus is a thief. *(Pulls out a chair and sits at the table)*

ELLA: What are we gonna do? It's Christmas and no turkey. *(Looks at NIKKI)* What are you gonna tell George?

NIKKI: What am *I* going to tell him. You mean *we*. You're not copping out on this, Mamma.

ELLA: *(Folds her arms and sits back in her chair)* Now wait just a minute, young lady. When I agreed to come down here, it was to help you with cleaning, cooking, and seeing after *(Points to MARIE)* this child. It wasn't for no 'plaining the disappearance of a turkey to your husband.

NIKKI: How can I tell him?

ELLA: Just say, George, we lost the turkey. You'll be eatin' crow today.

NIKKI: Come on, Mamma, you're being ridiculous now, and it's not funny.

MARIE: *(To both of them)* Well, I think the first thing we should do is find out what happened.

NIKKI: Marie's right, Mamma. You think we should call the police or somebody?

ELLA: What good would that do? It wasn't a break-in, the culprit is right under our nose.

MARIE: Granny, you're not accusing me of taking it, are you?

ELLA: No, no, child, there's other people living in this house besides the three of us.

NIKKI: I think you're trying to say something. *(Puts her hands on her hips)* So, come on out with it, Mamma. *(NIKKI and ELLA look at GEORGIA's door, then back at each other. They do a double take head swing back to the door, then look at each other again)* You don't mean. . . . *(Groping for words)* You're not trying to say that. . . . She wouldn't.

ELLA *and* NIKKI: She would.

ELLA: And why not? This summer didn't a full grown watermelon just disappear without any trace until it just turned up, out of the clear blue . . . *(Points finger to the floor)* right back in this very kitchen? *(Leans towards NIKKI)* Did you ever find out how come a watermelon this long *(stretches out her hands)* went from this kitchen to who knows where and back again, humph?

NIKKI: No, Mamma, I never did. *(Leans towards ELLA)* Did you?

MARIE: *(To NIKKI)* Mamma, did you ever find your nail clippers?

NIKKI: *(To MARIE)* No, I never found them. *(To ELLA)* And Mamma, did you ever find your silk scarf?

ELLA: It seems a lot of things around here have come up missing, never to be seen again.

NIKKI: I believe Grandma Freeman took the watermelon, but at least she brought it back.

MARIE: But, Mamma, what if she hadn't. It would have rotted in her room. And if she does have the turkey, think what will happen. Wow!

NIKKI: I know she takes some things. She doesn't mean any harm. She just doesn't know what she's doing. But now this.

MARIE: *(To NIKKI)* Well, let's face it. Grandma Freeman is senile.

NIKKI: *(To MARIE)* Where did you learn that word, Marie?

MARIE: *(To NIKKI)* I've been reading up on the subject ever since Grandma Freeman came to live with us. *(Slow and deliberate)* Psychology Today says many old people are unhappy in their daily lives. They get frustrated dealing with others and may feel rejected and worthless. They may even seek attention as a child would or even exhibit child-like behavior. And I think I can help.

ELLA: *(To MARIE)* You're smart, child, but let us

handle this.

MARIE: *(To both of them)* Okay, then, I'll go play with the rest of my toys. *(Exits)*

NIKKI: *(To ELLA)* You shouldn't send her away, she probably could help.

ELLA: A child's got no business doing grown people's work.

NIKKI: What can we do? We can't just go accuse the poor woman. What if she denies it? We can't just go search her room. That would be humiliating.

ELLA: You mean humiliating to you or her?

NIKKI: To her, of course. Old people have to be treated with respect.

ELLA: So, I guess you don't consider me an old lady. I could be unhappy and frustrated too. And all that other stuff Marie was saying about old people.

NIKKI: Oh, Mamma, you know what I mean, you're a young old. You're not senile . . . *(Rather tongue in cheek)* yet, that is.

ELLA: Well, enough of that. Back to the problem at hand, the turkey.

NIKKI: Yes, the turkey. What can we do?

ELLA: We'll just have to think up a way—a plan to go in there. *(Pauses)* Are you afraid?

NIKKI: No, I'm not scared, I just don't want to start any trouble. After all, she's my husband's mother. He'd never admit any imperfection on his side of the family. He has to keep up his front.

ELLA: That's right, humph, you're breaking your back helping him keep up his front, and his mamma is a real lunatic. Who's going to support you when all those people show up this afternoon for some real home cooking and they end up eating peanut butter sandwiches on Christmas? That's going to be awful humiliating for you.

NIKKI: I know guests are coming for dinner. So, we'll have to do what you said. *(Pause)* Get up a plan to go in there. What you got in mind?

ELLA: Well, let's see. *(Thinks)* I know, you go get her and take her up front to open her Christmas gifts. Then I'll go. . . . *(Stops and thinks)* No, I'll take her to the living room, and you go search the room. Now, that makes good sense.

NIKKI: No, it doesn't. I don't have to put up with this. *(Getting angry)* I'll let her son handle it.

(NIKKI exits stage right. ELLA sits alone in the kitchen, sighing. GEORGIA enters from her room. She is dressed in a long faded blue dress. She still looks frail, but jovial. She sits at the table and begins to fumble with the table cloth)

GEORGIA: *(To ELLA)* Ella, how long is it before Christmas?

ELLA: *(Looks at her, puzzled)* Today *is* Christmas, Georgia.

GEORGIA: Is it today? I thought it was a long ways off. It doesn't seem like Christmas at all. *(Turning to ELLA)* Does it to you, Ella?

ELLA: *(Sarcastic)* No, it sure doesn't, there're no Christmas smells in the house, you know, like turkey baking in the oven.

GEORGIA: You're cooking a turkey? Why, I don't smell it. *(Sniffs)*

ELLA: That's what I mean. There ain't no turkey smells 'cause there ain't no turkey. It disappeared during the night. Nobody's seen hide nor hair of it since then. *(Leans closer to her)* Have you seen the turkey, Georgia?

GEORGIA: No, I haven't seen a turkey. You mean you can't find it?

ELLA: That's just what I mean. It's gone. And with your children and grandchildren coming to dinner and all, I guess we'll feed them hash and water, wish 'em a Merry Christmas and a ho, ho, ho, and send them on their merry way. What'll you say to that, Georgia? *(Looks at her)*

GEORGIA: *(Indignant)* Don't look at me that way. You act as if I took the turkey.

ELLA: Didn't you? And the silverware too. You took the both of 'em.

GEORGIA: *(More indignant)* I got silver, the silver me and Ben, my late husband, had.

ELLA: *(Sarcastic)* You and Ben never had any silver. You probably ate out of the forks and spoons he carved in the penitentiary.

GEORGIA: Ben was never in prison, and you know it.

ELLA: *(Rises and goes over to the sink)* Well, the lunacy house, where you need to be 'cause you are one crazy old lady.

GEORGIA: You calling me old. I'm the same age as you, if not younger.

ELLA: *(Pacing the floor and wringing her apron)* Well, I still got my wits about me. I don't go around taking things that aren't mine.

GEORGIA: So why are you so nervous?

ELLA: *(Stops pacing)* I'm not nervous, *(Almost yelling)* I'm worried. You took the turkey, didn't you? Admit it. *(Coming towards her)* Why don't you bring it back in here so we can have a nice Christmas dinner. It'll defrost and won't be fittin' to eat, Georgia. You've done some weird things before, but this takes the cake, I mean the turkey. I mean you took the turkey. *(Sits down at the table)* Where is it? In that junk pile in your room?

GEORGIA: Now, I don't know what you're talking about. I told you once. I didn't take no turkey. I'm not telling you again.

ELLA: *(Pleading)* Come on now, I'll fix your hair up real nice so you can look good when your children and grandchildren come—So they can remember how you used to look when they were young. Just tell me where you hid the turkey and silver. Nobody will have to know what happened.

GEORGIA: *(Angrily)* You don't need to fix my hair. I'll still look a darn sight better than you could ever hope to look. *(She sits back and begins to reminisce)* My Ben said I was the prettiest woman he'd ever laid eyes on.

ELLA: Well, you know Ben never set foot out of Prairieville. So, he didn't have much chance to compare you with much of anything.

GEORGIA: *(Stares in space as if she didn't hear her)* Yes, I was the queen of the ball. *(Rises from the table, twirls in one place as if in a dance)* I danced with all the men at the Rain Drop Inn.

ELLA: *(Looking at GEORGIA)* Humph, the Rain Drop Inn, yeah, I remember it well. You always did frequent the questionable spots. Was that before or after you teamed up with that hooker Madam La Doux?

GEORGIA: *(As if in a daze, she dances around the room)* What's that you say, Ella?

ELLA: Never mind. *(Impatient)* Just tell me where the turkey is so I can cook. *(Throws up her hands)* My goodness, Lord, just look at her.

GEORGIA: *(Comes to the table and stands next to ELLA)* They used to call me sweet Georgia Brown, the vamp of the town.

ELLA: You mean the vampire of the town. Bloodsucking turkey thief. And get away from me, woman, with your sinful ways.

GEORGIA: *(Going towards her door)* That's right, Ella, you never had no fun at all. You just stayed in the church prayin' and waitin' on the Lawd. And he still ain't come yet! *(Opens the door and goes in her room. Stage lights come up in the bedroom. GEORGIA is still singing and dancing around)* That old Ella—thinks I'm crazy. I'm not crazy. I'm just old, that's all. Can't be old and crazy too. I have fun teasing that old Ella. Same way I had fun foolin' that pitiful Rufus Jones when he took me on that so-called hayride years ago. Call himself gonna take advantage of me. Yeah, I waited 'til he took off all his clothes. Then I pushed him out of that wagon, and I headed home. Never found out how he ever got out of the woods 'cause he never had the courage to look me in the eye—never again. Much less explain how he got out of fifteen miles of trees and snakes—huh—wid no clothes on. I tell you, those were the days. Then I met Benjamin Franklin Freeman. He was my man, and I was his Georgia Rose. He was a fine hunk of a man. The first time I saw him, he was feeding the chickens with his shirt off. The sun was glistening, making sweat run all down his back. *(Long pause)* I didn't know that bucket of water I threw on him was so cold—he almos' froze—right in his tracks. Yeah, I sho' do miss that old man. *(Pause)* We had three sons. First was Ben Jr., of course. Then Tom and last George. Of the three, George is the only one who offered me a home after Ben died. I'm grateful for that, too. Nothing's more pitiful than a forgotten old lady out in the cold—And on Christmas—of all days. Me and Ben sho' had some good Christmases. He'd kill a turkey. I'd cook corn bread and sweet potato pies, we'd eat and have a ball. *(Strong pause)* But those days are gone. *(Begins to sing in a blues fashion)* And I'm here all alone—my man's done gone—he left me to sing this song. *(There's a knock at the window. GEORGIA goes over and sees MARIE outside bedroom)* What are you doing out here, child?

MARIE: *(From outside)* Let me in, Grandma. It's cold out here.

(GEORGIA opens the window, and MARIE climbs through, clinging to her doll)

GEORGIA: Why'd you come through the window?

MARIE: *(Excited)* I want you to see my baby doll I got for Christmas. *(Shows her the doll)* Isn't she pretty? Her name is Akua.

GEORGIA: *(Takes the doll and sits in the rocking chair. MARIE sits on a foot stool near the window)* Akua, what a pretty name.

MARIE: It means the "cheerful messenger," Grandma. It's a Swahili name.

GEORGIA: She's a pretty little thing. *(Strong pause)* She's just like my baby.

MARIE: You got a baby, Grandma?

GEORGIA: Yeah, I got a baby, too.

MARIE: Can I see your baby?

GEORGIA: *(Hands MARIE her doll. Gets up and goes to the basket)* She's in here.

MARIE: *(Surprised)* In the clothes basket?

(GEORGIA begins taking the sheet and towels covering the turkey. She reaches down in the bottom of the basket and takes out the now rather soggy blanket containing the turkey)

GEORGIA: *(Turns to MARIE)* Here she is!

(MARIE takes the wet blanket. She opens the blanket and sees the turkey still wrapped in plastic)

MARIE: Why, Grandma, she *is* a pretty little baby. I know what we can do. Let's have a tea party, you and me and our babies.

GEORGIA: A tea party. That would be nice. And I got a silver setting. *(Pointing towards chest)* Look there, Marie, I believe it's in one of those drawers.

(MARIE opens each drawer until she finds the one with the sack containing the silver. She pulls the sack out. MARIE finds a small table and spreads a cloth over it. She places the turkey in the middle and places

some of the silver pieces on the table. She and GEORGIA *proceed to act out a tea party with youthful enthusiasm. They enter into a world of fantasy and reminiscence)*

MARIE: Care for some cream and sugar or lemon in your tea?

GEORGIA: I prefer lemon, if you don't mind. I always take lemon.

MARIE: I take cream and sugar in mine. I think it's healthier.

GEORGIA: Did I ever tell you how I could dance. Wow, how I could move on the dance floor. I could do a good time step, too.

MARIE: I take dance lessons, and we do time steps. But I prefer the modern dances. You can get a lot of exercise doing them. Watch this. *(Gets up and dances around the edges of the rug as she sings a tune. She moves to the center of the rug, stops, and goes into a singing rhyme and dance routine. Should be played as a show-stopper)*

They say I'm only ten, but I know I can dance and sing with the best of them.

Watch me strut my stuff.

I know how to slide, you bet I can glide.

I can make some folks wanna run and hide,

When I strut my stuff.

I can sing like Aretha Franklin wailing the Evil Gal blues,

Making the imitators really pay some dues,

When I strut my stuff.

Don't forget The Platters singing about the Great Pretender,

'Cause this little girl is a real contender.

Who coulda been the bride of young Tut,

But chose to be here with you . . .

(Quickly turns her back to the audience and looks over her shoulder)

Justa strutting my stuff!

(Spreads her arms out and bows. GEORGIA *gives applause for her talent)*

GEORGIA: You sure dance good, Marie. You must take after me.

MARIE: *(Seriously)* Grandma, why don't you let me take your baby and change her. I can wash your silver, too.

GEORGIA: Okay, but let me keep your baby to rock.

MARIE: You like Akua, don't you, Grandma Free-man. Tell you what, I'll let you keep her for always . . . if I can have the turk . . . I mean your baby and the silver.

GEORGIA: *(Elated)* It's a deal!

(They shake hands. GEORGIA *continues to rock while* MARIE *gathers up the silver and the turkey. She carries both into the kitchen. Lights fade to black in* GEORGIA's *room. Lights come up in kitchen.* MARIE *places the turkey back on the counter and removes the soggy blanket. She puts the silver on the table. She turns and reenters* GEORGIA's *bedroom. Loud voices can be heard offstage. The door at stage right suddenly opens. In comes* ELLA, *followed by* NIKKI *and her husband* GEORGE. GEORGE *is nicely dressed in casual clothes. He has one shoe on; he carries the other one in his hand)*

GEORGE: *(Loudly)* What do you mean, the turkey's missing? *(Goes directly to the turkey and points to it with his shoe)* Well, and what is this, a boa constrictor? *(*ELLA *and* NIKKI *look at each other in disbelief.* GEORGE *moves towards the table)* And here is your disappearing silver!

NIKKI: *(Groping for words)* But just a few minutes a . . . ago, th . . . they were gone.

ELLA: That's right. We couldn't make up such a thing, George.

GEORGE: *(Shaking the shoe at them)* I'll never understand women! They won't believe the things that they see, and make up things they want to see. Who in their right mind would take a frozen turkey out of the kitchen? *(Goes over to the door, and as he exits, he turns)* Tomorrow, I'm taking all the women in this house to have their eyes and their minds examined. Huh, some tale!

*(*GEORGE *exits.* GEORGIA *and* MARIE *enter)*

MARIE: What's all the shouting about? Did something happen?

*(*ELLA *and* NIKKI *are stupefied.* MARIE *and* GEORGIA *move toward center stage)*

ELLA: Well, what's everyone standing around for. We've got a turkey dinner to cook.

*(*NIKKI *brings four glasses to the table. She fills them with egg nog. The ladies raise their glasses high)*

NIKKI: To the miracle of Christmas! *(They drink)*

GEORGIA: To the turkey with a tale to tell! *(They drink)*

ELLA: To the grandmothers of the world! *(Drink again)*

MARIE: And to the child who shall lead them.

Lights fade

Curtain

Sea Urchin Press

This first edition
of Center Stage
was typeset in Bembo
and printed at
the West Coast Print Center,
first printing, 1981, 1,200 *copies,*
second printing, 1983, 2,000 *copies,*
for Sea Urchin Press, Publishers
P. O. Box 10503
Oakland, California
94610